Modern Drama by Women 1880s–1930s

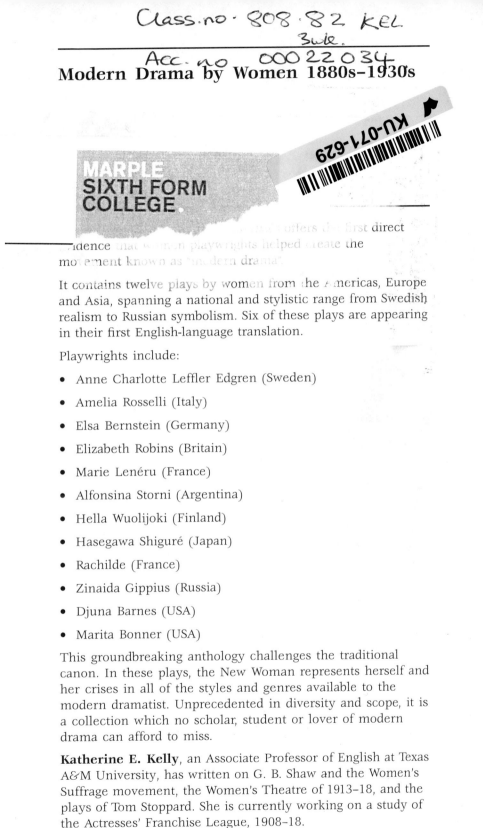

... offers the first direct evidence that women playwrights helped create the movement known as "modern drama".

It contains twelve plays by women from the Americas, Europe and Asia, spanning a national and stylistic range from Swedish realism to Russian symbolism. Six of these plays are appearing in their first English-language translation.

Playwrights include:

- Anne Charlotte Leffler Edgren (Sweden)
- Amelia Rosselli (Italy)
- Elsa Bernstein (Germany)
- Elizabeth Robins (Britain)
- Marie Lenéru (France)
- Alfonsina Storni (Argentina)
- Hella Wuolijoki (Finland)
- Hasegawa Shiguré (Japan)
- Rachilde (France)
- Zinaida Gippius (Russia)
- Djuna Barnes (USA)
- Marita Bonner (USA)

This groundbreaking anthology challenges the traditional canon. In these plays, the New Woman represents herself and her crises in all of the styles and genres available to the modern dramatist. Unprecedented in diversity and scope, it is a collection which no scholar, student or lover of modern drama can afford to miss.

Katherine E. Kelly, an Associate Professor of English at Texas A&M University, has written on G. B. Shaw and the Women's Suffrage movement, the Women's Theatre of 1913–18, and the plays of Tom Stoppard. She is currently working on a study of the Actresses' Franchise League, 1908–18.

Modern Drama by Women 1880s–1930s

An international anthology

Edited by Katherine E. Kelly

London and New York

First published 1996
by Routledge
11 New Fetter Lane, London EC4P 4EE

Simultaneously published in the USA and Canada
by Routledge
29 West 35th Street, New York, NY 10001

Routledge is an International Thomson Publishing Company I T P

Typeset in Veljovic by Keystroke, Jacaranda Lodge, Wolverhampton
Printed in Great Britain by Redwood Books, Trowbridge, Wiltshire

British Library Cataloguing in Publication Data
A catalogue record for this book is available from the
British Library

Library of Congress Cataloguing in Publication Data
Modern Drama by Women 1880s–1930s : An international anthology / edited
  by Katherine E. Kelly.
      p.   cm.
   Includes bibliographical references.
   1. Drama—Women authors. I. Kelly, Katherine E.
  PN6119.8.M63   1996
  808.82′0082—dc20   95–31553

ISBN 0–415–12493–X (hbk)
ISBN 0–415–12494–8 (pbk)

This anthology is dedicated
to women's friendship and women's work

Contents

List of illustrations   viii

Acknowledgments   ix

Introduction: The Making of Modern Drama   1
Katherine E. Kelly

REALISMS

1   **Anne Charlotte Leffler Edgren *True Women*** (Sweden)   17
    Translated and introduced by Anne-Charlotte Hanes Harvey

2   **Amelia Rosselli *Her Soul*** (Italy)   44
    Translated and introduced by Natalia Costa-Zalessow with Joan Borrelli

3   **Elsa Bernstein (Ernst Rosmer) *Maria Arndt*** (Germany)   80
    Translated and introduced by Susanne T. Kord

4   **Elizabeth Robins *Votes for Women*** (England)   108
    Edited and introduced by Joanne E. Gates

5   **Marie Lenéru *Woman Triumphant*** (France)   147
    Translated and introduced by Melanie C. Hawthorne

6   **Alfonsina Storni *The Master of the World*** (Argentina)   183
    Translated and introduced by Evelia Romano Thuesen

DEPARTURES

7   **Hella Wuolijoki *Hulda Juurakko*** (Finland)   214
    Translated by Ritva Poom. Introduced by Pirkko Koski

8   **Hasegawa Shiguré *Wavering Traces*** (Japan)   254
    Translated and introduced by Carole Cavanaugh

9   **Rachilde (Marguerite Eymery) *The Crystal Spider*** (France)   269
    Translated by Kiki Gounaridou and Frazer Lively.
    Introduced by Frazer Lively

10 **Zinaida Gippius *Sacred Blood*** (Russia)   278
    Translated by Mary F. Zirin and Catherine Schuler.
    Introduced by Catherine Schuler

11 **Djuna Barnes *The Dove*** (U.S.A.)   299
    Introduced by Cheryl J. Plumb

12 **Marita Bonner *The Purple Flower*** (U.S.A.)   309
    Introduced by Esther Beth Sullivan

Notes on translators and contributors   318

Illustrations

1 Anne Charlotte Leffler Edgren   17

2 Production photograph from *True Women*   40

3 Amelia Rosselli   44

4 Drawing of Elsa Bernstein   80

5 Elizabeth Robins   108

6 Marie Lenéru   147

7 Alfonsina Storni   183

8 Hella Wuolijoki with Bertolt Brecht   214

9 Production photograph from *Hulda Juurakko*   224

10 Hasegawa Shiguré   254

11 Plan of a present-day Kabuki stage   259

12 Rachilde (Marguerite Eymery)   269

13 Watercolour and photograph of
    Zinaida Gippius   278

14 Djuna Barnes   299

15 Marita Bonner   309

Acknowledgments

This anthology would not have been possible without the cooperation of archives, agents, and literary estates in Europe and the United States. We would like to thank the following institutions for access to their collections, for permission to reproduce photographs and to quote from manuscripts, and for other assistance: the Archive and Library of the Royal (Swedish) Dramatic Theatre, the Drottningholm Theatre Museum (Sweden), and the Royal Library (Sweden), for assistance with research on Ann Charlotte Leffler Edgren; the Finnish Literature Information Centre for subsidizing the translation costs for *Juurakkon Hulda*; New York University's Fales Library, "Elizabeth Robins Collection," for access to manuscripts and photographs of Elizabeth Robins; and Special Collections, McKeldin Library, University of Maryland, for the photograph of Djuna Barnes.

While we have made every effort to contact copyright holders, we wish to apologize to any we may have missed. The following individuals and publishers have greatly helped our efforts to return these playrights to print. We wish to thank: Aldo Rosselli, grandson of Amelia Rosselli, for permission to reproduce the photograph of the author and to publish the translation of *Her Soul*; Author's League Fund, 234 West 44th Street, New York, New York, as literary executors of the Estate of Djuna Barnes for permission to publish *The Dove*; Mats Bäcker for permission to reproduce his production photograph of Ann Charlotte Leffler Edgren's *True Women*; *The Crisis*, the official publication of the NAACP, for permission to reprint the photograph of Marita Bonner and the text of *The Purple Flower*; The Fonds Doucet and the Bibliothèque de l'Arsénal for newsclippings related to Rachilde; *La Nación*, the Argentine newspaper, for providing reviews of Alfonsina Storni's *Master of the World*;

Edith Silve for permission to publish Rachilde's *The Crystal Spider* and to reproduce the photograph of Rachilde; Mabel Smith, Literary Executor of the Elizabeth Robins Papers, for permission to publish the text of *Votes for Women*; Alejandro Storni, for assistance and information about the author, and the photograph of Alfonsina Storni; Mrs. Vappu Tuomioja and the Finnish Dramatists' Union for permission to translate and publish Hella Wuolijoki's *Juurakkon Hulda*, and to reproduce the photograph of Wuolijoki and Brecht; and Yamamoto Yukino of Fuji Shuppan publishers for permission to translate from the Japanese language text of Hasegawa Shigure's *Wavering Traces*. Hasegawa Massaru kindly provided the photograph of Hasegawa Shiguré.

The general editor would like to thank all of those who offered ideas and encouragement during the assembling of this anthology. Of the many scholars and theater professionals who helped, I especially thank the following, with apologies to any whose names I have omitted: Doris Abramson, Janet Benton, Viv Gardner, Melanie C. Hawthorne, The International Center for Women Playwrights, Tess Onwueme, Susan Pfisterer-Smith, Jenny Spencer, Sheila Stowell, Sue Thomas and Carla Waal. Jo Herbert offered invaluable assistance with correspondence related to this anthology, and Charles Snodgrass collected important evidence about the beginnings of modern drama. The support of Texas A&M University's College of Liberal Arts and English Department head, J. Lawrence Mitchell, helped ensure that this collection would be a full and representative sample of international plays by women. Finally, Talia Rodgers of Routledge showed humor, patience, and – above all – vision as she encouraged the evolution of this volume over months of development.

Introduction: The Making of Modern Drama

Katherine E. Kelly

Women are organising, speaking, working. . . .
It is now a crucial time, when our Western
help may give impetus and permanence to
the movement of Eastern women, and when
delay may mean a much longer continued
oppression of women. (Carrie Chapman Catt, 1913)

Women, rise up! Playwrights, sit down

The "crucial time" covered by this anthology of plays, especially the years 1890–1920, witnessed a massive increase in the direct participation of western European and U.S. women in politics, social policy, the professions, and the arts. The vastness of women's activism was disguised not only by its locally different forms but also by the hostility of established institutions. In England, France, Germany, the United States, Australia, Japan, Russia, Canada, and beyond, women agitated for the rights to vote, own property, raise the age of consent, and keep custody of their children in cases of divorce. Before, during, and after the First World War, women organized an international peace movement opposed to global warfare.[1] Women, that is, began to operate politically and in large numbers, enabled by the effects of higher literacy rates and improved health care.

Their political efforts met with aggressive opposition, both locally and internationally. A highly organized anti-suffrage movement in the U.S., England, Australia, and Canada, to name just a few English-speaking locations, attempted to defeat the drive for the vote, describing suffrage activists as neglectful mothers, rebellious wives, and unpatriotic citizens threatening the future of the race. Public ridicule, organized political opposition, and violent physical attack against women insisting upon greater autonomy were the overt methods used to silence them. Other, less obvious, forms of opposition have gone largely unremarked.

While the forces propelling this wave were gathering strength, what has come to be called Modern Drama debuted on selected stages in northern and western Europe, Australia, and the Americas. Henrik Ibsen, the so called "father of Modern Drama," won this title in part by creating dramatic portraits of middle-class women confronting the social, legal, and psychological limits of gender roles – the same roles being challenged by women activists in the late nineteenth and early twentieth centuries.[2] Nor was Ibsen alone in addressing the condition of women: scores of male dramatists but apparently few, if any, women found the subject compelling. The Nora struggling with "selfhood" was joined in Sweden by August Strindberg's Miss Julia tormented by sex role confusion, in Russia by Anton Chekhov's Nina suffering from artistic failure, in France by Eugène Brieux's Térèse crippled by employment discrimination, and in England by G. B. Shaw's Vivie Warren determined to have a professional career. These characters announced the arrival of a genre, we have been asked to believe, mastered solely by male authors. For many observers like Anthony Ellis writing in the London of 1909, male authorship of woman-centered plays actually defined the modern theater. In Ellis's view, Ibsen's "attempt to readjust ideals to modern conditions of life and modern thought" rested upon his "new charter of womanhood" (304). Writing in 1910, Louie Bennett described Ibsen's *Ghosts* as "essentially a woman's play, a woman's story addressed to women" (284), written, coincidentally, by a man.

This new theater created major roles for actresses, and may have expanded female audiences, but it apparently did little to encourage women as the authors of their emerging story. In spite of their presence everywhere as the defining object of modern plays, women seemed to have disappeared as writing subjects in the modern theater. A search of twenty-nine

1

anthologies, collections, and critical histories of "modern drama" published in both England and the United States between 1880 and 1940, for example, reveals only four women playwrights listed in more than one source. Why would these dramatists, so prolific and celebrated during the Restoration and eighteenth century, and writing in ever greater numbers in the nineteenth century, disappear at this "crucial time" of awakening?

The woman (dramatist) problem

A closer look at handlists of plays written in England and the U.S. during this period suggests that, far from deserting playwriting, more women than ever before were writing for the stage. James Ellis and Joseph Donohue list 189 women known to have written plays in England during the nineteenth century (1985: 301–02). Allardyce Nicoll's "Handlist of Plays 1900–1930" shows over 700 women writing plays in England during the first three decades of the twentieth century (1937: 451ff.). Frances Bzowski's recent checklist for the same thirty-year period in the U.S. shows 4,000 women writing plays of every variety, from "health plays" to pageants, to full-length tragedies. How could the work of 4,700 women writing in the U.S. and England – to cite two national examples – be mislaid? As we shall see, it took a sustained effort on the part of critics, historians, and producers to create the ghost effect.

Brander Matthews, one of the most influential U.S. sponsors of the new drama, devoted a separate chapter of his *Book about the Theater* (1916) to the "problem" of women dramatists. Why is it, asks Matthews, that women, successful as actors and as novelists, have failed to become as popular or as prolific as their male playwriting colleagues? Because, he answers, they lack the "inexhaustible fund of information about life which is the common property of men." They have succeeded as novelists, he explains, in the narrow realm of domestic fiction, where they need not "explore deeply . . . the great passionate crises of existence" (118). Furthermore, he continues, "we find in the works of female storytellers not only a lack of largeness in

topic but also a lack of strictness in treatment" (120). This lack Matthews traces directly to the "relative incapacity of women to build a plan, to make a single whole compounded of many parts, and yet dominated in every detail by but one purpose" (120). Deficient in "scientific imagination" (122), women are constitutionally unable to draw plans and execute them. Unaware of their shortcomings, women continued to write for the stage as determinedly as critics continued to ignore them.

Eight of nineteen critical histories of the "new," the "continental," and the "modern" drama published in the U.S. between 1910 and 1964 mention women dramatists of any kind. Those mentioned more than once are Elizabeth Baker, Lady Gregory, Susan Glaspell, and Githa Sowerby. Barrett H. Clark's encyclopedic *Study of the Modern Drama* (1925, 1928) devotes 1.5 of its 500 pages to considering the dearth of female dramatists on the modern stage. Clark draws particular attention to the absence of talented women playwrights on the continent. Aside from Marie Lenéru, he "can think of no woman who has written a really big play. . . . And Italy and Spain? . . . I have neither seen nor read a single play by a Spanish or Italian woman" (309). Clark's inability to think of a single woman playwright in these western countries – most of which are represented in this anthology – comments on the selection of plays for translation and production in English. "Is there any reason why a woman should not be as good a playwright as a man?" asks Clark. In answer, he echoes Brander Matthews's wisdom on woman's deficient "sense of structure" (309). Clark identifies fewer than seven "good" plays written by women, noting that all of them suppress evidence of the author's gender: "Do you discover in any of these the feminine note?" Clark asks rhetorically. "If so, what is it?" (309) To write "well" is to suppress the "feminine note," to write like a man.

Across the Atlantic, English critics also pointedly ignored women dramatists, remaining silent about all but three or four. Ashley Dukes's early critical study, *Modern Dramatists* (1912), codified the central works and cultural ambitions of "modern drama" in England. Dukes selected a total of seventeen (exclusively male) dramatists, most of whose plays had been translated and performed on English stages. Two or three playwrights from each of eight national locations served as exemplars of the "new," the "advanced," or the "modern" in drama.

Dukes's "Modern Drama" positioned England within a larger arena of continental art-making. Like drama canons in the early nineteenth century, it was created not only to direct students and teachers to carefully selected reading exercises but also to show them models of "modern" genius, virtue, and even citizenship, taken from beyond English borders. "What is . . . the hall-mark of modernity?" asks Dukes, "break[ing] new paths," creating characters who are "dynamic, developing, continually offering a criticism of [their] conditions, and so projecting themselves into the future and making history" (9). Modern Drama's contribution – to the individual and to the English nation – is to capture and activate the restless intellectual vitality of the twentieth century. Dukes associates such vitality on the English stage with only three playwrights – Bernard Shaw, Granville Barker, and John Galsworthy. In the anxious masculine arena of world drama preoccupied with representing modernity in the figure of a woman in crisis, plays by women were pointedly overlooked. Defining "world art" as the new field of play not only asserted the superiority of English as the language of world culture but also silenced women playwrights whose representation of the woman-in-crisis was markedly different from that of her male colleagues.

In the same year that Dukes's study appeared, the influential English critic of "new drama" and member of the Ibsen circle, William Archer, published a practical guide to writing for the theater. Responding to what in the introduction he calls the "constant demand for text-books of the art and craft of drama," Archer's *Play-Making* indirectly describes the prevailing norms of the London-based "new drama" movement and its relation to continental drama. "Thesis drama" – Eugène Brieux's *Maternité*, woman suffrage plays, capital and labor plays – fares badly in Archer's commentary by virtue of sacrificing illusion to assertion, humanity to abstraction (16–17). In its

documentary exactness, the Trafalgar Square suffrage rally in Act II of Elizabeth Robins's *Votes for Women* holds the audience "spellbound." But when the play's story is reintroduced, a fable revealing the interrelatedness of the personal and the political in the lives of two women, "the reality of the thing vanishe(s) and the interest with it" (20). Each of his chapters draws extensively on both English and continental examples – especially Ibsen's dramas – to assess the achievements of contemporary English playwriting. Like Dukes, Archer aims to position English new drama in the arena of European practice.[3]

Thirteen years after Dukes's and Archer's critical studies, Allardyce Nicoll's massive history of British drama perpetuated the male-author history of Modern Drama in England. Nicoll characterized the late nineteenth-century English dramatic revival as the product of Ibsen together with other (exclusively male) continental dramatists, among them Frederick Hebbel, Björnstjerne Björnson, Eugène Brieux, August Strindberg, Anton Chekhov, Leo Tolstoy, and Maxim Gorky. The gift of Modern Drama, in Nicoll's analysis, lies in shedding events and permitting stasis; in mimicking "inner life" rather than visible action; and in exploring the difficulties presented to men and women by the forces of sexual desire (1925: 42, 345). Nicoll's Modern Drama that is, undermines English insularity and encourages cultural expansion.

Did women contribute to this expansion? In his 50-page section on Modern Drama in England, Nicoll mentions in passing the contributions of three female playwrights to modernizing the drama: Clemence Dane, author of *Will Shakespeare* (1921), Elizabeth Baker, author of *Chains* (1909), and Githa Sowerby, author of *Rutherford and Son* (1912). Sowerby's bleak depiction of the hardness of a northern industrialist gains praise for its "expansive" effect: "(The) sense of the forces of social life, added to the grim majesty of John Rutherford . . . gives this play its intensity. . . . A broader spirit breathes from it" (384). Following Archer's and Nicoll's sanction of Baker and Sowerby, later critics in England and the U.S. would give passing mention to their works. But not until the 1980s and '90s have selected plays of Baker, Sowerby, Cicely Hamilton, Elizabeth Robins, and Florence Bell been returned to print (Fitzsimmons and Gardner 1991; Spender and Hayman 1985). Most subsequent histories and anthologies of English Modern Drama published through the 1940s and into the 1990s erased the contribution of women playwrights from the history of English dramatic modernism.

Cosmopolites only, please

Critics and historians turned a blind eye to the thousands of plays, some of them distinguished and commercially successful, written by women. Over time, this arrogance alone might have succeeded in effacing their work. But other cultural and material forces accelerated their disappearance. "Cosmopolitanism," the dominant ideological shaper of "Modern Drama," proved hostile to any but the most "universal" of playwrights. Cosmopolitanism surfaced in the late nineteenth and early twentieth centuries as a newly revitalized myth of portable culture capable of transcending national borders defining artistic taste and practice. Hardly a new invention in the history of western Europe, cosmopolitanism experienced a resurgence during the late nineteenth and early twentieth centuries when nationalism was on the rise. The variety of cosmo-politanism practiced by U.S. and English "new drama" producers, playwrights, and critics resembled what A. Hobson referred to in 1902 as the "old" or "humane" type – the reputedly beneficial by-product of a seventeenth-century ideal of world citizenship. Humane cosmopolitanism differed from "anarchic cosmopolitanism," which Hobson described as based on the economic self-interest of international financiers (10–11).[4] While apparently more benevolent than its counterpart, so-called humane cosmopolitanism asserted the superiority of cultural unity over difference, of the global over the local, and could thereby be used, as we shall see, to consign women's playwriting to the class of indigenous cultural products unqualified for professional production, for translation, or for exportation across national borders.

The need to mask one's difference in the face of an emerging "world spirit" of modern playwriting was a tacit rule of humane cosmopolitanism, whose nature and function was anatomized by U.S.

commentator, Archibald Henderson, author of *The Changing Drama: Contributions and Tendencies* (1914). Henderson draws on cosmopolitanism, evolutionary theory, and Benedetto Croce's aesthetic theory to situate drama squarely in the present and projected future of progressive, democratic culture. In Henderson's view, science has inspired cosmopolitanism:

> [S]cience has taught the artist that a consciousness of the feeling common to the citizens of civilized nations is more potent in winning the widest hearing and in attaining the most lasting repute than a consciousness simply of the feelings peculiar to his fellow-countrymen.
>
> (1914: 6)

Science transcends the national boundaries of "civilized" (i.e. selected western) countries by speaking an abstract "world" language. "Art and literature," adds Henderson, "are beginning to speak with the international mind, the cosmopolitan soul" (6). The expansion of English national literature anticipated by English critics through its contact with continental drama has become, in Henderson's formulation, a "world literature" written by "world authors" for a "world audience" (6). Along with its elevation to cosmic status, drama becomes a more exacting and demanding art:

> (T)he dramatist of to-day must possess not only wide knowledge of his art, but astute mastery of its technic. Above all, with a knowledge of human nature more circumstantial, more minute, than ever before . . . the contemporary auditor is quick to . . . condemn a lapse on the part of the . . . artist from the fundamental verities . . . of human experience and potentiality.
>
> (1914: 9)

As the ambitions of modern drama expanded under the aegis of cosmopolitanism, so did the obstacles to women's inclusion in that canon. Brander Matthews excluded female playwrights from the modern theater in the very terms Henderson used to describe the standards for "world drama": a deficiency in technique and a lack of information about life.

Barely citizens of their own nations (in many countries still unable to vote in national elections), women could hardly be admitted into the cosmopolitan fraternity, a select group of artists whose tastes and skills elevated them "above and beyond" their national borders. The normative cosmopolite was a man of science with a distinctly male "experience" of the world and a male exercise of "technique." The cosmopolitan canon of Modern Drama – exemplified in recent decades by the Block and Shedd *Masters of Modern Drama* (1962) – appeared expansive by virtue of promoting art and artists from across national divides. But the ideology of cosmopolitanism – the reinscribing of male-only, English-only culture in the context of a universalist view of human nature – promoted a new conservatism in the canon that precluded the eruption of voices speaking from multiple positions within a nation's borders.

Now you see them . . . Repertory selection and women's plays

The female-authored play that escaped critical condemnation and the growing preference for cosmopolitanism still faced the formidable barrier of repertory selection. The vast majority of plays by women – particularly those with a major part written for a woman – either failed to be produced or else appeared in theaters that would bring them neither profit nor acclaim.[5] The merest fraction of plays by women were blessed with professional production, without which neither a play nor its author had much chance to catch the eye of producers, critics, or publishers of the drama.[6] The disappearance of women's plays was secured by blocking them from the repertories of professional companies. But a fleeting moment of openness to female playwrights offered hope of a brighter future.

Two examples of repertory selection at self-styled "new" theaters in England and the U.S. suggest that, for a brief moment, female playwrights were welcome at the more "progressive" venues where the "new drama" was being constructed. The Independent Theatre Society in England, formed by Ibsen admirer J. T. Grein in 1891, and the Provincetown Players in the U.S., founded by George ("Jig") Cook and Susan Glaspell in 1915, initially opened their repertories to women writers. But after a brief welcome – encouraged by Elizabeth Robins in England and Susan Glaspell in the U.S. – women writers vanished from their stages. Six of the twenty-seven playwrights

produced by Grein's company over its six seasons from 1891 to 1897, were women.[7] This figure is 2.5 times higher than the percentage of all female playwrights in England over the period 1900–1930, when women composed roughly 10 per cent of the playwriting population (approximately 740 of 7,400).[8] But four of these six disguised their gender, choosing male pseudonyms or anonymity over open authorship. Even in the "progressive" London theater of this period, female authorship was a liability, inviting the dismissal or outright condemnation of professional theater critics and spectators. Nor were English women playwrights alone in disguising their sex. Female playwrights in Germany during this period routinely adopted male pseudonyms or opted for anonymity, suggesting the practice may have been widespread in western European theaters at this time (Kord 1994).

The opening for women writers on the stage of the Independent Theatre Society was modest and brief: when it dissolved in 1898, the Stage Society picked up the cause of the "new drama" but not its female authors. Three, or at the most four, of the 65 distinct playwrights produced on its stage from 1899 to 1914 were women – a meager 4.6 per cent. As women playwrights disappeared from the Stage Society, male continental playwrights emerged in full force – 23 of the 65 playwrights produced during this 15-year period (all of them male) appeared in translation. (Woodfield 1984: 181–89).

Across the Atlantic, a "new drama" stronghold took longer to form, but when it did, the Provincetown Players offered more opportunities to women playwrights than its English equivalent had fifteen years earlier. Women constituted 30 percent of the authors performed in the eight seasons from 1915 to 1922. When Glaspell and Cook left the Players in 1923, the number plummeted immediately to 1 and then to 0 (Bigsby 1982: 302–05). Following an exceptional period of early openness to diverse playwrights from the national arena, the repertories of both the Stage Society and the Provincetown Players narrowed sharply to feature exclusively works by men, divided in roughly equal parts between native and continental playwrights. Without powerful sponsors, women playwrights had little chance to be produced on even the experimental stages of both the U.S. and England. With the new goal of forming a "world" art, the makers of Modern Drama withdrew the brief welcome extended to women writers and reinscribed the narrow confines of a drama they sought to broaden.

Simultaneously fascinated and repulsed by the "new woman in crisis," Modern Drama placed her at the center of the drama's frame while removing her from the arena of the drama's making. How extensive was the erasure? Most of the evidence offered here to document the conditions under which women playwrights were briefly welcomed and then excluded from the formation of modern drama has been limited to England and the U.S. However, the introductions to the twelve playwrights included in this anthology suggest that the experience of English and U.S. women was repeated, with local – and sometimes significant – variations in other national locations. Within the space limits imposed by an anthology, each contributor has attempted a brief history of women's playwriting within the confines of her writer's national borders. We recognize these histories to be partial rather than exhaustive, exploratory rather than definitive: both in the selection of texts for recuperation and in the historical and political placing of writers and their works, this collection marks the beginnings of an effort, an invitation to other scholars to join us in recovering from silence and invisibility the female writing subject as a major – if unrecognized – force in the modern drama.

The plays: realisms and departures

[I]t was as if I was seeing ghosts. But I almost believe we are ghosts. . . . They must be haunting our whole country, ghosts everywhere – so many and thick, they're like grains of sand. (Mrs. Alving, Henrik Ibsen's *Ghosts*)

Assembling this anthology has been like hitchhiking to a mythical city: I stuck out my thumb and waited to see who would stop. And then I asked them, "Can you take me to where women wrote plays in Japan between 1880 and 1920?" "No such place," I was told. "But you might try the next town. I seem to recall somebody there

trying to find such a place. Good Luck!" (They always say, "Good Luck!") I had a strong hunch that this place existed, but I didn't expect any of my rides to take me there directly. Then, just when I'd decided to walk on in a vague direction, someone drove up, speaking Japanese, and said, "Yes, I know where you mean; I'll take you there." Just like that. In the end, I realized my destination was a ghost town, nearly forgotten by all but the *aficionados* of silenced writers, with a ghost stage in its pavilion, and ghost promptbooks opened on the floor. As other scholars stopped and then joined the search for something we hadn't seen in collections but knew existed, the gaps in the masters' canon became visible: the conversations before and after the head-of-household entered the room; the subtext of Hedda Gabler's fists raised in fury; the ghosts haunting Mrs. Alving; conflicted mothers torn between opposing desires; exuberant sexual fantasies; the careful cataloguing of professional disappointments; the flourish of moral indignation.

From symbolist one-act to political allegory to full-length *pièce-à-thèse*, these recovered works by women playwrights show them to have written in a wide range of styles and voices, a range that caught me by surprise as scripts and inquiries began arriving from the U.S. and abroad. In my very earliest imaginings, this was to have been an international anthology of suffrage dramas, until colleagues pointed (with great tact) to the peculiarly Anglo-American premise implicit in such a project. The suffrage movement, together with its theatricalized rallies, demonstrations, and propaganda plays, did not sweep the world in a single flash of light, but emerged unevenly in various places at various times. Nor did it produce a world literature by women; in some countries, like Denmark, it was feared that suffrage dramas would harm the suffrage cause by provoking the ridicule of male spectators.[9]

After hearing from many scholars and historians, it became clear to me that the writing of plays by women during this time occurred in response to many of the same provocations that produced plays by men. The Question in "The Woman Question" cut deeply into assumptions about citizenship, selfhood, and economic privilege. The

Question could be defined in terms of the franchise or the problem of surplus female labor. But however it was defined, it tacitly admitted the instability of sex and gender as cultural categories. Of course, not all women writers found "The Woman Question" attractive or compelling; in fact, several of the symbolist playwrights included here joined their male colleagues in dismissing bourgeois feminism as a ridiculously serious attempt by middle-class intellectual women to join a society that the symbolists despised. They sought an artistic identity that they believed would place them outside the bounds of middle-class law and custom in a "free" space marked by defiance and contempt for unreflective conformity. In spite of their attempts, few women appear to have been welcomed into the ranks of productive, avant-garde writers. Misogyny met women playwrights wherever they tried to work.

During the rise of nationalism in western Europe, when countries were defining their identity in terms of their differences from one another, the destabilizing of womanhood – often portrayed as the domestic anchor, or mother, of nationhood – must have caused profound anxiety. This anxiety would have fueled the growth of cosmopolitanism and its concomitant erasure of women artists. Most plays in the canon of Modern Drama in its early manifestations addressed the changing definitions of gender from within the patriarchy – the total system of world-wide entitlements and privileges that has, through individual acts of domination and exploitation, secured and perpetuated women's subordination (Lewis 1993: 20). But these plays demonstrate that such monoliths are a myth. They represent a small but significant gap in the patriarchy's lock on artistic representation. Framing their female characters and situations from the margins of patriarchy – from its servants' quarters, its subtexts, its nightmares – they speak not with an essential "female voice" but with a diverse energy united in its opposition to prevailing definitions of sex and gender.

Over time, a number of criteria emerged for selecting the plays to be included in the anthology. In addition to the obvious requirement that the play should, on the basis of its language and implied action, be of sufficient literary and theatrical quality to merit reading and/or production by contemporary actors, the plays selected for inclusion had to be authored by women; had to contribute to geographical and stylistic diversity; and finally, had to address issues of sex and gender difference from a critical vantage. Many important plays were excluded either for failing to meet one or more of these criteria or for being one of several worthy plays in the same language or from the same location to do so. All of the plays included here are spoken language dramas, although spoken dialogue was not a criterion for selection. Locating performance texts authored by women using sign systems other than recorded speech (dance dramas, folk dramas, etc.) proved more difficult than I had hoped. Such texts could not be recovered for this anthology, but there may now be sufficient interest to warrant the time and energy their recuperation would require.

In dividing these plays into two groups, "Realisms" and "Departures," I am both documenting the variety of realisms in the emerging modern drama and simultaneously demonstrating the non-realist (or "modernist" or "avant-garde") dramatic writing that flourished in small, coterie theaters.[10] In its diversity, this collection hopes to comment on the recent debate regarding the political efficacy of "realism" by providing further evidence of the feminist uses to which realist conventions were put not only on the Anglo-American but also on the western European and other stages. Theater historians routinely use this term to designate both a distinct theoretical movement established in 1853 by Jules-Husson Champfleury and a subsequent preoccupation with literature as an authentic record (rather than a re-presentation) of the material conditions of modern life (Brockett and Findlay 1992: chap. 1) Subsequent discussions of "realism" have become more nuanced as theorists have attempted to reconcile the assumptions of so-called naive realism (the view that writing mirrors or reflects the author's material and psychological conditions) with those of psychoanalysis and new historicism (the claim that writing can reveal internalized and institutionalized systems of repression).

Recent feminist arguments that realism has been and continues to be necessarily patriarchal in producing a seamless illusion of unmediated reality, in effacing its own status as a sign, and in privileging a narrative leading to closure, have provoked a reaction from historically based feminists who have demonstrated the nature and the uses of "realism" across time and location (Stowell 1992). Plays written during the early period of this anthology, such as the "realist" works of Githa Sowerby, Elizabeth Baker, Elizabeth Robins, and their actor colleagues, served attempts to shape both the production and the reception of representations of women as a class. The continuing recovery of women's writing offers a stimulus and check on theoretical speculation about what, as writing, it has been, is now, and might be.

Realisms

The passage from classicism to realism . . . correspond[s] to the invasion of fiction by "concrete details" of which history has always been so inordinately fond. (Naomi Schor, *Reading in Detail*)

The plural term "realisms" is intended to suggest both the variety of conventions associated with representational writing and staging and the aims these conventions tried to fulfill. Six plays in this collection use fable, dialogue, stage space, narrative, and action in ways characteristic of turn-of-the-century stage realism, with the difference that the realisms of this group of plays are gender-inflected: the "truthful" representation of the "real" (i.e. offstage, historical) world disrupts the apparently "natural" status of gender norms. The earliest of the plays, Anne Charlotte Leffler Edgren's *True Women* (1883), adopts the polemic of Georg Brandes – "Literature must submit problems to debate" -- by exposing the sexual double standard and its relation-ship to married women's legal right to retain control of their incomes. The sexual double standard – a social practice by which unmarried and married men sought the sexual companionship of women (typically from a class lower than their own) while, simultaneously, insisting that their fiancées remain sexually abstinent and their wives sexually faithful – figured prominently in plays by both men and women during this period.[11] As the play's Introduction notes, however, Edgren's treatment is unique in pointing to women's complicity with this

practice. The ironical title, "True Women," invites female and male spectators to consider their shared responsibility for sustaining an "ideal" of womanhood that encourages men to exploit women and encourages women to justify their exploitation as the suffering due to "angels of the household." The younger generation – Berta and Lundberg – suggest possible opposition to the double standard, an opposition staged variously in the several revised conclusions to the play.

Virtually all of the realist plays in the collection refer to the double standard in some way, but several of the plays following Edgren's show women and men attempting to resolve the contradictions it creates. Amelia Rosselli's *Her Soul* (1901) tells the story of Olga De Velaris, a painter abandoned by Silvio, her worldly fiancé, after she reveals to him that she is not a virgin, having been raped as a young woman. No longer pure of body, Olga takes comfort in being pure of "soul," but this purity does not interest her fiancé. Silvio's friend, Giorgio, befriends Olga and the two marry in a spirit of mutual respect. Silvio marries Graziana, a spoiled and idle young woman, who takes a lover soon after her marriage. The play concludes with the suicide of her cuckolded husband, Silvio, humiliated by his loss of male honor and despairing that he chose the wrong wife. The "realism" of this play both resembles and differs from the gender-inflected realism of *True Women*. In focusing on women's vulnerability in negotiating sexuality, love, and marriage; in referring to a topical issue (Platonic love) under discussion in Italy in that period; and in using informal, colloquial dialogue, the realism of *Her Soul* looks and sounds like that of *True Women*. But the structure of this play relies on argument and demonstration in addition to sudden melodramatic reversal. Act I concludes with Silvio breaking his engagement to Olga; Act II contains the climactic scene in which Olga arrives uninvited at Giorgio's male dinner party, deciding while there to auction her soul and her body, which Giorgio "buys" but refuses to exploit; and Act III closes with Silvio's suicide. The Act I exposure of Silvio's uncritical reverence for tradition and patriarchal privilege gives way to the Act II demonstration of Giorgio's respect for the person of Olga, which is followed, in Act III, by a description of the fruits of Giorgio's and Olga's mutual respect, and the bitterness of Silvio's marriage. Rosselli demonstrates the falseness of the double standard while arguing that women, like men, are capable of virtue – not the Victorian virtue of the (chaste) angel of the house but the intellectual virtue traditionally associated with male idealism.

Rosselli's use of space inverts that of male realists of this period. The action opens not in a traditionally female location (sitting room, bedroom, nursery, kitchen) but in Olga's studio, a professional space filled with models of her artistic productivity, including paintings of nude female bodies. In this space, she can reconcile the supposed contradiction between her "impure" body and her "pure" soul by producing her own representations of the body infused with soul. Silvio instinctively fears Olga's profession, "When we are together at last, I'll hide the brushes." But after her marriage to Giorgio, whose writing talent she has rekindled, Olga invites him to share her space, building a writing table for him inside her studio. Olga's model, Marietta, has earlier found refuge in the studio after being abandoned by her upper-class lover, the father of her child. The studio is an enclave outside of which the patriarchal ordering of relations remains intact. Olga runs headlong into that order when she arrives unannounced at Giorgio's male dinner party and decides to auction her soul (and body) to the highest bidder. This self-destructive act brings her close to social and psychological suicide, but Giorgio intervenes to save her and her reputation from harm, swearing his friends to secrecy and sending an escort to accompany her back to the contained safety of her home.

Marie Lenéru's *Woman Triumphant* (1922) also foregrounds the gendered nature of stage space, setting all three acts in successful author Claude Bersier's large office, an ambiguous, "immense" space, filled with "a forest of books," "cathedral-like nuances from the stained glass," and oriental carpets. She sits behind a "ministerial table," brokering literary politics, negotiating her failed marriage and her disintegrating love affair, and attempting to arrange her daughter's marriage. Her workplace is also her living place, where she produces a wide range of writing, from brilliant fiction to journalistic reviews, to personal letters. Like Olga, she has achieved professional and commercial success, which has given her an unusual degree of social mobility. But she embarked on a literary career by necessity rather than choice or idealism: "I am the man and the woman here . . . my husband, a former cavalry officer with no fortune . . . it's the deadly boredom of garrisons and a healthy impatience with our poverty that threw me into literature." In her office, Claude is free to write as well as men and to compete against them. She has achieved a degree of public success typically reserved for men, but this success costs her the love of the only man she cares for as well as the affection of her estranged and jealous daughter. By the play's close, her public literary reputation is at its height, but her private life is in shambles. The "triumph" of the play's title underscores the irony of women's success in the public realm: the greater the public triumph the more profound the private loss. The immensity of Claude's office speaks not only to her grand stature as a writer but also to her isolation as a woman.

In *Votes for Women* (1909), Elizabeth Robins deliberately creates a heroine without a fixed home. The play opens with Vida Levering visiting the Wynnstays, where she is comfortably but temporarily resting. Moving from place to place as her work demands, Miss Levering's social class and political skills enable her to travel with ease from drawing room to public gathering to ladies' clubroom. The second act shows her learning to perform on a public platform, the only character in the twelve plays to do so. In the third act, she meets in a private location with her former lover, Geoffrey Stonor, but uses the meeting to illustrate her understanding that the realm of the personal coincides with the realm of the political. Recalling their failed love affair leads Miss Levering to exact Stonor's promise of political support for the suffrage cause.

Most of the action of Alfonsina Storni's *Master of the World* (1927) occurs inside Margaret's home, an upper middle-class artistically decorated "intellectual" household like those of several other of the realist plays. In this home, women become engaged and unengaged, have sexual liaisons, and manage the lives of illegitimate children, servants, and men. The heroine, Margaret, adored her father enough to agree to raise his illegitimate daughter, but does not inform her own illegitimate child of her relation to him until the play's close. Margaret recognizes the overwhelming influence of her father upon her view of herself and her friends' opinions of her, mocking the special aura it gives her: "Even after death, his big shadow protects me. For you, for everybody, I live immersed in a spiritual atmosphere." Over the course of the play, Margaret begins to substitute her own sense of value for that she inherited from her father. By the play's close, she is preparing her son for a new beginning by confessing her relation to him, and by encouraging him to "study every-thing, understand everything." In claiming her maternity, she agrees to remake the future. Margaret concludes the play by leaving her father's house with her son to embark on a long journey together.

Other plays in the collection use stage space to underscore more insistently the entrapment of women in the multiple roles of mother, wife, and lover. Elsa Bernstein's tragedy *Maria Arndt* (1908), set in an old country house in a southern German town, shows the destructive consequences of the contradictory demands of motherhood, marriage, and sexual desire. Using ill health as an excuse, Maria has left her celebrated painter husband of sixteen years to bring her teenage daughter, Gemma, to live in a healthy climate, away from the decadent social life of Florence and close to the resources of an excellent German university. But the removal to Germany is not a removal from her husband's control: both the country house and its staff belong to him, and he is demanding her return. The town to which Maria has moved is also the birthplace of the man she secretly loves. Claussner, whom she has known for many years, epitomizes Romantic male freedom, ranging freely over Europe and Africa, collecting specimens of flora and fauna, and researching the sexual behavior of wild animals. When, at the play's close, Maria has become pregnant with Claussner's child, her entrapment is absolute: she can no longer return to her husband, nor can she admit to her daughter that she is a sexual being and has become pregnant, nor can she consent to abandon Gemma and elope

with Claussner. She has literally been erased from the positions she had thought she could occupy. She chooses suicide over betrayal or shame.

Some contemporary readers might object to what they view as the "defeatist" conclusions of many of the realist plays in the collection – a series of endings reinscribing the power of male law and privilege. But the tendency to dismiss them as such assumes that turn-of-the-century audiences confused art with life and narrative conventions with social inevitability. I have seen no evidence suggesting that readers and spectators were incapable of responding critically to drama and theater during this period. As spectators were well aware, the unhappy ending functioned as a hallmark of modernity. The Introduction to Edgren's *True Women* quotes Norwegian critic Mathilde Schjott, who attributed the play's "sad" conclusion to modern dramatic convention: "it must be [sad], since it is so modern." The conclusion through suicide became for a time the preferred ending for modern tragedies, including those by women writers. Two of the plays in this collection, Marie Lenéru's *Woman Triumphant* and Elsa Bernstein's *Maria Arndt* offer variant readings of suicide as an option for the modern heroine. In the case of the idealist Maria Arndt, the internalizing of absolute and absolutely conflicting demands left her without a subject position: she had no place from which to exist. Her suicide objectifies her erasure. The realist Claude Bersier, on the other hand, ironically describes suicide as an improbable option: "Women don't kill themselves. . . . They let themselves die." Women playwrights did not, by virtue of their gender, think or write identically or even in stylistically typical ways. But powerful writers active at this historical moment exercised the option to write critically about their status as women.

In their sense of an ending, in their treatment of the sexual double standard, their reference to offstage issues of contemporary interest, and their deployment of stage space, the six realist plays in the collection highlight in significantly different ways the constructed nature of gender norms in the "real" offstage world. But not all women playwrights wore the mantle of realism. Some, like Hella Wuolijoki, wrote social comedies; others, like Hasegawa Shiguré, wrote modernized versions of traditional dramas. The Introductions to these playwrights explain their choices of subject and style in reference to local dramatic practice. Here, I would like briefly to note how the form of these plays extends the collection's aesthetic and ideological range. Wuolijoki's *Hulda Juurakko* (1937) foregrounds the function of class in limiting a woman's social and economic range. As a working woman from the country rather than the city, the Hulda of the play's title is credited with being forthright and eminently educable. She demonstrates through her tenacity and good humor not only the virtues of country people but also the empowering effects of education. And while some readers of the play will conclude that her transformation from parlor maid to middle-class citizen destined to marry Judge Soratie at the play's close vindicates patriarchy, the closing scene offers other interpretive possibilities. The obligatory marriage imminent at the play's close is a political marriage between a populist, liberal parliamentarian and an orthodox, conservative politician. Wuolijoki's closure is both conventionally comic and playfully political. As the Judge orders Hulda to go to bed in preparation for their marriage the next day, Hulda comments: "[D]id I have to fall in love with such a dictator . . . if only I'd stayed in the party!" Her marriage and her political career occur simultaneously, because she, like Vida Levering in Robins's *Votes for Women*, recognizes that to be effective in the real world of politics, she must work successfully with men.

Hasegawa Shiguré's revision of the Kabuki tradition in *Wavering Traces* (1911) not only associates her play with a subgenre of the "domestic drama" in the "modern" Kabuki movement but also places the emotional emphasis of the action upon the female character. As the Introduction to the play explains, Hasegawa's writing for the Kabuki stage deliberately incorporated elements from western realism, placing it squarely in the "high modernist" practice of the East/West stage hybrid. The Chekhovian use of offstage sound and indirect lighting in the presentational frame of Kabuki offers an eastern counterpart to Yeats's adoption of selected Japanese conventions in an otherwise western stage milieu. Hasegawa's pastiche of eastern and western conventions exemplifies the falseness of the charge that women playwrights failed to reach beyond "local" artistic practices. But most importantly, Hasegawa's shift of focus from a husband's to a wife's heroism, while apparently a minor change, signaled a radical departure from the traditional Kabuki formula. Hasegawa's simple but powerful revision of a traditional form offers another model of women's playwriting in which gender, never mentioned explicitly, moves to the center of the artistic event. Merely shifting the focus from male to female within the confines of a highly prescribed theatrical form and fable can provoke the spectator to reconsider the gendered nature of conventions.

Still another group of playwrights in this collection selected symbolist and allegorical styles to celebrate the mysterious and ceremonial potential of drama, a celebration that evoked from women powerful writing with referents in history as well as dream, fantasy, and myth.

Departures

To the Twentieth Century events are not exciting. . . . The better the play the more static.
(Gertrude Stein, "How Writing Is Written")

Whether we take as our starting point Gertrude Stein's description of twentieth-century "static" playwriting, or Virginia Woolf's opposition of Edwardian materialism and Georgian spiritualism in her essay, "Mr. Bennett and Mrs. Brown," we arrive at the same point: a defined body of self-consciously "twentieth-century writing" shifting its representational center from the outside to the inside, from the natural/material realm to the ideational/mental realm as the crucial site of awareness. One of the most obvious symptoms of this shift in the modern theater occurred among the symbolists, a group of (primarily male) artists who rejected the realist claim of the knowability of the material world and substituted for that claim an interest in the non-logical processes of the human mind. Like realists, symbolists shared a stylistic common ground but also developed variants of the movement in agreement with their individual preoccupations. Women who chose to align their writing with symbolist practice faced formidable barriers to

production and publication. In spite –
or perhaps because – of the rise of the
bourgeois feminist movement, symbolists
demonized women by rekindling the latent
opposition between Nature (female) and
Culture (male). In this gendered view of
culture's operations, women and men were
thought to correspond to the secondary and
primary, minor and major, incidental and
essential, detailed and ideal. In their flight
from representing the natural world and its
aesthetic corollary, the detail, the symbolists
relegated woman to the unartistic, the
concrete, or what the cosmpolitanists would
call the local. This placed the woman
symbolist writers – the few of them who
ventured to work in such a hostile climate
– in a rather difficult position. As the
Introduction to Rachilde's *Crystal Spider*
explains, she recognized early on the
importance of fashioning herself in the
image of the writer, deliberately courting
scandal when she arrived in the Paris of
1881.

Like her contemporary, Oscar Wilde
(whose plays bear traces of her influence),
Rachilde cultivated a writer's persona,
dressing and behaving "artistically." She
threw herself into performing misogyny
with great gusto, calling herself "un homme
de lettres," mocking respectable feminist
intellectuals ("bluestockings") and wearing
men's clothes in public. She made her way
into the symbolist inner circle, but adopted
conventional women's dress after marrying.
Women writers like Rachilde and the
Russian symbolist, Gippius, subjugated
gender to their identity as "artist," perhaps
believing that the avant-garde coterie would
offer them better protection than "the
women's movement" from the restrictions
imposed on the more docile members
of their sex. They carefully distanced
themselves from the movement for women's
rights, seeking personal freedom and gender
flexibility under the auspices of avant-garde
defiance.

The inward turn of symbolist and non-
realist writing generated a new set of
conventions through which consciousness
could be explored and mimicked. The
normative became less interesting than the
deviant, the linear narrative less compelling
than static repetition, the unique individual
less attractive than the type. Owing to the
demands it made upon the spectator,

symbolist drama contracted, often taking the
form of a single act. Playwrights established
dramatic rhythm not through discursive
argument but musical phrase. Objects,
speech, and action became numinous.
Elemental facts of the body – blood, aging,
death – assumed a primary place in the
narrative. It is difficult to determine whether
the symbolist plays written by women
during this period differed from those by
men, but both Rachilde's *Crystal Spider* and
Zinaida Gippius's *Sacred Blood* (1901) place
female figures at the drama's center,
studying her effect on those she most loves.
The preoccupation with gender central to
the realist plays gives way to an evocation of
female sexuality as the power to create and
destroy. Both the Mother in Rachilde's play,
who nurtures and smothers her son, "Terror-
Stricken," and the Young Rusalka in
Gippius's play, who adores and eventually
murders her Christian adoptive father,
destroy what they most love. In this sense,
they behave like the female figures in male
symbolist drama. But there is a difference:
as Catherine Schuler notes in her
Introduction to Gippius's play, the Young
Rusalka's murder of Father Pafnuty will
only succeed in earning her a soul if
she commits his murder in a spirit of
unconditional love and if he prepares
himself to do God's will. With the murderer
and victim each in a state of spiritual
readiness, the murder takes on the quality
of Christian redemption, transforming both
of them through reciprocal sacrifice. The
Young Rusalka is joined to her friend and
fellow outcast through this final sacrificial
act.

Djuna Barnes's *The Dove* (1923), the most
enigmatic play in the collection, requires
biographical explanation to make sense of its
symbolist deployment of sexual reference
and taboo. Ann B. Dalton's linking of
Barnes's history of sexual abuse by her
father and grandmother to the text (and
subtext) of *The Dove* not only accounts for
the baffling emotional logic of the play but
also, through intertextual readings of
Barnes's other writing, begins to fill the
silences and expressive gaps in the play's
language and action (Dalton 1993: 117–39).
In Dalton's biographical reading, the
voyeurism of the two older sisters, Vera
and Amelia, for whom the young female
character called "The Dove" becomes an

object of desire, is linked through the text of Barnes's *Ryder* to sisters shamed by a history of sexual abuse, and further linked to Barnes's own abused childhood. Dalton also makes interpretive use of the painting mentioned in the play, Vittore Carpaccio's *Deux Courtisanes Vénitiennes*, an image of two lavishly dressed and bejeweled courtesans, staring listlessly ahead as they sit on a balcony surrounded by doves, a peacock, a raven, and two dogs. At the play's conclusion, Amelia becomes progressively more agitated, grasps The Dove's hand and squeezes it convulsively, following which The Dove bites her shoulder. The Dove exits with a pistol and a shot is heard. Amelia returns to the stage holding the Carpaccio painting in which a bullet hole can be seen and exclaims, "*This is obscene.*" We never know the precise meaning of the line nor do we know the fate of The Dove. Has she committed suicide? Has she repudiated her role in the sisters' unhappy lives? Has she learned to leave behind abusive and violent situations? In this play, as in the two already discussed, female sexuality is negatively charged with threatening and violent potential. When read biographically, the play can be construed as a salutary release of repressed rage and sorrow, the beginning of what Dalton has called Barnes's "lifelong writing cure." In Barnes's case, biography appears to be essential to interpretation; however, reading the play solely as disguised biography would reduce its play of meanings and flatten its complex tone. Cheryl Plumb's Introduction provides welcome production information about the play and attempts to account for the "multiple chords" it sounds.

The final play in the collection, Marita Bonner's *The Purple Flower* (1928), allegorizes African-American liberation in a heightened expressionist style. As an abstract rendering of historical forces, Bonner's play synthesizes two of the impulses in this collection – the centripetal force of various realisms with offstage referents in the material, historical world, and the centrifugal force of symbolisms, with referents in the interior realm of mind. The efficacy of Bonner's choice lies in the power of allegory to generalize the particular and to characterize the morality of the status quo. Her aestheticizing of rage simultaneously lays bare its causes and

meliorates its effects for readers who might otherwise turn from its face in fear. The play's references to blood and violence – "A New Man must be born for the New Day. Blood is needed for birth" – deliberately echo the Christian myth of salvation through Christ's sacrifice; but the call for blood originates from "Us's," all people of color who have built the White Devil's civilization and then found themselves forbidden from reaching the purple Flower-of-Life-at-Its-Fullest. Blood sacrifice in this play, unlike Gippius's, is based on a principle of justice rather than mystical communion. "You have taken blood," says the Old Man. "You must give blood." As in this passage, the gender of the play's characters is sometimes specified and other times left open. Bonner uses the generalizing power of allegory to describe the characters as representatives of groups in the African-American community: the older generation, the middle-aged, the young of both sexes; the average, the distinguished, and the innocent. Cornerstone, a middle-aged woman and the mother of Finest Blood, mediates the wisdom of age and the impatience of youth from her matriarchal position at center stage. She comforts Sweet, the young female adolescent, who is fondled by a White Devil hiding in a bush, and she watches her son exit at the play's close to exact the blood sacrifice.

Like many women writers in the U.S. and elsewhere at this time, Bonner wrote with a pragmatic sense of where and how her dramatic work would see print. Glossed "A Phantasy That Had Best Be Read," *The Purple Flower* appeared in *The Crisis* of January 1928, after winning the magazine's annual playwriting contest. Bonner's gloss also suggests that the controversial nature of her work precluded its public staging. It is tempting to speculate on Bonner's attraction to closet drama. As Beth Sullivan notes in her Introduction, the dramatist's first published play, *The Pot Maker*, is subtitled, "A Play to be Read." Was Bonner's eclipsing of public performance an ironical commentary on the inaccessibility of production for African-Americans (particularly women), or was it an example of what some feminist theorists have called the double-coding typical of women's writing? To write in a performance medium like drama with the foreknowledge that one's plays will not be staged is to call for a doubled reading aware of the text as both the presence of language and the absence of performance – an imaginary text too dangerous, too vast, or too impossible to be contained by an actual stage. Bonner's play stands apart from others in the collection by virtue of its synthetic realist/expressionist style, its closet form, and its representation of difference as a function of both gender and race. Her racial identity imposed other and different requirements on her expressive means and range. The publishing opportunities, artistic influences, and audiences for her works were inseparable from the Harlem Renaissance theater, whose goals, expressed by Montgomery Gregory in the early 1920s, she shared: "The only avenue of genuine achievement in American drama for the Negro lies in the development of the rich veins of folk tradition of the past and in the portrayals of the authentic life of the Negro masses of to-day" (Abramson 1969: 25). In her representation of ancient communal story-telling, future blood sacrifice, and present shared rage, Bonner's play complicates and enriches the corpus of modern drama by women.

Climbing what had been, in the Restoration and eighteenth century, a "new found path" of playwriting, these mothers of modern drama nevertheless found their way both steep and thorny. As a record of the plays they wrote, together with the circumstances under which they wrote them (and others erased them), this collection hopes to encourage the ongoing rediscovery of the ghosts of Modern Drama.

Notes

1 Women's history is also undergoing revision; however, many historians characterize the later nineteenth and early twentieth centuries as a period during which women worked hard and successfully to improve their condition as a class. See Genevieve Fraisse and Michelle Perrot (eds) (1993) *A History of Women in the West*, Cambridge: Belknap Press/Harvard University Press, 1993, especially chapters 17 and 18; and Jane Rendall (1991) "'Uneven Developments': Women's History, Feminist History and Gender History in Great Britain," in K. Offen, R. R. Pierson, and J. Rendall (eds) *Writing Women's History: International Perspectives*, Bloomington and Indianapolis: Indiana University Press.

2 Using the universalist rhetoric of cosmopolitanism, Ibsen dismissed the adoption of his plays by the women's movement insisting upon their "larger" scope. Speaking at a seventieth birthday banquet given in his honor by the Norwegian Women's Rights League, he clarified his position:

> I thank you for the toast, but must disclaim the honor of having consciously worked for the women's rights movement. . . . True enough, it is desirable to solve the woman problem, along with all the others; but that has not been the whole purpose. My task has been the description of humanity.
>
> (Ibsen, *Letters*, 337)

Ibsen's denial would echo for decades as critics, engaged in a "gentlemanly backlash" (Templeton 1989: 28ff.) against historically specific readings of the play, repeated Ibsen's statement to deny his implication in the women's rights movement.

3 But unlike Dukes, Archer draws brief attention to four women playwrights: his friend and colleague Elizabeth Robins; Elizabeth Baker, author of *Chains*; Lady Florence Bell, author of *The Way the Money Goes*; and Mrs. Pearl Craigie ("John Oliver Hobbes"), author of *The Ambassadors*.

4 For a discussion of "old" and "anarchic" cosmopolitanism among English liberals of this period, see M. E. Gibson, especially pp. 107–10.

5 The actor-manager system – a later nineteenth-century practice whereby the dramatic author wrote with a particular (usually male) actor in mind whose performance would then determine the success of the play – discouraged leading parts for women. Critic Clement Scott described a late nineteenth-century play, *Her Own Witness*, as "fatally, a woman's play" (qtd in Gates 1994: 33).

6 Brian Corman's discussion of the relationship between repertory and canonicity in Restoration and eighteenth-century drama offers a suggestive model for researching their interdependence in later periods.

7 These figures are based upon the Appendices to James Woodfield's *English Theatre in Transition*. The six female authors referred to include co-authors Elizabeth Robins and Florence Bell; therefore, the six writers averaged fewer than one play each.

8 This statistic is derived from the Handlist published with Allardyce Nicoll's *English Drama 1900-1930*. (This Handlist includes both published and unpublished plays.)

9 Ms. Britta Skovgaard, Research Librarian for the Danish Archives on Women's History, has written that Danish feminists and suffragists preferred forms of public agitation that included public "folk" meetings, speeches, debates, and recommendations to Parliament, but not stage plays. She notes, "In this period, Danish feminists could not afford the risk of laughter in public" (Private correspondence).

10 Astradur Eysteinsson's discussion of realism vs. modernity bears indirectly on this collection, particularly his characterization of the divergent "realisms" of modern novelists. The *Das Wort* controversy to which he refers is particularly interesting with respect to later developments in dramatic theory; however, for the most part, Eysteinsson ignores the effect of gender and genre in his discussion of realism and its variants. See especially chapter 5 of *The Concept of Modernism*.

11 For a well-researched discussion of the sexual double standard and its variants in England of this period, see S. K. Kent's *Sex and Suffrage*, especially pp. 35-37.

Bibliography

Abramson, D. (1969) *Negro Playwrights in the American Theatre 1925-1959*, New York: Columbia University Press.

Archer, W. (1912) *Playmaking*, Boston: Small, Maynard & Co.

Bennett, L. (1910) "Ibsen as a Pioneer of the Woman Movement," *The Westminster Review* 173: 278–85.

Bigsby, C. W. E. (1982) *A Critical Introduction to Twentieth-Century American Drama 1: 1900-1940*, Cambridge: Cambridge University Press.

Brockett, O. and Findlay, Robert (eds) (1992) *Century of Innovation: A History of European and American Theatre and Drama since the Late Nineteenth Century*, 2nd edn, New York: Allyn & Bacon.

Bzowski, F. D. (1992) *American Women Playwrights, 1900-1930: A Checklist*, Westport, CT: Greenwood Press.

Catt, C. (1913) "Our Cause Is One," address to the 1913 International Women's Suffrage Congress, *The Suffragette*, 4 July 1913: 637.

Clark, B. H. (1925, 1928) *Study of the Modern Drama*, rev. edn, New York: D. Appleton & Co.

Dalton, A. B. "'This is obscene': Female Voyeurism, Sexual Abuse, and Maternal Power in *The Dove*," *The Review of Contemporary Fiction* 13 (Fall 1993): 117–39.

Dukes, A. (1912, rpt. 1967) *Modern Dramatists*, Freeport, NY: Books for Libraries Press, Inc.

Ellis, A. (1909) "Woman in the Modern Drama," *The Englishwoman* no. 3 (April): 302–12.

Ellis, James (comp. and ed.), assisted by Joseph Donohue (1985) *English Drama of the Nineteenth Century: An Index and Finding Guide* (Readex Books), New Canaan, CT: Readex Microprint Corp.

Eysteinsson, A. (1990) *The Concept of Modernism*, Ithaca and London: Cornell University Press.

Fitzsimmons, L. and Gardner, Viv (1991) *New Woman Plays: Alan's Wife, Diana of Dobson's, Chains, Rutherford and Son*, London: Methuen.

Gates, J. (1994) *Elizabeth Robins: 1862-1954*, Tuscaloosa, AL: University of Alabama Press.

Gibson, M. E. (1985) "Illegitimate Order: Cosmopolitanism and Liberalism in Forster's *Howard's End*," *English Literature in Transition 1880-1920* 28, 2: 106–23.

Henderson, A. (1914) *The Changing Drama: Contributions and Tendencies*, New York: Henry Holt & Co.

Hobson, A. (1902, 1905, rpt. 1965) *Imperialism: A Study*, Ann Arbor: University of Michigan Press.

Ibsen, H. (1964) *Letters and Speeches*, ed. and trans. Evert Sprinchorn, New York: Hill.

Kent, S. K. (1987) *Sex and Suffrage in Britain, 1860-1914*, Princeton: Princeton University Press.

Kord, S. (1994) "Male Drama and Women's Theater: Gendered Genres in Germany," unpublished paper delivered at the 1994 Modern Language Association.

Lewis, M. (1993) *Without a Word: Teaching beyond Women's Silence*, New York: Routledge.

Matthews, B. (1916) *A Book about the Theater*, New York: Charles Scribner's Sons.

Nicoll, A (1925, 1947) *British Drama: An Historical Survey from the Beginnings to the Present Time*, 4th edn rev., London: George G. Harrap & Co. Ltd.

—— (1937) *English Drama 1900-1930: The Beginnings of the Modern Period*, Cambridge: Cambridge University Press.

Schor, N. (1987) *Reading in Detail*, New York: Methuen.

Spender, D. and Hayman, C. (1985) *"How the Vote Was Won" and Other Suffragette Plays*, London, New York: Methuen.

Stowell, S. (1992) "Rehabilitating Realism," *Journal of Dramatic Theory and Criticism* Spring 1992: 81-88.

Templeton, J. (1989) "The Doll House Backlash: Criticism, Feminism, and Ibsen," *PMLA* 104, 1: 28-40.

Woodfield, J. (1984) *English Theatre in Transition 1881-1914*, London: Croom Helm.

1 Anne Charlotte Leffler Edgren, 1849–92

True Women
Sweden

Anne Charlotte Leffler, Duchess of Cajanello.
Photograph provided courtesy of the Royal Library, Stockholm, Sweden.

Introduction

by Anne-Charlotte Hanes Harvey

In retrospect, the "modern breakthrough" in Scandinavia emerges as dominated by Ibsen and Strindberg. In the 1880s, however, the horizon was dotted with a number of lesser luminaries who, for a time at least, shone as brightly. Many of them were women. That they, like many other Scandinavian writers of the decade, borrowed some of their light from the major stars – Ibsen, Strindberg, and Björnson – was perhaps unavoidable. Particularly Ibsen's pervasive influence can hardly be overrated: even Strindberg – see, e.g., his satiric short story "A Doll's House" – picked up themes, ideas, and types from Ibsen. Female writers responded especially warmly to Ibsen's idealism and found their own careers as artists legitimized by his emancipatory arguments. One Swedish female writer whose dialogue with Ibsen positioned her in the thick of the 1880s' debate was Anne Charlotte Leffler Edgren. (Born Leffler and married Edgren, she is nevertheless often referred to as Edgren Leffler rather than Leffler Edgren. Following her second marriage, her full name became Anne Charlotte Leffler, Duchess of Cajanello.)

These women writers' clear indebtedness to Ibsen has sometimes been seen as a kind of female plagiarism, an expression of dependency and insufficiency. What has often been ignored – by male critics – is that some of the clearest invocations of Ibsen are responses, not echoes; challenges, not endorsements. Ibsen's female characters, particularly Nora, served these writers as models to be partly destroyed in a subversive dialogue with the master, ending in the construction of other, more "realistic" or pragmatic characters. (Leffler, and others with her, criticized Ibsen for being so "unrealistic" as to send his totally unprepared Nora out into the world, thus setting her up for failure rather than freedom.) Examples of direct responses to Ibsen are Leffler's short story "Tvifvel" (Doubts) (1882) and Alfhild Agrell's drama *Räddad* (Saved) (1882).

Typically, female writers of the 1880s chose as their vehicle the short story, the impressionistic sketch from everyday life, or – if more daring – the realistic drama. Anything to do with the theater – writing plays, having one's plays performed, appearing on stage – was of dubious respectability. On the other hand, nothing could confer instant notoriety or guarantee popular attention quite like being performed on one of the major stages of Stockholm, Copenhagen, Bergen, or Christiania. In order to, as the Danish critic Georg Brandes exhorted, "submit problems to debate," one could do worse than turn playwright.

Life

Born in 1849 into a cultured, tolerant Stockholm family of high achievers, Anne Charlotte Leffler was encouraged in her early writing efforts by her family – in 1869 her father published her first short stories, penned under the name "Carlot." But a conventional marriage, respectful but sexless, nearly derailed her writing career. On the other hand, her privileged social position and location in the capital gave her the opportunity in the 1880s to play hostess to "Young Sweden," the leading literary movement of the day. Anne Charlotte became a fixed point on their firmament, admired and respected. Although some of the fulsome praise from this circle may have been due to Anne Charlotte's social position and strong personality, she still showed to advantage compared with the circle's other female writers like Stella Kleve and Alfhild Agrell. As Ernst Ahlgren – pseudonym for the author Victoria Benedictsson from southern Sweden – said about Anne Charlotte upon visiting Stockholm: "There is something free, refreshing, and courageous about her that attracts. What a shame that she is rich!"

But her full potential she did not begin to fulfill until, at 39, she met the Neapolitan mathematician Pasquale del Pezzo, Duke of Cajanello, obtained a divorce from her husband, married the Duke, and settled in Italy. Passionate love, second marriage and the birth of a much-longed-for son (at the age of 42) introduced a richer, more nuanced emotional register into her writings. The titles of her last collection of short stories, published in 1889, read like prophetic shorthand notations for her personal odyssey: "Narrow Horizon," "Travel Abroad," "Marriage for Love," "About Marriage," "A Miracle," and "Equality."

What she might have accomplished with her new-found worldview and fulfillment we can only guess: she died in 1892 at the age of 43, of appendicitis.

Career

One of the most acknowledged women in the Swedish "modern breakthrough," Anne Charlotte Leffler was translated into Dano-Norwegian, English, German, Russian, and Italian. Ingeborg Nordin Hennel argues that Leffler's debt to Ibsen represented neither weakness nor subversion but a deliberate tactic in order to be heard. A desire to be heard prompted also Leffler's first plays *Skådespelerskan* (The Actress) (1873) and *Pastorsadjunkten* (The Curate) (1876), both anonymously submitted to protect her government-official husband and performed at the prestigious Royal Dramatic Theatre in Stockholm. Once *The Actress* – about a Nora-like choice between career and marriage – was accepted, Leffler went on to appear – still anonymously – in the play.

Carefully observed and nuanced dialogue is a hallmark both of her stories and her dramas. Throughout her writing career, Leffler kept returning to the dramatic form, though only one more time – in *Elfvan* (The Elf) (1880) – to the stage. Of her thirteen major works, eight are full-length plays, joining the Ibsen-inspired debate about, e.g., married woman's right to property, the double standard, and the tyranny of convention. *Sanna kvinnor* (*True Women*) (1883), her fourth, written under her own name, was her greatest public success on the stage.

True Women (1883)

Written and premiered in 1883, *True Women* was not only one of Sweden's first success-fully produced plays by a female writer but also Sweden's first major socio-realistic play dealing with the explosive "woman question," predated only by Leffler's own *The Actress* (1873). Norway had already seen Björnstjerne Björnson's *The Newlyweds* (1865), *The Bankrupt* (1874), and *A Gauntlet* (1883) as well as Ibsen's *A Doll House* (1879) and *Ghosts* (1881). In Sweden, Strindberg had published the breakthrough novel *The Red Room* (1879), but his short story collection *Married* (1884–86) and dramas like *The Father* (1887) and *Miss Julie* (1888) were yet to be written. At the time, Leffler was influential, admired, controversial: a member of society and a married woman who could expose the debauched upper classes and speak from experience about the conflict between marriage and career. In *True Women* she touched on two recent hotly debated developments: the passing in 1874 of a law allowing married women to dispose of their own income and the founding in 1878 of the British Federation against legalized prostitution.

Like Ibsen, Björnson, Agrell, Sonia Kovalevsky, Stella Kleve, Ernst Ahlgren, and the other socio-realist writers of the 1870s–80s, Leffler broke with literary tradition, depicted contemporary life, and aimed at lifelikeness. They all wanted to expose social ills and start a debate that would result in reform. Leffler was especially good at writing natural dialogue. Her focus was women in upper middle-class Stockholm, though she set a number of her short stories in other milieus. In *True Women* she examines the position of married women, but unlike Ibsen in *A Doll House*, she does not put all the blame on male-dominated society. She criticizes not only adulterous and self-centered husbands but also "true women," their eternally forgiving and self-effacing wives. The play was thus among the first in Scandinavia to attack both male and female attitudes. Also in contrast to *A Doll House*, which ends with an image of freedom for Nora, *True Women*'s naturalistic ending was felt to be "sad" – as the Norwegian critic Mathilde Schjött explained – "because it must be, since it is so modern."

The socio-realists broke also with theatrical tradition, deliberately challenging the then current notion of theater as an institution for amusement, escape, and socializing. As Leffler herself said about *True Women*, "the intent of this piece is not to 'be successful,' only to stir up a fight!" Nor was it wholly successful when it premiered in 1883: the critics rather liked it, the audience did not. Since that time, however, *True Women* has proven to be Leffler's most enduring work, revived at the Royal Dramatic Theatre no fewer than three times (1885, 1918, and 1988) and produced by Swedish Television (1974, repeated 1975 and 1978).

One reason for the play's warm reception in the late twentieth century – "watch out for Mrs. Leffler, the woman is still dangerous" – may be that it deftly exposes certain psycho-social dynamics and features of the dysfunctional family: absent and weak father, enabling mother, co-dependency, male dominance, workaholism, sibling rivalry, denial, martyr complex, mother fixation, and so on. If judged by more recent playwrighting standards, the plot may seem contrived and the characters two-dimensional: most of the men are conspirators and most of the women happy and cooperative victims of the male conspiracy. The heroine, Berta, and hero, the accountant Lundberg, are noble and self-sacrificial. The title "True Women" is explained several times in the course of the play. But the ending is deeply ironic: nothing has been solved, although – depending upon how the confrontation between Berta and Lundberg is played – the 1887 and 1918 texts support the possibility of a conventional "happy ending" for Berta and Lundberg.

Ibsen, Strindberg, Leffler . . .

Having *True Women* and several other plays accepted by the Royal Dramatic Theatre – Sweden's national and most prestigious stage – was quite a feather in Leffler's cap. In her lifetime she invited frequent and favorable comparison with both Ibsen and Strindberg – neither of whom had yet been accorded genius status. Her first volume of short stories published under her own name, *From Life I* (1882), was hailed as the "greatest work of modern Swedish literature after [Strindberg's] *The Red Room* (1879)" and the short story "Tvifvel" (Doubts) from that collection was recognized as a direct response to Ibsen's *Brand*. In the 1880s – much to Strindberg's chagrin and envy – her plays were more performed than his. In his original preface to *Married II* he attacked Leffler and aimed a special kick at the "monster" Berta in *True Women*.

For a time, women playwrights admired and emulated Leffler. Her plays were translated and personal friendships and strong shared interests joined her to a larger circle of politically enlightened women like Eleanor Marx and Annie Besant. But she had relatively little influence on the next generation of Swedish female writers. In part this may be explained by her failure to

leave the 1880s behind, in part by her move
away from Sweden and her premature
death. It is not until the twentieth century
that she has been rediscovered and given
the attention and appreciation she deserves.

Plays by Anne Charlotte Leffler

Skådespelerskan (The Actress) (1873)
Under toffeln (In Her Power) (1873)
Pastorsadjunkten (The Curate) (1876)
Elfvan (The Elf) (1880)
Sanna kvinnor (True Women) (1883)
Hur man gör godt (How To Do Good) (1885)
Kampen för lyckan (The Fight for Happiness)
(1887) double drama – with Sonia
Kovalevsky
Familjelycka (Family Happiness) (1891)
Moster Malvina (Aunt Malvina) (1891)
Den kärleken (That's Love For You) (1891)

Acknowledgments

For assistance with research in Stockholm,
Sweden, I would like to acknowledge the
staff at the Royal Library, Henrik Bramsjö
and Ulla Orre at the Archive and Library
of the Royal Dramatic Theatre, and Karin
Widegren at the Drottningholm Theatre
Museum. Thanks also to Jens Widestedt
of Folmer Hansen Theatre Publisher,
Linda Romanus, Peter Larlham, and,
especially, Susanna Nied.

Photo from the 1988 production *True
Women* at the Royal Dramatic Theatre taken
by Mats Bäcker. Reproduced with the
permission of Mats Bäcker and the Royal
Dramatic Theatre.

True Women

(Sanna kvinnor)

[A Play in Three Acts]
1883
Play translation by Anne-Charlotte Hanes Harvey

Anne Charlotte Leffler Edgren

Translator's note on the punctuation *

To avoid dulling or perverting the author's intention, the original emphases and punctuation have, as far as possible, been retained in the dialogue. (The punctuation in the stage directions, on the other hand, has been normalized.)

Particularly notable is the author's idiosyncratic and ungrammatical use of the period and exclamation mark to indicate a character's emotional involvement. Even where the sentence structure indicates a question, she often replaces the expected question mark with a period or exclamation mark. The period indicates downward inflection and relative control, the exclamation mark an outburst with relative lack of control.

The author uses single double dashes (--), double double dashes, even, in a few cases, triple and quadruple double dashes to help "direct" the action. Single double dashes indicate a quick breath or speech that is broken off by someone else, double double dashes represent a beat of thought or a longer break by the speaking character, and triple double dashes usually mark a longer, momentous break in the overall flow. (These are mere indications; obviously the sensitive actor and director will translate the rough signs on the printed page into nuanced action.) To avoid misinterpretation, I have chosen to retain the original system of double dashes rather than "translate" them into "m"-dashes and ellipses.

Characters *

BARK

MRS. BARK

BERTA ⎫
⎬ their daughters
LISSI ⎭

WILHELM, Lissi's husband

LUNDBERG, accountant

*The original also included LOVISA, the Barks' former housekeeper, and the non-speaking role of VILLE, Lissi's and Wilhelm's son.

[**Place**
The action takes place in the apartment of an upper middle-class family in Stockholm in the 1880s.]

Act I

A room furnished to serve as both dining room and living room.[1] In the back, door to the hallway [leading to the apartment's exterior door]; right [i.e., stage left--all directions are from the audience's point of view], we see the door to Berta's room; left, the door to her mother's. Left a desk, right a sofa and a small sewing table. In the center of the room a fair-sized dining table with matching chairs around it. In the back, a sideboard.

MRS. BARK *(Sitting on the sofa by the lighted lamp on the sewing table, rises and calls to the room right)* Berta dear! Aren't you going to bed soon? You know, you promised me not to stay up this evening.

BERTA *(Answering from inside her room)* But it's just a little past ten.

MRS. BARK Yes, but remember that you've been staying up till two and three in the morning the last few nights.

BERTA *(Appears in the doorway.)* But I have still more pages left to copy. I've never had a copying job that was as slow as this. The handwriting is so hard to decipher, and you know I promised to drop the whole thing off tomorrow morning early.

MRS. BARK *(Goes over to her and pats her cheek.)* Go to bed now anyway. I'll wake you up early. You look so tired -- and your eyes are red. Remember that we can expect Lissi any day now. She'll be upset if you look too peaked.

BERTA Yes, that's true. It will really be fun to see Lissi. *(Thoughtfully)* If only Wilhelm thought so, too!

MRS. BARK But, dear Berta, how can you say that. Why wouldn't he be happy to see his wife!

BERTA Wilhelm is so moody. If she comes at the wrong time, she won't get such a warm welcome, that's for sure.

MRS. BARK Shh, dear child, you're tired this evening, that's why everything looks so dark to you.

BERTA What time do you think Papa will be home tonight?

MRS. BARK He'll be here soon, you'll see.

BERTA Are you going to wait up for him?

MRS. BARK Yes -- you know I will.

BERTA Well -- then I'll go in and sit down and copy some more. *(Goes toward her room.)*

MRS. BARK No, Berta, don't, for my sake. You know that I *must* wait up for Papa. If he knew that everyone at home was fast asleep there is no telling how long he would stay out -- he always gets really angry with me when he comes home and finds me waiting up -- and why would he if he didn't feel that there was some kind of bond between us.

BERTA A very tiny bond, I would say. It was three o'clock when he came home last night.

MRS. BARK How do you know that? Your light was out. I thought you were asleep.

BERTA *(Jokingly)* When you're waiting up, I sleep like the proverbial cat when his mistress is churning butter -- with one eye open.

MRS. BARK *(Pats her lovingly and shakes her head.)* Will you go to bed now?

BERTA It depends on you, Mama. Will you?

MRS. BARK Yes, as you wish. Good night!
(MRS. BARK kisses BERTA; extinguishes the lamp. They go in separate directions, BERTA to the right, MRS. BARK to the left; nod to each other in the doorway, BERTA blows her mother a kiss. The stage is dark and empty for a moment.)

MRS. BARK *(Comes in with a candle in her hand, puts it down, tiptoes to Berta's door and looks through the keyhole. Opens Berta's door. Reproachfully)* Berta! Are you working again?

BERTA *(Comes running to her and throws her arms around her neck, imitating her tone of voice)* Mama! What are you doing up again? *(Runs back into her own room and calls out)* Look, now I'm blowing out the candle and getting undressed in the dark.

MRS. BARK Then give me the matches.

BERTA *(Appears again in the doorway, smiling.)* Here they are. My only ones. *(BERTA hands her a matchbox, kisses her, goes back into her room and closes the door. MRS. BARK goes back into her room and takes the candle with her. The stage is again empty and dark for a little while. BERTA comes out in the dark, dressed in a peignoir, walks stealthily on tiptoe over to her mother's door and looks through the crack. Knocks on the door.)*

MRS. BARK *(Gives a brief scream from the inside; opens the door)* How you scared me!

BERTA No more than you deserve, since you wanted to trick me. What's the meaning of this? You light your lamp and take out your work -- does this mean you are going to bed?

MRS. BARK *(Comes out with the candle.)* Oh, my darling, if you'd only let me do as I wish. I cannot sleep when Papa is out. I can't help it.

BERTA Oh, yes -- you're destroying yourself with this eternal night watch. Let Papa keep on gambling as much as he wants -- we can't do much about that any more. But for you to get sick with self-reproach and exhaustion -- that would be much worse.

MRS. BARK Ah -- if I have taken it for so long, I'm sure I can take it a few more years. And nobody knows what faithful, untiring love can do in the long run.

BERTA Love -- he isn't worth anyone's love any longer.

MRS. BARK You are a bit too harsh, dear Berta. I am sure you are fond of your father, a little, yes, deep down -- it would be unnatural otherwise -- but you mustn't talk about him so harshly -- it hurts me to hear it.

BERTA   I am not fond of him.

MRS. BARK   Berta -- he is your father!

BERTA   I don't owe him any thanks for that. I can't be fond of a person just because he happens to be my father. I have no fondness for somebody I don't respect.

MRS. BARK   That's because you don't understand the true nature of love itself. There is nothing hard about being fond of people whom we can look up to -- but the *forgiving* love, Berta dear -- that we may need, all of us, you see -- and that's why --

BERTA   Ah! It's just this *forgiving* love which makes me so furious! If it actually made people more upright -- yes, that would be different -- but when it just demoralizes! Just think, Mama, how kind -- how inexhaustible you've always been in your love -- and has Papa perhaps shown the slightest signs of improvement because of it?

MRS. BARK   You know that, in spite of his flaws, there are many people who are fond of Papa. He has so much natural charm -- -- -- --

BERTA   Hm!

MRS. BARK   You cannot deny that.

BERTA   It is precisely this charm that I can't stand.

MRS. BARK   Oh, Berta. When you know how good he is, deep down.

BERTA   Good -- yes, I know. Spineless characters are usually called good -- I find I'm developing a real contempt for goodness.

MRS. BARK   But -- Papa really has such good intentions. So often he has promised to try to conquer his unfortunate passion for gambling. And I really think that eventually -- -- --

BERTA   Ah -- these promises! these eternal lies!

MRS. BARK   Berta dear -- you're talking about your father.

BERTA   *(Embraces her)* But, Mama, it is only for your sake that I am so sharp with him. To see how he treats you -- and then to see you, always just as tender and loving -- to know what a love like yours is worth, and then to see it torn and walked on like -- like -- a weed that refuses to be killed.

MRS. BARK   You exaggerate. Papa has never treated me badly.

BERTA   No? Well, he hasn't beaten you, I think --

MRS. BARK   Oh -- Berta!

(The front door bell rings.)

MRS. BARK   *(Starts)* The doorbell! It isn't Papa, because he has a key. Who can it be this late! Something has happened to Papa --

(BERTA runs out [through the upstage door] and opens the front door. MRS. BARK listens apprehensively.)

BERTA   *(Is heard outside [in the hallway].)* Oh, Wilhelm, is that you? You gave us quite a scare. *(Looks in at the door)* Mama dear, it's Wilhelm.

MRS. BARK   Wilhelm! this late! What's the matter? -- Lissi? -- the children? *(Runs anxiously up to WILHELM, who enters in tails and white scarf, elegant, with buttoned-up gloves.)*[2] Tell me what it is! What is it? The children?

WILHELM   Goodness sakes -- if I'd had any idea I would scare you so, I wouldn't have come. I'm on my way from a dinner party, as you can see -- and when I walked past here and saw the lights on in the living room I had an impulse to pop my head in. One never quite knows what to do after a happy day like this. One is too excited to go to bed -- and at the same time one is a bit uneasy. *(Yawns)* What's so reassuring about this house is that the back door is always left open. One can tell that Papa-in-law is assistant caretaker.[3] *(Walks back and forth in the room, looks at himself in the mirror, whistles, sits down, then jumps up again.)* By the way, Lissi says hi. I had a letter from her yesterday.

MRS. BARK   We-ell! Then perhaps you know -- -- ?

(BERTA stops her with a look.)

WILHELM   Know what?

MRS. BARK   No -- nothing -- I mean -- that she is fine.

WILHELM   Yes, thank God! She doesn't seem to be suffering from any other illness than jealousy. But she is really afflicted by that one. Her letters are starting to get quite boring. Nothing but complaints forever. "Why do you write so seldom? Why don't you ever come home? Have you forgotten me?" and so on. She doesn't know the Stockholm life, she doesn't. Here one has other things to do than to sit down and write long sentimental letters to one's wife.

BERTA But couldn't Lissi come and visit you in town since the Committee will be in session for such a long time?

WILHELM And leave the children?! Or drag them along on such a long steamer journey at this time of year? No, spare me, and whatever you do, Berta, don't go inspiring her to do anything foolish.

BERTA If I were in her place, I would come and surprise you.

WILHELM Surprise me! That wouldn't occur to Lissi.

BERTA Why not?

WILHELM She knows I can't stand surprises.

BERTA If I had a husband who couldn't stand surprises, I would -- I think just because of that --

WILHELM I don't doubt it. But Lissi is fortunately not like you. Besides -- do you think she has the money to make such a long journey without my permission?

BERTA Doesn't she have any money? When you are away for so long?

WILHELM At the office, she is allowed to sign for a certain amount every month -- but not an *öre* above that. -- Listen, Berta, you'll help me get a really pretty dress for Lissi that I can take with me when I go home -- arrange to have it made by the smartest seamstress in town -- the one who sews for the aristocracy and the court --

BERTA But Lissi doesn't belong to the aristocracy. And does she really want to spend a couple of hundred crowns for a dress when --

WILHELM Does *she* want to! When I'm paying for it!

BERTA But she would be happy, I think, if you gave her the money instead and she could use it as she pleases.

WILHELM But *I* wouldn't be so happy, I tell you. I want to see my wife well-dressed -- I can't stand those small town get-ups any longer, now that I have been in Stockholm for so long. Here the ladies have a certain *je ne sais quoi* -- ah!

BERTA I don't know anyone who dresses as tastefully as Lissi.

WILHELM Tastefully -- oh, I suppose -- I don't mean to say that it's always so tasteful, the way they dress here -- but there is a certain style -- something sophisticated, exquisite, *piquant* -- even the café waitresses -- hm! [*To* MRS. BARK] Is Papa-in-law home?

MRS. BARK No, not yet. But I'm sure he'll be here soon.

WILHELM Listen -- you really should try to keep your eye on him a little.

MRS. BARK How so?

WILHELM I just heard someone mention him at dinner today -- they say that he has been losing heavily at the table every night for some time now.

BERTA How is it possible? He doesn't have any more money to lose.

WILHELM He is probably going into debt. [*To* MRS. BARK] And then you'll be the one who has to pay.

BERTA Mama can't do that. That's impossible.

WILHELM [*To* BERTA] It's unavoidable. It's been clear for a long time that he wouldn't quit until he had gambled away everything he owned.

BERTA He gambled away everything *he* owned a long time ago. Now it is Mama's money that's at stake.

WILHELM Well -- it amounts to the same thing. Of course at one time it was Mama-in-law's, all of it.

BERTA But the money that Mama still has left was given to her with the express condition that it would be her sole property.

WILHELM What good are such conditions, if he is in trouble now. Obviously, as long as there is any money at all -- -- Besides -- what are you going to do? Of course Mama-in-law can say no -- but for how long? In any case, she won't have any peace and quiet until she has given away her last crown.

BERTA That is true! I could see it all coming! And that's why long ago I came up with a plan to use in an emergency. Lundberg, the accountant at the bank, advised me to do it.

MRS. BARK How could you take him into your confidence about something like this!

BERTA He is a good man. Him you can really trust.

WILHELM (*Laughing*) What do you know, I think Berta has a *tendre* for him. You have strange taste, I must say. I've never met a worse bore in my life.

BERTA Bore. Yes, it's true that he doesn't talk as much as the rest of you. But he acts instead. The way he works and sacrifices for his mother and his brothers and sisters -- it is noble.

WILHELM   Noble! God knows, it's all the same to me. But in any case you surely can't marry a pauper who already has a large family to support.

BERTA   That's the noblest thing about him -- he has had to give up all thoughts of marrying, ever. And that's also why I safely can have him for a friend and confidant, without being misunderstood -- *(Playfully)* so that arrow missed its mark, dear sir.

WILHELM   Well, what a perfect match. You of course are also thinking of living and dying unwed.

BERTA   *(Patting her mother)* I will never leave Mama. -- But don't you want to hear my plan now? Those last few paltry bonds that are absolutely necessary for our continued existence -- you are going to sign them over to me as a gift, Mama, then I'll deposit them and see to it that Papa doesn't get at them.

MRS. BARK   Sign them over to you and Lissi, you mean.

BERTA   No, not to Lissi *(Jokingly)* because she has a husband.

MRS. BARK   But Berta --

WILHELM   *(Bows)* I'm most grateful for -- --

BERTA   I think you understand, Wilhelm -- if you were to manage this money, it would be as if Mama were receiving financial support from you -- and to secure Lissi's right I am also making a will.

WILHELM   No, really. You are too good. We will be most obliged. -- But don't you see that this whole transaction would be a kind of deception.

BERTA   Of whom?

WILHELM   Of whom! Of -- of -- Papa-in-law, obviously.

BERTA   The money is Mama's. She has the legal right to do with it whatever she chooses. Now when the law finally has done what it could to protect a wife's rights, you still want to remake the law and say she doesn't have any.[4]

WILHELM   All that -- that is just quibbling and hair-splitting. I don't get involved with things like that. But it would be cheating your Papa's creditors.

BERTA   When they agreed to gamble with him they knew very well that he didn't own anything.

WILHELM   Hare-brained modern ideas. The wife dispose of her own money! It is simply absolutely idiotic -- leads to the dissolution of the family.

BERTA   But it doesn't lead to the dissolution of the family if the husband uses up his wife's money by gambling and being extravagant?

WILHELM   No -- it doesn't have to lead to that at all. It is the wife who holds the family together, and if only she never forgets her duties, then the husband will surely return to home and hearth -- though he may have been a little extravagant for a while.

BERTA   *(Covers her ears with her hands)* Oh, Wilhelm, don't you hear how far off that is? Oh yes, you reason beautifully, you lords of creation.

WILHELM   *(Smiling)* Ah well -- even if I don't have as agile and sharp a tongue as my dear sister-in-law -- --

BERTA   *You*! I have never in my life had as agile a tongue as you. Do you think that I could utter all those pretty phrases about holding the family together and home and hearth and all that.

WILHELM   *(Jokingly)* Yes -- to have a debate with you -- is just like racing a skittish calf.

MRS. BARK   You're not misunderstanding her, dear Wilhelm? She is fighting for me -- and she means so well, although she likes to tease a little.

WILHELM   Yes -- I'll say! Phew! I am quite sweaty. -- Now why do you have to argue with me about business. I don't meddle in yours. Take it all, by all means. -- To ask for my advice, as if you ever cared about what I say! Do as you please -- the crazier, the better -- it's all the same to me.

MRS. BARK   No, Wilhelm, you mustn't be unfair to Berta. I think you know how she has worked and sacrificed during these last years -- how she has denied herself the smallest pleasure, the most insignificant expense for herself in order to lighten my cares. (BERTA *tries to interrupt her.)* No, let me finish. Oh, believe me, I know more than you think. I know how you used to worry and regret that your income wouldn't suffice to keep us all once Papa had finished off what little we still had left. *(Turns to* WILHELM*)* And I remember how happy, how really overwhelmingly, ecstatically happy she was last year when I got that little legacy with sole rights to a small sum of money.

WILHELM Yes, I remember that, too. And I remember how I thought then that my dear sister-in-law really was fairly -- how shall I put it -- fairly mercenary -- --

BERTA It was a big, big load off my mind that moment. Oh -- how I had been worrying about how to increase my income by just that small amount that suddenly seemed to rain down on me as if from heaven -- it was exactly what we needed to be able to live. But that Papa should now get his hands on this money and waste it all -- I can't bear to think about it.

MRS. BARK No, he won't, my girl, don't worry.

WILHELM No, that would really be too bad. Your plan may not be so bad after all, dear sister-in-law. You have your bright moments. You go ahead and talk to your friend from the bank. And now good night. In any case, I won't meddle in your arrangements. (Cuffs BERTA playfully) Are you angry, miss?

BERTA It doesn't pay to be angry with you. I am sure you sleep just as soundly anyway.

WILHELM (Yawns) I will certainly try. Good night. (Leaves)

BERTA (To her mother) We must take care of this without delay. First thing tomorrow morning I'll go to the bank and see Lundberg and ask him to come here to help us with the deed of gift.

MRS. BARK Only you're sure we're not doing anything that isn't right, Berta? A wife's property is also the property of the husband, you know.

BERTA No, Mama dear, that's the way it used to be, but it's not that way any longer now. And you were willed this modest sum by your Aunt with the express condition -- she would never have given it to you if she had thought it would go the same way as all the rest -- if so she would rather have donated it to charities along with the rest of her money. But now she gave it to you specifically so you wouldn't go without when Papa had spent all your money.

MRS. BARK Yes, Aunt Malla meant well by me -- but she never married and never understood what marriage means. She didn't understand that a wife must help her husband as long as she owns any-thing -- no laws in the world can alter

that fact. I don't understand laws and all that -- but what once was right will still be right, change the laws however much you like.

BERTA Just the opposite, I'd say. What used to be justice is now an injustice scream-ing to high heaven, at least as far as women are concerned. Now it is no longer a woman's greatest virtue to resemble a dog.

MRS. BARK A dog! But Berta!

BERTA Yes, precisely a dog. The more you beat it, the more affectionate it becomes. Now, when even the law has started to want to make women into human beings, they still cannot free themselves from tradition. They'd rather take kicks and no food than live without a master.

MRS. BARK You are right, my child. Your mother doesn't deserve anything but to be despised.

BERTA You, Mama! You are the best person on earth -- so loving -- so good!

MRS. BARK Why don't you say "weak"? You said just now that goodness is nothing but weakness.

BERTA Don't pay attention to all my stupid words -- I get so bitter sometimes when I think about -- but that's not important. No, goodness like yours, it is of an entirely different kind. You have a sense for what is right, and that I think is worth more than the usual so-called goodness. And that's why you must never agree to give Papa this money -- you will realize how unjust it would be. I work as hard as I can -- you know I do -- but I cannot support us all three by myself.

MRS. BARK No, no! my darling girl. But Papa will besiege me with pleas and threats -- it will be hard.

BERTA Yes, it is precisely to spare you all that that I want you to sign over the papers to me. He doesn't dare take them back from me.

(The sound of [a key in] the [front] door lock is heard.)

MRS. BARK Hush! Somebody at the door. Could it really be Papa already? Go then, my girl -- go, please.

BERTA I'd certainly like to give him a piece of my mind -- -- --

MRS. BARK No, for God's sake! He'd only get angry -- you won't gain anything -- --

BERTA Oh -- if I only got to speak out for once!

MRS. BARK Berta -- for my sake! I'd just end up having to pay for it later!

BERTA Yes -- that is true -- as *good* as he is -- *(Kisses her mother's hands; exits right but leaves the door ajar)*

(BARK comes in from the back.)

MRS. BARK *(Goes up to him, kindly)* Just imagine! Home already, my dear?

BARK *(Throws his hat on a chair)* Tonight I've gambled for the last time.

MRS. BARK Ah, Pontus -- if I could only believe that.

BARK If you could believe that -- but you have my word on it -- it is a vow of mine -- --

MRS. BARK But you've said that so many times before, my dear -- --

BARK You hear what I'm telling you: it's a vow -- don't you think I'm man enough to keep my vows! Besides, I have lost my taste for gambling -- I have had the most infernal bad luck -- --

MRS. BARK Soo -- you've lost?

BARK Yes.

MRS. BARK A lot?

BARK Well, it depends -- considering my assets, it is a not inconsiderable amount -- --

MRS. BARK How then were you able to pay?

BARK No -- I haven't been able to pay -- that's just it. I have had to borrow a little here and a little there from good friends.

MRS. BARK Ah, Pontus, you shouldn't have -- --

BARK What do you mean? Oh -- good, kind people -- they don't mind at all. But now the damned rascals have gone and finagled so that all the small debts are consolidated on one hand -- and then that scoundrel Lind comes and presents me with a bill this evening.

MRS. BARK Lind -- he's your good friend?

BARK Yes, of course he is -- a kind man -- the most honorable man in the world -- but how can I be sure he doesn't cheat me? One thing is sure, I didn't have any idea my debt could be up to such a big sum.

MRS. BARK How big a sum is it then?

BARK A bagatelle, on the whole. The stupid thing is I have to pay it tomorrow.

MRS. BARK Tomorrow! But isn't Lind well off?

BARK Nonsense. He! He's lost everything he ever had! And now the rascal says that he absolutely needs the money tomorrow.

MRS. BARK How much is it?

BARK Well -- if you absolutely must know -- just a paltry sum of a few thousand.

MRS. BARK A few *thousand!*

BARK Yes, it is unpleasant -- I admit. But then it won't happen to me again -- tonight was the last time I ever set foot in that gambling den.

MRS. BARK And where are you going to get the money?

BARK *(Cheerfully)* I thought I'd borrow from my little wife. 'Cause she is a capitalist.

MRS. BARK You know I don't have any ready money -- just a few bonds.

BARK Yes -- that is just as good. I thought I would borrow against the bonds from the bank for the moment.

MRS. BARK And when will you repay that loan?

BARK By and by.

MRS. BARK With what? If you decrease the capital, which is so small to begin with -- --

BARK Berta will have to contribute a little more to the household. It's no more than fair since I spent money on her expensive education.

MRS. BARK For the most part, Berta put herself through school. And she is already contributing everything she earns to the household.

BARK Well, then she'll have to work a little harder and get a better income.

MRS. BARK She works all day and sometimes she has to work nights, too.

BARK Does she really? Poor child! Well then -- things will work out, you'll see. I have been thinking a good deal about getting a job myself -- -- --

MRS. BARK My dear -- -- --

BARK What does that mean?

MRS. BARK I think you know that won't happen. You've been thinking about that for seven years now -- ever since we sold Bergfors Manor and moved to Stockholm.[5]

BARK Yes, you'll see, I'll make good my threat one day. But right now it's just a question of getting out of this temporary fix. Now get out the bonds right away so I won't have to wake you up when I go out tomorrow morning.

MRS. BARK I don't have them. They are deposited in the bank.

BARK Whatever for? Well, I suppose you have a proof of deposit, anyway?

MRS. BARK Berta has that.

BARK Berta! What on earth for, Berta! You are an unforgivably weak mother, Julie, I'm telling you straight out. You simply let Berta decide and take over in everything, as if she -- but I -- I don't intend to -- this beats everything! However, you tell Berta to give it back immediately -- --

MRS. BARK I'll go get her. (Goes toward the door right.)

BARK (Stops her) No, no, no! By all means! I have no desire to stand here like a supplicant before my lady daughter. You'll have to straighten this out with her by yourselves. You just tell her from me, if she makes a fuss or creates a scene or gives you any difficulties, it's not she who is the master of this house -- and I have to have the papers first thing tomorrow morning. Now good night, my dear. (Kisses her) If you want to, you can always tell Berta that I have resolved never to gamble again. And listen -- you can also tell her that I intend to get some kind of job so that I'll increase my income. That should please her.

(MRS. BARK smiles doubtfully.)

What -- what is this?

MRS. BARK Don't take this the wrong way, my dear -- but, you know, I don't want to pass on that particular greeting to Berta. She doesn't quite dare trust your promises. But if she were to see you act -- that would be a different story.

BARK Ah -- I don't need to be answerable to my own daughter, either in word or action. There is really something so unfeminine about Berta -- so -- off-putting -- so unpleasant. It is like I've always said, Aunt Malla all over again. Ah -- you certainly were something entirely different, you were -- in your youth -- yes, on top of that, even today you are far prettier than your younger daughter. Now Lissi -- she's something else again -- she resembles you -- she is a true woman, just like you. Speaking of Lissi, when is she coming?

MRS. BARK She couldn't say exactly. The steamer schedule is so irregular now in the fall.

BARK Well -- good night now, my dear. Now don't forget what I've said -- early tomorrow morning it all has to be ready. (Exits left.)

BERTA (Comes in from the right) Yes, tomorrow morning early it all has to be ready. Don't be so anxious, dear darling Mama -- I'll handle it all. As long as I live I won't allow him to ruin you.

(A ring at the front door.)

MRS. BARK There's the doorbell again! My God, Berta, how anxious I am. Just think, what if they're coming to collect! If they arrange for a foreclosure!

BERTA Oh, now Mama, don't be childish. (Runs out and opens the door.)

(LISSI enters, dressed in a traveling suit, followed by BERTA.)

MRS. BARK Lissi! It's you, my darling. (Embraces and caresses her) My little girl -- to think I have you here now. And Ville, where is he? And why are you arriving so late?

LISSI (Speaking all the time in an unnatural voice, stiffly) The steamer was stopped by fog in the archipelago. I left Ville and the maid onboard -- but I myself was too eager to stay -- I longed so to see Wilhelm.

BERTA Well -- why didn't you go straight home to him? He left here a little while ago.

LISSI He was here?

MRS. BARK Yes, he came from a dinner party and looked in on his way.

LISSI He didn't say where he was going?

MRS. BARK We thought he was going home.

LISSI (As before) I saw him.

MRS. BARK You saw him!

LISSI He was speaking to a woman.

BERTA Well?

LISSI Then they separated, and I hurried to catch up with him. It was right outside his apartment.

MRS. BARK and BERTA Well?

LISSI When he got to the door, she came up to him again. They went in together.

MRS. BARK Dear child, it must have been someone he knew, living in the same house.

LISSI That's what I thought, too. I couldn't believe anything bad, though I had a sense of foreboding. I rang the front doorbell.

MRS. BARK Well -- didn't the concierge open?

LISSI Yes. I asked for Wilhelm. Then she said --

MRS. BARK and BERTA What -- what?

LISSI Then she said that there already was one woman up there with him -- and then she called me a -- -- -- and sent me packing -- she'd send for the police, she said -- and then she slammed the door right in my face. (*Long pause. As before*) I thought of going down to the harbor and throwing myself in right away. But then I wanted to bring Ville here to you first.

BERTA Lissi! Oh!

MRS. BARK (*Embraces her, sobbing*) My child!

Curtain

Act II

Same room. Morning. The ACCOUNTANT *[*LUNDBERG*],* BERTA, *and* MRS. BARK *are all standing by the desk.*

MRS. BARK Dear Mr. Lundberg -- Berta puts such trust in your sense of what is right, I know that. You are quite sure that I have a right to withhold this money from my husband?

LUNDBERG (*Harshly*) Yes -- unless you consider yourself to have greater obligations to your husband's gambling companions than to your children.

MRS. BARK No, but -- it is considered a point of honor to pay one's debts.

LUNDBERG Quite right -- unless one takes from one party to pay the other.

MRS. BARK But this money is mine.

LUNDBERG Yes -- and given to you with the express condition that it was not to be used to pay your husband's debts but only for yourself and your children, wasn't it?

MRS. BARK Oh yes, that is true. But are such conditions absolutely binding?

LUNDBERG Allow me to ask -- if you now so nobly paid your husband's debts -- who would then, later on, pay yours?

MRS. BARK My debts! I've never had any debts.

LUNDBERG No, not so far. But when your husband has gone through all of your modest capital -- for if he now is given part of it, he will of course soon take the rest -- and when you thus have been reduced to living, all three of you, on Berta's income -- when you find that this is not sufficient, do you know what you will do then? You will be buying groceries on credit, go into debt for paltry sums in all the shops -- and then who will pay? (*Pause*) Forgive me for being so indelicate as to meddle in your business like this --

but Miss Berta has appointed me her financial adviser and I consider it my duty to speak out. And how do you think that your daughter will be able to hold up under all the worries and humiliations which you will be drawn into. She, too, will have to go into debt -- perhaps borrow from supervisors and fellow employees at the bank -- borrow though knowing that she will never be able to repay them -- but what does that matter, as long as your husband gets money for his gambling debts --

BERTA No, Mr. Lundberg, you go too far -- don't you see how you're hurting Mama?

LUNDBERG If, generally speaking, people were not so afraid of hurting each other, much evil in this world could be avoided.

MRS. BARK But what you're saying is absurd, anyway. My Berta is too proud by nature to ever humiliate herself like that -- borrow without being able to pay -- beg from her supervisors --

LUNDBERG Your daughter, Mrs. Bark, can do all for someone she loves, even humiliate herself.

BERTA (*Half jokingly*) Hush! I don't under-stand what has come over you, Mr. Lundberg. You are sounding so -- you assume an authority in this matter that -- --

LUNDBERG And have you not, by taking me into your confidence, given me the right to do so, Miss Berta? (*To* MRS. BARK) I know best how much your daughter does for you -- I, who see her daily at the bank. It has happened that she's been so tired when she's come in that she's been ready to faint -- --

(BERTA *tries hard to stop him.*)

LUNDBERG (*Pretending not to notice*) A couple of times she has had such severe headache attacks that she had to interrupt her work -- but no one was able to persuade her to go home since she didn't want to worry her mother -- --

MRS. BARK (*Embraces her, touched*) My dearest child! (*Eagerly to* LUNDBERG) Show me where to sign. (*Sits at the desk and looks at the paper.*)

BERTA (*In a low voice to* LUNDBERG) Well, you're certainly behaving like a gentle-man, Mr. Lundberg. What treason! And what a chatterbox you've become all of a sudden, you, who've always been so quiet. You have a gift of gab like -- yes, like Papa himself, I swear! Yes, you're right to look embarrassed! Now stand there and feel ashamed. *(Points a finger at him, playfully. He seizes it and kisses her hand.)*

MRS. BARK *(Turning)* Is this where I sign, Mr. Lundberg? [*Sits down and signs*]

LUNDBERG *(Takes his hat)* Good morning!

MRS. BARK But let us first thank you properly, dear Mr. Lundberg!

LUNDBERG *(Gruffly)* No need. Good morning. (LUNDBERG *gives a bow and leaves.)*

BERTA *(Embracing her mother and swinging her around)* Oh Mama, I'm so happy -- I'm so happy! You know, there comes over me sometimes in the middle of all my worries such an abandoned, ecstatic joy of life. I want to shout, I want to dance! I am so happy. But then I have won a big victory today. -- -- You look quite amazed, Mama. Do you perhaps think like Wilhelm that I am mercenary? Oh no, it's something other than a few bonds that I have won today. *(She pulls* MRS. BARK *over to a chair and sits down by her feet on a stool.)* You shall hear what it is, Mama. It is a confidence I will share with you.

MRS. BARK Ah, I understand, my child. He has proposed. So you really do like him?

BERTA *(Rises abruptly and crosses the floor, stops for a while with lowered head, shakes her head and returns to her place)* No Mama, you are mistaken -- that wasn't what I meant. It was only about you and me that I wanted to talk. *(Speaking with her face turned away, while playing with* MRS. BARK's *hand)* You see, ever since I started to think for myself there is one thing that has always bothered me. That thing is that you have had such a soft spot for Papa that you sacrificed us, Lissi and me, to satisfy his bad inclinations. I remember for example when Lissi had to stop her piano lessons because they were too expensive -- and at the same time Papa went through large amounts. And when I wanted so badly to study abroad for a year -- I thought it was so important for my future -- then you allowed Papa to waste the money that was specifically set aside for that purpose -- -- forgive me, dear dear Mama, for starting to stir all this up -- it is not to reproach you for anything, far from it; it hurt at the time but I have come to realize that it was not your fault -- Papa alone had the right to

dispose of your fortune and you couldn't legally do anything. But I just want to say that these bitter experiences have left a small thorn in my heart -- a persistent thought that Papa, for all his short-comings, meant more to you than Lissi and I and that you would be capable of sacrificing us for him. And I could not stand that, when I knew that I would be able to sacrifice everything, everything, all my personal happiness -- *(Pauses, appears to consider carefully; after a little while repeats emphatically)* yes -- all my personal happiness, for your sake. -- But then I've always kept my spirits up by thinking that if it really mattered, in a case where you *were* able to act, then you would have the strength to resist Papa for our sake -- or rather, for the sake of what is right. Now do you understand why I am so happy today? *(Jumps up)* Oh, but I nearly forgot. I have to deliver that clean copy. *(She goes to the desk, takes the deed of gift and exits to the right; returns right away with a changed expression.)* Oh, Mama, how frivolous I am.

MRS. BARK Whatever now?

BERTA I am surprised at myself. These violent, irresistible attacks of joy and jubilation often come over me when things around me are at their worst. I can't understand it -- it must be a reaction -- an absolute craving to live that is asserting itself. Just think, I had completely forgotten Lissi who's sitting in there crying -- just crying, and doesn't even want to look up.

MRS. BARK We must send for Wilhelm and ask him to come.

BERTA Yes -- I'll write a few lines. *(Writes; reads aloud)* "Come as soon as possible. We have important news from Lissi." *(Folds the letter and addresses it)* Now he ought to come. *(She rises, rolls up some written sheets of paper which she had brought from her room.)* I will send a messenger right away. *(Blows her mother a kiss)* I'll be back soon. If Papa should wake in the meantime, keep stalling him with evasive answers until I get back. It is only fair that I take the brunt of the storm when I am the one who has caused it all. (BERTA *exits upstage.)*

BARK *(Carefully cracks open the door left)* Is Berta gone now? Good -- I was waiting for that. *(Enters in dressing gown and slippers)* I don't want any scenes with my dear daughter. What kind of dire plots have you been hatching here this morning? I thought I heard Berta's friend, the accountant -- unpleasant fellow -- I've never been able to stand him -- has he too been dragged into our affairs, or what's going on?

MRS. BARK Now dear Father -- I think Mr. Lundberg is an excellent man -- and do you know -- I think he is in love with our Berta.

BARK In love with Berta! What peculiar taste. Well well, of course, Berta is a very clever girl -- but there is something so unfeminine about her -- Mr. Lundberg is an excellent man -- I've always liked him especially -- but he is as poor as a church mouse and has a whole family to support -- how do you think he'll be able to set up house.

MRS. BARK I imagine he could find a better position with a higher salary. He is supposed to be quite capable.

BARK Yes, very capable. Has he proposed already?

MRS. BARK Almost -- I think. But Berta doesn't seem to be able to make up her mind.

BARK Is the girl crazy? It's a real piece of luck that anybody wants to have her. You're not going to let her go do something stupid now.

MRS. BARK Berta has a head of her own -- --

BARK Yes, I sure know -- don't talk about it. I can't understand how she could have turned out like that -- with a mother who is such a true woman. But it's like I've said before -- she takes after Aunt Malla. Well, she'll come to her senses, I suppose. Now, dear old girl, please be a sweetheart and take out that deposit slip -- --

MRS. BARK Oh, Pontus, dearest -- our family is beset by misfortune. If you knew who is sitting in Berta's room this very moment, crying -- crying so that it rends your heart to hear it!

BARK What on earth now?

MRS. BARK It's our poor Lissi. She arrived in town late last night. Her husband wasn't expecting her and she has made a discovery -- a terrible discovery.

BARK A discovery! What do you mean?

MRS. BARK The bitterest discovery a wife can make. Wilhelm has forgotten her

during his assignment here in Stockholm and has gotten himself involved in some unworthy liaisons. The poor child is completely devastated.

BARK Ah, all that will pass. It is swinish of Wilhelm of course, and I'll certainly take him to task for it -- but what kind of mawkishness is this to take it so personally. Wilhelm is a jolly soul -- I am very fond of the boy -- though he is a rogue -- --

MRS. BARK Lissi says that she never wants to see him again -- --

BARK What twaddle! Who does she think will support her, in that case? Well, we'll talk about that later. I'll have it out with Wilhelm and I won't go easy on him, that's for sure -- but now I'm in a hurry -- give me the --

MRS. BARK But don't you want to say hello to Lissi?

BARK *(Hesitating)* Yes -- I would like to see her for a moment before I go out -- *(Approaching the door right)* crying, did you say?

MRS. BARK Yes -- she's sobbing and is quite beside herself.

BARK *(Makes an about face)* Then we'd better let her be. No tears, thank you -- I'm too kind, you see. I have never been able to watch a woman cry. And then I'm in a hurry -- --

MRS. BARK But I think she'd calm down if you came in to see her -- --

BARK No, I say! I don't want to see her crying -- Wilhelm is a scoundrel -- --

MRS. BARK Little Ville is here, too.

BARK *(Softening)* Ah! so the boy is here too!

MRS. BARK Shall I call for him? *(Goes toward the door.)*

BARK No -- I don't have time. Has he grown a lot? -- I don't have time, I tell you. I promised Lind to bring the money first thing in the morning. If I don't show up, that crook will make such a fuss -- --

MRS. BARK *(Tormented)* Dear Pontus -- think of the children -- should we rob them of the last -- and leave them only poverty for inheritance -- -- -- ?

BARK *(Increasingly angry)* Listen here -- are we starting in on that topic again? Didn't we finish that last night? I'll tell you something, my dear wife -- I am a kind man -- no one can deny that -- but there's a limit to my kindness -- and I am hotblooded -- so don't provoke me! I am sorry to have to insist -- but you force me to it with your stubbornness --

MRS. BARK *(Sinks into a chair, powerless)* Do with me what you will! I don't have the money any longer. I have given it away.

BARK *(Rushing toward her)* Given it away! Have you gone stark raving mad? Given away my money?

MRS. BARK Not yours -- mine.

BARK You are my wife, and everything you have is mine. What have you done with the money? -- answer!

MRS. BARK *(Pulling herself together, firmly)* I have given my money to Berta by a legal deed of gift, witnessed by Mr. Lundberg.

BARK To Berta, you say. Berta! She'll have to reckon with me. *(Clenches his fist threateningly)* In any case it is an illegal act that I don't care for. A wife has no property which is not also her husband's.

MRS. BARK Surely Mr. Lundberg knows about all that.

BARK Well, then I say that those are despicable laws that can allow such at thing -- it is shocking! -- there you see where these modern emancipation ideas are leading! A total dissolution of marriage and family life -- for what is marriage if the wife has the right to act so arbitrarily -- --

MRS. BARK Is it really so unreasonable that the wife has some means of protecting herself and her children?

BARK You talk as if man and wife were two enemy parties who have to be on guard against each other -- that's total hogwash — obviously all legislation should assume that man and wife are one and have the same interests at heart.

MRS. BARK But legislation must also think of those marriages where the wife might need protection against the husband -- -- --

BARK No, that's exactly what's wrong. By assuming that there may be such relation-ships, the law gives a kind of sanction to the woman who rises up against the man -- that is demoralizing in the highest degree.

MRS. BARK Berta, on the other hand, says that it's demoralizing for -- -- -- --

BARK Yes -- I know -- Berta! She has turned your head with her crazy unfeminine ideas! You, who used to be such a good wife -- just a look from me was all it took and you did what I wanted -- now you care little that I am

compromised, scandalized, brought to despair -- just as long as you have salvaged your money and preserved your independence, you're satisfied.

MRS. BARK Oh, Pontus!

BARK Yes -- and you even allow yourself to be lured into dishonesty and intrigues! -- --

MRS. BARK No, Pontus!

BARK Yes -- I won't mince words -- dishonesty -- an act of treason! It is betraying my creditors.

MRS. BARK They had no right to gamble with you for my money.

BARK *Yours -- yours!* I think you've gone mad with your "mine" and "yours" -- *your* money and *your* money -- I never hear anything else.

MRS. BARK I wasn't talking about "mine" and "yours," Pontus, when you had gone through my entire large fortune and everything had to be clubbed at auction -- our beautiful Bergfors [Manor], the silver, the linen -- you never heard me complain then, never reproach you in the least. No one can say that I didn't try to ease your burden as well as I could.

BARK Yes -- of course. You walked around at the auction with a phony smile on your lips and a happy, cheerful voice just to show all the neighbors what an angel you were and how badly I had hurt you. Oh, I sure know those tactics -- it was enough to drive a man mad! It is just like when you sit up waiting for me nights and instead of reproaching me, there you come, all smiles and concern, so I'll really feel like a criminal.

MRS. BARK *(Bitterly)* Yes, you're right. You have *much* to reproach me for.

BARK That's all one -- I am not reproaching you for anything -- you have now decided to dishonor me and drive me to despair -- I assume you have considered the consequences -- there's nothing left for me but to -- -- -- *(With emphasis)* quit the game.

MRS. BARK *(Attentive)* What do you mean?

BARK When the game's up, I will at least know how to die -- so I won't be a burden to you and the children any longer.

MRS. BARK Pontus!

BARK To hear that your voice still has such a tender note for me, Julie! Alas -- do you still remember the day when your father -- who, by the way, was always quite unfair to me -- required that there be a pre-nuptial agreement between us? -- how sweet you were when you then laid your hand in mine and said: "I don't ask anything more than to leave my fate in his hands." And then when your father -- a brutal, ruthless man, your father --

MRS. BARK Ah --

BARK Well, well, that is, he was of course an excellent man, my dear father-in-law, and I have always honored his memory -- then when he in a pretty insulting way suggested that I might spend it all and bring you to a beggar's staff -- ah, Julie, what a beautiful look you had when you said: "Even a beggar's staff I'll gladly receive from his hands." (MRS. BARK *is moved*) Yes, you see, Julie, then you were a woman -- a true woman, such as men adore and worship -- now you are much, much changed.

MRS. BARK Dear Pontus, I assure you -- it is not for my own sake -- as late as yesterday evening I was determined not to do it -- but when this thing with Lissi happened -- I thought --

BARK No explanations necessary, dear Julie. I know how it is -- your children are your idols -- you and the children, you have always meant so much to each other that I have been superfluous -- (*Visibly moved*) you will only feel it as a relief when I am gone.

MRS. BARK In God's name, Pontus, where are you going?

BARK I want to leave before Lind comes looking for me. I won't endure the shame of having to tell him that I have betrayed him.

MRS. BARK No, Pontus -- you mustn't -- you cannot.

BARK (*Weeping*) What better thing can I do than clear out of your way? You have never loved me -- and that is no more than fair, I admit. I have brought you from comfort and prosperity to poverty -- not even a wife can forgive such a thing, I do understand that. It is bitter that I wasn't given the opportunity to show you that I still *can* be exonerated -- I had hoped to be allowed to begin a new life -- but nothing is left for me now but to die with a spotted name.

MRS. BARK Pontus -- rather anything else -- oh, if I only owned something -- I would give you all -- all -- -- !

BARK (*Pushes her away*) That's just a manner of speaking -- an empty phrase. Nothing would be easier for you than to help me, if you wanted to.

MRS. BARK Just tell me what I must do!

BARK Where is that infernal deed?

MRS. BARK I don't know.

BARK Has Berta gone to the bank?

MRS. BARK No, not yet -- only to deliver some copy. She'll come back here before she goes to the bank.

BARK Then the paper is probably in there on her desk.

MRS. BARK Pontus -- you have no right to take it. A legally witnessed document -- --

BARK Me! Take it! I wouldn't dream of it. My fate is now completely in your hands. If you still had a spark of love for me you would of course revoke the whole thing -- destroy the deed of gift before Berta comes back.

MRS. BARK (*Anguished*) Can I do that, Pontus -- -- --

BARK Of course you can. Nothing is more common than for example changing a will. But don't make such a sacrifice for my sake. My life is not worth as much as that.

MRS. BARK (*Runs into* BERTA's *room, returns with a small briefcase in her hand*) It must be here. (*She searches eagerly, takes out the deed and tears it to pieces.*)

BARK (*Amazed*) But what will Berta say?

MRS. BARK (*With her hand on his shoulder*) I once promised to follow you all the way to a beggar's staff. I am keeping my word, as you can see.

BARK (*Embraces her*) You are an angel, Julie. A true woman! You won't regret what you've done. Even today I'll look for a position. We will work and save together, you and I. Ah, it will be a happy life! One hearth and one heart, Julie! -- Now find the certificate of deposit, too -- it's probably in the same briefcase -- (*Searches the briefcase, while his wife holds it [open]*) see there it is -- now you'll just sign this, so that I can collect those papers at the bank. (*He shows her where she must sign, stands leaning over her tenderly while she is writing.*)

MRS. BARK Is it right like this?

BARK (*Kisses her*) You are an angel, Julie. There is no other woman like you! (*Takes the papers and leaves.*)
(BERTA *enters at the same moment, meets him in the doorway.*)

BARK   Well -- good morning, my girl. Up and about so early!

BERTA   *(Stiffly)* Likewise. Already up, Papa?

BARK   Yes -- I have to go out on some business. *(Leaves)*

BERTA   *(Comes [farther downstage] into the room)* Who would have thought that he would wake up so early! Have you had to tell him everything now, Mama?

MRS. BARK   *(Who unobtrusively has hidden the briefcase in her desk)* Yes.

BERTA   Well -- and he didn't seem to be angry. He spoke to me quite kindly.

MRS. BARK   He was deeply hurt.

BERTA   I'm sure he was. -- -- Well, you just blamed me, didn't you?

MRS. BARK   Dear Berta, I don't think that we are doing right by him.

BERTA   Oh, you good, sensitive little Mama, can't you trust my sense of justice.

MRS. BARK   Yes, dear Berta, you certainly have a sense of justice, but you are too hard on your father.

BERTA   Well -- now I see how it is. He has caused a terrible scene -- you're still trembling all over. I really think I had better take the deed of gift and deposit it in the bank.

MRS. BARK   Why?

BERTA   Otherwise Papa is quite capable of -- oh, it's not worth talking about.

MRS. BARK   What do you mean?

BERTA   I don't want to hurt you, Mama -- and you don't like me to criticize Papa.

MRS. BARK   Say what you mean anyway.

BERTA   I mean that he would be quite capable of destroying the entire deed of gift -- he doesn't have enough sense of justice to realize that it would quite simply be theft.

MRS. BARK   Theft -- my God — how can you use such a word. Your father may have many shortcomings, but he would not commit theft.

BERTA   Actually, it would be far worse than theft -- but of course he doesn't understand that.

MRS. BARK   What do you mean by that? You're making me so nervous with all your insinuations.

BERTA   I only mean that if you, Mama, were now to be persuaded to go back on your promise to me, then I would no longer have a single person in the whole world to trust in.

MRS. BARK   *(Groping for a chair)* You mustn't trust too much in me, my child -- you know -- I am so weak -- -- *(Sinks down in the chair)* Would you give me some water. I am not feeling quite well.

BERTA   *(Runs up to her, supports her, and gives her water)* It is despicable how he treats you!

(WILHELM enters.)

MRS. BARK   *(Rises, addresses BERTA)* You must speak to Wilhelm. I can't take any more.

(BERTA greets WILHELM, then leads her mother off, right. One can hear the voice of little VILLE as the door is opened.)

WILHELM   *(Approaches BERTA as she returns)* What is the meaning of this? That was Ville's voice. What kind of mystery is this. Is Lissi here?

BERTA   Yes.

WILHELM   In there? How on earth did she get here?

BERTA   *(In a tired voice)* Please sit down. I have a few words to say to you.

WILHELM   What kind of ceremony is this? Has anything happened -- -- ?

BERTA   Lissi arrived on the steamer last night around ten o'clock. She had been looking forward like a child to giving you a surprise. When she came to your apartment building she saw you go in with a strange woman.

WILHELM   What! The concierge did say there was a lady whom she had turned away -- --

BERTA   It was your wife, Wilhelm.

WILHELM   *(Jumps up)* Damnation! I must talk to Lissi at once.

BERTA   *(Slowly)* She says that she never wants to see you again.

WILHELM   Ah -- she's overwrought -- it's not possible.

BERTA   There are some sensitive natures who can never get over such a blow.

WILHELM   That's possible -- but Lissi isn't one of them. She is so good -- she loves me -- she is a true woman -- she cannot cast off the father of her children.

BERTA   She is ashamed to look the father of her children in the eye after this, she says.

WILHELM   It's you who's putting her up to it.

BERTA   Yes -- I realize it must be hard for you men to grasp what a blow like this can mean to a woman. We like to put all our trust in those we love.

WILHELM   What do you know about that?

BERTA   That's how I love my mother and Lissi -- any others I have not really loved. But if one of them were to fail me in some way -- it would be like being betrayed by the whole world. All faith, all truth, all honor would be gone from this world, if *they* were to betray my trust in them. And that, I imagine, is how Lissi has been trusting you.

WILHELM   She has not.

BERTA   She has not?

WILHELM   She is not that hypersensitive -- her view of life is more realistic.

BERTA   Oh, realistic! She was 18 when she married you -- she didn't know life. I'll never forget how adorably sweet she was as a bride. I remember how I thought to myself, young though I was at the time: there is no man, no human being, who is worthy of her. Her husband may be ever so good -- he can still never live up to the image she has made herself of him. It isn't him she loves -- it is an ideal whom she has equipped with all that is pure and fine in her own nature.

WILHELM   Nonsense! You're supposed to have thought that! At 15!

BERTA   I didn't think it as clearly as I now say it -- but in any case -- it was still a feeling like this that made me beside myself when you put the ring on her finger and she promised to be yours for life -- perhaps you remember that I burst into tears and didn't want to show my face for the rest of the evening. (WILHELM *laughs.*) Are you laughing at that, Wilhelm? I really hadn't expected that.

WILHELM   Well, you see -- when I first fell in love with her, I thought, just like you, that she was much too good for any man -- and much, much too good for me. And when we were engaged and I kissed her for the first time -- oh, I'll never forget the shame over my past life that gripped me -- I would have given anything at that moment to be able to face her completely pure. I was seized by such disgust and self-loathing -- And still I certainly hadn't lived any worse a life than most men. Oh, you have no idea what a truly innocent and purehearted girl would be able to make of a man in a moment like that!

BERTA   A *truly* innocent girl, you say.

WILHELM   Yes -- now listen to this. My pangs of conscience drove me to make a confession to her -- not as if I would have wanted to soil her imagination by telling anything -- I merely hinted -- afraid to see her flee from me frightened at the first word --

BERTA   Well?

WILHELM   Well, she was interested -- wanted to hear more -- forced me to express myself more graphically -- she smiled, shook her finger at me and said with a bold look of admiration: "You're certainly a pretty one!" And then she threw her arms around my neck and whispered that she did not love me less because others had loved me first -- and then she made it clear that girls in general like those men best who have had some adventures -- it only makes them more piquant and fun than those inexperienced goody-goodies -- --

BERTA   *(Jumps up)* No -- it is not true -- --

WILHELM   Yes, do you know, my surprise was just as great. I pushed her from me and looked at her, and I assure you -- in that moment I thought the expression in her eyes was changed -- there was something knowing in them -- yes, I thought there was a certain boldness about that childish forehead -- I felt as if I had had a cold shower. From that moment on my love for her had lost its finest bouquet -- it was much cosier on the whole, for now I could be less inhibited with her in all respects. -- Well, was I so very wrong just now to call her "realistic"?

BERTA   Wilhelm!

WILHELM   Well!

BERTA   *(Grabs his arm hard)* I would like to hit you.

WILHELM   But Berta, have you taken leave of your senses?

BERTA   Yes, I have! It is shameful what you said just now, it is degrading -- to her, to me -- to our whole sex -- oh -- I can't bear it -- I can't bear it! *(Weeps with her face buried in her hands.)*

WILHELM   Dear Berta -- I don't understand you -- it is as I say -- you are so terribly high strung.

BERTA   *(Runs to the door right and pulls it open)* Lissi! Come out, Lissi! Your husband is here and expects you to come out and embrace him. Don't believe for a moment that he has insulted you -- on the contrary, he has only wanted to make himself more interesting in your eyes! He's expecting you to love him more than ever after this.

LISSI (Comes out, stiff, eyes red with weeping) What do you have to say to me?

WILHELM Oh, Lissi, how I regret my frivolity. It's this Stockholm life with eternal dinners and café-life in the evenings -- and almost nothing to do -- and then to live away from you. To satisfy a whim one goes ahead and sacrifices the best one has -- wife, children, all one's happiness. -- But Lissi -- you still must forgive me -- for the children's sake, Lissi!

LISSI (Weeping) The children -- the children -- you'll never see them again. I want to die -- I will never more be able to look anyone in the eye after this -- I've been so shamed -- but the children -- they won't learn from their father to be faithless -- they will be brought up by Berta -- as for myself, I'll just pray to God he'll let me die -- -- (Runs out crying.)

BERTA (Goes up to WILHELM, looks him in the eye) Now you see! You're despicable!

WILHELM (Grabs her by the shoulders) How dare you!

BERTA (As before) You are despicable, I say. Yes -- go ahead, hit me. You can't hurt me any more than you already have. (WILHELM slowly lets his hands drop, turns away and goes upstage. BERTA quickly buries her face in her hands and weeps.) Curtain

Act III

Same room. MRS. BARK and LISSI are sitting together, MRS. BARK on the sofa, LISSI on a stool with her head in her mother's lap.

MRS. BARK My dear girl -- you really mustn't take on so. Remember -- we women must endure and forgive much -- it is our lot. We won't be able to reform men -- we'll only make ourselves unhappy in the process. And without patience and mildness we cannot wholly win a man's heart -- you see! A man always quickly tires of a wife who makes scenes and reproaches him and -- --

LISSI Should men then be allowed to behave exactly as they please -- and we're just supposed to accept it with good grace?

MRS. BARK That's the way it's been since

the beginning -- my darling. And we ought not to grumble about it -- it is so sweet to forgive the one you love.

LISSI But Mama, you don't know what it is like -- when you have loved your husband like I have -- and then, this humiliation, this -- -- --

MRS. BARK I know what it is like, my child.

LISSI Yes -- of course I know that Papa has mistreated you many times -- but this -- --

MRS. BARK Yes, this. Don't imagine that I haven't been through this, too. More than once.

LISSI More than once? And still you have forgiven him?

MRS. BARK If I hadn't forgiven -- what would then have become of you? You would have grown up without a father but with a mother in the dubious position of a divorced wife. And also -- I have never stopped loving your father.

LISSI I love Wilhelm, too -- but I just want him to really regret everything -- to really feel how he has wronged me. Do you think he'll come again today, Mama?

MRS. BARK I guess it depends on what Berta has said to him. I fear she has portrayed you as completely unwilling to reconcile.

LISSI Yes -- that doesn't hurt. Oh, I want him to really be afraid of losing me -- to suffer as much as I have had to suffer. -- But I couldn't find out what he and Berta had said to each other this morning when Wilhelm had left -- she didn't answer me when I spoke to her -- she was so terribly pale and she shook all over -- finally she just said: "Now I'm going to work at the bank" and ran off.

MRS. BARK Poor Berta -- she empathizes so strongly with you -- -- --

WILHELM (Enters. LISSI jumps up) No, don't go, Lissi! Let me just say a few words to you.

MRS. BARK (Gets up) Stay, my girl. I'll leave you two alone! (Exits right.)

WILHELM I won't torment you with my presence -- I just wanted to tell you that I respect your wishes -- you have been shamed and wronged and I understand that it must now be repulsive to you to be my wife -- but I still wanted to beg of you, for the sake of the boys, not to insist on a legal divorce right away -- you'll take them and move in with your parents and

I get to have them with me in the country sometimes -- perhaps they can be a link between us and perhaps that day may come when you will send a greeting with them to me and say -- and say -- perhaps you'll say, Lissi, that your love for me isn't completely dead -- forgive me, I don't want to upset you -- but I wanted to tell you this myself -- and then I just wanted to be allowed to see Ville.

LISSI Wilhelm! listen! I am not so unreasonable as you think -- I was hasty, caught in --

WILHELM So you agree to my suggestion?

LISSI Suggestion? What -- ?

WILHELM That you stay here for the time being -- and that our home remains unchanged -- and that I can hope that -- one day -- --

LISSI Oh -- it is worse -- much worse than I thought -- you don't love me any more -- it isn't only as I thought that you had forgotten me for the moment -- you want to get rid of me to live your carefree single life unhampered -- --

WILHELM Lissi, now you're going too far -- you cannot misunderstand my sincere remorse like this -- --

LISSI Remorse! I don't care about your remorse -- I only care about whether you love me. And you don't if you can talk about a long separation as if it were the simplest thing in the world.

WILHELM Now I don't understand you at all.

LISSI No, you don't understand that if a man loves his wife, I suppose he can forget her in a moment of frivolity -- but to part from her for years -- --

WILHELM *You* were talking about divorce for life, if I understood you correctly.[6]

LISSI If you had understood me correctly, you would have seen that I was in despair and that you only needed to be a little loving to me to get me to forget and forgive everything.

WILHELM This is the second time I have been mistaken in you, Lissi.

LISSI Wilhelm -- then you don't love me the tiniest bit any more? What have I done to make you all at once so cold and hard to me? *(Tries to embrace him.)*

WILHELM *(Holding her back)* I want to be completely honest with you, Lissi! I want to tell you openly that I, at this moment, don't dare to promise that you will never again have anything to reproach me for. And that's why I wanted a temporary separation to test myself.

LISSI Oh, Wilhelm, if you knew what a wife's love means, you would realize that I'd rather suffer anything than live apart from you. *(Throws her arms around his neck)* Don't leave me, Wilhelm! You see how I love you -- how I am ready to forgive you everything -- *everything* -- both now and in the future -- if I only know that you still love me deep down.

WILHELM *(Pushes her away)* Do you know what this is? This way you are putting yourself on a level with this other kind of woman.

LISSI *(With a scream of despair)* Wilhelm! *(Runs to the door right)* Mama! *(MRS. BARK comes in.)* I think Wilhelm has gone crazy -- he is talking like -- like -- I don't understand him -- he's just accusing me in the most terrible -- --

MRS. BARK Dear child, I told you so. A wife must not insist on her right too much -- she must not test her husband's patience too hard.

LISSI But that's just exactly what he wanted, I think. He wants to drive me to go too far so that then he'll have a reason to leave me.

WILHELM Lissi has never been equipped with particular powers of ratiocination. Berta would not have misunderstood me like this.

LISSI Now he's reproaching me for that as well! How many times haven't you told me that you were glad I was not like Berta -- and that you appreciated my femininity a thousand times more than Berta's brains.

WILHELM Yes -- that is true -- you are a pretty and feminine little wife and I certainly don't want to trade. *(Caresses her)* If Berta were my wife she would force me to become a different person -- I don't know what I wouldn't do rather than lay myself open to her disapproval -- such a woman's disapproval is a bitter though bracing tonic -- but luckily my little wife isn't that kind of woman -- she is a true woman and permits me to slide as much as I want -- it is of course much more pleasant and makes life so much easier and more enjoyable -- long live true womanhood! *(Embraces her.)*

LISSI It is very mean of you to give it such an interpretation! If you have enough sense of justice to know what you owe your wife, it wouldn't make any difference whatever demands I made on you.

WILHELM No, that's right -- no demands -- that will be our motto. Full freedom -- isn't that so? That is, for me -- not for you, of course -- that would be turning the world upside down.

LISSI Shame, Wilhelm -- why are you talking to me in that mocking tone? Is this my thanks for loving you and wanting to forgive and forget all the sorrow you've given me.

WILHELM I regret all my unkind words. It all resulted from the fact that we men sometimes have a certain tendency to idolize our wives.[7] We would so much like to find in them the pure soul that we lack in ourselves -- childish stuff, of course -- old romanticism, left over from [that old epic poem] *Frithiof's Saga*[8] and our teens -- but women are more realistic, they are -- they know how to compromise their ideals and take life as it is.
(Embraces her.)
(BERTA enters [from the outside, upstage] -- starts when she sees WILHELM and LISSI together.)

WILHELM *(Cheerfully)* See there, welcome home, Berta. Now don't look so severe -- it doesn't suit you. It makes you look somewhat unfeminine. A woman should always be mild -- always loving and tolerant -- like my little Lissi.

BERTA Lissi -- what does this mean? I don't understand -- -- --

WILHELM Didn't I tell you already this morning that Lissi is realistic. It has always been a prominent feature in her character.

LISSI I don't know what you mean by "realistic." Is it your intention to mock me for that, too -- like you did just now because I am feminine?

WILHELM Mock you -- my little Lissi. How can you think that. *(Takes her by the chin)* To be realistic is a woman's greatest virtue. To be realistic, my dear Berta, is not to build yourself more sky-high mansions, known as ideals, but to build calmly and cosily in the valley a one-story building with fireproof tile roof and lightning rod. You'll never learn to be that realistic, I fear -- and that's why you'll

never find peace in the harbor of matrimony.

BERTA You seem to be very cheerful.

WILHELM And why shouldn't I be, when I've just received absolution for all my sins -- past, present, and future -- from the prettiest little wife imaginable.
(Embraces LISSI.)
(BERTA turns away — wants to go past them to exit right.)

LISSI Berta -- aren't you happy that we are reconciled?

BERTA Wilhelm said something about you this morning which made me beside myself -- now -- it's none of my business. *(Goes up to WILHELM and shakes his hand)* Forgive me, Wilhelm!

WILHELM *(Retains her hand)* Thank you, Berta -- no one has ever insulted me like you -- yes, if you had been my wife, Berta -- you would not have gotten away with insulting me a second time, I can assure you -- nor would you have had to -- you would have made me into quite a different man.

BERTA Oh -- I don't know about that -- whoever can't straighten himself out without the help of someone else -- he -- it must come from inside. *(She tears herself loose and goes to MRS. BARK)* Has Papa been home since I left?

WILHELM I must say hello to the boy.
(Goes out right with LISSI.)

MRS. BARK No, Papa hasn't been home.

BERTA That's good -- then you have escaped new scenes. Have you seen my keys -- I couldn't find them this morning and my drawer was locked. I want to get those papers.

MRS. BARK You don't trust your mother, my girl.

BERTA Not trust -- you, Mama? Then I wouldn't want to live any more. Now you are the only one I have left to believe in. *(Embraces her.)*

MRS. BARK *(Pulling back)* I wouldn't wonder if you didn't trust me, Berta. Not my good will -- but my powers of resistance. I am only a weak woman -- I, like Lissi. You mustn't judge us so harshly because we haven't been given your strength of character.
(BARK comes in, followed by ACCOUNTANT LUNDBERG and a DELIVERY BOY, carrying a couple of champagne bottles; receives the bottles and puts them on the dining table,

pays the BOY *while* LUNDBERG *greets* MRS. BARK *and* BERTA, *who returns his greeting very coldly.)*

BARK Good day -- my dear Julie -- good day, Berta. Where is your sister? I haven't had a chance to say hello to her yet.

MRS. BARK *(Opens the door right and calls)* Wilhelm and Lissi!
*(*WILHELM *and* LISSI *come in, his arm around her waist and her hand on his shoulder.)*

BARK Well -- what do you know. Everything fine and dandy again! Here they come, like two turtledoves. *(Kisses* LISSI*)* Welcome, baby Lissi. *(Softly to* WILHELM*)* You're a fine one, you are, Wilhelm. I had intended to rake you over the coals -- but now that *she* has already forgiven you, the whole thing is not worth talking about any more. Lissi is a true woman -- like her mother. -- Now do sit down, dear Mr. Lundberg. Now we'll have a good time. -- I wonder if you remember what day it is today. -- A double family celebration -- yes, indeed, I think you had forgotten! *(To* LUNDBERG*)* It is both our wedding anniversary and the children's.

LISSI *(Ingratiatingly, to* WILHELM*)* Don't you see that's why I wanted to be in town just today. And now it had slipped my mind with all this.

WILHELM What day would be better to celebrate our reconciliation.

BARK Now we'll have a festive moment and drink the toast of both married couples. Bring some champagne glasses, Berta!
*(*BERTA *takes out glasses and a tray from the sideboard upstage and puts them on the table.)*

BARK *(Pouring the champagne)* I asked our good friend, Mr. Lundberg, to join us -- since he has been the womenfolk's confidant in a few small family skir- mishes. You see, even in the happiest of families there may be little schisms sometimes -- nothing to speak about -- it looks like -- like some poet put it -- our great Tegnér, I think it was -- take a glass, old girl -- what was I saying -- oh, yes, it looks like a cloud in a rosy -- no, a rosy cloud in a -- no, not exactly rosy but anyway -- don't you laugh, Lissi! Ah, you rascal! -- I was saying -- a passing cloud like that only heightens the effect of the final reconciliation. My dear daughter

Berta has a somewhat hard and aggressive disposition -- well, it's not my intention to reproach you for anything, my dear Berta, on a day like today -- you also have great assets -- a firmness and a -- a -- a sublime -- well, briefly, your father is the first one to recognize your good qualities -- and I hope that you one day, through love, which is woman's -- I was going to say -- hm -- love, which is woman's -- *most precious jewel!* -- through love, I say, you will gain that feminine mildness which you now lack -- why don't you take a glass? -- well, suit yourself -- mildness and goodness, you see, they are woman's most precious jewel -- what now? What are you saying?

BERTA *(In a tired voice)* I just wanted to point out that it isn't *my* wedding anniversary today. I therefore don't understand why you address your speech to me.

BARK That was just a parenthesis. Am I not right -- just look how unfeminine it is to interrupt like that -- now I completely lost my mood -- what was it I wanted to say -- oh, I wanted to say -- it wasn't right of you, my dear Berta --

BERTA *(In a low voice)* Still addressed to me -- --

BARK It wasn't right of you to persuade your mother to do such a thing -- to give you the money which, by right, belongs to your father -- it was unfair also to your sister, for why should you have this money alone when Lissi has an equal right to it --

LISSI *(To* WILHELM*)* Has Berta done that?

BERTA You deliberately distort my motives. Even if you can believe something like that of *me*, you surely can't believe Mama would have agreed to perpetrate such an injustice against Lissi.

BARK Your mother, my dear Berta, might well have been misled for a moment by maternal weakness -- but she is too good a wife not to quickly realize her duties to her husband -- and since she now has destroyed this infernal document with her own hands, I have forgotten and forgiven all --

BERTA What do you mean? You're lying!

BARK *(Puts his glass down on the table, hard)* Lying! You're speaking to your father!

BERTA *(Filled with dread)* I have lost track -- I am quite turned around by all these

Scene from *True Women* by Anne Charlotte Leffler Edgren in the 1988 production directed by Gunnel Lindblom at the Royal Dramatic Theatre's Lejonkulan ("The Lion's Den"), Stockholm. Scenography: Gunilla Palmstierna-Weiss. BERTA (Agneta Ehrensvärd) and LUNDBERG (Johan Lindell) confront each other in Act III. In the background MRS. BARK (Margareta Byström), BARK (Axel Düberg), LISSI (Inga-Lill Anderson) and WILHELM (Jan Waldecranz). *Photograph Mats Bäcker. Reproduced by courtesy of Mats Bäcker and the Royal Dramatic Theatre.*

phrases -- I don't understand anything any longer. Explain to me, Mama!

MRS. BARK Forgive me, Berta! You mustn't judge me too harshly -- you *must* understand --

BERTA Mama! You too! No, I don't understand -- my head is spinning --

MRS. BARK No, Berta, no -- not like that! -- rather reproach me!

BERTA Reproach! Hard words! To you, Mama! No, don't stand there looking so criminal -- I can't stand it! -- Oh, if only I myself had committed the lowest, most despicable crime -- if you all were standing here to sentence me to the most shameful punishment -- -- rather that than this -- this!

BARK Come now, my dear Berta -- no theatrics now. Your mother has done her duty as a wife -- surely that's nothing to rant and rave about.

LUNDBERG (*Approaching* BERTA) Miss Berta!

BERTA (*Wheels on him*) You too! You knew how my father had gotten the money and still you didn't hesitate to let yourself be invited to this dishonorable celebration! Oh, isn't there a single person in the whole world with a sense of justice!

LUNDBERG It was for your sake -- I was hoping that I could be of some assistance to you -- that I came!

BERTA (*As before*) I do not like people to do shameful things for my sake.

BARK Let me tell you, my dear Berta, that your behavior is unsuitable. To disturb a family celebration like this. It is this unfeminine side of you that is so unpleasant -- --

LUNDBERG (*To* BERTA, *aside*) Miss Berta! I do not easily accept an insult, even from you. Won't you take back the unfair words you said just now?

BERTA Oh, by all means! I am the one who's wrong and you are all right. Honesty, faith, and truth -- they're just empty words -- one must be weak, then one is called good and loving -- one must pretend to have beautiful feelings, speak -- above all *speak* -- beautiful words -- --

LUNDBERG Miss Berta, may I tell you why I came here today -- I wanted to tell you this morning but didn't have the opportunity then -- I have been fortunate enough to get a position which makes me completely independent -- which makes it possible for me to make a home of my own without shirking any of my old obligations -- Berta, you understand -- you know what my aspirations and my longing must be at a time like this. Won't you let me try to make you forget your bitter experiences by a whole life's faithfulness -- teach you to believe in life again.

BERTA Oh, why are you telling me at a moment like this -- I cannot, I dare not trust anyone any longer.

LUNDBERG I still don't doubt that I will succeed. Just let me try.

BERTA I cannot, in any case. How could I possibly leave Mama!

LUNDBERG Oh, Berta, do you still want to sacrifice yourself for her?

BERTA *Still?* That's a word I had not expected from you. What has happened cannot change anything -- it can only make the sacrifice -- perhaps -- a little heavier. But she needs me -- and my work -- now more than ever. *(Clasps his hands)* Thank you anyway. And -- no, it is perhaps unfair to say it.

LUNDBERG Tell me just one thing. My love for you -- is it returned?

BERTA I have never dared ask myself that question. I just want to say -- don't forget me!

LUNDBERG This means almost the same as a yes to me. And since that is the case, nothing can make me give you up -- I will not permit that you sacrifice yourself -- --

BERTA If you reason like that -- why did you not offer me your hand a couple of years ago, Mr. Lundberg?

LUNDBERG But I couldn't. My income -- --

BERTA It was large enough to support your mother and your sisters. Why did you not leave them to starve and marry me? *(LUNDBERG starts.)* Then why do you now ask me to be less faithful than you have been. Am I not as needed by my family as you are by yours? No, one doesn't

build happiness by shirking old obligations, that is what you -- yes, you -- have taught me. Your life has impressed that upon me -- and I will try to hold on to that -- whatever happens. *(He kisses her hands repeatedly.)*

BARK *(Who has observed them, rises, takes his glass)* My friends -- I believe we'll have a triple celebration today -- -- *(LUNDBERG gestures "no.")* no? -- really -- well -- not yet -- well --

MRS. BARK *(Approaches* BERTA*)* Berta -- can't you forgive?

BERTA Forgive! It is so sad to have to *forgive* when one's whole soul longs to admire and believe and trust! *(*MRS. BARK *tries to pull back,* BERTA *stops her)* No, I don't want to push you away, Mama! not you, too. I will work for you -- I will try to be a good daughter to you. *(They embrace.)*

BARK Now there! That's what I like. Now one can truthfully say that this is a proper reconciliation -- didn't I say there's a germ of femininity also in Berta -- I said as much. *(Clinks his glass, solemnly)* My friends! My beloved wife -- my dear children -- let me propose a toast to true women! -- To true women! Hip hip hurrah! *(No one joins in.)*

The curtain falls quickly.

Notes

1 As is often the case in the domestic dramas of the late nineteenth century, the action takes place in a public area of a private home, bringing together issues from the male-dominated outer world with issues from the female-dominated domestic sphere in a semi-public space: the parlor or drawing room.

2 Wilhelm has been attending the kind of formal-dress dinner party thrown by Old Werle in Ibsen's *Wild Duck* and Judge Brack in *Hedda Gabler*, possibly presided over by a female hostess, otherwise exclusively male. These parties could be given in private homes or in private rooms of fashionable hotels and restaurants. In contrast to their British counterparts, Scandinavian men did not lead their social lives at city clubs.

3 Bark is a former landowner who lives on the interest from certain capital and investments. Bark's position as assistant caretaker of the building apparently does

not bring in any income—its point may be to show how he has come down in the world, possibly that he believes himself above moneymaking and therefore accepts the responsibility without pay. His son-in-law Wilhelm is apparently of some importance, as he is appointed to some unspecified standing [government] committee which meets in the capital [Stockholm] and has been in session "for such a long time."

4 The law referred to is the law passed in 1874, giving married women the right to hold private property. This law was still hotly debated at the time of the play, and Mrs. Bark is acutely uncomfortable about the freedom/responsibility it confers on her.

5 It is clear that the Barks are used to a grander style of living. Being forced to move seven years ago from a country manor into a city apartment indicates the extent of the family's financial decline. Over the years, Bark's carefree life and gambling habits have destroyed the family's economy: first he squandered Julia Bark's fair-sized fortune, then her family's country manor had to be sold at auction.

6 Divorce was possible in Sweden, though rare until the 1915 law recognizing "irreconcilable differences" as grounds for divorce. In the nineteenth century there were only between 100 and 300 divorces annually, mostly in the cities. Women usually filed for divorce on grounds of desertion, not infidelity alone, as men often did. In addition to being a social outcast, the divorced woman would probably be poor, unless she had a private fortune that had remained untouched during her marriage. Even if the husband were proven to have deserted her, in which case the woman was awarded custody of the children and the use of the home, the absence of alimony and lack of socially acceptable work spelled poverty.

7 Women were asked to harbor the pure souls men could/would not bother with for themselves. Thea Elvsted in *Hedda Gabler* poured "her pure soul" into the manuscript work with Lövborg, one reason why Lövborg suffers at the thought of the fate of the manuscript. In *True Women*, Wilhelm confesses to Berta that he has longed to be somehow cleansed by association with a pure woman, and that when he found his virginal 18-year-old fiancée to be sexually curious, he felt cheated and revolted. He betrays a wistful longing for a woman like Berta, who he knows would make demands on him, purify him by her discipline and her idealism.

8 *Frithiofs saga* (*Frithiof's Saga*) (1825) by Esaias Tegnér is Sweden's national verse epic, a Gothic-Romantic poem cycle based on an Old Norse saga mixed with Classical and Christian ideals. After a stormy life, the Byronic Viking Frithiof turns from plunder and desecration to atonement and reconciliation, winning the beautiful royal widow Ingeborg in the process. *Frithiof's Saga* became Tegnér's best-loved work and a staple in Swedish education from then on. The audiences for whom Leffler wrote had probably had to memorize the entire cycle, maintaining a kind of love–hate relationship with it through life.

Bibliography

As the primary sources and most of the secondary sources for studying Anne Charlotte Leffler are in Swedish, the list below does not reflect sources consulted. Instead it suggests readings that may inform an English-language discussion of *True Women*.

Algulin, Ingemar (1989) *A History of Swedish Literature*, trans. John Weinstock, Stockholm: The Swedish Institute.

Bradley, Harriet (1989) *Men's Work, Women's Work: A Sociological History of the Sexual Division of Labour in Employment*, Cambridge: Basil Blackwell.

Gustafsson, Alrik (1961) "Strindberg and the Realistic Breakthrough," in *A History of Swedish Literature*, Minneapolis: University of Minnesota Press.

Ibsen, Henrik (1965) *A Doll House*, trans. and ed. Rolf Fjelde, New York: New American Library. Originally published in Norwegian in 1879.

Kessler-Harris, Alice (1990) *A Woman's Wage: Historical Meanings and Social Consequences*, Lexington: University Press of Kentucky.

Salomé, Lou (1989) *Ibsen's Heroines*, trans. and ed. Siegfried Mandel, New York: Proscenium (Limelight Editions).

Originally published in German 1892.

Scobbie, Irene (ed.) (1988) *Aspects of Modern Literature*, Norwich: University of East Anglia Norvik Press.

Strindberg, August (1967) *The Red Room*, trans. Elizabeth Sprigge, London: Dent. Originally published in Swedish 1879.

—— (1973) "A Doll's House," in *Getting Married*, vols. I–II, trans. and ed. Mary Sandbach, New York: Viking Press, 167–84. Originally published in Swedish, vol. I in 1884, vol. II in 1886.

Sylvan, Maj (1984) *Anne Charlotte Leffler: En kvinna finner sin väg*, Stockholm: Biblioteksförlaget. Includes English summary.

Readers of Swedish are referred to ACL's unpublished letters in the Royal Library, Stockholm. Especially recommended are also:

Hennel, Ingeborg Nordin (1993) "Strid är sanning, frid är lögn: Om Alfhild Agrell och Anne Charlotte Edgren Leffler," in E. M. Jensen, *Fadershuset*, Höganäs: Wiken, 512–27.

Lönnroth, Lars (1988) *Den svenska litteraturen: De liberala genombrotten 1830–1890*, Stockholm: Bonniers, 200–299.

2 Amelia Rosselli, 1870–1954 _____

Her Soul
Italy

Amelia Rosselli in the early 1900s. *Photograph provided courtesy of Aldo Rosselli, the author's grandson.*

Introduction

by Natalia Costa-Zalessow

Women dramatists in Italy, 1400–1800s

Women writers have been a presence in Italian literature since the thirteenth century, when Compiuta Donzella wrote her sonnets. Italian poetry, considered nobler than prose, was widely cultivated. As a result, Italian women poets were honored during the Renaissance and Ludovico Domenichi published the first anthology of Italian women poets in 1559. Women took part in all literary activities, but not always with the same success. Modern scholars have discovered more women poets and novelists than playwrights. This is due to three major factors: Italy has relatively few great playwrights; plays are not very suitable for short selections; and the Italian stage has been in a serious decline since the advent of cinema. But Italian women wrote for the stage and, from the fifteenth century onward, contributed to the performing arts as actresses, singers, dancers, players of various instruments, and composers.

Religion lay at the center of daily life in the Middle Ages, and women held central positions in many spiritual movements. The first new theatrical genre to be born in Christian Europe was the devotional mystery play, cultivated from the fourteenth through the sixteenth century in Italy. Antonia Giannotti Pulci (born ca. 1452) occupies an important place among the writers of such mysteries. Four of her plays have survived, but *Santa Guglielma* is the best known and the most frequently

published. There were other women playwrights, now forgotten, such as Cherubina Venturelli, who published a play on St. Cecilia.

The Italian secular theater was born in 1480 with Angelo Poliziano's *Orpheus*. Patterned on the mystery play, it dealt with a well-known ancient Greek myth in a pastoral setting. What followed was a general imitation of Latin comedies and tragedies. While many works were written by various authors during this period, only Machiavelli's *The Mandrake Root* is considered original. Women did not write secular plays of this kind. But the sixteenth century offered another genre, known as spiritual comedy, which became popular after 1521, with a play by Antonio Alamanni. Other playwrights followed suit, until Federigo Della Valle bestowed on it a tragic dimension, and began writing plays for convents, which nuns performed during carnival, assuming women's and men's parts, and even dressing in stockings. Nuns subsequently wrote their own plays, but many of them have been lost. Other plays remain anonymous in manuscript form, while in some cases we have both the plays and the names of authors, such as the newly discovered *Amor di virtù* (Love of Virtue), composed ca. 1548 by Beatrice Del Sera.

The late sixteenth century saw the birth of other theatrical genres: the *commedia dell'arte* and the pastoral play, made popular by Torquato Tasso's *Aminta* (1573) and Giambattista Guarini's *The Faithful Shepherd* (1590). The *commedia dell'arte*, also known as Italian comedy, was improvised. The actors followed only a generic indication of the plot and always impersonated the same character using a mask. Actresses in general played an important role in the *commedia dell'arte*, but the most famous and respected actress of all was Isabella Canali Andreini (1562–1604), author of the pastoral play *Mirtilla* (1588), written in imitation of Tasso's *Aminta*. She wrote her play for the group of actors known as *I Gelosi*, to which she and her husband belonged. It went through six editions from 1588 to 1616, and was translated into French in 1602. But Maddalena Campiglia's *Flori* (1588), and Valeria (Neri) Miani's *Amorosa speranza* (Amorous Hope, 1604), were not as lucky.

In the seventeenth century, Margherita Costa wrote various works of Baroque extravaganza for the stage that included music and ballet, but her play *Li buffoni* (The Buffoons, 1641) is now cited as an example of the improvised comedy for which we have no texts. This period also gave us actresses such as Angiola D'Orsi, Orsola Biancolelli, and Brigida Bianchi (1613–1703), who translated or imitated Spanish plays. These works have established that women were acting as translators during this period, a profession they increasingly practiced. The translator Luisa Bergalli Gozzi (1703–79) is still remembered today for having published the first historical anthology of Italian women poets in 1726, while Elisabetta Caminer Turra (1751–96), who left some twenty volumes of translations, mainly of French plays, is important for her journalistic activities.

Women also wrote libretti for the opera from its birth in the late 1590s. Laura Guidiccioni Lucchesini wrote texts, now lost, for the music of Emilio de' Cavalieri. Petronilla Paolini Massimi (1663–1726) contributed libretti for operas and oratorios. The already mentioned Bergalli began her literary career with the libretto for *Agide*, set to music by Giovanni Porta and performed

in Venice in 1725. It was followed by *Elenia* with Albinoni's music and the oratorio *Eleazaro* with Bonno's, performed in Vienna in 1730. These works reflect the influence of her teacher, Apostolo Zeno, but her tragedy *Teba* (1728) has a more personal style. The comedy *Avventure del poeta* (A Poet's Adventures, 1730), is considered her best contribution to the Venetian stage. Teresa Bandettini Landucci (1763–1837), besides writing libretti such as *La caduta de' giganti* (The Fall of the Giants), wrote two tragedies, *Polidoro* (1794) and *Rosmunda in Ravenna* (1827). The pre-romantic poet Diodata Saluzzo Roero (1774–1840) wrote three tragedies, *Erminia*, *Tullia*, and the unfinished *Griselda*, but she burned her seven comedies.

Women dramatists, 1800s–1900s

The nineteenth century saw an increasing number of women writing for the stage, using themes dear to their period: patriotism (important at that time because it led to Italy's unification, achieved only in 1870), social injustice, and edifying morality. Their plays were either intended for performances by women's groups or girls' schools. The second half of the century is important for the debate on women's education, which had practical consequences in the 1879 passing of the law on compulsory elementary education for all. But Italy, once culturally ahead of the other European countries, was now decades behind the others, not only in industrial progress, education, and women's emancipation (the right to vote was obtained only in 1945) but also in literature and women's contribution to it. The plays by Luisa Marenco-Martini-Bernardi, Irma Melany Scodnik (b. 1857), and Gualberta Alaide Beccari (1850–1906) strike a contemporary reader as predictable, sentimental, and ingenuously plotted. Beccari tackled the problem of divorce in *Un caso di divorzio* (A Case of Divorce), performed in 1881. But this poorly constructed play fails to make a case for divorce, for the second "wife" was never married. (Divorce became legal in Italy only in 1970.) It is, therefore, the more surprising to find, at the end of the nineteenth century, a drama of the caliber of *Her Soul* (*Anima*) by Amelia Rosselli, the play chosen to represent Italian women playwrights in this anthology.

While Rosselli's plays were successfully performed, it is curious to note that the three great women novelists of the late nineteenth and early twentieth century made only a timid attempt at playwriting. Anna Radius Zuccari (1846–1918) wrote a comedy and had it staged, but withdrew it after a poor reception. Matilde Serao (1856–1927), and the Nobel prizewinner Grazia Deledda (1871–1936) collaborated with others in order to adapt their stories for the stage. Other women writers were more active in the theater. Clarice Tartufari (1868–1933) wrote plays dealing with passion, social and humanitarian problems, or reflecting breaks with tradition, as in *Modernissime* (1902) where she pokes fun at liberated women who don't always practice what they preach. Similarly, the dramas of Térésah, or Corinna Teresa Gray Ubertis (1877–1964), staged between 1907 and 1910, address either passion or extreme poverty leading to crime, recalling Giovanni Verga's naturalistic theater. On the other hand, two plays by Annie Vivanti (1868–1942), representing problems of war, are original in their dual interpretations. *L'invasore* (The Invader), performed in 1915 in Turin, deals with rape during World War I, where two women react differently, one aborting, the other not, while *Le bocche inutili* (Useless Mouths) exposes the tactics of war. Vivanti's patriotism left her room enough to present more than one aspect of these gripping problems.

A contemporary, Amalia Guglielminetti (1885–1941), preferred a very different style, however. Her first play, *L'amante ignoto* (The Unknown Lover, 1911), is a tragedy in the manner of Gabriele D'Annunzio, reflecting his decadent tone, refined and pompous settings, language, and depiction of strange passions. More original is her comedy *Nei e cicisbei* (Beauty-spots and Gallants, 1926), where two eighteenth-century lovers come back to life to create a parallel with two contemporary ones. Similarly, the feminist Sibilla Aleramo dedicated her *Endimione* (Endymion, 1923), to D'Annunzio and patterned it on his dramas, except that she used a woman's perspective. It was first performed in a French translation in Paris, in 1923.

The most original among the Italian women playwrights of the 1920s and 1930s is Paola Riccora (b. 1884), who began her career as a translator. She wrote plays not only in her native Neapolitan dialect, as in her first great success, *Viate a vvuie!* (Blessed You), that premiered in Rome in 1919, but also in Italian, as in *Nevicata d'aprile* (April Snow), that premiered in Florence in 1920. She continued to alternate successfully between Neapolitan and Italian, demonstrating a particular linguistic ability and originality. Her masterpiece, *Sarà stato Giovannino* (It Must Have Been Giovannino), performed by the De Filippo family of actors in Naples in 1933 and filmed with them in 1937, revealed Eduardo De Filippo's dramatic abilities. Using characters taken from the local bourgeoisie, Riccora introduced a more gentle type of comedy to the Neapolitan theater that traditionally had been based on bloody violence or slapstick comedy. Her plays, addressing family problems, sacrifice, and kindness, as opposed to ruthless egotism, continued to be performed throughout the 1950s. In 1958, she was awarded a prize for her theatrical activity, and in 1992 the actor Aldo Giuffré rediscovered her masterpiece and staged it in Rome.

Thus can we say that, while Italian women have contributed over hundreds of years to the stage, their contributions have gone largely unrecognized. Few of them are even mentioned in the major reference works describing the history of the theater. The time has come to reexamine history and to shed light on their forgotten works, one of which is Rosselli's *Her Soul*.

Amelia Rosselli: the life and works

Amelia Pincherle Moravia (1870–1954) was born in Venice, but moved to Rome in 1885. She married Joe Rosselli, whose family was famous for their patriotic ties to Giuseppe Mazzini. Her first play, *Her Soul*, won a national prize offered by the Italian state and was performed for the first time in Turin on October 29, 1898, at the Gerbino Theater, by the company of actors *Teatro d'Arte*, with Clara Della Guardia as the protagonist. It was written in answer to Giuseppe Giacosa's *The Rights of the Soul* (1894), discussed in the second act of Rosselli's play. Giacosa is considered the major exponent of the Italian bourgeois drama of the late nineteenth century. His play had been influenced by Ibsen's *A Doll House* (1879), in which Nora walks away from her husband and children in order to find herself. Giacosa's heroine also leaves her husband (but there are no children), in order to ascertain the right of a married woman to nurture a Platonic, or purely spiritual, love for a man who is not her husband. Platonic love enjoyed a certain popularity in those days. The writer Anna Radius Zuccari made great use of ideal platonic relationships in her novels. But Rosselli condemns this type of love and makes fun of it. Moreover, her play is an outright condemnation of how young men chose their wives at the turn of the century. First they fooled around with women who were not considered the marrying type, and then they picked a young inexperienced girl from a good family, either with the hope of molding her or simply for her dowry. However, some girls, kept too strictly at home and having received a very superficial education, made life for their husbands difficult with their continuous flirting, as is the case with Graziana in *Her Soul*. But Olga, the protagonist, who had been raped as a 15-year-old girl, represents not only the more intelligent and mature woman who had to hide her suffering but also the professional woman, a painter in her case, considered unsuitable for the role of a traditional wife by the majority of people.

Some of the points presented by Rosselli in *Her Soul* are still valid today, especially the trauma with which a rape victim lives, and the idea that a successful marriage must be based on mutual respect, common interests, perfect togetherness, and a spiritual understanding of each other's "soul." Her play deals essentially with Olga's serious problems, which are ably presented in parallel with those of her model, Marietta. Olga helps Marietta and gives her advice, but she is unable to apply it to her own situation, which unfolds immediately after. In this way, Rosselli presents us with two cases of women's destinies at two different social levels, both equally sad. Olga's despair reaches its climax in the second act, where Rosselli not only introduces the discussion of Giacosa's *The Rights of the Soul* but also makes use of the original expedient of making Olga auction off her soul and body. The dramatic

tension is cleverly interwoven with a sprinkling of humor in the dialogue of the minor characters, giving the play a varied tone.

Rosselli successfully continued to write for the stage, both in Italian and in the Venetian dialect of her native city. Her next play, *Illusione* (Illusion), premiered in 1901 in Turin and was published in 1906 together with *L'idea fissa* (The Fixed Idea) and *L'amica* (The Friend). *L'idea fissa* is the most interesting of the three, for the protagonist's discussion of his dual personality: he is alternately bad and good, gives two interpretations of everything, is tormented from within, cannot talk to anyone, and eventually throws himself from the window. When this play appeared, Luigi Pirandello had just started to write for the theater, though his short stories and novels had dealt with similar psychological problems.

Rosselli next wrote two Venetian plays, *El rèfolo* (A Burst of Wind) and *El socio del papà* (Daddy's Partner). The former, which premiered in Rome in 1909, is a vivacious comedy depicting the contrast of the melancholic old world with its stress on respect and submission, and the new generation, ready to fight for its rights. The latter, performed in Venice in 1911, is a comedy about the generation gap. Moreover, the four children in the play represent caricatures of the four types: a freethinker, a cleric, a spoiled mother's son, a liberated socialist woman, all in contrast with the conservative father and the typical house-wife mother. Rosselli's patriotic drama *San Marco* was performed for the first time in Milan in 1913. It deals with the 1848 revolution and the failed Venetian uprising against the Austrians, but is full of traditional clichés. Her last play, *Emma Liona* (1924), is the story of Lady Hamilton, depicted as the woman responsible for the persecution of Italian patriots in the late 1790s, through her influence on Admiral Nelson and the Neapolitan Court. Both of these plays reflect the patriotic fervor of the period of World War I, in which Rosselli lost her oldest son.

Besides plays, she published short stories, books for children, and translations from French. But she completely gave up her literary career after her sons, Carlo and Nello Rosselli, founders of the antifascist movement Giustizia e Libertà (Justice and Liberty), were assassinated in France, in 1937, by the French fascists or *cagoulards* on Mussolini's order. Carlo's daughter, born in 1930, not only received her grandmother's name but also followed in her footsteps, becoming a noted Italian poet. Aldo Rosselli, Nello's son, became a writer.

Her Soul

A Drama in Three Acts
Performed 1898
Published 1901
Play translation by Natalia Costa-Zalessow
with the collaboration of Joan Borrelli

Amelia Rosselli

Characters

OLGA DE VELARIS, a painter

SILVIO VETTORI, a lawyer

TERESA MAURI, former friend of Olga's
    mother

GIORGIO MAURI, Teresa's son

GRAZIANA MAURI, Teresa's daughter

MARQUIS BEI ⎫

CORRADO SALVELLI ⎬ Giorgio's friends

COUNT LORENZI ⎭

FERRANDI, a guest at the Mauri villa

VIRGINIA, Olga's old housekeeper

MISS BETT, Graziana's German governess

MARIETTA, Olga's model

PAOLO, Giorgio's butler

A PORTER

ANOTHER PORTER

Time and place
The action takes place in Rome at the end
of the nineteenth century.

Act I

OLGA's *studio*

*Entry to rear. To the left, a door leading to the
other rooms. The walls are full of sketches and
designs, many of which are studies of nudes.
To the right, prominently placed, an easel with
an unfinished painting depicting an ancient
Roman ruin. Here and there rugs, vases,
fabrics, etc., in artistic disarray.* OLGA *is
painting.* MARIETTA, *dressed as an ancient
Roman, poses before her.*

Scene 1

OLGA *and* MARIETTA; *later* VIRGINIA

OLGA *(Impatiently)* Up with that head. More
to the right . . . no. Too much. That's it
. . . and be still, if you can. *(Begins to paint
again)* It's impossible. What the devil's got
into you today? I can't do anything this
way. *(Angry, she sits down on the sofa.)*
You'd better go home. You've made me all
nervous . . . (MARIETTA *starts sobbing.)*
Oh, now she starts to cry! Come on, come
on, you know that when I'm nervous I no
longer watch my words. . . .

MARIETTA *(Between sobs)* It's not because
of that.

OLGA And why then? You don't feel well?
You could have told me; we could have
stopped sooner, no? Or . . . ?

MARIETTA *(Bursting out)* He . . . he left me.

OLGA Who? Leonardi? He left you? But
that's not possible. You must have had
one of your usual quarrels; it's common
among lovers. Go home, you silly girl,
and you'll find him there.

MARIETTA He's gone.

OLGA What do you mean, gone?

MARIETTA I'm telling you that he left two
days ago, and he took all of his things.
. . . Oh, he's not coming back. He isn't
coming back. I know him. If he had left
me suddenly. . . . I'd still hope; he's hot
tempered. . . . But he acted coolly, with
determination. . . .

OLGA But why? What did he say to you?

MARIETTA He told me . . . he told me that
just because things had gone well so far,
it wasn't any reason to suppose that
they'd go well in the future; that he had
to think about his own life, and I about
mine. . . .

OLGA How mean of him!

MARIETTA And then. . . . He treated me in
a way . . . as if I were a prostitute. . . .

OLGA Oh, you poor thing. Though I did
imagine it would end like this. I told you
not to trust Leonardi.

MARIETTA I loved him. . . .

OLGA He's an egotist. As long as it suited him, he kept you with him; now that he sees himself transported into another sphere, with the sudden success he's had with his painting, he doesn't need you any more. And you, silly girl, have so little pride that you show him, and everyone else, your weakness, giving him this last satisfaction.

MARIETTA Oh, what do I care about pride! . . . Where will it get me now that everyone can insult me to my face?

OLGA Oh, don't believe that all of a woman's virtue lies in. . . .

MARIETTA I swear to you, I never had any bad intentions. Even if I did what I did . . . I loved him, that was it. If I'd been more cunning, I wouldn't be just a model now.

OLGA And is that such a shame?

MARIETTA When I think of my child . . . I don't say that he should have pity on me, but on that innocent child that never did him any harm. . . . When I think of the day when he'll ask me about his father. What will I tell you, my darling?

OLGA The truth. (MARIETTA *hides her face in her hands.*) You mustn't be ashamed for having loved a man you considered worthy. It would be shameful had you *pretended* to love him, for a hidden purpose. . . .

MARIETTA (*Somewhat relieved*) Oh, bless you! Your words console me. And I did feel it, inside me, but I didn't understand. . . . I didn't know how to get it out. . . .

OLGA Poor Marietta. You know, we all have this voice inside us, which speaks to us, deep inside, to our heart. But it's difficult to silence the other voices and to listen only to this one. Be brave, and if you need advice or help, remember that I'm here. (MARIETTA *tries to kiss* OLGA's *hand, but* OLGA *takes her head between her hands and kisses her on the forehead.*) And now go get dressed. Hurry up, because I'm expecting guests.
(MARIETTA *steps behind a screen.* OLGA *begins to clean her brushes.*)

MARIETTA You want me back tomorrow?

OLGA Yes, but a little earlier, if you can?

MARIETTA Of course.

OLGA And if I can't . . . I'll send you a note to the usual address, okay?

MARIETTA Oh no, Signorina. I'm no longer there; I'm going there now to get my few things. . . .

OLGA Oh, are you moving?

MARIETTA How can I stay? My rent is paid only through today.

OLGA And the baby?

MARIETTA Thank God, it's still with the wet-nurse; as for me. . . . God will provide. . . . (*She reappears from behind the screen, dressed.*)

OLGA But where will you sleep tonight? Have you found a place?

MARIETTA (*In a hollow voice*) There's always somewhere to go, if worst comes to worst. . . .

OLGA Marietta!

MARIETTA Sorry. I just said it without thinking. . . .

OLGA You'll come sleep here, until you find a decent room.

MARIETTA Here?

OLGA Yes, I think it's best. . . .

MARIETTA I, here? Oh Signorina. But what will people say?

OLGA Don't worry about that. As soon as you've done what you need to do, come back here with your belongings. Understood?

MARIETTA (*Confused*) You're too kind. . . .

OLGA (*Calling*) Virginia! Virginia!

VIRGINIA (*Entering from the left*) You called me?

OLGA Listen. Marietta will sleep here for a few nights. Would you mind seeing that a bed is prepared for her in the last room, where I keep my canvases?

MARIETTA Then I'll be off. . . . My respects, Signorina. (*To* VIRGINIA) My respects.

OLGA Bye, see you later, Marietta.
(MARIETTA *exits.*)

Scene 2

VIRGINIA *and* OLGA

VIRGINIA But what's gotten into your head?

OLGA Why?

VIRGINIA Have her stay in your house with a reputation like that?

OLGA Oh. . . . What reputation? That she was Leonardi's lover?

VIRGINIA Was? . . . Isn't she any longer?

OLGA The hero has vanished.

VIRGINIA Poor thing! What scoundrels, these men!

OLGA I can't possibly leave her on the street, where she might end up. . . .

VIRGINIA No, but. . . .

OLGA   Be good. You certainly are eager to be bad. But you feel even more compassion for that poor girl than I do.

VIRGINIA   But it's unwise . . . especially in your case.

OLGA   Aren't *you* here?

VIRGINIA   Yes, yes, but it's not enough.

OLGA   Yes, it is. You're my dear little old lady, my friend, my guardian, my . . . everything. And then you have all the authority. . . . Aren't the portfolios of all the ministries in your hands? . . .

VIRGINIA   Except for that of Foreign Affairs.

OLGA   *(Jokingly)* Yes, I take care of foreign affairs.

VIRGINIA   It's easiest to make a mistake there.

OLGA   *(Still joking)* Did I ever meddle in your affairs? So don't meddle in mine.

VIRGINIA   But what will people say? That I'm an old crazy woman.

OLGA   Oh, listen. I'm fed up with this stupid world meddling in my private business. And I can laugh in its face.

VIRGINIA   Be careful, it's Silvio's world and he is bound to it, as you know.

OLGA   He, too! He is always worrying about what people will say. If only he loved me a little more. . . .

VIRGINIA   Thank Heaven, he's a young man with a good head on his shoulders, something you never had. . . .

OLGA   Oh, if only he thought the way I do. . . .

VIRGINIA   That's all we need! You have an excuse: you've been used to a free, independent life from early childhood. . . .

OLGA   It's a sad liberty, coming only from the death of one's parents.

VIRGINIA   . . . you grew up without the restraint of those few basic and vital rules. . . .

OLGA   Wrong rules . . .

VIRGINIA   . . . without which the world can't go on.

OLGA   For me it goes on just the same.

VIRGINIA   May God forgive your poor father. But to leave a girl for so many years in a mountain village, with a family of farmers. . . . It might be healthy, I admit, but not very reasonable, if the girl is destined to live in a big city.

OLGA   But you know, it's a serious threat to have been born of a mother dying of tuberculosis. And if anything can keep away this threat, it's a healthy, simple life in the fresh air of the countryside. And then. . . . *(Becoming uneasy)* Poor father, he did it for my own good. If he didn't succeed, it's not his fault.

VIRGINIA   You enjoy excellent health.

OLGA   Oh, I didn't mean that. . . . *(A pause. Then, as if talking to herself)* How come Silvio isn't here yet?

VIRGINIA   By the way, has he made up his mind? This uncertain, ill-defined situation is not ideal. . . .

OLGA   But there's plenty of time. Nobody knows anything at all.

VIRGINIA   That's what you think. Moreover, to speak frankly, I really should step in at this point.

OLGA   *(Vehemently)* Woe to you if you do!

VIRGINIA   But pray tell why?

OLGA   Because I don't want you to.

VIRGINIA   Don't I have . . . if not the right, at least the duty, to think of your future? Didn't your poor father entrust you to me?

OLGA   Yes, yes. . . .

VIRGINIA   I often ask myself whether I'm living up to the trust the poor man had in me; and it seems to me the answer is no.

OLGA   *(Affectionately)* Listen: I don't know if there is an afterlife. But if there is one, and if he, as well as my poor mother, can see us, they can't help but bless you.

VIRGINIA   But then let me. . . .

OLGA   No, no! You mustn't say a word. Look, I beg you.

VIRGINIA   But why?

OLGA   Don't ask. . . . I'm so happy the way things are. And you know. . . . There's a little bit of the peasant girl in me. . . . I'm superstitious. I'm afraid that if I change things just a little, something bad will happen to me.

VIRGINIA   In that case, it's up to you.

OLGA   Of course. Let me do it my own way.

VIRGINIA   I'm going to fix up that room . . . since things have to be done *your* way.

OLGA   *(Looking at the clock)* It's three o'clock already, and no sign of Silvio!

VIRGINIA   He probably went to the Exhibition. . . . *(Going toward the entry door, from which GIORGIO MAURI enters that very moment)* Oh, Mr. Mauri. Come in, come in. . . .

(GIORGIO MAURI enters. VIRGINIA exits.)

Scene 3

OLGA *and* GIORGIO

GIORGIO (*Approaching*) Am I disturbing you?

OLGA Not at all. What good luck brings you here? *Do* sit down.

GIORGIO Thank you. I was coming back from the Exhibition . . .

OLGA Oh, you went there.

GIORGIO . . . and passing by your place, I couldn't resist the temptation to come up a moment to tell you that your painting is a masterpiece.

OLGA Indeed!

GIORGIO Truly. And it was hung in the right spot for the light, which doesn't often happen. I tell you, it's a success!

OLGA So many compliments!

GIORGIO No, no, it's a fact. You know, I too can judge art, a little. . . .

OLGA Oh, more than a little. And if only you had had the desire to study. . . .

GIORGIO If I had had! . . . When a verb is conjugated that way, there's nothing one can do.

OLGA That's bad.

GIORGIO Are you serious?

OLGA Certainly.

GIORGIO Beware! If you say it to me once more in that way, I swear to you, I'll start to work. But perhaps it's too late. . . .

OLGA It's never too late. It's true, I was five years old when I took a pencil in my hand for the first time, or rather, a piece of charcoal. . . . I made certain scribbles, oh what beauty, on a rock, a big rock that was near a pine-tree, opposite the house, which served as a bench for my whole adoptive family in the summer evenings. I can still see them: Papa Tonio with his pipe, Auntie Marta with her braid, and us children gathered all around, like little chicks. And every evening my master-works were rubbed out. . . . Ah, I started out like Giotto, with the difference that, even if Cimabue had passed by, my scrawls would not have impressed him.

GIORGIO You're too modest. . . . Besides, it's a matter of talent, believe me. I, for example, belong to that class of individuals, so numerous and so useless, who feel beauty, goodness, and greatness, but who don't have the necessary ability to express these things in words, by writing, or by painting. I said useless: but then is that really true? You artists have in us your most fervent admirers and at the same time your most impartial critics; and criticism and admiration are hard to come by nowadays.

OLGA But I do not admit to the existence of a class of passive individuals. They don't exist in nature.

GIORGIO Forgive me, but in nature there do exist beings, bodies, call them whatever you like, which are active solely due to the cooperation of other beings, other bodies, and which achieve perfection only together. And can't this happen to humans? Plato believed it, so . . . ?

OLGA Just a minute. He believed that the union of two perfect souls formed a perfect being, not that the two parts, divided and distinct, could not separately perform a given job.

GIORGIO You're terrible. You don't give me a chance.

OLGA Simply because I'm sorry to see a talent like yours wasted. If I weren't interested in you. . . .

GIORGIO (*Lively*) It's true then . . . that you're interested in me?

OLGA What a question! Isn't it natural, given the friendship that ties me to your family?

GIORGIO (*Disappointed*) Ah, because of that!

OLGA What's the matter?

GIORGIO You have to admit that it's not the most flattering thing in the world to know that you're liked not because of yourself, but because of the more or less friendly relationship that exists between two families.

OLGA I get it. You want a declaration for your personal enjoyment? I can give you one, if you like.

GIORGIO That's a cruel joke.

OLGA Oh, you're not that serious as to get upset about a joke.

GIORGIO (*Getting up and looking at one of the paintings*) Tell me: this brilliant color, did you obtain it immediately, at the first stroke of the brush, or is it the result of several layers of various colors?

OLGA That's quite obvious..

GIORGIO So if I could remove the first superficial layer of color, I would find below it a less vivid color, and if I could remove that one too, I would find another still less brilliant, and so on. . . . Is that true?

OLGA   That's well known. Why? You want to learn?

GIORGIO   No, I want to teach you something. If you had bothered with me just once, you would have discovered that below this first brilliant layer of jokes and merriment there exists a second one, rather different . . . just like on that painting.

OLGA   Sublime! A treatise on living art.

GIORGIO   How cruel you are! And if I were to tell you that it hurts me?

OLGA   *(Turns serious all of a sudden)* Listen, my friend. Let's speak openly. Don't judge me either easygoing or cruel, if I poke fun at you a little. But lately I've noticed a change in you . . . and since I like you. . . . *(She smiles)* See, I even have the boldness to tell you so. . . .

GIORGIO   Precisely, because you don't like me.

OLGA   . . . I don't want you to suffer for nothing. It all seems so strange. You men are so restless. We were such good friends. We used to spend such pleasant hours together, without embarrassment, without illusions. No, sir! You couldn't keep it that way. You suddenly had to turn sentimental on me. . . .

GIORGIO   Is it my fault, if, little by little, without realizing it, the friendship which I had for you turned into something else?

OLGA   No, it's not your fault. But you have to stop it, immediately!

GIORGIO   *(In a trembling voice)* You love someone else?

OLGA   What's that got to do with it?

GIORGIO   Why don't you tell me frankly? Maybe you're no longer free? No, no, don't be afraid. I'm not one to make a scene, or to play the victim. I know how to suffer without bothering anyone.

OLGA   *(After a short hesitation)* Very well then . . . I want to be frank with you: yes.

GIORGIO   *(Turning pale)* Ah, you see.

OLGA   *(Makes a movement toward him)* But I assure you that. . . .

GIORGIO   For God's sake! No consolation, please. I'd hate it. Look: I'm not even asking his name. Only . . . it's too bad that you don't love me.

OLGA   But I do love you.

GIORGIO   Yes, yes, I understand . . . but in that other way. But I just can't imagine your finding happiness with anyone else. If you marry an artist, you'll end up being rivals and destroying each other; or – and you're capable of it – you'll humble yourself in order not to hamper his glory. If, on the other hand, you marry a middle-class man, you'll suffer and struggle a lot, because everything in you, your whole existence, is diametrically opposed to what's thought, done, and expected by the so-called good society.

OLGA   *(In a mocking tone, but somewhat upset)* So you would be the only one . . . ?

GIORGIO   It's ridiculous, I know. But you're too complex to be understood, and if understood, to be appreciated by the first man that comes along. There is in you some mysterious depth that needs to be respected; some surge of light so intense that it would burn the indiscreet eye of the unsuspecting gazer.

OLGA   *(Very upset)* Who told you . . . ?

(TERESA and GRAZIANA enter.)

Scene 4

Same, with GRAZIANA *and* TERESA MAURI

TERESA   Can we come in?

(The two compose themselves.)

GRAZIANA   *(Pointing to* GIORGIO*)* Look who's here! *(Exchange of greetings)*

OLGA   Oh, Mrs. Mauri. How nice of you. How are you? Hello, Graziana.

TERESA   *(Pointing at* GIORGIO*)* You rascal! What are you doing in the house of a respectable young lady?

GIORGIO   Well . . . the same thing you came to do, no more, no less.

OLGA   How nice of the two of you to come. We hardly see each other. . . .

GRAZIANA   Oh, do you really think so?

OLGA   I'm so busy.

TERESA   And we! We have a hundred things to do. . . . You know how many visits we are supposed to make today? *(She pulls out and shows her calling-card case.)*

GRAZIANA   Ten.

OLGA   Mercy!

TERESA   And then – can you imagine? – we were also at the Exhibition.

OLGA   Oh, indeed? And what do you think of it?

GRAZIANA   I saw your painting. Don't you think that the tie of that man is too narrow? Now that the wide ones are in fashion.

OLGA   *(Ironically)* My dear, I really didn't think of it.

TERESA It seems you've had a great success. . . . (GRAZIANA *starts to examine the studies on the walls.*)

OLGA Let's not exaggerate!

GIORGIO A great success, indeed.

TERESA At least that's what I hear. I, on the other hand, cannot judge. I don't understand your modern art at all.

OLGA It's not that obscure.

GRAZIANA *(Pointing at one of the designs)* This is the study for your painting, isn't it?

OLGA Yes.

GRAZIANA And this *(Pointing at a nude)*, what is it?

TERESA *(To GRAZIANA, angrily)* Don't look! There's no need to. *(To OLGA)* As I was saying: all this realism doesn't suit me. These are no longer exhibitions, but shops of human flesh. . . . Nudes here, nudes there. . . . And even flesh gone bad. *(She sniffs from a bottle of fragrance.)*

OLGA You're so proper.

GIORGIO Criticism based on smell.

TERESA Oh, yes. You, too, are modern. Moreover, I saw that you have bought a painting.

GIORGIO You like it?

TERESA Maybe it's very beautiful, but let's be clear: I don't want that painting in my house.

GIORGIO Don't worry. It's for my personal use and enjoyment.

GRAZIANA Where are you going to hang it?

GIORGIO I don't know yet. . . .

OLGA What painting is it? Tell me.

GRAZIANA Gianforti's *Bacchante*.

GIORGIO Indeed.

OLGA You've shown good taste.

GIORGIO You think so?

TERESA Yes, yes; but this is the last time you see me at an exhibition: at least with her *(Pointing to GRAZIANA, still busy looking at the nudes)*. Didn't you under-stand? I said not to look! *(To OLGA)* You, too, could show some respect, since this is your living room. . . .

OLGA *(Ironically, getting up)* Oh, so sorry. I really didn't think of it. *(She removes two or three of the studies of nudes to a corner.)*

GRAZIANA *(Getting angry)* Oh, come on! It would be better if you just locked me in a convent!

OLGA Poor Graziana. Here, now you can look.

GRAZIANA No more theater, no more exhibitions, no more books. . . .

TERESA Well. . . . It's not I who write immoral comedies and indecent books.

GIORGIO What an exaggeration.

TERESA *(Whispering to GIORGIO)* Oh really? But tell me if tomorrow a man and a woman were to walk down the street . . . in their . . . suits . . . you understand? Wouldn't there be a hundred policemen ready to arrest them?

GIORGIO What's that got to do with this?

TERESA Everything, because those who walk in effigy along the walls of exhibitions should be subject to the same surveillance . . . at least that's what *I* think.

GIORGIO *(Gets up to say goodbye)* That's what you think but not what others think.

TERESA Oh, yes, we know. You're superior. . . .

GRAZIANA *(To GIORGIO)* Are you going?

TERESA Are you coming home for dinner tonight?

GIORGIO Sorry, I have an invitation.

TERESA Then tomorrow?

GIORGIO You know that I am waiting for some friends.

GRAZIANA You never come. . . .

TERESA It's as if I never had this son of mine. A nice fashion, that young men must have an apartment of their own. In my day it wasn't so. In my day the sons received their friends in their parents' house; but nowadays . . . enough, let's forget about it.

GIORGIO You're wrong, it will be a most moral dinner.

TERESA We'd better not talk about it at all.

GRAZIANA Are there immoral ones, too?

TERESA Be quiet, tattler.

GIORGIO I can even tell you who'll be there: Marquis Bei, Vettori, the lawyer. . . .

TERESA *(Becoming interested)* Who? The one. . . .

GIORGIO Who was in Viareggio, yes. *(GRAZIANA blushes. OLGA observes her.)*

TERESA To tell the truth, he could have come at least once to look us up, after so much familiarity.

GRAZIANA *(To OLGA)* He comes to see *you*, doesn't he?

OLGA *(Slightly embarrassed)* Sometimes. . . .

GIORGIO So: Bei, Vettori, Salvelli. . . .

GRAZIANA The one involved with Miss Liuzzi?

OLGA You're well informed!

TERESA Silly girl! She repeats everything like a parrot. . . .

GIORGIO We are celebrating with Bei, who, after ten years, has finally got his law degree.

TERESA You choose your friends well!

GIORGIO (*Laughing, to* OLGA) Signorina, goodbye. (*Exchange of greetings*)

TERESA Good day, empty head!

(GIORGIO *exits*)

Scene 5

OLGA, TERESA, *and* GRAZIANA

TERESA (*To* OLGA) You know, nowadays I seem to be walking on ice, in danger of slipping at every step. And since I have to bring up one of these innocent girls . . . (*Pointing to* GRAZIANA) ah, my responsibility is great indeed. . . .

OLGA My dear lady, all of these problems would not exist if girls were brought up in a different way.

TERESA Ah, of course, your theories.

OLGA When mothers tell you: you know, there are two kinds of truths. Those that you can know and those that you must ignore. What happens? It so happens that you are not interested in the permitted truths, and instead, with a morbid curiosity, you are attracted to the forbidden fruit, which you are supposed to ignore.

TERESA But Olga, Olga. You take too much liberty with your language. . . .
(*To* GRAZIANA) Go ask for a glass of water. A little consideration, for Heaven's sake.

(GRAZIANA *exits*)

Scene 6

OLGA *and* TERESA

TERESA A dozen girls like you, and the world would be revolutionized. Indeed, you couldn't possibly think differently. . . . You don't want to listen to the advice of those who care about you. . . . What would your poor mother say, bless her soul. . . .

OLGA I always thought she would have brought me up the way I brought myself up.

TERESA Oh, no. She was a saintly woman. A sweet and docile person. . . .

OLGA She also was, and you told me so many times, incapable of a lie or of any meanness. She, too, adored truth and I don't think she would condemn her daughter for having taken truth as her faith and religion. . . . Tell me, am I really so bad the way I am?

TERESA Bad. . . . What an idea!

OLGA But would you mind if Graziana were to come here frequently?

TERESA No. It's only that you have such ideas. . . .

OLGA (*Suddenly becoming very serious*) You're right. You should never bring her here.

TERESA My dear girl. And yet, believe me, some good advice, once in a while, wouldn't hurt you. Young people have no experience. . . . they don't see danger. . . . No one knows better than I that you . . . but after all. . . .

OLGA But what? What?

TERESA For example, are you happy about what people are saying? That you're a liberated woman, that young men come and go as they please in your house. . . .

OLGA Ah!

TERESA A girl is easily compromised.

OLGA I am the one to worry about that.

TERESA Oh, sorry. Enough said. . . .
(*A pause*) By the way, that Vettori . . . do you know him well?

OLGA Why?

TERESA I'm asking. . . .

OLGA Yes.

TERESA Because I'd like you to. . . . (*Getting closer to* OLGA), if the opportunity arises . . . to speak to him about Graziana . . . to listen to what he says. . . . No, there's nothing. But . . . in Viareggio . . . he was courting her a little . . . and to tell you the truth . . . I would very much like not to let things cool down. Young men of that kind are hard to find nowadays. What do you say?

OLGA For Heaven's sake, don't give me tasks of that kind. I'm not a match-maker.

TERESA Psst! . . . (*Looks around*) I was just saying . . . but it doesn't really matter.

Scene 7

Same, GRAZIANA *and* SILVIO

GRAZIANA (*Enters, excited, with a glass of water in her hand, followed by* SILVIO) Mother, look who's here!

TERESA Give it to me, or you'll spill it all. *(Takes the glass.)*

SILVIO How are you, Mrs. Mauri?

TERESA *(To Silvio)* We have to come *here* to have the pleasure of seeing you.

SILVIO *(To OLGA, offering her a bouquet of flowers)* There should be some laurel leaves as well. . . . My congratulations.

OLGA *(Coolly)* Thank you.

TERESA *(To SILVIO)* Tell me, how come you've never been to see us?

SILVIO Forgive me. I am not a very sociable person. . . .
(Meanwhile OLGA retreats to the other side of the room on the pretext of arranging the flowers in a vase.)

SILVIO *(To GRAZIANA)* And how have you been? How did you spend the winter? Did you have a good time? Did you dance a lot?

GRAZIANA Not at all. Mother claims that I'm too young for social life.

SILVIO Your mother is right.

GRAZIANA I'm almost nineteen years old!

SILVIO Uh, that's old.

TERESA These blessed girls are always in a hurry.

GRAZIANA And are you coming to Viareggio this year?

SILVIO Oh, I don't believe so.

OLGA *(Ironically)* Why? They say the air is very healthy.

GRAZIANA *(Excited)* And then everyone has such a good time. Do you remember that boat ride that ended so tragically?

SILVIO Of course. *(Embarassed, looks now and then in the direction of OLGA)*

GRAZIANA My poor dress . . . I still have it, just as it was, all spotted by salt water. Do you remember?

SILVIO It had light blue and beige squares.

OLGA *(Ironically)* What a good memory!

SILVIO *(Vexed)* It's nothing out of the ordinary.

TERESA *(Gets up and approaches OLGA affectionately)* What are you doing?

OLGA *(Coolly)* Arranging the flowers.

TERESA *(Sees a bunch of loose sketches)* Oh, how many beautiful things.

OLGA They're studies of nudes, you wouldn't like them.

TERESA Show me, show me. *(She keeps OLGA busy by asking questions.)*

GRAZIANA *(To SILVIO)* You really won't be coming to Viareggio?

SILVIO I don't believe so. And you?

GRAZIANA It would be terrible if everyone were as unfaithful as you.

SILVIO You slander me.

GRAZIANA And why haven't you ever come to see us? Because you no longer care about me, confess!

SILVIO Oh, what accusations!

GRAZIANA If you'd have come only once to see if I were alive or dead.

SILVIO I knew from Giorgio that you enjoyed good health the whole time. . . . But I'll come by. It will be an exception, since I never pay visits. . . . *(To OLGA, approaching)* And don't we get to see anything?

OLGA *(Coolly)* They're designs you've seen already.

GRAZIANA And I'm not allowed to see them.

SILVIO *(Approaching the painting of the Roman ruin)* Ah, you've done some work on it.

OLGA *(Turning around)* Where? Oh yes, just three hours this morning.

TERESA Splendid!

GRAZIANA Magnificent!

OLGA Oh. . . . It's just a rough draft. . . . *(To SILVIO)* And you have nothing to say?

SILVIO Well . . . I wish that someone, perhaps you Miss Olga, would explain to me once and for all, what you admire in those four old stones.

GRAZIANA Wow!

OLGA Come on now.

SILVIO You ladies are shocked because I'm frank? Believe me, among those thousands of people who gaze at the Roman Forum for hours, contemplating, I'll bet there aren't ten who do it in good faith.

GRAZIANA That's what you say.

OLGA Silence, silence, these are heresies.

SILVIO Then help me understand.

OLGA My work certainly cannot aim that high. . . . But don't you see the spirit of things long dead reflected from among the stones?

SILVIO The spirit of things long dead? . . . And what else?

OLGA I think that's enough.

SILVIO Good grief, it's time to wake up! Do you know what impression your spirit of Rome makes on me? The same as that of a beautiful woman who, seeing her beauty fade, decides to assume a spiritual role, stressing her soul, all of a sudden.

I've had enough of it, to tell you the truth.

OLGA   That's really scandalous.

TERESA   Don't let anybody hear you.

GRAZIANA   Is that why you live up there, in the Macao district?

SILVIO   *(Laughing)* Precisely. Up there you can at least breathe freely. Of course, once in a while, a short visit down here, too . . . but for everyday living you need a healthy environment.

TERESA   As far as that's concerned, you're right.

OLGA   It remains to be seen if the houses of the new Rome, which have no other advantage except that they're new, would compensate me for the lack of fine estheticism which I find in my "four old stones," as you call them.

SILVIO   And the advantage of being new seems insignificant to you, in terms of a house? Look, I'm the first one to live in my apartment in the Macao district, the first one, you understand, since the house was constructed? Do you realize what a pleasure it is to know that those walls are virgin walls, untouched by others? No one's foot has walked on that smooth floor except mine. The virginity of a house! . . . Doesn't the word itself tell you that it refers to something precious?

OLGA   Precious! It depends.

SILVIO   What contradictions! *(To* TERESA*)* What do you say, Mrs. Mauri?

TERESA   Oh, stay in the company of Olga and you'll hear some good ones.
(Gets up)

OLGA   So soon?

TERESA   I told you we have so many visits to make. . . . *(To* SILVIO*)* Then come see us.

SILVIO   I certainly will.

GRAZIANA   Are you going to the Argentina Theater tonight?

SILVIO   Yes. . . .

GRAZIANA   We are too.

SILVIO   Then I'll take the liberty of paying my first visit to your box.

TERESA   Bravo! Number 12, first row. *(To* GRAZIANA*)* Let's go.

SILVIO   I'll remember. Speaking of theater, did you hear what happened to Mrs. Pattiani? *(*GRAZIANA *starts to giggle.)*

TERESA   It's late, we must go. . . .

SILVIO   No, no, listen first. It's a good one. They were performing *The Virgins.* Mrs.

Pattiani, judging the play by its title, took her daughters along.

TERESA   Brava!

SILVIO   Immediately, from the first few scenes, she realized her big mistake. . . . But what was she to do? Were they to walk out, everyone would notice, she thought, especially since they weren't in a box, but had orchestra seats.

TERESA   I would have walked out.

SILVIO   She remained, however, and resorted to an ingenious expedient.

OLGA   That is?

SIVIO   That of coughing at the most salacious points. Now . . . you are familiar with the play?

TERESA   No, but I've heard about it.

SILVIO   Well, this meant . . . a lot of coughing. The people seated nearby were annoyed and began to shush her. To make a long story short, the poor lady had to swallow her cough, to the great joy of her girls.

TERESA   How awful!

SILVIO   And this morning, at the Exhibition, they talked only about Mrs. Pattiani's cough, and someone even offered her cough drops. . . . *(They all laugh.)*

TERESA   That's how they encourage us to do our duty. Ungrateful people! You should be the first to protect us.

GRAZIANA   It was a big effort for nothing, the girls had already read the play in secret . . .

OLGA   You get it?

TERESA   Oh, these girls! . . . Come on, let's go, it's late.
(They say goodbye. TERESA *and* GRAZIANA *exit.)*

Scene 8

OLGA   Those are the supposedly *pure* girls! Ha! . . . Lilies that wallow in mud.

SILVIO   Why?

OLGA   Don't tell me you didn't notice how that flirt courted you.

SILVIO   Eh, if that's all. . . .

OLGA   Oh yes, you laugh about it.

SILVIO   Should I make a tragedy of it?

OLGA   So it seems nice to you, the way she carried on with you?

SILVIO   Neither beautiful, nor ugly, just natural. It's well known how it happens. We meet in a seaside resort. She is pretty, I have nothing better to do, so I flirt. We men come back to town, forget, but the poor girls don't. At the first encounter they blush, get confused, try to reestablish the former relationship, without realizing that it's out of place in the new environment. They secretly keep a faded flower, a spotted dress. . . . You would condemn them?

OLGA If it were only once! . . . But they do it all the time. Fifteen days ago all of Rome thought her engaged to a certain fellow, now she's clinging to you. . . .

SILVIO Come, come, the poor girl doesn't deserve all that anger.

OLGA Oh, indeed. Because, for you, the shortcoming is only . . . that one. On the other hand, for me it's the repeated prostitution of one's thoughts: today they belong to you, tomorrow they belong to someone else. But nobody is scandalized about the secret dedications of these flirts of the soul, and one must be careful what one says in front of them.

SILVIO That's a new one! So the purity of the body has no value?

OLGA Compared to that of the soul, certainly not.

SILVIO Soul, soul, what a word!

OLGA Sure, anything goes, as long as we remain materially pure. That's the great virtue, that's true chastity. And why? Did they perhaps tell you that it's this particular chastity and not any other?

SILVIO (Becomes serious) My dear, when an idea is passed on from century to century, when it is handed down from generation to generation and received as a most sacred heirloom, when the majority consider it an idea full of truth and justice, I have the right to believe in it and to proclaim wrong those who think otherwise.

OLGA During Galileo's time they also thought that way.

SILVIO But man could not live, not even for a moment, without these laws. They are, at the same time, his enslavement and his liberty, his weakness and his strength. One must accept them without discussing them. Just as discussion in religion creates an atheist, so the one who discusses this ends up putting himself beyond the common circle, where there is no longer any law, any right, any duty, any truth, any falsehood. (OLGA stands as if terrified and looks at him bewildered.) My

little rebel, you'd like to change nothing less than all the human laws. But why? It's people embittered by great sorrows who become great rebels. But you? . . . – And now you're crying? – Olga. – Come, lift your head. . . . Oh, how silly of us to lose time like this, when I have so many things to tell you.

OLGA (Forcing herself to smile) Forgive me, I'm a little nervous . . . maybe I worked too long.

SILVIO When we are together at last, I'll hide the brushes.

OLGA (Gently) I'll rebel. . . .

SILVIO Yes, you can rebel against me. – So listen. – I've made an agreement with Ciatti, the engineer.

OLGA Oh!

SILVIO The negotiations for that industrial installation are almost concluded. Ciatti and I will assume the administrative management. . . .

OLGA Here?

SILVIO In Berlin. – Would you mind very much leaving Italy? Of course, I understand. . . . But it would be, at the most, for two years. After which, if business is good, we'll open a branch in Italy, in Milan, for example, where I would be in charge. But we'll talk about that later. And now . . . for the best part. (He shows her a letter.) Look.

OLGA (Becoming uneasy) From your father?

SILVIO With his permission. – How happy I am. Because, although I was ready to marry you in any case, it would have bothered me to go against his will. . . . But why don't you say something?

OLGA The surprise. . . .

SILVIO I understand. His inexorable opposition has been hard on your pride. But you must forgive him. Old people have strange ideas. . . . My father was thinking of a quiet, plain, and insignificant wife for me . . . in short, a girl like Graziana and so many others like her. The idea of having an artist as daughter-in-law frightened him. Poor old man, it seemed impossible to him that the woman whose name is Olga De Velaris could adjust to an obscure family life . . . could be a good wife. . . . But you mustn't hold a grudge against him; now that he's convinced . . .

OLGA (As if to herself) But he was right. . . .

SILVIO You were saying?

OLGA   Nothing. . . .

SILVIO   Is this how you receive such news?

OLGA   Who knows what you must be thinking of me! *(Bursting out suddenly)* Do you love me?

SILVIO   You know I do.

OLGA   No, tell me . . . I must hear you say it. . . .

SILVIO   You are my dear love. . . .

OLGA   I love you too, you know. . . . Oh, why isn't there a stronger, a more intense word . . . a word never said before . . .

SILVIO   Darling. – And now we'll be happy, always together . . . always . . . always. . . .

OLGA   No, no, hush . . . you mustn't – you mustn't ask too much. . . . *(She leans her head against his shoulder)* Like this . . . forever. . . .

SILVIO   Angel. – I'll write to my father this very day, and when he comes here we'll be engaged, and in two months. . . .

OLGA   No . . . no. . . .

SILVIO   Because, you know, we must be in Berlin in September. And . . . the honeymoon. . . .

OLGA   *(Painfully straightening up)* Why do you say all these things? Aren't we happy the way we are?

SILVIO   *(Passionately)* Don't you want to be happier?

OLGA   *(As if dreaming)* Even happier?

SILVIO   We'll take a wonderful trip . . . to Switzerland. Would you like that?

OLGA   *(After a short pause)* Listen. Don't you think it would be better to wait and get married after you return?

SILVIO   Return from where?

OLGA   From Berlin. So we can settle down once and for all. . . .

SILVIO   What? Are you serious? Wait another two years! Is that the great love you have for me?

OLGA   You're right. . . . And then . . . it would be just the same.

SILVIO   Olga, what are you saying?

OLGA   *(Decisively)* Listen, I have to tell you something.

SILVIO   Let's hear.

OLGA   But you have to answer me truthfully, you know, just as if you were about to die.

SILVIO   How cheerful!

OLGA   *(Making an effort)* Do you really care about this marriage?

SILVIO   Olga!

OLGA   Answer me.

SILVIO   Are you hiding something from me? – Have you changed your mind?

OLGA   No, no, dear. . . .

SILVIO   You no longer love me!

OLGA   God knows how much I love you.

SILVIO   So?

OLGA   I've been thinking about it for a long time. . . . It's useless. I'm not the right wife for you. Today I'm really convinced of it.

SILVIO   But that's *my* problem. You have no say in it. I want you the way you are. If you weren't like this, I wouldn't love you.

OLGA   *(Painfully)* But will you have the strength to surmount so many prejudices, so many principles dear to you?

SILVIO   Which ones?

OLGA   The very ones for which your father hesitated to give his consent. . . .

SILVIO   Obviously, an old man has certain preconceptions. . . .

OLGA   You, too.

SILVIO   I?

OLGA   You, yes. Didn't you tell me so just a while ago?

SILVIO   Thank you. It's one thing to place oneself above the prejudice that demands, for example, that one receives his bride from her mother's hands, but another to trample on a sacred principle in order to obtain her.

OLGA   *(Gloomily)* And if you had to do it? – *(SILVIO stirs, looks at her.)* You see! Ah, leave me, leave me, before it's too late.

SILVIO   *(In a terrified voice)* What are you saying? What are you saying?

OLGA   *(Her voice fading, turning her gaze at her unfinished painting)* Silvio. I am. . . . I, too . . . am . . . a ruin. . . . *(She hides her face in her hands.)*

SILVIO   *(Not understanding at first, looks at her, then, suddenly, understanding, pushes* OLGA *away from him)* Ah . . . shameful woman!

OLGA   *(Falling to her knees in front of him)* No, no! I haven't done anything evil. I swear to you. I swear it to you on the memory of my dead mother. Listen to me. *(SILVIO draws back and tries to leave.)* No, for God's sake! Don't leave me like this. Silvio, let me explain first. . . .

SILVIO   *(Shaking her arm violently)* And what do you want to tell me, shameful woman, imposter?

OLGA   I know, I know, but it's not true. I

never had a thought for anyone but you. I have been more yours this way than had I been your lover. . . . Do you believe me? Do you believe me?

SILVIO *(Savagely)* I believe . . . oh! What have I done to deserve this! . . . *(He throws himself onto a chair, sobbing.)*

OLGA *(Dragging herself toward him)* Don't cry. I beg you not to cry. I should have told you earlier . . . it's true . . . but I always hoped that you were different than the rest . . . and then, I couldn't live without you. . . . It was my terrible destiny. . . . *(In a broken and agitated voice)* I was just an innocent girl, you understand? I was just fifteen years old. . . . What could I know? They took me, just like a flower is taken from a meadow. . . . just like that, just like that. Do you think I wouldn't tell you the truth, at this point? . . . Wait, I want to tell you everything. . . . *(She touches her forehead, confused.)* I was in the country . . . where they had sent me after my mother's death . . . oh, my saintly mother! . . . I was with good folks . . . They treated me like their own daughter. And to keep me busy, they made me tend a small flock, which I led to pasture every morning. . . . Oh, those long solitary hours. I thought about my dead mother . . . about my far-away father, about our house to which I hadn't returned, not even once . . . . What sadness. *(Pauses)* And he . . . he would come sometimes and sit next to me. . . . We didn't talk, overcome by the heat . . . oh, I remember! I remember! . . . *(She shudders.)* That day! . . . *(She pauses.)* All of a sudden I saw in the boy's eyes a dark flame which scared me. And without knowing why, I started to run. . . . But he ran after me . . . reached me. . . . *(She hides her face in her hands.)* – Oh Silvio, the horror of that act committed unconsciously; the disgust with myself, the terror of others, and that constant feeling of regret and of shame, the immense anguish over the irreparable evil. . . . Oh, how many tears of humiliation I shed! – But then, later, there was a sudden flash of light in the darkness of my childish mind. And from the bottom of my heart the echo of a voice, confused and terrible, calling out to me: "Why do you humiliate yourself, why do you humiliate yourself so? Don't you

still have something which no one can take away from you unless you want to give it away? Come on, lift up your head. You, poor crying girl, you still have a soul!" *(With a cry, getting excited)* A soul! . . . A treasure all mine, that I possessed without knowing, a sacred virginity over which I had to watch. Ah, no, no, don't cry. It seemed to me that I was able to see it, all white, all pure, innocent, and mine, only mine. And I swore to myself never to contaminate it. I had a maternal tenderness for it, a maternal pride, and I thought about the man who would receive it one day and who, as the first and only one, would write on it his adored name. . . . Yours, Silvio, yours and no one else's, ever! All my thoughts are for you alone. For you, all of them, including the most secret ones. . . . Who cares about the rest? – Isn't that right, Silvio? Why don't you answer? – *(With anguish)* Will you deny me that which God promised me when I was a poor ignorant girl? Silvio! Just one word! *(Silence. Then in a fading voice)* So I was right when I cried. . . . Ah, I was right. . . . *(SILVIO will have followed her narration first with distrust, with desperation, then with ever growing commotion. . . . At her last words he looks at her intensely for a long time, eye to eye, without saying a word. . . . Then, suddenly, he lifts her from the floor and draws her to himself. . . . OLGA, at first dubious, gives in little by litte, but then, understanding, she throws herself into his arms with a cry. – They remain in an embrace, and motionless in the twilight. A little later a knock on the door is heard. They stir as if awakening from a dream and just manage to compose themselves . As the door opens, light streams in.)*

Scene 9

Same, and MARIETTA

MARIETTA *(Entering)* Excuse me, Signorina. . . . I brought my things. . . .

OLGA Come right in.

MARIETTA If you permit, there's also the porter with my trunk. . . .

OLGA Yes, that's fine.

MARIETTA Shall I have him come in?

OLGA Yes, call Mrs. Virginia, she will show you. . . . *(MARIETTA exits)*

Scene 10

OLGA *and* SILVIO

SILVIO Who is she?

OLGA Didn't you see her? It's Marietta.

SILVIO In the darkness. . . . Your model?

OLGA Yes. . . .

SILVIO And what is she doing here, at this hour, with that trunk?

OLGA Poor thing. Don't you know? Leonardi left her suddenly. . . . And I offered to let her come sleep here, for a few nights. . . . Was that wrong of me?

SILVIO Oh yes, they told me. . . . He's marrying a young lady from Milan. He got engaged yesterday.
(A pause: during which SILVIO *looks around with the expression of a man who, waking up, returns to reality. Then he rises and takes his hat, which he had left on a chair when entering.* OLGA, *uneasy, follows each movement.)*

OLGA You're leaving? So soon? Silvio. . . .

SILVIO *(Coolly)* Let's not make a scene, okay?

OLGA *(With sudden anguish)* Silvio! . .

SILVIO Let me go peacefully. It's best for you and me.

OLGA *(Desperately)* Silvio!! Oh, you've changed your mind. You don't believe me!

SILVIO No!

OLGA But if I swear to you. . . .

SILVIO It's all the same. . . .

OLGA But then . . . just now . . . you lied! . . .

SILVIO I dreamed. And all dreams end in an awakening, sooner or later. Let me go.

OLGA What? . . . You're leaving me? You're leaving me?! Silvio!!

SILVIO Signorina, don't scream. What do you want? We were victims of an hallucination. . . . We thought the impossible possible. . . . Be reasonable. . . .

OLGA *(Dropping onto the sofa)* Oh, he no longer loves me! . . .

SILVIO *(Leaning over her, in a hoarse voice)* But I adore you . . . and if you want to. . . .
*(*OLGA, *with a terrible cry, falls face down on the sofa.* SILVIO *flees.)*
Curtain falls rapidly.

Act II

Living room in GIORGIO's *apartment*

On the right, a desk, next to it a section with easy-chairs, sofa, etc. To the left, bookshelves. *Also on the left, windows. At the far end, to the left, a china cabinet, to the right, a door leading to the bedroom, hidden behind a drape. The entry is to the right of it. In the middle of the room, a table set for five. On the desk, several photographs of women.*

Scene 1

GIORGIO *and* SILVIO; *later* PAOLO

GIORGIO But I am the one to thank *you*, my friend. And I can assure you that my father will receive your request with great pleasure. Graziana's happiness could not be better entrusted to anyone else.

SILVIO *(Uneasy)* I swear to you that I will do whatever is in my power to make her life as easy and happy as possible. . . .

GIORGIO My mother will be so pleased about it. And I, too, feel relieved of a great responsibility. . . . You know that I almost feel a paternal tenderness toward my sister. I am ten years older than she. And her future has been a terrible problem for me. I know too well what lives young men lead nowadays, and I was afraid that she might fall in love with one of those society Don Giovannis. . . .

SILVIO But we speak about all of this as if we were certain about it. . . .

GIORGIO You have doubts about her consent? But she always liked you, from the first day she met you! Didn't you realize it? In Viareggio everyone was talking about it. . . . And, you know, my mother talked to me about the possibility of a marriage. . . . Then, when we returned to town, seeing that things had stopped there, I thought that it had only been a flirtation. . . .

SILVIO Indeed, speaking frankly . . . I would be telling a lie if I were to say to you that I thought about her this winter. When I met her, down there, I immediately felt a strong liking for her. And during that time I really fell under her charm, but without thinking about marriage at all. . . .

GIORGIO Yes, yes.

SILVIO And then, having come back to Rome, I picked up my old habits; not only the old ones but I even started new ones. . . . And finally I threw myself once more into the whirl of a bachelor's life. . . .

GIORGIO   I see, I see. . . .

SILVIO   Then. . . . some unpleasantness. . . .

GIORGIO   Unpleasantness?

SILVIO   No, nothing important. But, you know, the moment comes when you realize how empty your life is. . . . Sometimes even a small matter is enough to tilt the scale, to make you scream: enough! And so, seeing your sister yesterday evening, I realized that the attraction had been there all the time, although hidden; and. . . .

GIORGIO   You stayed a long time in our box!

SILVIO   It seemed to me that her company was good for me . . . that ingenuousness, that freshness of imagination, all that purity, which we young men rarely come into contact with, impressed me. It acted like a balm on my irritated nerves. . . .

GIORGIO   And in order not to regret it, you did not want to delay?

SILVIO   I won't regret it, for sure.

GIORGIO   Certainly, marrying a girl like Graziana, you'll have the advantage of molding her into whatever you wish. And then . . . you know that the wife is always what her husband makes of her. *(Looking at the clock.)* Oh, gosh! It's five-thirty. . . . I need to go out for a minute. . . . I forgot to order something. What will you do? Will you stay? *(He rings.)*

SILVIO   I'll come with you. . . .

PAOLO   *(Entering)* Sir?

GIORGIO   My coat and hat. *(To* SILVIO*)* And . . . in the meantime I'll speak about it at home, okay?

SILVIO   Wait for two or three days. I would prefer. . . .

GIORGIO   *(Jokingly)* I understand. There is some business to attend to . . . some old game to finish. . . .

SILVIO   No, that's not it. . . .

GIORGIO   *(Still joking)* Come on, you want to tell me? There are not many who are ready to get engaged immediately. Most would ask for a month to be able to present themselves as white as freshly washed linen! *(Putting on his coat)* Only . . . watch it, eh?

SILVIO   *(Uneasy)* What an idea!

PAOLO   *(Whispering to* GIORGIO*)* We don't have any champagne. . . .

GIORGIO   I ordered some. *(To* SILVIO*)* These are things a guest should not know about.

SILVIO   Come, come, between the two of us! *(They exit.)*

Scene 2

PAOLO *and a* PORTER

PAOLO *finishes setting the table. A little later, the doorbell rings.* PAOLO *exits and returns immediately, followed by a porter carrying a basket on his shoulder.*

PORTER   Where shall I put it?

PAOLO   Over here. Easy, oh! Don't you see that there are glasses? *(The* PORTER *puts the basket on the floor and pulls out some bottles.)*

PORTER   *(Counting)* Two, four, six. And this is the bill.

PAOLO   Take it to the Mauri residence.

PORTER   And what is this here?

PAOLO   A branch: we receive here, but we don't pay.

PORTER   Then I'll take it over there. *(Taking the basket)* Giotto Street, right?

PAOLO   Number 12. *(PORTER exits. –* PAOLO *is busy with the table. – The doorbell rings again.* PAOLO *exits.)*

Scene 3

PAOLO, GRAZIANA, MISS BETT

GRAZIANA   *(Entering with* PAOLO *and* MISS BETT*)* Oh, he is not in?

PAOLO   No, Signorina. He left ten minutes ago.

GRAZIANA   Alone?

PAOLO   With Mr. Vettori.

GRAZIANA   Ah! *(Looking at the table)* Oh, oh, all set. What time is dinner?

PAOLO   Six-thirty.

MISS BETT   *(To* GRAZIANA*)* So, what are we going to do?

GRAZIANA   Let me think. . . . *(To* PAOLO*)* You said he will be back shortly?

PAOLO   Well, that's what I think, Signorina.

GRAZIANA   I'll wait for him. . . .

PAOLO   If you want to tell me. . . .

GRAZIANA   No, no. I prefer to wait for him. *(PAOLO exits.)*

MISS BETT   Well, if you are going to wait . . . I could take advantage of it and go next door. . . . I have an errand. . . .

GRAZIANA   *(Looking at her insistently)* That's fine with me.

MISS BETT   I'll be back in ten minutes.

GRAZIANA   Go right ahead.

MISS BETT   Don't tell your mother. . . .

GRAZIANA   Don't worry. *(To herself, as* MISS BETT *walks to the door)* As if I didn't know where you are going.

*(*MISS BETT *exits.)*

Scene 4

GRAZIANA *alone; later* SALVELLI, *and then* PAOLO

GRAZIANA   *(Seeing the photographs)* More than an exhibition! Here it would indeed be appropriate to say: don't look! What a choice! *(Picks up some and looks at them)* This one is rather pretty . . . but so skinny! . . . This one too. . . . It seems that Giorgio has a weakness for skinny women. There is a whole collection of them. . . . Oh, oh! What a provocative posture! I bet that every woman is attractive in such an outfit. Dressed . . . more no than yes . . . buried in fur and flowers . . . and then they expect young men to prefer us, poor devils. . . . *(Goes to the bookshelf, opens it, looks at the books)* Philosophy of Love. . . . What could that mean? *(Takes the book and returns to the front of the stage, toward the sofa . Passing near the desk she sees some cigarettes, takes one and lights it.)* Since no one can see me. . . . *(Stretches out on the sofa in a relaxed manner, and starts to read)* *(*SALVELLI *comes in and sees* GRAZIANA, *whose back is turned to him. He looks at her knowingly and then starts coughing.)*

GRAZIANA   *(Startled, turns toward him)* Oh my God!

SALVELLI   Forgive me . . . I am sorry to have frightened the young lady . . . I found the door open. . . .

GRAZIANA   The door open?

SALVELLI   Yes, perhaps the butler went out a moment. . . .

GRAZIANA   Are you looking for Giorgio?

SALVELLI   Right.

GRAZIANA   I, too, am waiting for him. . . . He'll be right back. Sit down, in the meantime. . . . *(Tries to hide the book)*

SALVELLI   Don't worry about me. . . . If you'll permit, I'll introduce myself Salvelli, Corrado Salvelli. *(*GRAZIANA *smiles meaningfully at him. He looks at her perplexed.)* You . . . Do I have the honor of being already acquainted with you?

GRAZIANA   No, but I've heard so much about *you*. . . . *(The book falls on the floor.)*

SALVELLI   *(Embarrassed)* Ah! . . . *(Picks up the book and reads the title)* Brava! *(Maliciously)* What would you say if we were to read it together? . . .

GRAZIANA   I know how to read on my own. . . .

SALVELLI   I was saying . . . because this type of book is better enjoyed if it it's read with someone else.

GRAZIANA   *(With faked ingenuousness)* I don't understand. . . .

SALVELLI   *(Looking straight at her)* In that case we will put it back in its place, okay? *(Gets up)*

GRAZIANA   That's best. If Giorgio should come. . . .

SALVELLI *(Looking straight at her)* Yes, he could think. . . . *(Puts the book away)* It surprises me that he never talked to me about you. He should not have done that to me. . . . What is he afraid of? I know the duty of a friend only too well.

GRAZIANA   What does it consist of?

SALVELLI   I could go with you to the end of the world without. . . .

GRAZIANA   Without?

SALVELLI   *(Shrugging his shoulders)* Without! . . . *(A pause)* Tell me, what do you think of Giorgio?

GRAZIANA   That's a nice one. You ask me? I should ask you that.

SALVELLI   Oh, no one can deny that he is kind, but. . . .

GRAZIANA   But what?

SALVELLI   You can't trust him. He is very unreliable.

GRAZIANA   Oh yes?

SALVELLI   Oh! . . .

GRAZIANA   Careful, don't say nasty things about him to me.

SALVELLI   On the contrary. I wanted to say . . . that, I, for example, am certainly not as rich as he is, *(Stressing his words)* but I am so faithful! . . .

GRAZIANA   What has that to do with it?

SALVELLI   Oh, I am sure you are above . . . but, after all, I was just saying. . . . Yes, you see, if it takes me some time to fall in love . . . but once I'm in love, that's it. Giorgio on the other hand. . . . And then that collection there . . . *(Pointing to the photographs)* proves it.

GRAZIANA   So he has many victims?

SALVELLI   I speak to you as a friend. . . .

GRAZIANA But not as Giorgio's friend.

SALVELLI But after all, everyone brings grist to his own mill. And Giorgio deserves it, you know. Oh, how he deserves it!

GRAZIANA What?

SALVELLI Look, I'll explain with an example. There's nothing wrong with an example, right? An example.

GRAZIANA Well?

SALVELLI A fellow walks into the house of another fellow and finds a forgotten treasure. Take notice – a forgotten treasure on a chair. He looks at it, right?

GRAZIANA (Ingenuously) I don't see anything bad in it. . . .

SALVELLI He looks at it insistently, with desire. . . .

GRAZIANA Go on.

SALVELLI He draws near, he touches it. . . . (Goes through the motion)

GRAZIANA Go on.

SALVELLI He takes it, puts it in his pocket and carries it off. Eh? (The doorbell rings.)

GRAZIANA Ah, that way. Let me see. . . . (She gets up, examines SALVELLI's pocket and then, with a malicious laugh) Another time I advise you to have a larger pocket made. (She walks toward the door, laughing.)

PAOLO (Walking in) Miss Bett is waiting for you downstairs.

GRAZIANA (To PAOLO) I'm coming. I see that Giorgio is taking his time. I can't wait any longer. You will give him this letter. Be careful where you put it, don't lose it.

PAOLO Don't worry.

GRAZIANA Give it to him as soon as he returns and tell him that Father is waiting for an answer; he wants it as soon as possible.

PAOLO Yes, Signorina.

GRAZIANA (Maliciously to SALVELLI) See you. (Walks out)

Scene 5

PAOLO and SALVELLI

SALVELLI (To PAOLO) Oh, listen! . . .

PAOLO Yes, sir.

SALVELLI (Whispering, pointing to GRAZIANA) Who is she?

PAOLO Signorina Graziana, my master's sister. But, excuse me, how did you get in?

SALVELLI (With comic terror) Giorgio's sister?!

PAOLO Yes, sir. But how did you get in?

SALVELLI Leave me alone! What a blunder!! And I am an expert! I would have sworn. . . . (Starts to laugh)

PAOLO (To himself) That wretched porter must have left the door open. . . . (Exits)

Scene 6

SALVELLI, PAOLO, LORENZI; then GIORGIO, SILVIO, BEI.

PAOLO shows LORENZI in.

LORENZI (To SALVELLI) Ah, you're here.

SALVELLI (Continues to laugh) Ah, leave me alone!

LORENZI What's wrong?

SALVELLI (As above) I pulled a great one! A famous one! . . .

LORENZI When you think. . . .

SALVELLI (Coming close to him, whispers) Imagine! I took her for a loose woman. (GIORGIO enters; SALVELLI coughs.)

GIORGIO Hope you'll excuse me. . . .

SALVELLI (To LORENZI) These are things that don't happen every day. You understand!

LORENZI May the devil take you if I understand a thing!

SALVELLI (Whispers) Be quiet, beast! (Loudly) That's a nice way to do things. The guests have arrived and the master of the house is not in.

GIORGIO That's your fault, because you came too early. I, on the other hand, am late because. . . . Can you imagine? I went out a moment to order something and coming back. . . .

SALVELLI I hope that at least you will serve us a good dinner. I didn't even have breakfast. . . .

GIORGIO You should not have done that. I'll tell Paolo to serve you last. So . . . what was I saying?

SALVELLI Nothing so far, except nonsense.

GIORGIO Oh, yes. I was just about to reenter when I saw – who do you think? Matilde – all in tears.

LORENZI The devil! The devil!

SALVELLI What happened? Has Varsaghi died?

GIORGIO Much worse: Sultan died.

SALVELLI and LORENZI (At the same time) Sultan died?

GIORGIO Sultan died! That's the horrible news I bring you.

SALVELLI But how?

GIORGIO In a very simple way . . . a predictable one. That idiot Varsaghi was training him for tomorrow. In jumping over a hedge, he gave him little go: Sultan fell and broke a leg.

SALVELLI Oh God! I told him to have Withe ride him! And they killed him?

GIORGIO Immediately. By now. . . .

SALVELLI And I had placed a bet!

GIORGIO And I? One ought to break his head. But then, he's broken it already. . . .

SALVELLI What? What? He got hurt?

GIORGIO He smashed his head.
(In the meanwhile SILVIO *enters. Exchange of greetings)*

SALVELLI A nice feat, that's all I say. And Matilde?

GIORGIO You should have seen her. I could not get away from her.

LORENZI Goodbye necklace!

SALVELLI Don't be afraid. She is not a woman who loses time. I bet tomorrow she will permit herself to be consoled. . . . Can you guess by whom?

SILVIO I think it must have been Luigi who advised Varsaghi to mount that horse. . . .

LORENZI What a discovery!

GIORGIO It wasn't such a bad idea. And now what will he do?

SALVELLI Who?

GIORGIO Varsaghi is ruined. . . .

SALVELLI Well, he still has two ways out: shoot himself or go to America to work as a streetcar driver.

SILVIO A nice future!

LORENZI *(To* SILVIO, *apart, while* SALVELLI *and* GIORGIO *speak to each other)* And so?

SILVIO What?

LORENZI That marriage . . . now that the consent has arrived. When will it take place?

SILVIO *(Breaking into a nervous laugh)* My dear sir, you are always late!

LORENZI What do you mean?

SILVIO It burst just like a bubble.

LORENZI You must be joking.

SILVIO Not at all. . . .

LORENZI But how . . . suddenly?

SILVIO So many things happen suddenly.

LORENZI It can only be a misunderstanding.

SILVIO No misunderstanding. But if you were really that interested in my marriage, console yourself. If the first one did not go well . . . I asked for the hand of his sister. . . . *(Pointing to* GIORGIO*).*

LORENZI You are out of your mind!

SILVIO No, no. My mind is as clear as can be.

LORENZI But how. . . .

SILVIO That's enough for now. Perhaps another time. . . .

LORENZI But pardon me. . . .

BEI *(Walking in)* Good evening, everyone.

EVERYONE Ohhh! . . .

BEI See what happens when you pass the exams? It brings bad luck! It's going to cost me twenty thousand lire.

SALVELLI Ah, ah, him too!

BEI That damned rascal!

PAOLO Ready.

LORENZI Who? Varsaghi or dinner?

GIORGIO Both. *(To* PAOLO, *pointing to* SALVELLI*)* You will serve that gentleman last.

SALVELLI That's too much!

GIORGIO Certainly, you eat for four. . . .

SALVELLI *(Sitting down at the table)* Well then. Blessed are the last ones, if the first ones are well bred!
(They all sit down at the table. PAOLO *serves them.)*

GIORGIO *(To* BEI*)* And so, if Professor Torni's wife hadn't been caught with Vittorio, you would have flunked for the tenth time!

LORENZI The fall of a woman prevents that of a student! . . .

BEI Strange, but true. Let me tell you. . . . Delicious, this "risotto."

SALVELLI *(In a doleful voice)* Blessed are the last ones, if the first ones are well bred!

BEI First of all I hope that you won't offend me by not believing me when I say that I tried my best to flunk. . . .

ALL OF THEM We don't doubt it.

BEI But what do you want? That poor man certainly had other things on his mind. . . .

SILVIO Who?

BEI *(To* SILVIO*)* Professor Torni. Don't you know? He recently discovered that his wife was betraying him. . . . And I, as if it had been done intentionally, wrote him a thesis on. . . . Oh, I say, it really was a farce.

SILVIO A new one?

BEI Not at all.

SALVELLI So still the old one. . . .

BEI On the legitimization of illegitimate children.

GIORGIO   Just the perfect topic! *(To
SALVELLI, who is emptying the plate)* Don't
stand on ceremony.

SALVELLI   I certainly won't, my friend.

BEI   But then I had corrected and enlarged
it, according to my latest experiences. . . .

LORENZI   Personal?

BEI   Ten years ago, when Professor Torni
was still a bachelor, I could not imagine
that ten years hence, Mrs. Torni not only
would have had a lover, but also the
insolence to tell her husband. . . . what
she said to him.

SILVIO   And so?

BEI   At a certain moment in the discussion,
I had the opportunity to quote right to his
face part of article 165 of the Civil Code
where it says that "the husband cannot
refuse to recognize a child as his, on the
pretext of adultery, unless the child's birth
was concealed from him."

ALL OF THEM   Ohhhh!

GIORGIO   Come, that's too much!

BEI   Just listen to this. I thought he would
have a stroke. He got all confused. He
groped, he stammered . . . and I took
advantage of it by rattling off a series of
blunders, until his colleagues, moved by
pity. . . .

SILVIO   For whom? For you or for him?

BEI   For both of us, obviously . . . by
sending me away with the highest marks.

GIORGIO   Really?

LORENZI   *(Getting up)* Friends, let's drink to
the health of husbands!

GIORGIO   Oh no!

ALL OF THEM   Down with husbands, down!

LORENZI   Long live husbands! Because if
not for husbands, there wouldn't be any
wives. Understood?

SILVIO   Bravo Lorenzi!

BEI   Speaking about husbands and wives.
What do you say about Bardi's marriage?
(SILVIO becomes uneasy.)

SALVELLI   Five-hundred thousand lire of
dowry. That says it all.

LORENZI   She is as ugly as can be.

BEI   What does it matter?
*(They continue to talk among themselves.
PAOLO, who had gone out a moment,
returns and says something in GIORGIO's
ear.)*

GIORGIO   What? She's here?

PAOLO   Yes sir.

GIORGIO   But what does she want? *(Gets up)*

PAOLO   She did not tell me. . . .

BEI   *(To GIORGIO)* Where are you going?

GIORGIO   Excuse me for a moment. . . .

SALVELLI   I get it. Have her come in!

LORENZI   *(Arguing with the others)* It's not
true. He had no obligations.

SILVIO   It would be a nice one if we had to
marry loose women!

BEI   I'll quote you the article. . . .

LORENZI   There's no article to support that!
*(While GIORGIO is about to exit, the door
opens and OLGA, who is very pale, appears
on the threshold.)*

Scene 7

The same and OLGA

*During the entire scene OLGA's behavior will
reflect a nervous, ill-repressed agitation, evident
from her banal discourse.*

GIORGIO   *(Confused)* Forgive me, the
surprise. . . .

OLGA   I thought you did not want me. *(She
shakes his hand and steps forward.)*

BEI   *(Whispers to the others)* Who is she?

SALVELLI   Gosh, what a beauty!
*(SILVIO is terrified. LORENZI looks at him
anxiously.)*

OLGA   I am disturbing you, it seems.

GIORGIO   *(In a shaking voice)* In my house
you can only be welcome – always.

OLGA   "A la bonne heure!" . . . Why don't
you introduce me to your friends?

GIORGIO   *(Offering her a chair)* Please. . . .

OLGA   Thank you. . . . No, no. Never mind.
I don't want to create confusion. *(Looks at
SILVIO, as if noticing him only at that very
moment.)* Oh! . . . You are here too? Good
evening. How are you?
(SILVIO, very pale, bows.)

GIORGIO   *(Introducing)* Marquis Bei, the
lawyer Salvelli, Count Lorenzi. . . .

LORENZI   I have already had the honor. . . .

OLGA   Yes, I recall. . . .

GIORGIO   Miss De Velaris. . . .
(They all look at each other, surprised.)

OLGA   Please, go on. . . . *(To GIORGIO)* It
surprises you to see me drop in like this?

GIORGIO   It's a pleasant surprise for one
who did not expect such a courtesy from
you.

OLGA   And yet it's quite simple. I was
alone, with an interminable evening
before me. I recalled that this evening
you would be at home, in good
company, and so I came. *(She takes off her*

cape. BEI *gets up to take it.)* Thank you, Marquis.

SALVELLI We admired you, yesterday, through your work. . . .

OLGA Oh, for Heaven's sake! Don't remind me of my misery. You know, we artists are like that. . . . There are moments when we would like to forget ourselves. . . . I don't know if you understand me. . . .

GIORGIO May I ask you to keep us company? . . . *(He offers her some fruit.)*

OLGA I hope you did not think I would pay you the compliment of coming here to eat?

SALVELLI We would have been most happy to share this miserable dinner with you.

OLGA *(To* GIORGIO*)* Is that flattering you?

GIORGIO Don't mind him. He is in the habit of not eating for twenty-four hours before an invitation. Therefore even the most Pantagruelian dinner is not sufficient for his voracity.

OLGA Indeed?

SALVELLI He covers his stinginess with a slander.

GIORGIO As if you yourself had not confessed that you haven't even had breakfast this morning.

SALVELLI But it's the most elementary act of courtesy to bring to the host's house a good, twelve-hour appetite. Had I known, I would not have sacrificed myself. . . .

LORENZI Poor victim!

SALVELLI It's a hard lot, in this world, to be misunderstood. Don't you think so?

OLGA I wouldn't know. . . . *(Ironically)* I always had the rare fortune of being appreciated and understood. . . .

GIORGIO Oh, you! That's natural. . . .

OLGA You really believe it!? You didn't always think so. . . .

SALVELLI It's a matter of being born under a lucky or unlucky star.

OLGA Precisely. And mine, in fact, was a very lucky star. A good woman, who was like a mother to me, used to tell me that when I was born, the entire sky was covered with dark, stormy clouds and only one tiny star was visible between two clouds, as if it wanted to spy on me. . . .

GIORGIO That's easy. Always victorious.

LORENZI Fond of danger.

OLGA And the good woman also used to say that I would be very happy, because I had a strong soul. *(She laughs bitterly.)*

BEI Why do you laugh about it?

OLGA Just so. . . . These old fables always make me laugh. And you, Vettori? . . . Let's hear your voice!

SILVIO I have nothing to say. . . .

SALVELLI Does the smoke bother you?

OLGA Look! *(Takes out her cigarette case)*

SALVELLI In that case. . . .

BEI *(Pointing to* SILVIO*)* Perhaps you don't know him well enough. He is a poor lad stricken to silence in the presence of beauty. Permit me. . . . *(He offers her a light.)*

OLGA Thank you.

BEI These strange effects can be seen in many individuals. . . .

OLGA Indeed?

BEI Certainly. I even intend to write an article about it.

SILVIO *(Annoyed)* He talks nonsense. . . .

BEI The subject makes you regain your speech. That's a bad sign.

OLGA You are indeed profound, Marquis.

BEI Oh, no science is unknown to me. I can give you lessons in physiology, alchemy, palmistry. . . .

OLGA Indeed? Then. . . . let's see how far your knowledge goes. Here, read my hand. *(Starts to take off her glove)*

BEI If you don't mind, I'll read whatever you want from your glove.

OLGA My glove?

GIORGIO The depth of his studies permits him to do even that!

BEI But . . . easy. Take it off straight, this way. . . . That's it.

LORENZI It's so obvious he just got his law degree two days ago!

BEI *(Scrutinizing the glove)* A black glove a rigid personality. The imprint of the nails is rather prominent, especially that of the thumb: a sign of authoritarian inclination. Look how the leather is worn, right here, in the hollow of the palm, that points to the habit of forming a fist: force of will. Oh! Oh! This is symptomatic!

GIORGIO What is it?

BEI I clearly see the marks of three nails in the form of a crescent. Look.

OLGA *(Annoyed)* I don't see anything.

BEI And yet . . . I bet that I can find the same signs on your hand. . . . You permit. . . . *(Scrutinizes* OLGA*'s hand)* Oh, oh! That's bad!

OLGA What wrong? Is there morc?

BEI It almost seems done on purpose! See

where this little nail mark is, the same as is visible on the glove?

OLGA Yes. . . .

BEI Halfway along the life-line! – (*In a mockingly serious tone*) You broke your life in half, in a moment of rage.

LORENZI Stop it, that's enough.

SALVELLI Charlatan!

OLGA (*Uneasy*) I advise you to study some more. You are not profound enough.

BEI I would be happy if I'm mistaken. In the meantime let me contribute toward healing that fatal sign. . . . (*He presses a long kiss on the palm of* OLGA's *hand.*)

GIORGIO I think you contribute a little too much!

BEI (*Returning to his seat*) I do the best I can.

SILVIO (*Getting up suddenly*) You must excuse me, but I really must go.

GIORGIO At this hour?

SILVIO Yes. . . . Didn't I tell you? . . . I have an appointment.

SALVELLI Not very gallant, my friend!

GIORGIO Come on, what appointment?

SILVIO But indeed . . . I assure you . . . at the Valle Theater.

OLGA (*Ironically*) Let him go. . . . Perhaps he does not feel well. . . .

SILVIO (*Holding himself back with difficulty*) You are mistaken. I feel fine. If I had had the least notion that you cared about my presence. . . .

OLGA Obviously. Isn't it natural, among old friends?

SILVIO (*Drawing close to* OLGA, *whispering*) Is this provocation?

OLGA (*Whispering*) Why?

SILVIO This is no place for you.

OLGA On the contrary! . . .

SILVIO Let's go. I'll accompany you.

OLGA What an honor. – I am staying.

SILVIO Mind you. . . .

OLGA You are threatening me? – You are forgetting that you no longer have any right to do so! (*Loudly*) What are they performing at the Valle Theater tonight?

SALVELLI It's the opening night of *The Rights of the Soul*.

LORENZI (*Whispers to* SILVIO) Come on, let's go.

SILVIO (*Whispers back*) No.

GIORGIO By Giacosa, isn't it?

BEI What a strange title.

GIORGIO It's a rather daring idea to propose that a woman can claim for

herself the right to be unfaithful in her thoughts, as long as she is not bodily. . . .

SALVELLI I think that's great.

BEI Me, too. That way there are two different civil statutes: one for the body, the other for the soul. For example, one would read in the newpapers: "Today the spirtual marriage between Mr. X and Miss Y took place. The bride's witness was her corporal husband Mr. Z. The groom's witness was etc., etc. The couple left for a Platonic honeymoon within the space of thought." (*They all laugh.*)

LORENZI As far as I am concerned, I would rather be the husband-witness.

SALVELLI Smart Alec, my friend!

GIORGIO And I . . . I would almost prefer to be the other. . . .

ALL OF THEM Eh, eh!

GIORGIO Yes, gentlemen. Since we disagree, we must establish first of all in which of the two ways a man actually and truly possesses a woman.

BEI (*Pointing to* OLGA) Here is one who can judge.

OLGA Mr. Mauri, don't talk nonsense, my friend. . . .

GIORGIO I am not!

OLGA (*Holding herself back with difficulty*) The soul. . . . Sentimentalism of days gone by. What do you say, Mr. Vettori? – You must know something about it, I believe.

SILVIO (*Beside himself*) Yes! I claim that the chastity of the body goes beyond every-thing else and that the soul is an obsolete pretext of those who cannot offer more.

SALVELLI Bravo!
BEI You are right!   } (*All at the same time*)
GIORGIO You are wrong!

OLGA (*Bursting out to* SILVIO) Oh, you think I really care about my soul? You think I am one of those who preserves it for the big occasion? Hah, hah! (*With a nervous laugh*) Do you want to see how much I value it? Here I am selling it! I will sell it to whoever gives me most for it!

ALL OF THEM Great! – Original!

OLGA Come on, how much do you offer?

SILVIO I've never bought souls.

OLGA But I'll give you the rest as a bargain. I hope it still has some value. Eh? (*To the others, who listen to this fast dialogue without understanding the hidden meaning*) You too. – Who will give the most?

SALVELLI Ten thousand lire.

BEI Twenty thousand.

GIORGIO (*Jokingly, but somewhat uneasy*) Fifty thousand.

OLGA (*Agitated*) Mr. Vettori, step forward. Are you afraid?

SILVIO (*Beside himself*) Shame on you!

OLGA Oh, oh!

LORENZI (*To* SILVIO) Let's go.

SILVIO Leave me alone. (*To* OLGA) And if you think. . . . (*Is about to throw himself at her*)

OLGA What? What?

LORENZI But Silvio, have you gone mad? (*Succeeds in getting him away from* OLGA)

BEI A hundred thousand.

SALVELLI Two hundred thousand.

GIORGIO Stop it!

OLGA (*Increasingly agitated, beside herself*) Let's go on. Vettori! (*At this point* SILVIO *is dragged out through the door by* LORENZI.)

GIORGIO (*In a powerful voice*) Everything I have!

OLGA Ah! . . . (*Exhausted, falls onto a chair*) Let me drink. . . . (GIORGIO *pours her a glass of water.*)

SALVELLI (*To* BEI, *only*) That's the end of it. . . .

BEI (*With comic desolation*) All we can do now is disappear. . . .

SALVELLI It's always like that: when two have a quarrel. . . . (*Meanwhile* OLGA *walks to the window and looks outside, without moving, with her back turned to the others.*)

BEI (*Whispering to* GIORGIO) My congratulations.

SALVELLI (*Also whispering*) Mine too. What an original idea! . . .

BEI Do you know what's behind it?

GIORGIO A moment of madness.

BEI Of which you took advantage.

GIORGIO You will do me the favor of going now and you will give me your word of honor not to utter a single word.

BEI Certainly.

SAVELLI We'll keep it under our hat!

GIORGIO Tell the other two. . . . I can trust you?

BEI Certainly.

SALVELLI I am surprised at you! Rascal! (*They exit laughing and talking among themselves. All this dialogue, just like the scene of the auction, must be performed very rapidly.*)

Scene 8

OLGA *and* GIORGIO

GIORGIO (*After having accompanied the two friends out, comes back, closes the door and looks, for some time, at* OLGA *who remains motionless. He slowly approaches her*) Olga . . . (OLGA *shudders, turns around, looks at him as if lost.*) What have you done? . . .

OLGA (*Becoming agitated again*) Oh yes! I know, I know!

GIORGIO Don't get excited. (*He goes to the door, as if to make sure that no one is listening.*)

OLGA (*Misinterpreting his intentions*) Don't be afraid. I am not going to run away, no. (*In a paroxysm of ever-increasing agitation*) Look at me, I am not moving. What are you waiting for? Am I not yours? . . . And when you have had enough of me, you'll throw me out . . . and I'll go to someone else . . . and then to another one. . . . (*She takes a few steps as if she were drunk. Suddenly she cries out*) Oh my God! What have I done! (*She is about to fall;* GIORGIO *runs up to her to hold her up.*) No, let me go! I don't want to! I don't want. . . .

GIORGIO (*Almost carrying her to the sofa*) For God's sake, don't yell so. . . . I am not going to harm you, look . . . I am not even touching you. You are in the house of a friend. Calm yourself. . . .

OLGA (*Looks at him steadfastly, then, in a trembling voice, like a frightened child*) Don't hurt me. Be kind. I am asking only for a minute, a minute only. . . .

GIORGIO Certainly, I am not touching you. . . .

OLGA I am suffering so much . . . here . . . listen. (*She takes one of his hands and presses it against her forehead*) Can you feel it? It's pounding. . . . No, no, don't take it away. (*Makes him hold his hand against her forehead*) It soothes me. It's so cold. . . . Why is your hand so cold? Ah, wasn't it horrible of him to tell me all those things? To me. . . . They said the same to Marietta . . . but she at least has a child . . . a child all her own. . . . You understand! I have no one, no one who loves me. Is it true that I did not deserve it? Tell me, Mauri, is it my fault if that shameless. . . . (GIORGIO *covers his eyes with one hand.*) You are crying! . . . Why are you crying? You feel sorry, because you are kind. . . . He did it purposely. . . .

To provoke me. Did you realize it? Purposely. . . .

GIORGIO (Forcefully) Where did you see him?

OLGA (As if sensing danger) Where? Did I say where? . . . What did I say? . . .

GIORGIO Here, in my place?

OLGA No, no! Far away.

GIORGIO It's Vettori! Tell me!

OLGA No, no!

GIORGIO It's him!

OLGA No!

GIORGIO Yes!

OLGA No, no!

GIORGIO (Pressing her arm) Then tell me who?

OLGA I don't know. . . . You're hurting me!

GIORGIO Tell me!

OLGA You are hurting me! (She frees herself and gets up.) And why would you care? Does one ask a creature like me the name of her first lover?

GIORGIO (Beside himself) Ah, you had a lover! (Correcting himself) That is not possible. . . . Why do you tell me things that are not true?

OLGA Things that are not true?

GIORGIO Yes, yes!

OLGA What do you know?

GIORGIO I know you. . . .

OLGA You know me? You! (With a bitter laugh) No one knows me.

GIORGIO (Passionately) Olga! You know that I . . . love you.

OLGA No! I beg you! Don't subject me to this last humiliation! . . . Oh, how horrible! How horrible! (She falls onto the seat again, crying.)

GIORGIO (Tenderly, whispering) The man who really loves, respects the woman he loves, even if she has fallen. . . .

OLGA (With painful irony) Respects! . . .

GIORGIO Yes . . . yes . . . respects. . . . Don't cry. I can't see you cry. . . .

OLGA But why do you treat me this way? Don't you understand that it is worse, . . . that. . . . Oh, don't I disgust you?

GIORGIO I love you. . . .

OLGA Tell me awful things. . . . Tell me. . . . But no pity, no, no!

GIORGIO You are offended by the pity of one who loves you? I know that you have suffered so much, my poor darling. . . . And I feel pity for you.

OLGA (As if lost) Who suffered?

GIORGIO You will tell me everything, one day.

OLGA Oh, yes. Everything! . . . To you. But now . . . I can't.

GIORGIO Not now. . . . One day. Whenever you like.

OLGA One day, yes. . . . Perhaps tomorrow. But when you know. . . . Ah! . . . You too, then. . . . (Becoming agitated again) Just like him!

GIORGIO No, no . . . calm down. It's enough for now. Step a moment in there to tidy your hair . . . your beautiful hair, all messed up. . . . (He caresses her with a trembling hand.) Come.

(He leads her towards the door of the bedroom, lifting the drape a bit. OLGA, after a moment's hesitation, enters. GIORGIO lets the drape drop and rings the bell..)

Scene 9

GIORGIO, PAOLO, then OLGA
PAOLO appears at the door.

GIORGIO (Takes OLGA's cape and hat and tells PAOLO with a choking voice) You will go call a cab and you'll accompany the lady home.

(OLGA, reentering, hears this, looks at GIORGIO with an expression of profound surprise and infinite gratitude.)

GIORGIO (Helps her put on her hat and cape, then, in a loud voice) I am grateful that you came. . . . I'll see you tomorrow, right? (Bows respectfully)

OLGA (Walks toward the door while looking at him; and on the threshold, in a voice profoundly moved, murmurs) You are so kind! . . . (Exits)

(GIORGIO, alone, sits down, dropping onto the sofa, exhausted, and covers his face with his hands.)
Curtain

Act III

A ground floor room in the Mauri Villa. At the far end, a glass door leading into the garden. To the right and to the left doors leading to the internal rooms

Scene 1

SILVIO, GIORGIO, and OLGA

SILVIO is seated in front of a desk in a corner, looking sad and depressed. GIORGIO and OLGA enter from the left and continue to talk

to each other without noticing SILVIO.
GIORGIO *is ready for departure.* SILVIO *watches them with an expression of painful envy.*

OLGA *(To* GIORGIO) But will you really come back tomorrow?

GIORGIO Certainly.

OLGA The house seems sad without you.

GIORGIO Do you think that I will be happy far away from you? But what can we do? We can't both leave our guests by themselves. . . .

OLGA Will you send me a telegram as soon as you arrive?

GIORGIO Yes. And you? Will you write me?

OLGA A big, ten-page letter.

GIORGIO Brava. And will you also remember to take a look at those galley-proofs?

OLGA I won't fail. It will be a way of passing time thinking about you. . . .

GIORGIO Darling! *(Kisses her. Turns around and sees* SILVIO) Ah! . . . Good morning. Nice to see you up. *(Shakes his hand)*

SILVIO *(Bowing to* OLGA) Oh, I didn't get up just now.

GIORGIO Good for you. The morning air is good for you. Where is Graziana?

SILVIO I think she is still in the bedroom. . . .

GIORGIO What a lazybones!

OLGA She has city habits. . . .

GIORGIO For the time being let her have her way. This first week she must rest. . . . But then I'll take it upon myself to wake her up at six. Dash it! This way she is missing the best hours. . . . *(Searching in his wallet and in his pockets)* Oh, my goodness! . . .

OLGA Have you lost something?

GIORGIO That receipt, of all things.

OLGA It's probably in the bedroom. Let me go see. *(Exits to the right)*

GIORGIO I could have sworn that I had put it here. . . .

SILVIO It must be in the bedroom, as Signora Olga says.

GIORGIO Let's hope so. . . .

SILVIO Are you coming back tomorrow?

GIORGIO Yes. . . . I am sorry to have to leave you, but I can't avoid it. . . .

SILVIO When it comes to business one must not stand on ceremony.

GIORGIO It's not really business . . . that is. . . . Now I'll make you laugh: I have an appointment with my editor. . . .

SILVIO With your editor! . . .

GIORGIO Yes. I have a book in print.

SILVIO You? Are you serious?

GIORGIO Yes. . . . A study on fifteenth-century art. . . .

SILVIO Wow! I would never have thought. . . . Congratulations.

GIORGIO Come on, come on, say it. You would never have thought that I would succeed in something, right?

SILVIO Let's make it clear: not because of lack of talent . . . but on account of laziness.

GIORGIO Yes, yes, it's true. I myself would not have thought it possible. It's all due to Olga. In fact, I needed to be pricked, spurred, like a reluctant horse. . . . Just imagine. It was a combination of things, one could say. One day, shortly after we were married, she cleaned one of my drawers and found among some old papers a draft I had written on that subject. You know that I have always written in my spare time. I threw down my ideas in whatever way they came to me, but then I let them rot in the drawer. Well, Olga read that draft and she liked it; and from that moment on she started to torment me, to tell me that the idea was good, that I should elaborate on it. In the end she said so much and did so much that she succeeded in making me cast aside my phenomenal laziness. I began collecting the necessary material for my work and, little by little, you know how it happens, I got pleasure out of it. . . . And then there was always Olga at my side to advise me, to help me. . . . Ah, to work that way is pleasant. She had a desk installed for me in her atelier. She would paint and I would write. . . . And now, after a year and a half of tireless work, I have done it. We are correcting the galley-proofs. It will come out in November.

SILVIO *(Listening to him avidly, but distressed)* Good for you! Good for you!

OLGA *(Returning and waving a piece of paper)* Didn't I tell you!

GIORGIO Ah, it was there?

OLGA It had fallen behind the chest of drawers.

GIORGIO That was lucky. Thank you. *(Puts away the receipt. To* OLGA) I was speaking about you. I was saying nasty things about you. . . .

OLGA *(Jokingly)* Shame on you!

GIORGIO Yes, I was saying to Silvio that if I have come to something it's all credit to you.

OLGA Eh, come on!

GIORGIO It's the truth. And one must always tell the truth, right?

SILVIO *(In an unsteady voice)* Certainly. . . .

OLGA *(Trying to change the subject)* Isn't it time to go?

GIORGIO She is sending me away!

OLGA The train won't wait for you.

GIORGIO There's time, there's time.

OLGA Let's see if the carriage is ready. . . . *(Steps out into the garden)*

SILVIO *(In an intensely sorrowful voice taking both of* GIORGIO'S *hands)* How happy you must be!

GIORGIO Yes. . . . I don't believe two people could get along better. . . . And to think that I had to fight hard to win her!

SILVIO *(In a trembling voice)* Fight? . . .

GIORGIO *(Hurriedly, passing on)* Oh, certain ideas of hers. . . . *(In a louder voice)* And then my mother: you can imagine! . . . But now she's changed her mind. Olga is an angel . . . You have to get to know her well: she has a withdrawn personality. Even to you she might seem cold, sometimes. She can't get used to sudden intimacy. . . . *(Noticing* SILVIO'S *agitation)* But what's wrong with you? You don't seem yourself. . . . Aren't you happy, too?

SILVIO Yes, yes, very happy. Why?

GIORGIO Silvio. Silvio . . . I am not blind. Nor does happiness make me an egotist to the point of not noticing those who are near me. Perhaps some business matters? . . .

SILVIO Oh, business is booming.

GIORGIO Then I don't understand. . . . *(Suddenly, looking at him)* Graziana?

SILVIO No, believe me . . . it's nothing . . . it will pass. . . .

GIORGIO For two nights now, instead of sleeping you have been walking up and down the study until dawn. . . .

SILVIO How do you know?

GIORGIO Your study is right above our bedroom. . . .

SILVIO I didn't know. I am sorry if I disturbed you. . . .

GIORGIO That's not what I meant. But it means that something is tormenting you. . . . And during the daytime you are always sad and taciturn. . . . Why? Tell me why?

SILVIO *(With an effort)* It's true: I am a little sad. . . . But no one is to blame except myself. It will pass. . . . I will find a way of getting better. . . . I will certainly find it. . . . *(As if talking to himself)* I am, indeed, out of place among the rest of you. . . .

GIORGIO No. But we would like to see you happy. . . .

SILVIO *(Gloomily)* I feel like a dark spot on your beautiful blue sky. *(Slowly, insistently)* And spots must be washed off.

OLGA *(From the garden)* Giorgio! It's getting late.

GIORGIO Here I am! Coming. *(To* SILVIO*)* See you.

SILVIO Goodbye. Have a good trip.

GIORGIO Greetings to Graziana. And take heart, what the hell!

SILVIO *(Pointing to* GRAZIANA*)* Look, here she is. . . .

Scene 2

The same and GRAZIANA

GRAZIANA *(Entering from the left, in a riding dress, to* GIORGIO*)* You're going away?

GIORGIO Lazybones! You've just got up, eh? I must run, it's late. Need anything from Rome?

GRAZIANA No, thanks. *(They kiss.)* Have a nice trip.

OLGA *(From outside)* Giorgio, you'll miss your train!

GIORGIO Coming. *(Goes out in a hurry)*

Scene 3

GRAZIANA *and* SILVIO

SILVIO *(To* GRAZIANA*)* Where are you going?

GRAZIANA Riding.

SILVIO By yourself?

GRAZIANA With Ferrandi.

SILVIO I would prefer that you don't go today, since Giorgio is away.

GRAZIANA Why?

SILVIO Because . . . you two alone. . . .

GRAZIANA I don't see anything wrong in it.

SILVIO Perhaps. But I beg you to give it up for today. If you don't want to do it for me, do it for the others. . . .

GRAZIANA But why? I don't get it.

SILVIO Because it seems strange, to say the least, that after two years of absence, instead of being eager to enjoy your family, you spend three-quarters of each day with a person who is neither your mother, nor your brother, nor your sister-in-law. And in fact, I am not the only one who's noticed it.

GRAZIANA *(Ironically)* Olga? Right?

SILVIO No, no, your mother. Yesterday evening, for example, seeing that you would not come back in from the garden, where you had been for over an hour with Ferrandi, she went to her room without saying good night to you.

GRAZIANA She had a headache.

SILVIO I know her well enough. She loves you too much to reproach you in front of me. But if you would really like to know, she went to her room painfully offended by your behavior.

GRAZIANA Fine. I'll ask her if it's the way you say it is.

SILVIO For Heaven's sake!

GRAZIANA That's a new one! I can't talk to anyone any more? – The same old story.

SILVIO *(Making an effort to be calm and gentle)* Don't make me look stupid. You know quite well what I mean. Look at your sister-in-law. . . .

GRAZIANA Not again! – My dear, when one has done what one wanted to before, one can easily be good later.

SILVIO *(Severely)* What do you mean?

GRAZIANA Come on! Did Olga ever have to put up with a mother or a brother?

SILVIO She didn't need to.

GRAZIANA As far as you know. . . .

SILVIO And besides, that doesn't concern us. *(With a sense of envy)* I see that Giorgio is happy. . . .

GRAZIANA You, obviously, are a poor victim.

SILVIO *(Still calm and full of dignity)* I hope you don't pretend to think that this is the way to make me happy. – The two of us are greater strangers to each other than if we had met yesterday. *(In a painful outburst, drawing nearer to her)* Is it possible that you don't feel the need for a more meaningful, deeper affection than these banal compliments offered to you by strangers?

GRAZIANA Here we go again!

SILVIO *(With anguish)* I can't go on like this, I warn you. I've told you so before. . . . I can't take it any more. I'm not the type to live like a machine. . . . I need to convince myself that I am alive, that I feel, that I love. I need companionship, and instead I feel so lonely. . . .

GRAZIANA *(Ironically)* Lonely? . . . There's a whole bunch of us. . . .

SILVIO *(Pointing to his heart)* Lonely here, Graziana . . . and I am afraid! . . . If only you knew how this constant mental loneliness hurts me. If you knew how bitter it is to have to say to yourself: you're called husband, son, brother, and yet you're lonelier than if you were living in a desert. How painful the certainty is that not one of those who surround you nurtures a thought about you in his soul. . . .

GRAZIANA I don't understand. You have strange ideas in your head. . . .

SILVIO That's the way it is. That's the way it is. That's what I feel. And then, you see, I experience bewilderment, anguish, it seems as if I'm dying, as if I were dead already. . . . And I suffer over the happiness of others. . . . Yes, I've even become nasty. . . . *(Jealously)* When I see those two, so close to each other, so happy, ah! . . . Graziana, help me . . . you can cure me, if you want to. We too could perhaps be happy, without envy and remorse. . . . *(Puts his head on* GRAZIANA's *shoulder)*

GRAZIANA *(Coolly)* Cure? Are you sick?

SILVIO Yes, very much so. . . .

GRAZIANA Call a doctor. *(Pushes him away)*

SILVIO *(Hardly restraining himself)* Ah! . . . *(A moment of silence. Then, in a cold and decisive voice)* Then we're agreed? You are not riding out this morning.

GRAZIANA I've already ordered the horses.

SILVIO That doesn't matter.

GRAZIANA What do you mean?

SILVIO You can go tomorrow, if you really care so much about it. Not today. Giorgio is not here today. . . . I want you to stay with me.

GRAZIANA It's a whim.

SILVIO Very well, let it be a whim. Aren't you going to humor me.

GRAZIANA No.

SILVIO Graziana!

GRAZIANA You've bothered me enough.

SILVIO Careful, if you don't listen to me, we shall go home tomorrow.

GRAZIANA Ah, is that what you were aiming at? Come on, was it this?

SILVIO It's not true.

GRAZIANA Yes, yes, now I understand.

SILVIO Don't go.

GRAZIANA I'm dying to see how this will end!.

SILVIO I forbid you to go!

Scene 4

The same and TERESA

TERESA *(Comes in hurriedly from the left)* But children, what's going on? *(To* GRAZIANA) My darling!

GRAZIANA He wants to leave.

TERESA But why? You have just arrived. Didn't you promise me you'd stay a month?

GRAZIANA Oh, what does he care about promises?

TERESA *(To* SILVIO) It that true? Do you want to take her away from me?

SILVIO Signora, I want to be listened to.

TERESA *(To* GRAZIANA) What is he saying?

GRAZIANA He's annoyed. . . . He's looking for an excuse to leave.

TERESA If you think I gave you my daughter so you can treat her this way! . . . My poor angel! . . . Look how pale she is. When she left me she was a flower. . . . *(To* SILVIO) Besides, may I remind you that you are not the only one to have authority over her. I am here too, and so is Giorgio. Let's see what he thinks of your plan.

SILVIO Giorgio knows perfectly well that no one has the right to intervene between me and my wife. *(To* GRAZIANA) So we have agreed. *(He moves toward the door on the left, but then returns, draws near to* GRAZIANA *and whispers to her beseechingly.)* Graziana . . . Graziana. . . . *(But* GRAZIANA *moves away vexed, whereupon* SILVIO *walks out, aggrieved.)*

Scene 5

GRAZIANA *and* TERESA, *then* FERRANDI

GRAZIANA Do you hear him?

TERESA But what is it? It's about Ferrandi, right?

GRAZIANA Yes, as if I were doing something evil.

TERESA He is not that wrong, you know.

GRAZIANA You too now!

TERESA No, bless you. Did you see how I treated him and what I told him? But . . . between ourselves . . . it's he who is right. You always leave him to himself. . . .

FERRANDI *(Entering from the garden)* Good morning ladies. How is everything?

TERESA Good morning, Ferrandi.

GRAZIANA Good morning. Where have you been hiding? I went all over the garden, up to the gate. . . .

FERRANDI If you had looked around the stables, you would have found me, because I was working for you. *(To* TERESA) Giovanni wanted to know if you had any commissions for him, because he is going to town.

TERESA Yes, yes. Where is he?

FERRANDI Out here. . . . Giorgio left?

TERESA On the eleven o'clock train. Excuse me. . . . *(Walks toward the door into the garden, calls)* Giovanni! Giovanni! Come see me after you hitch the horses. I have some letters to give you. . . . *(Exits to the left)*

Scene 6

GRAZIANA *and* FERRANDI

GRAZIANA Don't you think we should ask my sister-in-law if she would like to come with us today, since Giorgio is not here?

FERRANDI Oh, I beg you!

GRAZIANA You are not much of a gentleman.

FERRANDI Do as you like. But it will be a completely ruined ride. . . . I was hoping for such bliss from this unexpected tête-à-tête. . . .

GRAZIANA Don't be afraid, she won't accept.

FERRANDI So much the better. I know a certain little place, down there in the forest. . . .

GRAZIANA *(Singing)* "Down there, down there..." – Do you know that I am running a great risk going with you now?

FERRANDI A risk?

GRAZIANA My husband has threatened to kill *me*.

FERRANDI *(Worried)* To kill us?

GRAZIANA No, no. *(Stressing)* To kill *me*. Don't be afraid. . . .

FERRANDI *(Relieved)* Ah!

GRAZIANA And this, believe me, gives me

immense pleasure. I am like a war horse. The smell of gunpower excites me.

FERRANDI *(Looking at her)* How beautiful you are! . . . You are always beautiful, but this morning. . . . You know, I spied on you from my window; and I saw you for a moment as you were opening the shutters. You were all pink in that light dressing-gown. . . . You looked like dawn.

GRAZIANA A somewhat late dawn, admittedly.

FERRANDI *(Sadly)* You had the calm and happy expression of someone who has rested well. . . .

GRAZIANA Eight hours straight. . . . And you?

FERRANDI Oh, me! . . .

GRAZIANA Poor you! It's so annoying not to be able to sleep.

FERRANDI *(Anxiously)* So you, too, go through such torture, sometimes? The torment caused by a constant, sweet but terrible thought. . . .

GRAZIANA *(Maliciously)* Ah, yes. I remember once. . . . Oh, such a long time ago. . . . A little dog I adored died. I could not close my eyes all night long. It was such a darling. From that day on I swore not to have pets in my house. *(A pause. Then, looking at FERRANDI)* What's wrong with you?

FERRANDI Nothing.

GRAZIANA It seems that you mind that I sleep well.

FERRANDI Oh no. Sleep. Sleep. What do you care if there is someone who is awake, suffering in the darkness?

GRAZIANA You suffer?

FERRANDI You ask me? When I thought that I had succeeded in awakening an attraction in you, you dash my hopes with a cruel word. . . . Just like last night, for example.

GRAZIANA Well! Sometimes you are very imprudent.

FERRANDI When you look at me that way I lose my head. . . .

GRAZIANA *(Provocatively)* In what way?

FERRANDI As you look at me now. . . .

GRAZIANA Oh, then. . . . *(She covers her eyes with her hands.)*

FERRANDI You are too cruel. I'll leave today.

GRAZIANA And I command you to stay. . . .

Scene 7

The same and OLGA

GRAZIANA *(To* OLGA*)* Oh, good, I was looking for you. We wanted to ask you if you would come with us. . . .

OLGA Thank you, but I can't. . . .

GRAZIANA *(To* FERRANDI*)* I told you. Too bad. It's such an enchanting morning.

FERRANDI *(Meaningfully)* But there are some clouds in the air. . . . I would not be surprised if it rained.

GRAZIANA *(Maliciously)* Really? I didn't notice. *(To* OLGA*)* But why don't you want to come?

OLGA I promised Giorgio I'd copy something. . . . And if I don't start immediately, I won't finish on time. . . .

GRAZIANA In that case goodbye. *(To* FERRANDI*)* Are those blessed horses ready?

FERRANDI But of course, they have been for an hour.

GRAZIANA Then let's go. *(To* OLGA*)* See you later.

OLGA Will you be out long?

GRAZIANA Not at all. Just half an hour, time enough to have a good gallop. . . . *(GRAZIANA exits with* FERRANDI *into the garden.)*

Scene 8

OLGA *alone, then* SILVIO

OLGA, *after having watched them go, shakes her head and remains as if absorbed in thought.* SILVIO, *in the meanwhile, enters from the left, looks at her, uncertain whether to proceed or not. Then he makes up his mind and approaches.*

SILVIO Have you seen Graziana?

OLGA *(Startled)* Oh God! You scared me.

SILVIO Have you seen her?

OLGA *(Embarrassed)* Graziana?

SILVIO Wasn't she here?

OLGA Yes. . . .

SILVIO She went out, didn't she?

OLGA Yes, I think. . . .

SILVIO Yes. She went out with Ferrandi. So much the better. *(OLGA is about to go away.)* Stay a minute, I beg you. I must speak to you.

OLGA To me?

SILVIO Yes. *(Turning his eyes toward the garden, in a bitter tone)* What do you say about it? You can be happy about it!

OLGA   About what? I don't follow you. . . .

SILVIO   If your pride, in order to obtain satisfaction, wanted the ruin of the one who had offended you, it has received ample justice.

OLGA   (Very coldly) First of all, I don't see what right you have to recall a past that belongs to me alone. Secondly, I beg you to believe that my pride is not in the habit of asking for compensations of that kind.

SILVIO   In that case permit me to let you know that you are not very generous. . . .

OLGA   What do you mean?

SILVIO   You're always avoiding me. . . .

OLGA   I wouldn't have any reason to.

SILVIO   Always. Tell me whether in these eight days I've succeeded in seeing you face to face.

OLGA   Considering the fact that we have nothing to say to each other. . . .

SILVIO   Nothing at all! Don't you find that terribly sad?

OLGA   I would rather call it logical.

SILVIO   You're right. . . . But that's not why I am detaining you. I simply wanted to take advantage of this moment of solitude, which will not present itself again, to beg your pardon for having imposed my presence on you. . . . I think I will leave soon. . . .

OLGA   What?

SILVIO   On the other hand, I could not possibly avoid coming here without explaining. . . .

OLGA   (With cold courtesy) You are in the house of my husband, as husband of his sister. Your presence here is therefore quite natural.

SILVIO   But that doesn't make it less odious to you. . . . Don't deny it. It would be useless.

OLGA   Oh my God! Since this had to happen sooner or later, it's better this way. So we no longer have to think about it. . . .

SILVIO   Is that all? (OLGA looks at him.) You have nothing else to tell me? Not even a word, not a . . . nothing at all? (OLGA shakes her head.) Are we to separate like this, without a greeting, without an explanation. . . . (Bitterly) We are brother and sister, after all. Have you forgotten?

OLGA   (Laughing sadly) Brother and sister! . . .

SILVIO   Are you at least happy?

OLGA   Yes.

SILVIO   And you have forgiven me?

OLGA   (With subtle irony) Forgiven what? That you made me meet and appreciate a noble heart? One does not forgive this, one gives thanks for it.

SILVIO   You are cruel. . . .

OLGA   I should be more than grateful to you. . . .

SILVIO   At least don't use such expressions!

OLGA   Why?

SILVIO   Because it makes me suffer. . . . So you have not guessed what a torture these days have been for me? You have not understood how much I have suffered in this daily comparison between what my life is and . . . what it could have been? Ah, how I have been punished! Punished in the very way in which I hurt you. I deserved it, but it's painful. I discovered truth when error made me his forever, irremediably. . . .

OLGA   (Sadly) I knew that this day and this moment would come.

SILVIO   Ah, you might as well triumph about it! You deserved this revenge.

OLGA   (Very sweetly) I feel for you, Silvio.

SILVIO   (With a flash of hope in his eyes) So you don't hate me?

OLGA   No . . .

SILVIO   Oh, bless you!

OLGA   Was it perhaps your fault if you were immersed in prejudice, just like everyone else? What happened was destined. In order that you might recognize your error, it was necessary that you play havoc with my soul and that I undergo that painful experience. . . .

SILVIO   (In a tone of intense regret) Ah, your soul! I raised an altar to it in my heart, where I silently adore it and cry for it. . . .

OLGA   You could very well say that you killed it that evening! Nor did I believe that it would ever come back to life again. . . .

SILVIO   (Desperately) Now, now I understand the supreme advantage of possessing that and the futility of the rest. Now that I have lost it forever. . . . Ah, dear soul, which gave itself to me entirely, which I could feel beating within me, and with me it was happy, suffered, fought, and hoped. . . . Olga, Olga, how true were your words: "I was more yours than had I been your lover. . . ." Do you remember? Do you remember?

OLGA *(Uneasy)* What good is it to dig up the past?

SILVIO *(Impetuously)* But when we have no other consolation in life? When remembering is the only evidence that we are still alive? A single dear memory which animates my solitude and which lessens the anguish of my tormented heart, a memory which makes me live for you, just as I did in the days of our happy love. . . . Ah, let me have that! I don't ask for anything else.

OLGA You are forgetting that your thoughts no longer belong to you alone. . . .

SILVIO But does it really seem to you that Graziana would still have a right to be offended if she could see inside my soul? Don't you think that I've earned by now the right to dispose of it at will? Ah, you couldn't even guess! . . . But consider that not even for one minute in her life, since I married her, there has not been even one minute in which the soul of that girl has been mine! Even now, you can see her. . . . And yet I fought so hard to win her! I told myself, after committing that unforgivable madness, that it was not right to make her a victim of my error, and I tried, honestly, to find in myself a way of reconstructing my ruined life. . . . I felt that I could do it, if she helped me. I tried to get her interested in my work, by asking her advice, sharing my projects with her, talking about my future. I tried to establish between us that current of affection and thought, without which, ah, now I know it, there is no true possession. . . . But she! *(With an ironic laugh)* She did not understand me, or she would interrupt me to read me the poem Marquis B. had written in her album, or she would play me the song Mr. C. had composed for her. Rather than seeing in me her life's companion, her husband, she saw in me only the instrument of that liberty she fervently longed for. . . . *(A pause. Then, in a low voice, slowly)* Little by little, silence set in between us. You know, that silence of souls that persists even when lips speak. . . . I had moments of such profound anguish that I thought I was going to die. . . .

OLGA *(In a tone of intense pity)* Poor Silvio. Poor Silvio.

SILVIO *(Bitterly)* And yet, didn't destiny, ironically, give me what I had asked for?

The triumph, in my manly pride, to tell myself while looking at my wife: "no caress has passed over that body, except yours . . ." What a triumph! . . . And, with it, the pain of knowing that the soul that it hid was not mine, nor had it ever been. But that instead, the desire of a thousand men had passed over it just like a turbid wave of mud. . . . Then, then I understood the profound and sacred significance of true virginity, as I was kissing that chaste body, which was mine alone. I was consumed by rage at the thought that her soul, at that very same moment perhaps, was far away from me . . . was in the possession of someone else, was lover to another man. *(With a cry)* Ah, how I wanted to break open that pure forehead and discover the baseness, the betrayal! How I wanted the body to vanish, so that I could grab it with my hands, see it, and feel it, all contaminated! . . . *(A pause. Then, in a changed voice)* What awful misery! What awful misery!

OLGA Poor Silvio.

SILVIO You understand me. . . . You are the only one in the world to understand me. Ah, why did you destroy our happiness with your own hands? Why didn't you keep quiet that evening? Wouldn't merciful deceit have been better, until my eyes had discovered the truth for themselves?

OLGA I feel for you, Silvio, but the truth would have never come to you without your experience. . . .

SILVIO We would be happy now. . . .

OLGA Now you would be tormented by a more base and humiliating jealousy.

SILVIO *(With anguish)* Olga, Olga, what will become of me? Tell me what am I to do?

OLGA You need to be very patient and wait. Graziana is so young. . . .

SILVIO *(Dismayed)* Ah, I can't! I can't! I no longer have the strength. . . . I need you, in order to live . . . only you Olga! . . . Graziana! Let her have her fun as she pleases! But tell me that in your soul the memory of me has not died. . . . Tell me that in it there is a part of me that lives and still breathes. . . . Don't abandon me! I'll be happy with one of your tiniest thoughts . . . one tiny thought reserved for me. I am not asking you for more. . . .

OLGA You are asking for what I cannot give you. . . .

SILVIO Don't abandon me. Don't you too give me the horrible sensation of emptiness, of silence, and of death!

OLGA I am not abandoning you. You just said a few minutes ago that we are brother and sister. . . . I will help you. I'll do all I can to lead Graziana back to you. . . . But do not ask me for anything else.

SILVIO *(Jealously)* Ah, that's because you love Giorgio! Because you were able to forget and to love a second time!

OLGA *(Proudly)* Yes! . . . And you blame me for it? Instead you would have wanted to find me still as abject as when you left me? You have always been an egotist in your love. . . . And when he offered me his helping hand, you would have wanted me to refuse it and not to try to love him with that little bit of life that was still in me? Ah, but I wanted to find in myself some indescribably precious treasure in order to be able to offer it to him. . . . But instead . . . I didn't even have the consolation to give to him, who deserved it, the only virginity that was left to me! You had completely devastated everything in me, parched everything. . . . And now you are sorry that a flower has grown on this ruin? Ah, Silvio! Don't you think that I suffered enough because of you?

SILVIO *(Gloomily)* You are right. . . . Forgive me. I won't disturb you any longer with my presence.

OLGA Why are you saying these things?

SILVIO Because that's the way it is. . . . Because I am a burden to others. . . .

OLGA Silvio!

SILVIO Yes, yes, a burden to everyone. . . . *(Dejectedly)* For whom or for what am I supposed to live?

OLGA You know that there is someone who greatly needs you. . . .

SILVIO And what do I care? It's I who need you immensely, Olga. Tell me you still love me, ah, tell me so, if you don't want me to do something foolish.

OLGA *(Terrified)* Silvio!

SILVIO *(Beside himself, imploring)* Have pity on me. . . . Tell me something. . . . Just a kind word. . . . Is it possible, is it possible that you have forgotten? Olga! . . .

(The voice of GRAZIANA *is heard from the garden.* SILVIO, *who had grabbed* OLGA's *hand, lets it go and moves away. In his eyes there is a strange glare.)*

Scene 9

The same, GRAZIANA *and* FERRANDI

GRAZIANA *(From outside)* I'm famished! . . . Let's hope that lunch is ready. . . . *(Enters, her arms full of flowers)* Ah, you're here?

OLGA *(Trying to hide her own uneasiness)* What, back already?

GRAZIANA A storm is threatening. *(Drops the flowers on the floor)*

OLGA Really? *(Goes toward the door leading to the garden)*

FERRANDI *(Ill-humored)* Not at all! She got scared by a little, passing cloud. . . .

GRAZIANA He calls it a little cloud! I like that. *(To* OLGA *who is returning from the door into the garden)* What do you say?

OLGA The sky is all dark. . . . Some raindrops are starting to fall.

GRAZIANA *(To* FERRANDI*)* There you are! Who was right? *(Bends down over the flowers)*

OLGA Heavens, what a lot of flowers!

GRAZIANA Beautiful, aren't they? You should have seen. You know that little meadow in the forest? You can't see the green for the flowers. . . . Ferrandi, help me fill the vases. *(She divides the flowers into bunches and hands them one by one to* FERRANDI *who puts them into the vases.)* We even covered our horses. . . .

OLGA How beautiful they are. *(She takes one of them, which she will later drop to the floor distractedly.)*

GRAZIANA But Delfina ate those she could reach. She's quite right. The flowers of some of them are so sweet. Try this one.

OLGA No, dear, I don't eat flowers.

GRAZIANA But I like them very much. *(She sucks at one of the flowers.)* I'm so hungry I could devour them all. . . . What time do we eat?

OLGA Immediately, if you like. Let's call Mother. . . .

GRAZIANA Ah yes, let's go. *(She starts out toward the door to the left, followed by* FERRANDI.*)*

OLGA *(To* SILVIO *who, for the entire scene, remains motionless and gloomy)* Are you coming?

SILVIO *(Shudders)* In a minute . . . I'll be coming. . . .

(They all walk toward the door on the left. Only SILVIO *stays. From the room next door a confused noise of laughter, of chairs being moved, of plates, and of people calling each*

other loudly, can be heard. SILVIO *picks up the flower dropped by* OLGA *and kisses it with infinite passion. He remains absorbed in thought for a while, but slowly an expression of resolution forms on his face. Suddenly, he impetuously opens a drawer of the desk and takes out a small revolver. He looks at it for a moment, but then, as if changing his mind, he puts it back. He walks toward the door on the left and stops as if listening. In that moment* GRAZIANA'S *voice can be heard saying:* Come on, FERRANDI, come here. . . . SILVIO *backs away, laughing nervously, and returns to the desk. He opens the drawer again, grabs the revolver, and leaves desperately through the door into the garden.Right after, weakened by the distance, the shot of a revolver is heard.) The curtain falls immediately.*

Bibliography

Apollonio, M. (1982) *Storia della commedia dell'arte*, Florence: Sansoni.

Costa-Zalessow, N. (1982) *Scrittrici italiane dal XIII al XX secolo*, Ravenna: Longo.

—— (1989) "Italy" in M. Arkin and B. Shollar (eds) *Longman Anthology of World Literature by Women 1875–1975*, New York and London: Longman, 1143–51.

D'Amico, S. (1960) *Storia del teatro drammatico*, Milan: Garzanti.

D'Ancona, A. (ed.) (1872) *Sacre rappresentazioni dei secoli XIV, XV, e XVI*, Florence: Le Monnier.

Del Sera, Beatrice (1990) *Amor di virtù*, ed. E. Weaver, Ravenna: Longo.

Enciclopedia biografica e bibliografica italiana (1941–42) Series VI: Bandini Buti, M. (ed.) *Poetesse e scrittrici*, Rome: Istituto Editoriale Italiano.

Enciclopedia dello spettacolo (1954–62), Rome: Le Maschere.

Ferrone, S. (ed.) (1985) *Commedia dell'arte*, Milan: Mursia.

Giacosa, G. (1920) *The Rights of the Soul*, in F. Shay and P. Loving (eds), *Fifty Contemporary One-Act Plays*, Cincinnati: Stewart & Kidd, 201–12.

Reato, D. (1981) "Prefazione," in Amelia Rosselli *El rèfolo* (Serie Teatro Veneto), Venice: Filippi.

Rosselli, Aldo (1983) *La famiglia Rosselli*, Milan: Bompiani.

Rosselli, Amelia (1901). *Anima*, Turin: Lattes & Co.

Silvi, M. F. (ed.) (1980) *Il teatro delle donne*, Milan: La Salamandra.

Trevisani, G. (ed.) (1957) *Teatro napoletano*, Bologna: Fenice del Teatro.

Viviani, V. (1969) *Storia del teatro napoletano*, Naples: Guida.

3 Elsa Bernstein (Ernst Rosmer) 1866–1949

Maria Arndt
Germany

Elfa Bernstein
Nach einer Kohlezeichnung von Hans Müller-Dachau (1910)

Drawing of Elsa Bernstein by Hans Müller-Dachau, 1910. Reproduced from Albert Soergel, *Dichtung und Dichter der Zeit* (Leipzig 1911).

Introduction

by Susanne T. Kord

The life and the work

More than any other author, Elsa Bernstein can be seen as a representative of her era, since she participated in most major literary movements of her time. She wrote naturalistic dramas (*Three of Us*, 1891; *Twilight*, 1893; *Maria Arndt*, 1908), impressionist novellas ("Caprice," 1893), neo-romantic fairy tales (*Kingly Children*, 1894), a symbolistic dramatic requiem (*Mother Mary*, 1900) and neo-classical tragedies (*Nausikaa*, 1906, and *Achilles*, 1910). Aside from twenty dramas, of which eight were performed and twelve were printed, she authored numerous novellas and poems.

Elsa Porges was born in Vienna in 1866, the daughter of Jewish parents. Her father, who had come to Vienna to further his career as a musician and composer, moved to Munich in 1867, where he became a conductor at the court of King Ludwig II at Richard Wagner's request. Elsa received an education which left her dissatisfied, but demonstrated her literary talent early: at age 7, she began to write poems and dramas; her earliest publication is the play *Snowdrop: A Spring Play*, published in Isabella Braun's *Jugendblätter* in 1876. After a short but successful career as an actress (1883–87), which she had to give up due to her failing eyesight, she returned to writing. Her immediate success permitted her to run a literary salon of great renown, initially with her husband, the writer and lawyer Max Bernstein (1854–1925), whom she had married in 1890. In 1891, she adopted the pseudonym "Ernst Rosmer" under which she became famous; the only one of her works that did not appear under this pseudonym was her play *Johannes Herkner* (1904), which she published under her birth name. The bulk of her works was published between 1890 and 1910; after 1910, she stopped publishing almost entirely. Her last published drama *Fate* appeared in 1919, followed by only two published novellas ("The Old Woman," 1926, and "An Adventure," 1928/29). Until the Nazis forced her to move in 1939, she ran a literary salon together with her sister Gabriele. Bernstein received permission to emigrate to the United States but chose to stay since this permission did not include her sister. Both were deported to the concentration camp Theresienstadt in 1942, where Gabriele died after a few weeks; Bernstein survived the experience and went to live with her daughter in Hamburg, where she died in 1949.

Critical reception

Although Bernstein was initially considered one of the most promising dramatic authors of her time, her popularity began to wane around 1910. The history of Bernstein's reception as an author, as outlined by Pierce

(1988: 207-13), Zophoniasson-Baierl (1985: 57) and Giesing (1985), clearly shows that literary histories published after 1915 either presented her as a trivial author and dramatic dilettante or ignored her entirely, and that they tended to dismiss her on the basis of her gender. Whereas in 1911, Soergel praised her technical, dramatic, and experimental skill and her skill in evoking emotions (p. 360), he dismissed her as a previously overrated author in the second updated edition of the same work, which appeared in 1961 (Soergel/Hohoff, p. 223). In the 1911 edition, Soergel devoted an entire chapter to Bernstein, which was cut in the later edition. Similarly, Robert Arnold, who considered Bernstein "one of the few outstanding female dramatists of German as well as world literature" in 1912 (p. 304), revised his opinion of her in the second edition of 1925, in which he sees "the central dramatic flaw in her work as characteristic of all female-authored drama" (Pierce 1988: 210). Rudolph Lothar, probably the first critic to hold this position, set the tone for Bernstein's gendered reception:

> Because she has always been denied economic independence, woman lacks the sense, the capacity for action. She cannot differentiate between activity and action. But not activity, action alone is dramatic. . . . Woman, however, tends to confuse activity and plot, movement and action – in life as well as in art. . . . The desultory quality in female thinking, her lack of logic can be attributed to the same cause. . . . Banned from the world of things, woman was relegated to the world of feelings. Here, passivity assumed the appearance of action. Here, she felt herself as master, as queen. . . . For despite her dramas, she [Bernstein] has no idea what action is.
>
> (1905: 165)

The consistent dismissal of her work based on the author's *Weibnatur* (her "feminine nature," Lothar 1905: 167) perhaps explains Bernstein's decision to publish under a male pseudonym. Although this is hardly unusual – most women writers of the age tended to use male pseudonyms – Bernstein's case differs in one respect: her identity was known almost from the beginning, as frequent references to "Ernst Rosmer . . . she" (Meyer 1900: 893f.; Soergel, quoted in Zophoniasson-Baierl 1985: 25) or even "Frau Rosmer" (Lothar 1905: 166 and 167) attest. Although Bernstein's male pseudonym failed to give her literary credibility with her male

reviewers, it did obscure her to posterity. Today, she is virtually unknown. If she is remembered at all, it is under her pseudonym instead of her name (even recent feminist dictionaries, for example Brinker-Gabler *et al*: 1986, list her under her pseudonym), or as Engelbert Humperdinck's librettist instead of an author in her own right.

Bernstein's dramas are noteworthy for her thorough and unconventional characterization, especially of the female figures, her uninhibited language and treatment of taboo subjects, and her great attention to realistic detail (for her Greek tragedy *Themistokles*, 1896, Bernstein did extensive research, learned ancient Greek, and traveled to Greece to visit the sites she described in the play). A frequent subject of her plays is the culturally sanctioned oppression of women; her female figures are often torn between adherence to social norms and desires for personal autonomy. Bernstein's insistence on a realistic portrayal of her contemporary society is partly expressed in the fact that most of her autonomous heroines are forced back into conventional roles or uphold them voluntarily. The ambivalence and compromising nature of her dramatic endings has disappointed traditional and feminist critics alike. Her greatest success was *Kingly Children*, largely due to the incidental music written for the play by Engelbert Humperdinck (1845–1921; Humperdinck also rewrote the play as an opera). Stylistically, Bernstein experimented with many forms; her use of style defies analysis in terms of chronological or linear development: she worked simultaneously on her naturalistic drama *Three of Us* and on her neo-romantic fairy tale *Kingly Children*; her play *Maria Arndt*, a return to the naturalistic style, chronologically falls between her neo-classical tragedies *Nausikaa* and *Achilles*.

Maria Arndt and the naturalist legacy

Maria Arndt, published and performed in 1908, is her last naturalistic drama. It enjoyed a successful premiere at the Schauspielhaus in Munich on October 17, 1908, although many reviewers voiced their complaints about the play's "emancipation propaganda" (Pierce 1988: 246). The play was interpreted as the story of a mother who "leaves this world because, for her daughter's sake, she does not want to follow the man she has loved for a long time. But . . . the daughter is such an embarrassingly prudish creature that she succeeds in evoking no more than simple pity, rather than conveying the feeling of inner necessity" (Spiero 1913: 91). Modern scholars have criticized the play for its ultimate acceptance of patriarchal norms, which are apparently upheld, as far as women are concerned: "It is no coincidence that the emancipatory educational program is actualized in the subplot about the neighboring family's son, because the plot revokes the title figure's enlightening agenda for her own sex. . . . In the conflict between her lover and Gemma's needs, the child wins out, the mother kills herself" (Giesing 1985: 255).

Both interpretations assume that Maria, because she has raised her daughter Gemma as a person capable of making decisions independent from the patriarchal moral standard, would be free to follow her desire if she could take her own advice. But what Bernstein presents is not the traditional and clear-cut conflict between "duty" and "desire" that is implied in these criticisms, but rather a wavering between the two, "between magic and the law," as the play's motto states. Self-determination and self-fulfillment are not a possibility for Maria, who grew up in the "knit-your-stockings era," but a possibility for Gemma, albeit so remote that it is still relegated to the realm of "magic" – a magic to be ultimately attained through education.

The utopia of the play, which centers on Gemma rather than Maria – the dream of a woman who is empowered to make choices by exposure to "all knowledge," including academic subjects, physical and sex education – is pitted against the "law" governing the lives of women. In view of this law, emotional and ethical values lose their meaning. Claussner's as well as Gemma's love for Maria is revealed at the end of the play as their selfish desire to have Maria to him- or herself, without consideration for Maria's wishes or feelings: instead of granting her the choice of self-determination, both Claussner and Gemma merely try to subject her to the law that

determines women's lives in terms of their roles as lovers, wives, and mothers. Compared to this desire to force Maria to choose between the two roles offered her, that of wife and mother or that of lover – a choice already cancelled by her pregnancy – Claussner's and Gemma's "love" remains hypothetical, hence meaningless. Because the "law" eradicates both the possibility of self-determination and the meaning of feelings, it is unimportant, as Maria states, whether her pregnancy is the result of rape or love: as long as the consequences for her are the same, there *is* no difference between rape and love. For the same reason, it remains unclear to the end whether the boy with the torch portrayed in her study is Eros or Thanatos – the god of love or the god of death: the distinction between love and death, life-giving and life-taking, loses its meaning in view of the predetermined consequences.

Like many of Bernstein's dramas, *Maria Arndt* has been criticized, particularly by recent feminist critics, for its ambiguous ending: Maria's suicide seems to negate the educational values she tries to instill in her daughter. By committing suicide, by refusing to break the moral taboo and flee with Claussner, she implicitly upholds patriarchal moral values, thereby failing to practice what she has preached to Gemma. But the solution that is implied here – that Maria could find self-fulfillment if she abandoned her husband and followed her lover – is negated by Claussner's selfish attitude. Maria Arndt is not a feminist who relapses into traditional values, she is a woman who wishes to exercise freedom of choice over her future *and* remain within the bounds of social acceptability. Although Gemma's education is presented as a step towards self-fulfillment and self-determination, these ideals are as far removed from reality as magic. In accordance with Bernstein's much-cited realism, the play does not explore an emancipatory potential for which it sees no basis in contemporary social reality; rather, it portrays the restrictions put on female personal autonomy in direct and intentional contrast to men's possibilities for self-determination. This contrast is played out in the father–son conflict between Tucher and Otto, a reverse parallel of the relationship between Maria and Gemma: the men's cold and impersonal relationship is contrasted with the women's loving and jubilant one; Otto's predetermined course of life with Gemma's freedom and education; the men's failure to communicate with the women's ability to discuss even subjects that would have been considered extremely difficult and delicate. Finally, the law intervenes and the roles are reversed: the men communicate, ironically inspired to do so by the women, while the women fall mute. This complete reversal would be senseless if it did not intend to express a simple social reality: that Maria and Gemma are part of a cultural order that offers personal autonomy to men only.

It is this conclusion that distinguishes the play from other naturalistic dramas, like Gerhart Hauptmann's, or from other plays portraying puberty and advocating sex education, like Frank Wedekind's *Spring Awakening: A Children's Tragedy* (1891). As Pierce has argued, "In Hauptmann's plays, as in Wedekind's, the resolution hinges on the murder, arrest or disappearance of the main female character(s). Women are thus essentially removed from the drama in order to resolve the dramatic conflict" (1988: 208). In Wedekind's drama, which is more concerned with the awakening of sexual feelings in the male than in the female

characters, Wendla dies of a botched abortion, still unaware that she is pregnant. Although education is demanded in both plays, Bernstein contradicts Wedekind's premise that education alone is enough in view of the social position of women: in her play, which is in all likelihood the only contemporary play to portray such a scene, Gemma is fully informed of the sexual act and procreation; the religiously and morally inspired refusal to speak about "such things" that still prevents the implementation of sex education in some U.S. high schools plagues neither her nor Maria. Although the women, as witness their increased knowledge, awareness, and ability to discuss taboo subjects, are ready to transcend the traditionally exclusive roles of marriage and motherhood, society, here represented by Claussner and Gemma, refuses to accept them in any other roles. In her portrayal of Gemma as the symbol of the educational utopia *as well as* one of the figures unable to let go of the traditional roles women are assigned (the mother–daughter symbiosis), the author transcends the simplistic model of men-oppressing-women and makes the play a disturbing commentary about women's roles in the women's movement.

Maria Arndt

A Play in Five Acts
1908
Play translation by Susanne T. Kord

Elsa Bernstein (Ernst Rosmer)

We waver between magic and the law
And none is fully vanquished by the other.

Characters

FRAU MARIA ARNDT

GEMMA, her daughter

AGATA LOVERA, housekeeper at Frau Arndt's

THEKLA, maid

VON TUCHER

OTTO ⎫
⎬ his children
AMANDA ⎭

CLAUSSNER

Place

An old country house, named Rose Meadow,
in the upper-class neighborhood of a
university town in Southern Germany.

Time

Beginning of the twentieth century.

Right and left are assumed from the
spectator's viewpoint.

Act I

MARIA's *living room on the first floor. In the
middle, a large glass door leads out onto the
veranda. On the right a door leading into the
corridor and to* MARIA's *bedroom, on the left,
another door to* GEMMA's. *On the front left a
window and a large flat writing desk; on the
right a sofa and comfortable chairs. Behind the
sofa there is a renaissance table with a
Florentine mosaic top. Bookcase and fireplace
corner with smaller chairs. Carpet, curtains,
upholstery, and the polished wood of all
furniture are a greenish silver-grey. On the
walls some imitations of antique reliefs. The
largest portrays a boy extinguishing his torch.
Some very beautiful vases and stone chalices,
tastefully distributed. No knickknacks at all,
general absence of everything superfluous. The*
shutters *in front of the window and glass door
are closed. The room is lit weakly by a lamp
with a shade of white silk on the desk.*

MARIA *sits in an easy chair at the desk,
beside her two pages covered with writing,
hastily finishing the third. She is in a loose
white dress, her hair (chestnut brown with a
strong reddish gleam) tied in a loose knot at
her nape. After a decisive final stroke she lays
aside the pen, turns to face the front, her left
arm hanging over the side of her chair, leaving
her right on the desk. Her narrow, almost
colorless face wears an expression of deep
exhaustion. After she has stared into space for
a while, she takes the last sheet into her right
hand and re-reads it, her lips moving silently.
Her gaze remains fixed on the last page.
Slowly and bitterly reading to herself:*

"I see the necessity of returning – and
will resist no longer."

(She puts the sheet down slowly.)

"I will resist no longer – resist no
longer. . . . "

*(She folds the three sheets, puts them in an
envelope and writes the address. – Fast and
cheerful bangs at the shutter of the glass
door.)*

GEMMA's *bright voice:* Open – open – presto!
MARIA *(Her face lit by a melancholy smile)*
Gemma! *(Aloud, rising)* Yes, child,
immediately!

*(She is taller than average, slender and
feminine, with refined limbs and rhythmic
movements. She goes to the door and opens it,
then the shutters to the outside.* GEMMA *is
standing in the middle of the veranda. Fifteen,
slender and lanky, light blond but dark-eyed,
wearing a low-necked empire-dress[1] patterned
in a delicate green; her silk belt tied in a long,
fluttering bow in the front. In each arm she is
carrying a massive bunch of wild roses.
Behind her, the summer-green garden, brilliant*

84

sunshine, birds chirping. A light breeze blows the curtains of the door towards the inside.)

GEMMA   Mamma, Mammia, look! Roses, tons of roses! All from the garden! All the way back, behind the cave, there is a true wilderness – there it is, our Rose Meadow! *(She has entered.)*

MARIA   *(Carefully taking the bouquets from her.)* You didn't get pricked? There are so many thorns . . .

GEMMA   Adagio – my sleeves! And how I got stung! And I tore myself and I got stuck and I almost didn't make it out of the enchanted hedge, and if it hadn't been for the prince – no, there was no prince, only the boy from the second floor, young Tucher, he came to my aid.

MARIA   *(Busily distributing the roses into vases)* Oh, they have a son?

GEMMA   And a daughter. They only got home yesterday, they're on vacation, neither of them are educated at home, she's with the English governesses and he with the pages, the royal ones! Terrible, isn't it? Imagine if we weren't together, you and I! *(She stormily embraces MARIA and rocks herself at her shoulder.)* Oh Mama, Mamacomrade – do I love you!

MARIA   *(Her cheek resting on GEMMA's forehead)* And I you!

GEMMA   *(Releases her and puts both hands on MARIA's shoulders)* How did you sleep, Mother? Badly? Your eyes are very dark. And the lamp is still burning? And the shutters are still closed? You didn't stay up all night – ?

MARIA   No, no, calm yourself. I just got up very early. It was still too dark to write, so I turned on the lamp – *(She extinguishes it.)*

GEMMA   *(From behind the desk)* Who did you write to? Papa? These night letters cannot bring him joy.
(She turns around and opens the window and the shutters.)

MARIA   This one will. Because I wrote him – that we will return – in the fall – when the hottest part of the year in Florence will be over.

GEMMA   *(Turning in joyous shock)* Return? Really? Mammia! Will that be all right? Will that be all right with your health?

MARIA   It must be all right.

GEMMA   And my studies? My wonderful lessons?

MARIA   You will continue them. Even if we have to take a professor along.

GEMMA   *(Back with her, still in amazement)* Take one along . . . hm . . . I still can't believe – How did you suddenly decide . . . ? I can't believe. . . .

MARIA   Not suddenly, child. I already saw last winter – and even more in the spring – that you will never be at home here. And Papa wants us so much – that he even offered in his last letter to move here –

GEMMA   Here? Papa? That is impossible! How could he paint here? No light, no colors, and above all, not a single Botticelli! If I think how much even I missed all that! How I am looking forward to seeing our cathedral and our Gigante and our casa and our solemn garden of cypresses! And our Papa! Life is sure different with a man in the house. You and he and I – we are a family – the Holy Family.

MARIA   *(Turning away)* The Holy Family. . . .

GEMMA   Today, I'll have an appetite! May I ring for the tea?

MARIA   Please. *(She has taken a small watering-can from the mantle and pours water into the vases.)*

GEMMA   *(Who has rung the bell next to the corridor door three times)* Am I hungry, Mama! If you were ever this hungry! Sweet! Dear! Silly Mama! Look at me. Don't you notice anything? I have something for you – something – something – no, I can't tell you. I haven't slept half the night, I was so happy and excited. I was up at five, in the garden at six – finally, it got to be seven o'clock – but when will it be eight?! *(Glancing at the clock on the desk)* Is that one right?

MARIA   To the minute.

GEMMA   *(Sighing)* So, another whole long quarter hour.
(She walks around the room, humming to herself.)

M'è stato regalato tre viole,
Me le son messe sotto il capezale,
Tutta la notte ho sentito l'odore.

(To MARIA, impishly) Did you get it?

MARIA   Almost. . . . You smelled the odor all night?

GEMMA   What? You know that much Italian, even though you never really learned it? Aren't you curious at all, Mama?

MARIA   Not at all.

GEMMA   O Mother, you have completely stopped being a child.
(There is a knock at the corridor door.)
Avanti – Thekla with the tea!

THEKLA   *(Opens the door, puts down a two-level Japanese tea table, closes the door behind her and carries the table in front of the sofa. She is pretty, the domestic servant type, black English dress, white collar, white cuffs, white bonnet with a bow.)*
Good morning, ma'am, good morning, miss.

MARIA   *(Still busy with the flowers)* Good morning.

GEMMA   *(Right beside the maid)* You know, Thekla – through the garden at once – and in here, through the veranda –

THEKLA   Certainly, miss.

MARIA   *(Has approached them)* You look so pale, Thekla. Is anything wrong?

THEKLA   *(Stuttering)* Forgive me, ma'am – I have – I must have eaten something bad last night –

GEMMA   *(Laughing)* That must have been something very bad, considering how green you are.

MARIA   *(Cutting her off)* These things happen. Have the Signora give you some drops.

THEKLA   Thank you kindly, ma'am. *(Exits)*

MARIA   *(Sits down on the sofa, looking over the tea table.)* Why three cups? Is Agata having breakfast with us?

GEMMA   Oh no, she would never lay off her beloved caffè nero. And besides – we have already had our secrets today, the two of us.

MARIA   *(Pouring tea)* How can anyone have secrets with good old Agata!

GEMMA   I can't stand it if people aren't as excited and happy as I am! Thoroughly! Till you tremble with bliss all the way down to your little toe!

MARIA   If I didn't know that you also tremble with bliss when someone gives you a bar of very good chocolate –

GEMMA   Then you'd be curious now? O Mama, be just a little curious, at least guess, guess what it could be?

MARIA   Guess? All right! So – is it mineral? No? Vegetable?

GEMMA   *(Pointing at the third cup)* But Mama, it drinks tea!

MARIA   You may only answer with yes or no. Is it animal?

GEMMA   Yes, yes!

MARIA   Human?

GEMMA   Of course!

MARIA   Masculine?

GEMMA   *(Glancing into the garden with half an eye)* And how!

MARIA   *(Startled)* And how? None of your teachers?

GEMMA   Oh, those are all neuters. But this one – a tall, tough – no Rafael – a Dürer! You know it – I can see that you know it. *(Jumping up)* And there he comes, I can hear him, there he is, my amico!
(Exits through the veranda)

MARIA   *(Alone, pale into her lips, gazing at the floor. To herself, barely audible)* Him! *(Slowly, she turns her head toward the garden, rises and gazes toward the arrival with unshakeable calm.)*

GEMMA   *(Pulling CLAUSSNER behind her)* Here he is, Mama – here I am bringing him – there you have him!

CLAUSSNER   *(In a bright summer suit. Young-looking forties, tall sinewy figure. Full dark hair cropped short, lighter full beard. Hard, toil-worn face, dominated by forehead and eyes. He walks toward MARIA)* Yes, here he is, Frau Maria *(He takes her hand and pulls it to his lips.)* – and he is very happy.

MARIA   *(Friendly but with the same calmness)* Good day, Claussner. This is naturally a great surprise.

GEMMA   *(Who has stood in triumphant expectation)* Well? Is that all I get? I believed you would faint, at least. And now – like the snow queen! O Mama, I am dreadfully disappointed.

MARIA   *(Returning to the sofa)* Where would you like to sit?

CLAUSSNER   *(Putting his hat down)* Preferably near you.

MARIA   *(Pointing at GEMMA's seat next to herself)* Here.

GEMMA   And me? What about me? I belong in the middle!

CLAUSSNER   Well, well, Gemma. Still sitting on both sides of Mama?

GEMMA   To the right and to the left and front and back. I don't share her with anyone. But today I'll be magnanimous. You may sit next to her. You may speak with her. You may look at her. She is still exactly as she was way back in our Loggia – where Papa always painted her. The

Madonna with Tizian's hair! My beautiful Madonna!

(MARIA *makes an annoyed gesture.*)

GEMMA *(Laughing)* Look how she blushes! What about it? It's not your fault that you're beautiful. You just inherited that from me! Oh you – you – *(She kisses her.)* – you Gracious Silence, as the Black one there has named you.

CLAUSSNER Gracious silence – that is something your Mama did not inherit from you.

GEMMA Amico!! Ingrate! I'll take her away again – my Madonna. *(She sits down beside him.)*

MARIA *(Pouring tea for CLAUSSNER)* How do you take your tea? Still strong and without sugar?

CLAUSSNER Exactly. How well you remember.

GEMMA *(Pulling at his earlobe)* Yes – still strong and without sugar.

MARIA Do you have everything you need? Then I'd like to know –

GEMMA How this happened? Very simple. Almost too simple for such an événement. Last night we met him in town, Agata and me. He didn't recognize me, I recognized him at once. I wanted him to come along right then, but he had to go to a club and give a lecture about the family life of rhinoceroses. Mama! Rhinoceroses!

CLAUSSNER Better that than the family life of humans, I tell you.

GEMMA And then we arranged – I arranged with him! – that he would come for tea this morning at eight o'clock sharp.

MARIA How long have you been back in Europe?

CLAUSSNER Four weeks.

MARIA And here?

CLAUSSNER Fourteen days.

GEMMA And you're staying? How long?

CLAUSSNER Six months – a year – it depends.

GEMMA A whole year? Please, Mama, more *paste* – two! Wouldn't you lose your entire practice with the Negroes and the rhinos?

CLAUSSNER Which one do you mean? My medical practice? I gave that up a long time ago. I changed profession. A little late, Mama thinks. But still better than too late. I have realized that there is not a trace of the Good Samaritan in me. And to be a doctor, you need some of that.

MARIA And what are you – what do you do now?

CLAUSSNER This and that. I fertilize land, I go to war, I travel inland with caravans. In between, I hunt and climb mountains, especially those that nobody has climbed before me. That gives you the nicest surprises, for example, that these African glaciers can turn out to be burnt-out volcanoes. Research is much more rewarding than healing people. Because you really can't heal anything. But you can still research some things.

GEMMA And why have you come back now? Were you homesick?

CLAUSSNER Homesick? For whom? I have no relatives. No. The fever! I would like to get rid of it for a while. And save my collections. Most of which I will give away to appropriate researchers.

GEMMA You have collections? Many? You have to let me see them. I'm hot for stuff like that.

CLAUSSNER Cool down. So many rock layers, lichen, and mosses – completely uninteresting for little girls.

GEMMA That's where you're wrong, but completely, amico! I'll have you know, that I am studying, even university things, since we've been here – like a boy! I have professors, very strict ones, very old ones, and natural sciences are my favorite and I'm doing excellently. Shall I give you a lecture on directional particles and nuclear fission? See, now you're staring and admiring me! And pretty soon you'll feel sorry for me! At eight thirty, my Latin prof will be here and I haven't prepared at all! *(Rising, to* MARIA*)* But you don't have to be there today, I give you dispensation. *(To* CLAUSSNER*)* Too bad that I can't bother you any longer. *(Kissing* MARIA*)* Addio, Madonna! Don't be so pale! He'll think I'm treating you badly and not feeding you well. *(To* CLAUSSNER*)* Do you want one too? Or do you think I'm too old already? I don't! *(Kisses him)* Yech, you're scratchy with your barba di Giove! A rivederci! Pray for me, and for my verba! *(Exits hastily towards the corridor)*

CLAUSSNER *(Looking after her)* How utterly charming she is! What a delightful person she's become! Everything about that little creature just glows – fresh as the morning dew. Were you like that, Frau Maria?

MARIA I have never been so free.

CLAUSSNER Yes, yes, you grew up in the knit-your-stockings era. . . . But still, your father was an artist, a sculptor even –

MARIA Yes, but I was not allowed into his atelier until I was fourteen.

CLAUSSNER (Throwing up his hands) Not until fourteen! Of course, at that point it was too late.

MARIA Quite right. I was embarrassed by the nakedness that should have delighted me.

CLAUSSNER And then it goes on and on that way, and in the end, we think we could more easily do away with the body than with the dress. I know. Oh!! One cannot breathe in this Europe! – May I get up and look around a little? Things here are so different from Florence. Only a few old acquaintances. (At the bookcase) Darwin – I gave you that – right? And Plato? How do those two get along? The subtle smell of violets – (Pointing at the table) – and that one with his roses made of stone – Arndt's wedding gift to you – right? (He stops in front of the relief.) And the boy with the torch. Do the gentlemen of the fine arts still squabble whether it's Eros or Thanatos – love or death?

MARIA They still squabble.

CLAUSSNER I'm glad for them. . . . Who furnished this room for you?

MARIA I did.

CLAUSSNER (Looking around again) It is truly the room of a person – of this person in particular. Nothing left of the renaissance opulence of your former boudoir. Who always said that it did not suit you? I did! Only the silence – everything is so silent here – like an olive grove surrounding a small temple. (Returning to her) Is it just coincidence that we have found each other here – or is it the coincidence of inner necessity? Did you know that this educated little hole-in-the-corner town is my hometown?

MARIA (Not completely at her ease) I knew it.

CLAUSSNER How did you come to be here? You've been here for almost a year – Gemma said? Without your lord and master?

MARIA I have been frequently ill in the last few years – the climate in the South did not agree with me.

CLAUSSNER The climate in the South or the climate of the soul?

MARIA (Ignoring the remark) It was also for Gemma's sake.

CLAUSSNER For Gemma's sake – that I don't understand.

MARIA By Latin standards, Gemma is fully grown. I could not have kept her from moving in our circles. In circles – well, you know. All that is artistic and spiritual is turned into a personal luxury, especially in the case of women. Like a robe or a bracelet.

CLAUSSNER (Nodding) It is demeaned – yes.

MARIA And because a child cannot judge such circumstances, can only be confused by them –

CLAUSSNER When did you become so strict?

MARIA Not strict, just pensive. I would not for anything turn Gemma into a lady before she has grown into a woman.

CLAUSSNER (Both arms on his knees, looking at her from below) Go on, Frau Maria, go on. I can look at you like a woman and listen to you like a man.

MARIA Oh, Claussner, don't embarrass me. I have realized what my mission in life is, that is all.

CLAUSSNER And that is – what?

MARIA At the moment – to build a bridge for my child, a bridge on which she can directly and safely proceed from simplicity to knowledge.

CLAUSSNER To which knowledge?

MARIA To all knowledge – as far as human beings are granted it.

CLAUSSNER To all knowledge? Don't forget, Frau Maria, Gemma is a girl. And the son of God is a man.

MARIA Then I think it is time for woman to become God's daughter.

CLAUSSNER (Looks her full in the face. After a pause) What did you experience in these four years? Such thoughts don't come from reading – they come from experience. Your life's mission . . . But are you not more than a mother, aren't you a woman as well? How can he permit you to live separate from him?

MARIA (Rising) Dear Claussner, we have been married for seventeen years. We don't take these things all that seriously any more.

CLAUSSNER *(Also rising, increasingly upset)* Because you never took them seriously enough! Seventeen years! A life with you should just be beginning after seventeen years! But of course, he never loved your intrinsic value, he always just loved your effect. All right, he is a painter; for him, beauty is everything. I have never cared for your beauty. I have hated the fabrics and gems he used to dress you up as the show piece of his studio. You don't turn a swan into a peacock. And that was what finally drove me away, I just couldn't look at it any more –

MARIA Stop it, Claussner, you are as passionate and unjust as ever.

CLAUSSNER Passionate and unjust. . . . *(He approaches her.)* Frau Maria – you are excellent at withholding things – but a very bad liar. Just tell me this: has this last year not been a break from – a break with your former life?

MARIA *(Pointing at the desk)* There is the letter which determines our return for the fall.

CLAUSSNER *(Goes to the desk, reading.)* Signore Giulio Arndt, Firenze, Via dei Colli – And you will send this?

MARIA Today.

CLAUSSNER *(To himself)* Today. . . .

MARIA Claussner – you are planning something – what are you planning?

CLAUSSNER *(Taking up his hat)* To make you speak.

MARIA *(Her eyes downcast, her face completely closed)* Me?!

CLAUSSNER *(Directly beside her)* Yes, Maria – you.

(He exits quickly through the veranda. MARIA *stands immobile.)*

Act II

Bright midday, but no direct sunlight in the room. All vases filled with roses. The veranda door wide open. – MARIA *is standing in the middle of the room, wearing a loose unfashionable ivory-white summer dress. Beside her* AGATA *in a dark, tastefully modest dress. Pretty, elderly Italian, regular features, snow-white, wavy hair parted in the middle. Her figure a little stout, but not heavy. Speaks German very well and fluently, with the melodic and expressive tone of her mother language.*

MARIA But dearest Agata, what shall I do with Thekla? I cannot turn her out of doors.

AGATA *(With a troubled expression)* Ma – Signora! Gemma! It is impossible! The child is so smart – oh!! She sees everything – she will notice – she will ask – and then – what shall we say?

MARIA The truth! Yes, Agata! Simply the truth! Thekla will have a child and when she and her fiancé have saved enough, they will get married. It would have been better if the child had come after the wedding, as is customary. But whose business is it? Not mine, and not yours – it is their business exclusively. Thekla will be a good mother to the child, and as far as it's up to me, I will not make this more difficult for her. The few weeks that are left, she will have her good wages and her good food. We could tell Gemma something like that, don't you think?

AGATA The Signora could – I couldn't.

MARIA And do you see how everything in life is connected? Today it's the same story as it was seven or eight years ago, about the stork. You can't discuss this, you can't explain this to a child! And how simple it then turned out to be, and how moved the child was! Do you remember? She hugged me and kissed me and said, Mammia, now I know why mamas like their bambini so much! – I wish my mother had told me the same way.

AGATA Si, si. . . . *(Sighing)* But it gets more difficult all the time.

MARIA Would you rather have the child find out through coincidence – through ugly rumors – what we can tell her in a reasonable way? Why are you so taken with Ada Negri, why do you go to the women's club, if you shy away from – I have often thought – when I was so ill – if I turned Gemma over to your care I could lie down and die peacefully. But before then, you have to learn a lot – and unlearn even more.

AGATA *(In a low voice)* The Signora is more ill – in the last days?

MARIA Why, have you noticed anything?

AGATA *(Pointing at her desk)* The Signora has had made more polveri – the Signora does not sleep –

MARIA *(Has taken a small box from the desk and locks it in the left drawer)* Ah, yes . . . it's a habit, I just like to have it near. I didn't really need it. Really, Agata. I'm much better already. And just in case *(Jestingly)* I am struck by lightning – you will take care of our child?

AGATA E – il signore?

MARIA Her father – certainly – he adores her. But that is not enough.

AGATA Adores the Signora also.

MARIA And that was not enough, either. You don't understand? Do you think I always understand? But that doesn't change anything. *(She glances into the garden.)* Slowly, Gemma, slowly! How can you race like that?

GEMMA *(Hot and glowing, storms up the stairs and through the veranda)* Mother! Ten heaves! And twenty deep knee-bends at the end! I'm dead! Ecco! *(She throws herself full-length onto the sofa and crosses her arms behind her head.)* Say, has he still not gotten in touch with us?

MARIA Who?

GEMMA Who? The amico! Today, it's been four days! Unheard of! Agata, I suspect you're at the bottom of this. You tell him we're not at home, you don't let him in the door –

AGATA Gemma – oh! I would never presume –

GEMMA Be quiet! You don't like him! You've never liked him. You would not let him treat you for the world. I'm so upset with him! He's capable of leaving the country again, and in six months he'll send us three hairs from the beard of a lion!

AGATA *(Who has exchanged a few quiet words with MARIA)* Until the fifteenth of September – I will tell her immediately. Con permesso, signora.

(She exits through the corridor.)

MARIA *(From behind the sofa)* Don't you want to change?

GEMMA Let me lie down for a little while longer. I am so heavenly tired and lazy. What shall I wear? The pink one?

MARIA That is an evening gown, not something to wear at home. Wear your white one.

GEMMA But it suits me so well, the pink one.

MARIA But only if it also suits the occasion.

GEMMA Oh, Mama, you're so strict!

MARIA Strict? Since when have you found me strict?

GEMMA Since – since you have not always agreed with me.

MARIA Or vice versa.

GEMMA Mama, how old were you when you fell in love and became engaged?

MARIA Seventeen.

GEMMA And I'm sure you could wear whatever you liked then. See, and I'll be sixteen soon, I'm approaching the state of falling-in-love and getting-engaged and dressing-up –

(A knock)

MARIA Come in.

THEKLA *(Enters from the corridor with three cards on a majolika-plate, her eyes somewhat red)* The lady and the gentlemen would like to see you.

MARIA *(Takes the cards)* Cabinet Minister Von Tucher – Otto Von Tucher – Amanda von – how come they suddenly decided . . . ?

GEMMA *(Has jumped up, very embarrassed)* I forgot all about that, Mama. The young man asked me yesterday – in the garden – whether he and his sister would be permitted to pay their respects.

MARIA You should have told me that at once – I don't like such surprises. Now I can't help it. *(To THEKLA)* Show them in.

GEMMA *(Simultaneously plunging towards her room)* I'll go change, Mama.

(THEKLA exits.)

MARIA *(Looks after GEMMA and shakes her head slightly)* Hm . . . *(She takes one of the cards up again.)* His Excellency – Knight of the Royal Order. . . .

(THEKLA opens the door, shows VON TUCHER, OTTO and AMANDA in and closes the door behind them. TUCHER mid-fifties but looks like sixties, scrawny, medium height, grey hair, thin grey full beard. More distinguished than elegant. His dry character is softened by his upright attitude. He is wearing a black coat and carries a top hat in his hand. AMANDA seventeen, pretty, bird-like face, hair pulled tightly back from her face, fashion magazine figure. Institutional uniform made of dark grey serge, pelerine collar, flat yellow straw hat, soberly adorned with a black ribbon. White gloves, small mother-of-pearl handbag. OTTO nineteen, pretty Southern German nobleman type, wears some kind of uniform, dark grey service coat with a row of silver buttons, rapier at his side, cap in hand)

TUCHER *(Bowing deeply to* MARIA*)* My dear lady, I hope you will permit us as house-mates – I have long intended to – My daughter Amanda – my son Otto – Amanda keenly desires to improve her acquaintance of your daughter during the approaching vacation, assuming your consent as her mother. . . .

MARIA *(Who has shaken hands with the old gentleman and greeted the two youngsters with a nod of her head)* Gladly, Your Excellency – if the girls get along. *(She shakes hands with* AMANDA*.)* I have already seen you in the garden, dear Fräulein – with a big embroidery, almost as tall as you.

AMANDA *(Curtseying deeply)* Yes, madam.

MARIA *(Sits down on the sofa and invites* TUCHER *to sit beside her,* OTTO *and* AMANDA *on the chairs)* My daughter will be here at once. She is changing after her daily gym lesson.

TUCHER Daily? Isn't that a bit much for such a tender constitution?

MARIA I would like to make something sturdier out of it.

TUCHER Well, well – lately, some doctors have claimed – and I would not want to disagree entirely – you have gym lessons too, at the institute, Amanda?

AMANDA We have gym lessons once a week.

MARIA Isn't it very difficult for your wife to do without your daughter for most of the year?

TUCHER Dear lady, mothers are very rarely qualified as educators. And my wife has been unwell for many years. Nerves. In the institute of St. Theresa, the young ladies receive a very appropriate education. Especially languages are emphasized. Right, Amanda?

AMANDA Yes, we always have to speak French.

MARIA And what else do you learn?

AMANDA English, madam, and literature and physics and needlework and history and dance and religion –

TUCHER *(Interrupting her, a little nervously)* Classification, Amanda, organization! This is pure anarchy!

AMANDA But father, that's the way it goes – all day long, from one lesson to the next.

TUCHER *(To* MARIA*)* Girls will never have the ability to present something

coherently, or a sense of purpose. It's a good thing they don't need it. Women are supposed to be guided by their hearts, not by their heads.

MARIA And the heart should not learn to think a little?

TUCHER Doesn't hurt. But it's not neces-sary. In my opinion. Thinking is for the boys.

MARIA *(Trying to include* OTTO *in the conversation)* That means you, Herr von Tucher. Do you think a lot? These days, there are many opportunities for thought in the military.

OTTO I will not become a soldier, madam, I have to become a lawyer.

MARIA *(Pleasantly)* Oh! I would have suspected a future Moltke in you.

OTTO Me, too – at least that's what I would like to be.

TUCHER *(Sternly)* Otto! One always likes to be what one must like to be. *(To* MARIA*.)* Two of his cousins are already in the army – they were not particularly suited for the academic life – *one* Tucher must represent the family in the government service – and at our last family meeting, it was decided to uphold this tradition.

MARIA Tradition – ah, yes.

GEMMA *(Has come from her room. She is wearing a pink cambric dress, richly adorned with lace and volants, cut in the empire style, like her first one. She approaches them. Without looking at* MARIA*)* Here I am, Mama. *(*TUCHER *and* OTTO *have risen immediately.)*

MARIA *(After a short survey of* GEMMA*'s appearance)* My daughter, Your Excellency. *(To* AMANDA *and* OTTO*)* You know each other already?

GEMMA *(Giving her hand to the old gentle-man)* Buon giorno – pardon – good afternoon, Excellency.

TUCHER *(Holding* GEMMA*'s hand in his, with sincere, chivalrous admiration)* I am very pleased, little lady, truly very pleased. *(To his daughter)* Amanda – I hope you will be friends with the young lady – that you will try.

GEMMA *(Shaking hands with* AMANDA, *cordially)* That is not necessary. Mama, may we sit by the fireplace? Here, all seats are occupied.

MARIA Certainly, my child – I would just like to – come here for a minute – you've been too hasty – that one hook – *(She fixes something at* GEMMA's *belt.)*

GEMMA *(Comically embarrassed)* Oh, this mama sees everything.

MARIA *(Friendly, but with meaning)* Yes, Gemma, I see everything. *(She releases her.)* But please stay seated, Your Excellency. *(The three youngsters have gathered around the fireplace and started to chat eagerly, but in subdued voices.)*

TUCHER I would be much obliged to you, madam, if you would permit my children to associate with this exquisite creature. I have already mentioned that my wife is ill. For this reason, I have long since withdrawn from society – my sister-in-law represents me in the most urgent cases – and as for me, I do not regret this retiring life in the least.

MARIA I understand. Loneliness is not as bad as the wrong kind of sociability.

TUCHER Very true, madam, very heart-felt. However, for young people, things are different. They want diversion, entertainment, community –

MARIA Above all, I would think, with their parents?

TUCHER You're wrong, my dear lady, quite wrong. I have the fatherly feelings for my children that they can lay claim to – but I admit freely: I don't know what to do with them at all. As you may already have noticed, I have cultivated a small quantity of roses in our part of the garden. I assure you that this gives me more stimulation, more diversion, than my children do. I have awaited this vacation with downright discomfort.

MARIA I will try to take care of the young people.

TUCHER *(Rising)* If one is still so young oneself, my dear lady – *(He rises.)* I must take my leave – to my immense regret. *(He kisses her hand.)* Work on some files. The eight-hour-day is a thing for the Social Democrats. Will you permit my children to continue this visit?

MARIA Gladly.

TUCHER *(Turning)* Otto! Amanda! *(The three youngsters jump up.)* I am leaving! The lady of the house is so good as to permit you to remain. Do not forget anything when you leave, Amanda, as usual. *(To* GEMMA*)* My lovely Fräulein *(He kisses her hand tenderly.)* I hope to see you very often. *(To* MARIA*)* Madam –

MARIA I will see you out, Your Excellency. *(*OTTO *dashes to the door and opens it.* MARIA *and* TUCHER *exit.)*

GEMMA *(Somewhat relieved and very cheerful)* Now we are by ourselves! Shall we sit down again or stand around a little? Why don't you take off your coat and gloves, Fräulein Amanda? It makes it so much easier to move around. Tonight, when it's cool in the garden, we'll romp around!

AMANDA *(Taking off her coat)* You still romp?

GEMMA Passionately!

AMANDA I prefer embroidery. And I really must finish my blanket.

GEMMA How much longer will you need?

AMANDA Two or three weeks, at least.

GEMMA I can't embroider. I can only sew what's needed in the house. And cut patterns, a little. Mama says that you always have to be able to be your own maid.

AMANDA *(Examining her)* Where do you have your dresses made?

GEMMA At home, all of them.

AMANDA This one too? Very pretty, but out of fashion. The fashion now is very wide sleeves, and the skirts must be wide at the bottom. Why don't you dress according to fashion?

GEMMA Because Papa does not permit it. He says one has to dress according to one's personality, not according to fashion.

OTTO *(Laughing)* There you go, Amanda. What is your personality like – according to your dress?

AMANDA *(Offended)* I would know what to wear. It's not my fault I have to wear this uniform. We must wear it so as not to become vain.

OTTO You who can think of nothing but clothes!

AMANDA Still better than your naughtiness! *(To* GEMMA*)* A moment ago, you wished for a big brother. Do you still feel that way?

GEMMA *(Soothingly)* Oh, I think he doesn't mean it like that. Shall I show you something interesting? Mama gave it to me for Christmas. I just have to get it from my room, I'll be right back. *(Exits)*

AMANDA *(In a low voice to* OTTO*)* Impertinent, toi! First you bug me until I go to Father and pretend that I really want to associate with this Gemma –

OTTO Isn't it worth the trouble, though?

AMANDA To make such a big deal of her – no. "Mama says" – "Papa says" – . Everything is superficial.

GEMMA (*Returns from her room, carefully carrying a plate with wax models under a glass bell in front of her, which she puts down on the mosaic table*) Here it is. Do you know what this is? (*Since both of them shake their heads in surprise*) This is the development of the chick in the egg, from the first to the fourteenth day. (*She takes off the glass bell.*)

AMANDA All right – so what?

GEMMA So what? Isn't it strange – how it works – the origin of life, a little bit of Creation.

AMANDA What does this have to do with Creation? That's been finished for a long time.

GEMMA (*Somewhat confused*) I thought – it goes on and on.

AMANDA (*Patronizing*) But dear Fräulein! God created the world at the very beginning, in seven days.

GEMMA (*More confidently*) In seven days, that's impossible! If you need three weeks for your blanket alone! Every day must have lasted for thousands and thousands of years.

AMANDA A day, dear Fräulein, has twenty-four hours. You can ask whomever you like.

GEMMA What is your opinion, Herr von Tucher?

OTTO (*Embarrassed*) It is very difficult – our professors are in disagreement, too – at any rate – God's authority may not be questioned.

GEMMA That's not what I meant to do.

AMANDA (*Taking her coat*) Please, help me, Otto. (*Discreetly back over her shoulder*) She does not even have the basics. (*Aloud*) Dear Fräulein, we must go now –

OTTO (*In a low voice*) Amanda!!

AMANDA (*Decisively*) We must go now, it is twelve-thirty already. Please give my regards to your Mama. Adieu, Fräulein Arndt.

GEMMA Adieu, Fräulein von Tucher. (*She accompanies her to the veranda, where they stiffly say good-bye.*)

OTTO (*Presses GEMMA's hand and looks at her entreatingly*) Fräulein –

AMANDA (*Turning back*) Are you coming, Otto?

OTTO Yes, all right!

GEMMA (*Alone. She seems put out. She returns to the table and replaces the glass dome over the wax models. She has tears in her eyes. In a low voice to herself*) How stupid of me – stupid!

OTTO (*Returns hastily*) Pardon, Fräulein – my sister has left her pocket book with her cards –

GEMMA (*Looks around her*) The pocket book – (*She points to the mantle.*) There it is.

OTTO (*Takes it*) Thank you – thanks very much – Oh Fräulein – I would like so much to speak my heart with you, thoroughly – but this is impossible as long as Amanda is around – Could you not come into the garden again, early – or at night –

GEMMA No, that is impossible.

OTTO Why is it impossible?

GEMMA I don't know – it's impossible.

OTTO Fräulein Gemma – if you did, you would do a good work. You have no idea how lonely I feel – If you only knew – I am truly unhappy. Fräulein Gemma – come to the rosebushes tomorrow morning –

GEMMA (*Unsure*) To the rosebushes –

OTTO Yes – at six.

GEMMA Secretly?!

OTTO Why secretly – as long as nobody notices! Dear Fräulein Gemma – say yes – don't be hard – Will you come? – Gemma!

GEMMA (*In a very low voice*) Yes. . . .

OTTO (*Stormily kissing her hand*) You are an angel – I knew it – an angel! (*MARIA, followed by CLAUSSNER, opens the door at this moment. GEMMA and OTTO pull apart a little, startled.*)

OTTO (*Recovering quickly*) Excuse me, Madam, that I am still here – My sister forgot something – I was just about to take my leave. (*After a deep bow to MARIA and a smaller one to CLAUSSNER, he withdraws toward the door, where he bows to MARIA again. He exits through the veranda.*)

CLAUSSNER (*Without his hat, briskly and with a certain triumph*) Was that the son of the Excellency you just told me about? Mighty cultivated! A duo-decimo princeling! Good afternoon, Gemma. How are you, darling?

GEMMA (*Self-consciously, without moving an inch*) Thank you – I am well.

MARIA Well? Is that all?

CLAUSSNER *(Jovially)* She is proud today, Frau Maria. After such a distinguished visitor! Rapier at his side – silver buttons – and looking like Titania – let's just hope he won't turn out to be the ass – *(GEMMA winces.)* Uh oh, I didn't say anything, I didn't say anything at all!

GEMMA I don't care what you say.

MARIA Gemma!! How can you be so rude?

GEMMA Is he being polite to me? He's making fun of me!

CLAUSSNER If I see that you're sensitive, I'll –

MARIA But since when have you been so sensitive? *(Trying to take her hand)* *(GEMMA draws back her hand, covers her face with both hands, hurries into her room.)*

CLAUSSNER *(Amazed)* What was that? Is she being stubborn?

MARIA It would be the first time.

CLAUSSNER Hm. . . .

MARIA *(Nods and sits down at the desk)* You are right. I think that is probably so.

CLAUSSNER And how will you handle it?

MARIA Not at all. So harmless – with her. And quite serious – with me. Yes, here it comes – the first pain. There is a time for everything. *(She glances down thoughtfully.)*

CLAUSSNER *(Darkly, his jovial mood gone)* Wrong time for me. *(Pause)* What are you thinking?

MARIA How much the child needs me.

CLAUSSNER As long as she still is a child. But that won't be long.

MARIA No. Yes. . . .

CLAUSSNER *(Approaching her)* I have something to say to you, Frau Maria. Can you listen to me?

MARIA Now? I don't know. . . . My little Gemma. . . . Listen? What is it? Please.

CLAUSSNER *(Opposite her)* You have not mailed your letter, Frau Maria.

MARIA How did you know –

CLAUSSNER Because I went to Florence.

MARIA You went –

CLAUSSNER Yes indeed. On the same train that would have brought your letter. Instead it brought me – to my old friend Arndt.

MARIA *(Annoyed)* You were never his friend.

CLAUSSNER But I could be. I don't have anything against the man any more. He looks splendid, just as if he were the one

who is ten years younger. He still hasn't grown of course, he's still too short for you. Currently he's painting a Princess Borghese, and she is as much enchanted with his art as she is with his chivalry and his subtle melancholy. Unfortunately, he is not enchanted by her.

MARIA *(Trembling)* How dare you speak this way!

CLAUSSNER I'm speaking like a practical human being. And like an honest one: he's not thinking of the beautiful princess, he is still hoping for your return.

MARIA What is all this supposed to mean?

CLAUSSNER *(Takes a chair and sits down next to her)* That I know your story, Frau Maria. Don't be so shocked. I know you're no longer his wife, and haven't been for the past four years. Since the day I left Florence, my intuition tells me. And it tells me even more – it guesses from his confession now and my earlier observations: that in your innermost soul, you never were his wife. First you were cool and unenthusiastic – disappointed perhaps – later cold and hostile. Isn't that right? Isn't that right?

(MARIA is silent.)

You don't have to say yes, you can be silent as long as you want – I know anyway! *(Jumping up, with muted jubilation)* I know that I – that my silent wish woke you up from your deep slumber! Don't resist any more, Maria, don't resist – admit it!

MARIA *(Rising, softly, but with great effort)* And – if I admitted it – what would you gain? Either way – there is nothing for us but separation.

CLAUSSNER And – you will return to him?

MARIA *(Her eyes downcast)* I will never go to sleep again. And he will content himself to buy what remains of our togetherness with this one great renunciation.

CLAUSSNER *(Throwing up his hands)* Maria – do you want your life to end this way?

MARIA I'm not living for myself, I'm living for my child.

CLAUSSNER *(Right beside her, in a low passionate voice)* A woman like you should only have one child?

MARIA *(Tears welling up in her eyes)* I cannot permit myself to have a fate if I am to care for hers. I cannot destroy the concept of parents for her, the concept of motherhood!

CLAUSSNER *(Furiously)* The concept, the concept! That is idolatry, not worship! And you don't believe it – in your innermost heart you don't believe it – you're dying for the wrong cause!

MARIA *(With all her strength)* I believe it.

CLAUSSNER *(Beside himself)* Don't tell me this!

MARIA I believe it, and that's all I believe.

CLAUSSNER *(Falls onto a chair, crushed. After a long pause)* Well then – then it is not love – then I don't have the right – then return to him. *(He rises, slowly goes to the door, turns once more. With terrible bitterness)* To him, Maria. *(Exits)*

MARIA *(Alone. Her composure has left her. Weeping desperately, wringing her hands)* Not love! Not love!

Act III

Through the open veranda door, the darkening sunset and black clouds are visible. Dark red roses in all vases. OTTO *comes across the veranda in a Litewka-style jacket. Carefully glancing around, he tiptoes quickly to* GEMMA's *door and knocks.*

GEMMA's voice. Come in.

OTTO Gemma – it's me.

GEMMA *(Opening the door a moment later)* Dio mio – it is you?

OTTO *(In a low voice, passionately, drawing her into the room)* If you could just once call me *du*!² No, there is nobody here, nobody's coming. Your Mama is at the rose-bushes with my old man, they are having a lively conversation. All day long I have seen nothing of you – I can't stand this hellish courtesy any more! I tell you, Gemma, I'm going to be ill, or I'm going crazy!

GEMMA But what am I supposed to do, Otto?

OTTO *(Has sat down on the sofa and pulls her to him)* Be good, be sweet, let me look at you, let me adore you – *(He puts her head on his forehead.)* See, that alone works miracles! It cools me down! Calms me down!

GEMMA There will surely be a thunderstorm.

OTTO *(Putting his arm around her shoulders)* Where have you been all afternoon? What did you do this time? Did you read? Did you study? Oh, I hate your books! They take you away from me! You're always thinking of them!

GEMMA Oh, Otto, I can't think of anything any more. I do everything badly, all my exercises, I cannot concentrate on lessons any more –

OTTO Amanda said the other day that you will study, go to the university – that's not true, is it? A lady like you – among all the guys – the thought alone drives me insane! O Gemma, if I had you all to myself, all for me – on a deserted island in the middle of the ocean – *(He has gone down to his knees before her.)* – if I could hold you day and night, if I could just once – just once – Gemma, kiss me!

GEMMA No, no – everything is staring at me here.

OTTO But in the cave – when it gets dark – tonight – in half an hour –

GEMMA *(Listening)* There's something in the corridor – Mama – get up!

OTTO Only if you promise –

GEMMA Yes, yes – go now –

OTTO *(Jumping up)* Gemma – in half an hour – I'll die if you don't come. *(He exits through the veranda.* GEMMA *glides into her room.)*

MARIA *(In a black silk-crepe dress with a red rose in her belt. Entering, she notices* GEMMA *pulling her door closed. She starts, then looks over the veranda and into the garden. Nodding to herself)* Ah ha! *(She knocks at* GEMMA's *door.)* Gemma!

GEMMA *(From inside)* Mama?

MARIA Come on out.

GEMMA *(Opening)* Yes?

MARIA Didn't you just run away from me?

GEMMA But no! Run away from you? I'm at my books, I'm not stirring!

MARIA Who closed your door from the inside, a moment ago?

GEMMA My – door? *(She falls silent.)*

MARIA *(Shaking her head)* Oh Gemma! How silly! You don't need to play these games with me. – Did you write to Papa? Today is Friday.

GEMMA *(Startled)* Oh! – I forgot!

MARIA This is the second time. *(She sits down in her chair at the desk.)* Come here, my child. What is it with you? You haven't been yourself at all in the last few weeks. Sometimes you're irritated, sometimes cross – and something that's never happened before: your teachers have complained about you –

(GEMMA *bursts into tears.*)

But Blondie, why are you crying? I don't want to punish you, I want to examine this thing with you, reasonably, between comrades. What is going on? Is it too much for you to study in the summer? I thought – in the mornings in your cool room, and since you've never had trouble –

GEMMA *(Drying her tears)* No, it certainly isn't too much, Mama, and it would go pretty well if –

MARIA If?

GEMMA *(Pulling a stool to* MARIA'S *feet)* I've slept so badly – I feel a disquiet – I can't stick with anything. Everything bores me or upsets me – I am often so furious – at myself – at my thoughts – I'm ashamed. What can I do about this? What shall I do?

MARIA *(Stroking her hair)* Clear things up – become conscious –

GEMMA Conscious – of what?

MARIA Let me think a little – it's not that simple. . . . If you were a little Indian girl we wouldn't have to think about this much. You would be given to a man, to any man, you'd have children; ten years later, nature would have used up your strength and your life would be over long before you died. Well, you're not a little Indian girl, and you want things very different from an early old age and death. You want to turn into a being so particular and unique that she will leave a trace, an effect in the vast multitude of phenomena – beyond her lifetime. Do you follow me, my child?

GEMMA Yes – I can follow.

MARIA No dignity is more difficult to attain than human dignity. And most difficult of all, the dignity of women. Do you wish to give it up because of that? Every new joy is accompanied by a new sorrow and every new freedom by new restrictions. If you waste yourself on your first physical desires, you will be impoverished before your last intellectual ones. Your senses and your soul must decide over your fate in accord with each other, and not leave each other in darkness.

GEMMA In accord. . . .

MARIA Darling, your discomfort is completely natural. It's a little like your limbs hurt when you grow too fast. Everybody goes through this. And you can cope with it if you explain it to yourself, if you don't give yourself over to it in fear and in secrecy.

GEMMA In secrecy. . . . *(She begins to see the light.)*

MARIA You know so much, and I have very intentionally taught you how conception and reproduction happens in nature. How it changes and moves on a higher plane with the increasing perfection of creatures. The great magic which may have begun with two cells flowing together in the primordial sea and which ends in the love between man and woman.

GEMMA Mother!!

MARIA Do you remember, Gemma, how I explained to you, many years ago, how a child grows beneath the mother's heart, from a tiny cell? Today I must add that this cell can only develop when united with semen from the body of the other sex. In your womb, there are seeds that want to ripen, and that are supposed to ripen. One day, when you will find, when you will experience the complete physical and spiritual union with a man, joyfully and with conviction, not blindly passionate, but moved. And complete unity is divine – or it may well be.

GEMMA *(Has wrapped her arms around* MARIA) Mother – Mother! *(A pause)*

MARIA My child, I don't know what will be your fate. But I don't want it to be negligible and rash. A great fate can be very difficult – but it will never devalue you, exclude you from future exaltation – and that is your task, and that of humanity. *(She leans low over* GEMMA. *Long silence. Straightening)* We are completely in the dark now. Shall I turn on the light?

GEMMA *(Holding her)* Not yet.

MARIA All right, my child, all right. *(Humming to her in a low voice)*

Sleep, baby, sleep.
Outside, there are two sheep.
One's black, the other white.
And if the baby will not sleep
The black one will come *(She kisses her.)*
and bite.

GEMMA *(Returning her kiss)* Mother dearest
 – thank you.

MARIA *(Rising)* And now it's time for the
 lamps. *(She lights one.)* The days are
 already growing short.

GEMMA Mammia – I have to ask you for
 something – let me go to the cave for two
 – for three minutes. I just want to say –
 I must say – that I can't come
 – *(Lowering her voice)* – that I will never
 come again.

MARIA *(Gives her her hand and looks in her
 face)* Go, my child.
 *(GEMMA hurries through the veranda into
 the garden and disappears in the darkness.)*

MARIA *(Momentarily disquieted, follows her
 for a few steps. Turning around, sternly to
 herself)* Nothing can happen to her – not
 now. *(The wind has risen, the lamp flickers,
 she closes the window. A knock at the
 corridor door)* Come in.

AGATA *(With a letter)* For the Signora.

MARIA *(Extending her hand)* Thank you.
 *(She sees the address and changes color a
 little. Opening the letter)* Didn't you want to
 go out tonight?

AGATA Si signora – to the club. There will
 be a lecture – molto interessante: Duties
 to your child, duties to yourself. The
 Signora would not be interested?

MARIA, *(Still reading the letter, with a pained
 smile)* No. *(She puts the letter down.)*
 Claussner has announced his visit for
 tonight. To say good-bye. He will leave
 tomorrow.

AGATA *(Quickly)* Per Affrica?

MARIA Yes. . . .
 (AGATA cannot suppress a sigh of relief.)

MARIA *(Acts as if she had not noticed)*
 Please, tell Thekla to open for him. *(She
 turns to the garden, worried.)* Where is the
 girl?

GEMMA *(From afar)* Mammia! I'm coming!

MARIA *(Greatly relieved)* Thank God!

AGATA The Signora will permit me to go?

MARIA Take the carriage, Agata. The storm
 will be here soon. The leaves are shaking
 in the trees.

AGATA *(Exiting)* Grazie, signora, buona
 notte.
 (MARIA steps up to the veranda, waiting.)

GEMMA *(Rushing up and into her arms)*
 Here I am – here I am back with you –
 Mammia – what is it? What's in your
 eyelashes? Are you crying?

MARIA *(Smiling and drying her tears)* Well

yes – sometimes it's you and sometimes
 it's me. Shall we have tea now?

GEMMA Not me, Mama. I can't eat. I'm just
 tired – just want to sleep. Sleep in – that's
 all I want.

MARIA But will you – ?

GEMMA Oh Mama! Like a log. For three
 days in a row.

MARIA Good, my child.
 *(Both exit into Gemma's room. Heat lightning
 in the garden. Sound of rain. Short knock at
 the corridor door. A moment later, THEKLA
 opens and shows CLAUSSNER in.)*

THEKLA The madam will be in her room.
 *(She knocks at Maria's door. Since nobody
 answers)* Or in the Fräulein's room. *(She
 knocks at GEMMA's door.)*

MARIA'S *voice* Who is there?

THEKLA Madam, Herr Doctor Claussner is
 here.

MARIA Show the gentleman in, I'll be right
 there.

CLAUSSNER *(Stepping up to the door)* He is
 already here, madam, but he has time to
 wait.

THEKLA *(Closing the shutters and then the
 veranda door)* Don't you want to take a
 seat, Herr Doctor?

CLAUSSNER Can't you leave that open? It is
 so humid.

THEKLA I can't, Herr Doctor, the wind will
 blow the rain inside. *(Exits)*

CLAUSSNER *(Walks around slowly. He stops
 in front of the relief portraying the boy.
 Bitterly, from between his teeth:)* Oh Eros –
 Eros!

MARIA *(Entering, speaks over her shoulder)*
 And if you can't sleep, call me at once.
 Good night, my child. *(Closes the door and
 comes forward)* Good evening, Claussner.

CLAUSSNER *(In a low voice to himself)* And
 if you can't sleep, call me at once. . . .
 She has it good. *(He takes her hand.)* I
 don't know whether I should ask your
 forgiveness for coming again – maybe you
 even think it is a little – silly of me to
 come say good-bye. . . .
 (They sit down up front.)

MARIA When are you leaving?

CLAUSSNER Tomorrow morning at
 eight-thirty. Everything's been arranged.
 I even have my boarding pass.

MARIA And you will cross over
 immediately?

CLAUSSNER No. I have to waste four weeks
 in blessed Uleia with the gentlemen

scholars who are working on my findings. One has to talk to these people, writing doesn't work. I have to stop in Leipzig, Breslau, and Berlin. Then Hamburg, the steamship Wörmann – and the sea. The eternal sea.

MARIA You have received honors, I have read – from the German Scholars' Association.

CLAUSSNER They were so kind.

MARIA You were offered a teaching chair –

CLAUSSNER *(Interrupting)* Which I rejected. Do you think I could stand the High Priests of science even for eight days? I don't. I'm much better off with my Tschaggas. Besides, I sleep much better with the growling of lions than with the ringing of train bells. My faults and my strengths are better placed over there. You have to live and let *me* live – or let me die.

MARIA And if you can't stand it over there, in the long run?

CLAUSSNER How much longer can it be? The fever takes people, or some predator. . . . Let's not talk about the future. . . . That rose in your belt is beautiful – give it to me.

MARIA *(Taking it off)* It's already half withered.

CLAUSSNER *(Takes it, smelling it.)* But it smells – it smells – like only dying flowers do. *(He puts it into his briefcase.)* I usually don't like to save scraps. But the height of culture – on which you stand – can do it to a man. *(He rests his head in his hand and looks at her in silence.)* I have never seen you in black, Frau Maria – coal black – and your cheeks are so white, snow-white. . . . Like Patience on the monument, smiling at Grief – I always have an opportunity to quote Shakespeare at you. Why don't you say something? Something I can take along, over there – something I can think of when I lie in my tent again – and the smell of the earth wafts in – and the smell of the steppe – and the songs of the Blacks: Everything dies – God does not die. . . . Something, anything, Frau Maria. So that I can call you when I can't sleep – in my deepest night.

MARIA *(Looking up)* You shall have it, Gerhart. I just want to see first if the child is asleep. *(She rises, goes to GEMMA's door, opens it a little, and listens.)* Deeply.

– One breath like the next. She hasn't slept like this in a long time. *(She returns.)* It hasn't been easy, these last few weeks. Not for her and not for me.

CLAUSSNER It wasn't that fleeting then, the little disturbance? It went further?

MARIA *(Sitting down again)* Not visibly. But perceptible in hundreds of small creeping secrecies. It wasn't her frolicsomeness, it wasn't that she could have let herself be carried away in a game – a quick embrace or a hearty kiss. That would not have been a problem. A touch of fingers in the dark can be much more dangerous. And I began to fear something like that. I felt that Gemma was not completely honest any more – that she began to torture herself and to reflect, but did not know where to go with her reflections. So tonight, I took heart and gave the child my last mother-lesson.

CLAUSSNER What did you tell her?

MARIA I told her that the desire to reproduce that is alive in all creatures also awoke in her – and that it unites man and woman in one experience – the only one that brings the earthly close to the divine.

CLAUSSNER And you believe this?

MARIA *(Taking his hands, in a low voice, but transported with passion)* I believe it – because despite the distance and separation, I have experienced it – with you. Because through you, I have realized the truth in myself. Because through you, I have found the courage to rebel. How often have I asked myself whether that little bit of human dignity would be worth the pain I had to inflict on another – But if I hadn't dared – if I had not freed myself – there would have been no new life for my child, either. My misery has taught me to make a better life for her, to make her free and perceptive and proud. That I ever attempted it – and pursued it – and accomplished it – today – I have you to thank for, you alone, my only beloved!

CLAUSSNER Maria! Maria! You speak to me this way! – And we shall never see each other again!

MARIA Never again!

CLAUSSNER And never hear each other!

MARIA Never! Never!

CLAUSSNER How long will I have to live? What will I tell myself at the moment of

death? That I was a fool! What was mine
like nothing else in this world! What
belongs to me like nothing else! You –
you – (*He has jumped up and pulled her
up.*) You and I!

MARIA   (*Trying to struggle free*) I can't – have
mercy – I can't!

CLAUSSNER   Who – what is hindering you
now?

MARIA   Because it'll cost my life, Gerhart –
my life!

CLAUSSNER   It is worth my life – and not
yours?

MARIA   (*Senselessly, lost*) Everything, my
love, everything!

Act IV

*Gloomy day. Windows and door are closed. A
weak fire is burning in the fireplace. In all
vases bouquets of many-colored fall leaves.
OTTO is waiting in the middle of the room, in
full uniform, cap in hand.*

GEMMA   (*Returning from Maria's room, in a
light grey linen dress*) Mama regrets that
she cannot see you, she is too ill. But she
wishes you all the best on your way, and
if it ever should lead you to Florence –

OTTO   Thank you kindly, Fräulein – thank
you – I don't think I'll make it down
there any time soon – and now I will take
my leave.

GEMMA   (*A little closer*) Otto – I told Mama
that I still have to talk to you – of course
only if you want to –

OTTO   Oh Gemma – what else have I been
waiting for for four weeks!
(*They sit down.*)

GEMMA   You have avoided me at all costs.

OTTO   You yourself asked me to that night
– asked me in such a way – As a man of
honor, I had to honor your request like
the strictest order. How difficult that was
for me!

GEMMA   (*In a low voice*) It wasn't meant all
that strictly.
(*Pause. Both stare at the floor.*)

GEMMA   (*Searching for a way to continue the
conversation*) It has gotten quite cold.

OTTO   Quite cold.

GEMMA   Have you heated yet?

OTTO   No. Father does not permit it before
the first of October.

GEMMA   Do you think it will become nice
again?

OTTO   Oh, certainly. When the rain stops –
it can still be very nice in the garden.

GEMMA   Only the roses are all withered.

OTTO   Not all of them. The white ones are
still in bloom. If the frost doesn't kill
them before All Saints' Day. People
around here call them grave lights.

GEMMA   Grave lights – how sad.

OTTO   Everything is sad.
(*Another pause*)

GEMMA   Otto – did I offend you very much
that evening? Are you that mad at me?

OTTO   I can't be mad at you, Gemma. I just
didn't understand it. An hour earlier – I
guess it wasn't as serious for you as it
was for me.

GEMMA   Or much much more serious. And
someday, when we've both changed a lot,
you and I –

OTTO   Why should we change?

GEMMA   I don't want to stay the way I am.

OTTO   (*Bitterly*) Of course not! I know. You
want to be scholarly – very scholarly
– and look down on us –

GEMMA   I don't want to be scholarly and I
definitely don't want to look down on
anyone. I just want to go on, and on. . . .
So much had to come into being and
perish until I could exist – I want to be
grateful for that. I want to contribute my
part – I don't want to have received my
place in the world for nothing.

OTTO   Those new ideas, I don't get them. I
only know that you will achieve whatever
you want, and that that alone will make
you happy. But someone like me! Who
has to do something he doesn't like!
Something he can never be good at! Some
knowledge that is! Try running around
with that on your mind, and you'll soon
lose your gratitude.

GEMMA   I wouldn't do it.

OTTO   What shall I do about it? To whom
shall I turn? Mother is sick and Father is
working. And I cannot talk to him. He
cuts me off after the first word. I know
that much beforehand.

GEMMA   Still, you have to try.

OTTO   Tell me just one sentence I could
begin with!

GEMMA   First, I have to know – do you
really love your father?

OTTO   Yes. I do. Because I know the
burden he's borne for the past few years.
And how he has borne it. For our sake.
Amanda doesn't understand this. But I do.

He is a very special man. There aren't many like him. And I love him for that – despite everything.

GEMMA That's what you should tell him. That's how you'll start. Not with yourself. With him. He has to feel that he has your heart. And then you ask him – not to have your way – because you love him so much, because you want to do him honor in the future – and you'll tell him again and again, a hundred times: Father, I want to do this for you!

OTTO (*Extremely moved*) Gemma!! You are right. This way, it is possible! This way, I'll have the courage! This way, he won't be able to deny me! O Gemma, how I have to thank you and how I'll think of you for the rest of my life!

GEMMA (*In a low voice*) Me too.

OTTO (*Kissing her hand passionately*) You too? You will think of me?

GEMMA And of how beautiful they were – the first roses.

OTTO (*Rises with tears in his voice*) The first roses – I can't – Farewell – I can't. (*He hurries to the veranda door.*)

GEMMA (*After an internal battle of a few seconds, she rushes after him and takes his head into both hands.*) Addio, Otto – I loved you very much! (*She kisses him fervently on the mouth, tears herself from him, and flees into her room.* OTTO *stands for a moment as if thunderstruck, then hurries out with a sob.*)

AGATA (*Opens the door to* MARIA's *room, looks outside, then over her shoulder*) Nessuno, signora. (*She permits* MARIA *to enter.*)

MARIA (*In her loose white dress, exhausted and care-worn, falls onto the sofa at once*) When did the telegram say he would arrive?

AGATA (*Without looking at her*) Around twelve, Signora.

MARIA (*Tries to look at the clock at the desk*) And it is now?

AGATA One o'clock, Signora.

MARIA Do you want to tell Thekla –

AGATA Thekla left us yesterday.

MARIA Ah, yes – well, then tell the new one.

AGATA (*Leaving*) Anything else, Signora?

MARIA No, thank you. (AGATA *is already at the door. In a low voice*) Agata.

AGATA (*Politely, coolly*) Commandi, signora?

MARIA – – – Nothing.
(AGATA *exits.*)

GEMMA (*From her room*) Mother! You got up anyway? Is that a good idea?

MARIA It will be all right.

GEMMA (*Lifting her feet onto the sofa and covering them with a blanket*) At least let me make you comfortable. Are you warm enough? (*She leans over her and puts her cheek next to* MARIA's.) You worry me, Mother. Are you allowed to do that?!

MARIA Your face is wet – were you outside?

GEMMA I just washed my eyes –

MARIA Ah yes – Otto – how was it?

GEMMA Quite reasonable. I advised him to talk to his father today because of his profession. And he told me that he'll never forget me. And then we both cried a little – (*Hastily changing the subject*) Shall I read to you, Mama? From Phaedon? We didn't finish it yesterday. The best is yet to come. The death of Socrates. I read ahead, you see. When will I be able to sacrifice a rooster to Asklepios on your behalf? Maybe Claussner will have the answer. I can't believe he isn't here yet! I don't trust him any more, either.

CLAUSSNER's *voice in the anteroom* In the grey room? Thanks, Agata, thanks. (*Knocking and opening the door almost simultaneously*) Maria – Frau Maria – ah, Gemma – excuse me – but I heard that Mama is ill – or did Agata exaggerate? (*He shakes hands with* GEMMA.)

GEMMA Unfortunately not.

CLAUSSNER (*Approaches* MARIA. *When she moves to get up he puts his hand on her forehead.*) Don't move, Frau Maria, you need rest, rest, rest. (*He contemplates* MARIA *lying with her eyes closed. In a low voice to* GEMMA) Has it been like this for a long time?

GEMMA Certainly for two weeks.

CLAUSSNER (*To* MARIA) Why was I not told earlier?

GEMMA How did you get back all of a sudden?

CLAUSSNER My journey was prevented at the last minute. I still have something to do here. . . . Do you feel better now, Frau Maria?

MARIA Yes. . . .

CLAUSSNER (*To* GEMMA) Has Mama eaten anything today?

GEMMA Almost nothing. She hardly eats anything any more.

CLAUSSNER Let's try that, right now. Make a giardinetto, you yourself, not the servants. And do you have a glass of wine? Red wine? A good one?

GEMMA (*Nods*) L'abbiamo. (*At the door*) Is fifteen minutes all right?

CLAUSSNER Yes, Gemma.

(GEMMA *exits.*)

CLAUSSNER (*Waits until she has closed the door behind her, then leaning over* MARIA *in a burst of emotion*) I am here, child, I am here! Maria – for eight days your letter followed me – from one town to the next – yesterday, on board, it finally reached me. I didn't have time to finish reading it – I didn't until I was on the train – If that letter hadn't – If I hadn't found out— —!! I can't bear the thought! But now everything, everything will be fine.

MARIA Everything – fine?

CLAUSSNER (*Sits down on the sofa so that he can put his arm around* MARIA *and help her sit up*) And now have a good cry – have a good scream – your poor, desperate, helpless heart! Do you think I didn't read it between the lines – between these brave and uncomplaining words – I know you! I know my wife!

MARIA And do you know – what is going to happen now?

CLAUSSNER What is going to happen? There is only one thing that can happen. I've already planned it, all last night. I will go to him and tell him how it was, from the first moment to the last. And if you didn't think more highly of him than is right, just as I didn't think highly enough of him, then he'll make it easier for us, not harder. There's nothing else he can do.

MARIA And – and Gemma?

CLAUSSNER Gemma? That is your decision. Whether she shall be told now – and how much – or later –

MARIA (*Crying out in despair*) Never – never – I'd rather die first!

CLAUSSNER Maria! What is it? I don't know you any more. Where has my clear and gentle person gone? – But I understand. You're exhausted. The setback – the transition. It'll be over soon. And the separation too – the separation which Gemma would have initiated in a few years anyway.

MARIA She would have separated from me! But I separated from her – I did! And in such a way!

CLAUSSNER (*Soothingly*) It doesn't have to be at once! He won't mind leaving you together for a little while. And I will consent to everything. So – stay with her – somewhere – here –

MARIA Here? Here? Under his roof – with his servants – with Agata – who suspects – who knows – who would like to turn me out into the street like the servant who – and she is right!

CLAUSSNER Maria! You're beside yourself! What are you doing to me! Have morals suddenly become ethics for you? Are you saying that you prefer having been raped for years to having loved once?

MARIA (*Stares in front of herself. In a low, heavy voice*) Rape – love – but Nature does not make a difference and gives us the child. – I know that there is not one morality for everyone – but everyone must know what her morality is. I know that custom is not all – but custom is old and venerable, and she who breaks it cannot expect it to protect her any longer.

CLAUSSNER I will protect you. You don't need any other protection. (*In her ear*) Do you know, Maria, what has been my last desperate wish and fury for years, for many nights? Do you know the fervor of a prayer that cannot hope to be answered? And now that it has been answered, now that I shall have it all – the God who will take it away from me does not exist. What do you want? Do you want due course of the law? It'll be a long time – that I can tell you right now – a very long time. Outside of the law? We could elope just as well as they did thousands of years ago. The ship has not sailed yet – cut short what won't become easier if you drag it out – take your coat and go with me. (*He rises. Pause*)

MARIA Running away – running away from my child – no. I can't.

CLAUSSNER Then there is another way out. Let me speak to Gemma. I can do it. Because next to you, there is nothing dearer to me –

MARIA (*Sitting up*) No, no. Not you, either. If it has to be – if she has to know – then I'll tell her. And soon – and at once.

CLAUSSNER Not at once. When you have

gotten better – when you have gotten calmer – you have to wait that long.

MARIA I can't wait any more. The waiting is killing me. The fear of what may not be but must be – and today – today.

CLAUSSNER Then I want to be there.

MARIA You? Anyone? Be there? – – And I don't want to be rushed – I want to collect myself – You can't come back today. I don't know when I will find the right moment – now – or in the evening – or at night – when it is dark – completely dark –

CLAUSSNER I shall not see you any more today?

MARIA Tomorrow – as early as you want – tomorrow it will be over – tomorrow.

CLAUSSNER *(Vehemently)* I can't! I can't stand it!

MARIA If I can stand it?! I beg you – I implore you – until tomorrow! Then you can do with me whatever you wish.

CLAUSSNER *(Taking her into his arms)* Maria – are you mine?

MARIA *(Looking in his eyes)* Until death.

CLAUSSNER *(Laying her back tenderly)* Good.

GEMMA *(At the door)* May Gemma come in?

CLAUSSNER Gemma may always come in.

GEMMA Then please open the door for me, I don't have a free hand.

(CLAUSSNER goes and opens the door.)

GEMMA *(Carefully sets a large tray with wine, fruit, and sandwiches onto the mosaic table)* Ecco! I think this is good. Doesn't it have a touch of the Netherlands? What shall Mama start with?

CLAUSSNER *(Pouring wine)* With this. Drink up, Frau Maria.

(MARIA slowly drains the glass.)

GEMMA See – she heeds you.

CLAUSSNER And she will heed you, too. I'm going to my hotel now. The Deutsches Haus.

GEMMA *(Lowering her voice)* Do you know what's wrong with Mama?

CLAUSSNER *(Looking down)* It will be all right. Trust me. For now, she is your charge. Your charge, Gemma. *(He returns to MARIA.)* Something else I wanted to tell you – *(He kisses her hand, with a smile.)* The rest is silence. *(Extricating himself, with a last glance at the two women, in a strong voice)* Good-bye, you two! *(He exits through the veranda.)*

GEMMA *(Looks after him through the glass door)* How straight he walks – even straighter than usual. *(She steps behind the table and fixes a plate.)* If you don't eat the last bite – I'll be jealous. If you drank for him, you must eat for me. Mamachild! Are you my little toad? My house toad? Will you come out of your crack in the wall every day and eat with me from my plate? And if you're not good I'll whack you with the spoon and I'll take away your crown. *(She has given her the plate, pulls up a chair next to the sofa and sits down beside her.)* I just got a letter from Papa. Eat, Mama, eat. No breaks.

MARIA *(With some difficulty)* And what does he write?

GEMMA That it was very nice in Viareggio, especially bathing in the ocean, and that it is even nicer at home. That he has enjoyed very good company – but that he finally wants the best there is – ours.

(MARIA attempts to put down the plate.)

GEMMA *(Holding her back)* Don't even think of it! Three more bites! One for me – one for Papa – and another one for me. That's how you did it with me when I was little. A long time ago! On such foggy days as this one, you feel twice as old. I'm freezing for sunshine. . . . Tell me a story, Mother. Tell me about when you were young. Young and in love and engaged. What a beautiful bride you must have been! I would have loved to see you then. I would have loved even more to see through you.

MARIA You would not have found what you're expecting. There wasn't much there. Neither spiritually nor intellectually. I wasn't a child any more, but I was still childish.

GEMMA *(Drawing nearer to her)* What do you mean?

MARIA That I grew up neither here nor there. No longer in a convent – oh no. One was allowed outside the convent walls. But outside, there was no one to guide you. You will get married – that was the tone underlying everything you were told. Of course, you have to like him and he you. You were never really told what it meant to like someone. You were not told how great the task was that was expected of you. You weren't told that your choice in the matter might exist in appearance only. That it might be a sham based on birth and external considerations and satisfied vanity.

GEMMA   But it wasn't like that for you?

MARIA   It wasn't very different. Papa was famous – and I was a dependent little thing who marveled at him. And everybody said: how incredibly fortunate she is.

GEMMA′ *(Her breath caught in her throat)* But then – weren't you happy?

MARIA   I was far from grown up enough to be either happy or unhappy. After a year, you came and I was contented. And whenever it occurred to me that something in my life was not right, I warded it off. The threads that spin themselves around you are as numerous as days. They spin a net . . . and when you finally want to tear it apart –

GEMMA   *(Taking her hand)* Mother – can't it end differently? Can't one learn to love someone, to be friends with each other? Maybe later even better than at the beginning? There must have been some good in so many common experiences. Can't two people grow old together in peace? Can't they?

MARIA   Not everyone can. . . .

GEMMA   Why don't you want to tell me, Mother? You're afraid of going home. But it will be different from before. The year here made me grow up. You now have a big daughter who understands everything and with whom you can talk about everything. I can also talk to Papa, tell him how you should be treated, and that there cannot be another hour when you feel sad or irritated.

MARIA   And if – if it weren't possible – if you couldn't understand everything –

GEMMA   Not understand everything? *(She gets up, takes a few steps, returns, steps behind MARIA, leans over her. Very softly and tenderly)* I can understand everything – even things that cannot be spoken – ever. I'm thinking that everyone is holding back one last thing – a dream or a longing – that has never come true – even if it would have meant the most wonderful thing –

MARIA   *(Almost inaudibly, broken)* Gemma –

GEMMA   *(Hugging her)* And I don't know anything – I never want to know – because to tell – only in – – – And you can't let me forgive you anything! Forgive me that I can't lose you, leave you – that I'm demanding everything of you because you are everything to me – more than life

– my mother! *(Pause)* Will you go home with me?

MARIA   – Yes, Gemma.

GEMMA   Mama – you are sitting up – you're smiling – do you feel better?

MARIA   Yes.

GEMMA   Did I do that?

MARIA   Yes, you.

GEMMA   *(Blissfully)* What do I do? What do I do to make it last? Carry you around? No, no nonsense. Be quiet, quiet! Maybe read to you?

MARIA   Whatever you wish.

GEMMA   Phaedon? To the end?

MARIA   Yes – to the end.

GEMMA   *(Delighted, goes into her room)* I'll be right back – at once!

MARIA   *(Alone, turns her head, fixes her gaze onto the relief)* Death. . . .

Act V

Night. The lamp is down to a dying flicker which no longer illuminates the room but throws a weak glimmer over MARIA, who sits in her arm chair next to the desk. In her white dress, as in the first act, her right arm on the desk and her head resting in her hand, her left arm dangling over the side of the chair.

The glass door is open. A full moon over the veranda and garden. Slow steps can be heard on the gravel. The steps stop suddenly. Old TUCHER appears on the steps, hesitating, without a hat, in his house coat, a few white roses in his hand. He stops, advances again, and attempts to carefully close the door from the outside. MARIA's right arm falls on the desk at that moment.

TUCHER   *(Startled by the noise)* Pardon – is anyone there?

MARIA   *(Absent-minded, repeating mechanically)* Is anyone there. . . .

TUCHER   Who is there, may I ask?

MARIA   *(As before)* Who – me.

TUCHER   *(Advancing)* It is you, dearest lady? Then I ask a thousand pardons. I was still in the garden, I saw your door standing wide open and assumed a negligence on the part of your servants. To preserve at least the appearance of security, I attempted to close it from the outside – As I said, I ask a thousand pardons. *(He tries to withdraw. At that moment, the moon shines into the room, throwing light on MARIA who still stares silently in front of her.)* Excuse me, my dear lady – do you feel unwell?

MARIA *(Waking up, heavily)* Unwell – who feels unwell? Ah, it is you, Your Excellency – Yes – I feel well – I just fell asleep – or I wasn't awake – I don't know – Is it late already?

TUCHER It is past midnight, madam.

MARIA Past midnight –

TUCHER May I call your attention to the fact that the lamp will soon go out? Would it not be better to extinguish it altogether?

MARIA *(Slowly turning her head towards the lamp)* Extinguish – I wanted to wait until it goes out by itself – That long I wanted to wait – and then go to sleep.

TUCHER As you wish, madam. And so I wish you a most agreeable night.

(MARIA does not answer.)

TUCHER *(Bewildered)* My dearest lady – I do not wish to transcend the limits of discretion – but I do have the impression that something out of the ordinary – May I offer my assistance in any way?

MARIA *(Without looking at him, with tired friendliness)* Very kind, Your Excellency – very kind. But I wouldn't know how to make use of it. There are things with which one must cope alone – and one does cope with them.

TUCHER *(Approaching)* You are in such a serious mood?

MARIA *(Pleasantly, without losing her melancholy tone)* As it happens – sometimes more so – sometimes less – and sometimes very serious.

TUCHER *(With a deep sigh)* And sometimes very serious. Right. Since last night, I too have had something to put down in my files – May the good God preserve you from experiencing so.nething like this. From experiencing disappointment in your own child.

MARIA *(Looking at him for the first time)* In your son?

TUCHER *(Full of bitterness)* In my only son.

MARIA May I know –

TUCHER My dear lady – how could I bother you with this, and at this hour – Maybe you will grant me your attention some time in the garden, some evening –

MARIA I don't know that I will make it back to the garden that soon – *(With a glance at the lamp)* I guess I have another quarter of an hour – Take a seat, Your Excellency, and tell me what happened with your son.

TUCHER *(Takes a chair and sits down at a respectful distance)* If I really may – Well, the case is this: last night, my son has informed me, completely unexpectedly, that he does not intend to take up the career I have outlined for him.

MARIA Was that – really that unexpected?

TUCHER Well – I have already had occasion to notice – that his schoolbag is not very heavy.

MARIA Wouldn't it have been your turn to talk to him?

TUCHER My dearest lady, there is nothing to talk about. He has to do his duty by our traditions.

MARIA He can do that in different ways. Best of all in the way that makes him happy.

TUCHER My dear lady, he who cannot do his duty to the utmost, happily or not, is no real man. The best evidence for this is my own life. I have done without everything that makes a happy marriage – that can bring a man joy – for fifteen years. I know what it means to give up something, what it means to stand at your post, even where all is lost. I have not abandoned it, even for a moment; I have preserved the reputation of the family without blemish, and my son should take an example by this.

MARIA What if you had not done the right thing?

TUCHER *(Dumbfounded)* Not the right thing? Not the right thing? But what else is there? What other law, what other eternal truth?

MARIA Eternal truths, Excellency, can become everyday lies. You have done your duty and forgotten how to love. The effort you have had to extend on your traditions was so great that there was nothing left in you for your children. You have become hard, you have neglected your true duties.

TUCHER But what should I have done – how should I have lived instead?

MARIA Maybe it would have been better if you had separated from your wife – or if you had taken a mistress – a faithful person who could have helped you remain good and soft, even if it had been with the consciousness – of guilt. Because even that doesn't matter in the innermost heart – all that matters is how we bear our guilt, and what it makes of us.

TUCHER *(Greatly moved)* My dear lady – your words – your voice –

MARIA Don't let it get too late, Excellency. What did you say to your son? Did you tell him no? Go to him and take it back. Don't let him, too, become hard in this night of loneliness and helplessness. Love, Excellency, love! The letters of the law alone are not enough. Everyone should be allowed to search for that which is his own, that which will let him live – and if he can't hold on to it – that which will permit him to die.

TUCHER *(Deeply moved)* Amen, my dearest lady – Amen. *(He rises and comes to her.)* Thank you. . . . May I present you with these last roses – I wanted to save them from the frost.

MARIA *(Takes them and smiles)* White roses – how beautiful.

TUCHER And permit me to tell you that today, I have for the first time – received an ineradicable impression – from a woman. *(He kisses her hand.)* And now I will go to my son. Good night, madam.

MARIA Good night, Excellency.

(TUCHER exits hurriedly, closing the veranda door from the outside.)

MARIA *(Stares into the lamp for a while, one hand holding the roses in her lap, her head resting in the other.)* Still – it is still flickering – it will be too long. *(She rises, puts the roses on the desk and tiptoes to GEMMA's door. She presses her face and hands against it. In a low voice, heart-rending)* Wake up, Gemma, wake up — — — *(Turning away with great effort)* No! Sleep – sleep on, my child! *(She hurries to the desk, pulls out the drawer, takes the little box, shakes little envelopes filled with powder into her hand, counting.)* five, seven, eight – that will be enough. *(She blows out the lamp.)* Done – with everything. *(She goes to her door quickly, stands in front of it and casts a long glance over the room.)* And it was worth my life! *(Exits. She throws the bolt from the inside. The room remains empty for some time, after a while completely illuminated by the moon.)*

GEMMA *(In a long white nightdress, half opens her door)* Mama – *(She comes out.)* I thought – I felt like – *(She goes around the room, searching. She listens at MARIA's door.)* Mama – are you asleep? — — —

(In the meantime, a dark figure has appeared on the veranda, steps to the glass door and tries the handle. GEMMA whirls around, starts back, then, screwing up her courage, takes a few steps forward.) Who is there – who is out there?

CLAUSSNER's *calm voice* It is me, Gemma – open the door.

GEMMA *(Stupefied)* It is you – you?

CLAUSSNER Open the door – I beg you, open the door.

(GEMMA opens.)

CLAUSSNER *(Entering)* Is Maria asleep?

GEMMA Mama is asleep.

CLAUSSNER *(Taking a deep breath)* Ah! *(He throws his hat down.)* There is something cursed about fall nights. Death has invented them. It grabs you, it attacks you – like the second sight – it chases you out – It's a good thing that your gate isn't higher. Are you sure she's asleep?

GEMMA Quite sure. . . . Will you leave now?

CLAUSSNER Do you mind if I stay?

GEMMA *(After a stubborn pause)* Yes. *(Her voice trembles slightly.)* I know – that you have more rights than anyone – but coming here secretly – in the middle of the night –

CLAUSSNER But I've already told you – I am worried about your mother. I want to stay here and sit up. Why are you up? For the same reason? If I'm here you can stop worrying and go back to sleep.

GEMMA Oh, I can't sleep any more. I had such terrible dreams. I dreamed that someone was at my door and crying and I couldn't get up and couldn't open – *(She sits down on the sofa.)*

CLAUSSNER *(Puts a blanket over her)* Wrap yourself up, Gemma, it is cold, and with your bare feet – *(He sets a chair down beside Maria's door.)* Don't you want to look in?

GEMMA She would wake up at once. The old lock always creaks.

CLAUSSNER No, then we don't.

(Silence)

GEMMA *(Nervously)* Doesn't it smell like roses here? And there are no roses? I know I didn't bring any more.

CLAUSSNER Maybe the smell is coming from the garden. Isn't the door closed? *(He gets up and examines the door.)* It is closed, you must be mistaken.

GEMMA No, I am not mistaken. There is a

very strong smell – *(Quickly pointing at the desk)* and it's coming from there!

CLAUSSNER *(Goes to the desk)* Indeed, you're right. There are roses. Beautiful white roses. *(He brings them to her.)*

GEMMA *(Takes them, terrified)* White ones? But they're – who brought them?

CLAUSSNER What kind of roses are these?

GEMMA *(Shuddering)* They're roses for a grave.

CLAUSSNER Oh, Gemma – what you're imagining!

GEMMA *(Staring at the roses)* Who brought – them –

CLAUSSNER Agata – or someone else –

GEMMA Who else – who was here – who is here –

CLAUSSNER Child, child, you can't do this. You'll see ghosts next. *(He sits down again on his chair next to the door.)* We will talk about your mother, that will be the best remedy. How was she last night?

GEMMA Oh — — pretty cheerful. Only so veiled.

CLAUSSNER *(Nodding)* I know. And what did you talk about?

GEMMA A lot. Especially how we'll arrange things when we're back in Florence.

CLAUSSNER *(With disbelief)* When you're back – both of you?

GEMMA Yes – both of us.

CLAUSSNER *(After a pause)* Tell me, Gemma – haven't you noticed – you're quite perceptive – that your mother does not like to go back to Florence – to her former life? Such things can't be hidden.

GEMMA *(Tortured, to herself)* No – they can't be hidden.

CLAUSSNER And do you think it is right that she is forced to go?

GEMMA *(Pulling herself together)* I think it is right that everything should be done to preserve her for this life and for the two people who love her most in the world.

CLAUSSNER But you two don't love her most in the world.

GEMMA *(Blushing furiously)* We don't? And who should love her more than us?

CLAUSSNER I do.

GEMMA And you would expect her to make herself and us unhappy?

CLAUSSNER She has been unhappy for a long time.

GEMMA And will she be less unhappy if she leaves us? After seventeen years? Do you think those years can be eradicated like seventeen days?

CLAUSSNER Why should they be? Do two people who cannot love each other any more have to hate each other? And what do you think is nobler – a forced life together, forced by one of the two, or the fond remembrance of both, separated from each other?

GEMMA *(Passionately)* That can be true for man and woman! But not for my mother and me! You can't tear us apart! With no kind of love! With no kind of violence! With no power on this earth!

CLAUSSNER Only with magic.

GEMMA Not even with that! Not even with magic! Because to forget about me – to completely forget about me – she couldn't – not for a single moment!

CLAUSSNER What if she already had, for a single moment?

GEMMA *(Jumps up, beside herself)* That is not true! I want to hear that from her! Mother! Mother! *(She tries to open the door.)* Locked? *(She rattles the door.)* She's not answering? She doesn't hear? What is this? *(She screams.)*

(CLAUSSNER shoves her aside without a word, presses the lock in with both hands, pushes the door open and plunges into the dimly lit room.)

GEMMA *(Has broken down at the sofa. Paralyzed, whimpering to herself)* Mama — — Mama — — Mama — — —

CLAUSSNER *(Reappears in the doorframe. His face is grey and sunken. Tonelessly)* Come – come in, Gemma —

GEMMA *(With a helpless movement)* What – what is –

CLAUSSNER *(Goes to her, pulls her up.)* It is over, Gemma – she sacrificed herself for you –

GEMMA And she – loved you.

The End

Notes

1 The Empire referred to here is the Second German Empire, founded with the crowning of the Prussian King as German Emperor in 1871. Since the action of the play is supposed to be contemporary, Gemma's dress would be out of fashion by approximately thirty years.

2 In German, the informal *du* (as opposed to the formal *Sie* that is the normal form

of address between Gemma and Otto) was at the time reserved for intimate friends and family relationships.

Select bibliography

Primary works in English

Bernstein, Elsa (1910) *Kingly Children: Opera by Humperdinck*, trans. C. H. Meltzer, New York: Rullman.

—— (1911) *John Herkner*, trans. M. Harned, *Poet Lore* 22, Boston.

—— (1911) *The Royal Children: A Fairy Tale Founded on the Opera*, told for children by A. A. Chapin, New York: L. Harper & Bros.

—— (1912) *Twilight*, trans. P. H. Grummann, *Poet Lore* 23, Boston.

—— (1917) *Twilight. Drama in Five Acts*, *Poet Lore* Series 2: 369–443, Boston: Badger.

—— (1925) *The King's Children*, retold by J. McSpadden, *Stories from Great Operas*, New York: Cromwell.

—— (n. d.) *King's Children, a German Fairy Tale in 3 Acts*, by Ernst Rosmer [*sic*], New York: Rosenfield.

Secondary works

Arnold, R. F. (1912) *Das moderne Drama*, Strasburg: Karl J. Truebner.

—— (ed.) (1925) *Das deutsche Drama*, Munich: C. H. Beck.

Brinker-Gabler, G., Ludwig, K. and Wöffen, A. (1986) *Lexikon deutschsprachiger Schriftstellerinnen 1800–1945*, Munich: dtv.

Giesing, M. (1985) "Theater als verweigerter Raum: Dramatikerinnen der Jahrhundertwende in deutschsprachigen Ländern," in H. Gnüg and R. Möhrmann (eds) *Frauen Literatur Geschichte: Schreibende Frauen vom Mittelalter bis zur Gegenwart*, Stuttgart: Metzler, 240–59.

Kord, S. (1992) *Ein Blick hinter die Kulissen: Deutschsprachige Dramatikerinnen im 18. und 19. Jahrhundert*, Stuttgart: Metzler, 90–2, 204–9, 248f., 334f.

Kriwanek, G. (1952) "Das dramatische Werk von Elsa Bernstein," Dissertation, University of Vienna.

Lothar, R. (1905) *Das deutsche Drama der Gegenwart*, Munich: Georg Müller.

Meyer, R. (1900) *Die deutsche Litteratur des neunzehnten Jahrhunderts*, Berlin, n. p.

Pierce, N. J. F. (1988) "Woman's Place in Turn-of-the-Century Drama: The Function of Female Figures in Selected Plays by Gerhart Hauptmann, Frank Wedekind, Ricarda Huch and Elsa Bernstein," Dissertation, University of California, Irvine.

Scholtz Novak, S. G. (1971) "Images of Womanhood in the Works of German Female Dramatists 1892–1918," Dissertation, Johns Hopkins University.

Soergel, A. (1911) *Dichtung und Dichter der Zeit: Eine Schilderung der deutschen Literatur der letzten Jahrzehnte*, Leipzig: R. Voigtländer.

Soergel, A. and Hohoff, C. (1961) *Dichtung und Dichter der Zeit: Vom Naturalismus bis zur Gegenwart*, Düsseldorf: August Bagel.

Spiero, H. (1913) *Geschichte der deutschen Frauendichtung seit 1800*, Leipzig: B. G. Teubner.

Wiener, K. (1923) "Die Dramen Elsa Bernsteins (Ernst Rosmers)," Dissertation, University of Vienna.

Zophoniasson-Baierl, U. (1985) *Elsa Bernstein alias Ernst Rosmer: eine deutsche Dramatikerin im Spannungsfeld der literarischen Strömungen des Wilhelminischen Zeitalters*, Berne, New York: Lang.

4 Elizabeth Robins 1862-1952

Votes for Women
England

Elizabeth Robins. *Photograph provided courtesy of the Fales Library. Reproduced with the permission of Mabel Smith for the Backsettown Trustees.*

Introduction

by Joanne E. Gates

A new play for a new theater

The Court Theatre production of Elizabeth Robins's play, *Votes for Women*, in the Spring of 1907, identifies an important moment in theater history. After more than fifteen years of growing realism and attention to social issues in drama – most graphically marked, perhaps, by Janet Achurch's playing of Nora in the London production of Henrik Ibsen's *A Doll House* – this play addressed the politics of women's suffrage in an overtly didactic manner. Robins was well known as the actress who, early in the 1890s, had initiated a reappraisal of Ibsen with her independent productions of several of his plays. The play's director, Harley Granville Barker, is now regarded for his modernist directorial innovations. Prior to Barker's innovations, stage management had been in the hands of the actor-managers, and the theater had sacrificed artistic integrity to the star-status of the leading performer, who was also the principal investor.

Robins had lived with the frustrations of the actor-manager system during her first years on the American stage. In early 1882, James O'Neill had helped secure her first, non-speaking role, and he later employed her in his company. When O'Neill's *The Count of Monte Cristo* was assured a long future, Robins, playing a very impressive Mercedes, grew discontented with the repetition of a single, overly melodramatic role. She played scores of roles in her years with the Boston Museum Theater, 1883–86, yet seized upon an opportunity to seek acting opportunities in England when she traveled there in 1888. More than two long

years later, in the spring of 1891 (after sporadic work in small roles), her production of Ibsen's *Hedda Gabler* created a sensation. Yet the commercial actor-manager system limited her opportunities as severely as the narrow interest in what was perceived as Ibsen's decadence. Although she played as many non-Ibsen roles in the commercial theater, she repeatedly found the non-commercial theater opportunities a better outlet for her talents. She contributed to the efforts of the Independent Theatre and organized several independent series of her own: the Robins–Lea Joint Management (responsible for *Hedda Gabler*), a remarkable Ibsen Repertory Series in 1893, and the fund which supported Ibsen's *Little Eyolf* in 1896 and *Mariana* in 1897. She inspired the founding of the New Century Theatre, staged *John Gabriel Borkman* for them, and oversaw play selection. Her associations with the literati in London society during the 1890s inevitably led to her second career as a writer, which she very carefully disguised under the pseudonym "C. E. Raimond," until the 1898 publication of her male–female *Bildungsroman, The Open Question*, disclosed her American roots.

History meets drama

After her pseudonym was disclosed, Robins pursued diverse writing projects that took her as far afield as Alaska. In 1906 the actress Gertrude Kingston approached her with a proposal to commission a play that she could use to inaugurate her own acting company. Robins spent a good deal of time drafting a script for Kingston that would be centered around the impact in theatrical circles of the great tragic actress, Rachel, who reigned at the Comédie Française half a century earlier. Shortly after she began to attend the open-air meetings of the suffrage Union, Robins abandoned her original plot and worked furiously to complete a play that brought the street politics of the suffrage campaign onto the stage. The WSPU, or Women's Social and Political Union, had moved from Manchester to London in the fall of 1906. Led by Emmeline Pankhurst and her daughters, the WSPU's confrontational tactics injected a new urgency into a decades-long struggle. The more Robins became immersed in the work, the more she became converted to the cause. On November 1, 1906, she wrote to Millicent Fawcett, president of the more established National Union of Women's Suffrage Societies (NUWSS), that she was, for the first time, writing something "under the pressure of a strong moral conviction" (quoted in Gates 1994: 154). Eventually, Robins's anxiety that the issue might fade from importance and her awareness that Kingston was balking at the political nature of the drama led to legal arrangements which voided their contract. Within hours of the severing of negotiations with Kingston and Kingston's return of the script, on February 28, 1907, Robins had secured its production at the Court Theatre. By this time Robins had consulted an impressive band of dramatists – George Bernard Shaw, Henry James, Florence Bell, William Archer, and James Barrie – for reassurance that the play needed a substantial forum.

Using the debate over suffrage as a focal point, Robins documents the aspects of "sex antagonism" which had brought about women's resentment for being disenfranchised. The first act is set in a fashionable country home where the social elite gather for the weekend. Vida Levering, not well known by the other out-of-towners, has come to discuss her plans for a shelter for homeless women with the hostess. While she is offstage, one of the party tells of her earlier acquaintance with Vida, hinting at a secret in the younger woman's past. She had found Vida deathly sick in an old Welsh farmhouse after a visit from a crank doctor. The strong implication is that Vida had an abortion, yet the older women are careful to protect the innocence of Beatrice Dunbarton, a young heiress about to announce her engagement. Instead of heeding warnings to avoid Vida, Bee follows her to the open-air suffrage rally in Trafalgar Square, the setting of Act II. At the rally, in the presence of the man she's going to marry, Member of Parliament Geoffrey Stonor, Bee intuits from the look on Vida's face when she catches sight of Stonor that Stonor is the man in Vida's past. Act III is stirring for Robins's ability to make the action dramatically engaging by using politics to focus the personal crises for all concerned.

One of the most important features of the play is the second-act recreation of a Trafalgar Square suffrage rally. Reviews of the Court Theatre production complimented the staging for its realism and the force of its argument. On the page, the scene compares favorably to the town meeting scene in Ibsen's *An Enemy of the People*, which certainly must have influenced Robins. Robins's fiction had earlier demonstrated her ear for vernacular dialects, here commandingly displayed in speeches by the Working Woman and the hecklers in the crowd. As an American expatriate who had lived in England for close to twenty years, Robins showed a striking ability to capture the look and sound of a strictly English suffrage rally. Readers today may find the play's didactic purpose too blatant or its political attitudes strategically manipulated. But these qualities were a strong element in political public speaking and performing during this tumultuous period. The play's "recognition moments" are problematic for readers in that they are more visual than spoken. In Act I, Mrs. Heriot can only insinuate Vida's abortion with peripheral information. Bee must register surprise when she learns that Stonor somehow knows Vida's first name. In Act II, Bee's awareness of their past depends upon her monitoring their reactions at a moment of particular double entendre in Vida's lines, "Every woman who has borne a child is a Labour woman. No man among you can judge what she goes through in her hour of darkness." The final moment of Act III also depends upon the audience's recognition of the symbolic weight of Stonor's final action. Again, Robins understates this event in the manner of Ibsen.

Elizabeth Robins: writer as activist

The evolution of Robins's own political conscience, both in her overtly political service to the WSPU, and in her plays, novels, and stories, provides important insights into the militant suffrage movement that previous histories and analyses have not considered. Most striking to some will be the close working-class and Labour Party roots of the early phase of the movement. When the Labour Party and the WSPU split several years later, Robins was asked to serve on the board of directors of the WSPU. Despite the increasingly autocratic control of the Pankhursts, Robins maintained the importance of a women's movement that united across class lines. Her own dual career became one that contained her new feminist self and her artistic self. Especially in *Votes for Women* and in the novel retelling the same story, *The Convert*, her politics and her writing were in harmony. When she expanded her plot for the novel, she treated in detail Vida's life before politics. This extensive pre-history shows Vida's very gradual awakening to the convictions and tactics of the most vocal suffrage organization. Robins drew from her own experience to demonstrate that women were conditioned to behave in a way that won men's approval. The novel features four open-air suffrage rallies; the last one in the novel corresponds to the play's second act. At first, Vida attends out of curiosity; later, she puts on shabby clothing and pretends to stumble upon the rally. Even when Vida joins the Union, she is at first uncomfortable with the spontaneity of the occasion. Thus, the last few chapters of the novel form a cohesive epiphany to previous action and allow for both Vida and Stonor to be regarded as converts.

Within months of conceiving a heroine whose commitment to a cause propels her

to speak publicly, Robins herself was making platform speeches and lobbying for feminist political action. *Way Stations*, the collection of speeches, articles, and letters written to newspapers about the suffrage cause, testifies to her dedication to the movement. Christabel Pankhurst repeatedly begged her to contribute more generously, but Robins restricted her public speaking, agreeing to come to the aid of the Union only when a crisis developed. In contrast to the spontaneity of her characters' platform style, Robins usually wrote out, extensively revised, and practically memorized her speeches.

Even after the long struggle to secure the vote, Robins was recognized as a leading spokeswoman for feminist causes. She lobbied on behalf of many women's issues, and kept in close contact with fellow countrywoman Lady Nancy Astor as Lady Astor made her impact as the first woman Member of Parliament. Robins was on the Board of Directors of the all-women news weekly, *Time and Tide*, and she often contributed articles. When the Labour government regained power in 1924, she rushed into press a long treatise she had spent years developing, *Ancilla's Share: An Indictment of Sex Antagonism*.

Although *Votes for Women* was her only produced play, Robins had earlier perfected her talents as playwright with three finished pieces, all of which survive in her private papers, now available to scholars at the Fales Library, New York University. After *The Convert*, her next creative project was a drama about an American widow who befriends a promising young playwright. After consultation with Henry James, she decided to recast the play as a novel. Each of these plots, as well as *Votes for Women*, bears a vague resemblance to Henry James's *The Bostonians*, in representing a political or artistic older woman and a potential husband contending for the allegiance of a younger woman. Although there is no evidence that Robins was directly responding to James's earlier depiction of women's rights, she did begin work on a historical novel of the American stage, directly indicating that she was remedying a central flaw she found in James's *The Tragic Muse*. Probably the nearest Robins came to repeating the stage success of *Votes for Women* was her adaptation of her short novel exposing the evils of white slavery, *My Little Sister*, 1913 (published in Great Britain as *Where Are You Going To?*). Unlike her other play-novel projects, it was only as afterthought that she worked to dramatize her searing indictment of a profligate underworld that abducted young women. Just as Inez Bensusan's Women's Theatre prepared to stage the adaptation, the World War erupted and caused the production to be canceled. In America, prospects for a production were halted when the latest Rachel Crothers play did not measure up to commercial potential. Women playwrights' ability to draw audiences was still in doubt.

The version of Robins's play printed here has never appeared. Furthermore, it departs from other printed versions in important ways. Earlier publications of *Votes for Women* derive from the publication of a very limited edition by Mills and Boon, Ltd., in 1909. A few major differences distinguish that version and this one, based upon the script Robins submitted to the Court Theatre, where Harley Granville Barker was directing. Barker made annotations to Robins's typescript, but she did not see these until 1936. Nor did she consult his "prompt script," or director's copy of the play with notes for staging, when she rewrote the play as a novel and then revised the play for publication two years later. Barker's astute oversight of the production is best observed in close examination of the original prompt script. His annotations are of primary importance in understanding how carefully and precisely he staged the crowd interactions during Act II. For each of Robins's interjected comments, he assigns a specific character. In addition, he invented other dialogue and keyed line assignments to specific moments in the prompt script. While Barker must be credited with realistic staging innovations, this source text demonstrates how much Robins's writing laid the foundation for those effects.

When Robins revised the confrontation between Vida and Stonor for the final pages of her novel, she expanded the scene considerably. Although the narrative version allows for a closer sympathy for Stonor's viewpoint throughout, there is a decidedly harsher tone to Vida's logic in the last scene of the play as previously published. The ending as it was written for the Court Theatre, then, is available only in this edition. Other significant changes marked in the prompt script are worth noting. Robins had first entitled the play *A Friend of Woman*, which is the typed title-page, crossed out and amended by Barker. Barker proposed the new title, months before the WSPU periodical also adopted "Votes For Women" for their masthead. In addition, the play's original first name of Miss Dunbarton has been restored to Beatrice. The 1909 edition of the play as well as the novel give her name as Jean Dunbarton, no doubt taken from the name of the actress who played her at the Court, Jean MacKinlay. Reviews and the cast list of the first production, however, list her name as Beatrice.

Realism in *Votes for Women* is marked by several features that may not be present in other plays from the same period. Robins combined the private drawing-room courtesies of a class of people whose priorities depended upon maintaining the decorum of the status quo with some electrifying scenes of public political debate. In doing so, she exposed the economic divisions and the sexual double standard that stifled women. While she crafted her dramatic effects from the power of Ibsen's heroines – Nora, Hedda, and Hilda, in particular – she infused her play with a message that makes a powerful statement even decades after its most immediate context has evaporated. Although Great Britain's party politics of the early twentieth century may seem distant and women's right to vote is secure in the western world, the personal politics of women's empowerment are still of vital concern.

Votes for Women _____

1907

Elizabeth Robins

_____

Characters

LORD JOHN WYNNSTAY

LADY JOHN WYNNSTAY, his wife

MRS. HERIOT, sister of Lady John

MISS BEATRICE DUNBARTON, niece to Lady John and Mrs. Heriot

THE HON. GEOFFREY STONOR, Unionist M.P. (affianced to Beatrice Dunbarton)

MR. ST. JOHN GREATOREX Liberal M.P.

RICHARD FARNBOROUGH

MR. FREDDY TUNBRIDGE

MRS. FREDDY TUNBRIDGE

MR. ALLEN TRENT, Chairman of the meeting

MISS ERNESTINE BLUNT

MR. WALKER, a working man

A WORKING WOMAN

PERSONS IN THE CROWD; SERVANTS IN THE TWO HOUSES; and

MISS VIDA LEVERING

Place
Act I Wynnstay House in Hertfordshire
Act II Trafalgar Square, London
Act III Eaton Square

Time
Entire action of play takes place between Sunday noon and six o'clock the evening of the same day.

Act I

SCENE: *Hall of Wynnstay House. Twelve o'clock, Sunday morning, end of June. With the rising of the Curtain enter the* BUTLER. *As he is going with majestic port to answer the door left, enter briskly from the garden by lower french window* LADY JOHN WYNNSTAY, *flushed and flapping a garden hat to fan herself. She is a pink-cheeked woman of fifty-four who has plainly been a beauty, keeps her complexion but is gone to fat.*

LADY JOHN   Has Miss Levering come down yet?

BUTLER   *(Pausing)* I haven't seen her m'lady.

LADY JOHN   *(Almost sharply as butler turns left)* I won't have her disturbed if she's resting – *(To herself as she goes to writing table)* She certainly needs it.

BUTLER   Yes, m'lady.

LADY JOHN   *(Sitting at writing table, back to front door)* But I want her to know the moment she comes down, that the new plans have arrived by the morning post.

BUTLER   *(Pausing nearly at the door)* Plans, m'la –

LADY JOHN   She'll understand. There they are *(Glancing at the clock)* It's very important she should have them in time to look over before she goes –
*(*BUTLER *opens the door left)*

LADY JOHN   *(Over her shoulder)* Is that Miss Levering?

BUTLER   No m'lady. Mr. Farnborough. *(Exit* BUTLER*)*

FARNBOROUGH   *(Coming forward. He is twenty-six, reddish hair, high coloured, sanguine, self-important.)* I'm afraid I'm scandalously early. It didn't take me nearly as long to motor over as Lord John said.

LADY JOHN   *(Shaking hands)* I'm afraid my husband is no authority on motoring – and he's not home yet from church.

FARNBOROUGH   It's the greatest luck finding *you*. I wanted to see you about the Secretaryship.

LADY JOHN What Secretaryship?

FARNBOROUGH There *is* only one. There's only one man I'd give my ears to work for.

LADY JOHN *(Smiling)* I remember. Do you know Mr. Stonor personally? – or *(Smiling)* are you just dazzled from afar?

FARNBOROUGH Oh, I know him. The trouble is he doesn't know me. If he did he'd realise he can't be sure of winning his election without my valuable services. Forgive me, I know you're not interested in politics *qua* politics. But at this time now we've forced the Liberals to appeal to the Country. And it concerns Geoffrey Stonor.

LADY JOHN You count on my being interested in him like all the rest.

FARNBOROUGH *(Leans forward)* Lady John, I've heard the news.

LADY JOHN What news?

FARNBOROUGH That your little niece – the Scotch heiress is going to become Mrs. Geoffrey Stonor.

LADY JOHN Who told you that?

FARNBOROUGH Please don't mind my knowing.

LADY JOHN *(Visibly perturbed)* She had set her heart upon having a few days with just her family in the secret – before the flood of congratulation breaks loose.

FARNBOROUGH Oh, *that*'s all right. I always hear things before other people.

LADY JOHN Well, I must ask you to be good enough to be very circumspect. I wouldn't have my niece think that I –

FARNBOROUGH Oh, of course not.

LADY JOHN She will be here in an hour.

FARNBOROUGH *(Jumping up delighted)* What? To-day? The future Mrs. Stonor!

LADY JOHN *(Harassed)* Yes. Unfortunately we had one or two people already asked for the weekend –

FARNBOROUGH – and I go and invite myself to luncheon! Lady John you can buy me off. I'll promise to remove myself in five minutes if you'll put in a word for me.

LADY JOHN But you know Mr. Stonor inspires a similar enthusiasm in a good many young –

FARNBOROUGH They haven't studied the situation as I have. They don't know what's at stake. They don't go to that hole Dutfield as I did just to hear his Friday speech.

LADY JOHN Ah! But you were rewarded. Bee – my niece – wrote me it was 'glorious'.

FARNBOROUGH *(Judicially)* Well you know *I* was disappointed. He's too content just to criticise, just to make his delicate pungent fun of the men who are grappling – very inadequately of course – still *grappling* with the big questions. There's a carrying power *(Gets up and faces an imaginary audience)* – some of Stonor's friends ought to point it out – there's a driving power in the poorest constructive policy that makes the most brilliant criticism look barren.

LADY JOHN *(With good-humoured malice)* Who told you that?

FARNBOROUGH You think there's nothing in it because *I* say it. But now that he's coming into the family, Lord John or somebody really ought to point out – Stonor's overdoing his role of magnificent security.

LADY JOHN I don't see even Lord John offering to instruct Mr. Stonor.

FARNBOROUGH Believe me, that's just Stonor's danger! Nobody saying a word, everybody hoping he's on the point of adopting some definite line, something strong and original that's going to fire the public imagination and bring the Tories back into power –

LADY JOHN So he will.

FARNBOROUGH *(Hotly)* Not if he disappoints meetings – goes calmly up to town – and leaves the field to the Liberals.

LADY JOHN When did he do anything like that?

FARNBOROUGH Yesterday! *(With a harassed air)* And now that he's got this other preoccupation –

LADY JOHN You mean –

FARNBOROUGH Yes, your niece – the spoilt child of Fortune. Of course! *(Stopping suddenly)* She kept him from the meeting last night! Well! *(Sits down)* – if that's the effect she's going to have it's pretty serious.

LADY JOHN *(Smiling)* You are.

FARNBOROUGH I can assure you the election agent's more so. He's simply tearing his hair.

LADY JOHN *(More gravely and coming nearer)* How do you know?

FARNBOROUGH He told me so himself – yesterday. I scraped acquaintance with the agent just to see if – if –

LADY JOHN It's not only here that you
  manoeuvre for that Secretaryship.
FARNBOROUGH (*Confidentially*) You can
  never tell when your chance might come!
  The election chap's promised to keep me
  posted.
  (*The door flies open and* BEE DUNBARTON
  rushes in.)
BEE Aunt Ellen – here I –
LADY JOHN (*Astonished*) My dear child!
  (*They embrace. Enter* LORD JOHN *from the
  garden – a benevolent, silver-haired despot of
  sixty-two*)
LORD JOHN I *thought* that was you running
  up the avenue.
  (BEE *greets her uncle warmly but all the
  time she and her aunt talk together.* 'How
  did you get here so early?' 'I knew you'd be
  surprised – wasn't it clever of me to manage
  it? I don't deserve all the credit.' 'But there
  isn't any train between – ' 'Yes, wait till I tell
  you –' 'You walked in the broiling sun –' 'No,
  no.' 'You must be dead – Why didn't you
  telegraph? I ordered the carriage to meet the
  1.10. Didn't you say the 1.10? Yes, I'm sure
  you did – here's your letter –')
  (*Has shaken hands with* FARNBOROUGH
  and speaks through the torrent) Now they'll
  tell each other for ten minutes that she's
  an hour earlier then we expected.
  (LORD JOHN *leads* FARNBOROUGH *towards
  the garden.*)
FARNBOROUGH The Freddy Tunbridges said
  they were coming to you this week.
LORD JOHN Yes, they're dawdling through
  the park with the Church Brigade.
FARNBOROUGH Oh! (*With a glance at* LADY
  JOHN) I'll go and meet them.
  (*Exit* FARNBOROUGH)
LORD JOHN (*As he turns back*) That
  discreet young man will get on.
LADY JOHN But *how* did you get here?
BEE (*Breathless*) 'He' motored me down.
LADY JOHN Geoffrey Stonor? (BEE *nods.*)
  Why, where is he then?
BEE He dropped me at the end of the
  avenue and went on to see a supporter
  about something.
LORD JOHN You let him go off like that
  without –
LADY JOHN (*Taking* BEE'S *two hands*) Just
  tell me my child, is it all *right*?
BEE My engagement? (*Radiantly*) Yes,
  absolutely.
LADY JOHN Geoffrey Stonor isn't going to
  be – a little too old for you?

BEE (*Laughing*) Bless me, am I such a
  chicken?
LADY JOHN Twenty-four used not to be so
  young – but it's become so.
LORD JOHN Well, how spoilt is the great
  man?
BEE Not the least little bit in the world.
  You'll see. He so wants to know my best-
  beloved relations better. (*Another embrace*)
  An orphan has so few belongings she has
  to make the most of them.
LORD JOHN (*Smiling*) Let us hope he'll
  approve of us on intimate acquaintance.
BEE (*Firmly*) He will. He's an angel. Why,
  he gets on with my grandfather.
LADY JOHN *Does* he? He *must* have powers
  of persuasion – to get that old Covenanter
  to let you come in an abhorred motor car
  – on Sunday too!
BEE (*Half whispering*) Grandfather didn't
  know.
LADY JOHN Didn't know?
BEE I honestly meant to come by train.
  Geoffrey met me on my way to the
  station. We had the most glorious run!
  Oh, Aunt Ellen, we're so happy! (*Pressing
  her cheek against* LADY JOHN'S *shoulder*)
  I've so looked forward to having you to
  myself the whole day just to talk to you
  about –
LORD JOHN (*Turning away with affected
  displeasure*) Oh, very well –
BEE (*Catches him affectionately by the arm*)
  You'd find it dreffly dull to hear me talk
  about Geoffrey the whole blessed day!
LADY JOHN Well, till luncheon my dear
  (*A glance at the clock*), you mustn't mind if
  I – (*To* LORD JOHN *as she goes to writing
  table*) Miss Levering wasn't only tired last
  night, she was ill.
LORD JOHN I thought she looked very
  white.
BEE Who is Miss – ? You don't mean there
  are other people?
LADY JOHN One or two. Your uncle's
  responsible for asking that old cynic, St.
  John Greatorex and I'm responsible for –
BEE Mr. Greatorex – he's a radical, isn't he?
LORD JOHN (*Laughing*) Bee! Beginning to
  think in parties!
LADY JOHN It's very natural now that she
  should –
BEE Here they are! The Freddy Tunbridges!
  What? Not Aunt Lydia! Oh-h (*Looking
  reproachfully at* LADY JOHN, *who makes a
  discreet motion 'I couldn't help it'*)

(Enter the TUNBRIDGES. MR. FREDDY *of no profession and of independent means. Well-groomed: pleasant looking; of few words. A nice man who 'likes nice women' and has married one of them.* MRS. FREDDY *is thirty. An attractive figure, delicate face, intelligent grey eyes, over-sensitive mouth and naturally curling dust-coloured hair)*

MRS. FREDDY What a delightful surprise.

BEE *(Shaking hands warmly)* I'm so glad – How d'ye do Mr. Freddy.
(Enter MRS. HERIOT; *smart, pompous, fifty. Followed by* FARNBOROUGH)

MRS. HERIOT My dear Bee! My darling child!

BEE How do you do Aunt.

MRS. HERIOT *(Sotto voce)* I wasn't surprised! I always prophesied –

BEE Sh! *Please* –

FARNBOROUGH We haven't met since you were in short skirts. I'm Dick Farnborough.

BEE Oh, I remember. *(They shake hands.)*

MRS. FREDDY *(Looking round)* Not down yet – the Elusive One?

BEE Who is the Elusive One?

MRS. FREDDY Lady John's new friend.

LORD JOHN *(To* BEE) Oh, I forgot you hadn't seen Miss Levering – such a nice creature! – *(To* MRS. FREDDY) don't you think?

MRS. FREDDY Of course I do. You're lucky to get her to come so often. She won't go to other people.

LADY JOHN She knows she can rest here.

MRS. FREDDY *(Who has joined* LADY JOHN *near the writing table)* What does she do to tire her?

LADY JOHN She's been helping my sister and me with a scheme of ours.

MRS. HERIOT She certainly knows how to inveigle money out of the men!

LADY JOHN It would sound less equivocal, Lydia, if you added that the money is to build Baths in our Shelter for Homeless Women.

MR. FREDDY Homeless Women?

LADY JOHN Yes, in the most insanitary part of Soho.

MR. FREDDY Oh – a – really.

FARNBOROUGH It doesn't sound quite in Miss Levering's line.

LADY JOHN My dear boy, you know as little about what's in a woman's line as most men.

MR. FREDDY *(Laughing)* Oh, I say.

LORD JOHN *(Indulgently to* MR. FREDDY *and* FARNBOROUGH) Philanthropy in a woman like Miss Levering is a form of restlessness. But she's a *nice* creature – all she needs is to get some 'nice' fella to marry her.

MRS. FREDDY *(Laughing as she hangs on her husband's arm)* Yes a woman needs a balance wheel – if only to keep her from flying back to town on a hot day like this.

LORD JOHN Who's proposing anything so –

MRS. FREDDY The Elusive One.

LORD JOHN Not Miss –

MRS. FREDDY Yes, before luncheon. *(Exit* FARNBOROUGH *to garden)*

LADY JOHN She must be in London by two she says.

LORD JOHN What for in the name of –

LADY JOHN Well *that* I didn't ask her – But *(Consults watch)* I think I'll just go up and see if she's changed her plans.

LORD JOHN Oh, she *must* be made to. Such a nice creature! All she needs – *(Voices outside. Enter fussily, talking and gesticulating,* ST. JOHN GREATOREX *followed by* MISS LEVERING *and* FARNBOROUGH. GREATOREX *is sixty-two; wealthy county magnate and Liberal M.P. He is square, thick-set, square-bearded. His shining bald pate has two strands of coal-black hair trained across his crown from left ear to right and securely pasted there. He has small twinkling eyes and a reputation for telling good stories after dinner when ladies have left the room. He is carrying a little book of* MISS LEVERING'S. *She (parasol over shoulder) – an attractive, essentially feminine and rather 'smart' woman of thirty-two, with a somewhat foreign grace; the kind of whom men and woman alike say: 'What's her story? Why doesn't she marry?')*

GREATOREX I protest! Good Lord, what are the women of this country coming to! I *protest* against Miss Levering being carried off to discuss anything so revolting. Bless my soul! What can a woman like you *know* about it.

MISS LEVERING *(Smiling)* Little enough. Good morning.

GREATOREX *(Relieved)* I should think so indeed!

LORD JOHN *(Aside)* You aren't serious about going –

GREATOREX *(Waggishly breaking in)* We were so happy out there in the Summer-house weren't we?

MISS LEVERING Ideally.

GREATOREX – and to be haled out to talk about Public *Sanitation* forsooth! *(Hurries after* MISS LEVERING *as she advances to speak to the* FREDDY'S *etc.)* Why God bless my soul, do you realise that's *drains!*

MISS LEVERING I'm dreadfully afraid it is. *(Holds out her hand for the small book* GREATOREX *is carrying)*

GREATOREX *(Returns* MISS LEVERING*'s book with his finger in the place. She opens it and shuts her handkerchief in.)* – and we in the act of discussing Italian literature! Perhaps you'll tell me that isn't a more savoury topic for a lady.

MISS LEVERING But for the tramp population less conducive to savouriness don't you think, than – baths?

GREATOREX No, I can't understand this morbid interest in vagrants. *You're* much too – leave it to the others.

BEE What others?

GREATOREX *(With smiling impertinence)* Oh the sort of woman who smells of India rubber. The typical English spinster. *(To* MISS LEVERING*) You* know – Italy's full of her. She never goes anywhere without a macintosh and a collapsible bath – *rubber.* When you look at her it's borne in upon you that she doesn't only smell of rubber. *She's* rubber too.

LORD JOHN *(Laughing)* This is my niece Miss Beatrice Dunbarton, Miss Levering.

BEE How do you do. *(They shake hands.)*

GREATOREX *(To* BEE*)* I'm sure *you* agree with me.

BEE About Miss Levering being too –

GREATOREX For *that* sort of thing – *much too* –

MISS LEVERING What a pity you've exhausted the more eloquent adjectives.

GREATOREX But I haven't –

MISS LEVERING Well, you can't say to me as you did to Mrs. Freddy: 'You're too young and too happily married – and too –' *(Glances round smiling at* MRS. FREDDY *who, oblivious, is laughing and talking to her husband and* MRS. HERIOT*)*

BEE For what was Mrs. Freddy too happily married and all the rest?

MISS LEVERING *(Lightly)* Mr. Greatorex was repudiating the horrid rumour that Mrs. Freddy had been speaking in public; about – Women's Trade Unions, wasn't that what Mrs. Heriot said?

LORD JOHN *(Chuckling)* Yes, it isn't made

up as carefully as your Aunt's parties usually are. Here we've got Greatorex *(Takes his arm)* who hates political women and we've got in that mild and inoffensive-looking little lady – *(Motion over his shoulder towards* MRS. FREDDY*)*

GREATOREX *(Shrinking down stage in comic terror)* You don't mean she's really –

BEE *(Simultaneously and gaily rising)* Oh, and you've got me!

LORD JOHN *(With genial affection)* My dear child, he doesn't hate the charming wives and sweethearts who help to win seats. *(*BEE *makes her uncle a discreet little signal of warning.)*

MISS LEVERING Mr. Greatorex objects only to the unsexed creatures who – a –

LORD JOHN *(Hastily to cover up his slip)* Yes, yes, who want to act independently of men.

MISS LEVERING Vote, and do silly things of that sort.

LORD JOHN *(With enthusiasm)* Exactly.

MRS. HERIOT It will be a long time before we hear any more of *that* nonsense.

BEE You mean since that rowdy scene in the House of Commons?

MRS. HERIOT Yes. No decent woman will be able to say 'Suffrage' without blushing for another generation, thank Heaven!

MISS LEVERING *(Smiling)* Oh! I understood that so little I almost imagined people were more stirred up about it than they'd ever been before.

GREATOREX *(With a quizzical affectation of gallantry)* Not people like you.

MISS LEVERING *(Teasingly)* How do you know?

GREATOREX *(With a start)* God bless my soul –

LORD JOHN She's saying that only to get a rise out of you.

GREATOREX Ah, yes, your frocks aren't serious enough.

MISS LEVERING I'm told it's an exploded notion that the suffrage women are all dowdy and dull.

GREATOREX Don't you believe it!

MISS LEVERING Well, of course we know you've been an authority on the subject for – let's see how many years is it you've kept the House in roars whenever Women's Rights are mentioned?

LADY JOHN *(Entering)* Oh, *there* you are! I hope you slept – *(Greets* MISS LEVERING*)*

MISS LEVERING Very well thanks.

(To GREATOREX*)* Let me see, wasn't a deputation sent to you not long ago? *(Sits)*

GREATOREX Hm. *(Irritably)* Yes, yes.

MISS LEVERING *(As though she has just recalled the circumstances)* Oh, yes, I remember I thought at the time, in my modest way, it was nothing short of heroic 'of them to go asking audience of their arch opponent.

GREATOREX *(Stoutly)* It didn't come off.

MISS LEVERING *(Innocently)* Oh! I thought they insisted on bearding the lion in his den.

GREATOREX Of course I wasn't going to be bothered with a lot of –

MISS LEVERING You don't mean you refused to go out and face them!

GREATOREX *(With a comic look of terror)* I wouldn't have done it for worlds. But a friend of mine went and had a look at 'em.

MISS LEVERING *(Smiling)* Well, did he get back alive?

GREATOREX Yes, but he advised me not to go. 'You're quite right,' he said. 'Don't you think of bothering,' he said. 'I've looked over the lot,' he said, 'and there isn't a weekender among 'em.'

LADY JOHN *(At writing table)* Now you frivolous people go away. We've only got a few minutes to talk over the terms of the late Mr. Seddy's munificence before the carriage comes for Miss Levering –

MRS. FREDDY *(To* FARNBOROUGH*)* Did you know she'd got that old horror to give Lady John £8,000 for her charity before he died?

GREATOREX Who got him to?

LADY JOHN Miss Levering. He wouldn't do it for me, but she brought him round.

MR. FREDDY Yes. Bah-ee Jove. I expect so.

MRS. FREDDY *(Turning enthusiastically to her husband)* Isn't she wonderful?

LORD JOHN *(Aside)* Nice creature. All she needs is –

(MR. and MRS. FREDDY *and* FARNBOROUGH *stroll off to the garden.* LADY JOHN *on far side of the writing table.* MRS. HERIOT *at the top.* BEE *and* LORD JOHN *left)*

GREATOREX *(On divan; aside to* MISS LEVERING*)* Too wonderful to waste your time on the wrong people.

MISS LEVERING I shall waste less of my time after this.

GREATOREX I'm relieved to hear it. I can't see you wheedling money for shelters and rot of that sort out of retired grocers.

MISS LEVERING You see you call it rot. We couldn't have got £8,000 out of *you.*

GREATOREX *(Very low)* I'm not sure. *(*MISS LEVERING *looks at him quickly.)* If I gave you that much – for your little projects – what would you give me?

MISS LEVERING *(Speaking quietly)* Seddy didn't ask that.

GREATOREX *(Horrified)* Seddy? I should think not!

LORD JOHN *(Turning to* MISS LEVERING*)* Seddy? You two still talking Seddy? How flattered the old beggar'd be! *(Lower)* Did you hear what Mrs. Heriot said about him? 'So kind; so munificent – so *vulgar*, poor soul, we couldn't know him in London – *but we shall meet him in Heaven.'* *(*GREATOREX *and* LORD JOHN *go off laughing.)*

LADY JOHN *(To* MISS LEVERING*)* Sit over here, my dear *(Indicating chair in front of writing table)* You needn't stay Bee. This won't interest you.

MISS LEVERING *(In the tone of one agreeing)* It's only an effort to meet the greatest evil in the world.

BEE *(Pausing as she's following the others)* What do you call the greatest evil in the world? *(Looks pass between* MRS. HERIOT *and* LADY JOHN.*)*

MISS LEVERING *(Without emphasis)* The helplessness of women. *(*BEE *stands still.)*

LADY JOHN *(Rising and putting her arm about the girl's shoulder)* Bee darling, I know you can think of nothing but *(Aside)* 'him' – so just go and –

BEE *(Brightly)* Indeed, indeed, I can think of everything better than I ever did before. He has lit up everything for me – made everything vivider, more – more significant.

MISS LEVERING *(Turning round)* Who has?

BEE Oh, yes, I don't care about other things less but a thousand times more.

LADY JOHN You *are* in love.

MISS LEVERING Oh, that's it *(Smiling at* BEE*)* I congratulate you.

LADY JOHN *(Returning to the outspread plan)* Well – *this* you see obviates the difficulty you raised.

MISS LEVERING Yes, it's a great improvement.

MRS. HERIOT But it's going to cost a great deal more.

MISS LEVERING It's worth it.

MRS. HERIOT We'll have nothing left for the organ at St. Pilgrim's.

LADY JOHN My dear Lydia, we're putting the organ aside.

MRS. HERIOT (With asperity) We can't afford to 'put aside' the elevating influence of music.

LADY JOHN What we must make for, first, is the cheap and humanely conducted lodging house.

MRS. HERIOT There are several of those already, but poor St. Pilgrim's –

MISS LEVERING There are none for the poorest women.

LADY JOHN No, even the excellent Seddy was for multiplying Rowton Houses. You can never get men to realise – you can't always get women –

MISS LEVERING It's the work least able to wait.

MRS. HERIOT I don't agree with you and I happen to have spent a great deal of my life in works of charity.

MISS LEVERING Ah, then you might be interested in the girl I saw dying in a Tramp Yard a little while ago. Glad her cough was worse – only she mustn't die before her father. Two reasons. Nobody but her to keep the old man out of the workhouse – and 'father is so proud.' If she died first, he would starve; worst of all he might hear what had happened up in London to his girl.

MRS. HERIOT She didn't say I suppose how she happened to fall so low.

MISS LEVERING Yes. She had been in service. She lost the train back one Sunday night and was too terrified of her employer to dare to ring him up after hours. The wrong person found her crying on the platform.

MRS. HERIOT She should have gone to one of the Friendly Societies.

MISS LEVERING At eleven at night?

MRS. HERIOT – and there are the Rescue Leagues. I myself have been connected with one for twenty years –

MISS LEVERING (Reflectively) 'Twenty years'! Always arriving 'after the train's gone' – after the girl and the wrong person have got to the journey's end.

(MRS. HERIOT's eyes flash)

BEE Where is she now?

LADY JOHN Never mind.

MISS LEVERING Two nights ago she was waiting at a street corner in the rain.

MRS. HERIOT Near a public house, I suppose.

MISS LEVERING Yes, a sort of public house. She was plainly dying – she was told she shouldn't be out in the rain. 'I mustn't go in yet,' she said. 'This is what he gave me,' and she began to cry. In her hand were two pennies silvered over to look like half-crowns.

MRS. HERIOT I don't believe that story. It's just the sort of thing some sensation-monger trumps up – now who tells you these –

MISS LEVERING Several credible people. I didn't believe them till –

BEE Till –

MISS LEVERING Till last week – I saw for myself.

MRS. HERIOT Saw? Where –

MISS LEVERING In a low lodging house not a hundred yards from the church you want a new organ for.

MRS. HERIOT How did you happen to be there?

MISS LEVERING I was on a pilgrimage.

BEE A pilgrimage?

MISS LEVERING Into the Underworld.

LADY JOHN You went?

BEE How could you?

MISS LEVERING I put on an old gown and a tawdry hat – (Turns to LADY JOHN) You'll never know how many things are hidden from a woman in good clothes. The bold free look of a man at a woman he believes to be destitute – you must feel that look on you before you can understand – a good half of history.

BEE But where did you go – dressed like that?

MISS LEVERING – down among the home-less women – on a wet night looking for shelter.

MRS. HERIOT Bee –

LADY JOHN (Hastily) No wonder you've been ill.

BEE (Under breath) And it's like that?

MISS LEVERING No.

BEE No?

MISS LEVERING It's so much worse I dare not tell about it – even if you weren't here I couldn't tell about it.

MRS. HERIOT (To BEE) You needn't suppose, darling, that these wretched creatures feel it as we would.

MISS LEVERING The girls who need Shelter and Work aren't all serving-maids.

MRS. HERIOT *(With an involuntary flash)* We know that all the women who – *make mistakes*, aren't.

MISS LEVERING *(Steadily)* That is why *every* woman ought to take an interest in this – every girl too.

BEE Yes – Oh – yes!

(Simultaneously)

LADY JOHN No. This is a matter for us older –

MRS. HERIOT *(With an air of sly challenge)* – or for a person who has some special knowledge *(Significantly)* We can't pretend to have access to such sources of information as Miss Levering.

MISS LEVERING *(Meeting MRS. HERIOT's eyes steadily)* Yes, you can for I can give you access. As you might suggest, I have some personal knowledge about homeless girls.

LADY JOHN *(Cheerfully turning it aside)* Well, my dear, it will all come in convenient *(Tapping the plan)*

MISS LEVERING It once happened to me to take offence at an ugly thing that was going on under my father's roof. Oh years ago! I was an impulsive girl. I turned my back on my father's house –

LADY JOHN *(For BEE's benefit)* That was ill-advised.

MRS. HERIOT Oh course, if a girl does that –

MISS LEVERING So all my relations said. *(With a glance at BEE)* – and I couldn't explain.

BEE Not to your mother.

MISS LEVERING She was dead. I went to London to a small hotel and tried to find employment. I wandered about all day and every day from agency to agency. I was supposed to be educated. I'd been brought up partly in Paris. I could play several instruments and sing little songs in four different tongues.

(Slight pause)

BEE Did nobody want you to teach French or sing the little songs?

MISS LEVERING The heads of schools thought me too young. There were people ready to listen to my singing but the terms – they were too hard. Soon my money was gone. I began to pawn my trinkets. *They* went.

BEE – And still no work?

MISS LEVERING No, but by that time I had some real education – an unpaid hotel bill, and not a shilling in the world. Some girls think it hardship to have to earn their living. The horror is not to be allowed to.

BEE *(Bending forward)* What happened?

LADY JOHN *(Rises)* My dear, have your things been sent down.

MISS LEVERING Yes, I am quite ready, all but my hat.

BEE Well?

MISS LEVERING Well, by chance I met a friend of my family.

BEE That was lucky. *(Brightly)*

MISS LEVERING I thought so. He was nearly ten years older than I. He said he wanted to help me. *(Pauses)*

BEE And didn't he? *(LADY JOHN lays her hand on MISS LEVERING's shoulder.)*

MISS LEVERING Perhaps, after all, he did. Why do I waste time over myself? I belonged to the little class of armed women. My body wasn't born weak, and my spirit wasn't broken by the *habit* of slavery. But as Mrs. Heriot was kind enough to hint, I do know something about the possible fate of homeless girls – I found there were pleasant parks, museums, free libraries in our great rich London – and not one single place where destitute women can be sure of work that isn't killing or food that isn't worse than prison fare. That's why women ought not to sleep at night till this Shelter stands spreading out wide arms.

BEE No – no.

MRS. HERIOT *(Gathering up her gloves, fan, prayerbook, etc.)* Even when it's built – you'll see! many of those creatures will prefer the life they lead. They *like* it.

MISS LEVERING A woman told me – one of the sort that knows – told me many of them like it so much that they are indifferent to the risk of being sent to prison – '*it gives them a rest*' she said.

LADY JOHN A rest!

(MISS LEVERING glances at clock as she rises to go upstairs. LADY JOHN and MRS. HERIOT bend their heads over the plan covertly talking.)

BEE *(Intercepting MISS LEVERING)* I want to begin to understand something of – I'm horribly ignorant.

MISS LEVERING *(Looks at her searchingly)* I'm a rather busy person –

BEE *(Interrupting)* I have a quite special reason for wanting *not* to be ignorant.

(*Impulsively*) I'll go to town tomorrow if you'll come and lunch with me – or let me come –

MRS. HERIOT   Bee!

MISS LEVERING   I must go and put my hat on. (*Exit upstairs*)

MRS. HERIOT   (*Aside*) How little she minds talking about horrors.

LADY JOHN   They turn me cold. Ugh! (*Rising harassed*) I wonder if she's signed the visitor's book.

MRS. HERIOT   For all her Shelter schemes she's a hard woman.

BEE   Miss Levering is?

MRS. HERIOT   Oh of course *you* won't think so. She has angled very adroitly for your sympathy.

BEE   She doesn't look –

LADY JOHN   (*Glancing at* BEE *and taking alarm*) I'm not sure but what she does. Her mouth – always like this – as if she were holding back something by main force.

MRS. HERIOT   (*Half under her breath*) Well so she is. (*Exit* LADY JOHN *into the lobby*)

BEE   Why haven't I seen her before?

MRS. HERIOT   Oh she's lived abroad – (*Debating with herself*) You don't know about her, I suppose?

BEE   I don't know how Aunt Ellen came to know her.

MRS. HERIOT   That was my doing. But I didn't bargain for her being introduced to you.

BEE   She seems to go everywhere. And why shouldn't she?

MRS. HERIOT   (*Quickly*) You mustn't ask her to Eaton Square.

BEE   I have.

MRS. HERIOT   Then you'll have to get out of it.

BEE   (*With a stubborn look*) Then I must have a reason. And a very good reason.

MRS. HERIOT   Well, it's not a thing I should have preferred to tell you, but I know how difficult you are to guide – so I suppose you'll have to know. (*Lowering her voice*) It was ten or twelve years ago. I found her horribly ill in a lonely Welsh farm-house. We had taken the Manor for that August. The farmer's wife was frightened and begged me to go and see what I thought. I soon saw how it was – I thought she was dying.

BEE   *Dying?* – What was the –

MRS. HERIOT   I got no more out of her

than the farmer's wife did. She had had no letters. There had been no one to see her except a man down from London, a shady-looking doctor – nameless of course. And then this result. The farmer and his wife, highly respectable people, were incensed. They were for turning the girl out.

BEE   *Oh!* – but –

MRS. HERIOT   Yes. Pitiless some of these people are! I insisted they should treat the girl humanely and we became friends – that is 'sort of'. In spite of all I did for her –

BEE   What did you do?

MRS. HERIOT   I – I've told you, and I lent her money. No small sum either –

BEE   Has she never paid it back?

MRS. HERIOT   Oh yes, after a time. But I *always* kept her secret – as much as I knew.

BEE   But you've been telling me –

MRS. HERIOT   That was my duty – and I *never* had her full confidence.

BEE   Wasn't it natural she –

MRS. HERIOT   Well all things considered she might have wanted to tell me who was responsible.

BEE   Oh Aunt Lydia!

MRS. HERIOT   All she ever said was that she was ashamed – (*Losing her temper and her fine feeling for the innocence of her auditor*) ashamed that she 'hadn't had the courage to resist' – not the original temptation but the pressure brought to bear on her 'not to go through with it' as she said.

BEE   (*Wrinkling her brows*) You are being so delicate – I'm not sure I understand.

MRS. HERIOT   (*Irritably*) The only thing you need understand is that she's not a desirable companion for a young girl. (*Pause*)

BEE   When did you see her after – after –

MRS. HERIOT   (*With a slight grimace*) I met her last winter at the Bishop's. (*Hurriedly*) She's a connection of his wife's. They'd got her to help with some of their work. Then she took hold of ours. Your aunt and uncle are quite foolish about her and I'm debarred from taking any steps, at least till the Shelter is out of hand.

BEE   I do rather wonder she can bring herself to talk about the unfortunate women of the world.

MRS. HERIOT   The effrontery of it!

BEE   Or, the courage – (*Puts her hand up to her throat as if the sentence had caught there*)

MRS. HERIOT   Even presumes to set *me* right! Of course I don't *mind* in the least, poor soul – But I feel I owe it to your dead mother to tell you about her, especially as you're old enough to know something about life –

BEE   (*Slowly*) – And since a girl needn't be very old to suffer for her ignorance. (*Moves a little away*) I *felt* she was rather wonderful.

MRS. HERIOT   *Wonderful!*

BEE   (*Pausing*) – To have lived through *that*, when she was – how old?

MRS. HERIOT   (*Rising*) Oh nineteen or thereabouts.

BEE   Five years younger than I. To be abandoned and to come out of it like this!

MRS. HERIOT   (*Laying her hand on the girl's shoulder*) It was too bad to have to tell you such a sordid story to-day of all days.

BEE   It is a terrible story but this wasn't a bad time. I feel very sorry today for women who aren't happy. (*Jumping up*) Did you hear the car? That's Geoffrey!

MRS. HERIOT   Mr. Stonor!! What makes you think –

BEE   Yes, yes. I'm sure – (*Checks herself as she is flying off. Turns and sees* LORD JOHN *entering from the garden*)

LORD JOHN   Who do you think is coming round the drive?

BEE   (*Catching hold of him*) Oh dear! How am I ever going to be able to behave like a girl who isn't engaged to the only man in the world worth marrying!

MRS. HERIOT   You were expecting Mr. Stonor all the time!

BEE   He promised he'd come to luncheon if it was humanly possible. But I was afraid to tell you for fear he'd be prevented.

LORD JOHN   (*Laughing as he crosses to the lobby*) You felt we couldn't have borne the disappointment.

BEE   I felt I couldn't.
(*The lobby door opens,* LADY JOHN *appears radiant followed by a tall figure in a dust coat, etc., no goggles. He has straight firm features, a little blunt; fair skin high-coloured; fine straight hair, very fair; grey eyes set somewhat prominently are heavy when not interested; lips full but firmly*

moulded.* GEOFFREY STONOR *is heavier than a man of forty should be, but otherwise in the pink of physical condition. The footman stands waiting to help him off with his motor coat.*)

LADY JOHN   Here's an agreeable surprise! (BEE *has gone forward only a step and stands smiling at the approaching figure.*)

LORD JOHN   How do you do – (*He comes between them and briskly shakes hands with* STONOR.)

FARNBOROUGH   (*Appears at the French window*) What gigantic luck! Yes by Jove! (*Turning to the others clustered round the window*)
(*They crane and glance and then elaborately turn their backs and pretend to be talking among themselves, but betray as far as manners permit the enormous sensation the arrival has created.*)

STONOR   How do you do.
(*Shakes hands with* MRS. HERIOT, *who has rushed up to him with both hers out-stretched. Crosses to* BEE, *who meets him half way; they shake hands smiling into each other's eyes.*)

BEE   Such a long time since we met!

LORD JOHN   (*Observing the group half in half out of the French window*) You're growing very enterprising. I could hardly believe my ears when I heard you'd motored all the way from town to see a supporter on Sunday.

STONOR   I don't know how we ever covered the ground in the old days. (*To* LADY JOHN) It's no use to stand for your borough any more. The American, you know, he 'runs' for Congress. By and by we shall all be flying after the thing we want. (*Smiles at* BEE)

BEE   Sh! (*Smiles back and then glances over her shoulder, and speaks low*) – all sorts of irrelevant people here.

FARNBOROUGH   (*Unable to resist the temptation comes forward*) How do you do, Mr. Stonor.

STONOR   Oh – how are you?

FARNBOROUGH   Some of them were arguing in the smoking room last night whether it didn't hurt a candidate's chances going about in a motor.

STONOR   Well, I don't know – I've some-times wondered whether the charm of our presence wasn't counterbalanced by the way we tear about smothering our fellow-beings in dust and running down their pigs and chickens, not to speak of their children.

LORD JOHN *(Anxiously)* What on the whole are the prospects?

(FARNBOROUGH cranes forward.)

STONOR *(Gravely)* We shall have to work harder than we realised.

FARNBOROUGH Ah!

(BEE and LADY JOHN stand close together, the girl radiant, following STONOR with her eyes and whispering to the sympathetic older woman.)

STONOR *(Taking Sunday paper out of pocket)* There's this agitation about the Woman Question. Oddly enough it seems likely to affect the issue.

LORD JOHN Why should it? Can't you do what the other four hundred have done?

STONOR *(Laughs)* Easily. But you see the mere fact that 420 members have been worried into promising support – and then once in the House have let the matter severely alone –

LORD JOHN *(To STONOR)* Let it alone! Bless my soul, I should think so indeed!

STONOR Of course, only it's a device that's somewhat worn.

(Enter MISS LEVERING, with hat on; gloves and veil in her hand)

LORD JOHN Still if they think they're getting a future Cabinet Minister on their side –

STONOR It will be sufficiently embarrassing for the Cabinet Minister.

(STONOR turns to speak to BEE. Stops dead seeing MISS LEVERING)

BEE *(Smiling)* You know one another?

MISS LEVERING *(Looking at STONOR with intentness but quite calmly)* Everybody in this part of the world knows Mr. Stonor but he doesn't know me.

LORD JOHN Miss Levering.

(They shake hands. Enter GREATOREX, sidles in with an air of giving MRS. FREDDY a wide berth)

BEE *(To MISS LEVERING with artless enthusiasm)* Oh have you been hearing him speak?

MISS LEVERING Yes, I was visiting some relations near Dutfield. They took me to hear you.

STONOR Oh – the night the suffragettes made their customary row. *(Flying at the first chance of distraction shakes hands with MRS. FREDDY)* Well, Mrs. Freddy, what do you think of your friends now?

MRS. FREDDY My friends?

STONOR *(Offering her the Sunday paper)* Yes, the disorderly Women.

MRS. FREDDY *(With dignity)* They are not my friends, but I don't think you must call them –

STONOR Why not? *(Laughs)* I can forgive them for worrying the late Government. But they *are* disorderly.

MISS LEVERING *(Quietly)* Isn't the phrase consecrated to a different class?

GREATOREX *(Who has got hold of the Sunday paper)* He's perfectly right. How do you do. Disorderly women! That's what they are!

FARNBOROUGH *(Reading over his shoulder)* Ought to be locked up! – every one of 'em.

GREATOREX *(Assenting angrily)* Public nuisances! Going about with dog whips and spitting in policemen's faces.

MRS. FREDDY *(With a harassed air)* I wonder if they did spit.

GREATOREX *(Exulting)* Of *course* they did.

MRS. FREDDY *(Turns on him)* You're no authority on what they do. *You* run away.

GREATOREX *(Trying to turn the laugh)* Run away? Yes. *(Backing a few paces)* And if ever I muster up courage to come back it will be to vote for better manners in public life, not worse than we have already.

MRS. FREDDY *(Meekly)* So should I. Don't think *I* defend the Suffragette methods.

BEE *(With cheerful curiosity)* Still you *are* an advocate for the Suffrage, aren't you?

MRS. FREDDY Here? *(Shrugs)* I don't beat the air.

GREATOREX *(Mocking)* Only policemen.

MRS. FREDDY *(Plaintively)* If you cared to know the attitude of real workers in the reform you might have noticed in any paper last week we lost no time in dissociating ourselves from the two or three hysterical – *(Catches her husband's eye and instantly checks her flow of words)*

MRS. HERIOT They have lowered the whole sex in the eyes of the entire world.

BEE *(Joining GEOFFREY STONOR)* I can't quite see what they want – those Suffragettes.

GREATOREX Notoriety.

LORD JOHN Well, there's one sure thing. They've dished their goose.

(GREATOREX chuckles.)

I believe these silly scenes are a pure joy to you.

GREATOREX – Final death blow to the whole silly business!

BEE *(Clasping her hands with fervour)* Oh I hope they'll last till the election's over!

FARNBOROUGH *(Stares)* Why?

BEE Oh we want them to get the working man to – *(Stumbling and a little confused)* to vote for – the Conservative candidate, isn't that so?

(Looking round for help. General laughter)

LORD JOHN Fancy Bee!

GREATOREX The working man's a good deal of an ass, but even he won't listen to –

BEE *(Again speaking to the silent* STONOR*)* But he *does* listen like anything! I asked why there were so few at the long Mitcham meeting, and I was told: Oh they've all gone to hear Miss –

STONOR Just for a lark, that was.

LORD JOHN It has no real effect on the vote.

GREATOREX Not the smallest.

BEE *(Wide-eyed to* STONOR*)* Why I thought you said –

STONOR *(Hastily, rubbing his hand over the lower part of his face and speaking quickly)* I've a notion a little soap and water wouldn't do me any harm –

LORD JOHN I'll take you up. You know Tunbridge.

*(*STONOR *shakes hands. Exeunt all three)*

MRS. FREDDY Mr. Greatorex – *(*BEE *joins* MISS LEVERING*.)*

GREATOREX No – no – no – Farnborough, wait for me. I will not stay here unprotected.

(Exeunt FARNBOROUGH *and* GREATOREX*)*

MRS. FREDDY It's true what that old cynic says. The scene in the House has put back the Reform a generation.

BEE I wish I'd been there.

MRS. FREDDY I *was*.

BEE Oh, was it like the papers said?

MRS. FREDDY Worse. I've never been so moved in public – no tragedy, no great opera ever gripped an audience as the situation in the House did that night. There we all sat breathless – with every-thing more favourable to us than it had been within the memory of woman. Another five minutes and the Resolution would have passed. Then – all in a moment –

LADY JOHN *(To* MRS. HERIOT*)* Listen – they're talking about the female hooligans.

MRS. HERIOT No thank you! *(Sits apart with the 'Church Times')*

MRS. FREDDY *(Excitedly)* All in a moment a horrible dingy little flag was poked through the grills of the Woman's Gallery – cries – insults – scuffling – the Police – the ignominious turner out of the women – *us* as well as the – – Oh I can't *think* of it without – *(Jumps up and walks to and fro – pauses)* Then the next morning! The people gloating. Our friends antagonised – people who were wavering – nearly won over – all thrown back – heart breaking! Even my husband! Freddy's been an angel about letting me take my share when I felt I must – but of course I've always known he doesn't really like it. It makes him shy. I'm sure it gives him a horrid twist inside when he sees me placarded. But he's always been an angel about it before this. After the disgraceful scene he said: 'It just shows how unfit women are for any sort of coherent thinking or concerted action.'

BEE To think that it should be women who've given the cause the worst blow it ever had!

MRS. FREDDY The work of forty years destroyed in five minutes!

MISS LEVERING I thought I'd heard somebody say the Bill had got as far as that time and time again.

BEE Oh no. Surely not –

MRS. FREDDY *(Reluctantly)* Y-yes. A Suffrage Bill passed a second reading thirty-seven years ago. But we never had so many *friends* in the House before –

MISS LEVERING *(With a faint smile)* 'Friends!'

BEE Why do you say it like that?

MISS LEVERING Perhaps because I was thinking of a funny story – he *said* it was funny – a Liberal Whip told me the other day; a Radical member went out of the House after his speech in favour of the Woman's Bill and as he came back half an hour later he heard some members talking in the lobby about the astonishing number who were going to vote for the measure. And the Friend of Woman dropped his jaw and clutched the man next to him: 'My God!' he said, 'You don't mean they're going to *give* it to them!'

BEE Oh!

MRS. FREDDY You don't think all men in Parliament are like that!

MISS LEVERING I don't think all men are burglars, but I lock my doors.

BEE *(Below her breath)* You think, that night of the scene – you think the men didn't *mean* to play fair?

MISS LEVERING *(Her coolness in contrast to the excitement of the others)* Didn't the women sit quiet till ten minutes to closing time?

BEE Ten minutes to settle –

MISS LEVERING *(Quietly to* MRS. FREDDY*)* Couldn't you see the men were at their old game?

LADY JOHN *(Coming forward)* You think they were just putting off the issues till it was too late?

MISS LEVERING *(In a detached tone)* I wasn't there, but I haven't heard anybody deny that the women waited till ten minutes to eleven. Then they discovered the policemen who'd been sent up at the psychological moment to the back of the gallery. Then, I'm told, when the women saw they were betrayed once more, they utilised the few minutes left to impress on the country at large the fact of their demands – did it in the only way left them. *(Sits leaning forward reflectively smiling, chin in hand.)* It does rather look to the outsider as if the well-behaved women had worked for forty years and made less impression on the world than those fiery young women made in five minutes.

MRS. FREDDY Oh come, be fair!

MISS LEVERING Well you must admit that next day every newspaper reader in Europe and America knew there were women in England in such dead earnest about the Suffrage that the men had stopped laughing at last and turned them out of the House. Men even advertised how little they appreciated the fun by sending the women to gaol in pretty sober earnest. And all the world was talking about it.

MRS. FREDDY *(Lower, hastily to* MISS LEVERING*)* You're judging from the outside. Those of us who've been working for years – we all realise it was a perfectly lunatic proceeding. Why *think*! The only chance of our getting what we want is by *winning over* the men. *(Her watchful eye catches* MISS LEVERING's *little involuntary gesture.)* What's the matter?

MISS LEVERING 'Winning over the men' has been the woman's way since the Creation. Do you think the result should make us proud of our policy? Yes? Then go and walk in Piccadilly at midnight. *(The older women glance at* BEE.*)*

MISS LEVERING No, I forgot –

MRS. HERIOT *(With majesty)* Yes, it's not the first time you've forgotten.

MISS LEVERING I forgot the magistrate's ruling. He said no decent woman had any business to be in London's main thoroughfare at night unless she has *a man with her*. I heard that in Soho too. 'You're obliged to take up with a chap!' was what the woman said.

MRS. HERIOT *(Rising)* Come. *(She takes* BEE *by the arm and draws her to the windows where she signals* GREATOREX *and* FARNBOROUGH. MRS. FREDDY *joins her husband and* LORD JOHN.*)*

LADY JOHN *(Kindly aside to* MISS LEVERING*)* My dear, I think Lydia Heriot's right. We oughtn't to do anything, or *say* anything to encourage this ferment of feminism – and I'll tell you why: it's likely to bring a very terrible thing in its train.

MISS LEVERING What terrible thing?

LADY JOHN Sex-antagonism.

MISS LEVERING *(Rising)* It's here.

LADY JOHN *(Very gravely)* Don't say that! *(Enter* GREATOREX *and* FARNBOROUGH. BEE *has quietly disengaged herself from* MRS. HERIOT *and the group at the window, returns and stands behind* LADY JOHN *looking up into* MISS LEVERING's *face.)*

MISS LEVERING *(To* LADY JOHN*)* You're so conscious it's here, you're afraid to have it mentioned.

LADY JOHN *(Turning and seeing* BEE. *Rising hastily)* If it is here it's the fault of these women agitators –

MISS LEVERING *(Gently)* No woman *begins* that way. *(Leans forward with clasped hands looking into vacancy)* Every woman's in a state of natural subjection – *(smiles at* BEE*)* – no, I'd rather say allegiance to her idea of romance and her hope of motherhood: they're embodied for her in man. They're the strongest things in life till man kills them. *(Rousing herself and looking into* LADY JOHN's *face)* Let's be fair. Each woman knows why that allegiance died. *(*LADY JOHN *turns hastily.* LORD JOHN,

STONOR, and MR. FREDDY *enter by the stairs.* MISS LEVERING *has turned to the table looking for her gloves, etc., among the papers. Unconsciously drops the handkerchief she had in her little book)*

BEE *(In a low voice to* MISS LEVERING) All this talk against the wicked suffragettes – it makes me rather want to go and hear what they've got to say for themselves.

MISS LEVERING *(Smiling indifferently, as she finds the veil she's been searching for)* Well, they're holding a meeting in Trafalgar Square at three o'clock.

BEE This afternoon! That's no use to people out of town – unless I could invent some excuse –

LORD JOHN *(Benevolently)* Still talking over the Shelter plans?

MISS LEVERING No. We left the Shelter some time ago.

LADY JOHN *(To* BEE) Then what's all this chatterment about?
*(*BEE *a little confused looks at* MISS LEVERING.)*

MISS LEVERING The latest thing in veils. *(Ties hers round her hat)*

GREATOREX The invincible frivolity of Woman!

LORD JOHN *(Genially)* Don't scold them. It's a very proper topic.

MISS LEVERING *(Whimsically)* Oh I was afraid you'd despise us for it.

BOTH MEN *(With condescension)* Not at all. Not at all.

BEE *(To* MISS LEVERING *as* FOOTMAN *appears)* Oh they're coming for you. Don't forget your book.
*(*FOOTMAN *holds out a salver with a telegram on it for* BEE.
Why it's for me.

MISS LEVERING But it's time I was – *(Crosses to table)*

BEE *(Opening the telegram)* May I? *(Reads and glances over the paper at* MISS LEVERING) I've got your book. *(Crosses to* MISS LEVERING *looking at the back of the little volume)* Dante! Whereabouts are you? *(Opening at marker)* Oh the Inferno.

MISS LEVERING No, I'm in a worse place.

BEE *(Smiling)* I didn't know there was a worse.

MISS LEVERING Yes, it's worse with the Vigliacchi.

BEE I forget, were they Guelf or Ghilbelline?

MISS LEVERING *(Smiling)* They weren't either and that was why Dante couldn't stand them. *(More gravely)* He said there was no place in Heaven nor in Purgatory – not even a corner in Hell for the souls who had stood aloof from strife. *(Looking steadily into the girl's eyes)* He called them 'wretches who never lived' Dante did, because they'd never felt the pangs of partizanship. And so they wander homeless on the skirts of limbo, among the abortions and off-scourings of Creation.

BEE *(A long breath after a long look. When* MISS LEVERING *has turned away to make her leisurely adieux,* BEE's *eye falls on the open telegram.)* Aunt Ellen, I've got to go to London.
*(*STONOR *re-entering hears this but pretends to talk to* MR. FREDDY, *etc.)*

LADY JOHN My dear child!

MRS. HERIOT Nonsense! Is your grandfather worse?

BEE *(Folding the telegram)* N-no. I don't think so. But it's necessary I should go all the same.

MRS. HERIOT Go *away* when Mr. Stonor –

BEE He said he'd have to leave directly after luncheon.

LADY JOHN I'll just see Miss Levering off and then I'll come back and talk about it.

LORD JOHN *(To* MISS LEVERING) Why are you saying good-bye as if you were never coming back?

MISS LEVERING *(Smiling)* One never knows. Maybe I shan't come back. *(To* STONOR) Good-bye.
*(*STONOR *bows ceremoniously. They go up laughing.* STONOR *comes down.)*

BEE *(Impulsively)* There mayn't be another train! Miss Levering – *(Inadvertently drops the telegram)*

STONOR *(Intercepting)* What if there isn't? I'll take you back in the motor.

BEE *(Rapturously)* Will you? I must be there by three!

STONOR *(Picks up the telegram and a handkerchief lying near. Glances at the message)* Why it's only an invitation to dine – Wednesday!

BEE Sh! *(Takes the telegram and puts it in her pocket)*

STONOR Oh I see! *(Lower, smiling)* It's rather dear of you to arrange our going off like that. You *are* a clever little girl!

BEE It's not that I was arranging. I want to hear those women in Trafalgar Square – the Suffragettes.

STONOR (*Incredulous but smiling*) How perfectly absurd! Besides, (*Looking after* LADY JOHN) I expect she wouldn't like my carrying you off like that.

BEE Then she'll have to make up an excuse and come too.

STONOR Ah, it wouldn't be quite the same –

BEE (*Rapidly thinking it out*) She and I could get back here in time for dinner.
(STONOR *glances down at the handkerchief still in his hand and turns it half mechanically from corner to corner.*)

BEE (*Absent-mindedly*) Mine?

STONOR (*Hastily without reflection*) No.
(*Hands it to* MISS LEVERING *as she passes*) Yours. (MISS LEVERING *on her way to the lobby with* LORD JOHN *seems not to notice.*)

BEE (*Takes the handkerchief to give to her, glancing down at the embroidered corner: stops*) But that's not an L. It's V. I –
(GEOFFREY STONOR *suddenly turns his back and takes up the newspaper.*)

LADY JOHN (*From the lobby*) Come Vida, since you will go.

MISS LEVERING Yes, I'm coming. (*Exit* MISS LEVERING)

BEE *I* didn't know her name was Vida, how did you?
(STONOR *stares silently over the top of his paper.*)

Curtain

Act II

SCENE: *The North side of the Nelson Column in Trafalgar Square. The Curtain rises on an uproar. The crowd, which momentarily increases, is composed chiefly of weedy youths and wastrel old men. There are a few decent artisans: three or four 'beery' out o' works; three or four young women of the domestic servant or Strand Restaurant cashier class: one aged woman in rusty black peering with faded, wonderful eyes, consulting the faces of the men and laughing nervously and apologetically from time to time; one or two quiet-looking business-like women, thirty to forty; two upper middle-class men, who stare and whisper and smile. A quiet old man with a lot of unsold Sunday papers under one arm stands in an attitude of rapt attention, with the free hand round his deaf ear. A brisk-looking woman of forty-five or so, wearing pince-nez, goes round with a pile of propagandist literature on her arm. Many of the men smoking cigarettes – the old ones pipes. On the outskirts of this* crowd *of several hundred, a couple of smart men in tall shining hats hover a few moments single eyeglass up, and then saunter off. Against the middle of the Column, where it rises above the stone platform, is a great red banner, one supporting pole upheld by a grimy sandwich man, the other by a small dirty boy of eight. If practicable, only the lower portion of the banner is seen, bearing the final words of the legend, 'VOTES FOR WOMEN' in immense white letters. It will be well to get to the full the effect of the height above the crowd of the straggling group of speakers on the pedestal platform. These are, as the curtain rises, a working-class woman who is waving her arms and talking very earnestly, her voice for the moment blurred in the uproar. She is dressed in brown serge and looks pinched and sallow. At her side is the Chairman urging that she be given a fair hearing.* ALLEN TRENT *is a tall, slim, brown-haired man of 28, with a slight stoop, an agreeable aspect, well-bred voice and the gleaming brown eyes of the visionary. Behind these two, looking on or talking among themselves are several other carelessly dressed women; one better turned out than the rest is quite young, very slight and gracefully built, with round, very pink cheeks; full scarlet lips, naturally waving brown hair and an air of childish gravity. She looks at the unruly mob with imperturbable calm. The Chairman's voice is drowned.*

WORKING WOMAN (*With lean brown finger out and voice raised shriller now above the tumult*) I've got boys o' me own and we laugh at all sorts o' things, but I should be ashymed and so would they if ever they was to be'yve as you're doin' to'dy. (*In laughter the noise dies.*) People 'ave been saying this is a Middle-Class Woman's movement. It's a libel. I'm a workin' woman myself, the wife of a workin' man. I'm a Poor Law Guardian and a –

NOISY YOUNG MAN Think of that now – gracious me! (*Laughter and interruption*)

OLD NEWS VENDOR (*To the noisy young man near him*) Oh shut up, cawn't yer?

NOISY Y. MAN Not fur *you!*

OLD NEWS VENDOR I was afryde you'd 'ad 'alf a pint too much.

WORKING WOMAN You say we women 'ave no business serving on Boards and thinking about Politics. Wot's Politics? (*A derisive roar*) It's just 'ousekeepin' on a big scyle. 'Oo among you workin' men 'as the most comfortable 'omes? Those of you that gives yer wives yer wages. *(Loud laughter and jeers)*

VOICES That's it. Wantin' our money. Lord 'Igh 'Ousekeeper of England.

WORKING WOMAN If it was only to use fur *our* comforts d'ye think many o'you workin' men would be found turnin' over their wyges to their wives? No! Wot's the reason thousands do – and the best and the soberest – Because the workin' man knows that wot's a pound to 'im is twenty shillin's to 'is wife and she'll myke every penny in every one o' them shillin's *tell*. She gets more fur *'im* out of 'is wyges than wot 'e can! Some o' you know wot the 'omes is like w'ere the men don't let the women manage. Well the Poor Laws and the 'ole Government is just in the syme muddle because the men 'ave tried to do the national 'ousekeepin' without the women. *(Roars)* But like I told you before, it's a libel to say it's only the well off women wot's wantin' the vote. Wot about the 96,000 Textile Workers? Wot about the Yorkshire tailoresses? I can tell you wot plenty o' the poor women think about it. I'm one o' them and I can tell you we see there's reforms needed. *We ought to 'ave the vote:* (Jeers) and we know 'ow to appreciate the other women 'oo go to prison fur tryin' to get it fur us!
(With a little final bob of emphasis and a glance over shoulder at the old woman and the young one behind her, she seems about to retire, but pauses as the murmur in the crowd grows into distinct phrases. 'They get their 'air cut free'. 'Naow they don't that's only us.' 'Silly suffragettes' – 'Stop at 'ome' 'inderin' policemen – mykin' rows in the street.' Voices 'Ha, ha!' – 'Shut up!' 'Keep quiet cawn't yer.' General uproar)

CHAIRMAN TRENT You evidently don't know what had to be done by *men* before the extension of suffrage in '67. If it hadn't been for demonstrations of violence.
(His voice is drowned.)

WORKING WOMAN *(Coming forward again. Her shrill note rising clear)* You s'y woman's plyce is 'ome. Don't you know there's a third of the women in this country can't afford the luxury of stayin' in their 'omes? They *got* to go out and 'elp make money to p'y the rent and keep the 'ome from bein' sold up. Then there's

all the women that 'aven't got even miserable 'omes. They 'aven't got any 'omes *at all*.

NOISY YOUNG MAN You said *you* got one. W'y don't you stop in it?

WORKING WOMAN Yes, that's like a man. If one o' you is all right he thinks the rest don't matter. We women –

NOISY YOUNG MAN Lydies! God bless 'em! *(Voices drown her and the CHAIRMAN)*

OLD NEWS VENDOR *(To NOISY YOUNG MAN)* Oh take that extra 'alf pint 'ome and *sleep it off*!

WORKING WOMAN P'raps you aren't living old and young, married and single in one room. I come from a plyce where many fam'lies 'ave to live like that if they're to go on livin' *at all*. If you don't believe me come and let me show you! *(She spreads out her lean arms.)* Come with me to Canning Town – come with me to Bromley – come to Poplar and to Bow – No! You won't even *think* about the over worked women and the underfed children and the 'ovels they live in. And you want that we shouldn't think neither –

VAGRANT We'll do the thinkin'. You go 'ome and nuss the byby.

WORKING WOMAN I do nurse my byby. I've nursed seven. What have you done for yours? P'raps your children never goes 'ungry and maybe you're satisfied – though I must say I wouldn't 'a' thought it from the *look* o' you.

VOICE Oh I s'y!

WORKING WOMAN But we women are not satisfied. We don't want better things for our own children. We want better things for all. *Every* child is our child. We know in our 'earts we oughtn't to rest till we've mothered 'em every one.

VOICE Women – children – Wot about the men? Are *they* all 'appy? *(Derisive laughter and 'No! No! Not precisely.' ''Appy Lord!')*

WORKING WOMAN No, there's lots o' you men I'm sorry for, and we'll 'elp you if you let us.

VOICE 'Elp us? You tyke the bread out of our mouths. You women are black-leggin' the men!

WORKING WOMAN W'y does any woman tyke less wyges than a man for the same work? Only because we can't get anything better. That's a part the reason w'y we're yere to-d'y. Do you reely think we tyke

those low wyges because we got a *likin'*
for low wyges? No. We're just like you.
We want as much as ever we can get.
(*''Ear 'ear!' and laughter*) We got a gryte
deal to do with our wyges, we women
has. We got the children to think about.
And w'en we get our rights, a woman's
flesh and blood won't be so much cheaper
than a man's that employers can get rich
on keepin' you out o' work and sweaten'
us. If you men only could see it, we got
the *syme* cause, and if you 'elped us you'd
be 'elpin' yerselves.

OLD NEWS VENDOR   True as gospel!
(*She retires against the banner with the
others. There is some applause.*)

A MAN   (*Patronizingly*) Well, now, that wasn't
so bad – fur a woman.

ANOTHER   N-naw. Not for a woman.

CHAIRMAN TRENT   (*Speaking through this
last*) Miss Ernestine Blunt will now
address you.
(*Applause, chiefly ironic, laughter, a general
moving closer and knitting up of attention.*)
ERNESTINE BLUNT *is about 24 but looks
younger. She is very downright, not to say
pugnacious – the something amusing and
attractive about her is there, as it were,
against her will and the more fetching for
that. She has no conventional gestures and
none of any sort at first. As she warms to
her work she uses her slim hands to enforce
her emphasis but as though unconsciously.
Her manner of speech is less monotonous
than that of the average woman speaker, but
she too has a fashion of leaning all her
weight on the end of the sentence. She brings
out the final word or two with an effect of
under scoring and makes a forward motion
of the slim body as if the better to drive the
last nail in. She evidently means to be
immensely practical – the kind who is
pleased to think she hasn't a grain of
sentimentality in her composition – and
whose feeling when it does all but master her,
communicates itself magnetically to others.*)

MISS ERNESTINE BLUNT   Perhaps I'd better
begin by explaining a little about our
'tactics'.
(*Cries of 'Tactics! we know!' – 'mykin'
trouble' – 'Public scandal'*)
To make you *understand* what we've done
I must remind you of what others have
done. Perhaps you don't know that
women first petitioned Parliament for the
Franchise as long ago as 1866.

VOICE   How do *you* know?
(*She pauses a moment, taken off her guard
by the suddenness of the attack.*)

VOICE   You wasn't there!

VOICE   That was the trouble. Haw! Haw!

MISS E. BLUNT   – And the Petition was
presented –

VOICE   Give 'er a 'earin' now she 'as got
out of 'er crydle.

MISS E. BLUNT   – Presented to the House
of Commons by that great Liberal, John
Stuart Mill. Bills or Resolutions have been
before the House on and off for the last
thirty-six years. That roughly is our
history. We found ourselves at the
opening of this year with no assurance
that if we went on in the same way, any
girl born into the world in 1906 would
live to exercise the rights of citizenship
though she lived to be a hundred. So we
said all this has been in vain. We must try
some other way. How did the working
man get the suffrage, we asked ourselves.
Well, we turned up the records – and we
saw –
(*'Not by scratching people's faces' 'Disraeli
give it 'em.' 'Dizzy get out!' 'Chartist riots
she's thinkin' of.' 'Oh lord this education'
'Cahnty Cahncil scholarships' – noise in the
crowd*)
But we don't *want* to follow such a
violent example. We would much rather
not – but if that's the only way we can
make the country see we're in earnest –
we are prepared to show them.
(*'An' they'll show you! – Give ye another
month 'ard!'*)
Don't think that going to prison has any
fears for us. We'd go *for life* if by doing
that we got freedom for the rest of the
women.
(*Voices: 'Hear, hear!' 'Rot!' 'W'y don't the men
'elp ye to your rights?'*)
Here's someone asking why the men
don't help. It's partly they don't
understand yet – they *will* before we've
done. (*Laughter*) Partly they don't
understand yet what's at stake.

RESPECTABLE MAN   (*Chuckling*) They're a'
educatin' of us!

MISS E. BLUNT   And partly that the bravest
man is afraid of ridicule. Oh, yes, we've
heard a great deal all our lives about the
timidity and the sensitiveness of women.
And it's true. We *are* sensitive. But I tell
you ridicule crumples a man up. It steels

a woman. We've come to know the value of ridicule. We've educated ourselves so that we welcome ridicule. We owe our sincerest thanks to the comic writers. The cartoonist is our unconscious friend. Who cartoons people who are of no importance? What advertisement is so sure of being remembered?

POETIC YOUNG MAN I admit that.

MISS E. BLUNT If we didn't know it by any other sign, the comic papers would tell us we've arrived. But our greatest debt of gratitude we owe perhaps to the man who called us female Hooligans. *(The crowd bursts into laughter.)* We aren't Hooligans, but we hope the fact will be overlooked. If everybody said we were nice well-behaved women who'd come to hear us? *Not the men. (Roars)* Men tell us it isn't womanly for us to care about politics. How do they know what's womanly? It's for women to decide that. Let them attend to being manly – It will take them all their time.

VOICE Are we down'earted? Oh no!

MISS E. BLUNT And they say it would be dreadful if we got the vote because then we'd be pitted against men in the economic struggle. But that's come about already. Do you know that out of every hundred women in this country, eighty-two are wage-earning women? It used to be thought unfeminine for women to be students and to aspire to the arts – that brings fame and fortune. But nobody has ever said it was unfeminine for women to do the heavy drudgery that's badly paid, that kind of work had to be done by *some*body – and the men didn't hanker after it. Oh no.

(Laughter and interruption)

MAN ON OUTER FRINGE She can *talk* – the little one can.

ANOTHER Oh, they can all '*talk.*'

VAGRANT I wouldn't like to be 'er 'usband. Think of comin' home to *that!*

MISS E. BLUNT *(Speaking through the noise)* Oh no. *Let* the women scrub and cook and wash. That's all right! But if they want to try their hand at the better paid work of the liberal professions – Oh, very unfeminine indeed! Then there's another thing. Now I want you to listen to this because it's *very* important. Men say if we persist in competing with them for the bigger prizes they're dreadfully afraid

we'd lose the beautiful protecting chivalry that – Yes, I don't wonder you laugh. *We* laugh. *(Bending forward with lit eyes)* But the women I found at the Ferry Tin Works working for five shillings a week – I didn't see them laughing. The beautiful chivalry of the employers of women doesn't prevent them from paying women tenpence a day for sorting coal and loading and unloading carts, doesn't prevent them from forcing women to earn bread in ways worse still. So we won't talk about chivalry. It's being over-sarcastic. We'll just let this poor ghost of chivalry go – for a little plain justice.

VOICE If the House of Commons won't give you justice, why don't you go to the House of Lords?

MISS E. BLUNT What?

VOICE Better 'urry up. Case of early closin'. *(Laughter. A man at the back asks the speaker something.)*

MISS E. BLUNT *(Unable to hear)* You'll be allowed to ask any question you like at the end of the meeting.

NEWCOMER *(Boy of 18)* Oh is it question time? I s'y miss, 'oo killed cock robin? *(She is about to resume, but above the general noise, the voice of the man at the back reaches her indistinct but insistent. She leans forward trying to catch what he says. While the indistinguishable murmur has been going on,* GEOFFREY STONOR *has appeared on the edge of the crowd followed by* BEE *and* LADY JOHN *in motor veils.)*

BEE *(Pressing forward eagerly and raising her veil)* Is she one of them? That little thing?

STONOR *(Doubtfully)* I – I suppose so.

BEE Oh, ask someone Geoffrey. I'm so disappointed. I did so hope we'd hear one of the – the worst.

MISS E. BLUNT *(To the interrupter – on the other side)* What? What do you say? *(She screws up her eyes with the effort to hear and puts a hand up to her ear. A few indistinguishable words between her and the man)*

LADY JOHN *(Who has been studying the figures on the platform through her lorgnon turns to a working man beside her)* Can you tell me my man, which are the ones that a – that make the disturbances?

WORKING MAN The one that's doing the talking – she's the disturbingest o' the lot.

BEE *(Craning to listen)* Not that nice little –

WORKING MAN Don't you be took in, Miss.

MISS E. BLUNT Oh yes – I see. There's a man over here asking –

A YOUNG MAN *I've* got a question too. Are – you – married?

ANOTHER *(Sniggering)* There's yer chawnce. He's a bachelor. *(Laughter)*

MISS E. BLUNT *(Goes straight on as if she had not heard)* A – man asking if the women get full citizenship and a war is declared, will the women fight?

POETIC YOUNG MAN No really – really now!

(The crowd 'Haw! Haw!' 'Yes' 'Yes how about that')

MISS E. BLUNT *(Smiling)* Well you know some say the whole trouble about us, is that we *do* fight. But it's only hard necessity makes us do that. We don't *want* to fight as men seem to – just for fighting's sake. Women are for peace.

VOICE Hear, hear!

MISS E. BLUNT And when we have a share in public affairs there'll be less likelihood of war. But that's not to say women can't fight. The Boer women did. The Russian women face conflicts worse than any battlefield can show. *(Her voice shakes a little and the eyes fill but she controls her emotion gallantly and dashes on.)* But we women know all that is evil and we're for peace. Our part – we're proud to remember it – our part has been to go about after you men in war time and – pick up the pieces! *(A great shout)* Yes – seems funny doesn't it? You men blow them to bits and then we come along and put them together again. If you know anything about military nursing, you know a good deal of our work has been done in the face of danger – *but it's always been done.*

OLD NEWS VENDOR That's so. That's so.

MISS E. BLUNT You complain that more and more we're taking away from you men the work that's always been yours. You can't any longer keep women out of the industries. The only question is upon what terms shall she continue to be in? As long as she's in on bad terms, she's not only hurting herself – she's hurting you. But if you're feeling discouraged about our competing with you, we're willing to leave you your trade in war. Let the men take life! We *give* life! *(Her voice is once more moved and proud.)* No one will pretend ours isn't one of the Dangerous Trades either. And no one will pretend that we have shrunk from it. I won't say any more to you now because we've got others to speak to you and a new helper that I want you to hear.

(She retires to the sound of clapping. There's a hurried consultation between her and the CHAIRMAN *– Voices in the crowd: 'The little un's all right.' 'Ernestine's a corker.' etc.)*

BEE *(Looking at* GEOFFREY *to see how he's taken it)* Well?

STONOR *(Smiling down at her)* Well –

BEE Nothing reprehensible in what *she* said, was there?

STONOR *(Shrugs)* Oh reprehensible!

BEE It makes me rather miserable all the same.

STONOR *(Draws her hand protectingly through his arm)* You mustn't take it as much to heart as all that.

BEE I can't help it. I can't indeed, Geoffrey – I shall *never* be able to make a speech like that!

STONOR *(Taken aback)* I hope not indeed.

BEE Why, I thought you said you wanted me –

STONOR *(Smiling)* To make nice little speeches with composure – so I did! So I – *(Seems to lose his thread as he looks at her)*

BEE *(With a little frown)* You said –

STONOR That you have very pink cheeks. Well, I stick to that.

BEE *(Smiling)* Sh! don't tell everybody.

STONOR And you're the only female creature I ever saw who didn't look a fright in motor things.

BEE *(Melted and smiling)* I'm glad you don't think me a fright.

CHAIRMAN TRENT I will now ask – *(Name indistinguishable)* to address the meeting.

BEE *(As she sees* LADY JOHN *moving to one side)* Oh, *don't* go yet, Aunt Ellen!

LADY JOHN Certainly not. I want to hear another *(Craning her neck)* I can't believe, you know, she was really one of the worst.

(A big sallow Cockney has come forward. His scanty hair grows in wisps on a grey bony skull.)

VOICE That's Walker.

ANOTHER 'Oo's Walker?

ANOTHER If you can't afford a bottle of Tatcho, w'y don't you get your 'air cut?

MR. WALKER *(Not in the least discomposed)* I've been addressin' a big meetin' at

'Ammersmith this morning, and w'en I told 'em I wus comin' 'ere this awfternoon to speak fur the women – well – then the usual thing began! *(An appreciative roar from the crowd)* In these times if you want peace and quiet at a public meetin' – *(The crowd fills in the hiatus with laughter.)* There was a man at 'Ammersmith too talkin' about women's sphere bein' 'ome. 'Ome do you call it? You've got a kennel w'ere you can munch your tommy. You've got a corner w'ere you can curl up fur a few hours till you go out to work again. No, my man, there's too many of you ain't able to *give* the woman 'omes – fit to live – in too many of you in that fix fur you to go on jawin' at those o' the women 'oo want to myke the 'omes a little decenter.

VOICE If the vote ain't done us any good, 'ow'll it do the women any good?

MR. WALKER Any men here belongin' to the Labour Party? *(Shouts and applause)* Well, I don't need tell those men the vote 'as done us *some* good. They know it. And it'll do us a lot more good w'en you know 'ow to use the power you got in your 'and.

VOICE Power! It's those fellars at the bottom o' the street that's got the power.

MR. WALKER It's you and men like you that gave it to them. You carried the Liberals into Parliament Street on your own shoulders. *(Complacent applause)* You believed all their fine words. You never asked yerselves 'Wot's a Liberal anyw'y?'

VOICE He's a jolly good fellow. *(Cheers and booing)*

MR. WALKER No, 'e ain't, or if 'e is jolly, it's only because 'e's got you to swell his majority – *(Laughter in which STONOR joins)* – and to keep quiet while you see Liberal leaders desertin' Liberal principles. *(Voices in agreement and protest)* Show me a Liberal and I'll show you a Mr. Fycing-both-W'ys. *(STONOR moves closer with an amused look.)* 'E sheds the light of 'is warm and 'andsome smile on the working man and round on the other side 'e's tippin' a wink to the great landowners. That's to let 'em know 'e's standin' between them and the Socialists. *(General laughter in which STONOR joins)* The Liberal, 'e's the judicial sort o' chap that sits in the middle –

VOICE On the fence!

MR. WALKER Tories one side – Socialists the other. Well, it ain't always so comfortable in the middle – you're like to get squeezed. Now I s'y to the women, the Conservatives don't promise you much, but what they promise, they do.

STONOR *(To BEE)* This fellow isn't half bad.

MR. WALKER The Liberals – they'll promise you the earth and give yer the whole o' nothing.

(Roars of approval)

BEE Isn't it fun? Now aren't you glad I brought you?

STONOR *(Laughing)* This chap's rather amusing!

MR. WALKER We men 'ave seen it 'appen over and over. But the women can tyke a 'int quicker 'n what we can. They won't stand the nonsense men do. Only they 'aven't got a fair chawnce even to agitate fur their rights. As I wus comin' up 'ere, I 'eard a man sayin': 'Look at this big crowd. W'y, we're all *men*! If the women want the vote w'y ain't they here to s'y so?' Well I'll tell you w'y! It's because they've 'ad to get the dinner fur you and me and now they're washin' up the dishes.

VOICE D'you think we ought to st'y 'ome and wash the dishes?

MR. WALKER *(Laughs good-naturedly)* If they'd leave it to us once or twice per'aps we'd understand a little more about the Woman Question. I know w'y *my* wife isn't here. It's because she *knows* I ain't much use round the 'ouse and she's 'opin' I can talk to some purpose. Maybe she's mistaken. Any'ow here I am to vote for her and all the other women. *('Hear hear!' 'Oh-h!')* And to tell you men what improvements you can expect to see w'en women 'as the share in public affairs they ought to 'ave.

VOICE What do you know about it? You can't even talk grammar.

MR. WALKER I'm not 'ere to talk grammar but to talk Reform. I ain't defendin' my grammar – but I'll say in pawssing that if my mother 'ad 'ad 'er rights, maybe my grammar would have been better.

(STONOR and BEE exchange smiles. He takes her arm again and bends his head to whisper something in her ear. She listens with lowered eyes and happy face. The discreet love-making goes on during the next few sentences. Interruption. One voice

insistent but not clear. The speaker waits only a second and then resumes, 'Yes if the women' but he cannot instantly make himself heard. The boyish chairman looks harassed and anxious. MISS ERNESTINE BLUNT *alert, watchful)*

MR. WALKER Wait a bit – 'arf a minute. There seems to be a gentleman here who doesn't think women ought to 'ave the vote.

VOICE One? Oh-h! *(Laughter)*

MR. WALKER Per'aps 'e doesn't know much about women? *(Indistinguishable repartee)* Oh, the gentleman says 'e's married. Well then, fur the syke of 'is wife we mustn't be too sorry 'e's 'ere. No doubt she's s'ying: 'Eaven be prysed those women are mykin' a Demonstrytion in Trafalgar Square and I'll 'ave a little peace and quiet at 'ome for one Sunday in my life. *(The Crowd laughs and there are jeers for the interrupter – and at the speaker.)* *(Pointing)* Why you're like the man at 'Ammersmith this morning. 'E wus awskin' me: "'Ow would you like men to st'y at 'ome and do the family washin'?" *(Laughter)* I told 'im I wouldn't advise it. I 'ave too much respect fur – me clo'es.

VAGRANT It's their place – the women ought to do the washin'.

MR. WALKER I'm not sure you aren't right. For a good many o' you fellas from the look o' you – you cawn't even wash yerselves. *(Laughter)*

VOICE *(Threatening)* 'Oo are you talkin' to? (CHAIRMAN *more anxious than before – Movement in the crowd)*

THREATENING VOICE Which of us d'you mean?

MR. WALKER *(Coolly looking down)* Well, it takes about ten of your sort to make a man, so you may take it I mean the lot of you.

(Angry indistinguishable retorts and the crowd sways – MISS ERNESTINE BLUNT, *who has been watching the fray with serious face, turns suddenly catching sight of someone just arrived at the end of the platform.* MISS BLUNT *goes right with alacrity, saying audibly to* WALKER *as she passes: 'Here she is,' and proceeds to offer her hand to help someone get up the improvised steps.* LADY JOHN *has pushed in front of them amazed, transfixed, with glass up.* GEOFFREY STONOR *restrains a gesture of anger, and withdraws behind two big*

policemen. BEE *from time to time turns to look at him with a face of perplexity.)*

MR. WALKER *(Speaking through this last. Glancing at the new arrival whose hat appears above the platform right)* That's all right then. *(Turns to the left)* When I've attended to this microbe that's vitiating the air on my right –

(Laughter and interruptions from the crowd)

LADY JOHN Now there's another woman going to speak.

BEE Oh is she? Who? Which? I do hope she'll be one of the wild ones.

(WALKER retires in the midst of booing and cheers.)

CHAIRMAN TRENT *(Harassed and trying to create a diversion)* Someone suggests – and it's such a good idea I'd like you to listen to it –

(Noise dies down. STONOR *stares right, one dazed instant; at the face of the new arrival, his own changes.* BEE *withdraws her arm from his and quite suddenly presses a shade nearer the platform.* STONOR *moves forward and takes her by the arm.)*

STONOR We're going now.

BEE Not yet – Oh please not just yet *(Breathless, looking back)* Why I – I do believe –

STONOR *(To* LADY JOHN *with decision)* I'm going to take Bee out of this mob. Will you come?

LADY JOHN What? Oh yes, if you think – *(Another look through her glass)* but isn't that – surely it's –

(VIDA LEVERING appears on the platform right. She wears a long plain dark green silk dust cloak. Stands talking to ERNESTINE BLUNT *and glancing a little apprehensively at the crowd)*

BEE Geoffrey!

STONOR *(Trying to draw* BEE *away)* Lady John's tired –

BEE But you don't see who it is, Geoffrey – *(Looks into his face and is arrested by the look she finds there)* *(Noise dies down)*

CHAIRMAN TRENT – that a clause shall be inserted in the next suffrage bill that shall expressly reserve to each Cabinet Minister and to any respectable man the power to prevent a vote being given to the female members of his family on his public declaration of their lack of sufficient intelligence to entitle them to one.

VOICES Oh! Oh!

CHAIRMAN TRENT A lady will now speak to you who can tell you something of her impression of the administration of police court justice in this country.

(BEE *looks wondering at* STONOR'S *sphinx-like face as* VIDA LEVERING *comes to the edge of the platform.*)

MISS LEVERING Mr. Chairman, men and women.

VOICES *(Off)* Speak up.

(*She flushes, comes to the edge of the platform and raises her voice a little.*)

MISS LEVERING I just wanted to tell you that I was – I was – present in the Police Court when the women were charged for creating a disturbance.

VOICE Y' oughtn't t' get mixed up in wot didn't concern you.

MISS LEVERING I – I – *(Stumbles and stops)* *(Talking and laughing increases. 'Wot's 'er name?' 'Mrs or Miss?' 'Ain't seen her before')*

CHAIRMAN TRENT *(Anxiously)* Now see here, men, don't interrupt –

A GIRL *(Shrilly)* I like this one's 'at. You can see she ain't one of 'em.

MISS LEVERING *(Trying to recommence)* I –

VOICE They're a disgrace – them women be'ind yer.

A MAN WITH A FATHERLY AIR It's the w'y they goes on as mykes the Government keep ye from gettin' yer rights.

CHAIRMAN TRENT *(Losing his temper)* It's the way *you* go on that –

(*Noise increases.* CHAIRMAN *drowned waves his arms and moves his lips.* MISS LEVERING *discouraged turns, looks at* ERNESTINE BLUNT *and pantomimes 'It's no good. I can't go on.'* ERNESTINE BLUNT *comes forward, says a word to the* CHAIRMAN *who ceases gyrating and nods.*)

MISS E. BLUNT *(Facing the crowd)* Look here. If the Government withhold the vote because they don't like the way some of us ask for it let them give it to the quiet ones. Do they want to punish *all* women because they don't like the manners of a handful? Perhaps that's you men's notion of justice. It isn't women's.

VOICES Haw, haw!

MISS LEVERING Yes. Th-this is the first time I've ever 'gone on' as you call it, but they never gave me a vote.

MISS E. BLUNT *(With energy)* No! And there are one – two – three – four women on this platform. Now we all want the vote, as you know. Well we'd agreed to be

disenfranchised all our lives if they'd give the vote to all the other women.

VOICE Look here, you made one speech, give the lady a chawnce.

MISS E. BLUNT *(Retires smiling)* That's *just* what I wanted you to say.

MISS LEVERING Perhaps you – you don't know – you don't know –

VOICE *(Sarcastic)* 'Ow're we goin' to know if you can't tell us?

MISS LEVERING *(Flushing and smiling)* Thank you for that. We couldn't have a better motto. How *are* you to know if we can't somehow manage to tell you? *(With a visible effort she goes on.)* Well, I certainly didn't know before that the sergeants and policemen are instructed to deceive the people as to the time such cases are heard. You ask, and you're sent to Marlborough Police Court instead of to Marylebone.

VOICE They ought ter sent yer to 'Olloway – do y'good.

OLD NEWS VENDOR You go on, Miss, don't mind 'im.

VOICE Wot d'you expect from a pig but a grunt?

MISS LEVERING You're told the case will be at two o'clock and it's really called for eleven. Well I took a great deal of trouble and I didn't believe what I was told – *(Warming a little to her task)* Yes, that's almost the first thing we have to learn – to get over our touching faith that because a man tells us something it's true. I got to the right court and I was so anxious not to be late, I was too early. The case before the Women's was just coming on. I heard a noise, I saw the helmets of two policemen and I said to myself: What sort of crime shall I have to sit and hear about? Is this a burglar coming along between the two big policemen, or will it be a murderer? What sort of ruffianly fellow is to stand in the dock before the Women whose crime is they ask for the vote? But try as I would, I couldn't see the prisoner. My heart misgave me. Is it a woman I wondered. Then the policemen got nearer and I saw – *(She waits an instant.)* – a little thin half starved looking boy. Whàt do you think he was charged with? Stealing. What had he been stealing – that small criminal? *Milk.* It seemed to me as I sat there looking on, that the men who had the affairs of the world in their hands from the beginning and who've made so poor a business of it –

VOICES Oh! Oh! Pore benighted man! Are we down-'earted? *Oh no!*

MISS LEVERING So poor a business of it as to have the poor and the unemployed in this condition they're in today when your only remedy for a starving child is to hale him off to the Police Court because he had managed to get a little milk – well, I did wonder that the men refuse to be helped with a problem they've so notoriously failed at. I began to say to myself: Isn't it time the women lent a hand?

VOICE Would you have women magistrates? *(She is stumped by the suddenness of the demand.)*

VOICES Haw! Haw! Magistrates!

ANOTHER Women! Let 'em prove first they deserve –

A SHABBY ART STUDENT *(His hair longish, soft hat and flowing tie)* They study music by thousands, where's their Beethoven? Where's their Plato? Where's the woman Shakespeare?

ANOTHER Yes – what a' they ever *done*? *(The speaker clenches her hands and is recovering her presence of mind, so that by the time the CHAIRMAN can make himself heard with 'Now men, give this lady a fair hearing – don't interrupt' – she, with the slightest of gestures waves him aside with a low 'It's all right')*

MISS LEVERING *(Steadying and raising her voice)* These questions are quite proper! They are often asked elsewhere; and I would like to ask in return since when was human society held to exist for its handful of geniuses? How many Platos are there here in this crowd?

VOICE *(Very loud and shrill)* Divil a wan! *(A roar of laughter)*

MISS LEVERING Not one. Yet that doesn't keep you men off the register. How many Shakespeares are there in all England today? That is the question. Not one. Yet the State doesn't tumble to pieces. Railroads and ships are built – homes are kept going, and babies are born. The world goes on – *(Bending over the crowd)* – it goes on by *virtue of its common people.*

VOICES *(Subdued)* Hear, Hear!

MISS LEVERING I am not concerned that you should think we women can paint great pictures, or compose immortal music or write good books. I am content that we should be classed with the common people who keep the world going. But *(Straightening up and taking a fresh start)* I'd like the world to go a great deal better. We were talking about justice. I have been enquiring into the kind of lodging the poorest class of homeless women can get in this town of London. I find that only the men of that class are provided for. Some measure to establish Rowton Houses for women has been before the London County Council. They looked into the question very carefully – so their apologists say. And what did they decide? They decided that *they could do nothing.*

LADY JOHN *(Having forced her way to STONOR's side)* Is that true?

STONOR *(Speaking through MISS LEVERING's next words)* I don't know.

MISS LEVERING Why could that great all-powerful body do nothing? Because, if these cheap and decent houses were opened, they said, the homeless women in the streets would make use of them! You'll think I'm not in earnest. But that was actually the decision and the reason given for it. Women that the bitter struggle for existence had forced into a life of horror –

STONOR *(Sternly to LADY JOHN)* You think this is the kind of thing – *(A motion of the head towards BEE)*

MISS LEVERING – the outcast women might take advantage of the shelter these decent, cheap places offered. But the *men,* I said! Are all the men who avail them-selves of Lord Rowton's hostels, are *they* all angels? Or does wrongdoing in a man not matter? Yet women are recommended to depend on the chivalry of men! *(The two POLICEMEN who at first had been strolling about have stood all this time in front of GEOFFREY STONOR. They turn now and walk away leaving STONOR exposed. He, embarrassed, moves uneasily, and VIDA LEVERING's eyes fall upon his big figure. He still has the collar of his motor coat turned up to his ears. A change passes over her face, and her nerve fails her an instant.)*

MISS LEVERING Justice and chivalry – *(She steadies her voice and hurries on.)* – they both remind me of what those of you who read the Police Court news – I have begun only lately to do that. But you've seen the accounts of the girl who's been tried in Manchester lately for the murder of her child. Not pleasant reading. Even if we'd noticed it, we wouldn't speak of it in my world. A few months ago, I should have turned away my eyes and forgotten even the headline as quickly as I could. But since that morning in the Police Court, I read these things. This, as you'll remember was about a little working girl – an orphan of eighteen – who crawled with the dead body of her new-born child to her master's back door and left the baby there. She dragged herself a little way off and fainted. A few days later she found herself in court being tried for the murder of her child. Her master, a married man, had of course reported the 'find' at his back door to the police and hè had been summoned to give evidence. The girl cried out to him in the open court: 'You are the father!' He couldn't deny it. The Coroner at the jury's request censured the man and regretted that the law didn't make him responsible. But he went scot free. And that girl is now serving her sentence in Strangeways Gaol. *(Murmuring and scraps of indistinguishable comment in the crowd – through which only* BEE's *voice is clear)*

BEE *(Who has wormed her way to* STONOR's *side)* Why do you dislike her so?

STONOR I? Why should you think –

BEE *(With a vaguely frightened air)* I never saw you look as you did – as you do.

CHAIRMAN TRENT Order please – give the lady a fair –

MISS LEVERING *(Signing to him 'It's all right')* Men make boast that an English citizen is tried by his peers. What woman is tried by hers? *(A sombre passion strengthens her voice and hurries her on.)* A woman is arrested by a man, brought before a man judge, tried by a jury of men, condemned by men, taken to prison by a man, and by a man she's hanged! Where in all this were *her* 'peers'? Why did men as long ago as 1215 insist on trial by 'a jury of their peers'? So that justice shouldn't miscarry – wasn't it? A man's peers would best understand his circumstances, his temptation, the degree of his guilt. Yet there's no such unlikeness between different classes of men as exists between

man and woman. What man has the knowledge that makes him a fit judge of woman's deeds at that time of anguish – that hour – *(Lowers her voice and bends over the crowd)* – That hour that some woman struggled through to put each man here into the world. I noticed when a previous speaker quoted the Labour Party you applauded. Some of you here – I gather – call yourselves Labour men. Every woman who has borne a child is a Labour woman. No man among you can judge what she goes through in her hour of darkness –

BEE *(With frightened eyes on her lover's set white face – whispers)* Geoffrey –

MISS LEVERING *(Catching her fluttering breath goes on very low)* – in that great agony when even under the best conditions that money and devotion can buy, many a woman falls into temporary mania and not a few go down to death. In the case of this poor little abandoned working girl, what man can be the fit judge of her deeds in that awful moment of half-crazed temptation? Women know of these things as those know burning who have walked through fire.

*(*STONOR *makes a motion towards* BEE *and she turns away fronting the audience. Her hands go up to her throat as though she suffered a choking sensation. It is in her face that she 'knows'.* MISS LEVERING *leans over the platform and speaks with a low and thrilling earnestness.)*

MISS LEVERING I would say in conclusion to the women here, it's not enough to be sorry for these, our unfortunate sisters. We must get the conditions of life made fairer. We women must organise. We must learn to work together. We have all – rich and poor, happy and unhappy – worked so long and so exclusively for *men*, we hardly know how to work for one another. But we must learn. Those who can, may give money –

VOICES *(Grumbling)* Oh yes – Money! Money!

MISS LEVERING Those who haven't pennies to give – even those people aren't so poor they can't give some part of their labour – some share of their sympathy and support.

(Turns to hear something the CHAIRMAN *is whispering to her)*

BEE (*Low to* LADY JOHN) Oh, I'm glad I've got power!

LADY JOHN (*Aghast*) Power! – *You!*

BEE Yes, all that money –

(LADY JOHN *tries to make her way to* STONOR.)

MISS LEVERING (*Suddenly turning from the* CHAIRMAN *to the crowd*) Oh, yes, I hope you'll all join the Union. Come up after the meeting and give your names.

LOUD VOICE You won't get many men.

MISS LEVERING (*With fire*) Then it's to the women I appeal.

(*She is about to retire when with a sudden gleam in her lit eyes she turns for the last time to the crowd, silencing the general murmur and holding the people by the sudden concentration of passion in her face.*) I don't mean to say it wouldn't be better if men and women did this work together – shoulder to shoulder. But the mass of men won't have it so. I only hope they'll realize in time the good they've renounced and the spirit they've aroused. For I know as well as any man could tell me, it would be a bad day for England if all women felt about men *as I do.*

(*She retires in a tumult. The others on the platform close about her. The* CHAIRMAN *tries in vain to get a hearing from the excited crowd;* BEE *trying to make her way through the knot of people surging round her*)

STONOR (*Calls*) Here! Follow me!

BEE No – No – I –

STONOR You're going the wrong way.

BEE This is the way I must go.

STONOR You can get out quicker on this side.

BEE I don't *want* to get out.

STONOR What? Where are you going?

BEE To ask that woman to let me have the honour of working with her.

(*She disappears in the crowd.*)

Curtain

Act III

SCENE: *The drawing room at old* MR. DUNBARTON's *house in Eaton Square. Six o'clock the same evening. As the curtain rises the door left opens and* BEE *appears on the threshold. She looks back into her own sitting room, then crosses the drawing room, treading softly on the parquet spaces between the rugs.*

She goes to the window and is in the act of parting the lace curtains when the folding doors, centre, are opened by the BUTLER.

BEE (*To the* SERVANT) Sh!

(*She goes softly back to the door she has left open and closes it carefully. When she turns, the* BUTLER *has stepped aside to admit* GEOFFREY STONOR, *and departed, shutting the folding doors.* STONOR *comes rapidly forward.*)

(*Before he gets a word out*) Speak low, please.

STONOR (*Angrily*) I waited about a whole hour for you to come back. (BEE *turns away as though vaguely looking for the nearest chair.*) If you didn't mind leaving me like that, you might have considered Lady John.

BEE (*Pausing*) Is she here with you?

STONOR No. My place was nearer than this and she was very tired. I left her to get some tea. We couldn't tell whether you'd be here, or *what* had become of you!

BEE Mr. Trent got us a hansom.

STONOR Trent?

BEE The Chairman of the meeting.

STONOR Got us –?

BEE Miss Levering and me.

STONOR (*Incensed*) Miss L–

BUTLER (*Opens the door and announces*) Mr. Farnborough.

(*Enter* MR. RICHARD FARNBOROUGH – *more flurried than ever*)

FARNBOROUGH (*Seeing* STONOR) At last! You'll forgive the incursion, Miss Dunbarton, when you hear – (*Turns abruptly back to* STONOR) They've been telegraphing you all over London. In despair they set me on your track.

STONOR Who did? What's up?

FARNBOROUGH (*Lays down his hat and fumbles agitatedly in his breast pocket*) There was the devil to pay at Dutfield last night. The Liberal chap tore down from London and took over your meeting!

STONOR Oh? – Nothing about it in the Sunday paper *I* saw.

FARNBOROUGH Wait till you see the press tomorrow morning! There was a great rally and the beggar made a rousing speech.

STONOR What about?

FARNBOROUGH Abolition of the Upper House –

STONOR They were at that when I was at Eton!

FARNBOROUGH   Yes. But this new man has got a way of putting things! – the people went mad. *(Pompously)* The Liberal platform as defined at Dutfield is going to make a big difference.

STONOR   *(Dryly)* You think so.

FARNBOROUGH   Well. Your agent says as much. *(Opens telegram)*

STONOR   My – *(Taking telegram)* 'Try find Stonor' – Hm! Hm!

FARNBOROUGH   *(Pointing)* – 'tremendous effect of last night's Liberal manifesto ought to be counteracted in tomorrow's papers' – *(Very earnestly)* You see, Mr. Stonor, it's a battle cry we want.

STONOR   *(Turns on his heel)* Claptrap!

FARNBOROUGH   *(A little dashed)* Well, they've been saying we have nothing to offer but personal popularity. No practical reform. No –

STONOR   No truckling to the masses I suppose. *(Walks impatiently away)*

FARNBOROUGH   *(Snubbed)* Well, in these democratic days – *(Turns to* BEE *for countenance)* I hope you'll forgive my bursting in like this. *(Struck by her face)* But I can see you realise the gravity *(Lowering his voice with an air of speaking for her ear alone)* It isn't as if he were going to be a mere private member. Everybody knows he'll be in the Cabinet.

STONOR   *(Dryly)* It may be a Liberal Cabinet.

FARNBOROUGH   Nobody thought so up to last night. Why even your brother – *(Stops)* but I'm afraid I'm seeming officious *(Takes up his hat)*

STONOR   *(Coldly)* What about my brother?

FARNBOROUGH   I met Lord Windlesham as I rushed out of the Carlton.

STONOR   Did he say anything?

FARNBOROUGH   I told him the Dutfield news.

STONOR   *(Impatiently)* Well?

FARNBOROUGH   He said it only confirmed his fears.

STONOR   *(Half under his breath)* – said that did he?

FARNBOROUGH   Yes. Defeat is inevitable he thinks unless – *(Pause.* GEOFFREY STONOR, *who has been pacing the floor, stops, but doesn't raise his eyes.)* unless you can 'manufacture some political dynamite within the next few hours'. Those were his words.

STONOR   *(Resumes his walking to and fro,*

raises his head and catches sight of BEE's white drawn face. Stops short)* You are very tired.

BEE   No. No.

STONOR   *(To* FARNBOROUGH)* I'm obliged to you for troubling about this. *(Shakes hands)* I'll see what can be done.

FARNBOROUGH   *(Offering the reply paid form)* If you'd like to wire I'll take it –

STONOR   *(Faintly amused)* You don't understand, my young friend. Moves of this kind are not rushed at by responsible politicians. I must have time for consideration.

FARNBOROUGH   *(Disappointed)* Oh, well, I only hope some one else won't jump into the breach before you – *(Watch in hand)* I tell you *(To* BEE)* I'll find out what time the newspapers go to press on Sunday. Goodbye. *(To* STONOR)* I'll be at the Club just *in case* I can be of any use.

STONOR   *(Firmly)* No, don't do that. If I should have anything new to say –

FARNBOROUGH   *(Feverishly)* B-b-but with our party as your brother said – heading straight for a vast electoral disaster –

STONOR   If I decide on a counterblast I shall simply telegraph to headquarters. Goodbye.

FARNBOROUGH   Oh – a – g – *Goodbye*! *(A gesture of 'the country going to the dogs')* (BEE *rings the bell. Exit* FARNBOROUGH)

STONOR   *(Studying the carpet)* 'Political dynamite,' eh? *(Pause)* After all women are much more conservative than men – aren't they? (BEE *looks straight in front of her making no attempt at reply.)* Especially the women the property qualification would bring in –

BEE   Geoffrey.

STONOR   Yes.

BEE   I know her story.

STONOR   Whose story?

BEE   Miss Levering's.

STONOR   *Whose?*

BEE   Vida Levering's. (STONOR *stares speechless. Slight pause. The words escaping from her in a miserable cry)* Why did you desert her?

STONOR   *(Staggered)* I? I?

BEE   Oh, why did you do it?

STONOR   *(Bewildered)* What in the name of – What has she been saying to you?

BEE   Some one else told me part. Then the way you looked when you saw her at Aunt Ellen's – Miss Levering's saying you didn't know her – then your letting out that you knew even the curious name on the handkerchief – Oh, I pieced it together.

STONOR *(With recovered self-possession)* Your ingenuity is undeniable!

BEE – and then when she said that at the meeting about 'the dark hour' and I looked at your face – it flashed over me – Oh *why* did you desert her?

STONOR I *didn't* desert her.

BEE Ah-h! *(Puts her hands before her eyes. STONOR makes a passionate motion towards her, is checked by her muffled voice saying)* I'm glad – I'm glad! *(He stares bewildered. BEE drops her hands in her lap and steadies her voice.)* She went away from you then?

STONOR You don't expect me to enter into –

BEE She went away from you?

STONOR *(With a look of almost uncontrollable anger)* Yes!

BEE Was that because you wouldn't marry her?

STONOR I *couldn't* marry her – and she knew it.

BEE Did you want to?

STONOR *(An instant's angry scrutiny and then turning away his eyes)* I thought I did – *then*. It's a long time ago.

BEE And why 'couldn't' you?

STONOR *(A movement of strong irritation cut short)* Why are you catechising me? It's a matter that concerns another woman.

BEE If you're saying that it doesn't concern me, you're saying *(Her lip trembles.)* that *you* don't concern me.

STONOR *(Commanding his temper with difficulty)* In those days – I – I was absolutely dependent on my father.

BEE Why, you must have been thirty, Geoffrey.

STONOR *(Slight pause)* What? – Oh – Thereabouts.

BEE And everybody says you're so clever.

STONOR – Well everybody's mistaken.

BEE *(Drawing nearer)* It must have been terribly hard – *(STONOR turns towards her.)* – for you both – *(He arrests his movement and stands stonily.)* That a man like you shouldn't have had the freedom that even the lowest seem to have.

STONOR Freedom?

BEE – to marry the woman they choose.

STONOR She didn't break off our relations because I couldn't marry her.

BEE Why was it then?

STONOR You're too young to discuss such a story. *(Half turns away)*

BEE I'm not as young as she was when –

STONOR *(Wheeling upon her)* Very well then, if you will have it! The truth is, it didn't seem to weigh upon her as it seems to on you, that I wasn't able to marry her.

BEE Why are you sure of that?

STONOR Because she didn't so much as hint at it when she wrote that she meant to break off the – the –

BEE What made her write like that?

STONOR *(With suppressed rage)* Why will you go on talking of what's so long ended?

BEE What reason did she give?

STONOR If your curiosity has so got the upper hand – *ask her.*

BEE You're afraid to tell me.

STONOR *(Putting pressure on himself to answer quickly)* I still hoped – at *that* time – to win my father over. She blamed me because – *(Goes to window and looks out and speaks in a low tone)* if the child had lived it wouldn't have been possible to get my father to – to overlook it.

BEE *(Faintly)* You wanted it *overlooked?* I don't underst –

STONOR *(Turning passionately back to her)* Of course you don't. *(He seizes her hand and tries to draw her to him.)* If you did you wouldn't be the beautiful, tender, innocent child you are –

BEE *(Has withdrawn her hand and shrunk from him with an impulse – slight as its expression – so tragically eloquent that fear for the first time catches hold of him)* I am glad you didn't mean to desert her, Geoffrey. It wasn't your fault after all – only some misunderstanding that can be cleared up.

STONOR *Cleared up?*

BEE Yes. Cleared up.

STONOR *(Aghast)* You aren't thinking that this miserable old affair I'd as good as forgotten –

BEE *(In horror-struck whisper with a glance at the door left which he doesn't see) Forgotten!*

STONOR No, no. I don't mean exactly forgotten. But you're torturing me so I don't know what I'm saying. *(He goes closer.)* You aren't – Bee! you – you aren't going to let it come between you and me!

BEE *(Presses her handkerchief to her lips and then taking it away steadily)* I can't make or unmake what's past. But I'm glad at least that you didn't *mean* to desert her in her trouble. *(Moves to the door left)* You'll remind her of that first of all, won't you?

STONOR Where are you going? *(Raising his voice)* Why should I remind *anybody* of what I want only to forget.

BEE *(Finger on lip)* Sh!

STONOR *(With eyes on the door)* You don't mean that *she's* –

BEE Yes. I left her to get a little rest. *(He recoils in an access of uncontrollable rage. She follows him. Speechless he goes down right to get his hat.)*

BEE Geoffrey, don't go before you hear me. I don't know if what I think matters to you now – but I hope it does. *(With tears)* You can still make me think of you without shrinking – if you will.

STONOR *(Fixes her a moment with his eyes. Then sternly)* What is it you are asking of me?

BEE To make amends, Geoffrey.

STONOR *(With an outburst)* You poor little innocent!

BEE I'm poor enough. But *(Locking her hands together)* I'm not so innocent but what I know you must right that old wrong now, if you're ever to right it.

STONOR You aren't insane enough to think I would turn round in these few hours and go back to something that ten years ago was ended forever! Why, it's stark, staring madness!

BEE No. *(Catching his arm)* What you did ten years ago – that was mad. This is paying a debt.

STONOR Look here, Bee, you're dreadfully wrought up and excited – tired too –

BEE No, not tired – though I've travelled to-day as far as Tarsus is from Damascus and seen a sign in the heavens. I know you smile at sudden conversions. You think they're hysterical – worse – vulgar. But people must get their Revelation how they can. And Geoffrey, if I can't make you see this one of mine – I shall know your love could never mean strength to me. Only weakness. And I shall be afraid. So afraid I'll never dare to give you the *chance* of making me loathe myself. I shall never see you again.

STONOR How right I was to be afraid of that vein of fanaticism in you! *(Moves towards the door)*

BEE Certainly you couldn't make a greater mistake than to go away now and think it any good ever to come back. *(He turns.)* Even if I care to feel different, I couldn't *do* anything different. I should know all this couldn't be forgotten. I should know that it would poison my life in the end. Yours too.

STONOR *(With suppressed fury)* She has made good use of her time! *(With a sudden thought)* What has changed *her?* Has she been seeing visions too?

BEE What do you mean?

STONOR Why is she intriguing to get hold of a man that ten years ago she flatly refused to see or hold any communication with?

BEE 'Intriguing to get hold of'? She hasn't mentioned you!

STONOR What! Then how in the name of heaven do you know – that she wants – what you ask?

BEE *(Firmly)* There can't be any doubt about that.

STONOR *(With immense relief)* You absurd ridiculous child! – Then all this is just your own unaided invention. Well – I could thank God! *(Falls into the nearest chair and passes his handkerchief over his face)*

BEE *(Perplexed, uneasy)* For what are you thanking God?

STONOR *(Trying to think out his plan of action)* Suppose – I'm not going to risk it – but suppose – *(He looks up and at the sight of* BEE's *face a new tenderness comes into his own. He rises suddenly.)* Whether I deserve to suffer or not – it's quite certain *you* don't. Don't cry, dear one. It never was the real thing. I had to wait till I knew you before I understood.

BEE *(Lifts her eyes brimming)* Oh, is that true? *(Checks her movement towards him)* Loving you has made things clear to me I didn't dream of before. If I could think that because of me you were able to do this –

STONOR *(Seizes her by the shoulders and says hoarsely)* Look here! Do you seriously ask me to give up the girl I love – to go and offer to marry a woman that even to think of –

BEE You cared for her once. You'll care about her again. She is beautiful and

139

brilliant – everything. I've heard she could win any man she set herself to –

STONOR *(Pushing* BEE *from him)* She's bewitched you!

BEE Geoffrey, Geoffrey, you aren't going away like that. This isn't *the end!*

STONOR *(Darkly – hesitating)* I suppose if she refused me you'd –

BEE She won't refuse you.

STONOR She did once.

BEE She didn't refuse to *marry* you – (BEE *is going to the door left.)*

STONOR *(Snatches her by the arm)* Wait! – a – *(Hunting for some means of gaining time)* Lady John is waiting all this while for the car to go back with a message.

BEE That's not a matter of life and death –

STONOR All the same – I'll go down and give the order.

BEE *(Stopping quite still on a sudden)* Very well. *(Goes centre)* You'll come back if you're the man I pray you are. *(Breaks into a flood of silent tears, her elbows on the table, centre, her face in her hands)*

STONOR *(Returns, bends over her, about to take her in his arms)* Dearest of all the world –

(Door left opens softly and VIDA LEVERING *appears. She is arrested at the sight of* STONOR *and is in the act of drawing back when upon the slight noise* STONOR *looks round. His face darkens, he stands staring at her for a moment and then with a look of speechless anger goes silently out centre.* BEE *hearing him shut the door drops her head on the table with a sob.* VIDA LEVERING *crosses slowly to her and stands a moment silent at the girl's side.)*

MISS LEVERING What is the matter?

BEE *(Lifting her head and drying her eyes)* I – I-ve been seeing Geoffrey.

MISS LEVERING *(With an attempt at lightness)* Is this the effect seeing Geoffrey has?

BEE You see I know now. *(As* MISS LEVERING *looks quite uncomprehending)* – How he – *(Drops her eyes)* how he spoiled someone else's life.

MISS LEVERING *(Quickly)* Who tells you that?

BEE Several people have told me.

MISS LEVERING Well, you should be very careful how you believe what you hear.

BEE *(Passionately)* You *know* it's true!

MISS LEVERING I know that it's possible to be mistaken.

BEE I see. You're trying to shield him –

MISS LEVERING Why should I – what is it to me?

BEE *(With tears)* Oh-h, how you must love him!

MISS LEVERING Listen to me.

BEE *(Rising)* What's the use of your going on denying it? (MISS LEVERING *about to break in, is silenced.)* Geoffrey doesn't. (BEE *struggling to command her feelings goes to window.* VIDA LEVERING *relinquishes an impulse to follow and sits left centre.* BEE *comes slowly back with her eyes bent on the floor, does not lift them till she is quite near* VIDA. *Then the* GIRL's *self-absorbed face changes.)*

BEE Oh, don't look like that! I shall bring him back to you! *(Drops on her knees beside the other's chair)*

MISS LEVERING You would be impertinent *(Softening)* if you weren't a romantic child. You can't bring him back.

BEE Yes, he –

MISS LEVERING But there's something you *can* do –

BEE What!

MISS LEVERING Bring him to the point where he recognises that he's in our debt.

BEE In *our* debt?

MISS LEVERING In debt to women. He can't repay the one he robbed –

BEE *(Wincing and rising from her knees)* Yes, yes.

MISS LEVERING *(Sternly)* No. He can't repay the dead. But there are the living. There are the thousands with hope still in their hearts and youth in their blood. Let him help *them.* Let him be a Friend to Women.

BEE *(Rising on a wave of enthusiasm)* Yes, yes – I understand that too.

(As GEOFFREY *enters with* LADY JOHN, *he makes a slight gesture towards the two as much as to say: 'You see.')*

BEE *(Catching sight of him)* Thank you!

LADY JOHN *(In a clear commonplace tone to* BEE) Well, you rather gave us the slip. Vida, I believe Mr. Stonor wants to see you for a few minutes *(Glances at watch)* – but I'd like a word with you first, as I must get back. *(To* STONOR) Do you think the car – your man said something about re-charging –

STONOR *(Hastily)* Oh, did he – I'll see about it.

(As STONOR *is going out he encounters the* BUTLER. *Exit* STONOR)

BUTLER Mr. Trent has called, Miss, to take Miss Levering to the meeting.

BEE Bring Mr. Trent into my sitting room. I'll tell him – you can't go to-night.

(Exit BUTLER *centre,* BEE *left)*

LADY JOHN *(Hurriedly)* I know my dear, *you're* not aware of what that impulsive girl wants to insist on.

MISS LEVERING Yes, I am aware of it.

LADY JOHN But it isn't with your sanction surely, that she goes on making this extraordinary demand.

MISS LEVERING *(Slowly)* I didn't sanction it at first, but I've been thinking it over.

LADY JOHN Then all I can say is I am greatly disappointed in you. You threw this man over years ago for reasons – whatever they were – that seemed to you good and sufficient. And now you come in between him and a younger woman just to play Nemesis so far as I can make out.

MISS LEVERING Is that what he says?

LADY JOHN He says nothing that isn't fair and considerate.

MISS LEVERING I can see he's changed.

LADY JOHN And you're unchanged – is that it?

MISS LEVERING I've changed even more than he.

LADY JOHN But *(Pity and annoyance blended in her tone)* you care about him still, Vida?

MISS LEVERING No.

LADY JOHN I see – it's just that you wish to marry somebody?

MISS LEVERING Oh, Lady John, there are no men listening?

LADY JOHN *(Surprised)* No, I didn't suppose there were.

MISS LEVERING Then why keep up that old pretence?

LADY JOHN What pre –

MISS LEVERING – that to marry *at all costs* is every woman's dearest ambition till the grave closes over her. You and I *know* it isn't true.

LADY JOHN Well, but – Oh! It was just the unexpected sight of him bringing it all back – *That* was what fired you this afternoon! *(With an honest attempt at sympathetic understanding)* Of course. The memory of a thing like that can never die – can never be dimmed – *for the woman.*

MISS LEVERING I mean her to think so.

LADY JOHN *(Bewildered)* Bee!

(MISS LEVERING *nods.*)

And it *isn't* so?

MISS LEVERING You don't seriously believe a woman with anything else to think about comes to the end of ten years still *absorbed* in a memory of that sort?

LADY JOHN *(Astonished)* You've got over it then!

MISS LEVERING If the papers didn't remind me I shouldn't remember once a year that there was ever such a person as Geoffrey Stonor in the world.

LADY JOHN *(With unconscious rapture)* Oh, I'm *so* glad.

MISS LEVERING *(Smiles grimly)* Yes, I'm glad too.

LADY JOHN And if Geoffrey Stonor offered you – what's called 'reparation' – you'd refuse it?

MISS LEVERING *(Smiles a little contemptuously)* Geoffrey Stonor! For me he's simply one of the far-back links in a chain of evidence. It's certain I think a hundred times of women's present unhappiness to once that I remember that old unhappiness of mine that's past. I think of the nail and the chain makers of Cradley Heath, the sweated girls of the slums – I think of the army of ill-used women whose very existence I mustn't mention –

LADY JOHN *(Interrupting hurriedly)* Then why in heaven's name do you let poor Bee imagine –

MISS LEVERING *(Bending forward)* Look – I'll trust you Lady John. I don't suffer from that old wrong as Bee thinks I do, but I shall coin her every sympathy into gold for a greater cause than mine.

LADY JOHN I don't understand you.

MISS LEVERING Bee isn't old enough to be able to care as much about a principle as about a person. But if my half-forgotten pain can turn her generosity into the common treasury –

LADY JOHN What do you propose she shall do, poor child?

MISS LEVERING Use her hold over Geoffrey Stonor to make him help us!

LADY JOHN – help you?

MISS LEVERING The man who served one woman – God knows how many more – very ill – shall serve hundreds of thousands well. Geoffrey Stonor shall

141

make it harder for his son, harder still for his grandson, to treat any woman as he treated me.

LADY JOHN How will he do that?

MISS LEVERING By putting an end to the helplessness of women.

LADY JOHN (Ironically) You must think he has a great deal of power –

MISS LEVERING Power? Yes, men have too much over penniless and frightened women.

LADY JOHN (Impatiently) What nonsense! You talk as though the women hadn't their share of human nature. We aren't made of ice any more than the men.

MISS LEVERING No, but all the same we have more self-control.

LADY JOHN Than men?

MISS LEVERING You know we have.

LADY JOHN (Shrewdly) I know we mustn't admit it.

MISS LEVERING For fear they'll call us fishes.

LADY JOHN (Elusively) They talk of our lack of self-control – but it's the last thing they want women to have.

MISS LEVERING Oh, we know what they want us to have. So we make shift to have it. If we don't we go without hope – sometimes we go without bread.

LADY JOHN (Shocked) Vida – do you mean to say that you –

MISS LEVERING I mean to say that men's vanity won't let them see it, but the thing's largely a question of Economics.

LADY JOHN (Shocked) You never loved him then!

MISS LEVERING Oh, yes, I loved him – once. And then it was my helplessness turned the best thing life can bring, into a curse for both of us.

LADY JOHN (Rising and looking at her watch) I must get back – my poor ill-used guests –

MISS LEVERING (Rising) I won't ring. I think you'll find Mr. Stonor downstairs waiting for you.

LADY JOHN (Embarrassed) Oh – a – he will have left word about the car in any case. (MISS LEVERING has opened the door centre. ALLEN TRENT is in the act of saying goodbye to BEE.)

MISS LEVERING Well, Mr. Trent, I didn't expect to see you this evening.

ALLEN TRENT (Comes and stands in doorway) Why not? Have I ever failed?

MISS LEVERING Lady John, this is one of our allies. He is good enough to squire me through the rabble from time to time.

LADY JOHN Well, I think it's very handsome of you after what she said to-day about men. (Shakes hands)

ALLEN TRENT I've no great opinion of most men myself. I might add or of most women.

LADY JOHN Oh! Well, at any rate I shall go away relieved to think that Miss Levering's plain speaking hasn't alienated all masculine regard.

ALLEN TRENT Why should it?

LADY JOHN That's right, Mr. Trent? Don't believe all she says in the heat of propaganda.

ALLEN TRENT I do believe all she says. But I'm not cast down.

LADY JOHN (Smiling) Not when she says –

ALLEN TRENT (Interrupting) Was there never a misogynist of my sex who ended by deciding to make an exception?

LADY JOHN (Smiling significantly) Oh, if that's what you build on!

ALLEN TRENT Well, why shouldn't a man-hater on your side prove equally open to reason?

MISS LEVERING That part of the question doesn't concern me. I've come to a place where I realise that the first battles of this new campaign must be fought by women alone. The only effective help men could give – amendment of the law – they refuse. The rest is nothing.

LADY JOHN Don't be ungrateful, Vida. Here's Mr. Trent ready to face criticism in publicly championing you.

MISS LEVERING It's an illusion that I as an individual need Mr. Trent. I am quite safe in the crowd. Please don't wait for me, and don't come for me again.

ALLEN TRENT (Flushes) Of course if you'd rather –

MISS LEVERING And that reminds me. I was asked to thank you and to tell you, too, that they – the women of the Union – they won't need your chairmanship any more – though that, I beg you to believe, has nothing to do with any feeling of mine.

ALLEN TRENT (Hurt) Of course I know there must be other men ready – better known men –

MISS LEVERING It isn't that. It's simply that they find a man can't keep a rowdy meeting in order as well as a woman. *(He stares.)*

LADY JOHN   You aren't serious?

MISS LEVERING   *(To* TRENT*)* Haven't you noticed that all their worst disturbances come when men are in charge?

ALLEN TRENT   Well – a *(Laughs a little ruefully as he moves to the door)* I hadn't connected the two ideas. Goodbye.

MISS LEVERING   Goodbye. (BEE *takes him downstairs right centre)*

LADY JOHN   *(As* TRENT *disappears)* That nice boy's in love with you.
(MISS LEVERING *simply looks at her.)*
Good-bye. *(They shake hands.)* I wish you hadn't been so unkind to that nice boy!

MISS LEVERING   Do you?

LADY JOHN   Yes, for then I would be more sure of your telling Geoffrey Stonor that intelligent women don't nurse their wrongs and lie in wait to punish them.

MISS LEVERING   You are *not* sure?

LADY JOHN   *(Goes close up to* VIDA*)* Are you?
(VIDA *stands with her eyes on the ground, silent, motionless.* LADY JOHN *with a nervous glance at her watch and with a gesture of extreme perturbation goes hurriedly out.* VIDA *shuts the door. She comes slowly back, sits down and covers her face with her hands. She rises and begins to walk up and down, obviously trying to master her agitation. Enter* GEOFFREY STONOR*)*

MISS LEVERING   Well, have they primed you? Have you got your lesson – *(With a little broken laugh)* by heart at last?

STONOR   I have come to offer you amends.

MISS LEVERING   *(Quickly)* You've come to realise then – after all these years – that you owed me something.

STONOR   *(On the brink of protest, checks himself)* I am not here to deny it.

MISS LEVERING   *(Fiercely)* Pay then – *pay.*

STONOR   *(A moment's dread as he looks at her with set lips. Then stonily)* I have promised that if you exact it I will.

MISS LEVERING   Ah! If I insist you'll 'make it all good'! *(Quite low)* Then don't you know you must pay me in kind?

STONOR   What do you mean?

MISS LEVERING   You must give me back what you took from me: my old faith, give me that.

STONOR   Oh, if you mean to – *(Turns with a gesture of scant impatience)*

MISS LEVERING   *(Going closer)* Or give me back mere kindness – or even tolerance.

Oh, I don't mean *your* tolerance I mean mine. Give me back the power to think fairly of my brothers – not as mockers – thieves.

STONOR   I have not mocked you. And I have asked you –

MISS LEVERING   You knew I should refuse! Or did you dare to be afraid I wouldn't?

STONOR   I suppose if we set our teeth, we could –

MISS LEVERING   I couldn't – not even if I set my teeth. And you wouldn't dream of asking me if you thought there was the smallest chance.

STONOR   I can do no more than make you an offer of such reparation as is in my power. If you don't accept it – *(He turns with an air of 'that's done'.)*

MISS LEVERING   Accept it? No. . . . Go away and live in debt. Pay and pay and pay – and find yourself still in debt! – for a thing you'll never be able to give me back. *(Lower)* And when you come to die, pay all creditors but one.

STONOR   I'm rather tired, you know, of this talk of debt. If I hear that you persist in it I shall have to –

MISS LEVERING   What? *(She faces him.)*

STONOR   No, I'll keep to my resolution *(Turning to the door)*

MISS LEVERING   *(Intercepting him)* What resolution?

STONOR   I came here under considerable pressure to speak of the the future – not to re-open the past. My conscience is clear. I know – and so do you – that most men in my position wouldn't have troubled themselves. I gave myself endless trouble.

MISS LEVERING   So you've gone about all these years feeling that you'd discharged every obligation.

STONOR   Not only that. I stood by you with a fidelity that was nothing short of Quixotic. If, womanlike, you *must* recall the Past – I insist on your recalling it correctly.

MISS LEVERING   You think I don't?

STONOR   Not when you make – other people believe that I deserted you. *(With gathering wrath)* It's a curious enough charge when you stop to consider – *(Checks himself and with a gesture of impatience sweeps the whole thing out of his way)*

MISS LEVERING   *(Following him up)* Well,

143

when we do (just for five minutes out of ten years) – when we do stop to consider what –

STONOR Why it was *you* who did the deserting! Since you had to rake the story up you might have had the fairness to tell the facts.

MISS LEVERING You think 'the facts' would have excused you!

STONOR No doubt you have forgotten them since Lady John tells me you wouldn't remember my existence once a year if the papers didn't –

MISS LEVERING Ah, you minded that!

STONOR *(With manly spirit)* I minded your giving false impressions. *(She is about to speak, he advances on her.)* Do you deny that you returned my letters unopened?

MISS LEVERING *(Quietly)* No.

STONOR Do you deny that you refused to see me – and that when I persisted you vanished?

MISS LEVERING I don't deny any of those things.

STONOR Why I had no trace of you for years.

MISS LEVERING I suppose not.

STONOR Very well, then. What *could* I do?

MISS LEVERING Nothing. It was too late to do anything.

STONOR It wasn't too late! You knew – since you 'read the papers' that my father died that same year. There was no longer any barrier between us.

MISS LEVERING Oh yes, there was a barrier.

STONOR Of your own making then.

MISS LEVERING I had my guilty share in it – but the barrier was your invention.

STONOR It was no 'invention'. If you had ever known my father –

MISS LEVERING Oh, the echoes! The echoes! How often you used to say: if I 'knew your father'! But you said too, *(Lower)* you called the greatest barrier by another name.

STONOR What name?

MISS LEVERING The child that was to come.

STONOR *(Hastily)* That was before my father died. While I still hoped to get his consent.

MISS LEVERING *(Nods)* How the thought of that all-powerful personage used to terrorize me! What chance had a little unborn child against 'the last of the great feudal lords', as you called him.

STONOR You *know* the child would have stood between you and me!

MISS LEVERING I know the child did stand between me and you!

STONOR *(With vague uneasiness)* It *did* stand –

MISS LEVERING Happy mothers teach their children. Mine had to teach me.

STONOR You talk as if –

MISS LEVERING – teach me that a woman may do a thing for love's sake that shall kill love.

(An instant's silence)

STONOR *(Fearing and putting from him fuller comprehensions rises with an air of finality)* You certainly made it plain you had no love left for me.

MISS LEVERING I had need of it all for the child.

STONOR *(Stares – comes closer, speaks hurriedly and very low)* Do you mean that after all – it lived?

MISS LEVERING No, I mean that it was sacrificed. But it showed me no barrier is so impassable as the one a little child can raise.

STONOR *(A light dawning)* Was *that* why you –

MISS LEVERING *(Nods, speechless a moment)* Day and night there it was between my thought of you and me. *(He sits again, staring at her.)* When I was most unhappy I would wake, thinking I heard it cry. It was my own crying I heard, but I seemed to have it in my arm. I suppose I was mad. I used to lie there in that lonely farmhouse pretending to hush it. It was so I hushed myself.

STONOR I never knew.

MISS LEVERING I didn't blame you. You couldn't risk being with me.

STONOR You agreed that for both our sakes –

MISS LEVERING Yes, you had to be very circumspect. You were so well known. Your autocrat father – your brilliant political future –

STONOR Be fair. *Our* future – as I saw it then.

MISS LEVERING Yes, it all hung on concealment. It must have looked quite simple to you. You didn't know that the ghost of a child that had never seen the light (the frail thing you meant to sweep aside and forget – *have* swept aside and forgotten) – you didn't know it was strong enough to push you out of my life. (*Lower with an added intensity*) It can do more. (*Leans over him and whispers*) It can push that girl out. (STONOR's *face changes.*) It can do more still –

STONOR Are you threatening me?

MISS LEVERING No, I am preparing you. (*She walks away a few paces. He drops his face in his hands. She turns, takes in his attitude of hopelessness, comes back and stands beside him, looking down on the bowed head.*) After all, life hasn't been quite fair to you. (*He raises his heavy eyes.*) You fall out of one ardent woman's dreams into another's.

STONOR You may as well tell me – do you mean to –?

MISS LEVERING To keep you and her apart? No. But – I like that girl. I wonder what your two lives will be like.

STONOR You needn't be afraid, either for her or for her ardent dreams.

MISS LEVERING (*Smiles faintly*) Shall I tell you a secret? Her 'dreams' needn't frighten you, if she has a child. *That* – from the beginning it was not the strong arm – it was the weakest – the little – little arms that subdued the fiercest of us. (STONOR *stirred at her emotion puts out a pitying hand uncertainly towards her. She does not take it but speaks with great gentleness.*) You will have other children, Geoffrey – for me there was to be only one. (*Turns away*) Well – since men alone have tried and failed to make a decent world for the little children to live in – it's as well some of us are childless. (*Looking into vacancy*) Yes, *we* are the ones who have no excuse for standing aloof from the fight.

STONOR Vida, why should you think that it's only you these ten years have taught something to? Why not give even a man credit for a willingness to learn something of life – and for being sorry – profoundly sorry – for the pain his instruction has cost others. You seem to think I've taken it all quite lightly. That's not fair. All my life, ever since you disappeared, the thought of you has hurt. I would give anything I possess to know you – were happy again. (*With subdued cheerfulness*) And why shouldn't you be?

MISS LEVERING (*With a flash of scorn*) Ah, she couldn't help telling about Allen Trent – Lady John couldn't.

STONOR You're one of the people the years have not taken from but given more to. You are more than ever – you haven't lost your beauty.

MISS LEVERING The Gods saw it was so little effectual, it wasn't worth taking away.

STONOR (*He draws nearer and speaks with genuine feeling.*) You've shown me how little I gave and how much I took away. But I wish you'd give me something more. Let me hear when the day comes that brings happiness your way again. I begin to feel my own happiness won't mean much to me till then.

MISS LEVERING (*Brushes her handkerchief across her eyes*) One woman's mishap? – what is that? A thing as trivial to the great world as it's sordid in most eyes. But the time has come when a woman may look about her, and say: What general significance has my secret pain? Does it 'join on' to anything? And I find it does. I'm no longer merely a woman who has stumbled on the way. (*Looks out into space, controlling with difficulty the shake in her voice*) I'm one who has got up bruised and bleeding, wiped the dust from her hands and the tears from her face, and said to herself not merely: Here's one luckless woman! but – here is a stone of stumbling to many. Let's see if it can't be moved out of other women's way. And she calls people to come and help. No mortal man, let alone a woman, *by herself*, can move that rock of offence. But (*With a sudden sombre flare of enthusiasm*) if many help, Geoffrey, the thing can be done.

STONOR (*Gravely*) I begin to see my own future leading me that way.

MISS LEVERING Ah! (*Rises*)

STONOR The women need a friend.

MISS LEVERING We have four hundred and twenty already. (*Goes to the chair up left centre by the door where her hat and cloak are lying*)

STONOR (*Standing centre hands in pockets looking down at the floor*) But I mean a fighter – a fighter, a leader – one who can pull his party along after him.

MISS LEVERING Ah, if you could do that.

STONOR Why shouldn't I?

MISS LEVERING There's every reason you should – except one.

STONOR What is that?

MISS LEVERING Goodbye – we won't meet
again – But I shall be watching you!
(Ironically) I shall follow your career
with an interest I take in no other man's
– And when I've seen your Resolution –
and heard you support it – then I shall
know whether Woman has found at last
– a friend who doesn't betray her.

STONOR I shall support the cause not
because you or anyone else is watching
– but because I believe in it.

MISS LEVERING We shall see.

(Exit VIDA. STONOR *stands motionless an
instant; turns and walks across the room –
stops, raises his eyes, goes quickly to table
centre, draws the telegraph form to him and
writes as the curtain falls.)*

Curtain

Select bibliography

Cima, G. G. (November 1980) "Elizabeth
Robins: The Genesis of an Independent
Manageress," *Theatre Survey* 21: 145–63.

—— (1993) *Performing Women: Female
Characters, Male Playwrights, and the
Modern Stage*, Ithaca: Cornell University
Press.

Gates, J. E. (1979) "Elizabeth Robins: From
A Dark Lantern to *The Convert* (A Study of
her Fictional Style and Feminist
Viewpoint)," *Massachusetts Studies in
English*, Neglected Authors Double Issue
6, 3 and 4: 25–40.

—— (1988) "Stitches in a Critical Time: The
Diaries of Elizabeth Robins, American
Feminist in England," *A/B: Auto/Biography*
4, 2: 130–39.

—— (1994) *Elizabeth Robins, 1862–1952:
Actress, Novelist, Feminist*, Tuscaloosa and
London: University of Alabama Press.

Holledge, J. (1971) *Innocent Flowers: Women
in the Edwardian Theatre*, London: Virago.

Kennedy, D. (1985) *Granville Barker and the
Dream of Theatre*, Cambridge: Cambridge
University Press.

Raeburn, A. (1973) *The Militant Suffragettes*,
London: Michael Joseph.

—— (1976) *The Suffragette View*, New York:
St. Martin's Press.

Robins, E. (1907) *The Convert*, rpt: 1980, Old
Westbury, NY: Feminist Press.
Introduction by Jane Marcus.

—— (1907) *Votes for Women!* Harley
Granville Barker's Prompt Book of the
Court Theatre Production. Edited (1990,
unpublished), with an Introduction by
Joanne E. Gates.

—— (1913) *Way Stations*, New York: Dodd,
Mead.

Stowell, S. (1992) *A Stage of Their Own:
Feminist Playwrights of the Suffrage Era*,
Ann Arbor: University of Michigan Press.

5 Marie Lenéru, 1875–1918

Woman Triumphant
France

Marie Lenéru at 29 years of age. Reproduced from *Journal de Marie Lenéru*, vol. 2, Paris: G. Cres & Co., 1922.

Introduction

by Melanie C. Hawthorne

The life

"Marie Lenéru" is not a familiar name today, although in early twentieth-century Paris it enjoyed wide recognition. Lenéru was well known as a mainstream playwright, the author of works performed at the prestigious Comédie-Française. It is hard to believe that someone – especially a woman – who achieved such distinction should so quickly be forgotten, but in fact the trajectory of fame followed by oblivion is all too familiar in the careers of women writers.

Marie Lenéru was born in the naval town of Brest in Brittany, France, in 1875. Her father died at sea when she was only ten months old, so she was raised by her mother and her extended middle-class Catholic family.

Through this family, and in particular through her uncle, Lionel Dauriac, who became a professor at the Sorbonne in 1900, Marie was well connected to literary circles in Paris. She moved there from Brest in 1902 and began to publish. In 1905, she published a study of the French revolutionary St.-Just. She later turned to drama, and in 1907, she sent her play *Les Affranchis* (Free Souls) to Catulle Mendès. He became her protector, introduced her to other key figures in the world of theater, and in 1910 the play was performed at the Odéon, an unusual honor for a first play.

The work

Lenéru followed this success with another play at the Odéon, *Le Redoutable* (The

Redoutable). The play, set on board a ship, blends love interest with espionage in a combination that critics compared to the Dreyfus Affair. It opened on January 20, 1912, but suffered from the inevitable comparison with *Les Affranchis*.

Undaunted, Lenéru was soon at work on another play, *La Triomphatrice* (Woman Triumphant), which she aspired to have produced at the Comédie-Française, the leading theatrical company. To get a play accepted, one first had to get a committee to agree to hear a reading of the play, and then decide whether or not to accept it for their repertory. Lenéru used the influence of friends such as Léon Blum to put pressure on the famous actress Bartet to sponsor the play, which she readily agreed to do after she had read it. The committee met on February 9, 1914, to listen to Léon Blum's reading. They agreed to accept the play but made several suggestions for rewriting it, most notably that the third and fourth acts be combined into one. Hence the final version of the play has the classical three-act structure of exposition–crisis–resolution.

The verdict of the committee placed

Lenéru among distinguished company. Some have claimed that she was the first woman since George Sand to have a play produced at the Comédie-Française (see Lavaud 1932: 131). This is not strictly accurate, but it does not diminish Lenéru's achievement to acknowledge that, if not the first since Sand, she was still one of only a handful of women who could claim such distinction.

Unfortunately, before Lenéru's play could be produced, there would be complications. World War I broke out, and Paris theaters were temporarily closed. Eventually they reopened and preparations for *La Triomphatrice* continued, but in the meantime Lenéru had finished another play, *La Paix* (Peace). She wanted to substitute this latter play, far more topical, for the domestic drama of *La Triomphatrice*, but *La Paix* was judged too inflammatory. *La Triomphatrice* therefore opened on January 19, 1918. Despite positive reviews of the acting, the play was misunderstood (Lavaud 1932: 138–9). Times had changed considerably in the four years since the committee had accepted the play, and the issue of careers for women was considerably less important than it had been in the *belle époque* years before the war, as Mary Louise Roberts has recently argued. While World War I led to voting rights for women in Britain and France, French women would not vote until after World War II, and the French feminist movement shifted its emphasis from suffrage (and the related middle-class issue of careers) to the peace movement that embraced the fate of the nation.

Lenéru and pacifism

Lenéru made this shift, as *La Paix* demonstrates. The central character of this prophetic play is Lady Mabel Stanley, a "militant pacifist" (Whitridge 1924: 122). During the war, Stanley works in a hospital, but when it ends, she becomes what today we would call a political activist. She refuses to marry a French general on the grounds that a pacifist cannot marry a soldier, an example that causes a young lieutenant to resign his commission, thereby sacrificing the love of his fiancée. *La Paix* is interesting in a number of ways. Lenéru's choice to make her heroine British suggests the strong

influence of the British suffragist movement. The play also illustrates the asymmetrical experiences World War I offered to men and women, as described by Sandra Gilbert and Susan Gubar (1989). For men, the war was mutilating, as illustrated by the trauma of the lieutenant who discovers that his brother, killed by machine-gun fire, died a long, lingering death. For women, on the other hand, the war was paradoxically empowering. Stanley's work in a hospital gave her an important role, one that avoided entirely the debate about careers for women, and her public role brought her political power.

Marie Lenéru herself was a pacifist, and Natalie Clifford Barney credits her as inspiring her own pacifism (1992: 195). Barney organized a famous series of meetings of feminist pacifists at her Temple à l'amitié in 1917, which Lenéru attended. A pacifist is not the same as an anti-militarist, however. Lenéru's family had supplied naval officers for several generations, and Lenéru was not about to betray these family bonds.

Although Lenéru presciently described the post-World War I period in *La Paix*, she never lived to see the Armistice herself. In May of 1918, Lenéru and her mother fled Paris to escape the bombardment. They went to the port of Lorient, where troop ships brought the 'flu virus that spread in a deadly epidemic. Lenéru was one of its early victims; she died on September 23, 1918.

Assessments of Lenéru's achievement

One of the reasons Lenéru's career frequently arouses interest is that she accomplished so much in spite of the fact that she was completely deaf and virtually blind. (One of her earliest publications was an essay on Helen Keller.) Her deafness occurred as the result of childhood illness, and she was also plagued by eye problems which threatened her sight. She read slowly with the help of a magnifying glass. Reactions to her handicaps vary from astonishment that she could overcome them to an interest in her example of suffering (see Weinreis, for instance). It certainly was unusual for a woman to achieve such success, but it might also be that her handicaps made it easier for the public to accept her anomalous position as a successful woman playwright.

Lenéru enjoyed a second, posthumous, career in the 1920s. The wave of popularity began with the publication of her *Journal* in the *Revue de France* in 1921. Several of her plays were also published posthumously, including *La Triomphatrice*, which was published in 1922, along with the republication of her work on St.-Just. In 1925, Lenéru's remains were moved from Lorient to her home town of Brest, and a group of her friends began campaigning for the Comédie-Française to adopt *Les Affranchis*, and in 1927 it was indeed taken up. The critics were harsher in 1927 than they had been in 1910, but the play received widespread critical attention, a more telling indication of its importance. As Lavaud notes, only banal works are received with indifference (1932: 194). That same year, 1927, Natalie Barney devoted one of her Friday salons to a retrospective of Lenéru's work. Critical attention trickled in throughout the years, with the first book-length study – by Suzanne Lavaud – appearing in 1932. Writing in *Le Figaro* in 1927, another "forgotten" woman writer, Gérard d'Houville, offered a prophetic assessment of Lenéru's work: "Given another quarter of a century, this play [*Les Affranchis*] may appear surprisingly representative of one moment in the history of mores and matters of the heart" (quoted in Lavaud (1932: 196).

Lenéru's works continue to find readers not only because people wonder what someone deaf and blind could write, but because she created strong, vibrant characters and challenging moral dilemmas. Her plays frequently touch on women's issues, such as the question of careers in *La Triomphatrice* and pacifism in *La Paix*. *La Triomphatrice* foregrounds the twin themes of careers for women and the problems of the woman writer. These were popular topics of debate, since the Third Republic (which began in 1870) saw great strides in education, reform, and employment to the benefit of women. As Maugue and Perrot have shown, by 1906, 38.9 per cent of all women worked outside the home (including 20.2 per cent of married women), and the public perceived that women were advancing rapidly in the professions. In 1903, for example, there were already ninety-five

women doctors (the first M.D. granted to a French woman had been conferred only in 1875, the year of Lenéru's birth). Naturally, the question found its way into novels, and *La Triomphatrice* was compared to the novels of writers such as Colette Yver (Lavaud 1932: 135). Lenéru exposes the problems of women writers – it is hard to balance professional and personal life – but, as is characteristic of the "theater of ideas" school she followed, the exposition of the problem avoids assigning blame.

Woman Triumphant

Part of the interpretation of *La Triomphatrice* hinges on whether the character of Claude is autobiographical. Some critics have denied that Lenéru put anything of herself into her plays, but it remains difficult to overlook the evidence. The speech given to Claude in Act I, for example, in which she describes her struggles to become a woman writer is lifted directly from Lenéru's *Journal* for June 7, 1903:

> I arrived, like the Sibyl, at a time when I had all my future books in my hand. I was denied the prize, and three were thrown on the fire. With what was left, I made the same demands, and, faced with refusal, three more were burned. The Sibyl received the prize she had expected for all of them for the last three.
>
> (p. 217)

Regardless of the degree of autobiography, the play demands admiration for its rigorous construction. The first and last scenes represent the aspiring writer Miss Haller being received by the established woman of letters, Claude Bersier. At the beginning of the play, Claude encourages the young woman, while the same scene is replayed at the close of the play with a twist: Claude is now cold and discouraging. To Miss Haller, the change in Claude is inexplicable; the only difference Miss Haller is aware of is that in the meantime, Claude has been awarded the Nobel prize for literature. These two parallel scenes in which the audience sees Claude through the eyes of the public (Miss Haller) function like parentheses that enclose the rest of the play, depicting the private life dramas that explain the otherwise inexplicable change in Claude. While the public figure of the writer reaches the pinnacle of success, the private person descends into tragedy: her marriage unravels, she loses her lover, and her daughter runs away from home, all, so it seems, as a result of her writing. No wonder Claude tries to discourage Miss Haller from following in her footsteps.

Lenéru has been forgotten not only because she was a woman in a society that valued maleness but because the period in which she worked and the movement with which she was associated have been overshadowed by the long and dark shadows cast by subsequent theatrical movements. Lenéru was part of a school, led by her inspiration and mentor François de Curel, that called itself "the theater of ideas." It was not an experimental school, but a return to classicism after the excesses of the symbolist movement that dominated the end of the nineteenth century. The theater of ideas placed a debate on stage in which an insoluble problem was created to test the basically likeable and rational characters. (One critic has suggested that this staging of a public debate was Lenéru's revenge on her deafness.) But this brief moment of classicism was already in decline by the 1920s, a period which saw the beginnings of Artaud's "theater of cruelty" which inspired other modern theatrical developments such as existentialism and the absurd. Playwrights of the caliber of Sartre, Genet, Camus, Beckett, and Ionesco have dominated the picture of twentieth-century French drama, drawing the limelight away from numerous others who have remained in the shadows. To recognize Lenéru's talent is not to dilute aesthetic criteria but to recognize a talented playwright whose work has been over-looked.

Woman Triumphant

1914
Play translation by Melanie C. Hawthorne

Marie Lenéru

Characters (listed in order of appearance)

MISS HALLER

CLAUDE BERSIER ("Maître")

JEAN FLAHAUT

M. BRÉMONT

DENISE BERSIER, daughter of Claude

HENRI BERSIER, husband of Claude

MICHEL SORRÈZE, lover of Claude

CORALIE

AN AMERICAN

SERVANT

Act I

In the large office of Claude Bersier. It should convey immensity through height and depth. A forest of books. Cathedral-like nuances from the illuminated stained glass behind and oriental carpets.

Scene 1

CLAUDE, MISS HALLER

CLAUDE, *behind her ministerial table. Molded by a short black "princess"-style dress (a tight bodice with a full skirt), she looks like a young woman. Fashionable hairstyle, a tiny "Légion d'Honneur" rosette.*

CLAUDE   Well yes, you have talent, Miss Haller, and you will even have more. But, really, I don't know if I should encourage you to work. . . . Do you need to do this to live?

MISS HALLER   To live, yes. To subsist, no.

CLAUDE   Let's be clear. Do you have a dowry?

MISS HALLER   The kind you don't get married on, yes.

CLAUDE   Would it be indiscreet to ask who you are?

MISS HALLER   Oh! Mrs. Bersier, it's so kind of you to enquire. . . . The daughter of a former consul in Prague.

CLAUDE   *(All these questions are asked quickly.)* How old are you?

MISS HALLER   Twenty-six.

CLAUDE   Well! my dear child, as I was saying, the details aren't bad, and the style is already well-developed. . . . You have done some reading and you knew how to benefit from it. Sometimes that's worth more than having lived: yes, yes, when one lives, it's always a little at a time, and one overestimates, one hypnotizes oneself. It's very good to write as a disinterested party, especially for us *(Laughing)*. That teaches us to look at other women.

MISS HALLER   So I can continue?

CLAUDE   Keep an eye on your overall plan, compose, think of the public. . . . Already, if you cut out one or two chapters, I could perhaps talk to my publisher.

MISS HALLER   Oh! Mrs. Bersier, please don't think. . . . I didn't come to ask you a favor! It was just so wonderful to be read, encouraged by you. . . . We all admire you so much, we are so happy, so proud of your glory. . . .

CLAUDE   *(Cutting her off)* Don't you have anything else to show me?

MISS HALLER   No, nothing. Nothing I would care to show you but there will be, I promise you, there will be.

CLAUDE   *(Standing up to end the visit)* Well, we'll see, we'll examine it together. . . . but you will have to work, work regularly . . . not too much, not too little. . . . two hours a day, that's enough for you, since you have no mercenary tasks. . . . One can only work well when one feels at rest.

151

MISS HALLER But you work six hours a day!

CLAUDE Unless it's at night. But I'm writing copy, it's hackwork. I have a daughter to endow, you know.

MISS HALLER (With conviction) Jérôme Tiersot was not hackwork.

CLAUDE (Somewhat melancholically) That was a long time ago. . . .

MISS HALLER They say you have a book coming out in May.

CLAUDE (Smiling) Well, you'll tell me if it's as good as Jérôme.

MISS HALLER Your series in Débats and the Figaro are fascinating!

CLAUDE When you do this job, it won't fascinate you any more . . . my poor child, you have to do what you must, I am the man and the woman here . . . my husband, a former cavalry officer with no fortune . . . it's the deadly boredom of garrisons and a healthy impatience with our poverty that threw me into literature.

MISS HALLER Happy venality!

CLAUDE If we knew all the motives, the origins. . . . Writing is not as natural as you would think . Nature doesn't make blue-stockings. (Looking at her intently) Even you, yes, even you, if you were completely satisfied with your existence. . . .

MISS HALLER (Correcting her) I couldn't be satisfied by what it offered me.

CLAUDE (Laughing) I didn't mean that it has totally neglected you. . . .

MISS HALLER I have tried to be worth more than what existence was offering me.

CLAUDE (Brusquely) So you want me to like you?

(A young man enters familiarly, without a hat, cane, or gloves.)

Scene 2

The same, FLAHAUT

CLAUDE (Introducing them) Jean Flahaut, the author of The Barbarians, the last Goncourt prize-winner.

MISS HALLER (With a start) Ah! really, I'm delighted. . . . The Barbarians is very beautiful.

FLAHAUT You've read it then?

CLAUDE Remember the name Miss Haller. . . . You'll like what she writes. She will have talent like you and me.

FLAHAUT (To the young woman) And she knows what she's talking about. It's incredible the number of women who drop in every day here. Just because Claude Bersier is a lady, they think they are entitled to her patronage . . . well, this is the first time I've found her like this with a beginner.

BRÉMONT (Having entered, goes to greet CLAUDE and FLAHAUT who don't pay the slightest attention) Hello dear maitre. Well, so it's you, Flahaut?

MISS HALLER How good of you to tell me all that, and I just thought she was being nice.

CLAUDE Nice? Me? But I don't want to be nice, do you understand, I don't want to. Nothing is worse for people. Never say that I am nice!

FLAHAUT All right, you're a beast. When someone doesn't have talent you're a real lout.

CLAUDE (Crossing in front of the armchair where BRÉMONT is seated and turning her back on him pointedly) If someone brought you twenty manuscripts a month, Flahaut, and if, in those two thousand pages, you had never, never been able to discover, I won't say a writer, but just a living creature, with eyes, ears, a soul . . . or quite simply a body.

BRÉMONT (Seated) I'm telling you, I've accepted one manuscript in five years. (No one seems to hear him.)

FLAHAUT Yes, you have to teach them everything. We are the ones who give them sight, hearing, smell. . . . We are the ones who give them their love interests and even their sensuality.

CLAUDE (Thinking) Perhaps not. But there's really an incredible loss of intelligence as soon as one begins the writer's trade. One is always better than what one has done.

BRÉMONT That's very true.

FLAHAUT and HALLER (Together) Oh, no! Not you!

CLAUDE (Laughing) You are kind, what do you know about it? . . . Besides in fact I don't care. I'll leave some decent work. Materially speaking, and even from the point of view of glory, I've extracted from people everything they could give. . . . In the final analysis, that's what I wanted from them. . . . If it weren't for that, I would have been quite happy to live out my thoughts without writing.

BRÉMONT There is still the dream, the work of art to be realized.

CLAUDE *(Who, for the first time, seems to hear him)* The dream, the dream . . . oh! come on! The dream is to live. . . . We are not potters by predestination, machinists whose purpose is to produce well-made parts. It is miserable enough as it is to lock oneself up, to isolate oneself, to recollect one's life painfully, while life is there passing by our door without us. God preserve me from the writer who believes "that it happened" and who takes his "œuvre" tragically.

MISS HALLER You should take your own, however, with a certain seriousness.

CLAUDE Not at all. I'm doing this because women hardly have a choice. I was never very studious, myself, I was one of the active ones, one of the livelier ones. Sometimes I really reproach myself for the books I won't have read, the countries I won't have seen, the people I won't have known, because of these hours shut in a room, hidden hours, these hours which are wrong, no doubt, where I interrupt my short life for some imitation, for some false. . . .

FLAHAUT Oh! come on, don't turn off others! We need writers to savor life, to appreciate books, countries, and even people!

MISS HALLER It's odd. I never saw anyone so unliterary as literary people. Imagine listening to Claude Bersier disdain the writer's state!

CLAUDE Well, yes, it will always bother me to be a "novelist." You surely don't believe it's pleasant to read on your address the label "woman of letters"!

FLAHAUT *(Annoyed)* Then give up writing and don't associate with writers!

BRÉMONT Aren't you forgetting about glory!

CLAUDE *(Furious)* Oh! you, for once you're on target.

BRÉMONT I thought you knew what it was. Since you have courted it, too.

CLAUDE Why can't you be quiet, dear Brémont? Glory, "courting glory," no one uses clichés like that in my house. Glory? The admiration that everyone has for me in their own way, you mean? Brrr. . . .

BRÉMONT But there lies posterity. . . .

CLAUDE Absolutely not, it isn't in that. And this misconception is so important to me that I still prefer the most beastly of my contemporaries, one I have seen turn green with envy, to the most devoted celebrant of my centenary. If it would make my books more beautiful, I would agree that not one of them should survive more than an hour.

FLAHAUT So, my dear *maître*, why do you write and who for?

CLAUDE *(Seriously)* For you, Flahaut.

FLAHAUT You're right, we all write, we all live for each other.

BRÉMONT We also write for ourselves.

CLAUDE Come on! Do you think if I were alone on earth, I would write stories and novels? If no one were to read it, not even a diary, I assure you.

MISS HALLER I must be leaving, Madam, so glad I came. . . .

CLAUDE So, you'll come back?

MISS HALLER *(Laughing, happily)* All too often!

CLAUDE Never too often if, from time to time, you bring me something as good as that. *(She glances at the manuscript on her desk.)*

MISS HALLER I was forgetting to take it with me.

CLAUDE No, no, I need it, I'm keeping it. I hope that doesn't bother you?

MISS HALLER *(Leaving)* Good heavens! As far as I'm concerned, it has fulfilled its purpose. *(CLAUDE exits with her.)*

Scene 3

FLAHAUT, BRÉMONT

BRÉMONT *(to FLAHAUT, who is leafing through a book)* She can say what she likes, she's not rude enough.

FLAHAUT *(Ironically)* You think so?

BRÉMONT People bother her from morning till night.

FLAHAUT *(Not looking up from his book)* I couldn't agree more.

BRÉMONT She doesn't get anything done any more. Ever since *Jérôme*, she hasn't produced anything.

FLAHAUT Let's see what she does in May. We'll see the book.

BRÉMONT It took her three years to get through it. . . . There are always thirty people around her.

FLAHAUT *(Acerbically)* Like us, for example, so I wonder what we're doing here?

153

BRÉMONT   Oh! intimate friends, followers. . . .

FLAHAUT   Are you an imitator of Claude?

BRÉMONT   Come on, nobody imitates any more. But it's understood that she is the master, the leader of the young generation. . . . As for you, you derive more from Michel Sorrèze.

FLAHAUT   (To himself) Indeed! There's only the two of them.

BRÉMONT   Bersier is stronger.

FLAHAUT   No, and she's lucky, because, after all, she's a woman and I imagine that in these cases it must be cruel to expect nothing better than oneself.

BRÉMONT   Still she's ten years younger than him. The day he's finished she'll still be going strong. . . .

FLAHAUT   Bah! Sorrèze has climbed so high . . . he can look down on her.

BRÉMONT   Do you believe in that love affair? (Shrugging) Literature . . .

FLAHAUT   It's all they've got, and I imagine they're just like everybody else.

BRÉMONT   Sorrèze thought he owed it to himself to have the best there was in women, of every kind.

FLAHAUT   Claude is the last . . . she arrived rather late.

BRÉMONT   She knew how to make him wait for her. . . . They say she could have preceded Princess Czarhedine.

FLAHAUT   (With a certain bitterness) In any case, on her side, no one preceded Sorrèze.

BRÉMONT   Come on! What about Fréville?

FLAHAUT   Never.

BRÉMONT   Fréville wouldn't have killed himself. . . .

FLAHAUT   (Feverishly) Fréville told me a week before his death: what you lose, you've had. But what you lack, what you'll always lack, the thing no one realizes you have been denied, that's what brings ruin and catastrophe.

BRÉMONT   Fréville had talent. . . . In your place, I would simply ask Claude the truth.

FLAHAUT   I don't care to know it.

BRÉMONT   (After a moment) And then, your disdain for glory. . . . Come on! If someone told her that she was not going to walk off with the Nobel prize. . . .

FLAHAUT   195,000 francs.

BRÉMONT   195,000 francs. Yes, but in the meantime, Sorrèze is getting agitated; he was so disdainful up till now. . . .

Scene 4

The same, CLAUDE

CLAUDE   She is very nice . . . she seems like a well-brought-up woman.

FLAHAUT   And you don't come across many of those among us, eh my dear *maître?* Basically, you cannot forgive us for bringing you down in the world. . . .

BRÉMONT   You are getting a reputation for snobbery.

CLAUDE   They are right, I'm very snobbish. . . . I like things that are refined, elegant, removed. . . . I like rare flowers and thoroughbred animals, the manners of certain cavalry officers (To FLAHAUT) and the allure of your style.

FLAHAUT   Well, that harms you, my dear *maître.* . . . Oh! if you were one of the boys, if you addressed me informally, if you dressed as a man, and if you smoked like George Sand . . .

CLAUDE   But, I beg your pardon, I do smoke. (She passes the box of cigarettes to the others and lights one.)

FLAHAUT   Yes, but too simply, you smoke quietly . . . and you dress like everyone else! No "personal cachet," no "individual flair." Your dresses are fashionable and they suit you.

CLAUDE   I am a Philistine!

BRÉMONT   Did you like my article, Madam?

CLAUDE   Ah! yes, you sent it to me. . . . Thank you. . . . You say that I don't have any temperament.

BRÉMONT   (Frightened) I said that? You must be getting mixed up.

CLAUDE   Yes indeed, that was in another article . . . six weeks ago, another one that you didn't send me.

BRÉMONT   I have been unjustly accused, my dear *maître.*

CLAUDE   Don't keep calling me that! Flahaut, too, he thinks it's a sign of success. . . . I have never been able to take it upon myself to call a man thus. . . You can say "Madam." (Ironically) I am a woman of the world! Come along, say "goodbye, Madam."

BRÉMONT   (Bowing, pretentiously) Goodbye, Madam, and my most revered *maître.*

CLAUDE   (After he has left) Really, why does he come to see me? I have never asked him, I receive him badly, he can't like my books, I'll never be useful to him for anything.

FLAHAUT First, he is much too comfortable with you to need to be told to come. To imagine that you receive him badly he would need more self-doubt than he is likely to acquire any time soon. Your books? He is not even guilty of incomprehension: he hasn't read them. Finally, you are wrong and you are useful to him. He speaks ill or well of you, whichever, he isn't malicious, an echo is an echo, he gets paid the same either way.

CLAUDE Well then! Let him come. Anyway, I don't know what it would take to stop him.

FLAHAUT Besides, you know, his echoes . . . he isn't the only one. There's going to be an article on you in the *Revue de France*.

CLAUDE Another one. . . .

FLAHAUT An article by me.

CLAUDE Flahaut, that's the third one this year. You're not doing anything new.

FLAHAUT Say rather that I'm being methodical and showing continuity: "Claude Bersier and Style," "Claude Bersier and Women," . . .

CLAUDE And now?

FLAHAUT "Claude Bersier and Man."

CLAUDE That will be instructive.

FLAHAUT May I read it to you?

CLAUDE Well, since things have calmed down, go ahead.

FLAHAUT I didn't bring it with me: give me an appointment.

CLAUDE Have lunch with me tomorrow.

FLAHAUT With pleasure, my dear *maitre*, it's so pleasant here!

CLAUDE Well . . . that's a new refrain.

FLAHAUT You must be joking, it seems to me I spend plenty of time at your house.

CLAUDE You have done me the honor of cultivating me a great deal. But this time, my dear, if I heard you correctly, it's not your patron's house that you just complimented . . . it's a woman's house.

FLAHAUT Really? Is that what I led you to think. . . .

CLAUDE You looked like a nice house cat warming itself by my fire. . . . I'm going to re-read your first letters, when you were pontificating so rashly about marriage and about women. . . .

FLAHAUT So do you really think I'll let you marry me off?

CLAUDE Once upon a time, you believed in marrying young.

FLAHAUT I still do, in principle. . . .

CLAUDE I would like to see you rich. . . . Would you like a million, Flahaut? A very pretty girl . . . not mine.

FLAHAUT *(Lightly)* Too bad! . . . now don't go speaking ill of my good friend Denise. Let me tell you she is very pretty.

CLAUDE *(In the same light tone)* Denise isn't a good enough match for you.

FLAHAUT *(The same)* As a match, I beg you to believe I couldn't dream of better.

CLAUDE *(Laughing)* Don't tempt me, Flahaut, you're pushing politeness too far. *(Becoming serious once again, but as though she were changing the subject)* Denise is twenty. Unfortunately, I can only give her 200,000 francs, but while I'm alive I'll add an allowance of 20,000.

FLAHAUT *(Parenthetically)* You earn a lot of money, my dear *maitre*.

CLAUDE I work hard, more than would be necessary for glory. . . . I like luxury, and we had nothing. . . . Besides, it's for glory, too. . . . through sheer repetition. . . . If George Sand had been a woman of few books. . . . It's good to be an author who churns out paper. *(To her daughter, who opens a door, gaily)* Denise! what are you doing here?

Scene 5

CLAUDE, FLAHAUT, DENISE

DENISE Oh! Mother, I thought you were still alone.

CLAUDE It's Jean Flahaut, you can come in.

DENISE I didn't recognize him. *(To* FLAHAUT*)* Hello, Mr. Flahaut, when are you going to tell Mother to make me read your book?

FLAHAUT Why do you want to do that?

DENISE I'm dying to! And besides if you didn't read your friends' books. . . .

FLAHAUT Nothing could be more unnecessary, I assure you.

CLAUDE *(Roughly)* It's not for you. You wouldn't understand any of it.

DENISE You always tell me the same thing, even about yours. *(To* FLAHAUT*)* You can't imagine how backward the upbringing in this house is. Would you believe I have read nothing by Mother?

FLAHAUT I'll loan you her books.

CLAUDE *(Laughing)* If you accept full responsibility.

DENISE Come on, Mother, are you really as rigid as that?

CLAUDE (*Laughingly*) Oh! I'm not rigid: I'm worse than that.

FLAHAUT (*Smiling*) So Claude Bersier is a narrow-minded mother?

CLAUDE (*To her daughter*) What have you got there?

DENISE (*Quickly*) Nothing at all, Mother, I'll tell you later.

CLAUDE (*Taking a roll of paper from her*) A manuscript . . . a manuscript by you!

DENISE (*In agony*) No, Mother, no, I assure you.

CLAUDE Admit it, it's the smartest thing you can do. (*Highly amused*) Flahaut, a manuscript by my daughter!

DENISE Mother, you're cruel, don't show him!

CLAUDE (*Scanning the manuscript*) Ah! rest assured . . . no one will see this.

DENISE You're discouraging. . . . Why shouldn't I write literature like everyone else?

CLAUDE If you want to write literature like everyone else, you can take your laborious scribbling to the shop across the road. . . .

DENISE But Mother, with your name. . . . Your publisher would take me at once.

CLAUDE (*To* FLAHAUT) That's what she thinks!

FLAHAUT Denise, don't try this job. If you knew what trouble Claude Bersier and Michel Sorrèze went to get me published.

DENISE That didn't stop you getting the Goncourt prize.

CLAUDE Perhaps there is only one way to cure her, and that's to let her try it. I'll give you my card: "Claude Bersier warmly recommends a friend, Miss Denise Bersier."

DENISE But Mother, you're always telling us that we have only what you earn. Papa says that without you, we would be living under the eaves and making our own clothes. . . .

CLAUDE Do you want to be responsible for providing your own wardrobe?

DENISE I'd like to try.

CLAUDE Then become a milliner or a seamstress.

DENISE I prefer literature.

CLAUDE Flahaut, this is my punishment!

FLAHAUT Well, Miss Denise, why don't you show me what you're doing? I'll advise you.

DENISE Would you really do that?

FLAHAUT After all, you are the daughter of my master, I don't see why you shouldn't have some talent.

CLAUDE (*Giving the manuscript back to her daughter*) Are you quite determined to give it to him?

DENISE (*With defiance and solemnity*) I have as much confidence in him as in you, Mother.

CLAUDE (*Happily*) Ah! Flahaut, Flahaut . . . give her novel a good going-over for her, and try to make something out of it. . . . Here, go into the salon, both of you, and let me work.

DENISE (*Exiting with the young man*) Mr. Flahaut, as you'll see, it's an attempt at a psychological study.

(CLAUDE *follows them affectionately with her eyes and laughs softly while rubbing her hands. She is beginning to work when the doors opens.*)

Scene 6

CLAUDE, HENRI BERSIER

HENRI Are you working, Claude, am I disturbing you?

CLAUDE My morning is shot . . . no more disturbances . . . catch up tonight. . . .

HENRI You're working yourself too hard, it's absurd.

CLAUDE And the money?

HENRI We could easily spend half as much.

CLAUDE A dowry for Denise. . . .

HENRI There, my friend, I cannot help you . . . You earn exactly six times as much as my salary. . . . I suppose you think that's funny.

CLAUDE You have saved face, since personally you never agreed to owe me anything . . . so what is it to you if I earn the extra?

HENRI (*Muttering*) Denise's dowry, an extra? This 8,000-franc apartment, an extra, these servants and these entertaining expenses? . . .

CLAUDE If you had married a rich woman. . . .

HENRI (*Quickly*) It wouldn't have been the same thing! It would have been her father's money, or her grandfather's . . . a man's money.

CLAUDE Let's go back to the rue Notre-Dame-des-Champs.

HENRI *(Aggressively)* You loved me back then.

CLAUDE Do you miss those times?

HENRI *(Curtly)* Yes.

CLAUDE At least you're not going to pretend that it was for love of me.

HENRI As if the break-up wasn't your idea! *(CLAUDE remains silent.)* You were cynical. . . . Ah! don't talk to me about feminism . . . and you didn't even have a lover!

CLAUDE Is this what you came here to tell me, thinking you would disturb me?

HENRI You were just saying your morning was "shot". . . .

CLAUDE You aren't going to reproach me with my freedom.. it's been that way for ten years.

HENRI You can't trick a woman out of her freedom if she earns more than you. . . .

CLAUDE *(Annoyed)* Frankly, Henri, could you take your pride somewhere else? Do you want me to give up my royalties?

HENRI That's not the issue.

CLAUDE What then? I imagine it's not about your regrets. . . . Unless I'm mistaken, you hardly find me attractive, my personality horrifies you. . . . it is only out of revenge, out of masculine pride. . . .

HENRI Admit that that would be a start.

CLAUDE Not enough to upset the balance we have both committed ourselves to . . . and I assure you that, for some time, you have been restraining yourself less, your bad moods have been harder to tolerate. . . . Why don't you want to be good friends? I like you, Henri, I really do, because of the past.

HENRI It lasted for such a short time. You withdrew as soon as you believed in yourself.

CLAUDE *(With a sigh)* As soon as I thought our love . . .

HENRI It lasted you for a while. . . . I don't want to be disagreeable to you, my dear Claude, but for a few years, it is very probable that you loved me.

CLAUDE I think so too. . . . I was so different then.

HENRI I admit I've never really understood what happened.

CLAUDE If you had understood, we wouldn't have come to this. . . . Besides, you made your choice very elegantly, you quickly saw the advantages of the situation and since, obviously, I pleased you less and less. . . .

HENRI You did everything necessary for that. . . .

CLAUDE *(With serious softness)* Yes, I became more intelligent, more active and more balanced. I lost my apathy, my yawning and bad moods. . . . I didn't like boring conversations any more. . . .

HENRI So it was because I bored you?

CLAUDE No, quite the contrary, it was I who no longer amused you.

HENRI As I recall, I wasn't complaining?

CLAUDE I arranged it so that you had no cause . . .

HENRI How so?

CLAUDE By keeping quiet. . . . Oh! you didn't notice. You thought: Claude is exhausted, she is self-absorbed, she works too hard, when really I was biting my tongue to keep everything from coming out. *(Almost gaily)* Oh! what a disastrous meal, I remember! You criticized me for eating too fast. . . .

HENRI In a quarter of an hour . . . you were hurrying the staff. . . .

CLAUDE I was never so alive and never was expansion more forbidden to me. Oh! the joy of words spurting out and of laughter confidently shared! I was living in silence, the silence of old women. . . .

HENRI Lord! I would have been quite incapable of talking literature to you.

CLAUDE "Literature," it's true. . . . You think people "talk literature" like they talk Chinese. . . . When it comes down to it, I think we never exchanged many words, but I was the only one who noticed. And all the words I had to choke back, swallow, repress forever, like you repress tears, little by little they become cries, suffocation, anger, despair. I spent my days defending myself, keeping to myself, refusing you my soul, and even my carefree moments which were no longer yours, and at night you wanted . . . ah! wait, I should keep quiet again. *(Gathering herself, mastering herself)* I would have liked to be forgiven, to be a friend, be useful to you. . . . I didn't have the idiocy, my dear Henri, to hold a grudge against you, to think I was misunderstood. . . . It was up to me to understand. *(Softly)* That's what I did. *(A pause)* I forced myself by leading a discrete life. . . .

HENRI At first, I grant you, while . . . yes, I admit for seven years . . . but after!

CLAUDE Oh! excuse me. . . . You know it's a subject that can't be broached. We've dealt with it once and for all, loyally and clearly, we've discussed divorce. . . .

HENRI I would have opposed it with all my might.

CLAUDE I don't even know why. . . .

HENRI You're forgetting that I wasn't the only obstacle. Sorrèze is married too.

CLAUDE (Softly) Please. . . . Yes, there too a woman put her foot down. . . . We obeyed. . . .

HENRI You find such words!

CLAUDE Do you think it would have been enough for us to get together for the world to have applauded us. . . . Without love, without any reason, without conviction, two beings held us back . . . refused, even though it was time, to start their life over again somewhere else they preferred to the normal home, to the happy home they still could have created, their hatred for two creatures of another race, with whom they should have had nothing in common.

HENRI (Stiffly) Your duty was to remain with your daughter.

CLAUDE You know we could have come to some arrangement.

HENRI You'll never marry Sorrèze so long as I live.

CLAUDE Your spite will last forever, then?

HENRI I'd like to see you in my place!

CLAUDE I wouldn't have stayed in it.

HENRI It's too easy to get rid of the one in the way (Misogynistically) women, God forgive me, will know no limits.

CLAUDE So you stayed on principle?

HENRI I stayed because it pleased me to stay in my own home. I stayed because women don't yet repudiate their husbands . . . because I took your maidenhood and with my backward ideas, I feel responsible for you. . . .

CLAUDE (Standing) Say what you like . . . but leave out the hypocrisy!

HENRI You strayed from the path while under my roof, therefore I was a guilty husband, I didn't know how to keep an eye on you.

CLAUDE (With a loud bitter laugh) In a word, you are waiting for the return of the prodigal child to open your arms.

HENRI (In whom a vague feeling of revenge is rising up) A person can't go on showing off forever. . . . There comes a day when the masterpieces are less frequent, when the brain slows down.

CLAUDE You are waiting for softening and final penitence?

HENRI (With hostility) I demand to see the end.

CLAUDE God! All this is so base. . . . (She masters herself) Henri you didn't come here just to hurt me. Are you going out? Aren't you staying for lunch?

HENRI No, exactly, I came to let you know. . . . Excuse me. . . .

CLAUDE Well, on your way out, go through the salon. You'll find something nice there. Denise and Flahaut are working together on a manuscript by your daughter. Eh? Flahaut. . . . Didn't I do well?

HENRI You absolutely insist on marrying her to a literary type?

CLAUDE They are still the ones I know the best. Flahaut will go far, everything about him is distinguished, and he's a volunteer, a trooper.

HENRI It's really all your business. . . . Denise is young.

CLAUDE But Flahaut is too, and I'm afraid to wait. Better to snare him right away, when I know he's free as air. I've seen him every day these last few months . . . he's a charming boy. As a writer, he'll soon be worth the lot of us.

HENRI (Ironically) You are the head of the family, your daughter owes you everything.

CLAUDE Your insistence is in poor taste . . . well, go and see them and please take note of Flahaut's handsome face.

HENRI (Leaving) Another time, I'm really late.

CLAUDE (Hearing the bell ring) Fine! I won't have a minute's peace to work this morning.

Scene 7

CLAUDE, SORRÈZE

CLAUDE (With relief and happiness) Ah! (She goes to the visitor, takes his hand, and holds it to her lips.)

SORRÈZE (Forty-eight, in general the stereotype of a worldly man. But as for his face, it is intelligent to the point of suffering, to the point of neurosis.) Are you working?

CLAUDE Oh, God no! my book is finished
. . . just some copy to churn out.

SORRÈZE *(With sadness)* How I hate seeing
you do that. . . . Work for yourself,
Claude.

CLAUDE *(Melancholically)* You can see
perfectly well that in three years I have
completed one book . . . it used to take
me six months. . . . Bah! I no longer feel
the need to work.

SORRÈZE You'll never make me believe
that.

CLAUDE I'm doing fine without it, I assure
you, ever since. . . .

SORRÈZE Ever since?

CLAUDE Ever since I found happiness.

SORRÈZE *(With a hint of teasing)* And when
did you find happiness?

CLAUDE *(Seriously)* Three years ago.

SORRÈZE *(Impressed)* Only three years ago.
It's enough to make you shiver when you
look back. . . .

CLAUDE Don't be ungrateful towards my
predecessors.

SORRÈZE No, Claude . . . since they gave
me a sense of distance. *(CLAUDE makes a
movement.)* Rest assured, I won't say I
never loved anyone but you, but this love
is the culmination of my life, a love so
incomparable that it can face the past . . .
a past more unbearable in our eyes than
fatigue.

CLAUDE Michel! . . . and you want me to
produce literature, to take care of the life,
the needs, the loves of others . . . when I
have to avenge your past and mine!

SORRÈZE What would posterity say about
me if Claude Bersier's talent disappeared
on the day she fell in love with me. . . .

CLAUDE Posterity would say that you
undoubtedly changed her fate into that of
a happy woman.

SORRÈZE I shall make it a point of duty to
make you suffer so as to bring you back
in line. . . .

CLAUDE Go ahead, I challenge you!

SORRÈZE *(With curiosity)* Really? you
challenge me to make you suffer? You
told me that once . . . before you were . . .
what you were to become . . . when I
tried to make you jealous. . . .

CLAUDE *(Very seriously)* There is one
woman I am jealous of, however.

SORRÈZE Who?

CLAUDE Your wife.

SORRÈZE Ah! poor Claude. . . .

CLAUDE You yourself don't know everything you are to her. . . . Don't you see,
this woman who lives with you, whom
you kiss mechanically goodmorning and
goodnight, whose face is inseparable from
your past . . . this woman you call Marie
and who comes running for some lost
item or rumpled clothes. . . .

SORRÈZE Are you really jealous of that,
Claude, when you have all the energy of
the living person, when we have put all
our talent, which isn't small, into
penetrating each other's soul, into
possessing each other's heart and mind?

CLAUDE She will have been more than me!

SORRÈZE Dear Claude, aren't we, even in
the eyes of others, linked, blended
together? If one of us takes the path of
immortality, won't we both go down the
centuries shoulder to shoulder the way
we are now? *(He leans heavily on her.)*

CLAUDE I sometimes wonder if I haven't
been too scrupulous . . . if I shouldn't
have snatched you from the past, pitted
one marriage against another, home
against home. . . . We are among those
who can overcome anything.

SORRÈZE No, Claude, everything is better
this way . . . we must spare the weak. . . .
We were too strong.

CLAUDE They don't hate us any the less.
Perhaps they feel the daily insult even
more.

SORRÈZE I make every effort to mitigate
it. . . .

CLAUDE What about me? If you knew what
a comrade, what a friend I am to that
man who hates me and is jealous. The
wife and companion to which he had no
right, I let him have her as much as I
can. . . . I exert myself in the home the
way some wives do in society. If it
weren't for his vanity that suffers, he
should be happy.

SORRÈZE Sophist! You're just being a
sophist, Claude.

CLAUDE Oh! let's not talk about this any
more. Tell me the news about your book.

SORRÈZE No doubt it will come out at the
same time as yours. They have already
been announced.

CLAUDE Leaks . . . we can't do anything
about them. Do you think we are right to
appear together?

SORRÈZE That's up to our publishers. I
don't see what harm it could do.

CLAUDE Flahaut told me that it bothered you. Do you want me to tell them to wait until October?

SORRÈZE In that case, my friend, I would let you go first, but there is no problem with people talking about us together. That won't change their habits.

CLAUDE Are you quite ready?

SORRÈZE (Defensively) Yes, Claude. . . . (After a moment) Are you sorry? Admit that you don't like that book.

CLAUDE Less than the others.

SORRÈZE Honestly . . . is it good, yes or no?

CLAUDE Michel, some will say yes, some no. I won't be among them. All the same, it has your style . . . your style that attacks the mind, while other things attack the heart. . . . But I don't like your characters, I don't like their atmosphere, I don't like. . . .

SORRÈZE (Kissing her) Enough, enough! Besides, I have cause for complaint, too. (CLAUDE raises her head.) It's been two weeks since you came to the rue Michel-Ange. . . .

CLAUDE You didn't summon me.

SORRÈZE I left you to your book out of discretion.

CLAUDE (Sincerely) Michel . . . does a book count?

SORRÈZE Lord, it seems to me. . . .

CLAUDE You'll always be a man!

SORRÈZE You're not going to make me believe that you take no interest whatsoever in your achievements?

CLAUDE No, but we obviously do not bring the same convictions to them, or perhaps the same naivety, as you.

SORRÈZE You mean you don't share the same disinterested passion in art?

CLAUDE (With some doubt) Art. . . . Ah! I admit that what's most important is life. If I worked, if I had talent, it's because I found in that a more forceful way to exist, call it, if you like, a selfish love of art. If it excited me to be more than other women, superior in body, soul and mind, it was to be worth more love than them, it was to tear something stronger, some-thing more despairing out of you. . . .

SORRÈZE Claude. . . .

CLAUDE Ah! we don't come to art along the same path as you. . . . If you only knew the years I've been through, the first years of this marriage. . . .

SORRÈZE If you hadn't suffered, you wouldn't be what you are today.

CLAUDE (With a short laugh) There would be one less novelist on earth!

SORRÈZE (Reproachfully) And I wouldn't have met you!

CLAUDE (Moved) So I was right to suffer . . .

SORRÈZE (Murmuring) Revenge was approaching. . . .

CLAUDE Revenge? I had to forge it with the sweat of my brow. From twenty-five to thirty, I nearly died from the effort. My loneliness made me want to scream. . . . I was such a coward that I even tried to love my husband. A survival instinct saved me. You see, Michel, what you have to love about me is that I preferred despair to unworthy happiness. . . . That's when I wrote Jérôme. . . . I was thirty-one.

SORRÈZE (Very emotionally) And Jérôme gave you to me.

CLAUDE I came like the Sibyl, to a time when I had all my future books in my hand. I was denied the prize, and three were thrown on the fire. With what was left, I made the same demands, and, faced with refusal, three more were burned. The Sibyl finally received the prize she had expected for all of them for the last three. (Silence. SORRÈZE holds CLAUDE's hand and squeezes it hard. They do not look at each other.)

SORRÈZE What can I do to help you?

CLAUDE (With a cry of happiness) Be there .. be there for me to love.

SORRÈZE Ask anything of me. . . . You have never let me tell you my passion.

CLAUDE Hush! I'm so afraid of words. . . .

SORRÈZE What about the ones we'll never write, Claude? I remember . . . the first time I saw you, people would look at you and say: with her physique and superiority, it's too much.

CLAUDE (Passionately) It's never enough!

SORRÈZE I admit, Claude, the rival moved me at first. I understood at once that I would get no peace except by loving you: this person is my equal and a woman. She is everything I am and everyone will see it. She is equivalent to me, therefore she negates me. . . . What should I do? She is a woman, a woman that a man will love. . . . She smashes the glory I hold in my hands, she is dangerous, and a man will love her, will hold her in the close and tender disdain of love. She owes me humility, she will kneel before me, because she is woman, and because, no matter how great she is, I alone can fulfill her destiny.

CLAUDE *(Has kneeled in front of him and places her hands on those of* SORRÈZE, *as in hommage. Very moved, she laughs.)* There! Is the rival a real nuisance?

SORRÈZE In front of others, I am too proud of you, Claude, but between ourselves, I'm afraid of you becoming aware that you have such value, such force, I'm afraid of how you loved ambition, to the point where you wanted it in your own right, I'm afraid you will make comparisons and I'll suffer by it.

CLAUDE Michel, you haven't disappointed me. You've been my saviour, you've been a miracle. Without you, I was condemned. *(Ironically, bitterly)* What am I worth? What does that have to do with my happiness?

SORRÈZE In a normal love relationship, the man should come before the woman.

CLAUDE *(Firmly)* Yes.

SORRÈZE *(Scrutinizing her anxiously)* What if it were you, Claude, what if you were greater, stronger, superior. . . .

CLAUDE You were the foremost writer in France when I was a poor fashion page hack.

SORRÈZE *(With conviction)* Since then. . . .

CLAUDE *(Passionately)* Get out of my life and you'll see what's left of my glory and talent.

SORRÈZE Although my kingdom is not of this world, you are nevertheless a troublesome subject. I rule you only through love: if you were an inferior, I would rule through pride and self-interest. Oh! what a cruel love is ours. Since you have been mine, I have known no peace. I'm ten years older than you, Claude, and like women in love, I mustn't get any older. I must keep myself intact, I must keep myself whole for the struggle ahead: brain, work and success. Ah! you avenge women, and we shall know beauty that fades and love that we can no longer equal.

CLAUDE What an invalid you act like. . . .

SORRÈZE A lucid one.

CLAUDE You should have loved some little woman, a "true woman," the heroine so dear to your colleagues.

SORRÈZE Before, maybe, but after you. . . .

Claude, you have destroyed our former loves . . . are you sure of what you are giving in exchange?

CLAUDE *(Passionately)* If these former loves still made your heart really beat, we would have stayed the way we were . . . and we're the ones who can complain, Michel, it's your demanding desire which made us the women we are, it's your lassitude, your disdain for slaves, your very boredom with secular wives. Look, it will always be the most loved who live and survive, and the "woman of tomorrow" will be the most beloved of tomorrow.

SORRÈZE Well, let's let the others save themselves. I prefer to believe that you are a fortunate accident, hazardous, a little terrible, and, to my misfortune, one I love to love.

CLAUDE *(Seriously)* Michel, do you want me to do something? Do you want me to give up my job? If you only knew how work bores me, has always bored me, how lazy I am, how I would rather amuse myself. . . .

SORRÈZE *(Standing up)* I don't even have it in me to ask you that. . . . Your silence would be even more troubling to me. I want to know what is going on inside you, what is in your heart.

Curtain

Act II

Same decor

Scene 1

CLAUDE, DENISE

CLAUDE *is seated, she is tightly hugging her daughter, who is seated at her feet looking up at her.*

CLAUDE Is something making you sad, Denise, and you don't want to tell me?

DENISE I'm not sad.

CLAUDE For a week, you've been flitting around like a little shadow that never laughs, never talks, never listens. . . .

DENISE I don't have your vivacity, Mother, I'm not brilliant like you.

CLAUDE Excuse me! when I used to hear your voice while I was busy with others, I listened to you and it used to warm my heart.

DENISE *(Incredulously)* Oh! Mother, when you are with others, you don't think about me!

CLAUDE *(Moved)* Denise, have I ever neglected you? Have you ever suffered because your mother is a writer?

DENISE Oh! no, no, I'm not saying that. I know perfectly well that you love me. . . .

CLAUDE I was at home more than the mothers of other girls, and perhaps, because I was serious and attentive, I enjoyed mine more than other distracted mothers. . . . Weren't you often, very often, in the same room with me while I worked? You would play on the carpet with the dogs, and I never got angry, you could laugh and shout, and even growl and bark, and if I threw you out, it was always in laughter.

DENISE You were so patient, Mother.

CLAUDE I never left you. . . . I'm not just talking about your illnesses, every mother takes care of her sick daughter. . . . But we working women, we are under such suspicion. . . . I mean, dear, you never suffered on account of your mother's being famous. . . . If I had been like the others, I would have loved you less. . . . When you live with your heart, it develops like a strong muscle. . . . And then, we meditate like monks and we even replace them a little. Like them, we know that everything passes, that beings are merely loaned to us. *(She hugs her daughter with a shudder.)*

DENISE *(Very sadly)* Mother dear, you were very good.

CLAUDE *(With exasperation)* Well then, what's wrong with you? You're holding a grudge against me for something. You have that look. *(The girl makes an equivocal movement.)* Yes, that's it, the look of a nasty little enemy. *(The girl's face closes, hardens. She makes a move to break away. CLAUDE holds her back.)* Denise! Is it about that stupid manuscript . . . because I made fun of you?

DENISE No, Mother, you did the right thing. I know perfectly well that I have no talent.

CLAUDE *(With élan)* Do you want to have talent? Do you want us to work together? No one will know, no one will guess. . . . I'll disguise myself so well. . . . Well, do you want to? That would really be fun!

DENISE *(Very sadly)* No Mother.

CLAUDE Well then, what do I have to do. . . . . Denise? Are things not going well with Flahaut?

DENISE Mr. Flahaut is charming.

CLAUDE My dear child, why didn't you tell me?

DENISE *(Breaking away)* We don't understand one another, Mother. Rest assured that it's impossible for Mr. Flahaut to cause me any pain.

CLAUDE *(Standing up in discouragement)* I'm so sure he isn't the cause of your attitude that I'm going to question him when he arrives. . . . Only, Denise, the thing that causes me such incredible pain, the thing he can't tell me, is why you refuse so . . . cruelly to open up to me.

DENISE Yes, talk to him, that's it. *(Extremely upset)* And after, if you like, we can resume the conversation.

CLAUDE *(Stupefied)* What's the matter? What is the matter with her? Did Flahaut shock you somehow? He doesn't share your ideas. . . .

DENISE Mr. Flahaut shares your ideas, Mother. You didn't want them to be mine. . . .

CLAUDE *(Seizing the pretext)* So that's it? You don't agree on the big questions. . . .

DENISE *(With a very gentle indulgence)* Oh no, no, we haven't discussed any of that, we haven't gone that far.

CLAUDE You'll drive me crazy. . . . Denise, you were the first love of my heart, before you I cared about nothing. For ten years, all I had in the world was a little girl in a white dress who didn't like to be kissed. . . . Denise, I've heard the confession of thirty women, how can I see my daughter eaten up with pain?

DENISE *(With a little irony)* You're being too much of a psychologist, Mother. You're imagining something extraordinary.

CLAUDE I don't know if I'm being a psychologist, but I am convinced that idiot Flahaut is at the bottom of it, and he's going to account for what's happening. . . .

DENISE *(Gently resigned)* Don't speak to Flahaut. . . .

CLAUDE Don't speak to him? I'm terribly sorry to displease you. . . . He's not some stupid little girl. In five minutes, we'll know what we're up against.

DENISE *(Observing her mother)* You'll be sorry, Mother.

CLAUDE Among reasonable people, everything can be worked out. . . . Flahaut has confided in me on plenty of other occasions, there's nothing indiscreet on my part in asking him where things stand with you. He knows I want this marriage; if he didn't want to be a party to it, he had only to stay away. (DENISE *looks at her mother with strange eyes.*) Yes exactly, leave. I shall never be embarrassed to settle my daughter. By the way, it's one of the advantages of the job. Denise, do you want an artist, a writer, a millionaire or a marquis? Roquelaure, for example, would marry you right way.

DENISE (*Nervously*) Mother, leave my marriage alone, that's all I ask. I won't marry either some lord or some literary type.

CLAUDE (*With all the force of victory*) You shall marry who you like, I guarantee it!

DENISE (*Resigned*) Not that either, Mother, I probably shan't marry anyone.

CLAUDE Little ragamuffin! The way you let yourself go. . . . I'll get your Flahaut ready for you. Ah! Denise, kiss me, we shall have a good laugh tonight. (*The girl lets herself go, inert and without abandon.*) My foolish child, oh! the silly heroine, what an idiotic novel we could write with this young lady. . . .

(FLAHAUT *enters while* CLAUDE *is still rocking her daughter, whom she continues to hold in her arms during the first few exchanges.*)

Scene 2

CLAUDE, FLAHAUT, DENISE

FLAHAUT (*Emotionally, in a dull voice, with the devotion of a worshipper*) I'm very pleased with you, dear *maître*, what a book! I spent the night reading and re-reading you . . . what style! ah! the job is not dulling your edge! You are verve, force, life. I pity those geniuses who come after you. . . . There are some words, I don't know if I should hate you or love you for them, I'm so sure I'll never find them again.

CLAUDE (*Pretending to be distracted, her lips on the hair of her daughter, who has closed her eyes*) Yes, yes . . . it's all very well what he's saying. . . . He's not the first one, nobody knows how to flatter like that boy. . . . And then, he really does love beautiful things . . . all of which doesn't stop him from sometimes being blocked, blocked, limited. . . . (*The girl has pulled away, moved off, and exits during the following exchanges.*)

FLAHAUT (*Not in the least worried*) As limited as all that?

CLAUDE Go away, Denise. (*Sitting down and looking at the young man with concern*) Why are you hurting my daughter?

FLAHAUT Hurting your . . . but we are the best of friends!

CLAUDE Where do things stand, exactly?

FLAHAUT (*Surprised*) But . . . I am a trusted advisor, I assure you. I made her take out the beginning and change the end. The novel might make a very presentable short story.

CLAUDE (*Standing up, annoyed*) Tell me right away that I am the one who is blocked, blocked, limited! If you didn't want to marry Denise, why were you courting her?

FLAHAUT (*Sincerely*) I courted Denise?

CLAUDE You're always hanging around here. . . .

FLAHAUT I have been for five years, and it's the first time you've complained to me about it.

CLAUDE You never leave her side and you were quite capable of seeing that you upset her.

FLAHAUT (*Visibly bothered. After a pause*) You're an unusual mother. Denise received me like an old friend of the family and, these last few months, as a writer, as a writing teacher; we've worked a lot together, hence a closeness which might have seemed deceptive.

CLAUDE You can see just as clearly as me. You saw the feelings coming, that didn't displease you, you carried on the game, a parlor flirtation. . . . Oh! Flahaut. . . .

FLAHAUT (*His voice resonating*) Denise is the last woman I would dream of flirting with.

CLAUDE Come on! When a man amuses himself. . . .

FLAHAUT Do you want me to be honest? Indeed, how could I not see what was happening? When I saw certain inflections in your daughter's looks, I was flabbergasted, that's the truth, flabbergasted, you hear?

CLAUDE There was no reason to be.

163

FLAHAUT Yes there was, since I had categorically decided not to marry her, and since being chased away from your house seemed unacceptable to me.

CLAUDE *(Thinking)* I knew of your ideas about marriage. . . . I always saw you together. . . . I thought, without being an indiscreet mother. . . .

FLAHAUT *(His voice somewhat altered)* I couldn't marry your daughter.

CLAUDE But whyever not? Excuse me, Flahaut, we have told each other so much . . . I thought you were hiding nothing from me. I thought you were even counting on me . . . it was a small step to thinking of Denise. . . .

FLAHAUT *(In a strange voice)* There are limits to the most perfect foresight. . . . I think I should be going now.

CLAUDE As God is my witness, this isn't what I wanted. But since it is so impossible for you to marry Denise. . . .

FLAHAUT *(Sharply)* Perhaps if I loved Denise less, I would still marry her.

CLAUDE *(Bothered by his tone)* I don't think I understand you properly. . . .

FLAHAUT *(Same tone)* Because the last thing you could suppose is that the disciple who loves and admires you may have derived from your incomparable friendship a disgust for everything else which doesn't measure up to it. *(Very moved)* The impossibility of living anywhere else but in you.

CLAUDE *(Stricken)* Flahaut, you are forgetting my age!

FLAHAUT *(With a cruel laugh)* Go and look at your daughter next to you!

CLAUDE You are Sorrèze's friend. . . .

FLAHAUT *(Sharply)* Sorrèze is fifty years old.

CLAUDE So, not even you, not even you have understood with what passion we love one another . . . like the other gawkers we couldn't hide from, you only saw a scandal with a foregone conclusion!

FLAHAUT Don't hold such a grudge against me, Claude, it's hard, I assure you, it's hard to get used to you, to have the right, thanks to one's wit, to spend hours beside you . . . to watch you live, ardent, intelligent, and solemn, to hear your beautiful voice talking about what is dearest to me in the world, to know that such an atmosphere as yours exists nowhere else in the world *(Very thickly)* and to know that you are a woman, Claude, a woman who needs love. . . .

CLAUDE *(Questioning herself)* I haven't done anything . . . I'm no longer coquettish. With you I've always been a brother-in-arms, a friend, a comrade . . . I've never been a woman.

FLAHAUT The worst form of coquetry is to merit more love than the others. . . . When a person has dreamed about being loved by you, Claude, how do you expect a girl. . . .

CLAUDE I'm five years older than you. . . . Come on, Flahaut, don't confuse your spiritual loves with simple spasms of the heart.

FLAHAUT You are the only interest in my life. Warmth, daily energy, I find them only with you. . . . I go to sleep and I wake up with the passion of our wonderful conversations. . . . I've been coming here for five years, I can't stop myself from always coming back. . . .

CLAUDE You are very much to blame, you are, because you are more aware than many others, you are very much to blame for spoiling our beautiful friendship.

FLAHAUT No doubt you prefer men who don't like you!

CLAUDE *(Becoming more cruel as she gets more annoyed)* I prefer men who know that they can never rival Sorrèze.

FLAHAUT *(Following suit, out of control)* Sorrèze! But he isn't worthy of you! Look at his last book where he takes care to show off his beautiful soul. . . . Compare it to you! Head, heart, effort, will, you are a hundred times better than Sorrèze. . . . How can you not feel it? How can it not bother you? Ah! Claude, me, at least, you don't yet know who I am.

CLAUDE *(Who has indeed felt it and suffered, enraged)* Sorrèze is greater than all of us! And you are unworthy, Flahaut, unworthy as a friend and as a follower . . . a book can be a failure. . . . Sorrèze's past has killed any future for you!

FLAHAUT She doth protest too much . . . admit your disappointment! Sorrèze's triumph is that he had never spoken about love . . . now he's getting mixed up in it and I know perfectly well you have cried over it. *(Sarcastically)* There's nothing quite like loving a writer, you always end up knowing what's inside.

CLAUDE (*In much pain, reproachfully*) Yes, and they don't always even need to write.

FLAHAUT Forgive me, one fights you with whatever means one can, you are too strong.

CLAUDE (*Close to tears*) Too strong! I've been told that all my life. Too strong! Aren't we also weak, also begging . . . (*In tears*) You upset me, you wound me. . . . You can't do anything for me, you know that. . . . Why do you take it out on the only thing that has made my life acceptable . . . and that has made death something I can face. . . . Sorrèze doesn't talk about love as well as me, so what? What does that prove? Oh! prisoners that we are: more prodigies, more masterpieces.

FLAHAUT Claude, I'm here. Love Sorrèze, and when you suffer, when you have doubts, think of me. Tell yourself that another heart, as profound as his, another soul, as attentive as his, is paying the ransom you deserve through its fervor and its distress.

CLAUDE I don't suffer, I have no doubts. I won't allow anyone to doubt for me.

FLAHAUT (*Passionately*) If I didn't judge Sorrèze. . . . He cannot be all you'll ever have! Claude, one day you will open your eyes . . . that man will never love anyone but himself, he's our most famous egoist.

CLAUDE (*Brusquely*) Do I need the love of the devoted?

FLAHAUT You will suffer. . . . His book . . . it's you, it's your story . . . and look what he's done to it! . . . Oh! I'm not saying it's exploitation . . . it's worse: he's done nothing with it.

CLAUDE Well, yes, there I've had no peace . . . that book annoyed me, that book disappointed me, that book is a failure, let's forget it! It's my fault. . . . I must have been stupid. . . . You would have to have no feeling at all . . . it shouldn't have been written. . . . (*Ironically*) Oh! would I weren't a "woman of genius". . . .

FLAHAUT Don't deny yourself, Claude, because you are worth more than him. If you think we don't all know that . . . even he will suspect in the end! And when that day comes, ah! poor Claude, you'll see what a lover is worth!

CLAUDE Be quiet! If ever the shadow of professional rivalry, the shadow of that awful jealousy next to which everything else is a joy, were to come between us,

I would not wait an hour, do you hear me, to avenge the woman in me, to destroy that artificial being that boredom and idleness had caused to blossom in my mind.

FLAHAUT (*With a cry*) Claude, surely you don't mean. . . .

CLAUDE My talent! Ah! Lord have mercy, if you knew how little I care, if you knew how I've had it with writing. What is your admiration to me? What is glory for a woman, and even for a man? People admire us, Sorrèze and me, but no one lives to admire us. There isn't a single man, or woman, no matter how insignificant, for whom everyone wouldn't betray us. What do I care about the hearts I don't fill? The truth is that Sorrèze and I have only each other, and to think that he could be taken away from me for a circus act, for a wretched trick.

FLAHAUT That circus act, that wretched trick, he isn't about to give them up for you!

CLAUDE And I don't want that! (*Shivering*) But it wouldn't take two conversations like this one, old friend, for me to turn my back forever on a job to which I have given too much. (*She shivers for a long moment; they remain silent.*)

FLAHAUT (*With remorse*) I'm sorry, I'm sorry, I'm sorry. . . .

CLAUDE Later. . . . after you have left and come back again.

FLAHAUT (*As though stifling a curse*) No. . . .

CLAUDE (*Sad irony*) Ah! you'll have to give up a few habits. . . .

FLAHAUT Let me stay, Claude, even so! You know me . . . I guess I don't care about anything any more, I don't care about being and about being worthy. I believe, God forgive me, that if I have worked, it was to reach you, to bring together our distant existences. . . . Claude, you are my goal. Defend yourself, make yourself inaccessible. But let me pursue you, let me fight you. . . .

CLAUDE If it were up to me, I would keep you all the same, feverish, ill, incensed, whatever! I would try to remake your beautiful and balanced brain that I used to admire, the regular workman who was to outstrip us all. (*Smiling*) The "classical heart" I used to like so much. But there is my poor daughter; as for her, she must not see you here. . . . Flahaut, what I cannot forgive you for is that Denise guessed about you before me.

FLAHAUT *(With hardness)* You felt only through Sorrèze!

CLAUDE After him, I was most attached to you. I used to bless my job for having furnished my life with companions such as you, and you make me say goodbye.

FLAHAUT *(With an impatient gesture)* Relationships such as ours . . . it's not so simple to undo. You aren't just a woman who sends away a man received in intimacy. . . . You are my master, you don't have the right to abandon me.

CLAUDE I don't have the right to torture my daughter.

FLAHAUT All the evenings I used to spend next to you. . . .

CLAUDE Hush!

FLAHAUT You'll continue to speak, to live for others, Claude . . . you'll come to see me!

CLAUDE You'll work . . . you'll write beautiful things that will set my heart beating. . . . Away with you quickly, now, I have to think of my daughter. *(FLAHAUT falls to the ground and embraces her knees.)* Flahaut, I love you like a son. *(The door opens. DENISE enters and sees the young man only as she reaches mid-stage. She jumps slightly and stops dead in her tracks.)*

Scene 3

CLAUDE Flahaut, since you are leaving, say goodbye to Denise. *(FLAHAUT stands up, he is obstinate, pained, ill at ease.)*

DENISE *(Her eyes hostile, her voice sharp)* Don't feel obliged to send Mr. Flahaut away, I assure you there has never been anything between us.

CLAUDE *(Somewhat at a loss for words)* But I'm not sending him away, Flahaut does what he likes.

DENISE *(Same)* In that case I don't quite understand why I found him embracing your knees.

CLAUDE *(Somewhat sharply, to her daughter)* I'll tell you, we'll tell you, we'll explain it to you later. . . .

DENISE *(Woundingly)* I'm not asking for explanations.

CLAUDE Denise. . . .

FLAHAUT It is with great sorrow that I leave Mrs. Bersier. But I have just caused her a great disappointment, I have had to

decline an honor she wished to bestow on me. . . .

DENISE *(Nervously)* The honor of being her son-in-law! Mr. Flahaut, I'll take care of things myself. . . . My mother has been making up stories, that's her job. . . . It would never occur to me to look for a husband among her adorers.

CLAUDE Oh! . . . *(CLAUDE looks at her daughter with pained pity.)*

FLAHAUT *(Turning toward CLAUDE)* So, it . really is goodbye? *(She makes an imperceptible sign.)* And you, Mademoiselle Denise, don't forget that Claude is your best friend. *(Exit FLAHAUT.)*

Scene 4

CLAUDE, DENISE

DENISE *(Sharply and dryly)* He insists on going then? I thought I was going to take care of everything.

CLAUDE *(Very sadly)* My poor Denise, come here a moment.

DENISE Oh! please, Mother, no airs of commiseration! Can't you admit that a person can not be in love with Monsieur Flahaut?

CLAUDE What I cannot accept is the tone, the face, the attitude that you force me to adopt at the moment.

DENISE *(In despair, sincerely)* But do you think I have to try? Mother, do you think it's easy living with you?

CLAUDE *(Emotionally, indignantly)* My own daughter!

DENISE There's only enough breathing room for one woman in this house. Do I even exist here? Who looks at me, who loves me? I arrive in the world, which owes me happiness, I have all the rights of youth, and now it turns out that I am too late, the place is already taken . . . a woman has already ruined it for me, under her dangerous guidance I've lost everything. . . . My mother is my rival. . . .

CLAUDE *(The same)* Ah! you really are your father's daughter. . . .

DENISE But do you think it's the first time? You've always been against me. . . . Ah! I know only too well what you are worth, Mother. If I hadn't been your daughter, I would have worshipped you like the others . . . but it's impossible, Mother, it's impossible to be your daughter . . . it's impossible to be next to you and to be this poor infantile creature that can't speak, that can't write, that maybe can't even feel like you. . . . They know only too well that they would only stand to lose with me *(Bitterly, ironically)* Ah! they couldn't expect illustrious love affairs with me. What do you expect, Mother, you control their hearts and flatter their vanity.

CLAUDE *(Deeply)* Not as much as you think.

DENISE Flahaut, my God, I might have married him, perhaps, but he isn't the one *(Sharply)*, he isn't the one. *(She stops to breathe.)*

CLAUDE *(Resigned, immobile, frozen)* Let's see, who is it?

DENISE Two years ago, I loved with all my heart. I was naive, I was sixteen, he was twenty, he was always here. . . . By the way, Mother, you could have observed us . . . it's true that you knew what to expect. . . .

CLAUDE *(Increasingly immobile)* Go on, go on. . . .

DENISE You all admired him, said how charming he was, superior, full of promise. . . . Mother, you talked about him without stopping. I was stupid, I thought you were encouraging us. He used to look at you with such big eyes hungry for hope, Mother. . . . I thought he was expecting you to . . . ah! I'm not too bright, am I . . . to give him your daughter. *(CLAUDE is very somber.)* One day . . . *(With anguish)* one day I learned that Fréville had just killed himself because of you.

CLAUDE *(More like a statue than ever)* Who told you that?

DENISE One hears more than you think.

CLAUDE *(In a state of great reverie)* You were in love with Jacques Fréville?

DENISE That one, at least, I thought was closer to me than to you.

CLAUDE *(Sharp in turn)* You were mistaken. *(Immediately remorseful)* My poor, poor thing, you have just been very unreasonable . . . and so unfair.

DENISE No, Mother, I'm not unfair. Do I blame you for your actions?

CLAUDE Well then, finally, what are you blaming me for?

DENISE You, nothing . . . it's I who am in the wrong, for being your daughter.

CLAUDE You're back to that again, you poor ungrateful child. . . .

DENISE But you can see for yourself that my life is over, that you are suffocating me. . . . but what am I doing here, what am I hoping for? To marry one day someone of mediocre importance in your circle, a man of such restricted scope as to be able to aspire only to me?

CLAUDE God, what an awful girl. . . . Denise, thanks to you I have just treated harshly, cruelly my old friend Flahaut. It's possible he'll never do anything ever again. . . . He has no friends, no milieu. He came alive only here . . . perhaps I have just killed his talent. . . .

DENISE *(With irony and resentment)* That man will do like the others: he'll do without talent!

CLAUDE Ah! *(She gives in to rage for a moment.)* If you don't come and kiss me this instant, Denise, it's over. You'll horrify me, I won't be able to stand you. . . .

DENISE *(Like a little girl, worn out)* Mother, I'm sorry, I'm sorry!

CLAUDE *(Hugs her furiously like a lover)* Forget it, forget it, Denise, forget all about it! One can be happy with me, my darling, I loved you so much . . . you've said some monstrous things to me . . . you were in love with Fréville. . . . Ah! you were quite right, Denise. I forgive you because of that, that's the only good thing you've told me. And we'll find another, my child, there are a few like that. . . . I'll make myself quite small . . . and besides I don't count any more anyway. . . . Look at how white my hair is getting . . . now it's you who are my rival, it's you who only has to ask. . . . Ah Denise, as though I wanted to see you marry a cretin! *(The girl is immobile, hurt, closed.)* Well answer me, give me a good word, kiss me! *(Her daughter kisses her unwillingly.)* God! what a horrible kiss. . . . We'll have to teach her how. Come on, Denise, put more into it! *(The girl, discouraged, lets her arms fall around her mother's shoulders. CLAUDE covers her with kisses.)* My child, my only child. . . .

Scene 5

The same, BERSIER

BERSIER *(Mechanically)* Are you working, Claude? Am I disturbing you? *(The two*

women separate and try to compose
themselves. *With curiosity*) What's wrong?
Has Denise been crying?

CLAUDE It's finished. It's over, right
Denise?

DENISE *(With great sang-froid)* Completely
over. *(She moves off.)*

CLAUDE Where are you going?

DENISE I have to go out.

(CLAUDE follows her with her eyes, sighing.)

Scene 6

CLAUDE, BERSIER

BERSIER She doesn't look well.

CLAUDE Are you very friendly with
Denise? Do you chat with her often?

BERSIER Good heavens, my dear Claude
. . . I have always thought of myself as
the best of fathers. Denise lavishes signs
of affection and friendship on me, and as
for chatting . . . I would have thought that
it was more your concern.

CLAUDE It didn't work out just now. . . .
Denise bears me a grudge because it
didn't work out with Flahaut.

BERSIER Ah! that's unfortunate. . . . I had
got used to the idea . . . he was very
simple that boy. Has it failed completely?

CLAUDE Alas, yes . . . help me do better.
. . . My daughter will not forgive me until
she can no longer doubt my devotion. . . .
Ah! if only I could bring Flahaut back to
her.

BERSIER Why is that so impossible?

CLAUDE Flahaut is no longer at the age
where one falls for girls. . . . Denise is a
good girl, quite simple, not very brilliant.

BERSIER You certainly do eclipse her
somewhat.

CLAUDE *(Quickly)* We have the same bills at
the seamstress's.

BERSIER *(A brief burst of laughter)* Well, I
can see that Denise and I are in the same
boat. . . .

CLAUDE Henri. . . .

BERSIER We obviously are not the
aristocracy of the house. *(CLAUDE makes a
gesture of lassitude.)* Wait, since obviously
I'm reading Saint-Simon at the moment
. . . you can't always read your wife. . . .
Let me remind you what he says about
the Marshal de Villeroi . . . my dear
Claude, you act like a pneumatic
machine, you suck up all the air around
you.

CLAUDE *(Immobile once more)* Your
daughter just told me the same thing.

BERSIER Ah! her too, my word, that was
bound to happen . . . what do you expect
my dear, it's obvious you haven't lived
only for your husband and your child.

CLAUDE *(Shivers slightly and seems to be
dreaming)* With regard to Denise I do not
reproach myself. All the strength that I
drew from my work has maintained in
me an alertness, an ardor, a maternal joy,
the absence of which in other women has
often seemed to me chilling.

BERSIER With regard to Denise, let's say,
agreed. I have no difficulty in admitting
that you were a charming mother and the
child felt it . . . but there comes a
moment, my dear friend, when the task is
to charm a little less and to be a little
more self-effacing.

CLAUDE I don't understand the lesson
you're giving me there.

BERSIER I mean that the best mother is
the one you don't notice. . . . That's what
your daughter is missing . . . that child
has understood better than you, for all
your intelligence, the law that regulates
the generations, a mother is an abdicated
woman.

CLAUDE *(With tears in her eyes)* Good God!
but if my mother . . . if she had lived like
I did. . . . I don't want Denise to see her
life stifled at forty.

BERSIER That says it all, making your
daughter happy looks to you like a stifled
life.

CLAUDE *(Annoyed)* Ah! well then, let's see
her collaborate a little on this happiness
. . . so much the better.

BERSIER Saints preserve me from women
who make their own happiness.

CLAUDE Believe me they would prefer
someone else to take care of it.

BERSIER In that case, my dear, they have
more than one chance.

CLAUDE Ah! that's enough. . . . I must
really love life, despite your scenes,
despite your reproaches, despite your
tone of voice, and despite your looks, to
be able to face the daily prospect of work.
. . . Why don't you work, Henri, why
don't you work, Denise!

BERSIER Be quiet, I hear the doorbell . . .
that's Sorrèze's ring. *(Sarcastically)* Ah!
now there's a worker. *(CLAUDE is silent.)*
It's been a long time since I saw Sorrèze.

... How is his liver? (CLAUDE *maintains an impatient silence.*) Good Lord, my dear, what do you expect? one learns to live, one adapts to every situation ... what's rich is that it is you who are shocked.

CLAUDE *(Peeking outside)* I'm only shocked at your intentions. ...

Scene 7

CLAUDE, BERSIER, SORRÈZE

SORRÈZE *(He looks terrible; in his eyes one sees nervousness, worry, suspicion, unhappiness.)* Hello, Claude. ... Hello, Bersier. ... *(He throws on the desk a bundle of press cuttings.)*

BERSIER Hello, Sorrèze. Ah! you too ... the cuttings. I wonder why we keep getting them, Claude doesn't even read them.

CLAUDE *(Struck by SORRÈZE's appearance)* Are you upset?

SORRÈZE Worse than that, I'll tell you. ... *(He looks at BERSIER.)*

BERSIER How's the weather outside?

SORRÈZE Fine, I don't know ... it's not raining.

BERSIER Well, I'm going to take a walk with Denise, that will do us both good.

CLAUDE She left us quite abruptly, make her feel better.

BERSIER I can't promise anything like that with Denise. ... Goodbye Sorrèze, excuse me. ... I leave you to your colleague. I feel like a lady between the two of you.

SORRÈZE *(Who is thinking about something else, shakes his hand)* My regards to Denise.

BERSIER Goodbye, my dear friend, you don't have any errands for us? *(Exiting)* I plan to stop in at my seamstress and my milliner. ...

Scene 8

CLAUDE *(Crying with nervous irritation)* There's no end to those jokes. ... It's not that he's cruel, but he has the soul of an idler. When he's not with his register receipts – he calls that working! – he has nothing else to do in life. ... You're not listening to me, is it a serious problem?

SORRÈZE A savage attack by Flahaut.

CLAUDE No!

SORRÈZE Read it. ... *(After a minute she turns the page to see the signature.)* Ah! just like me, that's him all right. He signs only with his initials.

CLAUDE *(Reading)* The tone is measured. ...

SORRÈZE Only the tone.

CLAUDE *(The same)* It's not by Flahaut. ...

SORRÈZE Finish it. *(CLAUDE falls completely silent, she reads for a long time.)* Well?

CLAUDE I can't understand it. ... No one admires you more than Flahaut.

SORRÈZE I thought so. ... You can see we'll have to talk about it. ... I admit that upset me more than all the rest. *(He glances toward the cuttings.)*

CLAUDE *(Hesitating)* Perhaps I can explain. ...

SORRÈZE Flahaut's ingratitude? That's not what surprises me ... but that the thought of you didn't stop him, the certainty of hurting you. *(Bitterly)* Don't you realize all I owe you? But if I weren't your lover, my dear, if I weren't your weakness, you famous woman, you fashionable woman *(The phrase hits home and Claude makes a movement.)*, if people weren't afraid to displease you, I would have borne the brunt of all their insolence a long time ago.

CLAUDE Michel, Flahaut admires and likes you!

SORRÈZE He used to admire me, he used to like me ... since then, a different ideal, a different aesthetic. ...

CLAUDE *(Nervously)* Which ones?

SORRÈZE Lord, yours, I thought. Isn't Flahaut your follower?

CLAUDE In that case, you would be the master of both of us!

SORRÈZE *(With animation)* When were you ever my pupil? And I congratulate you for it, my dear Claude, don't bother with the formality of protesting. ... Have you ever imitated me? You know perfectly well that with our different paths. ...

CLAUDE That's the first time you have mentioned our different paths. ...

SORRÈZE Let the young generation have its way. It will take care of pointing them out to you.

CLAUDE This article by Flahaut is horrible.

SORRÈZE It isn't horrible, it's cruel. I had hoped that around you, within your circle, I would have found an understanding, an appreciation that was ... less parsimonious.

CLAUDE Michel, are you really going to think. ... Flahaut would never have spoken to me this way about one of your books.

SORRÈZE He added a little to your antipathies, that's all. . . . We don't understand each other any more, my poor Claude . . . it's almost inevitable, since we are two different people.

CLAUDE (Emotionally) We aren't two different people. . . .

SORRÈZE Yes we are . . . do you think I haven't felt it. . . .

CLAUDE (With animation) We are two different writers, that's quite likely, but the job has nothing to do with the single entity that we are. . . . Until now, it has never bothered us. . . .

SORRÈZE What do you know about it?

CLAUDE Would you have preferred. . . .

SORRÈZE Ah yes, finally, one suffers . . . if you think it's fun to watch thirty imbeciles flapping around you, thirty intelligent imbeciles, who understand you and admire you, who have your portrait at home, better than your portrait, an exact copy of your being your mind your heart, and all the rest, in the dozens of books in their legitimate and daily possession, which they re-read and judge to write articles, in which everything about you is made known, discussed, debated, your brain, your heart, and even your sensuality. . . .

CLAUDE (Convinced) Yes, it's true, it's annoying . . . but there are compensations.

SORRÈZE (Dryly) There aren't.

CLAUDE Michel, such an outburst, because you are upset about an article by Flahaut. . . .

SORRÈZE Such euphemisms. . . .

CLAUDE (Embarrassed) Well, this article, I wouldn't have dared to tell you . . . I'm beginning to understand it. It isn't the literary reasons that are making you Flahaut's enemy. Flahaut was here, not an hour ago. He left, he won't be coming back . . . for a while. . . . I asked him not to . . . we had had a conversation, he acted

SORRÈZE (Taking a deep breath, after a moment) It's better that way.

CLAUDE (Observing him, as though in a dream) Much better. . . .

SORRÈZE (As though to himself) Women always make everything more difficult.

CLAUDE (The same) Much more difficult. . . . Flahaut is a hothead, profound, dangerous . . . to himself.

SORRÈZE (Continuing to calm down) It's only natural that, smitten with you, he should resent me.

CLAUDE The absence will only exasperate him, but what else could I do? . . . I'll have to watch him when he comes back. . . .

SORRÈZE I should have seen it right away . . . this article reeks of bad faith. He did everything he could to misunderstand, worse than that, to seem to misunderstand.

CLAUDE (Who has been listening attentively) I like Flahaut a lot. I didn't want to tell you about the . . . troubling state he's in. I didn't want to complicate your relationship. Besides, he seemed to act the same toward you, there was nothing to explain.

SORRÈZE We'll see in the Revue de France, Flahaut has his fortnightly column. I'll be expecting him . . . send him to me tomorrow evening.

CLAUDE (Somewhat coldly) I just told you that I won't be seeing Flahaut again. . . . Write to him.

SORRÈZE After his attack? You have some funny ideas where my dignity is at stake.

CLAUDE What do you want then?

SORRÈZE For you to agree to send him to me.

CLAUDE (Emotionally) And at the same time, to ask him to come back here?

SORRÈZE That's another matter, you be the judge of it.

CLAUDE (Solemnly) The only judge, indeed. (Getting the better of herself) I'll send for him.

SORRÈZE (Preparing to leave, shaking hands with CLAUDE) Goodbye, Claude. (He leaves.)

Scene 9

CLAUDE, DENISE

CLAUDE leans back in an armchair, her eyes closed, her face a hardened mask. She recognizes the footsteps of her daughter.

CLAUDE Denise, is that you, my treasure?

DENISE Are you in pain, mother?

CLAUDE Come and sit down here, quickly my dear, I need you so badly.

DENISE Would you like me to ring for Emma?

CLAUDE No it's you I need, sit down here.

I'm going to put my head on your shoulder . . . it's a topsy-turvy world, isn't it? When you were little and I needed a good friend, I would stand you up on the table and I'd put my forehead on your collar, on your fragile little bird-like neck.

DENISE *(Moved, a little embarrassed)* Mother! *(Silence.* CLAUDE *has her head on her daughter's neck.)*

CLAUDE *(Without moving)* That's better already.

DENISE Headache?

CLAUDE A moment of great discouragement, Denise.

DENISE You! That's impossible, Mother, you must be mistaken. . . .

CLAUDE *(With a slight laugh)* And starting tomorrow . . . yes, starting tomorrow, I'm going to let myself go completely. . . .

DENISE You'll be bored, Mother, but I'm here and you can scold me again.

CLAUDE *(Intimately)* Denise, that's better. *(Confiding)* We hurt each other just now didn't we my dear. We have to dispel the misunderstanding. . . . Fréville? I wish so much that you would talk to me about him without . . . without any mistrust, Denise.

DENISE *(Hastily)* I'm not asking you for anything. Your business doesn't concern me, Mother.

CLAUDE That is a debatable point, but one thing is certain, my girl, is that yours concerns me. So, Denise, let me tell you something, and I think you have a heart and a mind open enough to sense that this should settle everything between us, let me tell you something, your love for Fréville is what I like best about you. He was exquisite, that boy . . . and my dear big girl understood that he was better than the others. She has forgotten nothing. For four years, while no one mentioned any names, she preserved the great, the painful memory. *(Softly)* Cry, my dear.

DENISE Fréville killed himself for you.

CLAUDE One can, alas, kill oneself for a woman who doesn't love you, who has never loved you. There was never anything but friendship between Fréville and me, my dear, never think anything else . . . even if others tell you so. Do you hear me, finally, little blockhead?

DENISE Fréville killed himself for you.

CLAUDE What can I say? What can I do?. . .

Fréville could hope for nothing from me . . . because he knew that I loved another.

DENISE You're just saying that to console me.

CLAUDE You don't believe me? . . . So, that's not enough? It's still not enough? . . . I've just done for you something a mother has never done. . . . To keep my daughter's heart, to console her, I've just made the kind of confession you make only on your deathbed.

DENISE I'm not judging you, Mother.

CLAUDE This is too much. . . . Very well, listen. Since you talk of judging, you'll hear me out, and I don't want any misunderstanding. Yes, you'll hear me out. *(She seizes her by both wrists.)* You see, my girl, there's nothing more beautiful than a happy marriage. You should be happy in marriage, having the husband of your life in your home. . . . I wish my daughter a life that is completely straightforward and simple. I want to prepare it for her with my own hands if I can . . . because here, you see, because here it's all a failure. . . . Your father loves you, we both love you . . . but your father and I are like two divorced people. . . . I was very unhappy, Denise, unhappy the way clever girls are sometimes, unhappy enough to die without ever opening my mouth . . . when my first book led me to meet Michel Sorrèze. (CLAUDE *shudders,* DENISE *is touched.)* And without a word, without a gesture and without any initiative, without anything really changing at that point, there was no more unhappiness, Denise, there was no more distress. *(Silence)* Then, some time passed . . . a long time. . . . I wasn't sure about Sorrèze, I didn't know anything about his life, when I arrived on the scene, with everything to gain. . . . Ah! if I hadn't seen there the elements of a serious and lasting union, happiness, when it is really big, is worth what it costs . . . but it's always a great misfortune to be happy on the sidelines of one's life . . . that was my painful happiness. I accepted it that way . . . so that you could grow up in peace. *(Rouses her daughter who seems overwhelmed, wiped out by the personality of her mother)* I put up with it that way so that, once you grew up, you could judge me and find me good . (DENISE *doesn't move.)* Well, Denise, were you worth that sacrifice?

DENISE (*Crushed*) Mother, Mother, I don't know.

CLAUDE No, that's not all. I had some unbelievable moments. Four years ago, Michel Sorrèze was ill, very ill, he nearly died. . . . I knew he was asking for me, and it was forbidden for me to see him. . . . There is no hell more frightening. To be somewhere else, anywhere else, when the one you love looks in agony. Then, when I saw him again, in the incredible joy of convales-cence, he ordered me to leave, to follow him home, to another home, and I had the courage, despite the look that said all day long: "I don't want to die without you," I had the cruelty to not budge, to stay attached to a man and a girl who, perhaps, didn't need me. . . .

DENISE (*On her mother's shoulder*) Mother, you are good.

CLAUDE (*In a very low voice*) And if, one day, Denise, you were all I had left . . . life is so monstrous. . . .

DENISE If Michel Sorrèze were to die?

CLAUDE In a word, if I were more unhappy than I've ever been. . . .

DENISE You are not the stuff the unhappy are made of.

CLAUDE No? And yet what is happening to me at the moment is so awful. (*Mad reverie*) I've asked too much of existence, I wanted a happiness that surpassed all others by far. . . . Well, if my little Denise has resented me, if she has found me too spoiled as a woman, if she has looked back upon it all . . . well done! Providence has heard her. . . . Ah! how she will be avenged!

DENISE Don't talk to me like that, Mother, what do you expect to become of me?

CLAUDE (*With a sigh*) Come along, I see I have to leave you. I had hoped for a word. . . . I don't know, and yet you are my daughter. . . . But here you are answering me like a poor little sheep that I'm torturing. (*She puts her head back on* DENISE's *shoulder.*) Come on, here, blow on my forehead. What are you waiting for? (DENISE *smiles and blows.*) She's my big girl, my faithful one. . . . We don't always understand each other, but we love each other. (DENISE *makes an instinctive gesture to break away.*) I'm boring you, my poor child, go on, go and amuse yourself, go and play. . . . Go and play the piano.

(*Affectionately*) What are you going to do, Denise?

DENISE (*With reticence*) I have to write. . . .

CLAUDE Fine, fine . . . you don't have to tell me who to. (*Impatiently*) Come on, off you go.

(*The girl leaves,* CLAUDE *bursts into tears.*)

BERSIER (*Holding a closed dispatch and without seeing the convulsions of his wife who sobs silently*) A dispatch . . . I opened it by mistake. . . . You've won the Nobel prize.

Curtain

Act III

Scene 1

Same decor

DENISE, CORALIE

CORALIE 2,130 francs, my lady. If I had gone to certain houses, I could have got more, but I didn't want to take my lady's jewels and dresses to. . . .

DENISE Yes, yes. . . . No one saw you? Did anyone see the dresses being taken out?

CORALIE By the back stair, in my own trunk. . . . Oh! no, my lady, no one suspects anything.

DENISE Were you able to hide from the chambermaid?

CORALIE Of course. My lady brought me up her dresses while Emma was doing Madam's hair, I only had to fasten the padlock.

DENISE And the valet?

CORALIE It was the concierge who carried the trunk down. My lady says she'll see I don't regret this. . . . I've been with Madam a long time. . . . If my lady weren't leaving all alone. . . .

DENISE (*Somewhat bitterly*) Who do you expect me to leave with?

CORALIE There is a young gentleman writer who was here to read his work to my lady. . . .

DENISE It must be contagious! Now Coralie is making up stories. . . . No, my dear girl, I'm leaving on my own, you'll drive me to the station, and you'll see for yourself. . . .

CORALIE If only my lady told me where she was going. . . .

DENISE (*Teasing*) Too late, Coralie, now that you've given me the 2,000 francs.

CORALIE   I won't be able to look Madam in the face.

DENISE   Don't be afraid, my girl, I'm going to Grandma's.

CORALIE   *(Stupefied)* The master's mother?

DENISE   Lord! As though I had two grand-mothers.

CORALIE   But they are angry at her.

DENISE   My mother, yes . . . but not my father, nor I.

CORALIE   So, my lady promises that's where she's going?

DENISE   Yes, and I'll even leave a letter with my address.

CORALIE   Ah, well, in that case. . . .

DENISE   Go ahead and take the 130 francs, Coralie; if it weren't that I need the rest. . . .

CORALIE   Oh, no, no, my lady, the journey is long, keep them, and then if there is extra, my lady will always know where to find her jewels again.

DENISE   An old watch and an opal. My mother's follies, I won't have enough to buy them back, take the 130 francs, Coralie.

CORALIE   Such a fine watch and such a pretty ring. . . .

DENISE   I wasn't attached to them.

CORALIE   Someone's ringing, my lady, I thank my lady, but with a heavy heart.

Scene 2

DENISE, FLAHAUT

DENISE   *(Dryly)* Have you come for my mother, Mr. Flahaut? I see with pleasure that you haven't left.

FLAHAUT   If it's with pleasure, then I'm a happy man. I thought you were a little vexed.

DENISE   And why would that be?

FLAHAUT   You haven't been very nice; you were a little agitated last time. . . .

DENISE   You must not pay too much attention to what goes on between my mother and me, we were both very worked up. *(Graciously)* I would be mortified if I gave you the wrong impression . . . *(Getting muddled)* an impression for which, to some extent, you might hold yourself responsible.

FLAHAUT   Of course not, of course not, Miss Denise, I'm not so dumb, I'm not mistaken. . . .

DENISE   And besides, I'm not your type, eh? We can certainly admit that . . . I lack substance, both physically and morally . . . that comes with age . . . but, Lord, we'd have to wait. . . . *(FLAHAUT remains silent.)* A piece of friendly advice, Mr. Flahaut, beware of this house, it wouldn't be the first time that it harmed someone.

FLAHAUT   *(Solemnly)* I fail to understand what use that recommendation might have for me.

DENISE   It's strange coming from me, isn't it? Is that what you mean? Let's not push it, my position is also a little strange. . . .

FLAHAUT   Your position is an enviable one, dear child, it should be among the happiest. You are the daughter of an admirable mother who adores you. . . . You have a tendency to forget that, watch out.

DENISE   Ah! my mother has set you up against me. *(With tears in her eyes)* You too, you cry ingratitude . . . and that's the way it will always be, I won't have a single person, not one on my side. . . . It's always my mother who will be understood, understood and admired. . . .

FLAHAUT   What do you have against Claude?

DENISE   Oh! I know, I don't have the right, I am in the wrong, it never looks good to complain about your mother. . . .

FLAHAUT   If you are unhappy, even on her account, you should tell her, she will understand. *(He goes to meet CLAUDE.)*

Scene 3

CLAUDE, FLAHAUT

CLAUDE   *(Surprised, happy)* Is that you, Denise? Were you two chatting? *(The girl slips away. CLAUDE, concerned)* Ah! that girl. . . . You see, Flahaut, I give up. . . . Someone else will have to help me, I'm counting on my husband. . . . *(Emotionally)* Denise doesn't love me.

FLAHAUT   At that age, they don't love anyone. . . .

CLAUDE   If only she were happy, at least. *(Very upset)* She's such a grump. . . . God knows, my life hasn't always been fun, but I never looked like that. *(Getting agitated)* I'll give some balls, matinees, cotillions, I'll invite all the youngest people, the silliest. It won't solve everything, but perhaps we'll have a laugh. I'll die of boredom if necessary, but Denise will have a good time, she'll have a good time at home with me!

FLAHAUT *(He is not listening to her, trembling, with a constrained voice full of expectation.)* You sent for me, Claude?

CLAUDE *(Sharply, ironically)* That initiative hardly proves my tenderness. . . . I am acting basely toward you, Flahaut, at least try to love me less for it.

FLAHAUT *(Hesitantly)* What do you want?

CLAUDE *(Same tone)* I sent for you to talk about Sorrèze.

FLAHAUT Explain what you mean.

CLAUDE *(Nervously)* You have just acted toward him like a novice, like a hostile and rude youngster.

FLAHAUT *(Wounded)* You are brutal, Madam.

CLAUDE We were stupefied, your article is an assassination.

FLAHAUT *(After a moment, seeming to weigh his words carefully)* I swear to you that there is no acrimony on my part, and I can't get over the effect caused by that little paper. It's not an attack, it is an analysis and an honest evaluation. Sorrèze isn't used to hearing the truth. I'm saddened that a man who wrote the admirable *Etudes* should be wounded by me. I admired Sorrèze with all my might, if he writes a mediocre, almost unlikeable book, it is my right as an admirer, it is my duty as a critic to put him squarely in his place.

CLAUDE These explanations are even more unacceptable than the rest, you know. You owed more respect to a master. Well, you see the result. If you don't want to break with our greatest French writer. . . .

FLAHAUT *(Calmly)* He isn't our greatest French writer.

CLAUDE *(Rapidly)* If you don't want to break with Sorrèze, keep an eye on the *Revue de France*, correct the impression it has created.

FLAHAUT My article is written. . . .

CLAUDE *(With emotion)* So, is it war?

FLAHAUT There will never be war between Sorrèze and me. My articles are among those he must accept, even from a friend. Come on, Claude, you've read it. . . .

CLAUDE It was harsh.

FLAHAUT But his novel was really bad.

CLAUDE *(With a sigh)* You had just devoted such a fine issue to me. . . .

FLAHAUT *(Coldly)* That's our business. You have fans at the *Revue*.

CLAUDE It was shocking. It seemed premeditated.

FLAHAUT *(Dryly)* We don't get into those considerations.

CLAUDE *(Unable to hold back any longer)* Ah! Flahaut, how you've hurt me.

FLAHAUT I only ask you to believe one thing. . . . All this dates from well before our conversation. . . . Remember, Claude, it was the same day that you were so hard that Sorrèze brought you the *Revue*. Don't think there was any cheap intention, I would be really upset. . . . Our opinion had already been formed about the two works that appeared.

CLAUDE *(With a long shudder)* Woman is not cut out for this. . . . See, Flahaut, it makes me ill! Happy the helpmeet who looks over her husband's shoulder, who admires and remains silent, happy the mercenary who copies and who serves, happy all the others, all the others. . . . *(She sobs.)*

FLAHAUT Claude, how can this be? When your career is so beautiful, your success so pure . . . when I thought you were full of satisfaction at your latest victories. Yesterday, the Nobel prize. . . . Tomorrow, the drama critic for our greatest daily paper.

CLAUDE *(Through her tears)* He asked me to. . . .

FLAHAUT There was absolutely no cause for that.

CLAUDE But he's going to hate me, and he will be right! It's not every day you find on your path the woman who claims to want your happiness . . . this is torture, this life is a living hell . . . and ever since I've stopped asking for anything, they are there after me. Wasn't it just the other day someone was talking to me about a promotion? *(She points to her "Legion of Honor" rosette.)* There was a ribbon to be awarded . . . ah! what madness, ah! how ridiculous. . . . Flahaut, Sorrèze isn't mediocre, no one else, in his shoes, would have had his patience, but it's too much, it's too much . . . what do you think will become of him? I am his exasperating, his unforgivable rival. He changes, and he has to . . .

FLAHAUT *(In a flat voice)* You are exaggerating your scruples.

CLAUDE No, it's terrible. He is changing terribly. In the beginning, he was the one who exaggerated. He respected me so chivalrously as a man, as a lover. He spoiled me, he made fun of himself, he said that husbands nowadays should learn another job, the most difficult of all, that of Prince Albert, that of prince-consort. Sorrèze was wonderful. Flahaut, he helped me . . . he had tireless patience, he was as much concerned with my manuscripts as with his. . . . He ran errands for me and took the initiative, he was the true husband to my career. . . . But he was sure of me . . . he knew that by serving me he was according me a grace. This prince-consort beside me, he had his own kingdom elsewhere. . . . and you are tearing it apart for him, you are contesting it, you are judging him and humiliating him! Sorrèze would have to have no dignity at all not to be hurt. . . . It is the most noble part of him that revolts. . . . Now he has reservations, he receives me like a woman who would betray him, like a woman one can't be sure of! . . .

FLAHAUT Yet surely he isn't jealous of you?

CLAUDE Jealous! No one was less jealous than he. No, he never will be. . . . It should be called something else . . . these sufferings are something completely new. I'm putting him in an impossible situation, that's all there is to it.

FLAHAUT (Sarcastically) You aren't going to insist that I feel sorry for him?

CLAUDE (Madly) Ah! you too? Everything turns against me, husband, child, love, friends, everything holds a grudge and accuses me. I've used up all my strength, I wanted to pull out of myself all the strength that other people admire there, I've expended myself for this world like saints do for the other. I was proud, I didn't value my happiness any less than their eternity. (Changing tone, sarcastically) My happiness! well, there it is, a complete fiasco. . . .

Scene 4

The same, SORRÈZE

SORRÈZE (His unpleasant expression of the last act has turned into his usual mask. He is cordial and sincere.) Hello, Claude. I was passing by, I wanted to congratulate you.

. . . The Nobel prize, that's quite a confirmation. It's a very fine success. You won it over two members of the Academy and . . . over yours truly. . . . (Suspiciously) Hello, Flahaut. I didn't see you, you didn't like my book?

FLAHAUT No, Sir, and Mrs. Bersier was telling me that my article did not have the good fortune to satisfy you. I can't say I was counting on it. I was hoping you would have seen beyond the reservations. . . .

SORRÈZE Ah, dear chap, you have the right to be unhappy, just as I have the right to make you unhappy.

FLAHAUT You know that the author of *Etudes* has no greater fan than I. . . .

SORRÈZE (Roughly) Les Etudes, Les Etudes, that was twenty years ago. . . . You are not encouraging, young Flahaut, take care that someone doesn't say to you some day: Ah! *The Barbarians, The Barbarians.* . . .

FLAHAUT I beg your pardon, Sir, I'm very sorry. . . .

CLAUDE (With animation, to FLAHAUT) Well, hope of French criticism, you'll be smarter next time.

SORRÈZE (Cuttingly) No hard feelings, Flahaut, come and see me some time, since it can be said you cultivate me, and Claude is right, we'll catch up some other time.

FLAHAUT (In a flat voice) I don't doubt it, Sir.

SORRÈZE When you choose to write sympathetically, you are among the best. Your article on Claude is certainly the best that's been done on her.

FLAHAUT (With bad grace) There have been others. . . .

SORRÈZE No one else was able to see the admirable virility of her mind and character. Claude is not only a great writer, she is close to being a great man.

CLAUDE (Surprised) How so?

SORRÈZE I mean that the woman in you, the woman with her weaknesses and her limitations doesn't exist. (CLAUDE makes a movement.) Firm and direct, intelligent and strong, you are a man, Claude, a man made for esteem and admiration.

CLAUDE (Bothered) Ah . . . so that's probably what it will say on my tomb?

SORRÈZE (Laughing) You can be absolutely certain of it, that's what it will say.

CLAUDE (Restraining herself, closing up) I

was so sure of it, I thought I was listening to my funeral oration – in your opinion, what exactly are these woman's weaknesses that I'm lacking? These weaknesses and limitations, what if they were attractions?

SORRÈZE Don't worry, you have your own attractions. . . . Admirably well balanced. (CLAUDE *shrugs her shoulders.*) You aren't high-strung, Claude, that's your first virile characteristic. . . . You will never flatter men's instinct to defend and protect.

FLAHAUT For me, Claude Bersier is very much a woman, she has never seemed virile to me.

SORRÈZE Watch out, my friend, beauty isn't always feminine. (CLAUDE *looks pained and stares off into the distance.*)

FLAHAUT *Jérôme Tiersot* is so much the work of a woman. Just think of the enveloping warmth of feeling. . . .

SORRÈZE Here we disagree, I can never take Claude for a woman in love. In love, no . . . as far as literature is concerned, you understand.

FLAHAUT (*After a silence, with uncertainty in his voice*) Aren't you going to protest, Madam?

CLAUDE (*Without conviction*) No. . . .

SORRÈZE (*Compensating*) Claude is more intelligent than us. She is the first to know what she meant to put in her books.

FLAHAUT (*Going to take* CLAUDE's *hand to kiss it*) I have quite misread you, Madam. A book by a woman has never troubled me the way yours have.

(*He leaves,* CLAUDE *doesn't move.*)

Scene 5

CLAUDE, SORRÈZE

SORRÈZE . . . There's someone who has really changed! After all, I had written other things besides the *Etudes* when he used to come every day to the avenue Marceau. (CLAUDE *nods energetically.*) You hold it against me, Claude, don't you? Say it then, you don't think I have been jealous enough in this matter? (CLAUDE *shakes her head energetically.*) What's the matter then? Why aren't you saying anything?

CLAUDE (*Standing up*) Because I feel like crying and it makes it hard for me to talk, so there!

SORRÈZE (*Makes a banal movement to caress and console*) You feel like crying. . . .

CLAUDE (*Pushing him away*) I'm not a woman. I don't get kissed.

SORRÈZE Ah ! now we're getting somewhere. . . .

CLAUDE If that's your complete retraction. . . .

SORRÈZE (*Seized once again by the hostility of a moment ago*) What sort of complaint is that?

CLAUDE (*Very simply*) That you are ungrateful.

SORRÈZE (*Nervously, getting carried away, with starts*) You have been a comrade, a marvelous friend, Claude (*More thickly*), a mistress too. . . . I don't deny that (*His voice resonates*), but a woman, never. (CLAUDE *turns away brusquely and takes a few steps, one senses impatience and distress.*)

SORRÈZE (*Melancholically, sincerely. One senses that he has found pretexts for his suffering.*) A quarrel that's been stifled for a long time . . . I loved you a lot, Claude. . . .

CLAUDE (*Still with her back turned*) It's over, then?

SORRÈZE (*Simply and movingly*) Not yet, alas, for us, but it looks bad. . . . Can two people like us look at each other without understanding everything?

CLAUDE (*Turning around*) So you understand that it's killing me?

SORRÈZE (*Animatedly, treacherously*) What is?

CLAUDE (*Surprised at first, after a moment's silence*) Your disaffection.

SORRÈZE (*Sincerely*) It comes from such disillusion.

CLAUDE That's what I can't stand. I live only through you, everything that isn't you is dismal. . . .

SORRÈZE An error, an error, an illusion . . . but it's not your fault, my friend, you couldn't know. (*With despair*) You would have had to have been a woman, and nature, endowing you with so many gifts, could not allow that humble science, Claude, to be revealed to you.

CLAUDE (*Opening her arms*) What does it take to be a woman?

SORRÈZE It's so hard to understand each other with words! We are making a quarrel, a painful quarrel out of what was at most a confession.

CLAUDE   The confession that our love has completely disappointed us! You are going to spoil both our lives and I almost feel that it's what you want. *(A* SERVANT *enters and presents a card.* CLAUDE *tears it up without looking at it.)* I'm not at home to anyone.

SORRÈZE   At least see what it is. . . .

CLAUDE   People are harassing me, it's gone too far, I don't want to see anyone.

SORRÈZE   This moment is too important for you. See what it is, Claude.

CLAUDE   No! I don't care what happens to me.

SORRÈZE   *(Goes and takes the card from the tray)* It's a reporter from the *New York Telegraph. (To the* SERVANT*)* Show them in. *(*CLAUDE *is seated, indifferent and distant.)*

Scene 6

The same. AN AMERICAN.

THE AMERICAN   *(To* SORRÈZE, *who steps forward)* Mrs. Claude Bersier? *(*SORRÈZE *gestures, the reporter greets her,* CLAUDE *replies vaguely.)*

SORRÈZE   You are here on behalf of the *New York Telegraph?*

THE AMERICAN   Mrs. Bersier is well acquainted with our newspaper. She has deigned several times to contribute material. On the occasion of the next Exhibition, we are organizing some lectures. All the most prominent figures in Europe have accepted our proposals. In Paris, we already have the agreement of the greatest writers. If we had the same assurance from Mrs. Bersier. . . .

(He turns toward her. CLAUDE, *in a painful attitude, squeezes and twists her handkerchief. She looks elsewhere and doesn't answer.)*

SORRÈZE   Mrs. Bersier is quite unwell. You were shown in because I was here. . . . You can deal entirely with me. I represent her.

THE AMERICAN   It's just that I would like to have it from Mrs. Bersier herself rather than a secretary. . . .

*(*CLAUDE *looks beseechingly at* SORRÈZE.*)*

SORRÈZE   *(Plainly)* Let's not tire her. What is your offer?

THE AMERICAN   We have contracted with these gentlemen 200,000 francs for ten lectures.

SORRÈZE   Of course, Mrs. Bersier will

choose the time . . . How long does the Exhibition last?

THE AMERICAN   Six to eight months.

SORRÈZE   Fine. The date remains to be discussed. Naturally, the travel expenses. . . .

THE AMERICAN   On our best steamers. Mrs. Bersier is guaranteed a luxury cabin. In addition, our newspaper would reserve the right to publish the lectures.

SORRÈZE   *(Interrupting)* How much?

THE AMERICAN   20,000 francs.

SORRÈZE   In Argentina, they did better than that: 30,000.

THE AMERICAN   Very well, 30,000. Our newspaper is prepared to make any sacrifice to get an exclusive with the great continental writers.

SORRÈZE   You can bring the contract. We ask for twenty-four hours to sign it.

THE AMERICAN   That's a lot. I leave the day after tomorrow.

SORRÈZE   Bring it tomorrow morning, and come back in the evening.

THE AMERICAN   We'll do as you wish. *(Toward* CLAUDE*)* I'm sorry that Mrs. Bersier is ill. I hope she'll get over it so that she can write many masterpieces. *(*CLAUDE *makes an imperceptible sign.)*

SORRÈZE   *(Seeing the journalist out)* Tomorrow, if Mrs. Bersier is better, she will judge and decide. You will have her definitive answer by evening.

*(*THE AMERICAN *nods lightly to* SORRÈZE *and disappears.)*

Scene 7

CLAUDE, SORRÈZE

SORRÈZE   That was too good to pass up, Claude.

CLAUDE   *(Still distant)* I won't go to America.

SORRÈZE   Yes, you'll go, my friend . . . because you need 200,000 francs.

CLAUDE   *(The same)* I don't need anything.

SORRÈZE   Excuse me! I don't want to criticize, but you are a big spender, Claude . . . and I wouldn't be surprised if you were poor. Admit that you don't have 200,000 francs.

CLAUDE   *(Like a child caught in the act)* No!

SORRÈZE   At least think of Denise.

CLAUDE   Why are you being so nice, since you don't love me any more?

SORRÈZE   *(Moved)* How could I not be a

friend? Did I say I didn't love you any more? I said I suffered on account of you, but so long as that is still possible, Claude. . . . *(His voice trembling)* So long as you haven't completely kicked me out, you'll find me at your side. . . . *(Trembling more and more)* You understand, don't you?

CLAUDE *(Still seated, holds her arms out to him; he leans over and they give each other a long hug.)* I'm sorry, I'm sorry. . . . I suffered so much just now because of that wretch who didn't recognize you. . . .

SORRÈZE Oh! dear Claude, that a journalist took me for your secretary, give me credit for not thinking I suffer on account of that.

CLAUDE *(Murmuring)* It's the last straw. I am more weary than you of this kind of situation.

SORRÈZE The fact is that for some time now we haven't had any peace, any confidence, any security. . . .

CLAUDE For some time now. . . . But for four years we have adored each other, each of us has been irreproachable, what has changed?

SORRÈZE What has changed? You ask me that when you are as pale as a corpse and I myself. . . . You can see for yourself what has changed. . . .

CLAUDE *(Hesitantly)* Michel. . . . Since Flahaut's miserable article.

SORRÈZE Yes . . . you've known me to be less susceptible, haven't you? I suffered so much from that rude young blow, because it passed between us like a snap of cold air. *(A moment passes.* CLAUDE *is thinking painfully. Low and fast)* I don't know how to reconcile male love and humility.

CLAUDE *(Struggling)* You have been an admirable friend. Words can't express the tact, the devotion . . . I felt through you, for the first time, masculine protection. Through you I've known the honor of giving in to what you love. . . . You are the one who has led me to where I am. . . . And the glory that is your work, what you wanted of me, what you loved in me perhaps, how could it be our enemy? It is our link, our kinship, our marriage. . . .

SORRÈZE *(Patiently)* I thought so, don't do me the insult of consoling my pride. That's not what is suffering. We could be doctors, lawyers, in business, the situation would be the same. . . .

CLAUDE *(Worn out)* I don't understand.

SORRÈZE Yes you do . . . you understand, you understand perfectly. When man and woman meet . . . even on a sports field. . . . What woman is going to fall for a nobody? Me, I'm a literary type . . . that's how I have to show my worth. But you, you who love me . . . you who judge me, you in whom I inspire such incomparable feeling.

CLAUDE That's not true!

SORRÈZE Ah! let me finish, since it's for the first and last time, one doesn't go through this sort of thing twice. . . . You are in torture, my poor Claude, you don't know how to heal, to erase . . . how to be forgiven for your ever-mounting glory. . . . and me, I don't know either how to congratulate you, to admire you strongly enough, to prove to you every moment, prove to the whole world that I'm not jealous. . . . Jealousy, what a fine thing, however, an appropriate thing, when your soul isn't base . . . or worse yet with a husband who gives up. If I weren't jealous of you. . . .

CLAUDE *(With élan)* Ah, if you were not miserable, I would tell you to be jealous with all your might. . . . I love your jealousy, really, it doesn't bother me!

SORRÈZE There is no possible solution. The very greatness of your renunciation would crush me. . . . There was one recourse: my equality. Ah! believe me, I wanted it . . . I was determined . . . no man has ever known such a struggle. The first emotional, conscious competition where I have understood that our love was at stake is this one. I have the feeling I'm being insulted, hit in front of you and that, still in front of you, reparation has had to be postponed. *(More harshly)* Reparation! Even other people, the whole world, requires it. . . . I can't be the only one without, next to your millions. *(His voice resonates.)* It's not up to me, Claude, to glorify myself in your love, you also have to take pride in me.

CLAUDE *(Adroitly and elusively, she looks at him with intense love and murmurs)* I love you this way, humiliated, in pain, wounded. . . .

SORRÈZE *(Troubled)* Don't love me too much. . . . We have to prepare ourselves. . . . We are too emotional today, but there will be other days. . . .

CLAUDE *(After a moment)* Michel, you drifted too far away from me, that's the source of the problem. . . . *(In a very low voice)* You forget too easily that I am a woman . . . like all the others. A woman with whom one can forget one's troubles. . . . *(She leans close to him, not daring to throw herself on his neck.)*

SORRÈZE *(Holding her back from this gesture)* No. . . .

CLAUDE Michel, that's the problem . . . once, just once, come with me. . . .

SORRÈZE *(Very sadly)* No.

CLAUDE *(Her head in her hands)* Why, why, why? Since with all my heart, with all my soul, I can't persuade you. . . . If you knew the degree of slavery. . . . I depend on you more in this awful trial than in all our past happiness.

SORRÈZE Spare me.

CLAUDE *(Stamps her foot in anger)* Ah!. . . . Why are you leaving me, why does it have to be me? I won't say another word, Michel, I won't respond to your worthless obsession, that you aren't there, at home. . . . If it ever comes down to a final scene between us . . . I accept it only where I can be completely myself. . . . When I feel the weight of your neck in my hands again, or when you take me by the shoulders with your wonderful threatening gesture, when I don't know if you are going to beat me or love me. . . .

SORRÈZE *(Bowled over)* You are seeking a holocaust for our pride, compensation? For henceforth our love can only be that; a compensation. . . . I don't want your body, which I used to hold in the new joy of equality, to become bait. . . . *(A moment of silence, they are on the verge of sobbing. Simply)* Come on, you can see it's over, goodbye. *(He holds out his hand to her.)*

CLAUDE *(Looking at him timidly)* Michel, you won't suffer any more . . . when you've left me?

SORRÈZE *(Plainly)* I'll suffer in another way that I prefer. . . . *(She is incapable of speaking.)* I'm leaving in time, I refuse to be present at my downfall, that's all . . . be quiet . . . remember what we were . . . and then, just now, with Flahaut, that flaming sword between you and me . . . no, no, no . . . the disappointment would become impatience and then tolerance . . . never, never. . . .

CLAUDE *(Mad with grief)* You are an inventor of torture . . . none of that exists.

SORRÈZE *(With authority)* Yes it does. . . . Man's love alone can diminish, woman's must increase. *(Darkly and brusquely)* I've told you everything. Let me leave while my departure can still hurt you, while you can still suffer on account of me.

CLAUDE You don't love me any more.

SORRÈZE *(Moved)* You still have a friend, Claude . . . it's better this way, believe me. *(He holds out his hand to her.)* You can humiliate a friend, but you can't humiliate a lover.
(CLAUDE, without looking at him, barely extends a hand, which he squeezes with a sort of relief. He picks up his briefcase and leaves rapidly. For a moment, CLAUDE is alone on stage.)

Scene 8

CLAUDE BERSIER, A SERVANT

SERVANT *(Entering)* Madam, ah Madam is back. We thought Madam was with the young lady. Should we remove the young lady's place setting . . . it's half past eight.

CLAUDE *(Without moving, distant)* Ask the young lady to come down. . . .

SERVANT But the young lady went out, not an hour ago, she hasn't come back. *(Voices in the antechamber)* I saw the young lady put a letter on the tray, I thought it was for the mail, but it has Madam's name on it.

BERSIER *(Entering)* Denise went out leaving a letter . . . shall I open it?
(CLAUDE makes a sign.)

BERSIER "Dear Mother, I shall surprise you perhaps less than I fear. You have often told me that it's your job to understand. I am leaving for Grandmother's. I'll stay there no doubt until I get married, if I get married. After what has happened between us, I don't think any explanation is necessary. I'm sorry to leave at a time when you are in such distress, it had been decided, I couldn't put it off. . . ." But has Denise gone mad, what are all these matters I knew nothing about? *(CLAUDE makes a gesture of discouragement.)* Were you aware of all this?

CLAUDE *(Unable to quit her lethargy)* She never said she would leave, that she wanted to leave . . . just yesterday . . . no, I would never have thought it!

BERSIER That's very informative of you . . . you would never have thought it, indeed! So what happened . . . scenes between the two of you?

CLAUDE Not even that. *(Shivering slightly)* That child didn't like me.

BERSIER And you think that's a good reason? First of all, why didn't she like you, you always petted and spoiled her. . . .

CLAUDE *(With great melancholy)* You can see for yourself that she's gone.

BERSIER Good Heavens! my dear, you talk about it as though it were an acceptable alternative. . . . I'll have her back to you in no time. . . .

CLAUDE *(Gently)* No. . . . leave Denise alone. *(As though regaining her vivacity)* Saints preserve me from keeping people against their will!

BERSIER But damn it, you are not the only one involved here, there's me to consider, how nice of Denise to think of me. You don't leave your mother and father just like that, especially when you've thought about it maturely, as Denise claims to have done.

CLAUDE *(Fatalistically)* Persuade her to come back.

BERSIER I shall, I promise you.

CLAUDE And if she refuses?

BERSIER You can give me your explanation . . . if I don't get it out of her first.

CLAUDE *(With great unhappiness)* Don't torment the child . . . let Denise be happy in her own way . . . since we've failed our way.

BERSIER She was an only child, showered with everything . . . much too spoiled. What we didn't do for her. *(He is so annoyed by the departure of his daughter that he forgets his former grievances.)* Even if your mother is a famous woman, that's no reason to just dump her. . . . Well, what are we to do?

CLAUDE *(Slowly, with tiredness)* The best thing . . . I'll write a letter, a long letter to Denise . . . I have no pride . . . I'll try, I'll explain to her . . . but not tonight, oh no, not tonight. . . .

BERSIER Very well, as you wish, let's give her time to reflect. As for me, I'm going to write to my mother.

CLAUDE Yes, that's it. . . . Don't get too worked up, think how happy Mrs. Bersier is going to be.

BERSIER *(Exiting, muttering)* Still, in Denise's place *(With conviction)* between my mother and you. . . . Hello, Flahaut.

Scene 9

CLAUDE, FLAHAUT, MISS HALLER

FLAHAUT *(Entering)* Excuse me for disturbing you, my dear *maître*. I took the liberty of bringing Miss Haller who is seeking news about her book. She's there in the gallery, and I'm returning Miss Denise's manuscript. Would you mind returning it to her?

CLAUDE *(Seated at her desk, her hands inert and idle, almost without intonation)* Denise has left.

FLAHAUT To go where?

CLAUDE She has run away.

FLAHAUT *(Stupefied)* With whom?

CLAUDE All alone. She was unhappy at home with me.

FLAHAUT *(Vehemently)* She was jealous of you, it's not the same thing.

CLAUDE *(Who is beginning to understand this)* First of all, it is the same thing, and secondly, when it comes down to it, maybe she was right.

FLAHAUT Are you very upset, Claude?

CLAUDE *(Still without gestures or intonation)* Me? I don't even think about it. . . . I've received quite another blow, I defy all the rest to bring me down.

FLAHAUT *(Observing her)* Sorrèze?

CLAUDE Yes.

FLAHAUT A scene?

CLAUDE Worse than that.

FLAHAUT Did you break up?

CLAUDE Yes.

FLAHAUT The wonder is that it took you three years to get around to it. You are going to experience a terrible crisis . . . and you'll overcome it. *(CLAUDE remains silent.)* Do you hear me, Claude, you will get over it.

CLAUDE *(With a sort of laugh)* Do I care about not suffering any more?

FLAHAUT You must make Denise come back home.

CLAUDE Her father will see to it. She doesn't need me.

FLAHAUT *(Gently)* It's you who need her.

CLAUDE *(Forcefully)* Denise can't do anything for me, and even if she loved me. . . . *(Shivering at the thought of the past)* You don't build you life around a heart that doesn't care about you. . . .

Scene 10

The same, MISS HALLER

MISS HALLER *(Coming forward awkwardly)* Mrs. Bersier? I didn't hear from you, I'm afraid my book must have displeased you.

CLAUDE *(Coldly, slowly)* Why do you persist in writing, Miss Haller? You have no talent, you never will have. . . . *(The two young people are dumbstruck.)*

MISS HALLER *(Squashed)* But you told me. . . .

CLAUDE *(Getting agitated)* I was mistaken, besides did I advise you to write in the first place? Have I ever advised a woman to write? I just let you carry on, that's all.

MISS HALLER So, it's no good? Should I start over?

CLAUDE *(Ambiguously)* You'll never do any better than this, leave it. . . . Learn tapestry and embossed leatherwork.

FLAHAUT Don't pay any attention, Claude isn't well.

CLAUDE *(With authority)* I've never been more lucid.

MISS HALLER *(With tears in her eyes)* Why are you discouraging me like this?

FLAHAUT Claude has a lot of problems. . . . She told me that your book was superb. . . .

MISS HALLER Is that true?

CLAUDE Obviously, you have style . . . like everyone. A certain originality . . . who doesn't? But it's lacking in volume. . . . I don't sense any future in what you are doing. You don't have any talent, you've no business here. . . . Go away! Go away!

MISS HALLER *(Trembling)* I didn't know it was the custom to inform people of those things so harshly.

CLAUDE You'll go on writing all the same. . . . Later on, you'll remember my advice. . . .

MISS HALLER *(Choking back her tears)* I must really have disappointed you. . . . Goodbye, Mrs. Bersier, rest assured, it will take me a long time to finish a new work.

CLAUDE *(Watching her go)* Goodbye Miss Haller.

Scene 11

FLAHAUT *(Indignantly)* Why did you do that?

CLAUDE Because she interests me, that girl.

FLAHAUT She might have believed you!

CLAUDE That's the best thing in the world she could do.

FLAHAUT Not every man is like Sorrèze.

CLAUDE *(Slowly, in a monotone)* You weren't there, you don't know. . . . It's not Sorrèze's fault.

FLAHAUT Let's see, if the roles were reversed, would you have stopped loving him if he had been your superior?

CLAUDE It's not the same thing. . . . *(Slowly)* But if I'd been a man, Flahaut . . . I've thought about it a lot . . . if I'd been a man, well then I would have suffered like Sorrèze, perhaps with less patience than him.

FLAHAUT Meanwhile, you're going to have to react and not just act negatively. . . . Don't behave the way you did with Miss Haller. . . . I'll bring her back in a week and you'll do me the honor. *(CLAUDE looks at him curiously and he stops.)* In a week. . . . *(CLAUDE laughs a little, as though she were shrugging her shoulders. FLAHAUT observes her very closely.)* Claude, promise me. . . .

CLAUDE *(As though she were answering her own thoughts)* Women don't kill themselves.

FLAHAUT *(Looking into her eyes)* Honestly?

CLAUDE *(Simply, the same)* They let themselves die.

Curtain

Bibliography

Barney, Natalie Clifford (1992) "Retrospective of Marie Lenéru by Magdeleine Marx Paz," in Barney, *Adventures of the Mind*, trans. and with annotations by John Spalding Gatton, New York: New York University Press, 191–98.

Duclaux, Mary (1920, rpt. 1966) "Mademoiselle Marie Lenéru," in *Twentieth Century French Writers: (Reviews and Reminiscences)*, Freeport, NY: Books for Libraries Press, 214–22.

Gilbert, Sandra M. and Gubar, Susan (1989) "Soldier's Heart: Literary Men, Literary

Women, and the Great War," in Gilbert and Gubar, *No Man's Land: The Place of the Woman Writer in the Twentieth Century*, New Haven: Yale University Press, 258–323.

Lavaud, Suzanne (1932) *Marie Lenéru: sa vie, son journal, son théâtre*, Paris: Société Française d'Editions Littéraires et Techniques.

Lenéru, Marie (1922) *Journal*, Paris: Crès.

—— (1928) *Pièces de théâtre* [*La Triomphatrice* and *Les Lutteurs*], Paris: Figuière.

—— (1988) *Saint-Just*, rpt., Paris: Editions du Trident.

Maugue, Annelise (1987) *L'Identité masculine en crise au tournant du siècle*, Paris: Rivages.

Perrot, Michelle (1987) "The New Eve and the Old Adam: Changes in French Women's Condition at the Turn of the Century," in Margaret Randolph Higonnet and Jane Jenson (eds) *Behind the Lines: Gender and the Two World Wars*, New Haven: Yale University Press, 51–60.

Roberts, Mary Louise (1994) *Civilization without Sexes: Reconstructing Gender in Postwar France 1917–1927*, Chicago: University of Chicago Press.

Waelti-Walters, Jennifer (1990) *Feminist Novelists of the Belle Epoque: Love as a Lifestyle*, Bloomington: Indiana University Press.

Weinreis, Sister Anne Marie (1942) "The Drama of Marie Lenéru," M.A. dissertation, Notre Dame, Indiana.

Whitridge, Arnold (1924) "Marie Lenéru," in Whitridge, *Critical Ventures in Modern French Literature*, New York: Scribner's, 119–40.

6 Alfonsina Storni, 1892–1938

The Master of the World
Argentina

Alfonsina Storni addresses spectators at the Poetry Festival in Mar del Plata. *Photograph provided courtesy of Alejandro Storni.*

Introduction

by Evelia Romano Thuesen

Alfonsina Storni is widely known as a poet, but little known as a playwright. Born in Switzerland in 1892, Alfonsina gained recognition and praise for her poems, and usually appears in photographs and anthologies among the well-known writers and intellectuals of her time in Argentina, which became her home country in 1896. She published her work between 1916 and 1938, the year in which she committed suicide. Alfonsina's life and works were contemporary with those of three other famous women poets from neighboring Latin American countries, the Chilean Gabriela Mistral and two Uruguayans, Delmira Agustini and Juana de Ibarbourou. The coincidence of these four talented personalities make this period and these writers particularly relevant for the study of Latin American women's poetry, and women's studies in general.

However, Alfonsina was unique in venturing into the theater, where she composed four plays for the general public and several others for children. While celebrated as a poet, she has been mostly neglected as a dramatist, although her plays constitute important and interesting documents in her creative evolution and in the literary and social history of Argentina during her lifetime.

Life and historical context

The personal life of Alfonsina illustrates the discrimination directed against unconventional women. After a short stay in San Juan, her family settled in the province of Santa Fe. Alfonsina's first encounter with the theater, not as an author but as a traveling actress, occurred during these formative years. Alfonsina's mother, Paulina, an amateur actress herself, introduced her to the company of José Tallavi in Rosario, with whom Storni toured the country for a little less than a year when she was 16 (Phillips 1975: 54). After this theatrical incursion, Alfonsina went back to her studies to become a teacher, and she graduated from the Escuela Normal de Coronda in 1910. In 1913 she moved to flourishing Buenos Aires, where life was economically and socially strenuous for the growing working and middle classes. In the case of Alfonsina, those hardships were intensified by her personal situation: she was a young, unwed mother who had to survive in a society with very conservative values. Her biographers have described this period of her life (Capdevila 1948; Etchenique 1958; and Delgado 1990).

At the turn of the century, the ideas of a group of socialist women led by Alicia

Moreau de Justo, Elvira Rawson de Dellepiane, and Sara Justo served as a springboard for a movement to improve women's working conditions and rights. Although women constituted a high percentage of the work force, that wasn't enough "to achieve any qualitative change from their secondary status" (Hollander 1973: 143). The efforts of women's movements and associations were rewarded in 1926 with the passage of legislation that recognized a woman's right to equal civil status with men. One interesting antecedent to this victory was the First International Feminist Congress of Buenos Aires, which focused on "education, child abandonment and infanticide, society in general, women's legal position and suffrage" (Jeffress Little 1978: 245). The Congress established that "feminists did not want to create a battle between the sexes; rather that women's rights be respected" and the need for "one moral standard for both sexes". Such concepts throw light on Alfonsina's theater. In fact, Alfonsina was an active participant in these early struggles for equality, as shown by the document cited by Andreola (1976: 137–41) and published in 1921 by the magazine *La mujer*, "Derechos civiles femeninos" (Women's Civil Rights), in which she denounces the unjust situation of women and advocates the adoption of social and political measures to overcome it.

Work and literary context

The battle of the sexes constitutes one of the thematic foci of Alfonsina's work. From the romantic and submissive tone of her first poems to the belligerence and irony of her final pieces, she expresses the contradiction between her desire for a meaningful encounter with the other sex and her awareness of its impossibility. She explored the world of women's feelings and psychology through her own experience, starting with her first books of poetry, and finally transcended her personal history to portray the general situation of women in some of her later poems, such as "Pudiera ser" (It Could Be) and "Veinte siglos" (Twenty Centuries).

After the publication of *Ocre*, her fifth book of poetry that appeared in 1925, almost ten years passed until the publication of *Mundo de siete Pozos* (World of Seven Wells) in 1934. During those years of poetic silence, Alfonsina applied her talent to the writing of plays, which showed her need of expression beyond the lyric.

The first two decades of our century are regarded as the Golden Age of the Argentine theater. Three authors, Florencio Sánchez, Gregorio de Laferrére and Roberto J. Payró are the most representative of the period (Ordaz 1963: 19–21), while women playwrights are non-existent. Actresses, however, played a principal role in the flourishing of the theater. Elba Andrade and Hilde Cramsie, in the introduction to their anthology *Dramaturgas latinoamericanas contemporáneas* (Contemporary Latin American Women Playwrights, 1991) mention the public character of the theater as one of the causes of the absence of women playwrights. Women belonged traditionally to the private sphere of the house. Actresses were usually regarded as belonging to a marginal class, and as representing other people's thoughts rather than making statements on their own.

Phillips (1975: 61) remarks on the declining quality of theater during the 1920s in Argentina, which must have deprived Alfonsina of valuable models. The most direct antecedent of Alfonsina's plays may have been a theater focused on female psychology and social situations, exemplified by the realist comedies of Iglesias Paz and the drama of ideas, such as *La mujer de Ulises* (Ulysses' Wife, 1917) of González Castillo and *Con las alas rotas* (With Broken Wings, 1917) of Emilio Berisso (Berenguer Carissomo 1947: 381–82). *The Master of the World* follows the line of the so-called "high comedy" (*alta comedia*) by Luis Ordaz. High comedy aimed at the critical representation of high society, relying on European-style intellectual games rather than on a psychological exploration of character (Ordaz 1965: 12).

Alfonsina's theater: *The Master of the World*

Alfonsina wrote four plays for adults, *El amo del mundo* (The Master of the World, 1927), *La debilidad de Mister Dougall* (Mister Dougall's Weakness, 1927), and *Dos farsas pirotécnicas* (Two Pyrotechnic Farces, 1931) consisting of *Cimbelina en 1900 y pico*

(Cymbeline in 1900 and Something) and *Polixena y la cocinerita* (Polixena and the Little Cook), and several other plays for children. Her theater for adults follows the same trajectory as her poetry, from confessional autobiography in *El amo del mundo* to a more objective experimentation in the two *Farsas*. These were written after her trip to Europe, where she became acquainted with post-war artistic movements, in particular with the ideas expressed by Ortega y Gasset in *La deshumanización del arte* (Phillips 1975: 91).

The Master of the World was the only one of the four plays performed while Alfonsina was alive. *La debilidad de Mister Dougall* was neither performed nor published in her lifetime, and the *Dos farsas . . .* were performed posthumously. The second play's theme resembles that of *El amo del mundo*, and, although the author considered it the intellectual equal of her first one, shows technical development (Jones 1979: 93). In the *Dos farsas . . .*, Alfonsina keeps her thematic focus on women's roles, but she achieves ironic distance and a more accomplished dramatic technique.

El amo del mundo was performed for the first time on March 10, 1927, at the Cervantes Theater in Buenos Aires. The play ran for only a few days, despite the opening night audience's enthusiastic response, according to the testimony of Alfonsina's son, Alejandro, who was present that night. Critics' harsh attacks were aimed more at the play's feminist themes than at its technical defects (Jones 1979: 87). In spite of the critics' attack, the play is essential to any history of women artists in Argentine society, as well as to a study of the evolution of Storni's literature and ideas. We should remember that women's civil rights had been recognized only one year earlier, and despite that victory, the "media had always portrayed the dedicated women who fought the battles for women's rights in less than sympathetic terms" (Hollander 1973: 146). Such was the atmosphere and prevailing attitude that Alfonsina's play encountered.

In her "Entretelones de un estreno" (Behind the Scenes of a Debut) published in *Nosotros* (April, 1927) and cited by Nalé Roxlo and Mármol (1965: 117–23), Alfonsina blames the failure of the production partially on the director and company, who,

according to her, changed parts of the script and misinterpreted characters. She also mentions (Nalé Roxlo and Mármol 1965: 120–21) several personal and external reasons for *La Nación*, *La Prensa*, and *Crítica*, the three most important newspapers of the time, giving the play a negative review.

The play repeats the argument of one of Alfonsina's best known poems, "Tú me quieres blanca" (Nalé Roxlo and Mármol 1965: 115) which denounces the moral double standard. The original title, "Dos mujeres" (Two Women), was changed because of the existence of a previous play with the same name and also with the hope of making it more appealing to the audience, shifting the emphasis from the female to the male characters (Jones 1979: 89). To answer the criticism that was based on her attack of the male sex in the play, Alfonsina in "Entretelones . . . " explains that she named the play "Dos mujeres" so that both good and evil would be represented by female characters (Nalé Roxlo and Mármol 1965: 120).

The autobiographical elements are obvious, since Margaret, the principal character, is an unwed mother. At the same time, the capricious attitude of Tendril also resembles the Alfonsina persona of some poems where she seems willing to play men's games for her own amusement or advantage, such as "Hombre pequeñito" (Little Man) and "Capricho" (Caprice). The male characters in the play are the more defeated, because they are trapped in their own beliefs, and unable to overcome the stereotypes of male behavior. Alfonsina's characters belong to the upper classes of the time: they live comfortable lives with no trace of economic worries. The lower middle class is represented by the servants: Emily, the waiters, and the doorkeeper. They share the same gender values as their masters, but ironically seem more aware of the limits of those values and their consequences in reality. The portrayal of the upper classes as dysfunctional may have contributed to the play's poor reception.

The thesis play, focusing on women's psychology and social situations, already existed and was even well received by Alfonsina's audience. But *The Master of the World* is the first Argentine thesis play in which a woman playwright represents her sex according to her own personal experience and values. This play established a significant precedent for other Argentine women playwrights and opened the proscenium to the woman's point of view.

Acknowledgments

I thank my colleague Thad Curtz for critically reading the translation and providing very useful suggestions.

The Master of the World ⸻

(El amo del mundo)

A comedy in three acts
1927
Play translation by Evelia Romano Thuesen.

Alfonsina Storni

Original text: published in *Bambalinas* (April 16, 1927), weekly theatre journal
Performed for the first time in the Cervantes Theatre of Buenos Aires, by Fanny Brena's company, on the night of March 10, 1927

Characters

Principal

MARGARET, 35 years old

TENDRIL, 18 years old

CLAUDIO, 43 years old

ERNEST, 21 years old

CHARLEY, 14 years old

EMILY, 30 years old

Supporting

CELIA, 24 years old

GIRL 1
GIRL 2 } around 20 years old
GIRL 3

WAITER 1
WAITER 2 } between 30 and 40 years old
WAITER 3

MISTER RODRíGUEZ, 40 years old

A GUEST, 50 years old

DOORKEEPER

A YOUNG MAN

SOME GUESTS WHO DO NOT SPEAK

Note

The original title of this comedy was *Two Women* (*Dos mujeres*). It is being published complete, including the detailed stage directions. Since it is a play of nuances, the expression of each character should be carefully considered.

Principal characters

MARGARET: Beautiful, with a proud appearance. Her hairstyle is sober and distinguished. She does not wear jewelry. Her eyes are penetrating and intelligent. In the first act, she is dressed in black, with a long-sleeved suit; in the second act, she is dressed colorfully, with a sleeveless suit. In the conflict, she is the woman who escapes from her environment.

TENDRIL: Delicate, with a sickly appearance; she possesses an unusual personal charm, moves like a squirrel, cold, faded-blue eyes. She is all imagination, calculation, affection, and cunning. Her way of talking is light, carefree, childish, and hides, intentionally, an uncommon intelligence serving her feminine interests. In the conflict, she is the woman who gets into her environment, adjusts to it, and profits from it. She pretends to be weak and uses that pretended weakness to dominate those who are stronger than her. She dresses fashionably, with lovely suits, short hair, necklaces, and amulets.

CLAUDIO: A natural, worldly elegance. Rich and bored with his life. For him, everything is merely worth a shrug of his shoulders. He is fast and categorical in his judgments. His overconfidence in his observations obscures the truth around him. Being a man, he believes he is the master of the world. A woman for him could be a whim, an amusement, even foolishness, but never another being with equal moral integrity.

ERNEST: The common modern young man; he is as polished, concerned, and proud of his appearance as a young, handsome sportsman could be.

CHARLEY: A precocious child, accustomed to an intellectual atmosphere.

EMILY: A good, common woman.

Act I

The scene presents the living room of a modern house, decorated with sober artistic taste. At the back, from right to left, run dark wooden stairs that lead to the first floor. At the right, a big sofa can be seen first, covered with Calchaqui[1] blankets and pillows. There are several expensive mats on the black and white ivory floor, and shelves with books on the walls. Under the stairs, there is an artistic piece of furniture, locked. To the left there is a small table. There are magazines and books on the furniture. The set suggests a tasteful intellectual atmosphere. At the left, a wooden door without glass leads to the open hall toward the street. At the right, two doors lead to the dining room and the library, whose interiors are partially seen. Several armchairs are placed to the right and left of the audience.

TENDRIL *and* CHARLEY

TENDRIL, *with a box of chocolates in her hand, talks on the phone and eats.* CHARLEY *draws, sitting on pillows, in front of a small easel.*

TENDRIL   Ernest? Hello! Ernest? Good morning. I had to make you get out of bed; it's already half past ten. Why? For the same reason as always, and this time I won't wait any longer. . . . Well . . . ? Are you going to give them to me or not? I'm asking if you will give them to me or not. No . . . no . . . I am not going! Go to hell! *(She hangs up the phone.)*
CHARLEY   What's wrong?
TENDRIL   Nothing.
CHARLEY   You look angry.
TENDRIL   I look like doing something crazy.
CHARLEY   Like . . . ?
TENDRIL   Killing. . . .
CHARLEY   A cockroach?
TENDRIL   A man.
CHARLEY   Tendril, remember you are even scared of mice. . . .

TENDRIL   Don't you think that animals are happier than we are?
CHARLEY   Why?
TENDRIL   Because they do what they please, and I'd like to do whatever I feel like doing.
CHARLEY   How boring!
TENDRIL   You act like a grown-up, always so solemn.
CHARLEY   And you pay too much attention to novels; you are constantly repeating phrases, like Margaret says.
TENDRIL   So what? Aren't phrases something nice? Chocolates, colors and phrases are the best things ever invented.
CHARLEY   What's your favorite color?
TENDRIL   Red.
CHARLEY   Why?
TENDRIL   Because it cheers me up.
CHARLEY   My dear Tendril, you have something loose upstairs.
TENDRIL   Maybe. . . . Do you know what I was thinking yesterday night? . . . That I would have liked to be a bird, if birds didn't have to lay eggs.
CHARLEY   What a thought!
TENDRIL   If birds didn't lay eggs, they'd be perfect. Work ruins everything, takes the beauty out of it.
CHARLEY   You're going to end up in a madhouse.
TENDRIL   And you'll come with me: in this house everybody is a little bit crazy.
CHARLEY   Except Margaret.
TENDRIL   Margaret is too nice. . . . Isn't that crazy enough? She is so nice, that if I did commit a murder, I'd confess it to her.
CHARLEY   But as you are not going to kill anyone. . . .
TENDRIL   Well, if I stole something, I would tell her.
CHARLEY   But as you are not going to steal anything. . . .
TENDRIL   Who told you that? Stealing is bad, but nice. Look: when you steal, you remember what you were in former lives. Listen: one day – I have it right here *(Points her forehead. With emphasis)* – I will write poems and I'll do what the modern poets do: praise robbery, but don't think I mean the wretched robbery by one man of another, I mean the robbery of species against species. . . .[2] You'll see.
CHARLEY   Poetry is the only thing you need. . . .

TENDRIL You're wrong; I need many other things. Charley, I want to get married. . . .

CHARLEY *(Singing)* "First comes love, then comes marriage. . . ."[3]

TENDRIL To the roughest man on earth.

CHARLEY I see: to Roger the chauffeur.

TENDRIL Idiot!

CHARLEY If you want rough. . . .

TENDRIL Rough but intelligent.

CHARLEY Look: tell all that to Margaret; let me work.

TENDRIL What are you drawing?

CHARLEY Nothing in particular.

TENDRIL *(Approaching)* A soccer player; aren't you ashamed?

CHARLEY You'd like me to draw Michaelangelo's Moses or something like that . . . right? I'm not a precocious genius.

TENDRIL You are adorable; give me a kiss.

CHARLEY I don't want to.

TENDRIL Come on, kiss me on my forehead.

CHARLEY I said I don't want to! Come on, stop it. *(Stands up and exits right)*

TENDRIL *(In loud voice)* I want a kiss right now, I want a kiss.

TENDRIL *and* CLAUDIO

CLAUDIO *(Entering from the street, through the door at the left)* Don't yell any more, I'll kiss you.

TENDRIL I am not joking: here I am. *(Runs toward* CLAUDIO *who kisses her in the hair. Joking)* This is what I call the tenderness of a father's kiss; it suits me well because I am a helpless person.

CLAUDIO Little devil! I'm determined to find you a husband as soon as possible.

TENDRIL Small task!

CLAUDIO What would you like him to be like?

TENDRIL Like you. *(They look into each other's eyes: she with a somewhat childish perversity, he with calm tenderness.)*

CLAUDIO You are a child.

TENDRIL *(In a caressing tone)* No. I'm a woman; I'm only 18 years old, but my years are worth double: the other girls are simply 18.

CLAUDIO And still, according to what I heard, you haven't learned how to make a bed.

TENDRIL Me? A bed? Or French fries? Daddy, you are humiliating me!

CLAUDIO Actually, beautiful hands like yours should be busy with other things; the hands are the aristocrats of the body.

TENDRIL Isn't that true? I spend an hour polishing my nails. *(Mocking)* I serve beauty in that prosaic way, daddy. . . .

CLAUDIO *(Grabbing her suddenly)* If you call me daddy again, I'll spank you!

TENDRIL *(Wickedly)* Ah, how nice! But hard, hard until it's bleeding. . . .

CLAUDIO *(Releasing her)* You don't know what you're saying. . . .

TENDRIL Yes, I do.

CLAUDIO *(Looking at her with deep, manly eyes)* You are a very promising woman. . . .

TENDRIL Why not an actual one?

CLAUDIO If you were aware of what you're saying, you'd be dreadful.

TENDRIL *(Pretending not to understand)* What?

CLAUDIO Nothing. *(Long pause)*

TENDRIL *(Going to pick up the box)* Want a chocolate?

CLAUDIO No, thanks.

TENDRIL *(Sits on the pillows of the sofa in an informal position, with her legs on the couch, and eats one chocolate after another. Adopts a naïve and pampered attitude)* What do you think is the best quality in a woman?

CLAUDIO *(Standing behind her)* The freshness of her ideas and feelings, total mental and physical innocence.

TENDRIL *(With hypocritical sweetness)* I'm innocent.

CLAUDIO You don't need to mention it: I know it, and I never make a mistake.

TENDRIL *(Suddenly, as a joke)* Is it true that innocence likes wisdom? Do you know which legendary character would have made me fall in love? King Solomon.[4] How nice it would have been to climb up his beard like a beetle. *(Giggles)*

CLAUDIO *(Checking out her morals)* What is your idea of love?

TENDRIL I don't know: I have no idea.

CLAUDIO I knew it: you think and talk boldly, but not on your own. You read too much.

TENDRIL *(Tenderly)* But I don't understand half of what I read.

CLAUDIO What a marvelous little head! *(Touches her hair)*

TENDRIL *(Closing her eyes, romantically)* It's nice to sleep!

CLAUDIO It's better to dream.

TENDRIL *(Laughing)* Do you know that if

anybody reminds me of King Solomon, that person is you?

CLAUDIO   Poor child! You have a frightening imagination!

TENDRIL   What are you saying?

CLAUDIO   Ah, poor girl, you never know what you're talking about!

TENDRIL   (*Furiously*) You're like all of them, you mistreat me and don't understand me! I hate you! (*Turns around like a small animal and bites his hand*)

CLAUDIO   Eh, brat! (*Pushes her away suddenly and she pretends to be pushed and falls on to the floor*)

TENDRIL   (*Crying*) Monster, monster! I hate you, go away!

CLAUDIO   (*Approaching her*) Are you OK? You threw yourself on to the floor on purpose. Come on! You know how hard you were going to bite me?

TENDRIL   (*Still crying*) How hard I *did* bite you.

CLAUDIO   Yes, you did.

TENDRIL   I don't want to talk with you any more. Go, go away!

CLAUDIO   Come on, stand up!

TENDRIL   I don't want to!

CLAUDIO   I'll pick you up. . . .

TENDRIL   I don't want you to!

CLAUDIO   But I do. (*Picks her up in one movement and keeps her in his arms as though she were a child; she smiles and cries at the same time.*) Are you better now?

TENDRIL   A little. Give me a chocolate.

CLAUDIO   With which hand? I have both full.

TENDRIL   A man can always do what he wants.

CLAUDIO   Now I can do what I want. See? (*Hugs her tightly against his chest*) You have to be still as long as I please and your tricks are worthless, little wild girl! I could just choke you slowly until you died. Do you want to die? Do you? (*She giggles again.*) See? Two fingers here, on your pretty throat! . . . Or I could kiss you on the mouth and instead of dying! . . .

TENDRIL   (*Provocatively*) Nobody ever kisses me.

CLAUDIO   Nobody?

TENDRIL   Nobody. (*Naïvely*) What's life about? I am dying of curiosity.

CLAUDIO   Be quiet! (*Kisses her on the mouth*)

TENDRIL   (*In a tone that is a mixture of shame, tenderness and slyness*) Is it true that Eve blushed? Ah, if I'd had a mirror!

CLAUDIO   Yes, you did blush.

TENDRIL   (*With a quick and graceful gesture, and with the intention of bothering him, pointing to his hair*) How many white hairs!

CLAUDIO   (*Puts her down roughly and starts to pace the floor*) Bah!

TENDRIL   (*Her eyes follow him with the ironic, happy, and intelligent look of a cunning hunter.*) What's wrong?

CLAUDIO   (*To himself*) Idiot!

TENDRIL   (*Bumping into him gracefully*) Why are you pacing the floor? Is this a cage? If this is a cage, which animal am I and which are you? It's useful to know.

CLAUDIO   Here it's only one that should be walking on all fours. . . .

TENDRIL   And that one, of course, is you.

CLAUDIO   Yes, it's me. (*He stops suddenly, looks at her short skirt and teases her back.*) Your skirt should be longer; you have too much calf to wear short skirts. (TENDRIL *looks at him in a mocking way. To scorn her*) I am waiting for Margaret.

TENDRIL   I know, she won't be long. (*Long pause*) Listen: do you want me to tell you something that's going to bother you? You don't deserve Margaret. Margaret is a wonderful woman. If I were as worthy as she is, I'd despise all men, no one would touch a single hair on my head. If I let you kiss me, listen, it's because I'm worthless. (CLAUDIO *looks at her with surprise, more confused than ever, and without saying anything touches his forehead in a gesture meaning that she is crazy.*)

CLAUDIO, TENDRIL, *and* MARGARET; *later,* EMILY

CLAUDIO   (*To* MARGARET, *who is entering from the street, wearing a hat*) Good morning to the most elegant woman on earth!

MARGARET   Hello.

TENDRIL   And the nicest!

MARGARET   (*Taking off her hat*) That's right, at least to you.

TENDRIL   I want to give you a hundred kisses, in your hair, your eyes, your hands.

MARGARET   Watch it, you're choking me!

TENDRIL   They call me "tendril." You yourself gave me that nickname. Put up with the consequences.

CLAUDIO Ah! You gave her the name! Good choice!

MARGARET What should we have called her? Since she came to live with me, almost five years ago, she's forgotten her real name.

TENDRIL And they call me "tendril"! It fits me perfectly, doesn't it? Tendrils are always begging, and use their hooks to hold on to firm things. Certainly it fits me well! Margaret, you are not telling me, but your love for me has a little bit of contempt also.

MARGARET But girl, when are you going to stop talking nonsense? What could be more charming than a tendril?

TENDRIL Yes, charming and soft, really soft. . . .

MARGARET Well, supposing that you are soft, as you say, I may add that even though you're soft, I support you with pleasure. Are you happy now?

TENDRIL You're bad, very bad! (Kisses MARGARET's hand)

MARGARET She's a handful.

CLAUDIO I've been waiting for you for a while.

MARGARET Were you waiting for me or my books? You don't go out in the morning, except on business.

CLAUDIO And sometimes to enjoy beautiful faces and beautiful souls; the vice of enjoyment is difficult to give up.

TENDRIL I've hidden all those big books. Here nobody breaks his skull against those rare books.

CLAUDIO What happened to your plan to donate your father's library to the medical school?

MARGARET One of these days I'll do it, although I'm so attached to those books that . . . I don't know!

TENDRIL I'm also interested in them. . . .

CLAUDIO A great father, your father, Margaret. . . .

MARGARET A great father and a great man! His place is still empty! Since he died, I've promised to change my life: I want to travel. I can't waste my time within these walls. I want to see the world on my own.

TENDRIL (Incisively) Maybe you won't go alone. (In a light tone) Listen, my dear Margaret, our friend Claudio has planned something wonderful: he wants to marry you. I guessed it. But I tell you: you

shouldn't accept. You know that I'm an absurd person with great common sense. . . . Now I'm leaving!

EMILY (Coming from the street door) Mr. Ernest wants to talk with the ladies.

MARGARET Bring him in. (EMILY exits.)

CLAUDIO Who's that?

MARGARET A young friend who lives next door.

CLAUDIO Ah, from the Jiménez family.

MARGARET Yes, Ernest.

CLAUDIO The one that won the last car race.

TENDRIL That one. The most handsome young man in Buenos Aires.

MARGARET And the most conceited.

TENDRIL, CLAUDIO, MARGARET, and ERNEST

ERNEST (Coming from the street door) Good morning, Margaret! How are you doing, Tendril? (Greetings)

MARGARET (Introducing them to each other) Mr. Claudio Ochoa, Ernest Jiménez. (They sit down: MARGARET and CLAUDIO in the couch on the right, ERNEST to their left on the armchair; TENDRIL stays standing up close to ERNEST.)

ERNEST I've wanted to meet you for a long time. Tendril has told me so much about you! She really admires you.

CLAUDIO Me? May I learn why?

ERNEST Tendril has a strange way of explaining things: she says that she admires you because you are one of Wilde's paradoxical characters.[5]

TENDRIL Placed in a harsh natural environment, you should add.

CLAUDIO Definitions continue: first Solomon, then one of Wilde's characters, now a rough man. . . . Clearly, I'm Tendril's creation, a futuristic creation of capricious lines and motley colors.[6] I'm thrilled to be reborn from such a wonderful imagination!

TENDRIL (Insolently) I speak inaccurately, but I think accurately, and I can assure you that what I say is too obscure for you who don't understand women.

CLAUDIO I don't understand women? More news. It's the second time that you, little girl, have described me according to your own imagination.

TENDRIL And I think that I'll keep on doing it, because you have many defects. You are very proud of being a man, Mr.

Ochoa. Proud of your low heels, of your cuffs and cufflinks, and of being the master of the world. . . .

MARGARET Tendril, I forbid you to talk any longer. You go too far with your jokes and mockery.

TENDRIL And the worst is that Mr. Ochoa is right to be proud of being a man. Sometimes I feel like crying. Margaret, the world has been poorly made. . . . *(Addressing* ERNEST*)* I don't want to be a woman, to be a woman is repugnant to me, I know what I'm talking about. . . .

MARGARET Stop it, shut up and go!

TENDRIL No, no, I'm sorry. I'll be more sensible. I promise you. Forgive me.

MARGARET *(Calmly)* What did you want, Ernest?

ERNEST Nothing important. Not very long ago, Tendril asked me on the phone to bring her the magazines with detailed pictures of my last race . . . and here they are.

TENDRIL Let me see. *(Approaches* ERNEST*, who stands up, and opens the magazines on a little table on the left)*

CLAUDIO *(To* MARGARET*)* We should control Tendril very closely, morally I mean. She is at a dangerous age. Censor her reading, choose it for her. We shouldn't let her imagination have free rein.

MARGARET Listen, Claudio: nothing that Tendril says is really important: her words, her gestures, like a child's, are just a game; she's all words.

CLAUDIO I know she has excellent morals; but at her age, the wrong book could be harmful.

MARGARET I don't think that books influence her so much. Tendril is a very strange girl.

CLAUDIO Doesn't her father come to see her?

MARGARET No. He gets more hopeless everyday, running from one gambling den to another. Her mother comes, but only once in a while. Tendril hates her.

CLAUDIO Tendril is partially right.

MARGARET Bizarre woman, Tendril's mother. You don't know how much my father loved her, and what is even more bizarre: because of his love for her, he brought Tendril home and put me in charge of her: because of his love for her and to protect Tendril from her.

CLAUDIO Yes, I knew it. Few daughters could have been more generous than you.

MARGARET You know, Claudio, I would have agreed to be burned alive for my father, and I adored his defects as much as his virtues.

TENDRIL *(In low voice, to* ERNEST*)* But. . . . Did you bring the papers?

ERNEST *(In low voice)* Come this afternoon for them. I'll be alone.

TENDRIL *(In low voice)* No, no, a thousand times no! *(Loudly)* Can I see this one? *(She picks up a magazine.)*

ERNEST *(In low voice)* You are capricious, but that doesn't work with me.

TENDRIL *(Loudly)* You look good in this one. *(Looking at a magazine)*

ERNEST *(Loudly)* So-so.

TENDRIL *(In low voice)* I'm going to shoot you. . . .

ERNEST *(In low voice)* OK, I'll send you a gun as a present.

TENDRIL *(Loudly)* This picture is great. *(In low voice)* I'd like to be a man so I could solve this with my fists.

ERNEST *(Loudly)* That's it. As you can see, the information is complete.

TENDRIL *(Loudly)* It's true. *(In low voice)* You'll pay for everything you've done to me. *(Foolishly)* Margaret, look at these pictures of our friend Ernest, last name Jiménez, great pilot, great body, great social life. . . . Two hundred women lie in a cold grave due to his sea-green eyes, green. . . . *(Laughs loudly)*

MARGARET Are you starting again, Tendril?

TENDRIL So? Can't I praise Ernest Jiménez, the sportsman? *(Makes such a funny face that* CLAUDIO, MARGARET, *and even* ERNEST *can't help but laugh)*

MARGARET *(Neglecting* TENDRIL'S *words)* Is it true, Ernest, that you are going out with Catty Miró? She's worth it, isn't she? It means. . . .

ERNEST Three million! Slander. No woman loves me.

MARGARET With shoulders and teeth like yours, three million succumb easily.

ERNEST Besides, Catty is ugly. I expect that in Buenos Aires more beautiful faces would be willing to serve me three million on a plate; we shouldn't rush serious commitments . . .

CLAUDIO . . . that one day become inevitable. It is said that at the age of thirty the symptoms of the diseases that lead to our death begin to appear in the body; transfer that to the moral order and. . . .

ERNEST I will find myself in possession of three million pesos. I accept. I ask: Are these symptoms frequent in a man's life?

MARGARET That depends on the quality of the individual, my friend. If the guy drives a car with elegance, maybe.

ERNEST I swear, Margaret, that I won't leave the wheel for a single moment.

TENDRIL (*Ironically*) Don't forget to always take that striped shirt that suits you so well.

ERNEST Your wish is my command. . . . Pleased to meet you, Mr. Ochoa. Bye-bye, Margaret. (*Mocking*) At your feet, my lovely Tendril. (*Exits through the street door*)

TENDRIL, CLAUDIO, MARGARET

(TENDRIL *sits in an armchair, with a set, serious, surprised look in her eyes.*)

CLAUDIO (*After observing her and trying her again*) Do you like going out, Tendril?

TENDRIL Yes, I do.

CLAUDIO How?

TENDRIL Any way at all.

CLAUDIO What do you prefer, train or car?

TENDRIL It's all the same.

CLAUDIO The car is more comfortable.

TENDRIL Yes, it's true.

CLAUDIO Do you like to drive or prefer the other person to drive?

TENDRIL I prefer the other to drive. I hate to work.

CLAUDIO Then you'd be happy, for instance, if you were in a car and Ernest were driving.

TENDRIL Psch! . . .

CLAUDIO You like Ernest, don't you?

TENDRIL Me? That pompous ass? How could you think such a thing? Defend me, Margaret, you know me. (*Cynically*) Isn't it true that I never flirt with anybody?

MARGARET You're mistaken, Claudio. The Jiménezes have been living next door for three years. Tendril is a good friend of the girls and we trust them. That's all. Besides, despite all her foolish behavior, I don't think Tendril is interested in wasting her time flirting.

TENDRIL (*Craftily*) You understand me, Margaret. (*Very affectionate*) Thank you. (*Suddenly*) Besides, what would I do with an empty man like Ernest? I'm empty and useless enough myself. On top of that, I'm poor; I'm stuck to Margaret. Do you think that Ernest's face doesn't have a price? How could I like a man willing to sell himself? (*Sincerely*) It's true he's so handsome that one feels like punching him, because such a nice face makes one crazy.

CLAUDIO Did you say crazy?

MARGARET Don't pay attention to those words please, Claudio. Yesterday, Mr. Valle said something similar here, and this silly girl is repeating it without rhyme or reason.

TENDRIL I'm very stupid.

MARGARET You expose yourself to being misjudged by others because of your mania for saying what you can't understand.

TENDRIL What I can't understand? (*Pretending*) Yes, yes, it's true, Ernest's face doesn't make me crazy, no. Ernest's face. . . . Well, I don't want to talk about him any more. I am going to disinfect my mouth since I have pronounced his name so many times.

MARGARET I hope you'll use a light disinfectant.

CLAUDIO And pleasing. Lipstick, for instance. It is the most suitable disinfectant for women's lips.

TENDRIL Then it's not good for me, because I'm not a woman: I am just a tendril. Find another kind better for me.

CLAUDIO For tendrils, copper sulfate, without doubt. . . .

TENDRIL That's the one I'm going to use.

MARGARET Go, silly, go and water your plants a little. You need some sun, too, don't forget it.

TENDRIL Until I get a hole in my lungs, I won't be perfect. (*With emphasis*) Margaret, I ought to die of a lung disease![7]

MARGARET I can't put up with you any longer. Go without saying a word. (TENDRIL *closes her mouth with two fingers, and with a comic gesture exits through the right, waving her hand.*)

CLAUDIO *and* MARGARET

(MARGARET *is sitting,* CLAUDIO *stands up and paces the floor; then talks, betraying his interest in* TENDRIL.)

CLAUDIO An original, Tendril!

MARGARET And pretty! (*Intelligently*) You like her very much, don't you?

193

CLAUDIO Psch! There are twenty women in the world whom I like as much as I like Tendril.

MARGARET *(Ironically)* And only one that you like as much as me.

CLAUDIO That is. . . .

MARGARET Do you know what you feel for me? Curiosity, a great curiosity.

CLAUDIO And everything else. *(Takes a book from a shelf and skims through it. Speaks carelessly)* Margaret, I am an unhappy man. I've just cashed in my new inheritance. It is a lot of money for only one man. Help me to deal with it.

MARGARET And what can I do?

CLAUDIO *(Always skimming through the book)* Marry me. I need an intelligent, strong partner more than ever. You are the only woman whose company never bores me.

MARGARET But you're so far from loving me, Claudio.

CLAUDIO *(Stopping his skimming through the book)* So are you, my good friend. We're two sensible people, able to create our happiness instead of waiting to be chosen by it.

MARGARET *(Sadly)* You're the man who knows me the least and the one who sees me the most frequently. How strange!

CLAUDIO It's not strange. You're a woman, that's all. . . .

MARGARET *(Bitingly)* Oh, yes! Eve, the obscure Eve! . . .

CLAUDIO But in you Eve is a little clearer than in the rest of women. You control the prompting of your heart very well. That's a start.

MARGARET *(With the dignity proper to a person not understood)* You mean that I'm somebody who obeys other people's commands, adjusts to the given model, crushes her heart, and destroys her real moral persona?

CLAUDIO You get prettier when you complain, so pretty that, despite my words and yours, I think that, maybe, I love you.

MARGARET *(Intelligent and sure of her words; a little sad, and ironic underneath)* No, Claudio, you don't love me. You are somehow attracted by the woman you imagine in me, let's call it a superior woman, and you surround me with a celestial halo. It's because of my father's influence. Even after death, his big shadow protects me. For you, for everybody, I live immersed in a spiritual atmosphere. Maybe it's due to my way of dressing, always in black; to my way of living, always inside the house; to the discipline of the people who work for me; to being up at six in the morning; and maybe – this is even stranger – to my habit of drinking tea without sugar.

CLAUDIO Maybe. But all that is superficial. The most attractive thing in you is that part of yourself that seems impossible to possess completely.

MARGARET Fairy tales.

CLAUDIO And something else. . . .

MARGARET *(Ironically)* My purity.

CLAUDIO Yes, your purity.

MARGARET *(Emphasizing her irony)* Of body and soul.

CLAUDIO Yes, of body and soul.

MARGARET *(Almost mocking)* It would be wonderful, in this late age, to awaken in me a surprising fire: the passion of a twenty-year-old; to see the frightened eyes that have been innocent before! . . . Oh, the sensuality of a refined man!

CLAUDIO Terrible sensuality, because you can understand it. . . .

MARGARET *(As a wicked act, because knowing him and knowing that she will be rejected, she prefers to provoke scorn rather than pity)* Fairy tales. Listen, in a couple of words I'm going to destroy everything your imagination has constructed. I will reveal to you what is inside yourself. I know you well, much better than you know me. . . . In a couple of words! . . . Here they are: Charley is my son.

CLAUDIO *(Turns to her as if bitten by a snake)* That's a lie! You are playing with me!

MARGARET *(Proud of having risked so much)* So, you don't even believe me, do you? You don't believe that I was able to love, to give life to another being and to keep him close to me to guide him in life, do you? Don't force me to despise you! I kept it secret up to now because of my father, only because of him. I didn't have the right to expose him to his enemies. But he knew it and he helped me to keep Charley with me. He also helped me to conceal all this from everybody. Someday, any day, if you want, I'll tell you the details of how it happened, but not so you'll forgive me. I don't want to be forgiven. I wasn't tricked into doing what I did; it was my choice, my decision, my own will, as a free being. What should I be forgiven for? I have committed only one crime: to keep Charley ignorant of the fact that I'm his mother. I'm really guilty of that. But I'm going to remedy that as soon as possible, despite and against everything. I confess to you first, who have been the least suspicious.

CLAUDIO *(Angry at her and with himself for being deceived and thinking that she was as he wished her to be)* I see that you are an excellent actress. I wouldn't have believed you capable of concealing such a thing so well.

MARGARET *(Bitingly)* But I won this round. In a couple of words I've torn down your love literature. See? I destroyed the chaste woman that you dreamt I was. You can't take my words back. . . . I am like any other woman. What could you call me? Come on! Give me a name! You could call me: despicable!

CLAUDIO *(Dryly)* There's no doubt that, like every woman, you are wicked. There's no doubt, either, that in every woman, the simplest or the most cunning, the silliest or the most intelligent, you can find all women.

MARGARET *(Scornfully)* Yes, and in any man, even in the most liberal one, all men! *(They take a challenging look at each other; he shrugs his shoulders and walks toward the main door; she follows him with her eyes, indifferently, without trying to stop him.)*

Curtain

Act II

The scene is the same as in the preceding act.

TENDRIL and EMILY

TENDRIL I'm telling you that it's very easy; haven't you, who go to the movies so frequently, noticed it? Listen: tomorrow, Sunday, nobody will stay home, not even the servants; I've made sure. I have the keys here. You don't have anything to fear.

EMILY But, Miss, I don't dare to go in; if they catch me, they'll think I'm a thief.

TENDRIL Nobody will catch you; I'll be watching from over here. It's so close,

Emily, so close and so easy, that in ten minutes everything will be done. Look. *(Approaching to the back door on the right)* That window, the one right next to the jasmine vine, is the room of Mr. Ernest. . . .

EMILY Yes, I know, but. . . .

TENDRIL But what?

EMILY I don't know, I wouldn't know; I can't. . . .

TENDRIL Why are you a maid if you don't know how to steal? What a way of carrying out your duties! You lack class. . . .

EMILY But Miss. . . .

TENDRIL I'm giving you a hundred pesos.

EMILY No, Miss, money is not the issue.

TENDRIL Idiot! I'll give you my gold bracelet, that's worth a lot more.

EMILY I wouldn't dare to enter somebody else's house for all the gold in the world.

TENDRIL Shut up! Shut up! You don't have the soul of a maid. You're a vulgar hired hand; a canned squid is more worthwhile because it's canned in its own ink. Don't look at me with that open mouth; I don't need you to look at me; I need you to know how to manipulate a chisel and bring me those letters.

EMILY Miss, I love you very much, but I can't do that; I don't dare.

TENDRIL You don't love me! Love is sacrifice! The old-time servants used to loot and rob to feed their masters.

EMILY Maybe, nowadays, servants have more shame, Miss.

TENDRIL Go away! Do you want me to believe that you never stole a thing, that you never forced the lock of a drawer? I'm telling you to go away!

EMILY *(Starts to go inside, but she turns back at the door)* I promise you that I won't say a word to anybody about this.

TENDRIL Who cares if you tell or not? Tell. I'll go in your place and do your job, because I do know how to steal, fool. Bring me a chisel, and I'll show you. *(THE MAID goes out right, and TENDRIL goes to the locked piece of furniture that is under the stairs and starts to pull out the drawer with rage.)*

EMILY Here it is. *(Gives TENDRIL a chisel)*

TENDRIL Look, you shove the blade of the chisel here and we pry the drawer open. Pull, harder! *(THE MAID pulls on the handle, while TENDRIL struggles with the chisel.)* Don't you have any strength?

EMILY But, Miss, I'm pulling. Don't you see that the wood is not giving?

TENDRIL It will. I swear it will give. Pull again! You are in my way.

EMILY This isn't as easy as it looks, Miss. This is a man's job.

TENDRIL I'll do it by myself, as soon as you leave, because you are nothing but a nuisance. Haven't you noticed that I always accomplish what I start out to do? Don't look at me with those stupid eyes. I'll sacrifice myself. You know perfectly well that I'm trying to save a girlfriend from an intrigue. Or did you think that I'm capable of getting in trouble like you? Don't you know this house? Don't you know me?

EMILY But I am not saying anything, Miss; you're the one making all this up!

TENDRIL Shut up and go to hell! (THE MAID *exits.*)

TENDRIL, MARGARET, *and* EMILY

TENDRIL (*Struggling again*) It has to burst, like it or not, it has to burst!

MARGARET (*Coming down the stairs, drawn by the noise*) What's that noise? What are you doing with that tool?

TENDRIL Nothing! Damn it! (*Throws down the chisel and bursts into tears*)

MARGARET What happened? Why are you crying?

TENDRIL Margaret, help me, only you can save me.

MARGARET What's happening?

TENDRIL I need to confess something serious to you, but very serious. I know how good you are, how understanding.

MARGARET But what?

TENDRIL Tell me, tell me, before I speak, if you'll despise me. Listen, Margaret, I'm a person – how can I put it? – with no morals! But I don't want you to despise me. I'm willing to deceive everybody but you. You are like a mother to me; even more, you are like a mother who's also a friend. I need you to know how miserable I am.

MARGARET Don't keep me in this suspense. Come and sit here. (*Brings* TENDRIL *toward the sofa*)

TENDRIL No, no, at your feet. (*Sits at* MARGARET'*s feet*) Let me rest my head on your lap; kiss my forehead, kiss it many times. . . .

MARGARET But, child, talk, tell me. . . .

TENDRIL Look, I. . . .

MARGARET What?

TENDRIL I'm being threatened.

MARGARET But what's threatening you?

TENDRIL Ernest is threatening me because – how can I tell you – ? He has some letters that compromise me to a great extent.

MARGARET Letters?

TENDRIL You are surprised, aren't you? Look . . . well I . . . to Ernest. . . . How can I put it? . . .

MARGARET Tell me, please. I'm dying to know!

TENDRIL Well, I kissed Ernest, a lot. Do you understand?

MARGARET When was that?

TENDRIL A few months ago; four, five. . . . You know how capricious I am. He's so handsome! Do you remember how I used to spend the afternoons at his house with his sisters? So many girls wanted him. . . . He's so conceited! You didn't notice anything because I'm a scoundrel and conceal things very well. . . . But the game went further than anything you could imagine.

MARGARET How far did it go?

TENDRIL Ay, how could I tell you? Everything happened, the most signifi- cant, the most serious thing that could happen between a man and a woman.

MARGARET But, where? . . . How? . . .

TENDRIL Don't torment me with questions; here, in his house, on the sly; I can't explain it. But it didn't have any conse- quences, Margaret, none.

MARGARET Oh, my God!

TENDRIL Look, now he's repugnant to me, and I'm repugnant to myself; but every- thing has already happened.

MARGARET And why is he threatening you?

TENDRIL Because he wants to have me in his power, to play with me, to humiliate me. He can't accept that I've rejected him. He threatens to give my letters to the first man that gets close to me. Talk to him, ask him for the letters!

MARGARET Haven't you asked him your- self?

TENDRIL Twenty times, but he sets a horrible price.

MARGARET Shut up, please!

TENDRIL Do you despise me?

MARGARET I told you to shut up.

TENDRIL Will you talk to him?

MARGARET Right now.

TENDRIL Margaret: since I started talking today, I need to keep telling you other things. Listen: I want to bury this episode of my life forever. I want to get married. I have a plan, a wish.

MARGARET Go on.

TENDRIL Help me, try to understand me. I'm in love with Ochoa.

MARGARET What else?

TENDRIL While I believed that Ochoa could marry you, I didn't dare to tell you anything, but now that I know you don't want to be his wife, I dare to talk, to ask you to help me; I'll thank you all my life.

MARGARET So you intend to conceal everything from him, do you?

TENDRIL (Vigorously) Ah, yes, yes; everything from everybody, except you! (Recovering herself) Do you think that I'm not able to deceive a man? Do you think, on the other hand, that men shouldn't be deceived? All women deceive them; all deceive them a little.

MARGARET You're wrong. Many women don't have anything to conceal from their husbands.

TENDRIL I am not saying that they conceal important things, but they do conceal many silly ones, like mine!

MARGARET And what do you call a silly thing or a serious one?

TENDRIL Look, our mind makes things serious. . . . The way we see things, we feel their weight in our lives. . . .

MARGARET And what could be heavy for you? Things affect you like water off a duck's back. Silly thing! Because of your "silly thing," other women kill themselves, others beat their chests all their lives, others reject love forever, others confess it trembling, as though they had skinned a child alive. But, yes, you're right: anything you do seems just chance, silliness. . . . Your actions take the color of your character; my actions take theirs from mine. . . .

TENDRIL Maybe, yes, but what do you want me to do? Should I destroy my life and be honest? And tell me: are men honest with their women and do they tell them, before marrying, of their lecheries? Why should we humiliate ourselves before them? Don't you see that it's a life or death matter? No, no; I don't want to tell

a single word to Ochoa; he has said twenty times that he's too much of a man to accept the love of a woman who has already loved. Don't you know that?

MARGARET Yes, I know it.

TENDRIL If he had the smallest suspicion about this, he'd stop loving me.

MARGARET Do you, perhaps, know that he loves you? Because you say you're in love, but what about him?

TENDRIL I have to tell you something else: two days ago I met him in the street. We had tea together. I can assure you he likes me more every day, because I understand these things very well. . . .

MARGARET (Looking at her with grief) You are such a case, Tendril.

TENDRIL You rejected him, didn't you? He told me. You did right; he doesn't deserve you.

MARGARET (Gloomily) No, I didn't reject him; life made us reject each other.

TENDRIL Help me, it shouldn't be hard for you. I know you wouldn't be able to do what I'm doing, but you are rich, in charge of your own life, and I'm alone: I don't have anything, not even good health. And I don't want to go back to my mother, never, never! Life is full of temptations, help me! You know I have a pretty bad disposition. (Noticing the cold look in MARGARET's eyes) No, no, don't despise me, not you. (Kisses MARGARET's feet, knees and hands)

MARGARET Tell the maid to go for Ernest: he must come immediately. (With pity) Ah, if only I could sacrifice myself to give you a fresh start! (TENDRIL presses the button to call the maid.)

EMILY (Entering) Miss. . . .

TENDRIL Go to the neighbor's, to Jiménez's house and tell Ernest, from Miss Margaret, to come right away.

MARGARET Go upstairs, to your room. I need to be alone; leave me alone.

TENDRIL Ay, Margaret, I know you well; don't get upset because of this. You don't know how to be happy; nobody can tell the truth all the time; sometimes, deception is a necessity.

MARGARET Listening to you drives me crazy; you take advantage of me, using your weakness; you exploit me with it, and the worst is that I understand it – see? – and I let you exploit me. . . .

TENDRIL But I admire you, Margaret, I

worship you, adore you: you are the only person I'd want to die for. . . .

MARGARET And you use me as an instrument of your plans, you implicate me in your misery, you offend me with your tricks, you force me, almost, to be your matchmaker!

TENDRIL *(Hot-headedly)* Give me your moral strength, then; here you have my veins, open them! Why aren't you opening yours up and sprinkling me with your blood! Yes, yes, give me your life, your soul, your nerves, your father, your mother. . . . Is it my fault that I suffered meningitis? Is it my fault that my mother has a different lover every month? Do you think I don't know all that? Why don't you pity me?

MARGARET Leave me, please, go upstairs, go away!

EMILY *(Entering)* Mr. Ernest is here.

MARGARET Bring him in. (THE MAID *exits left.)*

TENDRIL Don't be mean!

MARGARET Come on! Go upstairs!

TENDRIL I'm going. *(Runs upstairs)*

MARGARET *and* ERNEST

ERNEST *(Entering from the left, with his hat off)* Good afternoon! *(Offers his hand to shake, but* MARGARET *pretends not to see it and points to a seat for him)*

MARGARET Sit down.

ERNEST Do you need me?

MARGARET I have to talk seriously. *(Long pause during which* ERNEST *and* MARGARET *look at each other,* ERNEST *with curiosity,* MARGARET *harshly)*

ERNEST I suspect what's the matter; your attitude is telling me: I knew this would come sooner or later.

MARGARET And are you telling me that so calmly?

ERNEST Please, I'll ask you not to let Tendril's story give you the wrong impression. I certainly know her better than you. I'm sorry, but the people who are nearest to us are the ones we know the least. The comedian that lives within Tendril is not the usual kind. If she hadn't been under your protection, I wouldn't have had any consideration for her.

MARGARET And did you have any, at all? Do you imagine that Tendril has hidden anything from me?

ERNEST Yes, I had great consideration;

I did much less than any other man would have done in my place; but I can't talk to you about details that words don't let me describe.

MARGARET Talk, please, because I need to know everything.

ERNEST I can't, I don't want to. I assure you that I didn't trick her, that I didn't promise her anything. Everything that happened is her fault and only her fault.

MARGARET No, I'm not going to ask you to marry Tendril; don't defend yourself beforehand. I want to ask you, I want you to promise me, since you are a man, that you're not going to bother her at all, and that nobody, not even your shadow, will suspect what happened between the two of you; and, besides, that you'll give to me every little letter of hers that you have, at once.

ERNEST So, you believe I could use those letters despicably, don't you? Look: I kept them because of my resentment: I would have thrown them in the fire any day, but, it's true, I wanted to upset her. Margaret, you don't have any idea of the devil that lives within that girl when she is possessed by a whim: mockery, boldness, cynicism, everything combines within her to drive the most decent man crazy. She has taken advantage of my natural manly discretion, she has stirred up cruelty in me, and even rude behavior. It's true that I told her I'd give those damn letters to the first man that approaches her; but you would under-stand the use of those poignant words if you were a man and could see yourself manipulated by a hysterical girl.

MARGARET I know perfectly well that when there is a conflict between two people, both think of themselves as the victim. . . . The human condition is so weak. . . . Bah! I don't want to know about anything. You're a man and that says everything. I can't thank you for what happened, but I don't dare to reproach you either. I only insist on what I asked you before: you have to promise me absolute discretion, no matter what happens with Tendril in the future.

ERNEST I promise you seriously. You don't know how much I regret that you found out about this. Believe me, I'm very confused. Some men's actions can only be understood by other men.

MARGARET   Yes, maybe. . . .

ERNEST   You'll have the letters in a moment.

MARGARET   Have them delivered to me in person.

ERNEST   I'll make sure of that! Excuse me Margaret. *(He offers his hand, and he and* MARGARET *are shaking hands when* CLAUDIO *enters.)*

MARGARET, ERNEST, CLAUDIO, *and* EMILY

CLAUDIO   *(To* THE MAID, *who was leading him)* It's OK, I remember the way. *(*EMILY *exits.)* Good afternoon. How are you doing, Margaret?

MARGARET   Oh, what a surprise!

CLAUDIO   The maid told me that Jiménez was here. How are you?

ERNEST   Fine, as ever.

CLAUDIO   And Tendril?

MARGARET   She's resting; she had a bit of a headache.

ERNEST   I'll leave you; I was leaving when you arrived.

CLAUDIO   Stay, my friend; five minutes. . . . Would that be too much?

ERNEST   Not at all.

CLAUDIO   I feel like talking, nothing more.

MARGARET   Sit down . . . here.

CLAUDIO   *(Getting a cigarette from the top of the small table. To* MARGARET*)* I heard the news. Tendril informed me that you started smoking a month ago.

MARGARET   Ah, yes; it isn't important. No one knows why, for instance, we change perfumes or soap from day to day. I'm not prejudiced about petty things.

CLAUDIO   Why are you talking about prejudices? Smoking is good, entertaining. . . .

MARGARET   And it stains the fingers. . . . I'm still a poor smoker. *(*ERNEST *and* CLAUDIO *smoke;* MARGARET *refuses the cigarette that* CLAUDIO *offers her.)*

ERNEST   You needed me for some special reason, Ochoa. How can I be useful?

CLAUDIO   Young people are always useful; they exist and that in itself is useful; they speak, do something crazy, and that's useful too.

MARGARET   Actually, Ochoa, you have the mind of a writer. One of these days you'll surprise us with a novel, a drama. . . .

CLAUDIO   I have never written a line; I never will. I lack the essential vanity to believe that my observations are interesting to other people.

MARGARET   Sometimes, without being vain, one can feel the desire to talk aloud.

CLAUDIO   I don't feel that need.

MARGARET   Maybe that's why you're so bored.

CLAUDIO   Very bored; I'm so bored that more than ever I feel like doing something extravagant: becoming a pilot; traveling through the world on foot; taming wild beasts.

ERNEST   Women are more difficult. Don't you practice that sport?

CLAUDIO   There are no women left on earth; however, one of these days I'll marry the first one that stops my way. That will be fun! . . .

MARGARET   It isn't wise of you, Claudio, loving women who live in a gynæceum, to make a hasty choice.[8] Don't you know, Ernest, that our friend Claudio tenaciously pursues innocence? Do you think that he is such an original man?

ERNEST   I don't see the originality. All men pursue innocence; the problem is to get it.

CLAUDIO   One has to have a good sense of smell.

MARGARET   *(Deliberately)* There's nothing more cunning than a cunning woman.

CLAUDIO   *(Conceited)* Nor more sensitive than the nose of a man over forty.

MARGARET   *(Deliberately)* If we didn't have the pride that makes us see in others what we want to see. . . .

ERNEST   I agree.

CLAUDIO   I can see that you've surrendered to Margaret. . . .

MARGARET   *(Ironically)* Completely surrendered. Don't you know, Claudio, that I am about to fall in love with Ernest? It must be the syndrome of being thirty, such a dreadful age for women.

ERNEST   *(Following up* MARGARET*'s irony)* Margaret is so beautiful, so stately! Would it actually surprise you that I, or anybody, would be in love with her?

CLAUDIO   *(Lightly)* It's clear that I haven't been here for a while. *(Suddenly, showing that he was actually looking for her)* Isn't Tendril coming down?

MARGARET   *(Gloomily)* I'll call her.

ERNEST   *(Continuing the comedy)* I know you thought she was the reason I was visiting this house so frequently. What a mistake! She's not a woman; she's just a little girl.

CLAUDIO (*Sure of his words*) Actually, she's as childish and girlish as a woman could be. She speaks her mind to the four winds. And I'm never wrong.

ERNEST Maybe she can give you happiness, my friend Claudio. (MARGARET *gives* ERNEST *a look full of surprise, reproach, anguish, but when* CLAUDIO's *eyes meet hers, she closes her eyelids wearily.*)

CLAUDIO (*With an ironic smile*) Are you still living next door?

ERNEST Still. The villa is ours.

CLAUDIO (*Insinuating*) It's truly a dream house. I noticed the marvelous arbour when I passed by.

MARGARET (*Showing that she understood* CLAUDIO's *innuendo*) And so tempting! If you had seen it at two in the morning, full of spring roses and bathed by moonlight! What a scene for a future writer, my friend Claudio!

CLAUDIO (*Rudely*) And what a perfect nest for a devoted lover!

MARGARET Would you lend it to me sometimes, Ernest, now that I smoke?

ERNEST Are you thinking of taking our friend Ochoa there to listen to the crickets sing?

CLAUDIO It's true that that's the only thing I could do next to Margaret.

MARGARET You are, in fact, a man with a great sense of smell. You adjust to reality with marvelous precision.

ERNEST (*Looking at his watch*) Now I am leaving for real. I have an appointment in fifteen minutes.

CLAUDIO I appreciate your company. Come to see me. I need some entertainment. Let's see if we can go to Mar del Plata in my car or in yours, on the spur of the moment, sometime this week.

ERNEST Whenever you want, just give me a call. (*To* MARGARET) See you soon, Margaret.

MARGARET (*Goes with him to the door on the left, talking to him in low voice*) Don't forget your promise.

ERNEST (*In low voice*) I won't forget.

MARGARET *and* CLAUDIO

(MARGARET *gets a cigarette and sits down on an armchair to smoke it. Her attitude is dignified and negligent at the same time; she smokes gracefully;* CLAUDIO *watches her with desire.*)

CLAUDIO (*The suspicion that arose in the preceding scene has made him bold.*) You've changed a lot.

MARGARET You have too. In what ways do you notice change in me?

CLAUDIO I don't know. In your gestures, your dress, your cigarette. I never saw you with your arms naked before.

MARGARET I haven't seen this look in your eyes before, either.

CLAUDIO Me?

MARGARET Yes.

CLAUDIO What kind of look is that?

MARGARET A covetous one.

CLAUDIO Whom do I covet?

MARGARET (*She shrugs.*) You should know. (*Starts smoking again;* CLAUDIO *sits in front of her and watches her in silence, running his eyes over her and smoking as well; she suddenly stands up, throws away her cigarette, goes to him and speaks aggressively, with indignation.*) You could have been good enough to be my husband some day; you would never be good enough to be my lover.

CLAUDIO (*Indifferently*) What of that?

MARGARET (*Fiercely*) What about your eyes? Do you think you need to speak your intentions? They appear in your eyes as bright as lanterns.

CLAUDIO (*Brutally*) And what if I have intentions? Is it my fault the way you hold your cigarette, the way you cross your legs?

MARGARET (*With scorn*) You've never been so weak with me before.

CLAUDIO You've never been so insinuating. Why are you complaining?

MARGARET I'm not complaining; I'm observing.

CLAUDIO Observe.

MARGARET You couldn't stop being a man.

CLAUDIO I've always been a real man.

MARGARET (*Reflecting upon this with grief*) Do you know? Every day confirms for me the mental abyss between the sexes.

CLAUDIO Maybe.

MARGARET No, no; your right isn't my right; your piety isn't my piety.

CLAUDIO You need to remake the world.

MARGARET Why? It's all right as it is. (*Long pause*)

CLAUDIO (*Caustically*) So I'm not good enough to be your lover, but good enough to be your husband, am I?

MARGARET (*Calmly*) Yes, just the opposite

of a man's judgment. A man's logic would be: she can be my lover, but she isn't good enough to be my wife.

CLAUDIO Nevertheless, somebody was good enough to be your lover.

MARGARET *(Vehemently)* And I wouldn't have married him. My passion, the truth of my heart was too big. I loved a man for what he was, without caring about his intelligence, his social status, his background, his education; I loved him naïvely, sacrificially, to the point of losing or winning everything; that's the only justification for a lover in the life of an honest woman. A husband can be justified by need, by fear of being alone, by the desire of having a companion for the petty, daily things . . . bah! . . . ordinary things.

CLAUDIO Thank you.

MARGARET Don't mention it. *(Long pause)*

CLAUDIO Do you want me to tell you something that will move you deeply?

MARGARET Tell me.

CLAUDIO You're a wounded being that wants to get all her strength from her wound.

MARGARET You're wrong. I'm much more than a woman: I'm a human being. And facing you, since I don't need you, I'm free. And do you know the extent of my freedom? I'm free to the extent of not feeling offended by an act of love. I can look at you as an equal. I can talk to you as an equal. I can judge you as an equal. I feel the right to ask you if you thought you were worthy enough for me to receive your last name one day.

CLAUDIO The last name again. You insist on it too much. Come on, Margaret, free woman. You gladly would have been my wife, my honest wife, my bourgeois wife.

MARGARET *(Inaugurating the quarrelsome tone that will culminate at the end of the scene)* Never! Your manly conceit would have humiliated me. You would have thought of yourself as the clean one, the honest one who can forgive the miserable crime of a petty thief. Never!

CLAUDIO Why should we talk about this? Everything is dead. You killed it yourself. You lacked the ability, the tact to deceive me, to smooth things, to gild them. The disenchantment came from your attitude more than the facts themselves.

MARGARET I knew it; that's why I adopted that attitude. I don't want to have to dissimulate in front of the man destined to love me; to take advantage of his weakness would be repugnant to me; besides, I'm proud enough to aspire to be loved for what I am.

CLAUDIO Nobody will love you.

MARGARET So much the better.

CLAUDIO Hate, curiosity, eagerness to destroy you, to defeat you, to humiliate you, yes; but love, tenderness, the delicate tenderness of a lover, no. . . .

MARGARET So much the better! I can have the luxury of being the neutral audience of those things that always happen between a clever woman and a foolish man. Because men unwittingly appreciate cleverness in women, if that cleverness gives them some kind of pleasure, physical or mental. Do you think I don't understand?

CLAUDIO Do you know what the effect of intelligence in a woman is? It deforms her. She ends up a hybrid without the total, unbridled boldness of a man or the modesty and the coquetry of a woman, which are her strongest weapons. What use can philosophizing be to her? It just breaks her moral ties. . . . She can't be free unless she gets away from love because then she can philosophize, but nature burdens her with a child. . . . Why go on? Then comes what's impossible to understand in a free woman: concealing from the child himself that she's his mother, denying him the right to call her by her name.

MARGARET If I've done that, I did it for others: not for myself, but for others. And I'll remedy it.

CLAUDIO Life isn't just our own, but also other people's. How is it possible that an intelligent woman like yourself hasn't understood that?

MARGARET Then it's necessary to modify other people's lives; there is nothing more terrible than a man who believes he has a right that's being denied him. . . . The explosion of a right denied can blow up a mountain.

CLAUDIO As for the rest, when a woman thinks as freely as you do, one can't see her as a woman any more. . . . One can only see the comrade.

MARGARET Bah! You're just coming out of

the cave! ... For me the brutality of your words is much more pleasing and noble than your lustful desire a moment ago.

CLAUDIO   All the same, between a man and a woman my desire a moment ago is more natural than all this useless argumentation.

MARGARET   *(Despairing at his lack of understanding)* You are a man, a man to the marrow of your bones! ...

CLAUDIO   And you are so far from being a real woman, so separate, so distant!

MARGARET   What an aberration!

CLAUDIO   *(Without listening to her, despising her strength)* Do you know when intelligence is good in a woman? When she can use it to enhance her qualities, her natural talents; when it helps her to understand that she has come to the world to adjust to the man, and then her intelligence lies in her attraction, charm, affection. ...

MARGARET   *(Bursting with glee, because he, who is humiliating her, is at the same time giving her the opportunity to humiliate him)* Like Tendril!

CLAUDIO   Yes, perhaps, like Tendril!

MARGARET   *(Yelling, out of control)* Tendril! ... Come down! *(Without noticing her own yelling, continues her reasoning)* Besides, at that age, thinking hasn't deformed the natural character yet; hasn't twisted it, hasn't spotted it; the malice, the cunning haven't yet arisen. One can take a woman then and shape her as one pleases and order her intelligence to make her more of a woman. *(Yelling even more, in her desire to throw* TENDRIL *into* CLAUDIO's *arms as soon as possible)* Tendril! Tendril!

Enter TENDRIL *and* EMILY

TENDRIL   *(Coming downstairs, stops halfway and looks out from the handrail)* I'm coming! ...

CLAUDIO   Hello, Tendril!

TENDRIL   *(Waving to him)* Hello! Good afternoon!

CLAUDIO   *(Also yelling, from the bottom of the stairs, and with the intention of infuriating* MARGARET*)* Tell me, Tendril, blonde devil, would you marry me?

TENDRIL   *(Running down for the remaining steps)* Me? Right now! (CLAUDIO *goes to welcome her at the bottom of the stairs and they hold hands; they remain together until the end of the scene.)*

EMILY   *(Coming from the left, approaches* MARGARET, *who is upstage)* Mr. Ernest gave me this for you and asked me to give it to you in your own hands. *(Gives her a package of letters, tied by a lace)*

MARGARET   Very well. (EMILY *exits.)*

CLAUDIO   *(Turning around)* What's happening?

MARGARET   Nothing; something between Ernest and me.

CLAUDIO   *(Staying next to* TENDRIL*)* Ah! (MARGARET *bounces the package of letters in her hands, absent-mindedly, gazing into the distance.)*

Curtain

Act III

*A room with some leftover furniture, in disarray, as though the room had been half emptied to furnish other rooms and spare furniture had been brought in. There is an expensive carpet in the center of the floor and a luxurious chandelier. There is a big desk between the door at the back of the stage and the ones to the right. There is a small carved table in the center with some writing materials on it. There are some leather-covered armchairs and pictures on the walls. At the back, on the left, is a large glass window, closed and covered by a luxurious curtain. At the back, on the right, is a door to a hallway that runs parallel to the scene, from right to left.
The hallway ends in a decorative garden, illuminated by round lights at the top of low columns. There are some marble benches in the garden. At the right is the door to Tendril's dressing room; at the left is another door that leads to the room for the wedding gifts. The back and left doors are locked when the curtain rises. At the appropriate moment, one can see through the large window the movement of the wedding party in the hallway and the garden. It is nighttime.*

EMILY, DOORKEEPER, *and* TENDRIL

DOORKEEPER   *(Knocks on the door at the back:* EMILY *turns the key and he comes in with a jewel case and a letter.)* The presents won't stop coming! The messenger who brought this has orders to deliver it personally to Miss Tendril and to wait for an answer. Where is she?

EMILY   *(Pointing to the door at the right)* In that room, getting dressed. I'll tell her.

THE MASTER OF THE WORLD

(Knocking on the door) May I come in, Miss Tendril? I have a letter for you!

TENDRIL *(From inside)* Wait a second.

DOORKEEPER I have other presents, should I bring them here? There's no more space in the gift room.

EMILY Miss Margaret gave orders not to let anybody come in here, but I'll ask her again.

DOORKEEPER The young lady is setting herself up well, isn't she? According to my information, Mr. Claudio received a fat inheritance not long ago.

EMILY Even so, I'm afraid nothing good will come from this marriage.

DOORKEEPER If you say it's because of the short engagement, you shouldn't worry; it's useless to look at the outside of the fruit; 'til you cut it, you won't know what's inside.

EMILY Between the girl's whims and Mr. Claudio's temper!

DOORKEEPER Up to now, she's been in command. She's got what she wanted!

EMILY She wouldn't get married any other way. She got the altar as she likes it, the priest that she likes, the day that she likes.

DOORKEEPER Miss Tendril is that sort of woman.

EMILY You should have heard her complaining to Mr. Claudio because he didn't want to get married in church. . . . She made such a fuss! Saying she, more than anyone, deserved white flowers, poetry, chiffon, a white gown! Come on, she can fool him as she pleases.

DOORKEEPER That means happiness, lady, no doubt about it.

TENDRIL *(Entering from the right with white shoes and white petticoat and a very elaborate coiffure)* Where is it?

DOORKEEPER Here, Miss. *(Gives her the letter and the case and TENDRIL opens it)*

TENDRIL *(Disdainfully)* Ah! . . . Where's Miss Margaret?

DOORKEEPER Looking after the guests.

TENDRIL Tell her that I need her.

EMILY Miss Tendril, how much I'll miss you! You were the joy of this house; you always had a witty remark and an easy laugh; we'll be very sad.

TENDRIL *(In a light tone)* Emily, I've never hugged you, even when nobody helps to put stockings on as you do! Come here! Give me a hug!

EMILY Miss, you're making me cry!

TENDRIL *(Hugging her)* Come on, come on! *(Touching EMILY's cheek with one finger)* Crocodile tears! . . . *(Looking at her finger, joyfully)* A tear! Beautiful! . . . The first one tonight that anybody's shed for me.

EMILY That's not true; Mr. Charley has already cried.

Enter MARGARET, CLAUDIO later

MARGARET *(Through the back door; she is dressed in black for the wedding, with a hat. To TENDRIL)* But, child, what are you doing still half dressed? *(To EMILY)* Lock the door. *(EMILY locks the door again with the key.)*

TENDRIL I only have to get on the dress and the veil, please! Let me have a little rest from those tedious women: dressmakers, hairdressers, the manicurist. . . . I'm tired! I called you because my mother sent this with a letter . . . you can answer her; I wouldn't know what to say.

EMILY Miss, I have to ask you if we can leave the presents that don't fit in the other room in here and let people come into this room.

MARGARET Here? . . . But this is a mess!

EMILY It will be easy to tidy up. We can put the boxes on that desk. I can take care of it.

MARGARET *(Absent-mindedly)* Very well, do it. *(THE MAID goes out through the back, closing the door as she leaves, while MARGARET and TENDRIL are talking. EMILY and the DOORKEEPER carry presents and rearrange the armchairs; they bring some flower baskets; they always close the door as they enter.)*

TENDRIL Here's some paper and a pen.

MARGARET *(Standing close to the small table in the center, writes. TENDRIL stands close to her.)* I don't know what to tell her! . . .

TENDRIL My dear Margaret: a promise is a promise. I'm starting a new life. And what a life! You won't recognize me, Margaret. I swear I'll be an excellent housewife; you won't find a home as original as mine in the whole world! *(In a light tone)* Do you know that somebody promised to give me an adorable monkey?

MARGARET *(Looks at her with a little sadness)* Not a monkey?

TENDRIL Yes, Margaret, because I don't want any children.

MARGARET That sounds great: you'll dress

your monkey in red – I guess – and take him out for a drive with you and your husband.

TENDRIL You haven't forgiven me, have you? . . .

MARGARET I love you! . . . *(To* THE DOORKEEPER *who's going back and forth)* Give this to whoever brought that letter. *(Gives him a closed envelope)*

DOORKEEPER At once.

EMILY *(Showing a basket of flowers to* TENDRIL*)* This just arrived.

TENDRIL Beautiful! . . . Beautiful! . . .

MARGARET I haven't had any time to see anything.

EMILY There are some wonderful presents. *(Continues tidying the room)*

MARGARET How frivolous!

DOORKEEPER *(Reentering)* Mr. Claudio wants to see Miss Tendril.

TENDRIL No, no! I can't be seen. He won't see me until I have the veil on. I'll call you to put on the final touches. . . . Talk to him, you, my very bad, my very nice Margaret! *(Throws a kiss to her and runs to her room)*

MARGARET *(To* THE DOORKEEPER*)* Tell Mr. Claudio that I'm here, that he can come in. *(*THE DOORKEEPER *exits at the back.)*

CLAUDIO *(Entering from the back)* And Tendril? Isn't she ready?

MARGARET She doesn't want you to see her until she has the veil on.

CLAUDIO But she has to hurry up; it's already half past eight; we'll miss the train.

MARGARET We're a minute from the station; I think that everything will be over by nine, because I believe that everybody will leave after the ceremony.

CLAUDIO Everybody already knows that you're leaving tonight. *(Pause)* Why the trip?

MARGARET I want to have a change.

CLAUDIO *(Approaching to her and shaking her hand very cordially)* Friends?

MARGARET Friends!

CLAUDIO You deserve all the happiness in the world; somebody more sane than me will give it to you.

MARGARET Thank you.

CLAUDIO Maybe I'm wrong involving Tendril in my eccentricities, but what's done is done. Do you think I'm bad?

MARGARET We are as we are. . . .

CLAUDIO Neither better nor worse than anybody else.

MARGARET That's right; just different. . . .

CLAUDIO *(*EMILY *exits right.)* Do you know the story about a man that eats half a lamb, several dozen eggs, twenty cakes and doesn't die of indigestion, but of a mosquito bite?

MARGARET Why are you thinking of that?

CLAUDIO Because of my marriage, of marriage in general. One step more! . . . Like the toss of a coin, heads or tails!

MARGARET *(Interrupting him)* Don't forget to remind the people outside that I'm traveling tonight. As soon as you leave I don't want to be looking after anybody.

EMILY *(Enters from the right)* Miss Tendril wants to see you. . . .

MARGARET Go and see what she wants, Claudio.

CLAUDIO See you in a moment; try to speed things up. *(Exits at the back)*

MARGARET We'll be ready in five minutes. *(Exits right.* EMILY *gives the final touches to the room's arrangement: opens the curtain that covered the large window, unlocks and opens the door on the left, and exits through the back door, leaving it open. In the garden people dressed in gowns are walking, and some guests are sitting on the benches; through the opened doors come the laughter and talk of women; waiters go by with trays.)*

GIRLS *1, 2 and 3*

GIRL 1 *(Sticking her head out, on the left)* Look, there are more presents here.

GIRL 2 Let's see!

GIRL 3 *(Looking at a box)* Is it crystal?

GIRL 1 Make it sound.

GIRL 3 Can anybody see us?

GIRL 1 No!

GIRL 3 It's crystal!

GIRL 2 What's this?

GIRL 1 A gun.

GIRL 2 How scary! Is it loaded? . . .

GIRL 3 This must be Ernest's present.

GIRL 1 Then it's loaded for sure and the bullet is . . . for Tendril! . . .

GIRL 2 Don't talk nonsense. What does Ernest care about Tendril! He has as many women as he wants.

GIRL 1 Do you know what I saw in the garden?

GIRLS 2 *&* 3 What? What? Tell us!

GIRL 1 I'll whisper it to each of you, in

your ears. (*Goes to each of the girls and whispers something in their ears; the three of them laugh wildly.*)

GIRL 2 You invented that.

GIRL 3 I believe it.

GIRL 1 Poor them!

GIRL 2 (*Looking at another box*) Oh, perfume, and one of the best! It will suit the bride very well!

GIRL 1 If some day I get married, I'll start getting massages with perfume three months before.

GIRL 3 (*Scoffingly*) You're so Oriental!

GIRL 1 I'm convinced that a soft.skin is the best antidote against divorce.

GIRL 2 I'm an experienced person.

GIRL 1 I'm as experienced as you; don't play silly.

GIRL 2 Do you know what I read the other day in a magazine, in the feminine counseling section?

GIRLS 2 & 3 What?

GIRL 2 A reader asked if she could wear black lingerie the day of her wedding.

GIRL 1 Really?

GIRL 2 I swear it!

GIRL 1 What would you do if you were a man and you discovered that under her white wedding dress, your bride was wearing a black slip?

GIRL 2 I'd kill her!

GIRL 1 Sure, I'd kill her for being a fool. What a lack of common sense! What would you call a woman who does something like that?

GIRL 3 Hasty!

GIRL 2 Or spontaneous. (*They all laugh.*)

GIRL 1 That can only be accepted in a lover. . . .

GIRL 3 Or in a married woman, after being married for a while.

(*Enter* ERNEST, RODRÍGUEZ; *later a* YOUNG MAN)

GIRL 1 (*To* ERNEST *who is entering from the left*) Hello, irresistible! How could you let somebody steal your girlfriend?

ERNEST Tendril was never my girlfriend.

GIRL 1 She was almost your girlfriend.

RODRÍGUEZ (*Comes behind* ERNEST) Girlfriend? Who? . . .

GIRL 3 Tendril was Ernest's girlfriend.

RODRÍGUEZ It's understandable; Tendril is the kind of young woman that we men call dangerous.

YOUNG MAN (*Sticking his head out through the door at the back*) Beth, Lisa: the priest is here.

GIRL 2 Ah, how moving!

RODRÍGUEZ Are you moved?

GIRL 2 Weddings always impress me. The whole paraphernalia impresses me.

YOUNG MAN Come, girls!

GIRL 1 Watch your comments!

GIRL 2 See you later!

GIRL 3 We're coming, Jack. (*Exeunt* GIRLS *and* YOUNG MAN *through the hallway*)

ERNEST, RODRÍGUEZ, CELIA, *and* MARGARET

RODRÍGUEZ What do you think of the wedding?

ERNEST It's just like any wedding.

RODRÍGUEZ It's amazing what a middle-aged man will do to catch a fresh fruit!

ERNEST At least, sometimes, like this, the man gets what he was looking for.

RODRÍGUEZ "No one acts more foolishly than a wise man in love."[9]

ERNEST (*Sitting down*) And Celia?

RODRÍGUEZ She's over there, with a group of friends, looking at the presents.

ERNEST The presents are good, but perhaps not as good as the ones at your wedding; they must have amounted to a fortune.

RODRÍGUEZ But Celia has recently misplaced a marvelous pair of cufflinks, a wedding present from my business partner. . . .

ERNEST How did that happen?

RODRÍGUEZ She left her purse in a coffee shop the day she was taking them to the jewelry store to get them repaired.

ERNEST Bad luck. . . .

RODRÍGUEZ They were so fine! . . . With two top-quality diamonds, as big as the ones on your shirt buttons.

ERNEST Like these on my shirt?

RODRÍGUEZ Like those.

ERNEST How long since that happened?

RODRÍGUEZ A couple of weeks.

CELIA (*Enters from the left*) Honey, I was looking for you! How are you, Jiménez? Have you just arrived?

ERNEST Yes, not long ago; I've had a very busy day. May I tell your wife, Rodríguez, that she looks very nice?

RODRÍGUEZ She'll appreciate it very much.

ERNEST Being thinner suits you very much; I haven't seen you for four months.

CELIA Don't you notice I'm different?

ERNEST Maybe, a little. . . .

CELIA *(To her husband)* I'll tell him the secret. *(*RODRÍGUEZ *smiles.)* See? . . . I plucked my eyebrows.

RODRÍGUEZ She had me doing it today for an hour, pulling out hairs from her eyebrows with some tweezers. And she wept so much! Because it hurts; don't tell me it doesn't.

CELIA How funny! Oh, how many presents I haven't seen! *(To* RODRÍGUEZ*)* Why don't you go get Helen and tell her to come see this?

ERNEST *(Interrupting, to avoid* CELIA's *indiscretion)* I'll go look for her; don't bother, Rodríguez.

RODRÍGUEZ No, please, I'll go. *(Exits at the back of the stage)*

CELIA *(Looking around, goes by* ERNEST *and drops a paper in front of him)* Pick it up; I wrote it just in case I might not be able to talk to you. . . . Pay attention to what it says and don't fail me, scoundrel! I waited for you two hours on Saturday. Why didn't you come?

ERNEST I couldn't. Besides, we should be prudent. You take too many risks.

CELIA I do it for you. Are you reproaching me?

ERNEST You don't have any sense of discretion.

CELIA You should be the last person to complain about that.

ERNEST You are so bold! You disassembled a pair of your husband's cufflinks to give me these buttons, didn't you?

CELIA Who told you?

ERNEST I figured it out.

CELIA You don't have to feel any pity for me; you don't understand me; I would sacrifice anything for you and you treat me so cruelly. *(At that moment,* MARGARET *comes in through the door on the right and crosses the scene without saying anything; gives a harsh look to both* ERNEST *and* CELIA, *as she understands what is going on between them, and disappears left.)*

ERNEST *(After* MARGARET *disappears)* And you make me fed up with your jealousy!

CELIA You're terrible! You want every woman you see!

ERNEST That's what you think. At least – I suppose – you don't feel jealous of Tendril any more.

CELIA No! Do you think I don't suspect that Tendril was your lover? Do you think that I imagine that because she's getting married everything is over between the two of you? A fine rogue is Tendril!

ERNEST You don't know what you're saying. If I find out that you have even been hinting what you think to other people, I promise that you won't see my face any more. Would you like everybody to know what's going on between us?

CELIA Tell everyone about it! If I'm not the first one to shout it at the top of my voice! *(*MARGARET *crosses the stage again, from left to right, without saying anything.)*

ERNEST You're crazy!

RODRÍGUEZ *(Entering from the back of the stage)* I can't find her anywhere. Come on, come on, the wedding is about to start. *(They walk toward the back of the stage.)*

(Enter GIRLS *1, 2, and 3,* TENDRIL *and* MARGARET*)*

GIRL 1 People are coming and going!

CELIA Have you seen the bride yet?

GIRL 2 Not yet; we're dying of curiosity.

RODRÍGUEZ They're coming through the hallway; let's go and get a place. *(Exeunt* CELIA, ERNEST, *and* RODRÍGUEZ *at the back, toward the right)*

GIRL 1 Tendril! . . . Tendril! . . . *(Knocking on the door)* We've been told you're here.

TENDRIL *(Half-opening the door, without letting them see her)* I'm already dressed and I look beautiful!

GIRL 2 We can imagine! We want to see you!

TENDRIL The only thing I can show you is my foot. . . . *(Sticks her foot out the door)*

GIRL 3 *(Grabbing her foot)* Now we won't let you go. . . . We want to see you before anybody else; you can't deny that to your best friends.

TENDRIL Let me go. *(She strives to get her foot back, but all the girls hold on to it.)*

GIRL 2 Come out, just for a second. Let us see you!

GIRL 3 I won't let you go.

TENDRIL But it's open over there; other people could see me. . . .

GIRL 1 Close, close everything! *(*GIRL 2 *closes all doors and the curtain of the large window.)*

GIRL 2 Everything is closed. . . . Come out.

TENDRIL Really? *(Sticks her head out and sees that everything is closed)* Here I am. *(Comes out)*

GIRL 2   Ah, how pretty you look!

GIRL 1   How nice you smell!

GIRL 3   You look adorable!

GIRL 1   A real doll!

GIRL 2   Let us see the garters!

GIRLS 1 & 3   Yes, yes, the garters!

GIRL 2   *(Lifting* TENDRIL's *dress)* Let's see!

TENDRIL   Well, here they are. *(Making them sound)* Made out of white velvet. They are beautiful, aren't they?

MARGARET   *(Enters from* TENDRIL's *room)* But what are you doing? What an impossible child! You are the only one missing!

GIRLS 1 & 2   And we are too! . . .

MARGARET   Let's go once and for all! *(Grabs* TENDRIL's *arm and makes her go out through the right)*

TENDRIL   *(Going out)* Come, come through here!

GIRLS   No, we'll catch up with you in the hallway. *(Exeunt* ALL *at the back, rushing toward the right. They leave the door opened; other guests can be seen walking from left to right in the hallway; when the people disappear, one can see in the hallway three waiters who form a group close to the back of the stage.)*

WAITERS *1, 2, and 3*

WAITER 1   *(All waiters look inside for a moment, to the right, where the ceremony is taking place.)* They're getting married. Yes! Finally! How people gobble up the food at weddings!

WAITER 2   *(Entering)* Tell me if somebody is coming, because I want to sit down for a while, I'm beat.

WAITER 1   *(Entering as well)* I am too.

WAITER 3   *(From the hallway)* I'll peek from here.

WAITER 2   *(Settling snugly in an armchair, with his legs hanging over the arms of the chair)* I understand now why the rich don't get calluses on their behinds.

WAITER 3   On the other hand, you'll get them on your belly, since you're always lying on it.

WAITER 2   But not on these pillows; the advice from these pillows would lead me down the wrong road.

WAITER 1   You've already been down that road.

WAITER 3   If these pillows, or any pillow from these houses, could talk . . . !

WAITER 2   Well, about this bride, they'd have many things to say . . . !

WAITER 1   *(Getting closer)* Come on! Tell us what you know!

WAITER 2   My sister Eirene was a maid at the Jiménezes', the ones that live next door; and this girl in the white dress, at dawn, used to go to the neighbor's garden and the most delightful things in the world happened in an arbour over there.

WAITER 3   Do you find that surprising? I've seen so many things like that in all the houses I've been in!

WAITER 2   To write a novel! That's why houses have walls! . . .

WAITER 3   I have seen a fifty-year-old woman have an affair with her dying husband's male nurse, whom she'd known for only a week. . . . It's enough to spend one afternoon in a coffee shop where couples like to go, to realize how things are nowadays. . . .

WAITER 2   The funniest thing tonight is that the Señorina's husband, according to what my sister Eirene heard, spent his life looking for a woman who had never known another man . . . and he ended up with the most experienced!

WAITER 1   People who live in glass houses . . . look: take care of your own girlfriend!

WAITER 2   Dolt! Though you see me serving others, I'm not a jackass. I spend my free time burning the midnight oil over books, and I believe that women are flesh and bone like men, and I'm sure that my girlfriend has kissed other men and God knows what other things have happened to her!

WAITER 1   Come on! We congratulate you for your tolerance!

WAITER 2   Congratulate yourself as well, like it or not.

WAITER 1   Then, according to you, there's no honest woman, right?

WAITER 2   Yes, there are. How could it be otherwise? But you have to catch them! . . . I don't want to look so hard. A woman who takes care of our house, prepares our meals, and is faithful with us is enough. We shouldn't ask for more. . . .

WAITER 1   Well, if the world's like you say, look, it should be split in two.

WAITER 2   Precisely. But you'll never do it, because you have a slave's nature; yeah! You drool when you say "miss" or "mister."

WAITER 1   And you, why are you serving if you're so proud? You should be, at least, the chief of the social revolution by now.

Throw off your white servant's apron and go off to get impaled on a stake.

WAITER 2 You'll see me some day with my tongue hanging in one of the public squares, just wait!

WAITER 1 Please, take a good purge first; dirty tongues are disgusting, even if they belong to revolutionaries.

WAITER 2 Nobody can beat you at making jokes.

WAITER 1 You can beat me, because you *are* a joke! Trying to fix the world with a tray in your hand!

WAITER 2 You talk pretty poorly of the job that feeds you; in that regard, you're like some women. . . .

WAITER 3 *(During the scene, he has occasionally stood up to look out the back.)* They're coming, they're coming! *(They rush out to the left.)*

MARGARET, TENDRIL, CELIA, GIRLS *1, 2, and 3,* CLAUDIO, ERNEST, RODRÍGUEZ, CHARLEY, A GUEST, A YOUNG MAN, *ladies and gentlemen who interact with the main characters in different groups without talking; later* EMILY

TENDRIL *(Surrounded by friends, some of them kissing her and some others shaking her hand)* You're suffocating me; I'm just one woman.

CELIA *(Sweetly)* I hope you'll be very happy, Tendril.

TENDRIL I'll try to be.

ERNEST And for many years!

TENDRIL Ah, I don't know about that; I don't plan to live beyond forty; until then I have time to see the world.

RODRÍGUEZ You're an enchanting bride; your husband must be proud of you.

TENDRIL My husband? Oh, yes: I have a husband; I'll try not to forget! . . .

GIRL 1 *(Kissing her)* Tendril: you should behave like a married woman.

TENDRIL I assure you that deep inside I'm more serious than the grave.

GIRL 2 Despite your wild temper, you were shaking, weren't you? And your eyes were full of tears.

TENDRIL Look, look at my dress pearled with tears, as a poet would say.

A GUEST *(In a melancholic and solemn tone)* You have taken the most important step in life, Tendril; be as pure a wife as those white flowers in your hand.

TENDRIL *(Trying to hide her laughter)* If you're giving me that advice, I promise I'll follow your sensible words literally.

CLAUDIO *(Enters from the back of the stage with Margaret and other guests)* It's too early to start stealing my wife. Tendril, I have hardly seen you.

TENDRIL Here I am. *(She does a graceful movement like a manikin and steps forward toward* CLAUDIO.*)* Margaret, may I give my husband a second kiss? *(*MARGARET *nods affirmatively.)* Mister husband: kiss me on my forehead which is yours. *(*CLAUDIO *kisses her and everybody makes comments and claps hands at the scene.)*

CHARLEY *(Entering from the back)* I also want to kiss you, Tendril!

TENDRIL Charley, Charley! *(She bursts into tears when she hugs him.)*

CHARLEY Tendril, my pal, is leaving. . . .

TENDRIL But I'll come back.

CHARLEY We won't see you, because we'll be traveling to Europe.

TENDRIL But when you come back, I'll see you and you'll be a big sensible man, and we won't fight any more, my dear Charley.

CLAUDIO *(Looking at his watch)* We've got only fifteen minutes until the train leaves; hurry up, Tendril, go and change. . . .

MARGARET Only fifteen minutes? Then you won't have time.

CLAUDIO Just take off the veil and put a coat over your white dress; you can change on the train.

MARGARET Yes, yes, come on, quick. *(To* CHARLEY, *who's following them)* No, you stay here, don't make us waste time.

TENDRIL *(Waving to everybody)* See you soon, see you soon; excuse me, my friends.

MARGARET Excuse me. *(*CLAUDIO, MARGARET *and* TENDRIL *go inside to the left.* CHARLEY *goes to the large window and turns his back to the audience, with his face leaning against the vitraux, half-hidden behind the curtains.)*

ERNEST It would be wise for us to leave as soon as possible too, because Margaret is also leaving on a trip tonight.

GIRL 1 A wedding without music like this one is a little dead.

CELIA If there wasn't going to be any dancing, why have music?

GIRL 2 I think at least they should have played the wedding march.

ERNEST Margaret didn't want to; she was afraid people would stay to dance, and that's what would have happened if there had been a band.

GIRL 1 It's true she hates dancing; what a peculiar woman Margaret is! *(The guests start leaving, some sooner, some later, via the back of the stage toward the hallway, the left and the right.)*

CELIA I still don't understand this change of mind in Ochoa; we all thought that the marriage would be with Margaret; we found that the one getting married was Tendril.

A GUEST *(In the same melancholic tone as before)* That's because life is a mystery, lady, a serious mystery! . . .

CELIA *(Scoffingly)* Like the Holy Trinity, right?

A GUEST *(Solemn)* Or like the movement of the sea: flux and reflux! . . .

A YOUNG MAN *(Scoffingly)* And it never stops. . . .

A GUEST Never! That's why Shakespeare said about women: treacherous like waves![10]

CELIA Because they're always moving! . . . It's clear!

YOUNG MAN Who, women or waves?

A GUEST Waves move and women move, each in their sphere.

GIRL 3 *(She has been in a group looking out the back.)* The groom and bride are escaping.

GIRL 1 Let's go to say goodbye!

RODRÍGUEZ We should catch them at the door!

CELIA Let's go through the garden!

GIRL 1 *(Shouting)* Be careful not to lose a glass slipper.

(Everybody goes out at the back and runs toward the right. Other groups pass through the hallway, from right to left, shouting greetings like:) Bye, bye! Come back soon! Be very happy! Don't go off like this! *(CHARLEY stays in the same place, with his back toward the audience, lost in thought; EMILY enters from the right and touches him on the shoulder.)*

CHARLEY *and* EMILY

EMILY Mr. Charley, what are you doing?

CHARLEY Leave me alone!

EMILY Come on, don't cry any more! . . . Don't be sad. . . . Miss Tendril will come back soon.

CHARLEY I know she will, but we won't.

EMILY Maybe you'll get to see her when she comes back from the honeymoon.

CHARLEY No, when she comes back, we'll be on a trip to Europe.

EMILY Miss Margaret doesn't want to take me, why?

CHARLEY You know very well she doesn't want to take anybody from the house.

EMILY She doesn't want me to go with her to the country house either.

CHARLEY That's so close; just an hour and a half by train.

EMILY How can she go without a maid?

CHARLEY There are some maids in the country house.

EMILY But Miss Margaret has such demanding taste!

CHARLEY I don't know!

EMILY Don't be sad, Mr. Charley; you'll also get married some day.

CHARLEY I'm not sad because she got married; I'm sad because I'm sad.

EMILY You're too young to feel sad.

CHARLEY Do you think so? Other fourteen-year-old boys already make a living; but what do I do?

EMILY You'll do something. *(Pause)*

CHARLEY Did you play with paper boats when you were a child?

EMILY Sure I did!

CHARLEY Didn't you feel sad to see them heel over and sink?

EMILY I don't remember.

CHARLEY But I do.

EMILY Because you're very bright, like everybody else in this house. *(Pause)*

CHARLEY Did you get to know my mother, Emily?

EMILY No; your mother died in Europe. Besides, I've only been serving here for four years.

CHARLEY But your father was also in our service. . . .

EMILY He also entered the house service after Miss Margaret's father – God have him in His Glory! – came back from his last trip to Sweden.

CHARLEY I was born there. . . . I would have liked to know my mom's face; here we don't have any portraits of her.

EMILY Maybe Miss Margaret is taking you on this trip to see your relatives.

CHARLEY Precisely. *(Long pause. Talking to himself)* Anybody can fool a child.

EMILY What?

CHARLEY Do you remember being scared when you were a child, Emily? Waking up at night, how frightening! I remember seeing an Indian mummy on my dresser. I told people, and they said that I had tapeworms. But I saw the mummy, I saw it clearly, and the fear lasted in me for several days. But adults tell you you "shouldn't," shouldn't be scared! And if you are, they punish you.

EMILY   That's because the child has to be educated.

CHARLEY   Sure, what fun! Since the child cannot educate the adult, the adult educates the child. And if, for instance, the child dislikes some kind of food, he'll get it every day until he likes it; and the child will never like it, but he's frightened and eats it!

EMILY   And what about adults? Do you think that we don't eat what we don't like?

CHARLEY   If I were older, I wouldn't be so much of a coward. . . .

EMILY   When you're older! . . . Ah, I'd be a little bit scared of you. . . .

CHARLEY   Did I hit you ever?

EMILY   No, but you've looked at me in a way. . . .

CHARLEY   Bah, . . . in a home, nothing escapes the child, but nobody realizes that. It's the same at school. . . .

EMILY   All right! . . . What is?

CHARLEY   Look: I had a classmate who couldn't learn math. In the middle of the year we changed teachers and the new one taught him in fifteen days what he couldn't learn in six months.

EMILY   She must have hit him with a ruler.

CHARLEY   No; my classmate had an obsession: catching any animal he saw: lizards, butterflies, cats. He went crazy just from seeing them. I was attending an experimental school and we used to have class outdoors, in the garden.

EMILY   How much trouble the teacher must've had with that child!

CHARLEY   He drove the first teacher crazy; she couldn't make him stay quiet; he paid no attention, catching flies. But the new teacher decided to let him do what he wanted. He always had a baby bird in his pocket, but he wouldn't harm it: he caressed it. Don't you believe me? Having an animal close or in his hands, he started learning.

EMILY   We've all been children and we've all had to obey. . . . The world would be wild if children gave orders too!

CHARLEY   And in the same way as we take orders, they tell us stories. . . .

EMILY   Don't you like stories either?

CHARLEY   (Gravely) They've told me, just me, a good story, a very nice one. . . .

EMILY   They must have told you so many!

CHARLEY   But especially one. . . . (Long pause) Emily: don't you know anything about me? Don't you know why my father and my mother aren't with me, like in any other family?

EMILY   But Mr. Charley, your mother is dead!

CHARLEY   And is my father dead too?

EMILY   Honestly, I don't know. . . .

CHARLEY   Ah, if what I think is true!

EMILY   What do you think?

CHARLEY   I don't want to tell. If what I think is true. . . . Ah, I would be so happy and so unhappy! How I would cry! (During this scene, through the half-opened door at the back of the stage, one can see people with coats and hats on walking in the hallway, from right to left. Enter MARGARET)

MARGARET   (Entering from the left, without hat. To EMILY) Are my things ready?

EMILY   Everything is ready, Miss.

MARGARET   Turn off all the outside lights. Leave on as few as you can, the light annoys me!

EMILY   Don't worry, Miss.

MARGARET   (Walks nervously; suddenly she rushes toward the curtain of the large window and opens it; she opens the window all the way; through the opened window one can see the groups of round lights from outside as clusters of light; then she opens the doors all the way. At that moment, the lights in the garden go off. She herself turns off the luxurious chandelier and a faint moonlight invades the room.) Finally! Finally one can breathe! Clean air! (Drags an armchair toward the large window and lets herself fall into it, leaning her head backwards; the pale moonlight sharpens her face, already colorless from her emotions that night.)

CHARLEY   What has happened to you, Margaret?

MARGARET   I'm tired of so many people, so much noise, so much perfume, tobacco, flowers, stupidity! . . .

CHARLEY   I am too.

MARGARET   Come here, sit down here, close to me; bring a chair.

CHARLEY *(Sitting at her feet)* Like this?

MARGARET Yes, like this. *(Long pause)*

CHARLEY Tendril left.

MARGARET Yes, she did. . . .

CHARLEY Now we're alone, more than before; I have to love you more. *(Pause)*

MARGARET Do you know anything about the world, Charley?

CHARLEY Yes, I do.

MARGARET How do you see it? How's the world for you?

CHARLEY Look: I have an idea, but I don't know how to explain it. . . . The world for me is like the playing field of a game that everybody wants to win.

MARGARET Yes, everybody wants to win! Poor human beings! They are not guilty of anything. The most wretched human being is innocent! No, you cannot understand yet. They are miserable, dĕceitful, and confused, but they are innocent!

CHARLEY Teach me how to understand; you're all that I have.

MARGARET You're almost a man, Charley; I trust your heart. Tonight I've got my mouth full of burning words. I don't want to let another second go by without telling you a serious, terrible truth on which my whole life depends. I'm afraid of talking, afraid that you won't understand me, afraid that you won't love me, afraid of telling you, of scaring you, of driving you away instead of bringing you closer.

CHARLEY Tell me. Please, don't be afraid!. I almost know what you're going to say. . . .

MARGARET You almost know?

CHARLEY I'm fourteen already, Margaret. I understand everything, almost everything. Yes, Margaret, I go to the movies, read the newspaper, hear what is going on in other people's houses; I imagine; I think! . . .

MARGARET Give me a big hug, a long hug, that will last forever. *(CHARLEY hugs her, sobbing;* MARGARET *sits him on her lap and rocks him energetically; then puts her mouth close to his ear and tells him in a faltering, shaking, passionate way)* Charley, Charley, my dear: it's been fourteen years of lying to you, fourteen years of deceiving you, fourteen years of denying you, at night when you go to bed, in the morning when you wake up, the sweetness of calling me by my name.

You're mine, mine. My blood is your blood, my flesh your flesh. . . . I've lied to you. Forgive me. Listen. . . . Listen. . . . I am your mother. I myself.

CHARLEY *(Weeping)* I imagined it, I suspected it; but I didn't dare ask you; sometimes I doubted it; I didn't want to believe that you were lying to me, and, especially, I was afraid, afraid that I also, I don't know. . . .

MARGARET Afraid, afraid that I was your mother?

CHARLEY Yes.

MARGARET Why?

CHARLEY I don't know why.

MARGARET Then, you don't love me, do you?

CHARLEY I adore you; but you should understand: all this makes me sad; you told me something different, made me believe in unknown people. . . . I can't explain this well to you. But I adore you! You're so nice! I couldn't love anyone else more than you. . . .

MARGARET I'll explain it to you: I have to explain many things calmly, with precision; I want you to have an idea of life as it really is, not just of its appearances.

CHARLEY I really want that! I'm not a child any more, I don't think like a child. . . . *(Detaches himself from her arms and stands up)* When are we leaving?

MARGARET With the first steamship.

CHARLEY *(Reflectively)* Other people. . . .

MARGARET Yes, other people, other lives and other ways of seeing it, of feeling it, of fulfilling it. . . .

CHARLEY To Europe. . . .

MARGARET And from there we'll see the rest of the world. One should see everything, think everything, compare everything, study everything, understand everything.

CHARLEY I'll go with you wherever you want.

MARGARET If you knew how small the human soul is and how big, how sweet, how wide is life itself! *(Stands up and goes close to the large window)* Look: over there it's a river and beyond the river it's the sea. And over there, like over here, live millions of people and each of them, the most obscure, thinks he's the owner of the truth and doesn't understand the other, the other who is screaming in pain,

211

in despair, next to him. And if just one understands, forgives, tolerates, then that one is dragged down, humiliated, defeated, at least apparently. . . .

CHARLEY *(Contemplates her for a second, in silence)* Poor, poor Margaret!

MARGARET *(Goes toward him, seizes his head between her hands, combs his hair backwards with her hands, and gazes into his eyes)* The truth! . . . The truth! . . . Are you mine?

CHARLEY Yes.

MARGARET With shame or with pride?

CHARLEY With pride!

MARGARET Call me by my name! . . .

CHARLEY *(Throwing himself into her arms)* Mother, mom, mom!

MARGARET *(Glowing)* Listen, my child: the toughest way, but also the most fulfilling, that we can follow in life consists of living to make other people happy; it's learning to kill the ugliest things in human beings: their brutal selfishness, their greed, their terrible pride.

CHARLEY I want to learn from you; take me with you, take me with you! *(They exit hugging each other.)*

Curtain

Notes

1 The Calchaqui Indians were a subgroup of the Diaguitas who inhabited valleys of the Northwest provinces of Argentina. They used alpaca and llama wool for their textiles; therefore "Calchaqui blankets" refers to blankets made out of those or similar materials.

2 During the 1920s a new generation of poets, called the group of Florida, heirs of Spanish Ultraism, initiated a vanguard movement that published the journals *Proa* and *Martín Fierro*. They proclaimed the absolute reign of the metaphor in their manifesto and called for the elimination of ornamental elements and anecdote from their poems. Alfonsina adhered to some of their principles in her last two books of poetry. Simultaneously, the group of Boedo, another group of poets, who were opposed to the primary aesthetic concerns of the group of Florida, had a more social focus in their poetry. They described monstrosities and vices in their poems, and had a more combative attitude. Cf. Guillermo Ara's *Suma de poesía Argentina*, Buenos Aires, Guadalupe, 1970, vol. 1. This second group appears to be referred to as the "modern poets" in the text, although the reference is somewhat ambiguous.

3 In the Spanish text Alfonsina uses the first line of a very popular rhyme for children, "Arroz con leche," which expresses the desire to marry a woman who is able to carry out the principal chores of sewing, embroidering, and opening the door to go out and play.

4 Biblical king of Israel, a very wise and learned man. The legends of King Solomon focus on his wisdom and sense of fairness.

5 A reference to Oscar Wilde, poet and writer born in Dublin *(1854–1900)*. His witty comedies were probably well known by the time Alfonsina wrote this play, especially considering the economic and cultural influence of the British on Argentine society during those years.

6 Although "futuristic" indicates the modern and advanced quality of an object or process, Futurism has a very precise meaning. It was an artistic movement, born in Italy in the first decade of our century, which tried to express modern times and capture the essence of movement and speed.

7 Lung diseases, particularly tuberculosis, were related to romantic love in the popular mind, a connection which originated in the association of that disease with the consuming passion of characters and authors from the Romantic period.

8 Houses in Athens were divided into men's and women's rooms. The latter were furnished with locks and bars, and were called *gynæceum*. These rooms symbolized women's lack of freedom and the concern for preserving their good reputation.

9 We use this old Welsh proverb to translate the following saying in the original: "Zonzo el cristiano macho, cuando el amor lo domina." These words are taken from the *gauchesco* poem, *Martín Fierro* (1872) by José Hernández, a classic work of Argentine literature.

10 The inconstancy of women is frequently referred to in Shakespeare's theater.

Interestingly, one of the plays that insists upon women's changing nature is *Cymbeline*, on which Alfonsina's later farce *Cimbelina en 1900 y pico* (Cymbeline in 1900 and Something) is based.

Bibliography

Andrade, E. and Cramsie, H. (1991) *Dramaturgas latinoamericanas contemporáneas. Antología crítica*, Madrid: Verbum.

Andreola, C. A. (1976) *Alfonsina Storni: vida, talento, soledad*, Buenos Aires: Plus Ultra.

Baralis, M. (1964) *Contribución a la bibliografía de Alfonsina Storni*, Buenos Aires: Fondo Nacional de las Artes.

Berenguer Carisomo, A. (1947) *Las ideas estéticas en el teatro argentino*, Buenos Aires: Comisión Nacional de Cultura, Instituto Nacional de Estudios de Teatro.

Cambours Ocampo, A. (1952) "La creación literaria y Alfonsina Storni," *Indagaciones sobre literatura argentina*, Buenos Aires: Albatus, 53–66.

Campanas A. (1989) "Desde el cono Sur: Gabriela Mistral, Alfonsina Storni, Juana de Ibabourou," *Literatura chilena: creación y crítica* 13: 40–62.

Capdevila, A. (1948) *Alfonsina; época, dolor y obra de la poetisa Alfonsina Storni*, Buenos Aires: Centurión.

Castagnino, R. H. (1948) "El teatro pirotécnico de Alfonsina Storni," *Boletín de estudios de teatro* 6, 22–23: 101–03.

Delgado, J. (1990) *Alfonsina Storni: una biografía*, Buenos Aires: Planeta.

Estrella Gutiérrez, F. (1959) "Alfonsina Storni; su vida y su obra," *Boletín de la Academia Argentina de Letras* 24: 29–55.

Etchenique, N. (1958) *Alfonsina Storni*, Buenos Aires: La Mandrágora.

Giusti, R. F. (1938) "Alfonsina Storni," *Nosotros* November 1938: 372–97.

—— (1954) *Momentos y aspectos de la cultura argentina*, Buenos Aires: Raigal.

Gómez Paz, J. (1966) *Leyendo a Alfonsina Storni*, Buenos Aires: Losada.

Hollander, N. C. (1973) "Women: The Forgotten Half of Argentine History," in A. Pescatello (ed.), *Female and Male in Latin America Essays*, Pittsburg: University of Pittsburg Press.

Jeffress Little, C. (1978) "Education, Philanthropy and Feminism: Components of Argentine Womanhood, 1860–1926," in A. Lavrin (ed.), *Latin American Women: Historical Perspective*, Westport, CT: Greenwood Press.

Jehenson, M. (1982) "Four Women in Search of Freedom," *Revista / Review Interamericana* 12: 87–99.

Jones, S. (1979) *Alfonsina Storni*, Boston: Twayne.

—— (1982) "Alfonsina Storni's *El amo del mundo*," *Revista / Review Interamericana* 12: 100–03.

Koch, D. (1985) "Delmira, Alfonsina, Juana y Gabriela," *Revista Iberoamericana* 51: 723–29.

Lima, R. (1984) "Cumbres poéticas del erotismo femenino en Hispanoamérica," *Revista de estudios hispánicos* 18: 41–59.

Nalé Roxlo, C. and Mármol, M. (1965) *Genio y figura de Alfonsina Storni*, Buenos Aires: Editorial Universitaria de Buenos Aires.

Ordaz, L. (1963) *Breve historia del teatro argentino*, vol. IV, Buenos Aires: Editorial Universitaria de Buenos Aires.

—— (1965) *Breve historia del teatro argentino*, vol. V, Buenos Aires: Editorial Universitaria de Buenos Aires.

Percas, H. (1958) *La poesía femenina argentina (1810–1950)*, Madrid: Ediciones Cultura Hispánica.

Phillips, R. (1975) *Alfonsina Storni. From Poetess to Poet*, London: Tamesis Books.

Rivero Olazábal, R. (1932) "Dos farsas pirotécnicas, de Alfonsina Storni," *Megáfono*, June 1932: 186–89.

Rock, D. (1987) *Argentina 1516–1987: From Spanish Colonization to Alfonsín*, Berkeley: University of California Press.

Sánchez-Grey Alba, E. (1989) "Las farsas pirotécnicas de Alfonsina Storni," *Círculo: revista de cultura* 18: 205–15.

Storni, A. (1927) *El amo del mundo*, Bambalinas 470, 9: 1–39.

—— (1950) *Teatro infantil*, Buenos Aires: R. J. Roggero.

—— (1961) *Obra poética completa*, Buenos Aires: Meridión.

—— (1984) *Obras escogidas. Teatro*, Buenos Aires: Sociedad Editora Latinoamericana.

7 Hella Wuolijoki, 1886–1954

Hulda Juurakko
Finland

Hella Wuolijoki with Berthold Brecht. *Reproduced by courtesy of the Teatterimuseon in Helsinki.*

Introduction

by Pirkko Koski

Women dramatists in Finland, 1800s–1900s

Until the Second World War, women governed Finnish drama. Of the four most notable dramatists in the history of Finnish theater, only the first was a man. In the 1860s, at the turning point from romanticism to realism, Aleksis Kivi wrote the first significant Finnish language plays. Two decades later, in the 1880s, Minna Canth, following in the footsteps of the Norwegian Henrik Ibsen, depicted women both sympathetically and critically. Toward the end of her literary career, Canth's writing evolved from an indignant realism toward a sympathetic portrayal of women's spiritual life. Even though they might be the moral victors, her leading women characters nevertheless were left without power. Minna Canth was an active suffragette; however, her progressive and even radical ideas reflected her own time when a woman was squeezed between the demands of society and her husband. She was the product of others, searching for her own identity, pointing out social and gender inequities. Maria Jotuni's women, from the first decades of the 1900s, were already conscious of their subordinate position and ironic about it, but they were incapable of freeing themselves. What was new in these plays was that illusions were stripped away: a "happy" ending meant that illusions faded out as reality became inevitable. The women are strong because they acknowledge their marginality. Jotuni is linked to the artistic movement at the beginning of the century which has been characterized as sensual and colorful. Hella Wuolijoki depicted a new world in which women were not only conscious of, but also consciously governed, their own lives quite independently of men. They felt no need, like Nora in *A Doll House*, to go in search of their own identities. From the start, Wuolijoki's women knew who they were; the play's drama was not born of women's internal, but rather their external, struggle for acceptance as equals in work and at home. The nature of their struggle was inseparable from Finland. Unlike English drama of the late nineteenth and early twentieth centuries, Finnish women's drama does not demand women's political independence. This is understandable in a country that achieved suffrage early. From 1809 until its independence in 1917, Finland was an autonomous republic under Russian rule, with laws inherited from the Swedish period. The Great Strike of 1905 in Russia affected Finland as well, for it unified diverse political parties and portions of the population. The governmental reform initiated by the strike instantly changed Finland from a conservative, class society to one of the most modern societies in the world: whatever their economic circumstances everyone, including women, was given the right to vote in elections for the unicameral Parliament. A noticeably large number of women were, in fact, elected to the first Parliament in 1907. Hella Wuolijoki had become radicalized during the Great Strike and her dramas were guided by this social context and her own leftist ideology, although it is true that the influence of the latter did more to color her characters' opinions than to guide their actions. In Finland, many women attempted to enter Parliament, as Hulda does.

Wuolijoki's life and work

Hulda Juurakko (Juurakon Hulda) is Hella Wuolijoki's sixth full-length play. An Estonian, Wuolijoki came to study in Helsinki at the beginning of the century, married, and became a Finnish citizen. She wrote initially about Estonia in her native language, but at the beginning of the 1930s she began to write in Finnish and also sought her subject matter from her new homeland. She depicted the prosperous Finnish countryside, the newly evolved intelligentsia, and, toward the end of her career, the working people. Estonian and Finn overlap in Wuolijoki's portrayals, but this has not hindered the Finnish public from feeling that her plays convey the essence of Finnish character. *Hulda Juurakko* premiered and was published in 1937, one year after the breakthrough and unprecedented success of her play, *The Women of Niskavuori* (*Niskavuoren naiset*). It had already been twenty-five years since her first play, but the most distinctive characteristics of Wuolijoki's writing remained constant. She wrote a total of 23 plays, 17 of which are full length.

From the beginning, Wuolijoki wrote realistic, issue-oriented plays featuring romantic love and politics. She described what she knew best – the middle class and the transition period of her own time. Social issues govern her characters' decisive actions. All of Wuolijoki's main characters are women whose idealism is described respectfully. But this does not mean that Wuolijoki saw women only in a positive light. She extended her compassion to frank young women as well as independent-minded old women, reserving her most biting satire for idle society wives. In a number of the plays she wrote during the 1940s, she returns to the family histories of characters from her earlier, topical plays, but replaces those characters with more interesting figures. These are stalwart women who, in addition to being in conflict

with their environment, are also in conflict with themselves.

By 1920, having grown wealthy during the First World War and divorced from her husband, Wuolijoki was a businesswoman as well as the owner of an estate, but she also studied literature and the theory of drama, including Bertolt Brecht's epic theater. As a result, she wrote her plays intertextually, incorporating references to various other works. One of the most celebrated of her collaborations occurred in 1940, when she provided Brecht with a copy of her play, *The Sawdust Princess*, which they were together to revise for a Finnish Dramatists' League competition.[1]

Wuolijoki's plays were shaped less by theory than by the social and artistic life surrounding her, including theaters and the first directors of her plays. Foremost among these was Eino Salmelainen, who premiered the greatest number of Wuolijoki's plays written in the 1930s. Salmelainen praised Wuolijoki's realistic grasp of subject matter, but he showed little patience for the romantic tendency expressed in *Hulda Juurakko*. In fact, the linking of realism and romanticism may have contributed to Wuolijoki's success. She was able and willing to write for entertainment, yet even when doing so, offered a multifaceted, rich depiction of life, giving spectators access to her works at many levels.

Hulda Juurakko: the context and reception

Hulda Juurakko depicts a girl from a tenant farm who has come to Helsinki, Finland's capital, during the Depression years of the 1930s in search of work. She is a figure typical of her time, for the countryside was incapable of supporting the population. Wuolijoki was already familiar with this problem from her own childhood in Estonia. Hulda's companion, a tramp, has promised her a place for the night where his sister lives but instead steals her provisions and money, leaving Hulda sitting on a Boulevard bench. A jovial group of Parliamentarians on their way from dinner to the home of their bachelor colleague, Judge Soratie, notice Hulda on the park bench and decide to take her along, in order to interview her as "living material" for the Land Settlement Act then being drawn up. The group prophesies that, without a doubt, girls as pretty as Hulda end up on the capital's streets. However, as the evening ends, Hulda is hired to be Soratie's parlormaid, under the tutelage of his aunt and the cook. Hulda settles down in the household and demonstrates knowledge of a parlormaid's duties as well as the Land Settlement Act and politics in general. In the set of values represented by the men, the only way for her to avoid ending up on the street would be marriage. However, Hulda chooses another way, although the play does in fact conclude with a marriage. Wuolijoki transports her Hulda into the sphere of society governed by men.

A young woman similar to Hella Wuolijoki's idealized self-portrait became the leading character in many of her plays. As described by Wuolijoki herself, this was "a woman from a powerful tradition as are almost all my female types." Wuolijoki's previous leading female characters were the social and educational equals of the men in their community. Hulda appears to rank beneath Soratie, but finally proves his equal. Beginning with Wuolijoki's first play, the power relationship between a man and a woman follows a characteristic pattern. Wuolijoki wrote her first play, *The Children of the House* (*Talon lapset*), in 1912 (Finnish version, 1914). Performances of it were banned in both Estonia and Finland; both countries were under Russian rule and Wuolijoki's main character advocated ideas considered to be politically dangerous. This play shows love and ideology in conflict. The woman represents idealistic, leftist morality and the man, economic interests. In this first play, the woman leaves the man, but she clearly rises above him. This same conflict over ideology and social position between a radical, idealistic woman and a tradition-bound man is also central to many of Wuolijoki's later plays. In these plays the woman wins the moral victory and, after Wuolijoki's first play, also the romantic victory, for many of these plays end in marriage. This structure is reversed in only one of Wuolijoki's most important plays.

Hulda has a characteristically Finnish regard for education and social advancement through schooling. Minister Väinö Tanner especially supported these ideas, inspiring Wuolijoki to speak about

Tanner's formula in her play. Hella Wuolijoki and her husband were in fact the first generation in their families to receive an academic education, although their origins were more prosperous than Hulda's. Hulda's desire for knowledge and her goal-directedness are one key to the great appeal of *Hulda Juurakko* in Finland during the 1930s. Like Wuolijoki's other plays, *Hulda* offers a subject of interest to the Finnish public. Demonstrating the possibility of social advancement, the play pleased the first-generation city dwellers. In order to succeed, a Finnish play had to find favor with both the lower and the middle classes. *Hulda Juurakko* provided information about social structures and idealistic behavior, but it was also conservative in suggesting that social change could occur without rupturing social structures and norms. The "progress" described in the play is possible and acceptable in the extra-artistic world the play represents.

The play's cast of characters points to the many political parties typical of Finland. In 1937, the status of the countryside was higher than at any time before or since; the latter part of the 1930s even saw the first president elected from the ranks of the Agrarian Party. The position of the extreme left was weak, although the outright ban enacted at the beginning of the decade had been rescinded. *Hulda*'s "reds" represented the Social Democrats, not the Communists. Both the extreme left and the extreme right of the 1930s are missing from the play, which explains the amiable nature of the Parliamentarians' social dispute. A multi-party system must find compromises among its factions, compromises in which Hulda participates, demonstrating that democratic processes had reached even the daughters of rural crofters.

Hulda's social function dominates through the importance assigned to study and politics. In this sense, Wuolijoki was representing a different period than the earlier woman writers whose social thought was fixed upon the subordinate position of women in male–female relationships and upon the conflict between marriage and career. *Hulda Juurakko*'s working title, *Hulda Rises to the Top* (*Hulda nousee huipulle*), was the subject for a new play which the director, Salmelainen, suggested to Wuolijoki.

A manuscript in Hella Wuolijoki's archives sheds light on the genesis of the play. Wuolijoki wrote the text quickly to capitalize on the success of *The Women of Niskavuori* (*Niskavuoren naiset*) in marketing the new play. Initially Wuolijoki had constructed a play of six scenes. A scene summarizing Hulda's progress in her studies had been inserted in the middle of this text, apparently in place of the third scene. In the manuscript, the scenes are aptly named: "Hulda Arrives," "The Renaissance," "A Social Phenomenon," "Found on the Boulevard." The principles adhered to by Wuolijoki's 1930s director, Eino Salmelainen – dramatic concentration, emphasis upon rhythmic variation, and the adapting of expressive effects to realistic presentation – appear in Wuolijoki's revisions; i.e., acts are concluded more sharply and rejoinders are positioned to accelerate the action. Salmelainen strengthened the dramatic tension. The final version contains seven scenes focusing upon two time periods separated by a number of years.

Wuolijoki's popularity safeguarded her plays against censorship and official condemnation. In contrast to the three other notable Finnish dramatists mentioned earlier, Wuolijoki's breakthrough occurred at the Helsinki Folk Theater rather than the more traditional and conservative National Theater. She continued to be respected in theatrical and academic circles. Numerous specialized works have been written about her and museum exhibitions have been organized to draw attention to her plays. Approximately half of the works, including *Hulda Juurakko*, are found regularly among theater productions of Finnish plays from the inter-war period. Wuolijoki did not modernize Finnish dramatic form, but she deeply influenced theatrical content by including rural people and depicting them as a group on equal footing with the intelligentsia. The iconoclastic Hulda resembles her author who set the course for her own life and refused to conform to official doctrines.

Hulda Juurakko*

A comedy in seven scenes
1937
Play translation by Ritva Poom

Hella Wuolijoki

Pronunciation guide to names

Finnish is pronounced phonetically. The main stress is always on the first syllable. Each vowel in a Finnish diphthong is pronounced the same way as when it is a single vowel. The consonants *p*, *t*, *k* are always unaspirated.

Finnish i is like the i in "sit"
e is like the e in "set"
u is like the u in "pull"
o is like the o in "hot"
a is like the a in "father"
j is like the y in "yes"
Thus, the author's name is pronounced "Woolyocky."

Characters

JUDGE CARL CHRISTIAN SORATIE

PROFESSOR MAGNUS NORKO

PURTIAINEN, an editor (speaks in the garrulous Savo dialect)

ALI-LEHTONEN, country squire and member of the City Council

HULDA JUURAKKO

MISS CONSTANCE SANMARK (called "Auntie")

KAAVIO, Economic Counselor

MRS KAAVIO

MISS KIRSTI KAAVIO

MISS MATERO, actress

DOCTOR ALINEN

MISS SINIJÄRVI

* Performing rights controlled by Suomen Näytelmäkirjailijaliitto – Finnish Dramatists' Union. Address: Vironkatu 12 B, 00170 HELSINKI FINLAND, tel. 90–631 796, 90–628 191.

MIINA

THORMAN, Bank Director

MRS. KRONENSTRÖM

THE TRAMP

Place and time
The action takes place in the present. There are two weeks between the first scene and the second, a number of months between the second scene and the third, six years between the third and the fourth, approximately a week between the fourth and the fifth, a few days between the fifth and the sixth, and one day between the sixth and the seventh.

Scene 1

Judge Soratie's library-study. Elegantly furnished, functionalist in style. To the right, an open fireplace and, surrounding it, armchairs. To the left, a door open to a balcony; in the back wall, to the left, a door into a hall and, on the right, a door into a vestibule. To the right, in the foreground, a door to the Judge's bedroom. To the left, on both sides of the balcony door, two windows. The stage is dark as the curtain opens, only streetlights illuminate the room. The door to the hall opens. JUDGE SORATIE and PROFESSOR NORKO enter. The JUDGE first turns on the lights in the hall and then, wearing his overcoat, he comes into the study and turns the lights on there as well.

JUDGE (To the PROFESSOR *who stops at the door to the vestibule and speaks toward the staircase*) Shsh, quiet! Tell them over there to be quiet, shsh! They'll wake up the whole household! Old Mrs. Ravander, the Senator's wife, lives on the floor beneath us, she keeps track of every single step and whisper up here.

(From the staircase, commotion and the sound of a woman's voice)

PROFESSOR *(Speaks into the staircase)* Quiet over there! Remember our friend Soratie's reputation.

JUDGE Are they really bringing that woman along? Ali-Lehtonen seems quite drunk. Damn it, who told you to suggest continuing it here!

PROFESSOR It's a good thing he didn't bring that cab driver from the Market Square along, too.

JUDGE You might have suggested going on to a club.

PROFESSOR Hulda wouldn't have gotten into a club!

(BANK DIRECTOR THORMAN, PURTIAINEN, and ALI-LEHTONEN appear in the hall. The latter drags a resistant HULDA by the arm.)

ALI-LEHTONEN Come right in, little maid from Sääksmäki,[2] we could use some female companionship here as well. . . .

JUDGE Quiet, quiet, or you'll wake that Senator's wife downstairs!

BANK DIRECTOR Pardon us, Judge! This is a bit irksome, but the Councilman seems to be in such good spirits.

PURTIAINEN *(Doesn't hear)* Oh it's nice to have at least one bachelor on the committee, so we needn't concern ourselves about a lady of the house. Well, Miss Hulda, come right in!

ALI-LEHTONEN And Hulda, remember that the Squire himself, Ali-Lehtonen, even carried your "veneer luggage" upstairs.

HULDA Thank you, though I could very well have hauled the thing up by my own hand. Is this your place?

ALI-LEHTONEN No, it belongs to this Judge. But don't be shy, Hulda, even though we're men of such importance. You must keep us company here for a bit, Hulda, seeing as you're a member of my own constituency. We couldn't have left a girl from Sääksmäki on the Boulevard, sitting there with her bundles. No need to be afraid.

HULDA Oh I'm not, Sir. I'll get a glimpse of the gentry's doings since Ali-Lehtonen, the Squire, has come along. . . . I need a place to spend the night. Would the gentlemen have room for me here, so to speak?

ALI-LEHTONEN Oh, we'll take care of Hulda.

HULDA *(Looking around)* Would there be a chamber of some sort here?

ALI-LEHTONEN Isn't the gentry's chamber splendid?

HULDA We had fine rooms at the parsonage as well, and at Niskavuori Manor.[3]

PROFESSOR It's right that Hulda won't allow herself to be impressed.

HULDA I don't know what you mean by "impressed," but don't worry, Hulda Juurakko will hold her own and that's what Granny believed too when she sent me out into the world.

PROFESSOR Good, Hulda!

BANK DIRECTOR Clever girl!

PURTIAINEN Have the boys already given Hulda a hard time in the loft?

HULDA The loft! Why at our place we sleep in rooms just like people elsewhere. Have you gentlemen gotten this idea of a loft from museums and folk songs?

PROFESSOR *(Sings)* "Open, oh maiden, the door to your loft and I'll bring you raisins. . . ."

HULDA My, my, how childish the gentlemen are acting . . . !

ALI-LEHTONEN Good, Hulda! Hold your own against them!

PROFESSOR That Hulda is really nice.

JUDGE *(Has been to the dining room, and returns with glasses and a bottle of whiskey)* Maunu, come get some soda water and some more glasses!

ALI-LEHTONEN This is turning out to be a pleasant full session! Well, Hulda, take a load off your feet, come sit down here next to your host.

JUDGE Please, gentlemen, try to be a little more quiet, my old Aunt over there. . . .

ALI-LEHTONEN My, my, we'll all grow shy here, yet . . .

BANK DIRECTOR Pianissimo, pianissimo, gentlemen!

JUDGE Miss, come sit here at the table. Would the young lady also like some whiskey? Has she ever had such a drink?

HULDA I don't care for spirits of that kind.

ALI-LEHTONEN That girl's to my taste. Makes me feel as if I were back home at Sääksmäki. But now would Hulda tell us how she came to be there on the Boulevard?

PROFESSOR Yes, how did Hulda come to be there?

HULDA *(Angrily)* I was waiting for that

scoundrel of a tramp. He promised to find an apartment when we got to the city. He carried my crate there to the Boulevard and sat me down on a bench. It dawned on me that things weren't right when he started wheedling me for money though I'd even paid for his train ticket. Five marks he took from me, and that's all Hulda can be taken for. He lied that he was going over to a friend's sister's to get me a place, and that's the last I saw of him. I could tell he wasn't a real man or anything, just a tramp.

PROFESSOR *(Captivated)* Did you hear that, Purtiainen? A tramp! Fascinating! And that scoundrel abandoned Hulda?

PURTIAINEN It was nice of him to leave us Hulda. He didn't break Hulda's heart, did he?

HULDA No one simply abandons Hulda Juurakko that way, there was no one abandoning, no one abandoned. There was only a tramp.

ALI-LEHTONEN Well how did Hulda get involved with this tramp anyway? Did he promise to marry you?

HULDA I'm not one to marry a tramp.

ALI-LEHTONEN Well how did it happen then. . . . Have things gone a bit awry for you, Hulda?

HULDA *(A bit tearful)* No, they haven't, and they certainly won't either! And I'm not about to reveal my private life to just anyone who asks.

JUDGE Now don't tease Hulda. What can we offer Hulda now, shall I go get a little wine?

HULDA *(A bit tearful)* If the gentleman would give me a piece of a sandwich, it would suit me just fine. That scoundrel even took my food basket, my old mother's little basket, and I haven't eaten anything since yesterday evening because I felt a little nauseous on the train. I didn't even dare stir from the seat, or make it to the lavatory. . . .

JUDGE Good heavens! Hulda, come along, let's go into the kitchen. There's sure to be something to eat. But we must be careful not to wake Miina and my Aunt.

ALI-LEHTONEN How dreadful, poor girl!

HULDA Oh it's nothing to worry about, if I can just get something in my mouth.

JUDGE Well, come along, Hulda! *(Exits with HULDA)*

BANK DIRECTOR She's so genuine – the real thing, really the real thing.

PROFESSOR Yes, she's genuine alright, but now that she's come to town, in a few weeks she'll be walking along the Boulevard dolled up, her cheeks powdered, her hair frizzed.

ALI-LEHTONEN A bird ready for gentlemen to snare.

PURTIAINEN A nice girl, a breath of country air. . . . But. . . .

ALI-LEHTONEN Don't you . . . , now you keep your feet on the ground! But what the hell are we going to do with this girl? We must have been a bit tipsy out there to bring her along.

PURTIAINEN Yes, that was a bit stupid, but if you don't do something stupid once in a while, you're no real human being.

PROFESSOR What is such a girl's fate? The city will absorb her and melt her into its gray, proletarian mass.

PURTIAINEN Oh there's color enough in that mass, and there'd be even more if you didn't prevent it.[4]

JUDGE *(Returns)* The girl was really hungry. By the way, there in the kitchen it was fun to see her head almost straight for the pantry, without even glancing around, and grab some bread and butter as if she knew instinctively that the bread existed. As if she'd been walking about my kitchen for years. She found the bread, she'll probably always find it. Without the slightest hesitation, she even opened the exact drawer where the bread knife lay, and there she sits now, eating as if she were at home.

ALI-LEHTONEN Even a piglet will find its mother's teat as soon as it drops to the straw.

PROFESSOR A powerful metaphor, indeed!

JUDGE Would you like some more whiskey? Now, here's a problem for you. Let's return to our discussion of the population issue. There are now two additional unemployed hands and a hungry mouth in Helsinki, for the municipal government to support!

PROFESSOR That girl doesn't need to support herself by her own hand, with a figure like a flower stem.

JUDGE Hulda is our quintessential demographic dilemma. There's a shortage of dairymaids in the countryside, but Hulda prefers to come and sit on a

Boulevard bench, and tomorrow she'll go looking for work, which she won't find, and the day after tomorrow she'll be looking for a government handout.

PURTIAINEN Or she'll gravitate toward a particular slave market which is also overcrowded. But society is obliged to take care of Hulda. Hulda demands it, Hulda is one of the downtrodden, Hulda is always right. Don't you worry, Hulda, just be carefree. Those who represent the downtrodden are looking out for you. Cheers, Parliament!

PROFESSOR A Hulda such as this has ended up in Parliament's care. Here's to you, cheers, Judicial and Economic Committee! What initiatives have been launched concerning Hulda's fate? By what factors and clauses will Hulda's future be gauged? Here's to you, legislators!

JUDGE Hulda is a problem to be tabled until the next session!

ALI-LEHTONEN Hear, hear, an invocation! And she's such a plump, soft problem too!

PURTIAINEN A definite rural problem!

(HULDA *has entered during the previous remarks and is standing at the door.*)

HULDA I'm no "problem," I'm just Hulda Juurakko, and the gentlemen needn't concern themselves about me. Oh I'll take what's mine, wherever.

(The gentlemen, each in his own manner, shout: Good, good!)

JUDGE Does Hulda know what a problem is?

HULDA I've had enough grammar school and even a bit of folk high school in the parish. And I've certainly read about problems, even in the study circle at the Workers' Association. So, gentlemen, out with it!

ALI-LEHTONEN My, my, so Hulda's even been to the Workers' Association? Could it be that Hulda is a Socialist like that Purtiainen?

HULDA I am what I am, and I haven't asked the Squire for work yet.

PURTIAINEN Well, well, Hulda's snapping.

JUDGE Look, Hulda, we're all placid Parliamentarians here and we've just taken up population and housing issues in our committee, and the question of why the population is moving from the country to the cities. Couldn't Hulda enlighten us a bit and tell us why she, too, has moved to the city?

HULDA There were too many mouths at the Juurakko cottage. There wasn't enough bread. My brother was a mechanic in town. He lost his job and came back home with his children. So someone had to leave. Many of us have left Juurakko for Tampere, Hämeenlinna, and Helsinki like rabbits from their warren, and never returned again.

ALI-LEHTONEN Wasn't there any work to be found in that part of the parish?

HULDA There certainly was, in the summertime. Even I earned ten marks a day last summer, I'm a pretty energetic worker. But I was supposed to be content with that . . . until I reached the Sääksmäki graveyard. . . . My brother brought his radio with him from the city. I twisted the dial this way and that at night, sometimes. All the world hissed and crackled there, such a wide forest of a world. And there I was, just sitting alone in a corner at Juurakko. Then once, on the radio, I heard a song saying that the people should rise up, and so I, Hulda, decided to rise and now here I am.

PROFESSOR Good. And here Hulda is now! What next?

HULDA Just a minute, I left that devil of a coffee pot boiling. Even Miina woke up, and there's cream, so I thought I'd make the gentlemen a little coffee. It'll be ready soon!

PROFESSOR Ha, ha, ha.

(The others also laugh, except for the JUDGE.)

JUDGE What in the world is that Miina thinking?

PROFESSOR Let Hulda take care of it. Splendid to get some coffee! We're out of whiskey, in fact.

JUDGE All we need now is for my Aunt to wake up as well!

PROFESSOR The immaculate Soratie reputation is lost, no doubt. But I'll think of something. In fact, let's interview Hulda here as an expert committee witness. Cheers! Long live Hulda who has simply decided to rise up this way from the night of oppression! Hulda is no "problem." Hulda is a fact, take her or leave her! It seems to me that we are problems for Hulda. Would Hulda in fact acknowledge that our existence is necessary?

ALI-LEHTONEN Splendid! Let's ask Hulda what they think of Parliament at Juurakko and what they know about it there.

PURTIAINEN Well, Parliamentarians! Hulda is the voice of the people. Let's hear the people's voice. Let Hulda decide our fate! Is Hulda going to toss us into the trash, or does she support the flag of democracy?

JUDGE *(Gets a bottle of brandy from the cabinet)* Leave that girl in peace. A Hulda such as this is a very sad phenomenon during a time of unemployment. Even the tobacco factories are cutting down their work force, not to mention the work stoppages in all other fields. Among women the rate of unemployment is increasing day by day because smaller families no longer employ servants during these hard times. If you take a look at recent statistics, they're downright shocking. It is extremely sad that Hulda is lost to us as a citizen! Street-walkers don't vote! Hulda is so pretty that, at least according to the statistics, she cannot be saved . . . from the street. . . .

(HULDA arrives with the coffee serving tray and hears the entire rejoinder. She stops at the door, the tray quivers a bit in her hands. For a moment it seems as if she intends to fling the whole tray on the table. The JUDGE is first to notice her, and he is embarrassed.)

HULDA I see . . . so the gentlemen sentence me to the streets? . . . Here's some coffee for the gentlemen. That Miina there is a nice person. She even promised me a place for the night if only the Judge will permit it. And since the Judge has no parlormaid, wouldn't Hulda do? I was second maid at Niskavuori Manor and at the Deanery as well for two years. I even have a letter of recommendation with me from the Dean's wife. Customs at those houses are just as refined as they are here at the Judge's. And in this way, the Judge could save me from the streets.

PROFESSOR Good! Hulda is not a problem, Hulda is fact!

JUDGE Hulda can discuss this with my Aunt. I know nothing about these household matters.

HULDA Well, in fact Miina has already told me that, but I thought I'd mention it to the master of the house in any case.

BANK DIRECTOR My good gentlemen, as there already exists a famous operetta, *Daughter of the Regiment,* I propose that Miss Hulda be made "daughter of the Parliament."

PROFESSOR Let us support the Folkpartiet, the Swedish-language bourgeois party! Let us support them! A splendid operetta! I have always taken an interest in operettas!

PURTIAINEN But first we must conduct that interview . . . with our future daughter.

JUDGE Here's some coffee for Hulda, too!

HULDA Oh, I'll not drink with the gentlemen. Besides, I already gulped down a cup in the kitchen. I'll have some back there with Miina. I'm no "daughter of the Parliament," just a parlormaid.

PURTIAINEN *(Takes a chair and places it in the middle of the floor)* Hulda, dear, sit down here, an important proceeding is about to begin. The Parliament has decided to interview Hulda about a significant matter. What do they think there at Juurakko? Is this Parliament needed?

HULDA The gentlemen probably intend to take me for a bit of a fool, but never mind. I'll tell the gentlemen about it as well as I'm able. My departed grandfather used to say we need that Parliament to keep the government in line, otherwise the government will begin ordering Parliament and us around, and that would never do, for this is a Democracy.

JUDGE Now, in Hulda's opinion, is there anything wrong with Parliament?

HULDA So the gentlemen intend to take me for a fool. My grandfather used to say that's because you there in Parliament and the government tend to forget whose servants you are. Grandpa Juurakko used to say: the people's bread is bitter bread, the bread of many masters, and it demands a great deal of humility.

JUDGE Excellent, Hulda, out with the truth! My opinion, exactly!

HULDA It always infuriates me when I see such government gentry go past me in a cloud of dust and I can't help thinking, you're nothing but our servant! We've given you your position, and don't forget it!

PURTIAINEN A moving speech! We'll put this in the papers.

ALI-LEHTONEN Well, Hulda is good at ranting! But listen, Judge, most of this fell into Purtiainen's sack. Actually we're all ready to serve so pretty a Hulda. *(Far off, the sound of a bell)*

JUDGE What's that?

MIINA *(Thrusts her head in through the dining room doorway)* The doorbell rang like the devil. Can't get any peace here at night. Would Hulda go and open it? *(HULDA intends to go.)*

JUDGE No, I'll go see what's the matter there, myself.

PROFESSOR Who the devil, at this time of night. . . .

JUDGE *(Opens the door to the vestibule. The tramp enters, drunk)* What do you want?

HULDA That . . . tramp!

BANK DIRECTOR This is annoying, gentlemen!

TRAMP *(Lunges past the JUDGE to the study door)* So here you are, girl, with the gentry!

HULDA So I am.

JUDGE *(Steps in front of her)* How dare you force your way in here! What do you want? You're drunk.

TRAMP I've come for that girl. She's my girl, came with me from the country.

HULDA Never in the world have I been your girl.

PROFESSOR Now you listen here, Mister, leave while the going's good . . .

JUDGE . . . or else we'll call the police about this.

TRAMP Go on, call, if you gentlemen are prepared for a scandal.

JUDGE Did you break the downstairs door? How did you get inside?

TRAMP Oh the tramp has his ways.

BANK DIRECTOR Well I'll be. . . . This is outrageous!

JUDGE Does Hulda want to go with him?

HULDA *(Backing away)* No, never!

ALI-LEHTONEN See here, Hulda, this could turn into a slightly awkward tale. If Hulda's promised him. . . . *(ALI-LEHTONEN speaks to the PROFESSOR.)*

HULDA No, never!

PURTIAINEN Hear that, tramp, Hulda's against it. Now off with you.

ALI-LEHTONEN Here's a bit of drinking money for the tramp. . . .

JUDGE Never mind, Ali-Lehtonen. Are you leaving or. . . . *(Takes the struggling TRAMP by the collar and brings him to the door. The TRAMP is*

shouting loudly for HULDA. *The* PROFESSOR *and* ALI-LEHTONEN *go to the door, likewise* PURTIAINEN *who is first to return.* HULDA *stands, motionless.)*

PURTIAINEN Hulda's quite in demand!

ALI-LEHTONEN So that's how that Judge expropriated the Sääksmäki girl. *(HULDA stands, motionless. She simply stands and looks at the JUDGE, who is straightening his cuffs.)*

PROFESSOR Now then, Hulda, that was that! *(AUNT CONNIE appears at the dining room door in her dressing gown and nightcap.)*

AUNT Good evening, gentlemen! Pardon me, Carl Christian, what is this? Up until now you've kept your home in order. *(The gentlemen bow,* HULDA *curtsies.)*

BANK DIRECTOR We are really extremely sorry, Miss Sanmark.

JUDGE There's nothing to be concerned about, Auntie. The situation looks worse than it is. This is a defenseless country girl whom we found on the Boulevard. I woke Miina, who promised her a place for the night in the parlormaid's room.

HULDA *(Curtsies)* Miss, you needn't think badly of me although I came in here with the gentlemen. I am a proper person. *(Gets her papers from her purse)* And Miina said that the household lacks a parlormaid. I came to Helsinki to find a job and that . . . that tramp left me sitting on the Boulevard. I'm Hulda Juurakko from Sääksmäki. *(AUNT quickly looks* HULDA *up and down, and takes the papers)*

ALI-LEHTONEN Sorry now, Miss, about that bit of commotion here.

PURTIAINEN Sorry to have disturbed you, but we were having a rather jolly good time.

HULDA Miina there said you're very good at teaching, Miss. If you'd only take the trouble, I do indeed promise to obey and to do everything as it should be done.

JUDGE We'll discuss that later. Let her stay on. *(Briefly)* You may stay.

HULDA Thank you, Miss! Thank you, Judge!

ALI-LEHTONEN So they've expropriated the Sääksmäki girl. If you don't happen to like it, Hulda, Squire Ali-Lehtonen's place will do just as well.

HULDA It will not.

PROFESSOR Good night, Miss, and pardon us for disturbing your sleep.

223

BANK DIRECTOR So the "daughter of the Parliament" will remain under the Judge's jurisdiction.

(PURTIAINEN *and* ALI-LEHTONEN *say good night. The* JUDGE *sees the gentlemen to the vestibule.*)

AUNT Bring your things to the parlormaid's room, Hulda, and take the tray away

HULDA (*Takes the tray, curtsies*) Yes, Miss. (*Exits*)

JUDGE (*Returns*) I held a dinner for the committee members. Squire Ali-Lehtonen found that girl from Sääksmäki on a Boulevard bench and, naturally, asked her along . . . without my permission.

AUNT Listen, Carl Christian, you don't have to explain. That girl knows how to curtsy. That's sufficient for me. In the old, traditional way. Aunt Anna used to say to me: "Remember, Constance, a parlormaid must know how to curtsy correctly, and she must know to whom to curtsy." That Martta, that pearl you hired, dear Carl Christian, she had two fire fighters as sweethearts, one in April and one in May.

JUDGE (*Yawns*) At separate times, Auntie Connie? Actually I thought they were at the same time. But I take no responsibility for this Hulda.

AUNT You don't know women, Carl Christian.

JUDGE But Auntie, how could I! I've only been divorced once. Besides a parlormaid isn't a woman, she's a parlormaid.

AUNT That's the most comforting thing about you. When I recall your late father and his brothers. . . . Oh how particular your mother had to be about choosing parlormaids. . . .

JUDGE And they certainly were scarecrows! Haven't you noticed that I'm a renegade in the Sanmark clan? Good night, Auntie Connie. . . . But take note, that Hulda is interested in parliamentarianism . . . and in Parliament.

AUNT My! My!

Curtain

Scene 2

A few weeks later. A late summer morning. The JUDGE *is coming from the bathroom, wearing his bathrobe.* HULDA *is cleaning the room.*

Emmi Jurkka as Hulda. *Photograph reproduced by courtesy of the Teatterimuseon in Helsinki.*

JUDGE Good morning, Hulda!

HULDA Good morning, Judge!

JUDGE Will you never learn to remember that I don't wish to be scalded in the bathtub every morning, Hulda!

HULDA Yesterday morning the Judge complained about freezing.

JUDGE Thirty-eight degrees Celsius. Can't you read the thermometer, Hulda?

HULDA But water tends to cool in an hour. The bath was drawn at eight o'clock and yesterday the Judge awoke at nine.

JUDGE Hulda's always got something to say. There's so much Hulda here.

HULDA Oh dear, oh dear!

JUDGE (*Looks at her. Curtly*) If the Professor comes, send him into my bedroom, Hulda.

HULDA Yes, Judge.

AUNT (*Inside*) Carl Christian, do you have time for the household accounts?

JUDGE Auntie dear, spare me the accounts. Call the office if you need money.

AUNT But Carl Christian!

JUDGE Some other time, when there's not

such a rush. I have a committee meeting at twelve o'clock. Has my tuxedo been sent to be pressed? I'll need it this evening.

AUNT   It has, Carl Christian.

JUDGE   Yes, and there'll be four of us gentlemen at lunch.

AUNT   My dear Carl Christian, today is window washing day.

JUDGE   *(By the desk)* That's your business, Aunt Connie. . . . Where has that yellow envelope disappeared to? I have told Hulda that she must not touch my papers.

HULDA   And, in fact, I haven't touched them. Isn't that envelope on your night table, Judge?

JUDGE   Very well. *(Exits)*

AUNT   You must remember, Hulda, when cleaning the desk, that papers have to be returned to exactly the same spot.

HULDA   Even if there are ten copies of the same land reform proposal scattered helter-skelter?

AUNT   Whether it is a land reform proposal or some other book, you have no permission to read it, Hulda.

HULDA   I do have eyes, I can't help but see.

AUNT   In this room, your eyes are to concern themselves only with dust and order, Hulda. My old aunt taught me: cleanliness and order are the pillars of a woman's life. She who is clean and orderly outwardly is so inwardly as well.

HULDA   *(Dusting)* My, my, Miss Connie, your aunt must have been a wise woman.

AUNT   So she was, and she was very precise. She always awoke at precisely six o'clock in the morning.

HULDA   *(Working)* But what if she couldn't fall asleep until four in the morning?

AUNT   She always fell asleep. She was always asleep by ten o'clock at the latest. Her clear conscience and faith in God served as her pillow.

HULDA   Good grief! You mean she never had a bad conscience?

AUNT   No, never, because she never did anything, she simply was.

HULDA   *(Laughs gaily)* So that's how. . . .

AUNT   Hulda dear, one must never laugh so loudly here, it's not good manners. And you mustn't speak too loudly either, Hulda. That disturbs the Judge. Look, you must act as if you don't exist, Hulda. You must act as if everything cleaned itself and put itself in order. You mustn't speak unless you are asked something, Hulda.

HULDA   To always be silent . . . and alone.

AUNT   And keep out of others' way. The less people touch each other and brush against each other, the better they get along.

HULDA   But may I speak with Miina and you, Miss?

AUNT   Certainly.

HULDA   You're so alone here, too, Miss Connie. Have you been with the Judge long, Miss?

AUNT   Ever since my departed sister's death. That's already twenty years ago. Although I was away for a few years.

HULDA   Yes, while the Judge was married?

AUNT   Yes, three years. But he called me back immediately when his Mrs. left. . . . You must remember to handle these vases with great care, Hulda. They are of very expensive glass!

HULDA   Why did his wife divorce him? How could she simply leave her husband that way? Such things don't happen very much where we live, except for that Master of Niskavuori.

AUNT   Hulda mustn't ask . . . so much.

HULDA   Pardon me, Miss. . . . Are these windows to be washed today?

AUNT   Only the windows in this room. *(The doorbell rings.)* Hulda, would you please go and open it. I'm going to the kitchen. *(Exits.* HULDA *opens the door for the* PROFESSOR, *who enters.)*

PROFESSOR   Well, Hulda! How are you enjoying yourself?

HULDA   Very well. But how can I enjoy myself? The work here is just so childish.

PROFESSOR   Come, come! Are you still asking about the Land Reform Law, Hulda? Or are you familiar with it, already?

HULDA   *(Angrily)* So even the Professor has heard about that? Never mind me, but since the gentlemen here are always discussing that Land Reform Law, I couldn't help but ask about those clauses. It affects all of us from Juurakko a great deal. But the Judge got angry and advised me to remember the "dusting law."

PROFESSOR   *(Laughing)* Yes, I heard about that, but you mustn't take offense, Hulda. After mulling over that law in Parliament for twelve hours a day, one can't bear dealing with it at home, too. You can simply read the newspaper accounts and the Parliamentary minutes, Hulda.

HULDA Oh, I'll certainly find out about it. I'll read all those minutes once more – and in fact I'll even learn to stop asking.

PROFESSOR You can always ask me, Hulda.

HULDA Yes, you're always kind, Professor.

JUDGE (From the door to his room) Well, Magnus, do you intend to flirt with Hulda all day, or are you finally going to come in here?

PROFESSOR I'm coming. Hulda's not flirting. She's interested in the Land Reform Law. (He exits, laughing. HULDA angrily watches him leave. The doorbell rings. HULDA goes to open it. There is a fine lady in the vestibule.)

LADY Is the Judge in?

HULDA (In a memorized tone) Who may I say is calling?

LADY Mrs. Kronenström.

HULDA Please come in, Madam. (HULDA knocks on the JUDGE's door. Opens it) Mrs. Kronenström would like to see the Judge.

JUDGE (From the door) What does she want? I'll be there right away.

HULDA (Turns back and goes over to MRS. KRONENSTRÖM) The Judge would like to know what this is in reference to?

MRS. KRONENSTRÖM It's a private matter. Please tell the Judge that the matter is private in nature.

HULDA (At the JUDGE's door) Mrs. Kronenström is here on a matter private . . . in nature.

JUDGE (Comes quickly, buttoning his jacket) How can I help you, Mrs. Kronenström?

MRS. KRONENSTRÖM (Bowing) Pardon me, Judge, but I would like to recommend an exceptional vacuum cleaner for you.

JUDGE I don't want to buy a vacuum cleaner. Hulda would you be so kind and see the lady out. (HULDA sees the LADY to the outside door. The JUDGE stops at his bedroom door, his hands in his pockets.) Haven't you learned even yet to ask what business those ladies have? Haven't you been instructed a hundred times during the past two weeks to do so? Won't that penetrate your thick skull, Hulda?

HULDA But good Lord, she was a fine lady and she said she was on business private . . . in nature.

JUDGE It doesn't matter if she were the Queen of England or the Empress of India, you must find out what she wants, Hulda, and inform me. And if nothing less will suffice to make you understand, Hulda, I shall wring your neck.

HULDA (Gritting her teeth) Oh I understand. (The JUDGE slams the door shut. MIINA enters with a basin of hot water, a chair in her other hand.)

MIINA Well, here is the window washing equipment now. Don't fall.

HULDA I won't fall. In fact, this work is a bit nicer than that dusting and rug scraping. You even see some results, and looking at the world from up there puts you in a better mood. Oh, Miina, I can't learn these city ways and all these details about opening the door. And all these people trying to meet with him!

MIINA Oh, you'll learn. Here's a bottle of varnish and some rags for you. Now be careful climbing up there. First wash both of them on the outside and then on the inside.

HULDA (Climbs up to the window) Oh what fun to watch that hustle and bustle of people from up here. And the sea! It's just like being on a boulder on top of Käpälä Mountain and looking down at the lake.

MIINA You're not getting dizzy are you, Hulda?

HULDA Me? I'd like to lie on an airplane wing and look down, so I could feel the wind in my hair! (Wipes the outside of the window, holding on to the window frame with only one hand, her skirt billowing in the wind. MIINA goes out. HULDA leans backward and looks down, singing.)

And again it came, came again to our shore
that white-capped wave.
In the evening, the girl was
a stranger at the door,
come morning, a family member. . . .

(The JUDGE and PROFESSOR enter the room. Both suppress a cry of horror.)

JUDGE (To the PROFESSOR, who wants to rush forward) Don't frighten her, stay calm!
(HULDA, who has finished washing one half, moves to the other. The JUDGE steps nearer and suddenly seizes HULDA by the waist, lifting her down.)

JUDGE Damn girl, on the sixth floor! Do you have a brain in your head, Hulda?

HULDA *(Frightened)* What now, Judge?

PROFESSOR Good God, don't you get dizzy at all, Hulda?

HULDA *(Laughing)* Me? Never!

JUDGE And I tell you, Hulda, don't ever do this again. Good God, going and standing outside the window on the sixth floor!

HULDA Well, those windows can't be left dirty either!

JUDGE A way must be found to clean them from inside. All kinds of brushes exist. But you will not go stand outside. Do you understand?

HULDA I don't get dizzy over a little thing like that. But whatever the Judge wishes. I don't know if Miina has any such brush. *(HULDA exits. The JUDGE leafs through his papers. Both gentlemen have their backs to the dining-room door.)*

PROFESSOR Nevertheless, that certainly was a fine sight. Beautiful legs and, all in all, a fine fistful.

JUDGE So you were quick enough to examine her legs.

PROFESSOR Not just her legs, her whole torso's like a flower stem. *(HULDA has returned.)* In my opinion, it's nice to have such a Hulda around, and she's easily available.

JUDGE *(Leafing through papers)* Smells of sweat and yellow soap, no doubt. My taste is: first of all, beautiful hands, and then, starting with Houbigant and Fleur du Soir, the whole range of scents. Even if she were Venus, herself . . . sweaty and with rough hands! Impossible! Not for me.

PROFESSOR At your age, I had already returned to nature.

JUDGE *(Turns and sees HULDA, who has been listening, agitated)* Hulda has a charming way of always appearing at an unsuitable moment.

HULDA *(Curtsies)* I'll try to mend my ways. *(Begins to wash a window)*

JUDGE *(Whispering to the PROFESSOR . . .)* We certainly must get an expert's opinion about this for the committee. . . . *(The doorbell rings. HULDA goes to open it. Two women enter the vestibule.)*

HULDA Who may I say is calling?

MRS. Mrs. Kaavio, wife of the Economic Counselor, and Miss Kaavio.

HULDA May I ask what this is in reference to?

MRS This is a personal matter.

HULDA Yes, but may I ask the nature of this personal matter? The Judge will not receive you otherwise.

MISS KAAVIO This is outrageous! Please go and announce our names.

HULDA I cannot go and announce anyone without, at the same time, stating the reason for their call.

MISS KAAVIO This is impossible! Here are our cards, take them inside immediately.

HULDA *(Enters, quietly hands the cards to the JUDGE)* There are two women, here are their cards, but they're vacuum cleaners again, no doubt.

JUDGE *(Looks at the cards)* Hulda's an ass! *(Goes to the door)* I beg your pardon, Mrs. Kaavio, Miss Kaavio. This Hulda of ours is a bit inexperienced.

MRS. KAAVIO This was a somewhat unexpected welcome, indeed, but one experiences such things quite frequently when going about tending to those missions of mercy.

JUDGE May I invite you into the drawing room. There's a massive housecleaning in process here, supposedly. May I introduce Professor Norko.
(The PROFESSOR greets them, the JUDGE escorts the ladies into the drawing room.)

PROFESSOR *(Last, to HULDA quietly)* Not vacuum cleaners, but money sweepers! *(He also goes into the drawing room. HULDA remains standing in her place, thinking, and she then begins to wash the windows again. MIINA comes inside.)*

MIINA Aren't you done yet?

HULDA There are so many people running around, here.

MIINA Let me wash it from inside now.

HULDA *(Looking at her hands)* Miina, do I have terribly ugly hands?

MIINA Who looks at working people's hands? That dishwater and washing eats at them.

HULDA And weeding turnips and rutabagas. And turning up cabbages doesn't help them, either. A working person's hands, but work shouldn't spoil the human body, God's creation, should it?

MIINA Be grateful that you're not yet hunched over, like me!

HULDA That young lady who lives on the floor below us has rubber gloves.

MIINA My, my, what foolish talk is this? *(The sound of laughter from the next room)* Who's there?

227

HULDA A Mrs. Kaavio, the Economic Counselor's wife, and Miss Kaavio.

MIINA Ahaa, is that who it is? I wonder if she's flirting with the Judge, too? They're all trying to become mistress here. But that Judge of ours isn't such an easy catch any more. He's already singed his fingertips once. Besides, he's no man, he's nothing but law and order.

HULDA Yet he was kind to me and let me stay here.

MIINA Now girl, don't you start eyeing that man! Though there's no snaring him here at home.

HULDA (After a silence) Good God, how they despise us, our sweat and our hands!

MIINA Don't talk nonsense! Do your work! Or Miss Connie will get upset.

HULDA I'd like to learn, Miina, I want to learn everything that they know, so they can't always despise people like us. Dear Miina, will you help me? So I could stay here, so I could work and study at the same time. I want to know what they know. They get it from books. First I'll go to the Workers' Association. You speak to Miss Connie on my behalf too, so I can get an evening off now and then, when there aren't any guests.

MIINA Well, of course I'll help you, you're a tidy girl. Go ahead and study, if you like. But what's the use of studies when there's no money? Downstairs, that young wife, with a husband who has a Master's degree, cares for her children herself.

HULDA Miina, they said something in clear Finnish and I didn't understand a thing, not a thing. I want to learn the kind of Finnish they speak. What is the "primitive culture" the Judge was discussing with those gentlemen yesterday?

MIINA Well study then, study. If you'll just help me with this daily cleaning and see to the laundry.
(The PROFESSOR and MRS. KAAVIO come out of the drawing room, having an animated conversation.)

MRS. KAAVIO The municipal government must give us assistance. Our institution is just as important as Milk for Children, the organization which gives mothers aid.

PROFESSOR It would be best for you to discuss this with Tulenheimo and Frenckel.

MISS KAAVIO (Follows them with the JUDGE) The highest expression of Renaissance humanism was, nevertheless, discovered by Leonardo. And they say that the artist, Vaahtonen, has Leonardo's brush.

JUDGE And Miss Kaavio is said to be his Mona Lisa.

MISS KAAVIO Who's told you that? I like artists and actors, they call me their muse . . . but that's because of my father's wallet, no doubt.

JUDGE What a cynical notion! But as far as a picture of that speaker of Parliament goes, I can whisper to you that your favorite, Vaahtonen, has the greatest chances. Unless they suggest Järnefelt at the session.

MISS KAAVIO It's very kind of you, Judge, to promise to support him. He's come up with a new explanation for Mona Lisa's smile.

JUDGE That's exciting! What is it?

MISS KAAVIO Come see my picture!
(The PROFESSOR and the JUDGE see the women out. The PROFESSOR returns to the room to get his papers.)

PROFESSOR A real hen!
(MIINA has finished her work and leaves.)

JUDGE Yes, so she is, but the girl isn't bad. Would you get my top hat, Hulda, and brush my coat.
(He puts on his overcoat. HULDA brings a top hat and a brush, she brushes the overcoat.)

HULDA What is . . . ? (Stops suddenly)

JUDGE (Smiles) Ahaa, go right ahead and ask, Hulda.

HULDA (Swallows her question) Pardon me.
(The JUDGE goes out. The PROFESSOR has taken his overcoat and hat.)

PROFESSOR Well, Hulda, what is what?

HULDA Mona Lisa?

PROFESSOR Oh you poor dear, Mona Lisa is a beautiful picture and you are too, Hulda. (Pats HULDA's cheek. AUNT enters.) Good morning, Miss Constance! Don't look at me so crossly. I was only joking a bit with Hulda. Good day. (The JUDGE and the PROFESSOR exit, laughing.)

AUNT Hulda must not allow such games.

HULDA Miss Connie, who is Mona Lisa?

AUNT Why are you asking that, Hulda?

HULDA And who is the Renaissance?

AUNT In my time, young girls didn't know about things like that. I attended the girls' school in Vaasa, we weren't taught such things. But this much I can say, if the gentlemen are discussing it, it is undoubtedly something unseemly.

Curtain

Scene 3

A few months later. The same room. HULDA *is cleaning the room with a vacuum cleaner. She comes to the desk, stops, and turns off the vacuum cleaner. She takes a document folder from the desk and begins to read it.* MIINA *enters from the kitchen wearing an apron and holding a soup ladle.*

MIINA   Won't you ever stop clattering about, girl, the potatoes aren't even peeled.

HULDA   Oh, Miina dear, forgive me, this is about that League of Nations. . . . *(Turns on the vacuum cleaner; it drones.)*

MIINA   *(Shouts)* What League of Nations?

HULDA   *(Shouts as the vacuum cleaner drones)* Well, the one that's supposed to create peace, that world peace. They gave us a lecture about it at the Workers' Association. . . . I should be giving a presentation about it too at the club after Christmas, so I still intend to snitch the presentation the Judge made there at the Economics Institute.

MIINA   You don't mean to say that you're really going to speak there . . . come on now . . . is our Hulda really going to give a speech! You know, I'm such a softy that I'm about to cry. . . . Oh, if only I too could come and listen when our Hulda speaks!

AUNT   *(Enters.* HULDA *throws the document folder on the desk.)* Are you tampering with the Judge's papers again, Hulda? You must not touch the Judge's documents! Can't you learn that, Hulda?

HULDA   But it's about that League of Nations! *(Turns on the machine again)*

AUNT   What League of Nations? Why is Miina blubbering?

MIINA   Well, you see, Hulda's going to give a real speech after Christmas.

AUNT   How so? Where? What are you going to talk about, Hulda?

HULDA   *(Turns off the machine)* The League of Nations. We take turns giving presentations at that club of ours, so we can learn to make speeches.

AUNT   Then if only you would become as good a speaker as Aleksandra Gripenberg and Hilda Käkikoski, Hulda!

MIINA   Miina Sillanpää too is such a fine speaker that. . . .

AUNT   Well, I haven't heard that Minister Sillanpää speak, but I do recall how poor departed Elvira and I once listened to Aleksandra Gripenberg. That was when women's right to vote was being discussed. Perhaps even Hulda will get into Parliament some day.

MIINA   My, my!

HULDA   *(Looking far off)* Perhaps. . . .

AUNT   But how are things going with the vacuum cleaner, Miss Parliament?

HULDA   Oh, pardon me! *(The vacuum cleaner begins to drone again.)*

AUNT   And what about you, Miina?

MIINA   Well, I was coming to get Hulda. . . . *(Exits)*

AUNT   *(Listens)* The doorbell is ringing, Hulda!

HULDA   *(Leaves the vacuum cleaner)* Yes, it's that never-ending doorbell! *(Goes to open the door.* MISS SINIJÄRVI *enters.)*

MISS SINIJÄRVI   Good day! Isn't the Judge home yet? He told me to come wait here with these papers.

HULDA   No, the Judge isn't home yet.

AUNT   Come right in, Miss Sinijärvi, and sit down. The Judge and Professor Norko will be here for lunch shortly. Hulda, try and finish as quickly as possible. *(AUNT CONNIE leaves.* MISS SINIJÄRVI *enters and sits down.* HULDA *continues her work, then suddenly stops in front of* MISS SINIJÄRVI.*)*

HULDA   Listen, Miss Sinijärvi, you know English well, don't you? The Judge said that you write English language letters for him.

MISS SINIJÄRVI   Yes, I do know it.

HULDA   Would you give me English lessons?

MISS SINIJÄRVI   Why not, but it's going to be a bit expensive for you, Hulda. Why don't you attend those evening courses?

HULDA   There they instruct people as if they were little children. I'm in a hurry. I want to understand books, not just that children are playing in the yard, and here are a table and a chair. If I pay ten marks an hour, will that be enough?

MISS SINIJÄRVI   Perhaps I could do it for that, if you have time to come over to my

229

place, Hulda. *(The* JUDGE *and the* PROFESSOR *come into the vestibule.* HULDA *continues her work with the vacuum cleaner.)*

JUDGE *(Inside)* Good day, Miss Sinijärvi! Hulda, you could certainly stop that blaring now.

PROFESSOR Good day, Miss Sinijärvi! Good day, Hulda! *(*HULDA *curtsies.)* Well, Hulda's at her favorite task again.

HULDA *(Looks at him angrily and gathers her dustcloth and the vacuum cleaner)* The Professor is always teasing.

PROFESSOR *(Laughs)* That's my cheerful nature, Hulda. The world isn't improved by melancholy.

HULDA Or by dusting, either.

PROFESSOR You mustn't disparage dusting. Look, Hulda, I too dust. But we have a division of labor: Hulda wipes dust off furniture, while Purtiainen and I attempt to wipe it off people.

(The JUDGE *has been speaking with* MISS SINIJÄRVI *in the meantime.)*

JUDGE *(To the Professor)* Could you perhaps relinquish Hulda to Aunt Connie and Miina over there?

PROFESSOR Couldn't Hulda wipe the dust of law and order off the Judge, in fact?

*(*HULDA *exits.)*

JUDGE Here's a cigar, read this report while I finish with the young lady here. *(The* PROFESSOR *sits down. The* JUDGE *to* MISS SINIJÄRVI*)* If you would take these official documents to the Cabinet offices, Miss Sinijärvi, and then I have a letter here, and another letter to be taken to Miss Kaavio, Economic Counselor Kaavio lives in Kaivopuisto Park. Are you familiar with it, Miss Sinijärvi?

MISS SINIJÄRVI Certainly, Judge.

JUDGE Here's the letter, but what's happened to that book? It was here on my desk just a few days ago. *(Searches for the book)* Well, this is astounding! Is this Hulda's organizational genius again? Look on that shelf, Miss.

MISS SINIJÄRVI What book was it?

JUDGE Gobineau's *Renaissance.*

*(*MISS SINIJÄRVI *searches the bookshelf. The* JUDGE *rings a bell on the desk.* HULDA *enters.)*

HULDA You rang, Judge?

JUDGE Hulda, have you seen a book with a blue binding here on my desk? Gobineau's *Renaissance*? Have you taken it, Hulda? What sort of trick is this, again?

HULDA No . . . no I . . . I don't know. . . .

JUDGE Then who's taken it? Well, Hulda, look for it! *(*HULDA *begins searching reluctantly.)* Hulda, go see whether it's on my night table! It is absolutely astounding that a book would disappear from my desk in this manner.

PROFESSOR *(Smoking a cigar and looking at documents)* It happens. Don't get upset!

HULDA *(Comes from the bedroom)* It wasn't there!

JUDGE *(Looking in the drawers)* Incomprehensible . . . and there was even a letter inside it.

PROFESSOR *(Absorbed in reading)* Well, well, is that how you treat the young lady's letters?

JUDGE This is absolutely maddening! Nowhere! *(Goes to the door of the drawing room, shouts)* Aunt Connie! Would you come here, Aunt!

AUNT *(Inside)* Oh my, what's the trouble now?

JUDGE Have you taken a book from here, Aunt Connie, a book with blue binding, Gobineau's *Renaissance*?

AUNT Good heavens, not I . . . by no means. . . .

JUDGE Try to look for it now, Auntie.

PROFESSOR *(Gets up)* Good day, Miss Connie! What extraordinary books you do take an interest in, a mature person like yourself! The *Renaissance*! Very appropriate reading matter, indeed for a barrister. Why not the Galdean *Book of Dreams* or a book of sermons?

JUDGE Stop laughing! Damned hens, sending me all kinds of books!

PROFESSOR Ahaa, it's the interest that Economic Counselor's daughter takes in the arts. Ahaa, on account of that artist, Vaahtonen's, *Renaissance*?

AUNT *(Searches, looks at* HULDA *now and then)* Renaissance . . . hmmm, *Renaissance*. . . . You haven't seen such a *Renaissance* have you, Hulda?

HULDA *(Avoids looking at* AUNT CONNIE*)* No. *(She is searching through the bookshelf. The* PROFESSOR *looks at* HULDA *sharply.* HULDA *turns away, embarrassed.)*

PROFESSOR Listen, Carl, don't bother looking for the damned thing! Why don't you just buy that girl a new book.

JUDGE Damn it! Of course the book must be found in this house, now!

AUNT CONNIE Oh dear, oh dear, this is so

unpleasant! You really haven't seen that book, Hulda?

JUDGE (Gives MISS SINIJÄRVI money) Miss Sinijärvi can certainly go and buy a new book at the Academic Bookstore. And then come take this letter.

MISS SINIJÄRVI Thank you, Judge! Goodbye! (Exits)

JUDGE But now! You must find that book, Hulda.

HULDA (Anxious) Oh dear, dear. . . . I'll try to find . . . the Judge needn't buy it. . . .

PROFESSOR Listen, forget this book business!

JUDGE (Angrily) This matter must be clarified. Hulda certainly has permission to say where the book is!

AUNT Oh, Carl Christian, all because of one book. . . .

JUDGE I want to set my house in order. The book has to be here. Hulda, the matter will not be left at this. Where is the book?

HULDA (Petrified) I don't know.

AUNT CONNIE Well now, it would be best for Hulda to confess. I saw Hulda with that book.

HULDA (Raises her hands to her face) I took it. . . . I didn't mean to steal it. . . . I was reading it . . . because I wanted to know what that Renaissance is . . . but I was ashamed. . . . I was so terribly ashamed when the Judge began asking . . . and I was afraid.

PROFESSOR Poor Hulda. . . .

AUNT Hulda, you must always speak the truth.

JUDGE You must certainly understand that this is impossible! Hulda, you will leave and this very day, in fact! I cannot tolerate this kind of thing in my house! (Kicks the trash basket over. Papers scatter across the floor.)

HULDA Because of one book . . . ?

PROFESSOR Because of the Renaissance! Gobineau should have left it unwritten!

AUNT Carl Christian, perhaps this matter can still be resolved!

PROFESSOR Oh, I'd take Hulda to our place, but that Mrs. of ours is one of the most malicious ladies in Helsinki, not at all like Miss Connie. Hulda wouldn't get to snitch books there and, even less, to read them.

HULDA Because of one book. . . . (Looks at the JUDGE. Suddenly) I liked it so much

here, Miss Connie. . . . I was able to study . . . here everything was different . . . it was just as if the windows were open . . . to somewhere . . . and yet . . . never mind, maybe I'll get a job in a factory somewhere and study at night . . . and yet. . . .

AUNT Carl Christian, be a human being!

PROFESSOR It's a matter of form!

JUDGE Well, alright, this time! If you promise not to touch my desk or my books any more without permission, Hulda, and that there will be, so to speak, somewhat less of you here. Then you can stay, this time, Hulda.

HULDA I won't touch them, and yes I will learn to act as if I don't exist at all. (Tears in her eyes)

AUNT Oh, we'll manage Hulda here!

PROFESSOR Now, now, just hold your head up, Hulda! That Judge really isn't the tiger he appears to be.

AUNT And now I invite you all to lunch. Hulda, gather the trash back into the waste basket and empty it in the kitchen. (All three go to the door of the drawing room.)

JUDGE (Turns) And Hulda remember to act . . . as if you don't exist! (Exits)

HULDA (Lifts the papers back into the wastepaper basket, sits down on the floor weeping, her hands clenched) Just wait. . . . I'll show them . . . just wait. . . .

Curtain

Scene 4

Seven years after the first scene. HULDA *is lying on a large easy chair in front of the open balcony door. On the smoker's table beside her, a lamp is turned on. The table is covered with books and papers.* HULDA *is wearing an old-fashioned, feminine dressing gown with wide bands of lace at the neckline and sleeves. Her hair is disheveled and her knees are bare. The* JUDGE *enters from the vestibule, suitcases in his hand. He casts his overcoat and hat on the chair and approaches Hulda, whose face is illuminated by moonlight. The* JUDGE *remains looking at her. In complete silence, he moves to the other easy chair opposite* HULDA *and, still looking at the sleeping girl, he lights a cigarette. He silently examines* HULDA's *books and papers.* HULDA *notices him, and suppresses a cry of astonishment. She remains motionless.*

JUDGE *(Lightly)* Good evening, Hulda! (HULDA *doesn't answer, she is entirely motionless.*) Did I frighten you?

HULDA This is a dream, you're in Paris. . . .

JUDGE *(Laughing)* Unfortunately, I'm here. A governmental crisis is imminent. But I did send a telegram.

HULDA I was at the seashore in the afternoon and got tired. I haven't received a telegram. Pardon me. *(Attempts to rise)*

JUDGE *(Hindering her)* Just remain seated, Hulda. We've something to discuss. You're a very beautiful sight, Hulda. *(Frightened,* HULDA *covers her knees with the hem of her dressing gown.)* Never mind, they're very beautiful knees! (HULDA *attempts to get up again.)* Hulda just sit now and tell me what's the meaning of all this. Political science texts, finance texts! Have you written this report yourself, Hulda?

HULDA *(Still fighting off sleep)* I have. *(Stammering a bit)* I'm studying for exams at the College of Social Sciences. And that's why your Aunt left me in the city.

JUDGE What? You've been attending the College of Social Sciences there in Sörnäinen where Ruutu's the rector?

HULDA Yes I have, for four years. First I studied at the Workers' High School, then I passed my secondary school examinations and went on to the College.

JUDGE Good God, when? While working in this house? And I knew nothing about it.

HULDA As far as I know, parlormaids' private lives have never been of any interest to the Judge. But I've always done my work. And you have been abroad so much, Judge, and I've had a lot of time.

JUDGE Why haven't you ever told me about your studies, Hulda?

HULDA Your reactions to my questions about the Land Reform Act were very unfriendly, at first. I didn't dare. Don't you remember, Judge, that I was supposed to act as if I didn't exist? But I've asked you for a book now and then, anyway. And the rest I've taken without asking.

JUDGE But when have you studied, Hulda?

HULDA Nights.

JUDGE And slept?

HULDA It doesn't make much difference. Besides, I should be able to stay awake for a few years, because the people of Juurakko farm have been asleep for centuries.

JUDGE I still don't understand how all this has been possible. Does my Aunt know about it?

HULDA Both Miina and Miss Connie have helped me. Miina has often done my work, and because my salary is always spent on books and school fees, Miina has bought me a skirt now and then with her own funds, so that I wouldn't have to feel ashamed among the others. Not to even mention Miss Connie, who has also helped me in many ways. Don't look at my morning gown so suspiciously. It's a gift from Miss Connie and belonged to your late mother, no doubt. It's very old-fashioned and feminine.

JUDGE Charmingly feminine! I can almost recall seeing it as a little boy. What surprises one finds upon arriving home at night unexpectedly! Although it could certainly have been worse!

HULDA Pardon me for working here in your room. Your Aunt left me in the city to work and also to keep an eye on the house. The servants' quarters, which you've probably never seen, are nine feet by six and the courtyard absolutely stinks in the summertime. It's been just wonderful to work here and to read whatever I wanted . . . all the summers. I never felt lonely in this room. Your books . . . were here . . . perhaps you even left some of your thoughts to keep me company.

JUDGE This has become a friendly room for me as well. Because of your thoughts perhaps, Hulda. . . . Why don't you move into the room beside my Aunt's, at least for the summer?

HULDA That's the guest room!

JUDGE Even so. Move in there immediately, Hulda.

HULDA I don't think your Aunt would like that.

JUDGE But I would.

HULDA Dictator!

JUDGE Yes, of course, in this house! (HULDA *laughs.*) Go on, laugh. Sometimes I've been amazed at how silent you've become, Hulda. Your temperament must be a bit smothered by this studying?

HULDA It's merely been reined in a bit, Judge.

JUDGE Tell me, Hulda, why this passion

for studying? What are you striving for? What are you aiming to become? Are you looking for a job in an office somewhere, Hulda?

HULDA I'll be quite satisfied with my job as a parlormaid until I get a job somewhere as a lecturer, perhaps. The Department of Social Sciences certainly hasn't made me a worse parlormaid, has it?

JUDGE But why go to all the trouble? And those sleepless nights?

HULDA Because I wanted knowledge in order to help those who've stayed at Juurakko. Because I wanted to live a life as rich as yours. I'm familiar with your Land Reform Law now, your primitive culture, your El Greco, and your Leonardo. I've studied your mathematics, your logarithms and your logic. I've learned to think and to see, and even to do, in fact.

JUDGE And all this without my knowing about it, under my very own eyes?

HULDA You've never seen me. To you I've been a piece of furniture, one number in your statistics. Do you remember, according to your statistics I was supposed to end up on the street?

JUDGE Hulda, dear, before you sits a great sinner. I do recall that situation, almost. And that's been weighing on you, Hulda?

HULDA "Weighing on" is an exaggeration.

JUDGE (Gets up) And yet. . . . Do you know, people have been a statistical subject for me . . . that habit of constantly thinking in terms of society . . . of overlooking the individual. . . .

HULDA (Also gets up) The Judge must certainly be tired. Would you like some tea? I'll put your bed in order.

JUDGE I had dinner at the Kaivohuone Restaurant. Would you bring a bottle of port here, Hulda?

HULDA If you'll allow, Judge, I'll get dressed and return immediately.

JUDGE Just stay in that comfortable dressing gown. Sit back down in that chair, Hulda. I should even have some wine here in the cabinet and some glasses as well. (Takes a bottle of wine and glasses from the bar cabinet, puts them on the table. Hulda sits silently, looking out. The JUDGE pours wine into the glasses and offers HULDA a glass.) To your health, Hulda. Welcome to our ranks!

HULDA What "ranks" are you inviting me into?

JUDGE The "ranks" of the cultured people in this country.

HULDA (Distrustfully) The "cultured"? My mother sang Whitsuntide hymns and my father taught us about honor and integrity at the workplace, although his customs include eating with his knife. The "cultured"! (Suddenly) I was without knowledge and I've obtained it here in this house . . . as well as something from Miss Connie. . . .

JUDGE I deserved that box on the ears. Give me your hand. A strong hand . . . but smooth. . . . (Kisses her hand and keeps it in his)

HULDA (Slowly) No one has ever kissed my hand, or my mother's hand, either. . . . I'm probably a bit sleepy and tired, and I'm talking nonsense. . . .

JUDGE (Paces back and forth) Empty your glass, Hulda!

HULDA I've never tasted wine. . . .

JUDGE What? And we always have wine on the table!

HULDA Miss Constance won't allow Miina or me to touch wine. All the leftover wine is saved for sauces. And besides, Miina is a teetotaler.

JUDGE How have you lived here all these years? When did you become like this? I know nothing at all about you. We live in the same house, within hand's reach, and we know nothing about each other!

HULDA I know a great deal about you. I know that you prefer Houbigant and Coty perfumes to sweaty parlormaids with chapped hands. I know about your work and your interests. Sometimes, when brushing your coat, I've found a blond hair, sometimes a dark one. I know why you didn't join the Kivimäki cabinet. I know all the propositions you put forth during the Land Reform proceedings . . . and I know about your sense of duty. . . . I even know that you suppress your doubts with that sense of duty.

JUDGE Extraordinary powers of observation! Damnation! (Walks, stops suddenly) How are things with that tramp? What happened to him?

HULDA Ahaa, and what else do you know about me?

JUDGE I know that you've boxed certain

gentlemen on the ears a few times here in our vestibule.

HULDA It's strange that gentlemen don't know how to hold their tongues!

JUDGE Besides, all those boxes on the ear have been laid to my account or, more precisely, it's said that they are because of me.

HULDA What do you mean, Judge?

JUDGE The gentlemen consider Hulda my personal property. Hasn't anyone mentioned this to you, Hulda?

HULDA Well, your friends certainly have little understanding of your taste, Judge, or your principles regarding parlormaids!

JUDGE So they do. They have no idea that Hulda may be boxing those ears because of that tramp. Or do you have someone else, Hulda?

HULDA Is that how it should be according to the statistics? Being a servant girl in this house, I couldn't possibly have even the most rudimentary instinct for self-preservation. I've never been considered a live human being here, merely a social phenomenon. I know that all three of us women in this house, Miss Connie, Miina, and I, we've never been anything to you but social phenomena.

JUDGE (Gets up) My world is full of categories, social phenomena, laws, work, obligation . . . and crap.

HULDA I know. There isn't the slightest bit of wonder in your life. You never stop in front of something, amazed, your heart in your throat. How bleak a life is with no surprises!

JUDGE I'm just listening, Hulda. Keep on talking. In recent years I've often been amazed at how quiet you've become. In the beginning your presence was felt in the house, Hulda, and then somehow you grew imperceptible.

HULDA As if Hulda didn't exist, in fact. . . . Isn't that called loss of individuality? Or, more precisely: Hulda became furniture.

JUDGE Listen, Hulda, for years you've been following my life with those wise eyes of yours. You've made my bed, ironed my shirts, organized my desk, offered me your companionship. Tell me straight out: how have your really felt about me?

HULDA My attitude toward you has been approximately that of an old-fashioned marriage in which the wife's sole task is to serve her master. That was how things were at the Deanery, where the Dean's wife served her husband, and it was the same in another place where I worked for a little while. There, too, the wife prepared her husband's bath, brought him his morning coffee, organized his desk, kept the household accounts, and was silent when there were guests. She was just as necessary a piece of furniture as I am. Just as accustomed to her master. But I have no bittersweet memories of a time when my master treated me better, and I've had the freedom to attend lectures at the College of Social Sciences on the average of five times a week. You've treated me well. And I've heard you express very interesting opinions sometimes, although not to me. I'm sorry you've never bothered to speak with me as you're doing now . . . as a person . . . but I've learned a great deal from you, nevertheless. . . .

JUDGE I've been a fool. (Sits down again) But sometimes I've even seen a smile in your eyes, Hulda, and then I've wanted to find out about that smile, that very provocative smile. But you've always behaved so oddly. Do you remember last Christmas, Hulda, when I was sitting here alone and you brought me some glögg? I wanted to speak with you, but when I caught your wrist, you tore yourself away, Hulda. Then I was even more alone. . . .

HULDA You caught me by the wrist because I was wearing a white cap and a lace apron. And because life has always been served to you on a tray.

The sun is already rising. . . .

JUDGE (Bending over her) Not always on a serving tray. Good God, how blind I've been. Here you've been walking beside me, wise, flowering, full of vitality . . . a beautiful, live human being! And I've walked past you, blind. Should I begin to reassess certain values?

HULDA This has been a very pointless conversation. I must go now and put your bed in order.

JUDGE Empty your glass, Hulda. I hope you'll consider me your friend. Let me take a little care of you.

HULDA (Gets up from the chair) You took me into this household once . . . that's sufficient.

JUDGE (Paces back and forth, stops before

HULDA *and seizes her by the arms)* We're completely alone in this house, isn't that so? Why are you trying to be a stranger to me?

HULDA *(Laughs brightly, backs to the balcony door)* We're not alone. The Land Reform Law, the finance text and Lombart's *History of Socialism*, over there, are with me.

JUDGE And a warm summer night . . .

HULDA *(Backs to the door on the left)* . . . Which will soon become a summer morning. . . . *(Speaks mischievously and softly)*

"Oh you Creator, you,
why didn't you create
longer summer nights. . . . "

Now I'm going to get the sheets and put the Judge's bed in order.

JUDGE Hulda, come here! *(HULDA goes to the left quickly. The JUDGE lights a cigarette, walks back and forth, stops at the balcony door, pours a glass full of wine, drinks it quickly. He casts himself down on the armchair, stretches out his legs. HULDA enters from the left, dressed in a maid's uniform. She goes to the right, toward the JUDGE's bedroom door. The JUDGE watches her, not moving his eyes, and then he says coldly.)* You forgot shoes and stockings. Slippers are not appropriate to that uniform.

HULDA *(Stops, looks at the JUDGE, drops the sheets on a table, intends to return to the left)* Pardon me!

JUDGE You have very beautiful legs. Go on, get my bed in order. *(HULDA takes the sheets and the suitcase, goes to the right. The JUDGE sits, motionless, then he shouts into the next room.)* Hulda, take out my black, silk pajamas!

HULDA Yes, Judge!

JUDGE You've become a very proper maid. Is that also thanks to the College of Social Sciences?

HULDA *(From the other room)* . . . Work methods and critical capacity. . . . *(The JUDGE rises and approaches the bedroom door. HULDA comes out. The JUDGE seizes her by the wrists and pulls off her cap.)*

JUDGE A useless masquerade and irritating! Hulda, the night is brief.

HULDA Judge, please. . . . *(The JUDGE pulls her onto his lap and kisses her for a long time. Initially HULDA is quite limp, then she wrenches herself free.)* Let me go!

JUDGE Hulda, you sweet. . . . *(Approaches HULDA)*

HULDA Don't touch me!

JUDGE Nonsense, Hulda! I know you like me. We're all alone, don't be difficult. . . .

HULDA *(Backs behind the chair)* I will not come. Don't you touch me!

JUDGE Hulda, stop that, it's absolutely useless! I know that you like me. . . . I saw how you caressed my pillow, once. . . .

HULDA You don't understand . . . leave me alone!

JUDGE The whole world thinks you've been mine for many years, already.

HULDA Is that so, and now it's about time . . . don't speak to me that way. You're mistaken.

JUDGE Oh, quite seriously?

HULDA I'm not one of those women who can be taken to bed this way!

JUDGE Is that so. . . . *(Paces back and forth)* Even the most charming woman has her price. What's your price, Hulda?

HULDA *(Startled, she raises her hands to her face.)* So, I too have a price. . . .

JUDGE What is it? A lovely wedding ring, perhaps?

HULDA Perhaps even that. . . .

JUDGE Too expensive . . . there are less expensive women.

HULDA Everyone has their own price.

JUDGE So Hulda is that expensive.

HULDA I am what I am.

JUDGE There are also those women who don't think about their price, because they like a certain man.

HULDA Perhaps that depends on the man.

JUDGE This situation certainly does have its humor.

HULDA So it does. But it also has its sad side. According to the present labor regulations, I must give two weeks' notice. But surely the Judge will allow me to leave tomorrow?

JUDGE Listen, Hulda, let's not turn this into a tragedy . . . where would you go, Hulda?

HULDA You needn't worry, Judge. Not to the street, at any rate.

JUDGE I am indeed keeping to that old labor regulation . You must give two weeks' notice, Hulda. Aunt Connie is arriving tomorrow and she will need a parlormaid.

HULDA I don't want to be here! You can't force me!

JUDGE   I am accustomed to observing the law.

HULDA   Except for tonight.

JUDGE   A warm night such as this imperils all principles. . . . And how you will yet regret this night!

HULDA   You too will regret it. If you dare touch me. . . .

JUDGE   I don't dare, but you will certainly remain here for two more weeks, Hulda.

HULDA   Alright, I'll stay.

JUDGE   You needn't lock your door, Hulda. I've no need to take you by force. (HULDA *stands, infuriated, her hands clenched. The* JUDGE *is laughing.*) Don't you trust my word, Hulda? They trust it, even in Parliament.

HULDA   (*Restraining herself*) Oh I'll certainly last those two weeks. (*Takes the tray with its glasses and bottles. The* JUDGE *quickly goes to the door of his room and opens it.* HULDA *goes toward the dining room with her tray. The* JUDGE *opens his door.*) And the leftover wine will be used for fish sauce! (*Exits*)

JUDGE   Damn you! (*Slams his door shut*)

Curtain

Scene 5

The same room about a week later. Late at night. The JUDGE, *the* PROFESSOR, *and* PURTIAINEN *are sitting around the coffee table with papers before them.*

JUDGE   You forgot the comma in front of the words "new legal arrangement."

PROFESSOR   You're still under the influence of Setälä's comma antics. Well all right, it's finished at last! This certainly was a report. I must say, remembering departed Rautapää, that the quality of the committee secretary certainly has deteriorated. . . .

JUDGE   The state of laws is such nowadays that previous jurists must be turning over in their graves.

PROFESSOR   Yes, it's all the fault of those Purtiainens. Just try, now, to get those illogical laws into logical order.

PURTIAINEN   Now listen, Conservative Party, this is merely your spiritual inertia.

PROFESSOR   If only there were more of my sane conservatism against this flood of laws! Who the devil is ever going to be able to make head or tail of them any more!

PURTIAINEN   Oh he who needs them will. Give it here, let me make those changes on my copy.

JUDGE   Is that arguing about to begin again now that you're free of the report? (*The telephone rings, the* JUDGE *goes to the telephone.*) Hello . . . this is the Soratie . . . are you still sitting there . . . ? No, we've finished. . . . (*Continues the conversation*)

PROFESSOR   Too bad we had to leave the Café Pörssi so early, it's only taken us two hours to finish here.

PURTIAINEN   (*Lights his cigar; quietly to the* PROFESSOR) I don't understand what upset the Judge so much this evening, either. . . .

PROFESSOR   Well I do have an idea. (*The* JUDGE *puts down the receiver, but he remains at the desk searching for some papers.*)

JUDGE   Wait a moment, I'll get the original text for you.

PURTIAINEN   Listen, I remember something now. We were here at Soratie's place with Ali-Lehtonen a few years ago, the time we brought that girl along with us from the Boulevard. What's become of that girl? Didn't she stay on here as a parlormaid?

JUDGE   (*Still at the desk*) Yes. She's still here.

PROFESSOR   She's turned into an absolutely charming girl, in fact. She was already threatening to start studying back then and now she's been studying at the College of Social Sciences and what all. She even speaks foreign languages. And she seems to be active in your party, in fact.

JUDGE   What do you mean? What party is she active in?

PROFESSOR   Do you mean to say that you don't know anything about Hulda's doings? (*The* PROFESSOR *looks at the* JUDGE *sharply.*)

JUDGE   No, I really haven't had time to keep track of the parlormaid's doings.

PROFESSOR   Listen, Kalle, don't bother pretending you don't know that Miss Hulda Juurakko was lecturing at the Workers' Association all last winter and that she has spoken at all kinds of meetings. . . .

PURTIAINEN   Is it that Hulda, in fact? Well damnation, Hulda, is that so! I've even seen her at women's meetings now and then. The women cheer her on and she appears to have a great deal of support. . . . Hulda Juurakko . . . well. . . .

JUDGE *(To the* PROFESSOR*)* Is that so. . . . How is it you're so well informed about Hulda?

PROFESSOR I am indeed. . . . I've always followed Hulda's development with a great deal of interest, even though . . . well . . . I'm not Hulda's master.

JUDGE *(Takes a whiskey bottle from the cabinet)* I'm going to see if there's any soda water to be had in the kitchen. . . . *(Exits)*

PROFESSOR Some whiskey would certainly be good after this report. . . . The girl was sitting across from us at the Café Pörssi with a young gentleman. That must have been more than her master's nerves could take.

PURTIAINEN You don't say. And we sentenced her to the street. Damn, I remember how she came in with the coffee tray, pale as a sheet. . . . And now she's one of us. . . . She probably won't stay on here as a maid any longer, will she? Or does she already have some other tasks here? Damnation, this is a juicy story! Did the gentry greet each other? Such are the modern times!

PROFESSOR Of course! The master bowed with extraordinary politeness and the girl responded like a princess.

PURTIAINEN Damn, this is fabulous! These are the modern times, this is democracy! Master and servant encounter each other at Café Pörssi. What a headline! It makes my fingers itch. *(The* JUDGE *returns with a bottle of soda water.)* Why didn't you tell me at the Café Pörssi that Hulda was there too? I would have gone and said hello to her. It's been such a long time. And Ali-Lehtonen was sitting there with the heads of the Agrarian Party.

PROFESSOR And you could have pointed Hulda out to me as well. I did see you greet someone, but only as we were leaving did I notice Hulda going to dance. And how she does dance!

JUDGE Yes, Hulda dances well. It's a good thing you didn't notice her earlier. It's unlikely that Hulda would have been terribly overjoyed at such an encounter and, even less so, the young Ph.D. who was accompanying her.

PURTIAINEN Quite so. Who was that young man?

JUDGE Alinen, a young Ph.D. in literature.

PURTIAINEN Do you think he knows who Hulda is?

JUDGE I think this is enough about Hulda, already. Hulda is a young, cultured woman who is employed in my household and I would appreciate it, Purtiainen, if you didn't make an issue of this.

PURTIAINEN Absolutely not, although this is, in fact, a new cultural phenomenon.

JUDGE *(Pushes a chair out of his way abruptly)* Damned social phenomena! Go try and tell Hulda that she's a phenomenon!

PURTIAINEN A magnificent phenomenon! Those below are beginning to rise. Watch out, gentlemen! Just imagine, when they all begin studying in their free time, all the Huldas and Miinas, the Kaisas and Tyynes, when they all go to Workers' Associations and to study circles. And the boys from the factories follow along, all the stockmen and the street cleaners! The cafés in Sörnäinen, the workers' district, will empty and, likewise, all the dance halls and grade B movies. The theaters will present *Crime and Punishment*, *Othello*, *The Wonders of Verdun*, and Arvid Järnefelt's *Tiitus* for sold-out audiences. All editions of history and economics texts will be sold out and, likewise, classical literature. And the personnel at the state liquor stores will be decreased by half. The young people will stand as a wall in front of Parliament and demand additional Workers' Associations, libraries, and books, additional lecture halls for the University. How would that be, my good gentlemen?

PROFESSOR Don't paint the devil on the wall, that would be an outright revolution! What will become of us if all the female students strive to become parlormaids and young men with Master's degrees, cooks. Ali-Lehtonen is right, limits must be set on the flood of students to the universities. What will happen if farmhands begin to speak foreign languages and put on airs before their masters?

JUDGE Nothing except that the farmhands will then begin to civilize their masters. Something of them will even rub off on their masters!

PROFESSOR I have always been of the

237

opinion that Gutenberg was the arch devil, in fact. Down with Gutenberg, down with typesetting, printing presses and those damned funds for culture! Here one is supposed to preserve and take care of the society and, at the same time, appropriate cultural funds for schools, libraries, and all kinds of cultural institutions. And they're nothing but cradles of revolution, all of them! Your health, gentlemen! Through my mouth speaks a wholesome conservatism! Down with your progressive stance, down with Purtiainen's Socialism!

PURTIAINEN Yes, a dangerous tale, this cultural business.

PROFESSOR Long live the catechism, contentedness, and comfort! Let's stick our heads in the sand and our tails toward the sun!

PURTIAINEN And though, out of decency, I preach to the young: girls and boys read so that, via elections, you will reach Parliament, via Parliament you will reach the government and, via the government, better circumstances, in accordance with Tanner's formula. Yes, it would clearly be a revolution if all of them, or 300,000 of them for instance, began to read.

PROFESSOR Hail, Purtiainen, the revolutionary! I too am a revolutionary, I vote cultural grant funds. (The JUDGE paces back and forth, upset.) Why are you so upset, brother Carl? It seems as if you're afraid of losing a good parlormaid. But soon we will be losing all our servant girls. Don't be upset!

PURTIAINEN As far as women like that are concerned, it's the same old story as with trams: don't run after them, there'll soon be another.

JUDGE Listen now, gentlemen, stop this. We were supposed to discuss the clauses of that Land Reform Law a bit.

PURTIAINEN It is my fundamental belief and isn't it yours as well, fine Professor and friend, even though you are in fact from the Coalition Party: no horse-trading after midnight. Our group is such that it can sense at what time of day which deal has been made. And then there is also that mamma of mine waiting at home and . . . suspicious.

PROFESSOR Well, we're not leaving here with parched throats even though that progressive is in a bad mood because he seems to be in danger of losing Hulda.

JUDGE Stop babbling! (The sound of the hall door. The JUDGE gets up.) Ahaa, there's Hulda. We've been awaiting Hulda's return here.

PROFESSOR (Charges toward the door) Greetings, oh Hulda! (Leads HULDA in, half forcefully)

PURTIAINEN Well, I had no idea that "Hulda" was actually Hulda Juurakko.

HULDA (Calmly) Pardon me. Thank you, gentlemen. My overcoat belongs on the kitchen side, but I've forgotten the kitchen key.

PROFESSOR Come sit here with us. We've all been waiting for you, Hulda.

JUDGE Would you be so kind and make us some tea, Hulda, and then come in to talk with us?

HULDA If the Judge would like some tea, I'll be glad to make it. Talking is a different matter, that's not part of a parlormaid's duties.

PROFESSOR You mustn't be rigid, Hulda. Purtiainen and I are a bit like your godfathers.

HULDA Quite right. Mr. Purtiainen also participated in "rescuing" me from the Boulevard. I'll bring some tea right away. (Exits)

PURTIAINEN She certainly is pretty, but her tongue's a bit sharp.

PROFESSOR (To the JUDGE) You've always had good taste in women's dresses, simple and stylish.

JUDGE Listen, my good man, Hulda takes care of her own dresses, with her own salary.

PROFESSOR That's the modern system!

JUDGE Listen, this really is enough.

PURTIAINEN No fighting over Hulda. Soratie has a monopoly. We'll leave Hulda to him.

HULDA (Enters during the last remarks, carrying a tea tray. She intends to say something but lowers the tray calmly to the table.) Yes, that's just what the gentlemen did, in fact. And here's some tea. Miina woke up when the Judge went to get soda water and she made some tea. Help yourself.

JUDGE (Gets up and offers HULDA a chair) Please sit down, Hulda. There's no cup set for you here.

HULDA I'm not used to drinking at the gentry's table.

JUDGE Except at the Café Pörssi.

HULDA   I forgot to add: at the gentry's table
   – in this house.
JUDGE   Then it's time to begin.
PROFESSOR AND PURTIAINEN   Good! We
   agree! Hulda must stay here to our
   delight.
HULDA *.(Pours tea)* Actually . . . why not.
   . . . I should also learn a bit about the art
   of socializing.
PROFESSOR   Oh, Hulda certainly knows
   about that! So, you too are going to
   become a candidate for Parliament,
   Hulda?
HULDA   I don't like titles.
JUDGE   Except for one.
HULDA   And what would that be?
JUDGE   Mrs.
PROFESSOR   How old-fashioned!
HULDA   The Judge is mistaken. There's
   another title I like even more.
JUDGE   Ahaa, and what is that?
HULDA   Member of Parliament, the most
   honorable title on earth. Unfortunately
   those who hold it aren't always aware of
   its obligations.
PROFESSOR   Good, Hulda, just belt it out!
   You were already instructing us when
   you had just arrived here from
   Juurakko.
PURTIAINEN   It seems that Hulda is still
   faithful to the principles of our party, she
   holds Parliament in esteem.
HULDA   So I do.
JUDGE   Have you become a judge of
   morals, Hulda? Is this Dr. Alinen's
   influence . . . at the Café Pörssi?
HULDA   No, yours.
PROFESSOR   The Judge is jealous. We're all
   jealous. By the way, they say that you
   have a great many supporters, Hulda. You
   will probably also soon be sitting there in
   Parliament.
HULDA   That institution could use some
   humor. I wonder if I have enough of it.
   From what I've heard, sitting up in the
   galleries, listening, I've noticed that
   humor unifies the parties much more
   than patriotism does.
PROFESSOR   Hulda, where have you learned
   that?
HULDA   From my master . . . as I have so
   many other . . . paradoxes.
JUDGE   This woman has been observing my
   weaknesses for six years. Can you
   imagine anything more horrible?
HULDA   I have a famous, noble forefather:

Figaro, who was a great factor in toppling
France's old regime.
   May I have a cigarette, Judge?
JUDGE *(Offers* HULDA *a cigarette)* A
   cigarette doesn't suit you, Hulda.
HULDA   If I myself smoke, I'll suffer less
   from the gentlemen's smoking.
JUDGE *(Instinctively)* We apologize.
HULDA   To me? Why I'm only Hulda.
JUDGE   Did that Ph.D. there in the Café
   Pörssi know that you're "only Hulda"?
HULDA *(Looks at the* JUDGE*)* Do you mean
   to say, "your Hulda"?
PROFESSOR AND PURTIAINEN *(Laughing)*
   Good, good!
HULDA   Pardon me, "your maid Hulda."
   I don't know, I haven't asked him.
JUDGE   Does he have serious intentions?
HULDA   Most certainly. He treats me as if
   I weren't Hulda, but a better person of
   some sort.
JUDGE   Haven't you been treated well in
   this household?
HULDA   This household will get the best
   testimonial from me.
PROFESSOR   We all treat Hulda well. If you
   are not well treated here, I'll take you
   under my wing for protection. Never
   mind that clause man.
PURTIAINEN   I'd even take Hulda under my
   care if I didn't have an ill-tempered lady
   at home.
HULDA   Thank you, gentlemen, but I'm not
   a trophy, just an old-fashioned servant. I'll
   stay with my old master . . . *(Winks at the*
   JUDGE*, quietly)* . . . at least for another
   week. . . .
JUDGE   Hulda's learned to flirt at the Café
   Pörssi.
HULDA   I'm practicing more easy-going
   manners, in case I should happen to need
   them.
PROFESSOR   That Carl is soon going to
   marry a shoe factory. (HULDA *grows rigid.)*
   So, Hulda, do remember that it's I who
   has the first date. Not Doctor Alinen. It's I
   who will sit with Hulda at the Pörssi.
HULDA   I'll remember, Professor, unless you
   also soon find a shirt factory, for example.
PROFESSOR   Yes. But I'm not striving for
   the presidency like that progressive, who
   only marries wives suited to the presidency.
JUDGE   Listen, Magnus, you're talking
   rubbish.
PURTIAINEN   I'm also of that opinion.

Listen, Mr. Conservative, you're talking trash, you're talking about private matters. We only discuss social phenomena.

PROFESSOR A shoe factory and a shirt factory are social phenomena.

HULDA So they are. But tomorrow is my last big cleaning day. Thank you very much for all your kindness and humanity, Professor. . . .

PROFESSOR But joking aside, are you really leaving here, Hulda?

HULDA That's my master's wish. In a week. This is our fate as servants, we grow accustomed to a house's nooks and crannies, we learn to like a particular doorway or, for example, that balcony window from which I have so often looked at the moonlight on the lake. And then we have to leave. *(The JUDGE stands, his arms crossed at his chest. The PROFESSOR swallows something, PURTIAINEN looks at his whiskey glass.)* The only consolation is in leaving yesterday for tomorrow.

PROFESSOR *(Coughs, clearing his throat)* It's not appropriate for me to meddle in other people's affairs. . . .

JUDGE It isn't, indeed.

PURTIAINEN No, never. Come along, Conservatives!

PROFESSOR But if Hulda hasn't got a job, I'll certainly try to get work for her. Look, Hulda, I'd like to make you a little speech. I'm merely an ill-tempered Conservative, who can also say of himself that he's been in politics for thirty years . . . and always on the wrong side. *(Attempts to regain his humor)* But it's a damn shame, Hulda, that you didn't end up here on the Conservative side. Here you would have been cared for and you would have risen to your rightful place. *(Unintentionally serious)* You would come to represent the vitality of our people's lower strata. *(Tries to speak jokingly)* But if you go with that Marxist bunch, you'll be lost there. No one there will notice that you're . . . *(Earnestly again)* . . . the image of our people's tenacity, energy, and vitality, the prototype of integrity and honor. But now it will be my duty as well to hurl abuse at you in the future, Hulda.

PURTIAINEN Look, my good friend, in our party, everyone is that way. It's just that you haven't noticed how well we represent our people's fundamental characteristics. It's good you noticed Hulda, at least.

HULDA *(Laughing)* Purtiainen is right. But you're a dear, Professor.

PROFESSOR But that progressive isn't saying a word. It's true that, in his deepest self, he acknowledges Hulda, but he's afraid of the Conservatives.

JUDGE Not this time.

HULDA Thank you, gentlemen, for all your kindness and good will. Good night! *(Extends her hand to the PROFESSOR, who kisses it, and then to PURTIAINEN)*

PURTIAINEN *(Kisses HULDA's hand)* I know how to do that, too.

HULDA My, my, comrade Purtiainen, that was really unnecessary. *(Curtsies to the JUDGE, who nods his head at HULDA. HULDA exits.)*

PURTIAINEN Sorry that things were a bit loud here. But it's about time now for me to get back home beside Kaisa. Well, good night, gentlemen!

PROFESSOR Cheer up, old fellow! It happens in even the best of families.

JUDGE Good night! And try to rein in your imaginations.

PURTIAINEN Of course, of course. *(The gentlemen leave. The JUDGE paces back and forth angrily. Then he rings a bell on the desk. The bell is heard ringing off in another room. HULDA enters with a tray in her hand.)*

HULDA Good heavens, Judge, I'll come with a slight ring. Just don't wake Miss Connie and Miina. *(She opens the window and begins to gather cups and glasses onto the tray.)* Good night!

JUDGE *(Coldly)* Put the tray on the table. What kind of a maneuver was that? Why did you act like a disreputable woman, Hulda? Why did you give them the impression that you're my mistress? And that I'm sending you away, Hulda? Like some sort of a scoundrel!

HULDA You were acting rather oddly, yourself. Why didn't you explode for once, you whited sepulcher!

JUDGE Hulda dear, for many generations my family has been taught not to explode . . . or to swear . . . that too is a way of dealing with things. By the way, I didn't care for your behavior with that man at the Pörssi, either . . . especially if you're thinking of trying for Parliament.

HULDA I haven't asked for your opinion, but it's fun to hear it!

JUDGE Where have you gotten that stylish dress? From that man?

HULDA No, from you. Last month's paycheck plus a few articles and a few lectures at the Youth League. If you weren't the master of this house, I'd box you on the ears.

JUDGE And I'd deserve it, Hulda. But I was beside myself because of those men. You certainly have created a stew this evening!

HULDA (Picks up the tray again) There's no shame in a man keeping mistresses. Did you notice, Judge, that you said I acted like a disreputable woman, like your mistress? In other words you consider your mistresses disreputable women? (Curtsying) Good night!

JUDGE I said, put that tray back on the table. Or I'll throw it down.

HULDA That is a very powerful and convincing argument. (Lowers the tray to the table)

JUDGE You are the most devilish woman I have ever met in the world. (Grabs HULDA by the arms) Every damned one of them has been disreputable, and if you don't watch out, you will be, too! (HULDA tries to free herself. The JUDGE thrusts her onto the chair and goes to his room.)

HULDA (Furious, she remains seated and shouts.) And what about that shoe factory! (She jumps up, takes the tray, notices that the windows are open, closes them, takes the tray again and leaves.)

Curtain

Scene 6

The same room a few days later. Grand festivities at the JUDGE's home have concluded. The sound of laughter and the buzz of conversation in the adjacent room and the room next door. MISS SINIJÄRVI is typing. HULDA is preparing the coffee table and then she sits down beside the desk.

HULDA Will you be finished soon, Pinnebergska?

MISS SINIJÄRVI Why do you always call me Pinnebergska?

HULDA Because you're not yet Larssonska.

MISS SINIJÄRVI Who are Pinnebergska and Larssonska?

HULDA Haven't you read about them?

MISS SINIJÄRVI No. I've just been reading Iris Uurto's *Longing for the Body* and Hilja Valtonen's *Little Wife*, wonderful books! (Finishes writing)

HULDA My, my, Pinnebergska! Come into the kitchen and eat! They'll soon be finished with lunch and come in here for coffee.

MISS SINIJÄRVI I don't know. . . . I'm feeling a bit shy. . . .

HULDA But you live entirely on coffee, oh I'm well aware of it. Come have some decent food for once!

MISS SINIJÄRVI Oh, I'm feeling a bit shy . . . how could I just go into the kitchen like that?

HULDA Listen, Pinnebergska, I'm angry today. Still, it's much better to be a servant girl than an office assistant. (The telephone rings, MISS SINIJÄRVI answers.)

MISS SINIJÄRVI Judge Sorotie's residence. . . . Certainly, I'll call the Judge. . . . Hulda, ask the Judge to the phone.

HULDA As you wish, Pinnebergska. (Leaves)

MISS SINIJÄRVI (Gathers her papers. The JUDGE enters.) The telephone for you, Judge.

JUDGE (On the telephone) Helloo, Soratie. . . . Good evening, Dr. Alinen. . . . Yes, those regulations are ready here. . . . (Turns) Aren't they, Miss Sinijärvi?

MISS SINIJÄRVI Yes, Judge.

JUDGE (Into the telephone) They're ready. If the Doctor could stop here, even tonight, for instance. I have guests here. The dinner is over, but the Doctor could have some coffee . . . there are even some acquaintances of the Doctor's here. . . . Good. Welcome! (Hangs up the telephone. To MISS SINIJÄRVI) Are you ready? Thank you. You may go now and you can come to the office a bit later tomorrow.

MISS SINIJÄRVI Thank you. Good night.

JUDGE Good night. (The JUDGE leaves. HULDA comes toward him, a tray in her hand, she steps aside for the JUDGE. The JUDGE stops, looks at her as if he wished to say something but he leaves nevertheless.)

HULDA Aren't you going to come eat in the kitchen?

MISS SINIJÄRVI Well, the Judge didn't ask me!

HULDA Him? Remember a social phenomenon? . . . Well, good night then, Pinnebergska!

MISS SINIJÄRVI Good night, Hulda! (Leaves)

JUDGE *(Returns and intends to say something to* HULDA *again)* Hulda . . . Dr. Alinen. . . .

HULDA And, once again, you allowed that social phenomenon to go home without eating, Judge!

JUDGE Damn it . . . ! Why didn't you remind me, Hulda?

HULDA I don't want to come between you and social phenomena, but I'll call her back. *(Shouts)* Miss Sinijärvi. . . . *(The* JUDGE *exits.* AUNT *enters.)*

AUNT They're already in the drawing room. Is the coffee table ready? Cigars, matches, candles? The brandy tray is ready in the pantry.

HULDA *(Suddenly stops in front of* AUNT*)* Miss Connie, I'm exhausted. Couldn't Liisa serve the liqueur?

AUNT Liisa? Who hasn't poured a glass of wine without spilling it?

HULDA I can't serve such stupid people.

AUNT Hulda, you must. Often in life it seems as if we can't any more, that all the threads on the skein are hopelessly tangled. But then you sit down for a moment and begin to rewind it . . . and then, once again, you have the strength.

HULDA I'm leaving here, Miss Connie, tomorrow!

AUNT You're not leaving, Hulda, you haven't a place yet.

HULDA I'll get a place at the Women's League.

AUNT Let's talk about this later.

HULDA You and Miina have been so kind to me. When the Judge gets married you can both come and live at my place. Then neither of you will have any cares, and I have no one, even my mother is dead.

AUNT Hulda, dear. Now you go fetch the tray, they'll be here soon. *(HULDA exits, the* JUDGE *opens the door.)*

JUDGE Please come in. *(MRS. KAAVIO and* MISS KAAVIO *enter, followed by* MISS MATERO, *an actress, then* MR. KAAVIO, *the Economic Counselor, the* PROFESSOR, *the* JUDGE, *and* THORMAN, *a bank director.)*

AUNT Can I offer you some coffee? Please sit down here on the sofa, Mrs. Kaavio.

MRS. KAAVIO Thank you. It's very comfortable here. What a fine reading room and such a beautiful view, but it's so high up, and I don't like elevators. I always get such a funny feeling in my chest when I'm in them. That's why I must always live on the ground floor, in fact. But when you live in your own building, you can arrange matters as you wish.

AUNT That elevator certainly is uncomfortable. Would you like some cream? And sugar?

MRS. KAAVIO Thank you, thank you! *(MISS KAAVIO and* MISS MATERO *are conversing.)*

JUDGE *(Offering the* BANK DIRECTOR *and the* ECONOMIC COUNSELOR *cigars)* Would you care for a cigar?

BANK DIRECTOR Thank you. This cigar is exquisite. I don't understand how people can smoke tobacco wrapped in paper.

MR. KAAVIO Hah, ha, ha. Those paper-wrapped cigarettes are a bit childish. They're really not appropriate for elderly gentlemen like the bank director and myself, with our substantial cigar bellies.

MISS KAAVIO Daddy has a sense of style. I've tried to smoke those long, thin cigars. I saw Princess Radziwill smoking them in Biarritz, but they made me ill. And yet they cost 15 francs apiece. But tell me, Judge, doesn't this cigarette holder suit me extremely well? *(Displays a very long cigarette holder)*

JUDGE Most suitable . . . for a woody vine.

MISS KAAVIO Would you like some coffee?

JUDGE *(Takes the coffee cup)* Would you like some, Miss Matero? And you, Miss Kaavio? Let's sit here. *(They sit apart around a table to the right.* HULDA *enters with a liqueur tray. She serves the older women and men first.)*

AUNT Would Mrs. Kaavio like some liqueur? *(They continue their conversation.)*

MISS KAAVIO My, this is Cointreau, in fact. I can't abide Cointreau, could I have a glass of Benedictine?

JUDGE Pour some of the monks' brew, Hulda! *(HULDA lowers the tray to the table, pours Benedictine into a glass, and offers it to* MISS KAAVIO.*)*

MISS KAAVIO I've always been told that my taste in liqueurs is masculine.

MISS MATERO You like men's liqueur as much as you like men themselves.

MISS KAAVIO I like men too much, in fact. Do you know, I could never be satisfied with just one man. I'd always need several. I'd have morning coffee with one, with another I'd go riding, with a third I'd have lunch, with a fourth, I'd drink tea, with a fifth I'd have dinner. *(Quietly)* My night I could spend with them all. Mamma didn't hear that, did she?

MISS MATERO Isn't she delightfully frank? That's why I like her. There's an artist in her.

JUDGE Marvelous! To your health, Miss Kirsti! Could we have some more cognac, Hulda!

MISS MATERO Only society ladies can speak in such a manner, of course. The morals of our work slaves, the actresses, are closely guarded by both the Board of Directors and the Administrative Board.

MISS KAAVIO Oh, one of the greatest faults of this country is that we have so few people who don't work. As if it were a merit of some sort for a person to be a work slave. My daddy has worked so that I might enjoy myself. I am the product of my daddy's work. We children of the rich are oppressed in this country. Here it's the custom to be doing something. I'm always being asked what I do. I want to be, not to do. My daddy's done enough. My job is to enjoy life.

JUDGE Not alone, hopefully?

MISS KAAVIO Not at all. I intend to marry a man who can build a career with my help, and then I intend to take pleasure in his career.

JUDGE The modern woman has a great deal of style, indeed. Her talk is as low-cut as her dress. And what about the other men?

MISS KAAVIO Hah, they're for my amusement. My husband won't have time to amuse me . . . at least not in the daytime.

JUDGE Hopefully, he won't be . . . shall we say . . . too tired in the evening.

MISS KAAVIO *(Looks at him)* Do you think so?

MISS MATERO Judge, haven't you noticed that she's courting you?

JUDGE I'm afraid I'm so old-fashioned that I'm unable to grasp all the fine points. But Miss Kirsti is a charming creature!

MISS KAAVIO You wish to say "refined," no doubt!

HULDA Would you like some more coffee, Miss?

MISS KAAVIO No more coffee, you can get yellow spots on your back from coffee. Oh, Judge, would you look and see if I have a yellow spot on my back?

JUDGE No spot at all, only the captivating contour of your backbone.

MISS KAAVIO Thank you so much. Such a compliment! The men here really are quite incompetent.

MRS. KAAVIO Is that Kirsti having her back scrutinized again? My, my, is that the fashion in the great wide world these days?

MISS KAAVIO Mamma mustn't constantly scold me.

JUDGE Even though little Kirsti has been very wild, indeed.

MISS MATERO *(To the* PROFESSOR, *who has approached their table)* We actresses really aren't interested in politics, but Kirsti is constantly nagging me to go along with her and watch you in Parliament. But, I'm afraid to sit with her up there in the galleries, because she's sure to loudly discuss those Aaltonen statues[5] and compare them to the people sitting below.

PROFESSOR I too am of the opinion that some of the people down in the lower chamber would be better suited to those pedestals.

MISS KAAVIO Above all, the Professor himself. But, Judge, we will definitely be coming next week, and then you must explain to us about the laws and the regulations, and who those bald papas are.

PROFESSOR *(Derisively)* Very good. In fact, popular presentations comprehensible to the public are his specialty. All in all, he's becoming a charmer! A real Casanova!

MISS KAAVIO My, what a recommendation! Papa always says that he'll become a minister in the government. When will you become a minister, Judge?

JUDGE Ask the President.

PROFESSOR Fine! Every progressive will someday become a minister or President and this, then, will bring an end to the Party. *(HULDA serves liqueur.)* Isn't that so, Hulda?

HULDA Right.

MISS KAAVIO I shall ask the President, in fact. Papa's a good friend of his.

BANK DIRECTOR Listen, Carl, come give us a bit of advice over here. Just in case there are no experts on the banking committee. . . . *(Continues the discussion enthusiastically)*

MISS KAAVIO And that's how our suitors are always spirited off, to all manner of international banking discussions. Not that the Judge would be much of a flirt. *(The doorbell has rung, meanwhile.* MIINA *shows* DR. ALINEN *inside.)*

JUDGE *(Who has heard Miss Kaavio's last sentence)* But in fact here comes a young man who is skilled at flirting. Greetings, Doctor. May I introduce Doctor Alinen, Miss Kaavio and Miss Matero.

MISS MATERO Oh, I know Dr. Alinen extremely well.

ALINEN Yes, I am a great admirer of both Miss Matero and Miss Kaavio. It was very cordial of you, Judge, to invite me here. *(Greets the others.* HULDA *comes in through the door with a tray.)*

JUDGE Hulda, would you bring some coffee here, additional guests have arrived. *(Looks mischievously at* HULDA *who, smiling ironically at the* JUDGE, *approaches* DR. ALINEN *with the coffee tray.)*

HULDA Please, Dr. Alinen.

ALINEN Good heavens, Miss Juurakko! Good evening! How are you, Miss Hulda? Resting on your laurels?

HULDA Good evening, Doctor! Does this look like I'm resting on my laurels?

JUDGE The gentry are acquainted with each other, no doubt.

ALINEN Of course. Miss Juurakko has been my best student at the College of Social Sciences.

HULDA Thank you for the good grade, Doctor.

ALINEN And Miss Hulda was awarded her degree last week. The two of us went dancing at the Café Pörssi. She wouldn't agree to celebrating in any other way.

PROFESSOR And Hulda never said a thing. We would have joined you, too. Congratulations on our behalf, Hulda.

HULDA Thank you. Would the Professor like some liqueur? And you, Judge? A glass of cognac?

JUDGE Did you know that Hulda works here, Dr. Alinen?

ALINEN Certainly. The entire faculty is aware of that. It is just splendid, Judge, that you have arranged Miss Hulda's work schedule so that she has been able to study.

JUDGE Has Hulda portrayed me as a noble benefactor?

ALINEN Yes, indeed.

PROFESSOR Good!

JUDGE This has been more my Aunt's doing, in fact.

HULDA The Judge is too modest.

ALINEN In any case, it is very rare for someone to have received their degree in so short a time. She's even studied languages. Hulda's German is better than mine.

HULDA You mustn't exaggerate, Professor.

ALINEN And next week Miss Hulda is making a presentation about Land Reform Laws and agricultural issues at our club. So it's worth coming to listen.

HULDA *(Smiling)* If you draw the audience from the city's fine salons, I'll cancel my entire lecture. *(Leaves with her tray)*

ALINEN But Miss Hulda!

AUNT You mustn't offend Hulda.

ALINEN Miss Juurakko is a magnificent speaker, by the way. I've heard her speak at various study circle gatherings. And she's said to have a great deal of support in the Social Democratic Youth Alliance. I am certain that Hulda, too, will become a parliamentary candidate in the next elections.

MISS MATERO That's exciting! Even Ida Aalberg was a railway guard's daughter. . . .

ALINEN So she was. How would it feel, Judge, to sit on the same committee with Miss Hulda? Such are the modern times!

MISS KAAVIO Where has the Judge found such a parlormaid? Our maids certainly don't have time to take examinations – they have better things to do, in fact. But in bachelor households such as these, things get out of hand.

MISS MATERO Oh, such bachelors' households are infamous!

JUDGE This is not a so-called "bachelor household." My Aunt looks after my house and my servants.

MISS MATERO It's common knowledge. Such households are comfortable. Even Rebecca West was a housekeeper. *(HULDA returns with a cup of coffee.)* Besides, Hulda's very pretty. So this is why Judge Soratie has remained a bachelor for so long.

JUDGE The young lady has a remarkable imagination.

ALINEN Miss Hulda, would you accompany me to the theater tomorrow evening? Would you promise to come?

HULDA Thank you very much, but the evenings I have free depend upon whether the Judge has guests and whether Miss Connie will permit me to go out.

JUDGE I have a meeting tomorrow. Hulda will be quite free. I won't be coming home for dinner.

HULDA Thank you, I'll be glad to go to the theater. *(Gathers the coffee cups from the tables and exits into the kitchen. The JUDGE and MISS KAAVIO converse quietly.)*

MISS KAAVIO *(Abruptly)* Yes, but where did you find such a Hulda?

PROFESSOR *(In a cheerful mood)* We found her on the Boulevard. *(HULDA returns at that moment, stops at the door. She looks at the JUDGE, then comes over to the table and calmly begins to gather the dishes. The PROFESSOR turns, notices HULDA's silence and the silence of the rest of the guests. During this time only the quiet conversation of the BANK DIRECTOR and the ECONOMIC COUNSELOR is audible. But AUNT and MRS. KAAVIO are listening to the conversation at the other table.)*

MRS. KAAVIO Goodness, what?

PROFESSOR *(Abruptly)* Yes, yes, Hulda had come from the country and we came across her at night on the Boulevard.

MRS. KAAVIO Good heavens!

HULDA *(Smiling at the PROFESSOR)* Do you still remember that, Professor? I was wearing a yellow hat with a red feather in it. My train was six feet long and I had a feather boa around my neck, isn't that right?

PROFESSOR *(Stammering)* Of course, a hat . . . Hulda was wearing some sort of hat. *(HULDA goes to the door, the tray is quivering in her hands.)*

ALINEN May I take the tray, Miss Juurakko?

HULDA Thank you. *(Opens the door. ALINEN leaves with HULDA. AUNT follows them.)*

AUNT Pardon me, Mrs. Kaavio.

JUDGE That was quite inexcusable, Maunu. Actually, Hulda was newly arrived from the country and she didn't know where she should go. We did find her on the Boulevard, as a matter of fact, and my Aunt took her in as a parlormaid. *(AUNT returns and sits down beside MRS. KAAVIO again.)*

MRS. KAAVIO But how did you dare to hire her? *(AUNT responds quietly.)*

MISS KAAVIO We base our trust on even less. Gentlemen are always so helpful and polite – on the Boulevard. Isn't that so, Mirja?

JUDGE Miss Matero cannot possibly have any knowledge of that?

MISS MATERO Or of you, Judge!

PROFESSOR I'm absolutely impossible. It's only now that I understand what I've done. I've probably offended Hulda for life. There was nothing to it. We compelled her to come with us.

JUDGE Listen, Maunu, don't mouth any more rubbish, you're only making matters worse. Hulda doesn't get angry. Hulda is a person with a sense of humor. *(ALINEN returns.)*

MISS KAAVIO Well, were you able to console Hulda?

ALINEN I was.

MISS KAAVIO But if she is such a remarkably able person and has earned her degree, why doesn't she seek another kind of position? Is it, perhaps, that she has a bit too much of a past. . . .

ALINEN I think Hulda already has another position in mind.

JUDGE Is that so? Actually she hasn't been dismissed, yet.

ALINEN *(Amused)* Do you hold to the old-fashioned labor regulation, Judge?

JUDGE Hulda is an old-fashioned person.

ALINEN Have you verified this yourself, Judge?

JUDGE I have.

MISS KAAVIO Mirja, have you noticed that the gentlemen's interest is focused entirely on the parlormaid? Apparently we can't compete with a parlormaid. We don't have so interesting a past. Therefore, it would be best for us to be on our way.

PROFESSOR But Miss Kirsti, you're greatly mistaken. Hulda is a social phenomenon. We are interested in her purely as a social phenomenon.

MISS KAAVIO Did you hear that, Mirja, we are not social phenomena!

JUDGE Miss Kaavio, you are a most interesting social phenomenon!

PROFESSOR A charming phenomenon!

ALINEN A social rarity!

MRS. KAAVIO Kalle, isn't it time we left?

MR. KAAVIO Yes, actually, tomorrow is a work day.

BANK DIRECTOR A pity, that was such an interesting plan.

JUDGE *(Gets up and leaves while they are talking)* Pardon me!

MR. KAAVIO It will be utterly impossible to pry you away from the womenfolk then. Kirsti still seems to have charm, heh, heh, heh. . . . *(They talk among themselves.)*

MISS KAAVIO Professor, you certainly were indiscreet . . . but how could such a person ever even be considered for Parliament?

MISS MATERO Even someone straight from the Boulevard suits those Socialists just fine.

PROFESSOR Oh, Miss Kirsti, don't think ill of the one closest to you. I swear that Hulda was a completely innocent country girl who was sitting on the Boulevard. . . .

MISS MATERO It's true, isn't it, that those innocent country girls leave the Boulevard with men?

MISS KAAVIO This certainly would create a scandal in Parliament! Mama knows some of those Socialist women on the municipal commission. She'll have to call this to their attention, of course.

MISS MATERO Oh, Kirsti, that's not. . . .

PROFESSOR Miss Kaavio, you are gravely mistaken. That would be heartless. Hulda is a most upright person.

MISS KAAVIO Perhaps, but we are such great patriots that we take Parliament's honor into consideration, even though the gentlemen do not do so.

PROFESSOR Miss, you are mistaken, I swear it.

MRS. KAAVIO Farewell, then, and we hope to see you at our place soon!

AUNT I so seldom leave home. Thank you, nevertheless!

MRS. KAAVIO But that parlormaid must go. It would be best. They can err again. I know . . . I understand . . . it is sweet of you to try and protect her.

MR. KAAVIO The old lady is pressing forward even with this.

BANK DIRECTOR Goodbye, Judge Soratie, I will certainly see to that expert opinion. Mr. Kaavio is especially well versed in the regulations of economic law. *(General farewells)*

ALINEN But that regulation proposal, Judge. Perhaps we can come over some time to discuss that journal of ours?

JUDGE *(Hands over a paper from the table)* I'd somewhat forgotten that. *(ALINEN and the PROFESSOR help the women with their outer garments. AUNT stands at the door,*

and the JUDGE helps MISS KAAVIO with her evening cape.)

JUDGE I hope to see you soon again.

MISS KAAVIO *(Looks over her shoulder coquettishly at the JUDGE)* Invite me to tea sometime – but without maid Hulda. I think we'd have something to discuss between us. At home, Mother is always meddling.

JUDGE May I telephone you, Miss?

MISS KAAVIO You may.

PROFESSOR Next week let's go to dinner at my summer cottage, but . . . *(Motioning to the others)* . . . without these old fogies. And there this tedious issue can be completely clarified. So you must forget it, isn't that right?

MISS MATERO It shall be forgotten.

MISS KAAVIO We'll try! *(The guests leave, except for the PROFESSOR. AUNT leaves.)*

PROFESSOR I certainly have created a fine stew now!

JUDGE So you have. And by tomorrow everyone in town will know about this already. Did you hear what that old, full-blooded hyena said: they can err again.

PROFESSOR Social phenomena!

JUDGE Good God, you ass!

PROFESSOR I'll try to do something. I'll certainly think up something.

JUDGE Don't think up anything, Maunu, you just thought up that Boulevard story.

PROFESSOR Well, good night! I'll call Hulda tomorrow and maybe even go talk to those monkeys. Good night! *(Leaves)*

JUDGE Good! *(Lights a cigarette. AUNT comes and clears away the dishes.)* Where is Hulda?

AUNT In bed, and she'll stay there.

JUDGE The situation is becoming absolutely impossible. Is she leaving?

AUNT She wants to leave. She hopes to find a place.

JUDGE Under no circumstances can she leave here before she has a place to live and a means of making ends meet. You must see to that.

AUNT Oh Hulda will certainly find a place, if this gossip doesn't ruin her reputation.

JUDGE And she herself does nothing to dispel suspicions!

AUNT What should she do? *(Sits down)* Carl Christian, you've been very nice, allowing me to stay at your place and live on your charity . . . since Elvira passed away. . . .

JUDGE That is idle chatter, Auntie. You've

kept my home in exemplary order and you've worked in our family your entire life. I've always been so fond of you, Auntie.

AUNT You're very kind, but I know that I am not indispensable. I once had to leave your household because your wife couldn't tolerate me, and I know that I shall have to leave again if, for example, you marry that Economic Counselor's daughter. I've never learned to do anything else in life but to care for my relatives' households. No man took a fancy to me, I was ugly, and I had no skills. I've been like a mouse in my relative's household, quiet and unobtrusive, so that you would be able to tolerate me. I've been happy to be given obligations. Even to have been able to care for you when you've been ill. I've never dared wish for a life of my own. There are many like me. Miina there in the kitchen is similar. During my lifetime, I've seen hundreds like me off in people's corners. But then along came Hulda who wasn't satisfied with being thrust into a dark corner. Instead, she took life into her own hands, worked, studied at night, lived like a human being. I too was able to give her something of the little I know. Little customs, which the present generation has forgotten, a little help. Well, Carl Christian, this has been the longest speech of my life. Don't touch Hulda!

Curtain

Scene 7

The same room, a day later. Ten o'clock in the evening. AUNT *is mixing cocktails.* MIINA *is setting glasses on the table.*

MIINA And where in the world is Hulda?

AUNT I don't know. But, Miina, it would be more appropriate for you to call Hulda "Miss." She's no longer of your rank, Miina. . . . She almost has a Master's degree, just like Lars' brother, in fact.

MIINA Oh, Hulda isn't like that. . . . How many glasses should I bring in there?

AUNT At least ten, that should be enough. The Judge and the Professor are coming here from Parliament along with Miss Kaavio and that actress. Perhaps some of the Professor's friends will come here as

well to wait for them. They are all driving to Gustavelund for dinner.

MIINA In the middle of the night?

AUNT These modern customs.

MIINA (HULDA *enters through the drawing room door in a low-cut evening gown, her hair curled and an evening cape over her arm.*) Good God, Hulda!

AUNT Hulda, what's the meaning of this?

HULDA It means that Hulda is going out for dinner and dancing before she departs this gentrified existence and goes to Sörnäinen.

AUNT Where have you gotten that dress, Hulda?

HULDA Borrowed it from the girls at Stockman's Department Store, of course. And listen now, would you be so kind and do the serving, Miina, if anything is to be served. The Doctor has invited me out to dinner and I'm going. Auntie, dear, I've found a place and I'm leaving tomorrow. (*Hugs and kisses* AUNT *on the cheek*) Hulda is leaving and you can both come along, if you wish. (*Whirls* MIINA *around the room*) Miina, Hulda's happy, Hulda's leaving! I've found an editorial job and I'll get my own place to live. You and Miina can both come to my place, if only you want to. Don't look at me like that. Why aren't you joyful along with me? (*Turns her back to* AUNT) Auntie, dear, you can't see that miserable slip there in back at the neckline, can you?

MIINA Oh, my dear child, you're certain to get chilled, you'll catch your death. And how do you dare – a stark naked back – be sure to keep that cape on.

HULDA I'm going to a costume party. (*Sits on the arm of the chair*) Miss Sandmark, how do you like my dress? Lord Gossip will certainly take a fancy to me and Prince Radziwill will come kiss my hand. Good heavens, I forgot perfume, I couldn't get that on loan. A drop of Coty's "Violet" – they stole twenty marks for it at Stockman's! Won't you take a look, Aunt Constance, is my back alluring?

AUNT Hulda, you're out of your mind!

HULDA Shocking. Hulda's merely attempting to portray a woman of the world. What can I do about the fact that women of the world are absurd? (*The telephone rings,* HULDA *goes to answer it.*) It's for me, no doubt. Sylvi-Kyllikki promised to call me from the association meeting, to tell me whether I've been verified as a candidate for Parliament in the party vote. Oh, Auntie dear, oh, Miina dear, how have things turned out for me? *(Lifts the receiver)* Hello . . . Hulda Juurakko here . . . is this Sylvi-Kyllikki . . . ? Yes, how did it go . . . ? I was rejected? Why? What is this . . . ? How is that possible . . . ? Yes, for what reason? *(Pause)* Picked up on the Boulevard . . . yes, be direct . . . a woman with a bad reputation living in a bourgeoise home, yes, quite so . . . yes, quite so . . . in both organizations, then . . . yes, thank you, yes of course I believe that you defended me, although I shouldn't have needed defending . . . They have no right to start accusing me . . . We won't talk about that now. Thank you, Sylvi-Kyllikki, I'm not angry at you. . . . Good-bye. . . . (HULDA *slams down the receiver, remains motionless beside the table.)*

AUNT What now, Hulda?

HULDA *(Wipes her hands across her eyes)* I'm not a suitable candidate for Parliament because the mamas there have heard that I was picked up on the Boulevard, and that I'm living here . . . as the Judge's mistress. You understand, of course, Auntie? Such news travels extremely quickly, in only a few days. . . .

AUNT Oh, poor Hulda, this is unheard of, this must be cleared up. . . .

HULDA Cleared up . . . how can Auntie clear this up?

MIINA *(Weeping)* Oh, oh, Hulda dear!

HULDA Cleared up, how. . . . Wasn't I brought here from the Boulevard, in fact? Haven't I lived in this house for seven years with an unmarried man who is a well-known womanizer? Isn't everyone well aware that I've been a favorite in this household and that my work hours have been organized so that I've been able to study? Quite right. . . . isn't every single scoundrel of a man who enters this house certain that I'm Soratie's mistress? Because my face isn't pockmarked and I don't weigh 200 pounds? (HULDA *grows furious as she paces back and forth.)*

AUNT Dear child, this must be cleared up. Carl Christian must do something. He must clarify. . . .

HULDA Him?

AUNT Now you just sit here, Hulda, and stay calm.

MIINA *(To herself)* Hulda cannot be trampled down in this way, can she?

HULDA No . . . Hulda's going to do something horrible today. . . . So they've rejected me, have they? Good! What if Hulda shows them that they're right, in fact!

MIINA Hulda, poor thing. Now don't you start drinking like Ville, that brother of mine, when he wanted to show the gentlemen. . . .

HULDA Miina, dear, I'll soon drink and soundly. Actually, I should have had a yellow hat with a red feather, but this nakedness may do just as well.

MIINA Aren't you ashamed!

HULDA No, actually I'm not ashamed. Oh I'll certainly try to keep that cape on.

AUNT Oh, Hulda dear, what's going to come of this? It will bring no good.

HULDA Certainly not, and there's no reason it should. *(The doorbell rings.)* Oh, Auntie dear, my perfume, my shoes, my handkerchief! Miina will come tell us when they've all arrived. I'll enter last – as gentry!

AUNT I will not stay to watch this.

HULDA Good night, Auntie. Don't stay! *(Rushes out. AUNT waits but leaves when she notices that it is ALI-LEHTONEN and the PROFESSOR who are arriving.)*

PROFESSOR Well, Miina, where's Hulda?

MIINA Hulda isn't at home.

ALI-LEHTONEN And I came expressly to see what's become of that girl from my area of the country. They're saying astounding things about her. Well dammit, so she isn't home.

PROFESSOR Hulda certainly hasn't eaten her words yet, has she? There isn't anyone here yet, is there? *(The doorbell rings. MISS KAAVIO and MISS MATERO enter.)* Welcome, my fair ladies!

MISS KAAVIO Good evening.

PROFESSOR *(Introducing)* Parliamentarian and municipal counselor Ali-Lehtonen, Miss Kaavio, Miss Matero.

ALI-LEHTONEN Good evening. Well, well, the Economic Counselor's own daughter. Oh the Economic Counselor is well known.

MISS KAAVIO I suppose so. Isn't the Judge at home?

PROFESSOR I sent my car back to fetch him. He stayed on at the Speaker's meeting and asked me to receive the guests. Then we'll all go to Gustavelund in the same car. It's only a half hour's journey. And this should be a smashing evening, indeed. I've even arranged a surprise.

MIINA Miss Connie requested that these drinks be served. (MIINA *exits.*)

PROFESSOR Fantastic! And here are martinis, already prepared, in fact!

MISS MATERO This is marvelous! I caught a chill waiting for Kirsti to get out of the elevator.

MISS KAAVIO I had a bit of a tiff with Mamma. She was afraid I was going to the Artists' Club.

PROFESSOR Greetings, young ladies! Your mamma was right, Miss Kirsti, we too are artists here – tightrope dancers, primarily.

MISS MATERO Oh, Professor!

JUDGE (*Enters with* PURTIAINEN) Good evening! Pardon us for being late. (*Kisses the women's hands*) Has that Maunu been a capable host?

ALI-LEHTONEN We have marvelous drinks in hand. No problems here.

JUDGE We must wait a bit. (*To the* PROFESSOR) I sent the chauffeur to get my car from the garage too. We certainly won't all fit into the same car. Greetings, beautiful young lady!

PROFESSOR I see that you want to divide the group into two. But there is one guest still missing . . . our guest of honor . . . our surprise.

HULDA (*Has appeared at the door*) Hopefully the Professor is referring to me. (*Everyone turns, shocked.*)

JUDGE Hulda! . . . What does this mean?

PROFESSOR Excellent, Hulda! (*Quietly to the* JUDGE) A delightful surprise. Misses Kaavio and Matero, modern women with no prejudices, have expressed their desire to become better acquainted with her.

JUDGE Of course. So this is your brilliant contrivance.

PURTIAINEN Damn Hulda! She certainly does know how!

ALI-LEHTONEN Well, just look at that girl from our district! Is this really the right Hulda?

HULDA (*First greets* ALI-LEHTONEN, *then the* PROFESSOR *and* PURTIAINEN, *nods her head at the women and at the* JUDGE) I am indeed, Squire, what news from Sääksmäki?

ALI-LEHTONEN Well what the devil would

the old mistress of Niskavuori say if she could see Hulda now?

HULDA She'd scold me about this finery, no doubt. She'd say that Hulda Juurakko, who was so good at scrubbing floors and even used to rake the field like everyone else, is now showing off on a drawing room floor like a peacock of some sort! Useless people, aren't they?

ALI-LEHTONEN Good heavens, that Hulda certainly does have the knack! Listen, Professor, shall we take Hulda into our sleigh? The Judge will still be left two fine pearls. May I continue to address you as Hulda?

HULDA As the Squire wishes.

PROFESSOR Of course Hulda will come in our car.

JUDGE Which company she chooses depends upon Hulda, herself, of course.

HULDA I'm interested in the Land Reform Law. In six years' time, the Judge hasn't been able to explain it to me. I notice that I must change the basis of the data. Besides, the question of the rural economy is a stepchild in the Progressive Party's platform. I have never understood what they mean, but the program of such a straightforward Conservative Party member is different. It is obvious that I, as a representative of the landless people, must maintain precisely the opposite position.

JUDGE Well, you mean you haven't explained your political views to me yet, Hulda?

HULDA I was afraid of terror at the workplace.

JUDGE Aren't you afraid any more, Hulda?

HULDA No, because I intend to leave my job as a parlormaid today.

ALI-LEHTONEN and the PROFESSOR Good! Good!

(MISSES KAAVIO *and* MATERO *are discussing something between themselves.*)

JUDGE Pardon me, my good ladies, but Hulda has been quite a surprise to us this evening.

MISS KAAVIO We certainly have noticed that.

PROFESSOR A cocktail for Hulda, as well. . . .

HULDA And a cigarette! Miss Kaavio, pardon me for having learned from you. I need to, and do intend to, conquer at least two men today, both the Professor and the Municipal Counselor. I'm in such a good mood that I definitely need another kiss on both my right and left hands.

PROFESSOR *(Kisses* HULDA's *hand)* Hulda is enchanting.

ALI-LEHTONEN *(Kisses* HULDA's *other hand)* Hulda is fabulous!

HULDA Can't the gentlemen come up with something more alliterative? Hulda is holy, Hulda is hysterical. . . .

PROFESSOR Hulda is heady!

ALI-LEHTONEN Hulda is a handful!

HULDA Hulda is a novelty, isn't that so?

PROFESSOR Hulda is going to our heads, no more cocktails.

JUDGE Would you come over here for a moment, Hulda? I have something to say to you.

PURTIAINEN No secrets.

ALI-LEHTONEN Quite right.

HULDA Since the master is making the request, Hulda will comply.

PROFESSOR *(To* MISS KAAVIO*)* Look, Miss Kirsti, we've gone a bit mad over Hulda.

MISS KAAVIO That's quite obvious. We're not really sure whether we should go at all. The car hasn't even arrived yet. It will be so late.

PROFESSOR The young ladies mustn't take offense. Hulda has given us quite a surprise. This is her debut among the women of the world.

MISS MATERO This has been almost like theater!

JUDGE *(On the right, quietly to* HULDA*)* Hulda, what's the meaning of this?

HULDA I intend to have a good time. This is my last night in your house, Judge!

JUDGE You mustn't drink, Hulda!

HULDA I'll soon be ripe to become your lover. My price is going down!

JUDGE I don't know whether I care about price, any more.

HULDA There are others who do. *(Begins to return to the group by the sofa)*

JUDGE *(Angrily)* Listen, Hulda, that dress of yours alarms me. *(Looks at* HULDA *brazenly)* What keeps it up on you, actually?

HULDA Your incomparable self-control, Judge.

JUDGE Actually, you deserve a thrashing.

HULDA The only sensible words this evening. *(Returns to the table)*

JUDGE You don't hear the car yet, do you? *(Goes over to the window)*

PURTIAINEN *(Leaves the group conversing at the table and goes over beside the Judge. Quietly to the Judge.)* Poor Hulda . . . I'm merely an onlooker here . . . I'm beginning to feel sorry for the girl. . . .

JUDGE How so?

PURTIAINEN Well, those Social Democratic women are so narrow-minded. They had a meeting today about candidates for Parliament and the moral mammas voted Hulda out. Hulda herself doesn't know it yet.

JUDGE What do you mean to say by this, Purtiainen?

PURTIAINEN Well, it was made explicit at the meeting that Hulda is a parlormaid here at my good friend's, and a bit more than a parlormaid, in fact. Stories even circulated that she'd been picked up on the Boulevard and, no matter how much I explained, nothing helped.

JUDGE That is intolerable! Trash! Every single word of it, slander!

PURTIAINEN Now don't get upset, my good friend. Look, no matter how they themselves may act, they're such damned moralists.

HULDA *(Sits on the arm of the chair)* Of course, we women of the people have a different goal in life. The young ladies will forgive me if I don't know how to socialize in accordance with all the fine rules of etiquette.

PROFESSOR Miss Kaavio, smile your Mona-Lisa smile for me!.

HULDA And about Mona Lisa! Do you know why Mona Lisa was smiling, Professor? Take note, now, that I wish to dazzle you with my knowledge!

MISS MATERO *(Rises)* Pardon me, Professor, but my friend and I don't wish to wait for the car. We're going home, instead.

MISS KAAVIO Quite so. Besides, we are unaccustomed to being in the company of snobbish "parlormaids" . . . *(Sarcastically)* . . . who've been picked up on the Boulevard.

HULDA This is precisely what I've been waiting for, like a tiger. Stay where you are, Miss, now I'm going to have my say. The entire city now knows that the gentlemen picked me up on the Boulevard and that, in this household, I've been Judge Soratie's lover. Even the working women rejected my candidacy today for this very reason. Every effort has been made to shame and slander me. What do you, who have not eaten bread moistened with tears, know about life . . . ? And even if I had in fact been picked up on the street, what business is it of yours? And even if I had in fact cohabited with all of those men who have groped at my arm, what business is it of yours? Haven't I fulfilled my personal obligations, haven't I done my work? Good Lord, how much I am needed in the world! Every stone in the street calls out: Hulda, come and help! All human life is in disarray. Like wild animals, people are ready to turn on each other. Everyone should come and help. And I have done my work. In order to be able to help my fellow human beings, I have sat up nights reading until I couldn't see any more, and those women don't approve of me! A wall has been raised up against me. But with all ten of my fingernails I will tear down that wall. I will not simply be cast out onto the street, for I have a life in other people's lives, a social existence, just as you men do! Long ago the devil sat on Käpälä Mountain, and cast stones, and blew frost onto the Juurakko fields, but there was "sisu" in the Juurakko fists, saying: And now! A flood came and took the grain, and the people's "will" said: And what next! Death and war came, they took brother, father, and the people's "will" said: And what next! We'll take what's ours! Although I was found on the street, and although I've slept in this man's bed for six years, those people from among whose ranks I have come will still accept me.

JUDGE This is enough, now, Hulda. Your speech was a bit too long. If Hulda has slept in my bed, unfortunately she has been there alone. But that mishap will certainly be rectified, for in a few weeks Hulda will become my wife. She is one of those old-fashioned girls. The Professor has organized this small dinner in order to celebrate our engagement.

HULDA *(Startled. Sits calmly smoking her cigarette)* That is an absolute lie. Chivalry!

JUDGE Don't pay any attention to what Hulda says. She loves a martyr's crown, but she loves me even more.

HULDA I don't. . . .

ALI-LEHTONEN Thank heavens! I like this. . . . I really like this. . . .

PURTIAINEN Done like a man!

PROFESSOR You certainly knew how to handle that, Carl! Well now, for once even the parties are all of the same mind! Although I don't understand why it's you Hulda had to fall in love with.

MISS KAAVIO Pardon me, Miss Juurakko! But this is a rather odd way to announce an engagement. I would like extend my congratulations!

MISS MATERO Congratulations! Your speech was fantastic, Miss Juurakko! We actresses too are constantly being oppressed. Despite everything, I like you.

HULDA *(Looking at the JUDGE)* He's pretending now. He did this to crush me throughout the land. *(Raises her hands to her eyes)*

JUDGE *(Takes hold of her hands. Quietly)* Hulda, dearest, you've won! *(The sound of an automobile outside)*

PROFESSOR Hulda is nervous, and it's no wonder. But let's go! I'm hungry, in fact. And yet! Hulda, smile at your old friend.

HULDA Pardon me, I'm too tired. I wish the gentry a fun-filled evening! Good night!

PROFESSOR But Hulda an event such as this must certainly be celebrated. You'll have time enough for arguing, too.

HULDA I beg your pardon, but I have a headache. Good night! *(Leaves)*

JUDGE Since my fiancée is not going, I must stay home as well. Pardon me.

PROFESSOR Now you're deserting your company.

ALI-LEHTONEN We protest.

PURTIAINEN There's nothing to be done about it, young love!

THE WOMEN *(Take their evening cloaks, make farewell bows)* Good night, Judge!

PROFESSOR It would have been better if you had given that Hulda orders. If it starts out like this, you're going to be completely henpecked.

ALI-LEHTONEN And so, in fact, a lady of the house was brought into the Judge's household! Good night! *(The guests leave. The JUDGE closes the door, comes back into the study, turns on the light in the drawing room, listens by the drawing room door. HULDA comes through the drawing room door wearing a maid's uniform, a tray in her hand. She begins to gather glasses onto the tray.)*

JUDGE Now what is this supposed to mean? I thought I'd have a chance to study your beautiful back freely, for once, though I'll probably have time enough for that.

HULDA *(Suddenly sets the tray on the table)* Are you still continuing that same joke?

JUDGE Taking into account the social talents you've just displayed, a ring isn't an expensive price for you, in fact.

HULDA No doubt a ring even from you would be suitable for a wise young maiden's collection. . . . So you actually believe that I want a ring from you? Your fiancée, little Miss Juurakko! Never, do you hear, absolutely never! For seven years, with your stranger's eyes, you've been measuring me in this household as if I were an unfamiliar horse and I've listened for your footsteps like a madwoman. And I don't know why in heaven's name I care for you! Your politics are narrow-minded and two-faced! I, myself, have wept with joy when you've been good to me and other people at times. Maybe I like you because, despite it all, you're a good person. But I don't want to become your wife. I want to live my own life, I want to fight on behalf of those people from amongst whom I have come.
I want to smash this damned wall which has risen up before me, myself.

JUDGE You're not so brainless as to reject my help in this. That's women's logic. If this is what's holding you back and not your own feelings, if even the street stones call you, then use me for your benefit now, too.

HULDA But what if you begin to stand in my way?

JUDGE I'm not about to block a volcano, at most I'll organize a channel for its lava flow. *(Grasps* HULDA *by the arms)* Look, I care for you . . . too much . . . and even though you're making a terrible fuss now, people have always done stupid things on account of love. You're struggling in vain, you understand that yourself. Tomorrow the announcement will be posted on the courtroom bulletin board, your name together with mine, and there's no escape, do you hear?

HULDA I hear.

JUDGE *(Kisses her)* Now be good and go to sleep, otherwise things will go awry for you.

AUNT *(Comes inside)* Good Lord, didn't Hulda go? And you're home too, Carl Christian!

JUDGE Auntie, dear, I've decided to marry that Hulda despite everything . . . that's how things have turned out . . . but she won't send you out of this house . . . there has to be someone here who will take care of the children while Hulda is trying to better the world of Parliament. . . .

HULDA My God, did I have to fall in love with such a dictator . . . if only I'd stayed in the party!

AUNT *(Sits down on the chair and wipes her eyes)* Well, my dear children . . . I'm so happy. Oh, Carl Christian, I have never forgotten how, at my brother's place, the departed Professor Juhana Wilhelm Snellman always used to tell us young girls that a woman's role in the family is to tend to family traditions. Hulda will certainly do that. . . .

Curtain

Notes

1 According to editorial notes in *Brecht Collected Plays Vol. 6*, Brecht's notion of collaboration meant reconstructing Wuolijoki's play in "epic" form. When Wuolijoki read the reworked script Brecht gave her, she found it "unfunny" and "undramatic," but translated it into Finnish for publication. Brecht made extensive subsequent revisions to the play, titled *Puntilla and Matti, His Hired Man*, but was not always careful to credit Wuolijoki as author of the original play upon which *Matti* was based. Ralph Manheim and John Willett describe the Wuolijoki–Brecht collaboration from a point of view sympathetic to Brecht. See *Brecht Collected Plays Vol. 6*, pp. 423–30 (Vintage, New York, 1976).

2 Sääksmäki – a locality in Häme, a province of south-central Finland.

3 Niskavuori – the name of a manor familiar to Finnish audiences from Hella Wuolijoki's previous play *The Women of Niskavuori* (*Niskavuoren naiset*, 1936).

4 For a period in the 1920s the activities of the Communist Party, including display of its bright red flag, were forbidden in Finland.

5 Unclothed statues by A. Aaltonen in the hall of Parliament.

Bibliography

Primary sources

Hella Wuolijoki's archive. Finland's State Archive.

Helsinki City Theatre's Archive.

The Theatre Museum of Finland, Archive, [Newspaper reviews]

(Wuolijoki, Hella) Tervapää, Juhani (1937) *Juurakon Hulda. 7-kuvaelmainen huvinäytelmä*, Jyväskylä and Helsinki: K. J. Gummerus.

Wuolijoki, Hella (1937?) "Hulda. 7-kuvaelmainen huvinäytelmä" (Manuscript, Finland's State Archive).

Secondary sources

Ammondt, Jukka (ed.) (1973) *Hella Wuolijoki kulttuurivaikuttaja. Vuosisata Hella Wuolijoen syntymästä*, Jyväskylä: Jyväskylän yliopisto (Jyväskylä Studies in the Arts 29).

— (1980) *Niskavuoren talosta Juurakon torppaan. Hella Wuolijoen maaseutunäytelmien aatetaustaa*, Jyväskylä: Gaudeamus (Jyväskylä Studies in the Arts 14).

— (1984) *Hurma ja paatos. Näkökulmia 1920- ja 1930-luvun kirjallisuuteen*, Turku: Turun Yliopisto. Kirjallisuuden ja musiikkitieteen laitos (A:9).

Häikiö, Martti (1992) *A Brief History of Modern Finland*, Helsinki: University of Helsinki, Lahti Research and Training Centre.

Koski, Pirkko (1987) *Kansan teatteri. 2. Helsingin Kansanteatteri*, Helsinki: Helsingin Teatterisäätiö.

— (1992) *Teatterinjohtaja ja aika. Eino Salmeaisen toiminta Helsingin Kansanteatterissa 1934–1939*, Helsinki: Yliopistopaino.

— (1993) "The Dramatic Arts," in Pävi Molarus (ed.), *From Folklore to Applied Arts. Aspects of Finnish Culture*, Helsinki: University of Helsinki, Lahti Research and Training Centre.

Laurila, K. S. (1938) *Taistelu taiteesta ja siveellisyydestä*, Helsinki and Porvoo: Werner Söderstöm.

Salmelainen, Eino (1957) *Hurma ja surma. Muistelmia tavallaan*, Helsinki: Tammi.

8 Hasegawa Shiguré, 1879–1941

Wavering Traces
Japan

Hasegawa Shiguré. *Photograph provided by courtesy of Hasegawa Masaru.*

Introduction

by Carole Cavanaugh

Kabuki at the century's end

When Hasegawa Shiguré wrote her first play for a Tokyo newspaper contest in 1905, the richness and vitality of Japanese theatrical performance not only sustained traditional dramatic forms but also encouraged experiments in the more realistic dramatization of contemporary problems and situations. The performance arts at the turn of the century included a standard repertoire of Kabuki plays staged and acted almost as they had been for two hundred years, new melodramas (*shimpa*), modern plays (*shingeki*) strongly influenced by western theater, and productions of translated works by Shakespeare, Ibsen, and Chekhov. But within this variety, Kabuki still dominated; its familiar plots, lush costumes, stunning make-up, and extravagant style secured the form's popularity against serious competition from newer kinds of drama. Intellectual writers famous for their prose but amateurs in the world of Japanese performance attempted fresh plays for the Kabuki theater, dramas that reflected their interest in the unified structure and theatrical realism of the West. The most famous of the literati who participated in the revision of popular Japanese drama was the critic and scholar Tsubouchi Shōyō (all names are given according to Japanese convention, surname first). His academic study of western drama and translations of Shakespeare's complete works transformed Tsubouchi (1859–1935) into an innovator who championed reform in Kabuki action and characterization, and a

pioneer in the development of modern drama in Japan. It is not surprising then that he was the judge for the *Yomiuri* newspaper contest that prompted Hasegawa to write *Kaichō'on* (The Sound of the Morning Sea). More remarkable is that the dean of literary critics in the almost entirely male realm of Japanese theater recognized the emerging talent of a woman in her twenties with little formal education and no pretensions to the aesthetic conventions of western drama. Hasegawa Shiguré's work was striking, despite its flaws, because it expressed, for the first time within the dramatic structure of the Kabuki theater, the emotional conflicts of women in a patriarchal society.

Hasegawa's early life and work

Middle-class merchants, like the Hasegawa family who lived in the bustling downtown area of Tokyo, were the heart of the Kabuki audience. Urban shopkeepers, artisans, and tradesmen preferred the traditional theater's flamboyant dramas of unflinching courage, deadly swordplay, and doomed love to the subtler psychological conflicts of realistic characters portrayed by actors in drab modern dress and in everyday settings.

Hasegawa's father, a solicitor and small-time politician, was an especially avid Kabuki fan; he regularly gathered at his home a group of *aficionados* who discussed plays, new productions, and the nuances of their favorite actors' performances. Yasuko (she would take the pen name Shiguré in 1902) grew up in an aura of enthusiasm for Japanese music and performance. When she was very young, her father took her with him to the theater where, whether or not she understood the convoluted plots and historical references, she must have been delighted by the spectacle of Kabuki. Actors moved through the audience on the *hanamichi* (flower path), a raised passage-way adjoining the stage, appeared and disappeared on trap-lifts, and effected sudden changes in mood or character through outer costumes that fell away with the pull of a few threads. Even the stage itself revolved (a 1758 Japanese invention) and, in some theaters, a second, inner stage could revolve again in the opposite direction.

Theater-going was an all-day event: matinées began before noon and ended around five in the evening. When Yasuko grew tired, she was left to amuse herself in the theater tearoom where she leafed through the periodical *Kabuki News* (*Kabuki shinpō*), a magazine she would remember as having had more influence on her interest in drama, music, and dance than did the performances themselves. First published in 1879, *Kabuki News* was printed, octavo, on heavy Japanese paper and issued three times a month. The most important theater magazine in its day, the periodical published essays on Japanese and western drama and translations of European plays. Too young to read articles by critics and scholars, Yasuko colored in the wood-block pictures of her favorite actors, enlivening the black-on-white prints in a way that anticipated the tinge of personal sensibility she would later bring to Kabuki's traditional outlines.

As she grew older, the chance to gaze at a magazine full of pictures or read a popular work of fiction became a rare indulgence. Though Japan had reassessed many of its values and institutions in the decades following the Meiji Restoration of 1868, the expectation that girls prepare themselves to become obedient wives remained entrenched. The oldest of seven children,

Yasuko was given little time to indulge her passion for illustrated stories, and when she was discovered reading, her mother was known to rip the book to pieces in front of her and burn it in the garden. Despite her mother's antipathy to her interest in fiction, Yasuko and a group of friends produced a little magazine of their stories and poems called *Autumn Brocade*.

Hasegawa was typical of most girls from middle- and lower-class families in ending her education with graduation from the sixth grade. But during her adolescence, a university student who boarded with her family enabled her to enter a new world of literary possibility. An editor of a student magazine, Usawa Akiakira, often brought his fellow literature students to the Hasegawa home where their enthusiastic exchanges on Japanese classics, western novels, and plays were Hasegawa's first introduction to writing with more depth and intensity than the popular fiction and traditional tales she had loved as a child. Yasuko reclaimed some of the education that society, her family, and her circumstances had denied her by devouring every night the notes Usawa brought home from that day's lectures.

In 1894, when she was 15, she became a kind of literary apprentice to the poet and scholar Sasaki Nobutsuna. This tutorial arrangement was not unusual for young women who wanted to write, but for Hasegawa it was short-lived. Her mother, who held that preparation for marriage was more important for a daughter than preparation for a literary avocation, arranged a live-in domestic position for her with a wealthy family named Ikeda. Despite her mother's request to her employers that her daughter not be given anything to read, Hasegawa managed to peek at the newspapers used to wrap the milk cans delivered to the Ikedas each day. She found an advertisement for "The Women's Correspondence Course" and, with her first monthly wage, sent away for the lectures and studied them secretly at night.

Her stay with the Ikeda family was meant to polish and train her for the duties of marriage. In December of 1897, at the age of 19, her parents arranged for her what they regarded as an excellent match. The Mizuhashi family was well-to-do, but her young husband, a carouser and womanizer, had little interest in her. Hasegawa was freer now than she had ever been, with money to buy books and the leisure to read them. Her husband's parents eventually wearied of his dissolute behavior and cut him off financially, but they would not agree to her request for a divorce, a legal matter that required them to remove her name from their family register. Trapped in a loveless, nearly penniless, marriage, Hasegawa began to write.

Her first slim work, "Uzumibi" (Embers), was published in *Jogaku sekai*, a magazine for women, in 1901. The story articulated a theme she would return to again and again in her fiction and later in her plays – female endurance under the crushing force of the patriarchal family. Japanese feminism was just awakening to a sense of the injustices marriage and family imposed on women, but the movement had not yet arrived at a workable response that could reconcile individuality, sexuality, motherhood, marriage and women's roles in societal institutions. Factions within the Japanese feminist movement would grapple with these issues for the next several decades, and indeed, the debate continues to this day. Around the turn of the century, women's writing was just finding its way into newspapers and magazines. The mere expression by women of the suffering they experienced under a male-centered family system that had underpinned the hierarchies of Japanese society for centuries, though tame by today's standards, was, in itself, revolutionary.

Japanese feminism had grown out of the Jiyū minkan (Movement for Freedom and Popular Rights) of the late nineteenth century. Government suppression of feminist activity was intense: after 1890 women who organized politically, demonstrated, or joined political associations were fined and imprisoned. As a result, Japanese feminism in the early twentieth century abandoned political reform and concentrated on social issues. The feminist literary journal *Seitō* (Blue Stocking), launched in 1911, provided a forum for debate on women's concerns. Though the periodical shied away from political controversy, an entire issue of the magazine devoted to a production of Ibsen's *A Doll House* drew such a wide response from its readers that *Seitō*'s editors were compelled to debate seriously the problems of women that the play addressed (Sievers

1983: 170). When he noticed that the Ibsen play brought tears to the eyes of a woman in the audience, the playwright and critic Ihara Seiseien in his review coined the phrase "new woman" (*atarashii onna*) to describe her. It was a term that would divide the *Seitō* writers in their debate over feminism as a demand for legal equality, for special protection, or for liberation through socialism (Rodd 1991: 176). The woman in the audience that Ihara could only describe as "new" was Hasegawa Shiguré.

In the years between her first work of fiction and the Ibsen play that sparked unexpected controversy in feminist thinking, Hasegawa embarked on a life style that was extraordinarily unconventional by contemporary standards. Japanese society had for centuries expected women to live their lives under the authority of male family members. Girls were subordinate to fathers and brothers, wives to husbands, and widows to eldest sons. Poor rural and urban women in the labor force lived under legal contract within economic structures controlled by men, such as textile-mill dormitories or brothels. Hasegawa was one of a tiny minority of Japanese women in the early twentieth century, most of them writers, who tried to make a life for themselves outside the economic and social conventions of the patriarchal family, either in living arrangements with other women or with men not chosen by their families. Their essays, poems, and short stories, published in magazines and newspapers, earned them only a meager living but rewarded them with independence. Literary talent gave some women admission to bohemian coteries of poets and novelists, dominated by university-educated men who questioned the purposes of literature and argued the comparative merits of western and Japanese modes of expression. Hasegawa, who eventually divorced her husband, associated with a group that included Uno Kōji, one of the most prominent writers in the I-novel genre. Within that circle she also met, and eventually fell in love with, Mikami Otokichi, a struggling young writer who had just graduated from Waseda University. In 1915, Hasegawa, then 36, and Mikami, 25, married. Their relationship greatly influenced the course of her writing career; eventually, in order to support him and herself, she abandoned drama, after a string of successful plays, for a more dependable market. Hasegawa turned her attention to romantic fiction and pieces for popular magazines, items meant to sell and to entertain rather than to explore literary, feminist, or political issues.

Hasegawa's later work

Between 1905 and 1914 Hasegawa devoted herself to the theater. In 1908 her play *Hanomaru* was staged at the Kabuki-za by an important troupe, the first play ever produced in Japan written by a Japanese woman and performed by Japanese actors, to enormous fanfare. Hasegawa was famous overnight. She wrote several more plays that won a measure of acclaim but her first big success was *Sakura fubuki* (Blizzard of Blossoms), a monumental drama in five acts, produced in 1911. Set in feudal Japan, the play dealt with revenge, a typical Kabuki theme. *Sakura fubuki* is different from the traditional *jidaigeki* (historical drama) in that the avengers are women rather than men. In Hasegawa's play the dead man's wife and mistress, previously rivals, join forces. Though some casts of Hasegawa's plays included actresses, *Sakura fubuki* was performed in conventional Kabuki style with *onnagata*, men who play only women's parts, taking the lead roles. Four of the seven dramas Hasegawa wrote during these years were staged. She also formed her own performance company and published a short-lived theater magazine with a group of colleagues, and continued to write *butō kyoku* (musicals) until 1940, the year before her death. Kabuki, however, began to resist experimentation. By the 1920s, new Japanese plays and new ideas found a more congenial home in the realist drama dominated by western-educated intellectuals. Caught between two theatrical forms – one old and one new but both monopolized by men – Hasegawa was no longer economically able to continue writing plays for the Kabuki stage. She remained an energetic and active writer of fiction and essays almost until the day she died of leukemia, on August 22, 1941. Today in Japan she is hardly remembered.

The art of Kabuki

Kabuki is an entertaining and complex performance art that presents, rather than represents, narrative through a combination of acting, music, mime, and dance. Kabuki does not share the western preoccupation with the reproduction of reality, but works instead to display, for artistic effect, the intense emotions of characters thrust into extreme circumstances. The distinction between representation and presentation is important. Kabuki makes no effort to convince the audience that the stage is not a stage and the actor is not an actor (Ernst 1974: 19), but, instead, strives for visual impact through emphasis on theatricality. Make-up is garish or starkly obvious; costumes are usually elaborate, and even the plain lines of the simplest ones are stunning on stage. Because realism is not a priority, stage assistants who help actors negotiate their elaborate costumes in energetic scenes, or who handle props, move on and off stage as necessary. Covered from head to toe in black, they remain "invisible." Perhaps the best example of Japanese theater's aversion to literalism is the concept that only *onnagata*, male actors who specialize in women's roles, can achieve Kabuki's idea of the aesthetic essence of womanhood. When asked why women do not appear on the Kabuki stage, the noted actor Nakamura Kichiemon, aghast at the question, replied, "But that would be too real!" (Ernst 1974: 23).

Kabuki is a theater of actors rather than playwrights, of technique rather than text. Dialogue, except in domestic scenes, does not attempt to mimic an exchange of colloquial conversation. The actor isolates his speeches by declaiming, rather than speaking, his lines and often coordinates the pace of his utterances to the rhythm of his movements. Kabuki essentially plays to the audience, and so, even when two characters are engaged in conversation, they seem at times not to "hear" each other. A third character may interject dialogue for which there is no preparation in the script, because Kabuki is less interested in representing natural transitions than in presenting a series of critical moments. The disconnections or empty spaces within dialogue inhibit forward progression; consequently, characterization is not achieved, nor does plot advance appreciably through verbal interchange, as usually occurs in western theater.

The effect of Kabuki is sculptural: the individual actor is almost always surrounded by space, and contact with other actors is rare. The actor moves and gestures according to stylized patterns dictated by character type, dramatic situation, and his role's particular performance tradition. The high point of Kabuki performance is the *mie*, an artificially tense pose struck at a climactic moment. The *mie* culminates as the actor snaps his head and glares into the distance (Leiter 1979: 232) to form a carefully composed tableau. The *mie* usually elicits enthusiastic cheers of appreciation from the audience, well versed in the subtlties of performance. Only a master can bring artistry and an original style to plays where the pacing of every line and the timing of every gesture are prescribed. The actor strives for intense rapport with his audience; the responsiveness of spectators completes the circuit of aesthetic communication that Kabuki hopes to achieve.

Wavering Traces and the Kabuki tradition

Hasegawa wrote *Chōji midare* (*Wavering Traces*) in 1911. Two years later the play was staged at Tokyo's top theater, the Ichimura-za, to full houses during its run. Onoe Kikugorō IV, the greatest star of his day, played the lead. Kikugorō (1885–1949) was renowned as a *kaneru yakusha*, one of the rare actors in Kabuki skilled in playing both male and female roles. He was a pioneer in the development of modern Kabuki and excited audiences with his special sensitivity for the characters in its new dramas (Leiter 1979: 295). Kabuki plays are divided into two broad genres: *sewamono*, "domestic plays" about the merchant class, usually set in the Edo period (1600–1868); and *jidaimono*, "period pieces" set in the Kamakura (1185–1333) or Muromachi (1333–1600) eras. *Sewamono* usually center on the emotional conflict of a man who has fallen in love with a courtesan; *jidaimono* are action plays filled with violence and gore. *Wavering Traces* falls into a subgenre called *jidai-sewamono*, plays that dramatize domestic conflict in the period setting, but is different in that its emotional focus is on the woman and not her husband. Hasegawa may have chosen a

remote time to defamiliarize the play's modern issue: a striving husband's inability to recognize his wife's self-sacrifice. It is tempting to speculate on the effect *A Doll House* may have had on Hasegawa's writing (she saw Ibsen's play the year before she wrote *Wavering Traces*) but there is no direct evidence of influence. In any case, the "feminism" of *Wavering Traces* evoked wild appreciation from its spectators. On the last day of the play's run, the audience, in an affectionate gesture unprecedented in the memory of the Kabuki theater, literally covered the stage with flowers as a tribute to the play's author and its star.

The title *Wavering Traces* refers to the unique file traces, a kind of signature, that a sword-maker leaves on the blades he forges. The sword that figures so prominently in the play, like other properties in Kabuki, is carried on stage at the moment called for in the action, not by a character, but by a stage assistant, and is removed when no longer needed. Kabuki is famous for its tricks: red coloring, inserted in the sword ridge, flows like blood when a character is struck. Hasegawa used conventions like these but also incorporated newer elements into her play, like innovative lighting and off-stage sound. Kabuki lighting is flat and is not reduced for night scenes. Hasegawa's attention to the effect of cross-lighting on the fallen leaves and to the setting sun, rising moon, and gradually darkening night in her stage directions indicates a modern use of lighting closer to the representational theater of the West. Her use of sound also broke the boundaries of Kabuki, where only the observable limits of the stage have theatrical significance (Ernst 1974: 65). Sounds occur on stage, or, when offstage sound effects are used, they correspond to onstage action. A thematic element in Hasegawa's play, however, is the recurring offstage cry of the fox kitten. The author clearly grasped the theatrical potential of sound to penetrate unseen space in her use of this effect and others, such as the ring of the hammer, the trickle of water, and the voices of characters prior to their entry.

Ghosts, demons, and other-worldly beings are frequent in Kabuki, but Hasegawa treats the supernatural with subtlety. In a scene that seems to have nothing to do with the rest of the play, the sword-smith Masakuni notices a young man and woman outside his window. They are running away together in order to marry, against their parents' wishes, just as he and his wife Hatsushimo did years ago. Although the couple is "real," they also figure both as a ghostly visitation from Masakuni's past, and as a dramatization of his own vivid memories. Whether real or imagined, these secondary characters materialize the play's subconscious desire in a way that recognizes Kabuki's traditional treatment of unexplainable apparitions and odd coincidences.

Wavering Traces is a melodrama – a term with a bad reputation in the West, almost synonymous with soap-opera, but one that Peter Brooks has suggested can be more effectively applied as a description rather than as a pejorative dismissal. Melodrama is the theater of hyperbole and excess. In it "characters assume primary psychic roles, father, mother, child and express basic psychic conditions" (Brooks 1976: 4). Recent film theory has also recognized melodrama's tendency to give prominence to the experiences, emotions, and activities of women and has noted the genre's potential to expose patriarchal ideology (Dissanayake 1993: 2). Understood in these terms, Hasegawa's play becomes a more fruitful exploration of women's emotional lives embedded in a particular culture and a particular time.

Wavering Traces pits female love against male ambition. In Japan, where marriage is arranged by parents and where romance in marriage is seldom nurtured and rarely valorized, spectators can immediately recognize that Masakuni and Hatsushimo's marriage-for-love is an escape from the patriarchal family. Unresolved feelings about their irrevocable break with parents fire both his obsession to triumph in his craft and Hatsushimo's intense desire to be the only person who can help him succeed. The characters enact the inclinations that directed Hasegawa's writing for the Kabuki stage: her devotion as a writer to the traditions of her craft and her impulse, as someone excluded from the lineage of those traditions, to interrogate and redefine them.

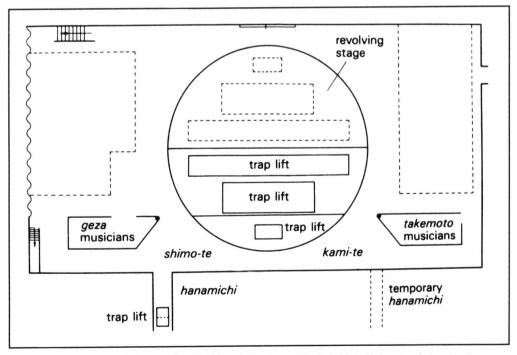

Plan of a present-day Kabuki stage by Chiaki Yoshida. From *The Kabuki Guide* by Masakatsu Gunji. *Copyright © 1987 by Kodansha International Ltd. All rights reserved. Reprinted by permission.*

Wavering Traces _____

1911
Play translation by Carole Cavanaugh

Hasegawa Shiguré

Characters

RAI MASAKUNI, a sword-maker

HATSUSHIMO, his wife

ICHIWAKA, their eight-year-old son

SOMEGO, their one-year-old daughter

MASAKI MORITO, a masterless samurai

A BUDDHIST MONK

KOROKUTA, sword-smith's apprentice

A YOUNG MAN AND WOMAN, eloping
  together

Time

The play takes place on a single night in
late autumn sometime during the feudal
Kamakura period (1185–1333) in the
province of Musashi no kuni.

Place

Outside a sword-smith's workshop, the living
quarters of the sword-maker Masakuni; a
Buddhist temple to Kannon in the forest.

Scene 1

*At stage left is an old, bare ginkgo tree. Beyond
it, spreading under the eaves of a sword-
smith's shop is a creeping vine. A large
window wraps around the smithy. From the
eaves are suspended sacred Shinto straw
festoons. At stage right, at the far wall of the
sword-smith's living quarters is a tattered
paper, sliding-door, closed, at the entrance to
the kitchen. On either side of the house are
bamboo groves, near the kitchen entrance is
the well-sweep. The fading sunlight glances off
the fallen leaves piled on all sides. In the
middle of this scene the sun sets; in the next
scene the moon comes out and a misty night
falls. When the curtain rises,*
HATSUSHIMO *is taking down laundry. When*

*she is finished, she goes back into the kitchen.
From the darkness of the forest comes*
ICHIWAKA's *voice singing a lullaby.*

ICHIWAKA *(Singing)* When night comes to
  the little grove behind the house, the fox
  kitten born last night is softer than the
  inside of a flower, warmer than dried
  grass; mother holds me to her breast and
  whispers, "Go to sleep."
  *(*HATSUSHIMO *comes out once more and,
  listening to the song, draws some water from
  the well.* ICHIWAKA's *singing continues.)*
ICHIWAKA *(Singing offstage)* The sun pierces
  the little grove behind the house, the fox
  kitten that sang last night, cries though it
  has not even opened its eyes; mother
  who asked "Do you want some milk?" was
  captured in a trap and carried away by
  the hunter. . . .
  *(*ICHIWAKA, *singing and carrying* SOMEGO
  on his back enters, guiding a BUDDHIST
  MONK.*)*
ICHIWAKA *(To the monk)* My mother is
  right there.
HATSUSHIMO Waka, you're back? Somego
  must have been fussy.
ICHIWAKA Mother, we went into the grove
  and fed the fox kittens our rice balls.
  Then we gathered acorns, and Somego
  was fine.
HATSUSHIMO Well then, you both deserve
  praise. Will you take good care of her for
  me tomorrow too? She was safe and
  sound today. And aren't you clever! You
  made Somego a pinwheel from maple
  leaves to entertain her! *(To* SOMEGO*)*
  Look, look! Can you see this?
ICHIWAKA *(Pointing to the* MONK*)*: Mother,
  there's a monk waiting for you over there
  who says he has come to see you about
  something.
MONK I beg your pardon, when you hear
  the sound of that hammer, you don't have

260

to ask if this is the house of the sword-smith who lives in this forest.

HATSUSHIMO *(Untying the cords that hold up her long, wide sleeves)* Oh my, how rude of me, please forgive me. What can I do for you? That is, if my naughty son has played some prank. . . .

MONK No, no, nothing of the kind. I was entrusted with a parcel from the sword-sharpener in town.

HATSUSHIMO A parcel, you say. The sword?

MONK He said he has finished polishing it. See for yourself.

HATSUSHIMO So he has finished it, then!

MONK Here it is.

HATSUSHIMO *(Takes the parcel and, closing her eyes, carefully removes the sheath. She opens her eyes in spite of herself and looks at the sword.)* Aah, it's finished! – it's as though a misty aura arises from it – the patina of the polish, its aroma! Please, look!

MONK Can you see all that?

HATSUSHIMO I can't help but appreciate the fine work my husband forges! Even if I were blind, if someone brandished one of his unsheathed swords before me I would surely know his workmanship.

MONK The sword-polisher said it was a rare piece of work.

HATSUSHIMO The sword-polisher said so, too? Ha, ha, ha, listen to me – sounding so proud of my own husband! Ha, ha, ha.

MONK Hatsushimo, your husband the sword-smith does not seem so satisfied with himself. *(Sound of hammering against metal.)* Even my poor monk's ears are not deaf to the sound of the blows of his hammer filled with passion. Whom does he favor with that single-minded concentration?

HATSUSHIMO *(Dispirited)* It doesn't come by someone's favor. He won't let even his darling children near him. He washes with the frost in the morning, and at night, when he sleeps at all, the hammer is his pillow. Day and night he hammers away. No matter how much he beats his swords, they're not good enough for him. He exhausts himself fretting over the temperature of the water he uses for tempering. He's grown terribly thin.

ICHIWAKA Late at night Mother goes off alone, Reverend, and hides from Father.

MONK Where?

ICHIWAKA To the lonely forest.

MONK Why does she go there?

ICHIWAKA To pray, for one hundred nights.

HATSUSHIMO Tonight is the last night. I vowed to perform this secret penance because I wanted *this* sword to be a masterpiece. I thought it would console my husband's heart.

MONK And tonight you will fulfill your vow?

HATSUSHIMO My hundred-night pilgrimage to the temple in the woods will pass tonight like the dream of a single night.

MONK I'm a monk of meager virtue but since it was I who carried the sword wrapped in my shabby sleeves, I must tell you that the blade of this splendid masterpiece you have been praying for is the devil's sword of victory.

HATSUSHIMO This sword then carries an evil omen?

MONK I came here as an unworthy messenger, poor and humble as I am, to warn you of its evil. When I passed in front of the sword-polisher's workshop, I heard him say, as he gazed upon that sword, that it was a work of art, a masterpiece! Then, suddenly, I noticed that it brimmed with murderous intent.

HATSUSHIMO What?

MONK I was not going to tell you what I suspected, but now, hearing of your devotion to your husband, I think withholding what I have witnessed will be far more dangerous. Look, the misty aura, as you call it, arising from that sword is an ominous cloud hovering over it.

HATSUSHIMO This cannot be. . . .

MONK Do not wander from the path of virtue. The sword-smith, being the man that he is, will not stray. He will continue his single-minded fervor with no regrets for this sword, this harbinger of evil.

ICHIWAKA *(Tossing acorns, in a sing-song voice)* One is for Somego and one is her age. Somego is a girl. I'm her big brother and I'm a boy. One is for Mother; one is for Father; one is for the Reverend Monk; one is for the fox kitten. The acorns I gathered one by one – one by one I toss them.

(As ICHIWAKA *tosses the acorns, the* MONK *draws the boy's hand toward him, counts the acorns, frowns, and closes his eyes.)*

MONK *(Gloomily)* What an omen, what an extraordinary sign has appeared!

Hatsushimo, take it to heart when I tell you that you must never show that sword to anyone. Especially since your husband is so agitated, never show that sword to him.

HATSUSHIMO I am pleased to receive your advice.

MONK Tomorrow, perhaps, a true masterpiece may arrive, and when you compare them you will agree with me. Until then I will pray for your well-being.

ICHIWAKA Reverend, are you leaving now?

MONK My good child, farewell.

(Saying his beads, the MONK *begins to leave.)*

HATSUSHIMO I was so sure of myself. I was so convinced of my husband's fine workmanship.

*(*HATSUSHIMO *puts her hand on* ICHIWAKA's *shoulder, and watches intently after the departing* MONK. *Night begins to fall.)*

He is a holy sight. These words have not been wasted on me, I will remember them – aah, now I have even more worries!

ICHIWAKA It's already dark. Let's go in and you can feed Somego.

HATSUSHIMO Oh, I forgot! Her crying will disturb your father. Well, well, now, let's go.

ICHIWAKA There, there, don't cry. If you cry the demons will come and take you away.

(They go into the house together. Silhouetted on the paper window of the smithy is the shadow of the sword-smith working his hammer and its sound echoes forth. At stage left a young MAN *and* WOMAN, *wearing sedge hats and clothes for travel, emerge stealthily from the shadowy grove.)*

MAN No one will see us in this place. And it's already dark. Why don't we rest here?

WOMAN But it's getting late.

MAN Are you afraid? I thought you were ready and eager for traveling along the dark roads at night.

WOMAN I'm not afraid, it just feels eerie.

MAN I need just a little rest – your delicate legs have made *me* tired. We haven't even had a sip of water since we left the inn today. Aren't you thirsty, Somoji?

WOMAN *(Rubbing her feet)* I *am* thirsty.

MAN *(Standing up)* This is a sword-smith's, isn't it? I heard the sound echoing back in the woods. Let's just ask – I'm sure it's

not much more than a couple of miles from here. *(Going up to the window)* Hello! *(The hammering inside stops.)* Sorry to bother you, but how far is it to Azabu from here?

(From inside the window comes the voice of the young apprentice.)

KOROKUTA Well . . . less than two miles. If you go very quickly you'll get there this evening.

MAN Much obliged. Sorry to have interrupted your work. *(Moving away from the window he says to himself)* I guess we won't make it before late at night. *(Aloud)* Ahh, a crescent moon has come out. *(Going over to the young* WOMAN*)* It's only a little way now so let's go, just a little faster.

WOMAN I'm thirsty.

MAN Now that the end is in sight, you're relieved enough to give me a little trouble, eh?

WOMAN Uhh. . . .

MAN All right then. There's a well over there. Let's go have a little water. Come here.

(The MAN *draws some water. In her cupped hands the* WOMAN *scoops some of it and drinks. Scooping some more, she offers it to the* MAN. *He drinks thirstily. In the dim light coming from the papered window of the back door, they take each other's hand and depart. Just then the window of the work-shop opens a bit;* MASAKUNI, *a look of exhaustion on his face, looks out and spies the pair. The stage revolves to reveal the inside of the house. At stage right is the smithy on the ground level. To the other side and one step up are the living quarters with a rustic kitchen to stage left. There is a hearth between the kitchen and the living area. A sliding paper screen separates the living quarters from the smithy.)*

ICHIWAKA *(Playing with a shadow puppet in the lamplight)* Mother, when I put the shadow puppet up close to the lamp even though it is a little devil, its shadow looks dark and fierce. When I go like this, it's big but blurry and not so scary. Tell me why.

HATSUSHIMO *(Holding* SOMEGO, *stoking the hearth fire)* I'll tell you, but first go see what Father is doing.

ICHIWAKA Nowadays, even when I'm not near Father he scares me. I hate it when he scolds me.

HATSUSHIMO Call Korokuta then.

ICHIWAKA Korokuta won't come either. He's afraid because if he just lays down his hammer, Father scowls at him.

HATSUSHIMO Well, then I won't ask you to call them, you won't listen.

(HATSUSHIMO stands up and puts SOMEGO down to sleep behind a folding screen. ICHIWAKA tiptoes to the smithy and peeks in through the screen.)

ICHIWAKA How strange, Mother! Father is standing near the window and he seems worried about something. Korokuta is cleaning up and putting out the fire.

(The forge fire is out in the smithy, only a votive candle is burning on a shelf before a small shrine.)

ICHIWAKA Korokuta, if you're finished work, won't you come here.

KOROKUTA *(Entering the living quarters)* I have to go on an errand, Ichiwaka.

ICHIWAKA Where are you going?

KOROKUTA To buy metal, from that devil who sells it.

ICHIWAKA So then you can't play with me? I'm lonely.

HATSUSHIMO You must be tired, Korokuta. You stopped earlier than usual, so even if you rest a bit, you won't be leaving very late. You must be hungry. You'd better eat some dinner before you go.

KOROKUTA No, if I eat dinner, I'll get sleepy and feel too full to walk a step.

HATSUSHIMO Night and day, whether lying down or sitting up, you temper the steel. You're just the same as he is – you never put down your hammer, so you must be exhausted. I'll go on the errand for you and you eat and get some sleep.

KOROKUTA No, please, let me go. I haven't seen my mother for a long time and I don't know when I'll be able to go there on an errand for work again, so I would like to call on her.

HATSUSHIMO In that case, you may go. But what will your mother think when she sees how thin and worn out you look? Apologize to her for me for not doing well enough by you.

KOROKUTA Don't worry. I'll just tell her that I ran over in the middle of a very busy time.

HATSUSHIMO Is your mother ill?

KOROKUTA She's elderly and is always coughing.

HATSUSHIMO I'd like to send her

something – you so rarely have a chance to visit her. Ichiwaka, are there any chestnuts in that basket?

ICHIWAKA Not really, these are all the chestnuts I have. *(He shows her the basket.)* There's hardly any barley either.

HATSUSHIMO Haven't I told you not to tell what you are not asked?

KOROKUTA *(Toward MASAKUNI who stands by the window)* Will that be the only errand?

(MASAKUNI nods.)

Well, then, I'm on my way.

(KOROKUTA bows and leaves; MASAKUNI leaves the window and comes into the room.)

ICHIWAKA *(Happily)* Father, are you done for the day?

(MASAKUNI nods.)

MASAKUNI *(To HATSUSHIMO)* Give me a drink of water.

HATSUSHIMO Yes, of course.

(She hurries to the back. MASAKUNI follows. ICHIWAKA puts chestnuts on the hearth fire. SOMEGO begins to cry. ICHIWAKA goes to her, pats her and calls HATSUSHIMO.)

ICHIWAKA Mother, Mother!

HATSUSHIMO *(Entering)* Oh, did she wake up?

(She takes ICHIWAKA's place and comforts the baby. MASAKUNI enters and sits down. ICHIWAKA tentatively offers MASAKUNI some roasted chestnuts. MASAKUNI gently pulls ICHIWAKA toward him and hugs him.)

MASAKUNI Has Somego fallen asleep?

HATSUSHIMO *(Cheerfully)* She was good all day – Ichiwaka carried her on his back and she slept a good while, but now she's restless and she's as wakeful and fussy as she usually is at night.

MASAKUNI Do you know that she cries every night?

HATSUSHIMO What?

MASAKUNI If you're right there next to her, I would think nursing would settle her down.

HATSUSHIMO Uh . . . does her crying disturb you?

MASAKUNI It disturbs me that she cries for you night after night. . . . It torments me.

HATSUSHIMO Has she cried that much?

MASAKUNI Don't you realize that she cries as though you're not here?

HATSUSHIMO . . . I never dreamed. . . . I had no idea she slept so fitfully. From tonight on I'll be more attentive.

MASAKUNI Sometimes she cries at midnight, sometimes at dawn. My muscles are tired from hammering night and day, when I doze off, it's as though I can hear the sound of someone's sandals – someone running away, stepping on my chest. I have painful nightmares. And at the same time every night Somego cries.

HATSUSHIMO (Lightly) Your stress and fatigue are giving you nightmares. Well, well ... Ichiwaka can have dinner with you – he hasn't done that in a long time.

MASAKUNI Hatsushimo, is there any wine?

HATSUSHIMO Just the sacred wine for offering.

MASAKUNI I'll drink that.

ICHIWAKA (As though suddenly remembering something) Papa please let me see you smile a little!

MASAKUNI Why? What did you think of just now?

ICHIWAKA Father's fierce face – I hate it that Mother always looks so sad, and I hate it that you work at the forge all the time and look so angry. I forgot how your face looks when you smile.

MASAKUNI (Taking the wine from HAT-SUSHIMO, smiling sadly) Once you grow up, you can't be laughing all the time. When you were born, Mother and I smiled all the time for no reason at all and passed the days just looking at each other.

HATSUSHIMO (With a faraway look) Father was kind-hearted in those days. . . .

MASAKUNI Your Mother still wore a long-sleeved kimono then, her teeth were bright ... she was an innocent bride devoted to her husband.

HATSUSHIMO You eloped with me and took me away from Kamakura. As we escaped along the road at night I was happy and afraid. I was so frightened by the howling wind, I clung to you. I cried when I couldn't see you, and then laughed with you.

MASAKUNI Happy or sad, our hearts were one. That was a long time ago. Now autumn has fallen in our hearts. What's worse, Ichiwaka feels sad.

ICHIWAKA No, no, I'm not sad. Tonight I'm happy. (He lays his head on MASAKUNI's knee.)

HATSUSHIMO Not a bit sad. I can take a life of poverty – I haven't sold my mirror, because I want to put on a face for you better than this one worn by daily cares.

MASAKUNI (Sardonically) A woman would paint her lips just as she is about to die.

HATSUSHIMO But those are the feelings of a wife for her husband, after all.

MASAKUNI Would you like to return to the dream of those bygone days?

HATSUSHIMO Yes, even if my life must be taken with the cold blade of a sword. If you would take me warmly in your arms once more, I should die with no regrets.

MASAKUNI You don't say?

HATSUSHIMO You never spoke that way to me before or looked at me with those cold eyes!

MASAKUNI Are you blaming me for that? Look into your own heart. When the red flowers bloom in one place, they fade and fall in another. Melted in a different crucible, old metal doesn't take on a new sheen. Until her mirror fails to compliment her, a woman can live in a dream-world. I have no time for that.

HATSUSHIMO I know that well.

MASAKUNI I want to leave this world a masterpiece made by me, Rai Masakuni, that's what this victor in love has come to. But even if you step on my face with your muddy clogs in the night when you go away – if I am utterly disgraced – my arms, tempered by resentment, will rise again. Is that not also passion? (He holds ICHIWAKA and lies down heavily.)

HATSUSHIMO You're angry. I'm the only one you have to let out your frustrations on and I am the one who has made you what you are now. (She clears away the wine bottle and cup, takes out their bedding and covers them both. MASAKUNI and ICHIWAKA sleep.) You're worn out. I can't wait to see your happy face when you've finished your work and feel completely satisfied with it. I want to be comforted by your smiling face, the way it used to be, just once more. Ichiwaka's face, smiling in his sleep! There, there, hold on to your Father and don't let him go. (The faint sound of the bells marking the hour echoes from afar.)

HATSUSHIMO (To herself) Tonight is my last night of prayer, but somehow I don't want to go. Maybe I should reveal everything to him before I leave – but no, no, the reverend monk said I should not show the sword to him. *(She looks at the sword.)* How happy he would be to see this work that he has made. I'll do it all tomorrow. *(Whispering to the sleeping* MASAKUNI*)* Please, please . . . it is just this one last night – let me go for just a little while. *(As* HATSUSHIMO *starts to go out the door,* SOMEGO *begins to cry. As she pauses and begins to close the door,* SOMEGO *quiets down.)*

MASAKUNI *(Opening his eyes)* Hatsushimo, Hatsushimo, Somego's crying.
(He gets up and looks all around as though he suspects something. He suddenly notices the sword by his pillow. Just as he is about to touch it, he hears the sound of footsteps stealing through the fallen leaves piled outside. Listening, he glares in the direction of the door, turns up the lamp wick, takes the sheath from the sword and stares at it.) The wavering traces left by my file, the sword-smith's signature on the blade, are opaque as the morning frost. They rise like the mist and gather into clouds – this seems to be my work but . . . no, no, it is not mine. The patina of its polish, its tempering – it is not the ordinary kind of sword that I forge with my dull arms. Though I am obscure, my vision is not clouded. As I slip it from its sheath, the edges of this work of art flow like a double stream of water in autumn. How loathsome! Whose work has been placed here? – Has frenzy killed my emotions? Though I am just over thirty, has romantic love extinguished my soul? Hatsushimo! Hatsushimo, where have you gone? Who has done this, this act that speaks contempt for me, this act meant to humiliate me? I want to know!
(Carrying the sword, MASAKUNI *goes out the door.)*

MASAKUNI *(In the shadows)* Where have you gone? Hatsushimo! Hatsushimo!
*(*ICHIWAKA *wakes up and weeps softly.)*

Curtain

Scene 2

In the forest. When the curtain opens there is the sound of a light wind through a stand of cedars, in the center of the stage is a huge oak reaching toward the sky. Within the wood is a weathered, run-down temple to Kannon, the Buddhist female deity of mercy and compassion. There is no moon and the woods are gloomy and dark. Under the huge tree, MASAKI MORITO, *a masterless samurai, is raking a fire he has made of fallen leaves. Beside him stands the* MONK.

MONK I wasn't startled. Such a thing has happened to me before.

MORITO I can see the results of your ascetic training. Now as for me, I'm far from being a monk.

MONK I am like a leaf blown by the wind. Apart from loneliness, I have no fear or trepidation. Encounters such as this make people believe they've seen a ghost, but I suppose, after all, I was snoring loudly, though I was only dozing.

MORITO Ha, ha, ha. In all my many travels I thought I had disciplined myself but I'm no monk like you. To tell the truth, a little while ago I heard a baby's cry in the woods and was frightened. I thought it must mean something, and so I stopped here and made a fire. The "coo, coo" cried through the firelight.

MONK Hmm, maybe it was a fox.

MORITO If it was a fox kitten, its eyes are not even open yet.

MONK The sword-smith's boy was saying there was a fox kitten whose mother was captured by a hunter.

MORITO A sword-smith in the woods back there?

MONK You know of him?

MORITO I *have* made a mistake then! Let me tell you why I'm camping here tonight. The truth is, last night I lost my way and came upon the forest path. From somewhere came the sound of hammering clear as frost. I could tell it was hammering with full concentration; I did not know who it was, but the effort was splendid. My heart quickened at the thought that, though he may not be a famous sword-smith, he will create a masterpiece! The strange thing was, though, all of a sudden the hammer missed a beat. I wondered why, when, before I knew it, a black shadow slipped by me without a sound and disappeared into the darkness.
*(*MONK *nods knowingly.)*
Do you know what that was?

MONK First, go ahead and tell me more.

MORITO Well, I couldn't go any further

265

since I didn't know my way on the dark road. I was still curious, but I never found out what it was. Going about my business today I walked around this area and realized that this grove must have been the place where I lost sight of that shadowy figure. I was concerned about the sword-smith, so I decided to spend the night here. When I saw you stir under the eaves of the temple just a little while ago, I thought *you* were the one I had seen last night and so I startled you. I'm terribly sorry.

MONK   That shadow was the sword-smith's wife.

MORITO   What? His wife?

MONK   She said tonight is the last night of her one hundred nights of prayer in the temple. I am a monk, but, even so, I thought I might be in her way and I was just about to leave the temple when you came along and surprised me.

MORITO   Why is she praying?

MONK   For her husband's work.

MORITO   (*Hitting his arm*) Last night I had my hand on the hilt of my sword, as usual not thinking a thing of it, and just now I was ready to draw it. I'm dim-witted and heedless and so eager to show my courage. Reverend, if I had not met you, I might have thought that virtuous wife was a ghost haunting the sword-smith tonight, and would have surely killed her!

MONK   (*Sadly*) She does carry with her the sign of death by the sword.

MORITO   What's that you say?

MONK   And what's more, the sword her husband made was filled with a murderous air.

MORITO   Did you warn her of it?

MONK   I who am so poor in virtue can only preach about the future. I lack the power to rescue anyone from the sufferings of the present.

(*There is the sound of someone performing ablutions in the temple. From within the forest comes the faint sound of a woman's voice.*)

HATSUSHIMO   Buddha, please wrap him in the sleeve of your benevolence. Let him make a true work of art.

(*MONK and MORITO look surprised.*)

MORITO   (*Whispering*) Do not worry, tomorrow I will examine that sword for myself. Throughout this night I will

protect this virtuous wife who has fallen under an omen of death.

MONK   (*Opening his palms*) Merit beyond measure. It is in your power to rescue the present.

MORITO   I humbly accept this task.

MONK   I will trust you to accomplish it. Now I feel the clouds of my apprehension clearing a bit. I will leave you to take care of matters here while I go to the sword-smith's.

MORITO   Farewell.

(*MONK tips his hat and disappears into the woods.*)

HATSUSHIMO   Please let my husband know the joy of the answer to my prayers. Hail, Kannon, in the morning and in the evening!

(*MASAKUNI enters running with the sword in his hand. MORITO sees him, follows him and then hides behind the tree. Without noticing MORITO, MASAKUNI looks around, goes to the fire and in its light gazes at the sword.*)

MASAKUNI   (*Loudly*) Aha! This *is* my work and it is splendid! There is no signature on this sword but the wavering traces of the file are indeed the distinctive marks of the line of sword-makers from which I myself descend! Where is Hatsushimo? Hatsushimo! Look at this! Hatsushimo!

(*He gazes admiringly at the sword in the light of the fire. HATSUSHIMO, hearing her husband, emerges and approaches MASAKUNI. She silently looks at his face and at the sword. MASAKUNI does not notice her, and with a proud smile on his face suddenly swings the sword.*)

HATSUSHIMO   Aaa!

(*Struck unawares, she falls bleeding to the ground. MASAKUNI sees the blood on the sword and, shocked, drops it.*)

HATSUSHIMO   My husband!

(*MASAKUNI, surprised to hear her voice, trembles as he holds her.*)

MASAKUNI   Who? Who are you?

HATSUSHIMO   My husband!

MASAKUNI   Oh, no! Hatsushimo! Where is the wound? Where?

HATSUSHIMO   (*With difficulty*) My husband, the sword?

MASAKUNI   (*Without answering he looks for the wound.*) Where is the wound?

HATSUSHIMO   I was told the sword-finisher said it was a masterpiece.

MASAKUNI   (*Hurriedly*) You can tell me

about the sword later – where are you cut? You must tell me! Don't give up!

HATSUSHIMO *(Clinging to him)* Are your doubts gone, my husband? *(Pointing to the temple)* Tonight is the last of my one hundred nights of prayer.

MASAKUNI Do you think I struck you with the sword because I doubted your fidelity? It was an accident!

HATSUSHIMO I wonder if the sacrificial blood cleansed by these one hundred days has purified the sword of evil.

MASAKUNI What do you mean by sacrificial? I never dreamed of becoming famous by sacrificing you!

HATSUSHIMO I had not known that I would be the one to test the sharpness of the sword that holds both our hearts.

MASAKUNI It was not a test – don't say such a scornful thing! How heartless!

HATSUSHIMO *(Getting weaker)* What I scorn is what men do for the sake of their honor. The word honor is what I despise!

MASAKUNI Aah, my heart became the home of an evil demon. Without realizing how foolish I was, I worried about producing a masterpiece and am about to lose my beloved wife. There is no masterpiece, no honor, if I've killed you. Our names that were sung together in love will be our legacy.

(MASAKUNI draws the sword close to him. HATSUSHIMO clings to his arm, looks up at him and smiles. A fox kitten cries in the distance.)

HATSUSHIMO Aah, my son . . . Somego.

(MASAKUNI, losing heart, gazes at HATSUSHIMO.)

HATSUSHIMO Where is Somego? And Ichiwaka?

(She falls down lightly. Quickly, MASAKUNI embraces her.)

MASAKUNI Hatsushimo!

HATSUSHIMO My. . . . *(She dies.)*

MASAKUNI Is this my cruel punishment? Even the fire has gone out. Let me see you one more time, even in a vision. Please say something! Hatsushimo, Hatsushimo! How will I tell our children? *(Taking the sword he is about to kill himself when MORITO comes out and grabs his hand.)*

MASAKUNI Who are you? How cruel not to let me die when I have every good reason.

MORITO I understand your torment but didn't you hear her say your children's names with her dying breath? If you die, you will escape your own suffering, but you must think how long your children will suffer. I don't think she would want that.

(MORITO pulls the sword away and MASAKUNI falls onto HATSUSHIMO.)

MASAKUNI *(Holding her body)* Forgive me! *(MASAKUNI sobs quietly. MORITO wipes the blood from the blade and peers at the sword in the dark. A fox kitten cries in the distance.)*

Curtain

Bibliography

Brooks, P. (1976) *The Melodramatic Imagination: Balzac, Henry James, Melodrama and the Mode of Excess*, New Haven: Yale University Press.

Dissanayake, W. (ed.) (1993) *Melodrama and Asian Cinema*, Cambridge: Cambridge University Press.

Ernst, E. (1974) *The Kabuki Theater*, Honolulu: The University Press of Hawaii.

Gunji, M. (1987) *The Kabuki Guide*, trans. C. Holmes, Tokyo: Kodansha.

Hasegawa, S. (1993) *Hasegawa Shiguré zenshū*, 5 vols, Tokyo: Fuji shuppan.

Homma, H. (1959) *Tsubouchi Shōyō*, Tokyo: Shohakusha.

Keene, D. (1976) *World Within Walls: Japanese Literature of the Pre-Modern Era, 1600–1897*, New York: Holt, Rinehart & Winston.

—— (1984) *Dawn to the West, Japanese Literature in the Modern Era: Poetry, Drama, Criticism*, New York: Henry Holt.

Kenny, D. (1974) *On Stage in Japan: Kabuki, Bunraku, Noh, Gagaku*, Tokyo: Shofunotomo.

Leiter, S. L. (ed.) (1979) *Kabuki Encyclopedia: An English-Language Adaptation of* Kabuki Jiten, Westport, CT: Greenwood.

Pronko, L. C. (1984) *Guide to Japanese Drama*, 2nd edn, Boston: G. K. Hall.

Rodd, L. R. (1991) "The Taishō Debate over the 'New Woman,'" in G. L. Bernstein (ed.), *Recreating Japanese Women, 1600–1945*, Berkeley: University of California Press.

Sievers, S. (1983) *Flowers in Salt: The Beginnings of Feminist Consciousness in*

Modern Japan, Stanford: Stanford University Press.

Smith, J. L. (1973) *Melodrama*, London: Methuen.

Toita, Y. and Yoshida, C. (1982) *Kabuki*, trans. D. Kenny, Osaka: Hoikusha.

9 Rachilde (Marguerite Eymery), 1860–1953

The Crystal Spider
France

Rachilde (Marguerite Eymery). *Photograph reproduced by courtesy of Bibliothèque littéraire Jacques Doucet, Paris.*

Introduction

by Frazer Lively

The symbolist theater

Rachilde wrote her first plays for the Théâtre d'Art, the avant-garde symbolist theater founded by the young poet Paul Fort in 1890. Antoine's naturalist Théâtre Libre had just created a sensation in Paris with its new, super-realistic staging. Subscription audiences marveled at the acting, which seemed close to real life, and at scenery like the butcher shop with actual dripping carcasses of beef. Antoine's methods were an improvement over the predictable mediocrity of most commercial nineteeth-century theater, but the symbolists wanted a theater of the soul, in which a mystical inner life would transcend the corporeal world. They believed that realistic sets and even the bodies and voices of live actors could interfere with achieving a state of reverie.

When the symbolists did produce plays, they tried new styles. Lights were dim. Pauses were long; Maeterlinck theorized that in the spaces between the words, the supernatural could enter. To heighten the desired atmosphere of the unknown, a gauze curtain might separate the audience from the stage. An evening might include several plays, poetry readings, scents sprayed into the audience – and often ended with a brawl about literary style. Many plays showed neurasthenic characters, like Terror-stricken in *The Crystal Spider*, who seem to exist partway between the real world and the beyond, and whose fear of a vague menacing force gradually infects the other characters with terror. Theater was a "pretext for a dream."

In their reaction against what they perceived as the vulgarity of turn-of-the-century existence, and in their quest for the rarefied life of artifice and art, many symbolists equated "women" with "nature" and despised both. The word "feminism" had just been coined and suffragists were agitating for the vote, but woman existed in symbolist art as the Other, an invention to fuel masculine fantasies of female power, helplessness, or perversity. Paris theater was nearly closed to women playwrights. A partial exception was Rachilde (pseudonym of Marguerite Eymery, 1860–1953). The only woman writer who had a position of influence in the early avant-garde French theater, Rachilde wrote over twenty plays, which were performed in Paris, St. Petersburg, Belgium, Germany, and Scandinavia. She worked behind the scenes to encourage the directors and playwrights of the first "Art theaters" in Europe, where her plays were famous in their day among the earliest attempts at non-realistic drama. A self-declared anti-feminist who nevertheless peopled much of her writing with strong women and passive men, Rachilde had a major influence on the new styles which sparked the modern theater and the theater of the absurd.

Rachilde's life and work

Rachilde cultivated a scandalous persona when she arrived in Paris in 1881, determined to make a living as a writer and to become a member of the misogynist symbolist clique. She cut her hair short, called herself a "man of letters," and applied for permission from the prefect of police to wear men's clothes in public. Her most famous novel, *Monsieur Vénus*, disrupted gender conventions and brought her early notoriety. "A pornographer, well and good! But so very distinguished," said Barbey d'Aurevilly of her when the two novelists met (Dauphiné 1991: 74). The Tuesday salon at Rachilde's apartment became an important gathering place for young symbolist writers, who called her "Mademoiselle Baudelaire" and "the queen of the decadents." She continued to write best-selling fiction, much of which focused on sexuality, gender reversals, and death.

When Rachilde married Alfred Vallette in 1889, she promptly let her hair grow long and resumed women's clothes. Her first biographer wrote that her personal life ended with her marriage: "the legend of the amazon died away on the threshold of the hearth. The history of Rachilde became no more than the history of her books" (Gaubert 1907: 17). But Rachilde refused to settle comfortably into the role of the bourgeois wife. Although she had one daughter, she disliked motherhood and put her energy into the *Mercure de France*, which Vallette founded in 1890. She now held her salon at the newspaper; her connections and reputation helped the *Mercure* succeed as the premier avant-garde journal out of the hundreds of small periodicals circulating in Paris.

One of the goals of the *Mercure* was to foster a symbolist theater. Rachilde helped choose plays for Paul Fort and defended the Théâtre d'Art against attacks by mainstream critics. Her own play, *Madame la Mort* (Lady Death), produced by Fort in 1891, intrigued reviewers as a novel effort to reveal the supernatural on stage. In this "cerebral drama," the first and third acts were essentially realist. Rachilde's innovation was to try to show a subjective inner truth by locating the second act inside the protagonist's mind. Act II takes place in a mysterious garden where two women, the incarnations of Death and Life, argue for possession of Paul after he has attempted suicide. Life, in the guise of his mistress Lucie, clings to Paul and reminds him of their passion, but he recoils from her to worship the "veiled Woman." Death calls Lucie a "slut" who "poisons love with the idea of procreation" (Rachilde 1891: 88). Paul chooses to fall asleep beneath the enigmatic folds of Death's veil.

The Crystal Spider

Georgette Camée's unusual acting style in the title role heightened the dreamlike atmosphere of the garden scene. Rachilde praised her ethereal gestures and chant-like, poetic voice, but she hated the over-melodramatic misinterpretation by the lead actor. Even though she was Franck's good friend, she refused his plea to play Terror-stricken in her next "cerebral drama" (Franck, letter: 1892). Instead, she offered *The Crystal Spider* to a new symbolist theater. The Théâtre de l'Œuvre came to owe its continuing existence to Rachilde's encouragement. She acted as a buffer, a go-between, a soother of ruffled feathers, and a morale-builder for the often despondent young director, Lugné-Poe, whom she advised to "take the motto of our courageous directress: onward!" (Rachilde, letter: 1893). One of the Œuvre's most pressing problems was the dearth of French plays for the repertory. The nationalistic Rachilde complained that there was only one Ibsen, and although she admired and imitated Maeterlinck, he was a Belgian. She led the passionate search for French symbolist playwrights; her best-known recommendation was Alfred Jarry's *Ubu roi*, the play which made Jarry famous. Rachilde's memoirs of Jarry are the source of several false anecdotes, since she "made up incredible lies"(Severini, interview: 1993).

The Crystal Spider, produced in February 1894, was the first French play performed at the Œuvre. It starred Lugné-Poe as the frightened son and Berthe Bady as his devoted, devouring, sensual mother. Both actors had succeeded in unlearning some of their traditional training and were beginning to define a new symbolist performing style, including the intoned vocal techniques pioneered by Camée, but reviews suggest that the performers had not yet achieved the slow pace which became a hallmark of symbolist acting. One critic wrote that Rachilde's "poem" was "interesting" but that "Lugné-Poe rushed too much. He should have acted out all that fear in a crescendo of horror" (de Gachons 1984: 177). All the other reviewers praised the star's acting. Lugné-Poe showed "incontestable talent" in the "eerie episode à la Edgar Poe" ("Hamlette"). *The Crystal Spider* was "an eerie and a strange evocation of cerebral morbidity with a poignant effect. M. Lugné-Poe and Mlle. Bady were admirable in the role of the Mother and Terror-stricken" (Albert 1894). The short play served as curtain raiser before the major piece of the evening, Bjørnson's *Beyond Human Power*. Rachilde's play received just a few lines at the end of the long reviews of the Scandinavian work. Her play attracted more interest in September when the company took it on tour to Belgium; Lugné-Poe later recalled that Rachilde's prestige was greater outside of France (Lugné-Poe 1931: 107).

The Crystal Spider first appeared in print in the *Mercure de France* in June 1892, one of several fantastical plays, prose poems, and stories that Rachilde republished in *The Demon of the Absurd* (1894). More carefully composed than much of Rachilde's work, the collection includes some of her finest writing. It proved to her most critical contemporaries that a woman "can have phases of virility" (de Gourmont 1896: 117). For Rachilde herself, "woman writer" was an oxymoron. She wrote extensively about why she disliked women of letters, bluestockings, and women in general. She continued to call herself a "man of letters" and yet to conform to the sensuous "Mademoiselle Baudelaire" image. The uncomfortable contradictions of these real-life masquerades show up in all her plays. Issues of sexuality, fear, and death permeate Rachilde's work; she claimed to be an anti-feminist, but her ambition and her drive for status belied her surface beliefs, and her sneers at "*les bas-bleus*" came from a desire to secure her position in the decadent milieu. In her plays, her concerns about gender and power make it clear that she couldn't help being part of the debate she pretended to mock.

The Crystal Spider uses motifs that were common to symbolist writers: the horror of women as the embodiment of sexuality, the morbid interest in aberrant psychological states, the connection of fear with a mystical world, the obsession with death, the dangerous enchantment of mirrors. Rachilde's personal twist on these themes changes the Narcissus legend from the story of a beautiful youth who falls in love with his own reflection to a play about a young man who confuses mirrors with women and is afraid of both. "Invite all the mirrors you please, and hang up all the women of the world on the wall," he says. Terror-stricken (l'Epouvanté) is himself a reflection of his mother, "like a dead man who resembles his own portrait," and her psyche mirror sends out light instead of reflecting it. Next to him, her languorous sensuality is full of life, but even though she has "lively eyes, a tender mouth, a young face," she sees an "old woman" when she looks into a mirror. This response to aging is the only moment Rachilde allows sympathy for the female character; otherwise, the author and audience identify with the son, a fusion of male/female. Deceptively sweet and maternal, she is the universal, nameless Mother who demands a sick intimacy: "resolved to meddle in everything," she insists on owning his thoughts, his feelings, his body, his sex. "If my own flesh were sick . . . we would take care of ourselves," she tells him, in a prudish reference to syphilis. She accuses him of an unimaginable "dreadful vice," probably homosexuality, which clearly she *has* imagined.

The Mother goads Terror-stricken into telling the nightmare experience that has scarred him. The "moment of silence" after he confesses his fear of mirrors should be unnaturally drawn out; for the symbolists, the "supernatural" enters here. To understand the mood of his long speeches, it is helpful to remember the conventions of melodrama. The emphasis on the internal battle of an individual, the milking of emotion, the buildup of pathos, and the climactic closure before the final curtain were all familiar theater experiences for audiences of Rachilde's time (and for soap-opera fans today). But she shows a more modern impulse in her awareness of the unconscious. From the opening stage directions to the son's monologues, looking for examples of the "inner" and the "outer" will provide a way to fathom *The Crystal Spider* at the depth the symbolists intended.

In our translation, we have tried to provide an idiomatic text suitable for performance, but we have kept the poetic strangeness of Rachilde's dialogue between these two non-human characters.

The Crystal Spider

1892
Play translation by Kiki Gounaridou
and Frazer Lively

Rachilde

To Jules Renard

A large drawing room in which one of the three windows opens over a terrace full of honeysuckle. Very bright summer night. The moon illuminates the space where the characters sit. The back remains dark. One can barely discern shapes of heavy, ancient furniture. At the center of this half-darkness, a tall psyche mirror in empire style, supported on each side by the long necks of swans with brass beaks. A hazy reflection of light on the mirror, but, seen from the lit terrace, this reflection does not seem to come from the moon; it rather appears to emanate from the mirror itself like a light which might be its own.

THE MOTHER, *aged 45, lively eyes, a tender mouth; a young face under gray hair. She wears an elegant black robe and a shawl of white lace. Sensual voice.*

TERROR-STRICKEN, *her son, aged 20. He is thin, as if floating in his loose shirt of pure white twill. His complexion is wan, his eyes are fixed. His straight black hair gleams on his forehead. He has even features which recall his mother's beauty, a little like a dead man who resembles his own portrait. Heavy, slow voice.*

The two characters sit in front of the open door.

THE MOTHER Well, my dear, what are you thinking about?

TERROR-STRICKEN But . . . nothing, mother.

THE MOTHER *(Stretching out in her armchair)* What an aroma this honeysuckle has! Do you smell it? It makes you dizzy. It is like a lady's liqueur. . . . *(She smacks her lips.)*

TERROR-STRICKEN A liqueur, the honeysuckle? Ah? . . . yes, mother.

THE MOTHER You are not cold, I hope, in this weather? And you don't have a headache?

TERROR-STRICKEN No, thank you, mother.

THE MOTHER Thank you for what? *(She leans over and looks at him attentively.)* My poor little Sylvius! Admit it then, it is not amusing to keep an old lady company. *(Breathing in the breeze)* What a sweet night! It is useless to ask for the lamps, is it not? I told François that he could go for a walk, and I am sure he has gone to flirt with the maids. We shall stay here until the moon goes down. . . . *(A moment of silence. Gravely, she begins again.)* Sylvius, you are defensive for a reason, love has broken your heart. The more you go on like that, the more you waste away. . . .

TERROR-STRICKEN I have already explained to you, Mother, that I love no one but you.

THE MOTHER *(Moved)* Nonsense! Now then, if she is a princess of a girl, doubtless we could have her. And if she is homely, provided you don't marry her. . . .

TERROR-STRICKEN Mother, your teasing plunges needles into my ears.

THE MOTHER And if this is all about a debt, a huge debt, so what? You know I could pay it off.

TERROR-STRICKEN Debt again! But I have more money than I can spend.

THE MOTHER *(Lowering her voice and drawing her armchair closer)* Well then . . . you are not going to be angry, Sylvius? Oh yes! You men, you have more shameful secrets than illicit passions and debts. . . . I have decided to interfere with everything . . . you hear me? If my own flesh were sick . . . well, *(Delicately)* we would take care of ourselves. . . .

TERROR-STRICKEN *(With a gesture of disgust)* You are insane, Mother.

THE MOTHER *(With an outburst)* Yes, in fact I am starting to believe that I am losing my mind just by looking at you! *(She stands up.)* Don't you realize that you frighten me?

TERROR-STRICKEN *(Shuddering)* Frighten!

THE MOTHER *(Turning back and leaning over him, sweetly)* I didn't mean to hurt you, my Sylvius! *(A pause, then she gets up again and speaks vehemently.)* Oh! Who is the despicable slut who has taken my Sylvius away from me? Because there is a slut, that's certain. . . .

TERROR-STRICKEN *(Shrugging his shoulders)* Let's say . . . several, if that suits you, Mother.

THE MOTHER *(Still standing, as if talking to herself)* Or perhaps a dreadful vice, one of those vices which *we* cannot even imagine, we, honest women, cannot. *(She addresses him directly.)* Ever since you have been like this, I have been reading novels trying to fathom you, and I have discovered nothing yet I did not already know.

TERROR-STRICKEN Oh! I rather thought so.

THE MOTHER It's decided! Tomorrow, we shall invite women and young girls. You shall see Sylvia again, your cousin. Once you used to follow her like a little dog, and she has now become rather charming. A bit coquettish perhaps but so special with her imitations of all the fashionable singers! . . . Oh! darling, woman ought to be the sole preoccupation of man. After all, love makes you handsome! *(She caresses his chin.)* You will be able to look into your dressing-room mirror again! . . .

TERROR-STRICKEN *(Standing up with a gesture of terror)* My dressing-room mirror! . . . God! Women, young girls, creatures with reflections of mirrors at the back of their eyes . . . Mother! You want to kill me. . . .

THE MOTHER *(Astonished)* What! Still those ideas about mirrors! Then it is serious, that obsession? My word, he has ended up imagining he is ugly. *(She laughs.)*

TERROR-STRICKEN *(Glancing furtively behind him, toward the psyche which the moon illuminates from far away)* Mama, I beg you, let's abandon this discussion. No, my physical state is not the point here. . . . There are moral reasons. . . . Oh God! You can see very well I am suffocating! . . . Can you understand? . . . Oh! for the last eight days, it has been an incessant persecution! You are crushing me! No, I am not ill! I need to be alone, that's all. Invite all the mirrors you please and hang up all the women in the world on the wall, but do not tickle me to make me laugh. . . . Ah! that's too much, that's too much! . . . *(He falls back into his armchair.)*

THE MOTHER *(Putting her arms around him)* You are suffocating, Sylvius, to whom are you saying this? I am dying of grief myself to see you with this silent look. Try a little, I am capable of understanding you, come on . . . because I adore you! . . . *(She kisses him.)*

TERROR-STRICKEN *(Exploding)* All right! yes, here it is, I am afraid of mirrors, have me put away if you want! *(A moment of silence)*

THE MOTHER *(Softly)* We shall put the mirrors away, Sylvius.

TERROR-STRICKEN *(Holding out his hands to her)* Forgive me, Mother, I am rude. Perhaps I should have spoken sooner, but it's torture to imagine that people will laugh at you. And this kind of thing can hardly be explained in a couple of words. . . . *(He passes his hands over his forehead.)* Mother, what do you see when you look at yourself? *(He breathes with difficulty.)*

THE MOTHER I see myself, my little Sylvius *(She sits back down sadly and lowers her head)*, I see an old woman! Alas! . . .

TERROR-STRICKEN *(Glancing at her with compassion)* Ah! You have never seen anything *in there* but yourself? I am sorry for you! *(Becoming animated)* As for me, it seems to me that the inventor of the first mirror should have gone mad with terror in the presence of his creation! So, for you, an intelligent woman, nothing exists inside a mirror except for simple things? In that atmosphere of the unknown, have you not seen an army of phantoms suddenly rising? On the threshold of these doors to dream, have you not unraveled the magic of the infinite lying in wait for you? But it is so very frightening, a mirror is, that I am stunned, every morning, to see you are still alive, you, women and young girls who look at yourselves incessantly in the mirror! . . . Mother, listen to me, it is quite a story, and I must go far back to expose the reason for my hatred of mirrors, because I was predestined, I was first *warned* when I was a child. . . . I was ten, I was down there, in the lodge in our garden, all alone, and, in front of a great grand mirror that has not been there for a long time now, I was leafing through my school books, I had homework to do. The stifling room, the drawn curtains, gave me the feeling of a pauper's home. It was furnished with garden chairs all eaten away with dampness, and a table covered with a dirty, worn-out rug. The ceiling leaked, I could hear the rain rattling on a half-torn down zinc roof. Only the grand mirror hinted at luxury, oh! so big, tall like a person! Mechanically, I looked at myself. Under the limpidity of the glass, there were dismal marks. Like lilies growing on still water, and further on, in a remote darkness, undefined forms stood up like ghosts moving along the stream of their slimy hair. I remember that, as I was looking at myself, I had the bizarre sensation of going up to my neck inside that mirror, like in a muddy lake. I was locked up, I was being punished, and so, like it or not, I had to stay in that dead water. Fixing my eyes on the eyes of my image, I distinguished a bright dot in the middle of those mists, and at the same time I perceived the light sound of an insect coming from the place where I was seeing the dot. Gradually the dot radiated into a star. It sparkled like intense lightning in the middle of that sensation of sleep, it buzzed like a fly against a window-pane. Mother! I saw it and I heard it! I was not dreaming. There was no possible explanation for a ten-year-old boy, not even for a man, I swear to you! I knew that the lodge adjoined a shed where the gardening tools were kept; but no one lived there. I said to myself that, in all probability, some spider of an unknown species was going to jump on my face. I couldn't move. The white spider kept moving forward, it turned into a small crab in a silver shell, its head starred with dazzling ridges, its legs along my reflected head, it invaded my forehead, cracked my temples, devoured my pupils, slowly effaced my image, decapitated me. For a moment I saw myself standing there, arms twisted with horror, carrying on my shoulders a monstrous animal with the sinister look of an octopus! I wanted to cry out. But as in all nightmares, I could not. After that, I felt myself at the mercy of the crystal spider who sucked out my brain! And it kept on buzzing like an animal

determined to finish off its enemy once and for all. . . . All of a sudden, the grand mirror shattered under the tremendous pressure of the monster's tentacles, and this entire vision collapsed into sparkling fragments. One of them slightly cut my hand. I let out a rending cry and fainted. . . . When I regained consciousness, our gardener, who had entered my prison in order to reassure me, showed me the brace he had been using, *on the other side of the wall,* just to drive in an enormous nail! Penetrating the wall, he had also penetrated the mirror, unaware of me, pursuing his work accompanied by the grinding of the tool. My injury was not serious. . . . The good man was afraid there might be a scene . . . and I promised to keep quiet. . . . From that day on, mirrors have strangely absorbed me, in spite of the nervous aversion I felt for them. My brief existence is all infused by their satanic reflections. And after the first physical blow, I received many other mental shocks. . . . Here is the grotesque memory of the head I had beneath my scholastic laurels. And there is the transparent photograph of my dissolute life. . . . There is a mystery in this pursuit by the mirror, in this hunt for the guilty man directed against myself alone! (*He dreams for a moment, then begins again, becoming more and more agitated.*) Against myself alone? . . . But no! Believe it, Mother, those who see *clearly* are as terror-stricken as I am. After all, does anyone know why this piece of glass that we cover with quicksilver suddenly assumes the depths of an abyss . . . and doubles the world? The mirror is the problem of life perpetually thwarting man. Does anyone know exactly what Narcissus saw in the fountain and what it was that killed him?

THE MOTHER (*Shivering*) Oh! Sylvius! You frighten me. You are not just telling me stories? You . . . honestly think about such things?

TERROR-STRICKEN Mother, at this moment, would you dare go look at yourself in a mirror?

THE MOTHER (*Turning toward the back of the drawing room, very troubled*) No! No! I wouldn't dare. . . . If we lighted a lamp. . . .

TERROR-STRICKEN (*Forcing her to sit down again*) There . . . I knew that you, too, would be afraid! In a moment, you will see quite clearly! Why do you women obstinately insist on crowding our apartments with those cynical delusions that compel me never, *never* to be alone? Why do you throw at my head that spy who has the talent of shedding my own tears? I saw, one evening, while leaving a ball, as I put a fur coat over your shoulders, I saw a lady smiling voluptuously in the mirror, a lady who resembled you, Mother! . . . And one morning, while waiting for my cousin Sylvia, shivering behind her door, a bouquet of orchids in my hand, I saw through that half-open door, in an immense mirror, the reflection of a beautiful naked girl in a provocative pose! . . . Mirrors, Mother, are abysses where the virtue of women and the serenity of men founder together.

THE MOTHER Stop it! I don't want to hear you any more.

TERROR-STRICKEN (*Gripping her arms and getting up*) Mother, have you ever encountered those stalking mirrors that seize you while you cross the streets of the big cities? Those that drop down on you abruptly like a shower? The mirrors in shop windows mounted on false frames, with rouge and jewels like creatures for sale? Have you seen them offering you their gleaming flanks where one after the other each passer-by went to bed? Infernal mirrors! But they torment us from all sides! They rise from the oceans, the rivers, the streams! Drinking from my glass, I see my hideousness. The neighbor who thinks he has only one ulcer always has two! . . . Mirrors are informers, and they transform a simple unpleasantness into infinite despair. They lie in the dew-drop in order to change the heart of a flower into a sobbing heart. By turn full of false promises of joy, full of shameful secrets (*and sterile like prostitutes*), they can hold neither an image nor a color. Even if *she* has slipped into the arms of *another* man in front of the mirror which I contemplate, it is always myself that I see in the place of the *other*! (*Furious*) They are hateful torturers who remain impassive, and yet, endowed with the power of Satan, if they saw God, Mother, they would look just like him! . . .

THE MOTHER (*In a suppliant tone*) Sylvius! The moon is at the corner of the wall. Go get a lamp, I want to look in there. . . .

TERROR-STRICKEN (*Once again with a hollow voice*) Oh! I tell you these things because you force me to! I am not really qualified to become the fatal informer, but it is only right that blind women discern, by accident, the frightening situation which they create for men who can see, even in the darkness. Sumptuously you install those pitiless jailors in our homes, and we must tolerate them for your love. And in return for our patience, they slap us with our own image, our foulness, our absurd gestures. Ah! Damn them, your doubles! Damn them, our rivals! Between you and them, there is a diabolical pact. (*In a desolate tone*) Have you seen those birds, on some snowy winter morning, those birds that turn round and round over the trap that glistens and lures them to the phantom of a heap of silver oats or golden corn? Have you seen them, as they fall, and fall, one by one, from the height of the skies, the broken wings, the bloody beak, the eyes still dazzled by the splendors of their delusion! There is a mirror to catch skylarks and there is a mirror to catch men, a mirror that lurks at the dangerous turn of their dark existence, a mirror that will watch them die with their faces crushed against the icy crystal of their enigma. . . .

THE MOTHER (*Clinging to him*) No! Enough! I am suffering too much! Your voice is killing me! Anxiety grips me by the throat. Have you no pity for your mother, Sylvius? I wanted to know, I was wrong. Forgive me! Go get the lamps, I beg you! (*She kneels down, clasps her hands.*) I feel paralyzed. . . .

TERROR-STRICKEN (*Staggering*) Me, I dread the mirror concealed in the dark, your grand psyche, Mother. . . .

THE MOTHER (*Exasperated*) Coward! Am I not even more frightened than you are! Will you obey me now!

TERROR-STRICKEN (*Getting up again, beside himself*) All right, fine! I will go get your light!

(*He launches himself with rage in the direction of the psyche mirror and of the drawing-room door behind it. For a moment, he runs into the deep night. . . . All at once, the terrible jolt of an enormous piece of furniture, the resonant sound of shattering crystal, and the dismal howl of a man whose throat is cut. . . .)*

Curtain

Note

Gallimard has recently published editions of *L'animal*, *Nono*, and *La tour d'amour* by Rachilde. Also forthcoming by Johns Hopkins University Press, Performing Arts Journal Publications, is *Seven Plays by Rachilde* (working title), trans. Kiki Gounaridou and Frazer Lively.

Bibliography

Selected primary sources

Rachilde (1884) *Monsieur Vénus*, Brussels: Brancort; trans. Liz Heron (1992), Sawtry: Daedelus.
— (1891) *Théâtre*, collected plays, Paris: Savine.
— (1893) Letter to A.Lugné-Poe, February 15, 1893, (Société des auteurs et compositeurs dramatiques, Paris).
— (1894) *Le démon de l'absurde*, Paris: Mercure de France.
— (1900) *La jongleuse*, Paris: Mercure de France; trans. M. Hawthorne (1990) *The Juggler*, New Brunswick: Rutgers University Press.
— (1919) *La poupée transparente*, one-act play, *Le Monde Nouveau*, March 20, 1919.
— (ca. 1920) "Répulsion," one-act play, MS n.d. (Fonds Doucet, Paris).
—(1921) "La femme peinte," one-act play, *Mercure de France*, August 1, 1921: 642–52.
— (1928) *Alfred Jarry ou le surmâle des lettres*, Paris: Bernard Grasset.
— (1928) *Pourquoi je ne suis pas féministe*, Paris: Editions de France.
— (1947) *Quand j'étais jeune*, Paris: Mercure de France.
Albert, H. (1894) "Théâtre de l'Œuvre," *Mercure de France*, March 1894.
Franck, P. (1892) Letter to Rachilde (Fonds Doucet, Paris).
de Gachons, J. (1894) "Autour des théâtres," in *l'Ermitage*, March 1894.

de Gourmont, R. (1896) *Le livre des masques*, Paris: Mercure de France.
Severini, R. (1993) Personal Interview, July 26, 1993, Paris.
Theatre records for the Théâtre d'Art and the Théâtre de l'Œuvre, 1890–99 (Includes article by "Hamlette") (Bibliothèque de l'Arsénal, Paris).

Selected secondary sources

Birkett, J. (1986) *The Sins of the Fathers: Decadence in France, 1870–1914*, London: Quartet.
David, A. (1924) *Rachilde, homme de lettres*, Paris: Editions de la Nouvelle Revue Critique.
Dauphiné, C. (1991) *Rachilde*, Paris: Mercure de France.
Deak, F. (1993) *Symbolist Theater*, Baltimore: Johns Hopkins University Press.
Gaubert, E. (1907) *Rachilde*, Paris: Sansot.
Gerould, D. (ed.) (1985) *Doubles, Demons, and Dreamers: An International Anthology of Symbolist Drama*, New York: Performing Arts Journal Publications.
Hawthorne, M. C. (1989) "The Social Construction of Sexuality in Three Novels by Rachilde," *Michigan Romance Studies* 9: 49–59.
— (1991) "Rachilde (1860–1953)," in E. M. Sartori and D. W. Zimmerman (eds) *French Women Writers*, Westport, CT: Greenwood.
— (1992) "To the Lighthouse: Fictions of Masculine Identity in Rachilde's *La tour d'amour*," *L'Esprit Créateur* 34.2: 41–51.
Kiebuzinska, C. (1994) "Behind the Mirror: Madame Rachilde's *The Crystal Spider*" *Modern Language Studies* 44.3: 14–43.
Kingcaid, R. A. (1992) *Neurosis and Narrative: The Decadent Short Fiction of Proust, Lorrain, and Rachilde*, Carbondale: Southern Illinois University Press.
Organographes du cymbalum pataphysicum, April, 4 1983: 19–20.
Santon, N. (1928) *La poésie de Rachilde*. Paris: Le rouge et le noir.
Ziegler, R. (1990) "Fantasies of Partial Selves in Rachilde's *Le démon de l'absurde*," *Nineteenth-Century French Studies* 19.1: 122–31.

10 Zinaida Gippius, 1869–1945 _____

Sacred Blood
Russia

Introduction

by Catherine Schuler

The life and work of Zinaida Gippius

Zinaida Gippius, poet, playwright, prose writer, essayist, and literary critic, was born in Russia, in 1869 and died in Paris in 1945. The oldest child of Nikolai Romanovich and Anastasiia Stepanovna Gippius, by the turn of the century she was, according to one critic, "the most talented of our woman writers (*pisatel'nitsa-zhenshchina*)," "a genuine virtuoso of the word" (Bezrodnyi 1990: 3). Although educated at home, Gippius read

Watercolour of Zinaida Gippius by Leon Bakst, 1905. *Photograph: source unknown.*

widely and, even as an adolescent, wrote prodigiously. At age 10, already confident of her talent, she asked her Russian language teacher rhetorically: "Do you know another little girl who can write like me – without a single mistake?" (Bezrodnyi 1990: 3).

In 1889, she married Dmitri Merezhkovskii and moved to St. Petersburg. Like that of Virginia and Leonard Woolf, their relationship was based primarily on Platonic mutual affection and intellectual compatibility, rather than sexual attraction. Gippius and Merezhkovskii moved in circles that included the most prominent Russian decadents and symbolists, among them Vyacheslov Ivanov, Aleksandr Blok, Andrei Belyi, and Valery Briusov. Gippius published poetry, short stories, and plays in the most prominent progressive and symbolist journals, including *The Northern Herald* (*Severnyi vestnik*), *The World of Art* (*Mir iskusstva*), and *The Scales* (*Vesy*). In 1901, she and Merezhkovskii began organizing gatherings at their home, which were intended to foster discussion among intellectuals and academics of current theological, philosophical, and social issues.

The plays

Although Gippius's work is located firmly in the *belles-lettres* tradition, conditions in late Imperial Russia were not conducive to political passivity. Even the relatively apolitical decadents and symbolists, many of whom sought to rise above vulgar reality through appeals to ideal truth and beauty, could not transcend the social and political dissension that eventually tore their country apart. Although she was not a political activist and consistently disparaged "civic poetry," following the failed revolution of 1905, Gippius became more interested in topical issues. In her *Petersburg Diary* (*Peterburgskii dnevnik*), she wrote: "Politics – the conditions of the autocracy – were of vital interest to us, for every cultured Russian, whatever side he [*sic*] was on – and whether he wanted to or not – inevitably collided with political questions" (Gippius 1991: 10).

Thematic changes in her work after 1905 suggest an evolving political consciousness, but Gippius was never a political pragmatist; rather she saw political revolution as a means to spiritual transformation. The revolution of 1917 failed to fulfill her expectations: a supporter of the moderate Social Democratic movement, she was dismayed by the Bolshevik victory. For that reason, Gippius and Merezhkovskii fled to Poland in 1920, where they engaged in anti-Bolshevik activities. Soon after, they settled in Paris and resumed their literary, philosophical, and theological pursuits.

Although Gippius's fame rests on her poetry and short stories, she wrote four plays between 1901 and 1914: *Sacred Blood* (*Sviataia krov'*), *The Red Poppy* (*Makov svet*), *No and Yes* (*Net i da*), and *The Green Ring* (*Zelenoe kol'tso*). Although Gippius published all four plays, only *The Green Ring*, directed in 1915 by Meierhold, was actually realized in production. Written in 1901, *Sacred Blood*

reveals the influence of Dostoevskii on Gippius's early work. Like Dostoevskii, she believed that knowledge and moral perfection could be achieved only through voluntary suffering and intense spiritual torment. Like many Russian symbolists, Gippius was preoccupied with matters of theology. From a strictly biographical perspective, *Sacred Blood* reflects Gippius's own zealous pursuit of inner freedom through mystical Christianity. Perhaps inadvertently, it also reflects the intellectual ambivalence of an "advanced woman" about the nature of institutionalized Christianity and the relationship of women to the Orthodox church.

Sacred Blood

The plot of *Sacred Blood* concerns the quest of a young *rusalka* for an immortal soul. Although *rusalka* is usually translated as mermaid and the protagonist of *Sacred Blood* does bear a resemblance to Hans Christian Andersen's mermaid, the Russian *rusalka* is not the familiar, benign fish woman of western folklore. Irresistibly beautiful, Russian *rusalki* are, according to Natalie Moyle, the "feminine version of the unquiet dead" (Moyle 1987: 222). *Rusalki* are once mortal women who die untimely or unnatural deaths; most are suicides who drown themselves after becoming pregnant outside of wedlock. They tend to congregate near water and their principal occupation consists of luring men (not necessarily the man who caused their misfortune – any male will do) into their watery abode to drown. *Rusalki* embody both the terror and fascination of the "other world." For male humans, who cannot resist the beauty of their bodies and voices, they are a "fatal attraction." According to Moyle, a *rusalka*'s ugliness "is not that of appearance, for she is gorgeous, but that of sin" (Moyle 1987: 222).

In Russian symbolism, "Otherness"[1] is a necessary attribute of the "eternal feminine," and in the hands of men like Blok, Sologub, and Annenskii, the "eternal feminine" is represented by an alluring, otherworldly siren of great beauty and frigidity. By positioning a *rusalka* as the protagonist of *Sacred Blood*, Gippius, like her male colleagues, opposes human (male) and supernatural (female) worlds, and toys with the female demonic and with "Otherness." But by positing an alternative to the standard demonic "eternal feminine" of Russian symbolism, Gippius challenges the hegemony of the traditionally masculinist aesthetic. The differences lie not only in the characterization of the young *rusalka* but in the way Gippius reconciles the opposition between the female/demonic and the male/human.

In conventional folktales, *rusalki* evince little interest in issues of Christian doctrine, but in Gippius's hands, the folkloric *rusalka* is positioned in the center of a quest for Christian redemption through self-sacrifice and suffering. Rather than a sexually alluring siren of great physical beauty, Gippius's *rusalka* is a thin young woman of frightening intensity. She is still "almost a child," but has no interest in the childish games of her companions. Indeed, in her single-minded passion, she resembles nothing so much as the ascetic female university students (*kursistki*) and other fanatical young women of the intelligentsia who joined radical reform movements like the People's Will, the group that assassi-nated Aleksandr II. Like her nonfictional counterparts, the *rusalka*'s idealism and obsessive devotion to her cause is so great that she uses any means to achieve it – even murder.

In her quest for a human soul, the *rusalka* bonds with Father Pafnuty, a Christian ascetic with decidedly pantheistic inclinations. Strongly attracted by the *rusalka*'s simplicity, natural goodness, and desire for Christian redemption, Pafnuty comes to regard her as his "heaven-sent daughter" (*bogodannaia dochka*). Alike in their simplicity and unwillingness to accept orthodoxies, whether it be the hegemony of the Orthodox church or the absolute condition of marginality,[2] Pafnuty and the *rusalka* seek alternatives. It is through their spiritual bonding that Gippius offers an alternative to the masculinist aesthetic of symbolism which requires a demonic "eternal feminine" and an epiphany consisting of the death of the male hero at the hands of the Other. For although the *rusalka* kills Father Pafnuty, his death can only be accomplished through unconditional love. The epiphany of Gippius's drama implies the transfiguration and regeneration of both Pafnuty and the *rusalka* through mutual self-sacrifice.

Although Gippius offered what might be called a feminist alternative to the decidedly masculinist aesthetic of traditional Russian symbolism, it was not intentional. Her diaries suggest that she was intensely aware of herself as a gendered subject, but like many Russian women, Gippius was hostile to the objectives of what she and other mem-bers of the intelligentsia disdainfully called "bourgeois feminism."[3] If her work is not feminist in any obvious (or perhaps western) sense, it does offer an important instance of opposition to the patriarchal ideology of Russian orthodoxy. On a more personal level, the *rusalka*'s passionate desire for acceptance into the human world of Christian suffering and redemption mirrors Gippius's own frustration with issues of sex and gender and her struggle to be accepted by her fellow symbolists as a "human being" (*chelovek*) rather than a woman.

Sacred Blood ─────────────

1901
Play translation by Mary F. Zirin and
Catherine Schuler

Zinaida Gippius

Scene 1

*Before the curtain rises, the distant,
intermittent tolling of a bell is heard. A forest
wilderness. A smooth, flat, shining lake, not
very large. On the right bank, overgrown with
rushes, is a glade, and beyond it the dark
forest begins. A waning moon hangs quite low
in the sky, still illuminating the lake and the
glade with a faint, dull reddish light. A swarm
of pale, misty, naked rusalki moves very
slowly in a circle around the clearing, holding
hands. Their song is also slow and even, but it
is not sad. Their voices rise above the bell,
which keeps on tolling steadily. When the
rusalki fall silent for a few moments it is
much more audible. Not all the rusalki are
dancing: some, the older ones, sit on the bank
dangling their feet in the water, and others are
wandering through the reeds. At the edge of
the glade, close to the forest, an old, rather fat
rusalka sits under a large tree, slowly and
efficiently combing her hair. Beside her is a
very young rusalka, almost a child. She sits
motionless, her thin arms clasping her naked
knees, looks at the glade with a steady gaze,
and the entire time seems to be listening for
something. It is very late. The sliver of a
moon, however, is not setting, but rising. The
fog spreads over the water like a living being.*

OLD RUSALKA *(Sighing)* Your hair gets
   tangled, all tangled in the eddies, and you
   can't comb it out. *(After a silence, to the
   young one)* And why are you just sitting
   there? Why don't you dance? Go on, frolic
   with the others.
   *(YOUNG RUSALKA remains silent and
   motionless, looking at the glade.)*
OLD RUSALKA *(Indifferently)* She's turned to
   stone again! And what a strange child she
   is! Even the moon doesn't seem to warm
   her.
   *(She continues on combing her hair. The
   slow and quiet singing of the rusalki is*

audible, in time with their measured, gliding
movements.)*
RUSALKI
We are the white daughters
of the shining lake,
we were born of purity and coolness.
Foam and mire and grasses caress us,
light hollow rushes fondle us;
in winter under the ice like under warm
   glass,
we sleep and dream of summer.
   All's good: life! reality! and sleep!

*(The singing breaks off, the circle moves in
silence for a moment, neither speeding up
nor slowing down. The bell is more audible.)*

We do not know, we have not seen,
the lethal, scorching sun;
but we know his reflection,
we know the tranquil moon.
She's moist, meek, sweet, and pure,
all golden in the silver night,
she – like the *rusalka* – is benign . . .
   All's good: life! and us! and the moon!

*(Again the circle moves in silence for a few
moments. The bell tolls.)*

On the bank, amid the rushes,
the pale fog glides and melts away.
We know that summer gives way to
   winter,
winter once more to spring,
and the mystic hour will come,
– blessed like all hours –
when we will melt into the white fog,
and the white fog will melt.
And there will be new *rusalki*,
and the moon will shine for them,
and they too will melt with the fog.
   All's good: life! and us! and the world!
   and death!

OLD RUSALKA *(Painstakingly running the
   comb through her sparse hair)* What's

wrong? Why don't you join in the song? Go on. The moonlight's almost gone. It will soon be dawn.

YOUNG RUSALKA *(Gazing steadily)* I don't want to, Granny. The song is so depressing.

OLD RUSALKA *(Displeased)* Depressing is it! It's a good song. What kind do you want?

YOUNG RUSALKA What I wanted to ask you, Granny, is this: it says in our songs that we live and look at the moon, and then we melt into the fog and it's like there never was a *rusalka*. Why is that?

OLD RUSALKA Why is there any why about it? The hour comes for each of us, and then we melt. We have an easy, long life: we live for three hundred, sometimes even four hundred years.

YOUNG RUSALKA And afterwards we melt into the fog?

OLD RUSALKA Yes, into the fog.

YOUNG RUSALKA And there's nothing more?

OLD RUSALKA Nothing. Why do you want more?

YOUNG RUSALKA *(After reflection)* Is it the same for all living creatures, Granny?

OLD RUSALKA *(With conviction)* Yes. *(Silence)* No, wait, I forgot. Not all of them. I did hear from my aunt that it's not the same for all of them. There are humans. I've seen them. And you've seen them, too, at a distance. It's said that *they* don't vanish with the fog. They have an immortal soul.

YOUNG RUSALKA *(Wide-eyed)* They never die?

OLD RUSALKA No, no! They die. And their life is terribly short, they don't last a hundred years. A human body decomposes in the ground, but that doesn't matter, because a human has an immortal soul, and the soul stays alive. I think it's even better and easier for humans after they die. When they're alive, their bodies are dense and heavy and full of blood.

YOUNG RUSALKA But the soul is light like us?

OLD RUSALKA Perhaps even lighter. After all, we die, but the human soul doesn't.

YOUNG RUSALKA *(After a silence, unexpectedly, imploring)* Granny! Dear one! Tell me everything you know about us, about humans, about their souls! You're old, you know, and I was born not long ago. I could melt into the fog like I am now,

and I don't know anything, and I want to know!

OLD RUSALKA *(Astonished)* What a child you are! Why do you want to know? I'll tell you. Give me a chance to think. I heard it a long time ago. *(She stops. The* YOUNG RUSALKA *has turned toward her and is looking her in the face as intently as she looked at the meadow earlier.)* I don't know much, child. I did hear that once, long ago, there were both humans and other living creatures – *rusalki* and such – in the world. Humans with a heavy body, with blood, with a short life, and with death, and we, *rusalki* and the other creatures of water and forest, of meadows and deserts, with a light and immortal body.

YOUNG RUSALKA An immortal body? And humans had an immortal soul?

OLD RUSALKA No, wait, don't confuse me. At that time humans didn't have an immortal soul. And as time went by, humans found out that we alone were immortal, and they worshipped us and humbled themselves before us. But with their short life and their death, their lives were dismal, and they only pretended to be humble and behind our backs they complained and had other thoughts. Then there was born among them a Man whom they called God, and He shed His blood for them and gave them an immortal soul.

YOUNG RUSALKA Blood?

OLD RUSALKA Yes, His blood.

YOUNG RUSALKA He shed it for them? For all of them?

OLD RUSALKA Yes, yes, for all the humans. But from that time we knew we were not immortal, and we began to die. Our lifetime is long, our death is easy, but – we have no souls to give us immortality.

YOUNG RUSALKA And so He – that Man or, as you said, God – brought us death and humans life? Why should we have death because of His blood?

OLD RUSALKA Blood for blood. We have no blood.

YOUNG RUSALKA Granny! Are humans kinder than us? Do they live better?

OLD RUSALKA How should I know! I have heard that they are evil, that they are hostile, envious, and full of hate . . . You don't understand: we don't have any of that. We are good.

YOUNG RUSALKA Then why did the Man bring them life and us death, if we are better than they are?

OLD RUSALKA I have no idea. My granny told me that humans are not just evil and full of hate, they have something else, and that, she said, is why the Man brought them life, but I don't remember what it's called. Now "hate" I remember, but I've forgotten the other word. We don't have that, either. Yes. My memory's gotten bad.

(Silence)

The moon is turning pale. It'll be morning soon. It's time for sleep.

YOUNG RUSALKA (As if waking up) Granny, dearest! Don't you know anything else?

OLD RUSALKA Not that I can think of.

YOUNG RUSALKA And you don't know . . . if it's possible somehow . . . for one of us . . . a rusalka, say . . . to do something to get a human immortal soul, too?

OLD RUSALKA I don't know. What a persistent child you are! It's good to be born a rusalka and live out your life. Why do you want more?

YOUNG RUSALKA Then there's no way at all? It's impossible?

OLD RUSALKA I tell you, I don't know! Wait – I've heard something about a way to do it, but no, I don't remember.

YOUNG RUSALKA So who does remember? Who knows?

OLD RUSALKA If you really want to know, ask the Witch. She lives in the woods, she was human, and I've heard that she sold her soul to someone for a long life. She's five hundred years old already. She knows everything. She crawls here, to our lake, every night, to drink the water. We never see her because she shows up just at dawn when the sky is already pink. That's a frightening time for us, because we don't dare see even the outermost edge of the sun.

YOUNG RUSALKA When the fog is thickest?

OLD RUSALKA Yes, that's right. When I was a bit younger, I was a bold one. I would stay to the very last moment. And I saw the Witch. She's not the sun, she can't do anything bad to us. So if you're not afraid – stay, wait for the Witch. She'll tell you everything. But it's time for me to go back into my water, into my mire, for a rest. My old bones are aching. Over there our folk are already tumbling into the water.

(The rusalki vanish one after another into the water. The moon turns pale and then pink. The fog is livelier and more dense.)

OLD RUSALKA (Getting up heavily) I'm going. Morning is not far off.

YOUNG RUSALKA I'm not afraid, Granny. Perhaps the Witch will come. I'm going to stay.

OLD RUSALKA (Indifferently) She'll come, she'll come. All right then, stay.

(She leaves, making her way through the rushes which bend and crackle. A splash is heard. The YOUNG RUSALKA sits down by the tree, presses close to the trunk, and waits, motionless, with arms clasping her knees. The bell falls silent. Quiet. The sky grows pinker, the fog rises higher. A crooked little old woman, wrapped in rags, creeps soundlessly out of the forest. Her large jaundiced face is turned to the ground. Crawling over to the lake, she lies on the bank and takes a long drink. Not a sound is heard. Finally the old woman rises slowly, sniffs the air, and looks all around. The RUSALKA has also risen and stands, gripping a small branch. The old woman turns toward her and raises her hand to her eyes, shielding them from the pink light of dawn.)

YOUNG RUSALKA (Timidly) Greetings, Granny.

WITCH Greetings. Only I'm not your granny. I'm the Witch.

YOUNG RUSALKA I know, Granny Witch. I'm here . . .

WITCH I see you're here. I see what you are, too, little fish. Why have you stayed so late? The dear little sun will be rising soon. And it's harsh on you, the sun. You don't dare make a mistake.

YOUNG RUSALKA You're late, Granny Witch. And I've been waiting for you.

WITCH Me? Why should you wait for me? Do you need something from me, is that it? Speak quickly, don't mumble. The sun will rise any minute now.

YOUNG RUSALKA (In a rush) I'll be quick, Granny. Just now I heard all kinds of things about us, the rusalki, and about humans . . . I heard that we die – and the fog comes from us, and that's the end of it. But humans, I heard, have an immortal soul, because blood was shed for them. Is that true?

WITCH   That's true. What else?

YOUNG RUSALKA   And so I wanted to ask you – after all, you know – is it possible to make it so that a *rusalka* could have an immortal soul? Tell me, Granny, dear! You know!
(The WITCH *looks at her and suddenly begins to guffaw noiselessly, body quaking. The young rusalka is silent and frightened, but she does not look away.)*

YOUNG RUSALKA   Why are you laughing? Why are you laughing? Is it impossible?
(The WITCH *guffaws.)*

YOUNG RUSALKA   *(Quivering and raising her voice)* So there's no way to do it? It's impossible?

WITCH   It's possible, it's possible! Ooh, you're funny, little fish! It's a long time since I've had a laugh. I've been waiting for a little fish like you for a long time. Why should it be impossible? Wait a second, I have to catch my breath.

YOUNG RUSALKA   *(Joyful and pleading)* Granny! Dearest! That means I can? Teach me how! Afterward I'll do what you want . . .

WITCH   Hold on, hold on. If I say it's possible, it's possible. I'll teach you. And you and I don't need any special knowledge.

YOUNG RUSALKA   You're kind, Granny Witch.

WITCH   What's kindness got to do with it? I'm helping you because I get my fun that way. I help everyone. Little fish like you and humans, whenever I can. Whenever anyone wants something – I provide it right away – there, take it! And I never ask for anything in return: it's my bit of fun, that's enough for me. I will teach you how a *rusalka* can get an immortal soul, since that's what you want. Let's sit down, girl, my legs aren't young any more. The sun will wait.
(They sit down on the bank amid the rushes.)

WITCH   *(Wheezing and wrapping herself up)* It's cold at dawn. The fog is thick. The sun will be bright. *(Silence)* Now then, little fish, you really want an immortal soul?

YOUNG RUSALKA   *(Raising her eyes)* Yes.

WITCH   You're hurt, are you, because . . . He shed his blood for humans, and not for creatures like you?

YOUNG RUSALKA   *(Thinking)* I don't know. . . . I guess I'm hurt.

WITCH   So now listen, girl: I'll teach you how. You have to go to the humans.

YOUNG RUSALKA   *(Startled)* To the humans? But I don't know where to find humans.

WITCH   Listen, I'll tell you. I know. There are humans not far from here. Go through the clearing, and you'll come to a cell, a kind of little wood house, a human dwelling. And close by, on a little hill, there's a chapel; you'll know it by the tall bell-tower. Go there tomorrow night. Not at this time, but earlier, when it's darker. Only make sure the bell isn't tolling. When the bell tolls, it means they are saying their morning prayers and won't be asleep.

YOUNG RUSALKA   Granny, I'm frightened. Are there many of them? And how can I speak to them?

WITCH   If you're frightened – that's your business, don't go. I'm only telling you what to do. There are two humans there: an old one and a young one. At first you won't have to speak to them. You just go into the cell, and make sure that they don't see you, that they're asleep, and nestle up to the one who's closer and warm yourself, and just to make sure he breathes on you, touch him. He will wake up and he won't know what to make of it, he'll start saying words over you, he'll chase you away, maybe he'll start beating you – and don't you do anything, bear it and don't go away. He will breathe on you·and touch you – and you will get a body like humans have, with blood. And then you can see the sun.

YOUNG RUSALKA   *(Loudly)* And I'll have an immortal soul?

WITCH   Come, come now, you're awfully impatient! You won't have an immortal soul. And your blood won't be warm like humans' but cold.

YOUNG RUSALKA   *(Downcast)* Then why do I need it?

WITCH   Because for a human soul you have to have a human body. Without a body that looks human, humans won't let you come near them, and the Man who shed warm blood won't give you a soul.

YOUNG RUSALKA   All right then, and afterward, Granny, when I have a body – what do I do then?

WITCH You have to get the humans to baptize you.

YOUNG RUSALKA What's that, Granny – to baptize?

WITCH To make a kind of sign. Humans will accept you among them, your blood will become warm, and the Man will give you an immortal soul.

YOUNG RUSALKA Humans are kind then? So tomorrow I'll ask them to baptize me.

WITCH Wait a second, silly girl. Kind or not, they won't baptize you. To them you are unclean.

YOUNG RUSALKA (Sadly) Unclean?

WITCH Yes. They don't know much and so they're frightened of lots of things. In the beginning don't say anything to them, don't tell them anything, or else they'll get frightened and won't accept you. But you just go on living with them and warming yourself, and get used to your body. And then one of them will be . . . one of them will be very kind to you and you will be kind to him – that's when you confide in him and ask him to baptize you.

YOUNG RUSALKA I'm kind to everybody.

WITCH But that doesn't count. You need to be especially kind to one in particular.

YOUNG RUSALKA And then he will agree to baptize me?

WITCH I don't know. He might not agree no matter what. Then you won't get an immortal soul.

YOUNG RUSALKA Granny Witch! You darling! How could that be? But if he shouldn't agree – then isn't there any other way?

WITCH Settle down! You even startled a frog. And stop interrupting, because we are almost out of time, we have only the merest minute. I didn't say he wouldn't agree. I only said . . . something might happen. . . . But then there's another way. . . .

YOUNG RUSALKA (Joyfully) Truly? There is? There is?

WITCH Yes, but it's not for you. I know you kind little fishes. Well, for now I'm not going to tell you that method. Try this first. What, are you still frightened?

YOUNG RUSALKA No.

WITCH Apparently you really do want warm blood and a human soul?

YOUNG RUSALKA Yes.

WITCH (Laughs long and noiselessly and finally stops) Very well then. You're very amusing, little fish. Go tomorrow. Remember: warm yourself, warm yourself up near them! They'll start asking where you're from – tell them you've forgotten! They'll start telling you things – listen!

YOUNG RUSALKA You say there are two of them in the cell. Which one should I approach first, the old one or the young one?

WITCH It doesn't make any difference. (Thinking it over) Better the young one, he'll be sleeping more soundly and you'll have better luck inhaling his breath. And he's strict about temptations besides. He'll stand firm. He'll wake up – and he'll beat you good and hard. And that's just what you need! Let's hope he doesn't beat you to death. (She guffaws.)

YOUNG RUSALKA (Considering, seriously) He won't beat me to death. Thank you, Granny Witch.

WITCH Don't thank me, don't thank me! I love my fun. If you need anything, girl, I'm not far away. I gather herbs in these parts. Oh, yes! I almost forgot! If he tries to beat you to death – cross yourself and he'll let up. . . .

YOUNG RUSALKA How do I do that? What is it?

WITCH Also a sign. I can't show you how. But I can tell you. Take three fingers. . . . Not those, these! That's right. Then put them to your brow, then to your breast, then to your right shoulder, and then to the left. What a stupid girl you are! That's it, that's the way. Once more. Good. Don't forget. And now, my dear little fish, you must hurry. The sun's rising right now!

(Birds have set up a clamor. The sky is red. The bell is audible, faster and a little louder than at night. The YOUNG RUSALKA tries to say something more, but the WITCH waves her hand, and the YOUNG RUSALKA leaps into the water and vanishes. That very second the sun rises. The WITCH looks at the circles spreading in the water and guffaws noiselessly, quaking.)

WITCH How she leaped, just like a froggy! What a funny child! Well now, what are my little monks going to say? I always help them. I show them the way. Let them save an immortal soul. That's their business.

(She shuffles into the forest, continuing to laugh and mutter something. The bells keep getting louder.)

The curtain falls softly.

Scene 2

Early morning, foggy, sunless. The forest. A hewed out clearing. A wooden cell on the right. Farther off a corner of the chapel is visible. On the left is a narrow road at the end of which the lake glints faintly. The YOUNG RUSALKA *is lying, curled up in a ball, in a corner between the wall and the open door of the cell. Her face is covered with disheveled, rather short hair.* FATHER PAFNUTY *stands, bending over her. He wears an old monastic cassock and a small skullcap. He has a small, shining, wrinkled face and a gray, sparse, wedge-shaped beard. At a distance is* NIKODIM, *a novice, standing with lowered arms. His face is young, pale, and stony, with sunken cheeks and thick, knitted eyebrows.*

FATHER PAFNUTY She's alive! The little girl's alive, Nikodimushka! You almost killed the child, you know! She's barely breathing. How cold she is. A girl, just a little girl!

(The YOUNG RUSALKA *is silent.)*

FATHER PAFNUTY *(Bending closer and pushing back her hair)* Honestly, you almost killed her. What if we had destroyed a Christian soul! So, Nikodimushka, what did you think you saw? Were you dreaming, was that it?

NIKODIM *(Evenly)* It was a temptation for me.

FATHER PAFNUTY Temptation! What are we, saints, that we should be tempted! You have to merit temptations from the Lord God. Temptations are for real ascetics, not for the likes of us. But you in your pride almost beat a child to death, a little girl who doesn't know better, a living person! Just take a look, she's a splendid girl! She got a bad fright.

NIKODIM *(Taking two steps)* Father Pafnuty, give me your blessing to cover her.

FATHER PAFNUTY Of course. There's an old, short cassock of mine on a nail in the cell. Bring it here.

(NIKODIM exits.)

Don't be afraid, little girl. We won't harm you. Tell me, where do you belong?

(The YOUNG RUSALKA *slowly raises her eyes to him and remains silent.)*

FATHER PAFNUTY What's your name? Are you a Christian?

(NIKODIM returns with the cassock. FATHER PAFNUTY tries clumsily and tenderly to dress the YOUNG RUSALKA. NIKODIM *stays out of it.)*

NIKODIM She's not wearing a cross.

FATHER PAFNUTY So what? She must have lost it. We'll make her a cross.

NIKODIM If she's not a Christian, it's impossible.

(The YOUNG RUSALKA *is watching and listening. The last words apparently remind her of something and, raising her hand, she attempts to make the sign of the cross.)*

FATHER PAFNUTY *(Joyfully)* You see, you see, she's crossing herself, she's a Christian! God's soul. I told you so! And you in your arrogance almost killed her. Sit up, sit up, little girl. Don't be afraid. There now, that's right.

(The YOUNG RUSALKA *hugs* FATHER PAFNUTY *and clings to him.)*

She's snuggling up to me, just like a child. Can she talk or can't she? Maybe she doesn't know how. She must have tried to snuggle up to you the way a child does, and you run on about temptation! Are you mute, little girl? Can you speak?

YOUNG RUSALKA *(Barely audibly)* Yes.

FATHER PAFNUTY *(Cheerfully)* That's a blessing. Tell us, don't be afraid, where did you come from?

YOUNG RUSALKA I . . . don't know.

FATHER PAFNUTY How can it be that you don't know?

YOUNG RUSALKA I don't remember.

FATHER PAFNUTY And you don't remember where you belong?

YOUNG RUSALKA I don't remember.

FATHER PAFNUTY And what's your name?

YOUNG RUSALKA I don't remember.

FATHER PAFNUTY So all you can say is "I don't remember!" You try, you'll remember. What do they call you? Annushka perhaps?

YOUNG RUSALKA Yes.

FATHER PAFNUTY If you're Annushka, that's a blessing. So that's what we'll call you. See if you can remember anything else.

NIKODIM It's all black magic.

FATHER PAFNUTY That's enough of that!

Black magic! This is a child of God. God deprived her of wisdom and set her among the blessed. She makes the sign of the cross, and you say it's black magic. *(To the* YOUNG RUSALKA*)* Annushka, don't be afraid. Let me stroke your head. Isn't that cassock too big for you?

NIKODIM Father Pafnuty, give me your blessing to ring the bell for mass.

FATHER PAFNUTY Hold on, hold on. Do we have any bread left? Bring it, please: she may be hungry. Are you hungry, Annushka?

*(*NIKODIM *disappears silently and returns with the bread. The* YOUNG RUSALKA *takes the bread from* FATHER PAFNUTY'S *hand and eats greedily.)*

NIKODIM She didn't cross herself before she ate.

FATHER PAFNUTY Do you know how to pray to God, Annushka?

YOUNG RUSALKA To who?

FATHER PAFNUTY To God. Don't you know who God is?

YOUNG RUSALKA God? Yes, I know. The one who shed His blood for humans?

FATHER PAFNUTY *(Joyfully)* Do you hear, Nikodimushka? She knows Christ, our true God! She knows that He, Our Little Father, shed his blood for us. Blessed little fool, she doesn't remember her name, but she remembers that. Can you pray to Him, do you know what prayers are?

YOUNG RUSALKA *(Softly)* No. You'll teach me, tell me.

FATHER PAFNUTY Yes, I'll teach you, child. Of course, you must pray to Our Heavenly King. If you're lost, we'll give you bread, we'll teach you a prayer, and then we'll take you home, if you remember where you live.

YOUNG RUSALKA I don't remember! I don't know! I never lived anywhere. I want to live here, with you. You'll teach me a prayer.

NIKODIM We should turn her out into the forest.

FATHER PAFNUTY *(Reproachfully)* You never give up! How can we turn the child out in the forest? Christ said: Suffer the little children to come unto Me, so I should drive a child, and a hungry and cold one besides, out into the forest? Do as you wish, Nikodim, but I won't lift a hand. We should take the child in, warm her up, and teach her. If she hasn't a home, let

her live with us to the glory of the Heavenly King, He who is Protection, Power, and Mercy!

NIKODIM *(Evenly)* Amen!

FATHER PAFNUTY *(Stroking the* YOUNG RUSALKA *on the head)* If you have no refuge, little girl, live here, God bless you.

NIKODIM Give me your blessing, Father Pafnuty, to ring the bell for mass.

FATHER PAFNUTY Wait a minute. *(To the* YOUNG RUSALKA*)* So you don't know your prayers, Annushka? What do you know? Can you do anything? Try and remember.

YOUNG RUSALKA I . . . know songs. I sang lots of songs in the glade. I'll sing for you later.

NIKODIM Instead of prayers – she knows silly games.

FATHER PAFNUTY What of that? Songs are prayers, too. To each his own. To a pure soul everything is pure. Do you think that the lark in the heavens isn't praying to the Creator? And how vibrantly and merrily it breaks into song. All earthly voices are praise to God. Go on, Nikodimushka, the Lord bless you, it's time to ring for the service.

(Without a glance at the YOUNG RUSALKA, NIKODIM *approaches for his blessing and goes off toward the chapel.)*

You truly don't remember your father and mother, Annushka?

YOUNG RUSALKA Father and mother? I don't know. We only have grannies. . . . *(Quickly)* I had a granny.

FATHER PAFNUTY So. And where is she now?

YOUNG RUSALKA I don't know.

FATHER PAFNUTY You poor thing! You've never known the affection of parents.

YOUNG RUSALKA And there were granddaddies, too. . . . Little old ones, like you. Only you're better, kinder! There wasn't anyone as kind as you are! I will stay with you forever. Teach me to pray, Grandfather! And, if you like, I'll teach you my songs.

FATHER PAFNUTY *(Laughing)* What a quick little one you are! We have our own songs, songs of prayer. *(Thinking it over)* Don't be afraid of Nikodim, Annushka. He's given his soul to Christ. His penance is a strict one. He serves out his novitiate and is probably more righteous than his superiors. The Lord in His wisdom reveals Himself to him, he reads holy

287

books, and knows every word of God.
And in my simplicity I praise my God,
the blades of grass rise out of the earth,
and I listen and rejoice in life and think
of the Creator. Perhaps the Lord will not
condemn my simplicity.
(The bell begins to toll. FATHER PAFNUTY
crosses himself. YOUNG RUSALKA *looks at
him and does the same. The bell sounds
even louder, stronger, and more frequently.
Without being aware of it,* FATHER
PAFNUTY *starts to sing in a quavering, soft
old man's voice. At the end, watching him
closely and trying to remember the words,
the* YOUNG RUSALKA *barely audibly begins
to sing with him.)*

We praise You, Creator of earth and
    heavens,
we sing glory to You, the Almighty.
Your mercy, strength, and power
are blessed and will endure through the
    ages;
in You is light, hope, and life,
and Your name will go throughout Your
    land,
we praise You, Creator of earth and
    heaven.

(The bell sounds.)

Curtain

Scene 3

*The same place in the forest near the cell. It is
the hottest time of the afternoon.* FATHER
PAFNUTY *is sitting by the wall of the cell,
using a heap of rushes as a kind of bench,
and, with difficulty, weaves a bast sandal. At
the edge of the clearing,* NIKODIM *stands and,
putting his hand to his eyes, looks attentively
far off toward the lake.*

FATHER PAFNUTY What are you looking
at, Nikodim? What is there to see? Is
someone coming, perhaps?
NIKODIM *(After a silence)* No, nobody. Only
she seems to be bathing again.
FATHER PAFNUTY Annushka? So let her
bathe, Christ bless her. The weather is
hot. . . .
NIKODIM Whenever you look in that
direction, there's always something white
on the lake. She's always bathing. She's
always hot. She even bathes after vespers.
Yesterday the stars had already begun to

shine, there was dew on the grass, and
she – went to the lake. She's always hot.
FATHER PAFNUTY There's no sin in God's
water! Let the child bathe in God's grace.
You're full of strange ideas, Nikodim. I
can't make out what you're thinking, but
only that something's bothering you. Let
it go, isn't it the devil confounding you?
It's from our heart that the invisible ones
send us temptation.
NIKODIM *(He is silent, looks, and then lowers
his arm and takes two steps toward*
PAFNUTY.*)* No, Father. . . . And yesterday I
was thinking about you and me. We lived
in the village. . . . People came to you.
You helped them and prayed with them.
And the Lord loved you for your saintly
life and gave you the power to heal those
who suffer. . . .
FATHER PAFNUTY *(Frightened, waving his
hands)* What are you saying! Stop! That's a
sin! What kind of saint am I? I'm a great
sinner.
NIKODIM *(Not listening)* And you chose the
strictest penance. You chose to withdraw
from people and renounce your worldly
self so your prayer would rise more
directly to the Lord. And I, too, was
seized by a desire for that same penance.
You didn't reject me and I became a
novice. We lived in peace and quiet and
we worked. And now people have found
us, and there isn't the same sweetness
and austerity in our penance. What do
you think about that, Father?
FATHER PAFNUTY *(Setting down the sandal)*
Are you talking about Annushka? *(After a
silence)* Here's what I would say to you,
Nikodimushka. Forgive me, I'm telling
you in all simplicity. You say that I chose
a penance and withdrew to the cell. I
don't know, Nikodimushka. I didn't think
about that, but I started dreading being
with people, I dreaded living with them.
What kind of saint am I? How do I dare
to heal people? It's high time for me to
atone for my sins with prayer. Here my
heart is merry, and there's no work too
hard for me, but it's all very easy. Maybe
you know better, maybe it's a sin, but it's
only that my heart loves the dear sun and
the water and every blade of grass and
the Lord God Who created it all, to Him
and Him alone praise forever and ever.
NIKODIM Amen. Father Pafnuty, people
are also His creation. And if you

renounce people for anything but the most onerous labors. . . .

FATHER PAFNUTY I haven't renounced people, Nikodimushka. I tell you – I dread being around them! It's dreadful, there are so many of them, and they have gone away from God, and I, an unworthy one, am too weak to teach and admonish them. Christ brought a sword to earth, and I am only his slave, and no teacher. My heart is full of anguish. Perhaps I went away into the wilderness not from strength but from my weakness. The Lord created my soul without cunning, and he will not condemn my weakness.

NIKODIM I took the novitiate on myself not out of love but out of zeal.

FATHER PAFNUTY I know, Nikodimushka, I know. Your penance is strict. Maybe you are much worthier than I. The Lord revealed His wisdom to you. Every word of God is familiar to you from books. You don't spare yourself in the Lord's work. Yes, from you much is asked, because much has been given. Be strict in your penance, Nikodimushka.

NIKODIM Once we choose to be alone with God – we have to avoid all human seducements. And another seducement came to us – and you took it in.

FATHER PAFNUTY You're talking about Annushka again? Is she really a person? She is God's child. She lives like a blade of grass, rejoicing in the stars and the water. Can you really be frightened of her? She's not a person at all.

NIKODIM Maybe she's not human.

FATHER PAFNUTY What has she done to you? Why do you persecute the child? No, you're not thinking clearly, Nikodim. I am a great sinner before the Lord, but the child has a pure soul. I won't let you harm her. How can I drive her out in the name of God? You know yourself, it's said: I will have mercy and not sacrifice.

NIKODIM It's also said: He that does not leave his mother and his father and his home and follow Me – he is not worthy of Me.

FATHER PAFNUTY (Mournfully) The books of wisdom are open wider for you than for me. But just the same don't you hurt Annushka. Leave her alone. . . .

NIKODIM Give me your blessing, Father Pafnuty, to draw water from the well.

(At that moment the YOUNG RUSALKA runs on, merry, with wet hair down to her shoulders. She is in the same old cassock, and there are water grasses and flowers in her hair. She holds a wreath plaited out of yellow globeflowers. Not noticing NIKODIM, she rushes directly over to FATHER PAFNUTY.)

YOUNG RUSALKA Grandfather! My dear kind grandfather! You're weaving sandals? I was at the lake. And just look, Grandfather, I brought. . . . (Suddenly she sees NIKODIM and stops, not daring to continue.)

FATHER PAFNUTY (Hastily) Go for water, Nikodimushka. The bucket's at the well. In the name of the Father and Son and Holy Spirit!

NIKODIM Amen. (He approaches to be blessed and leaves.)

FATHER PAFNUTY (Affectionately) Well now, Annushka? What are you thinking about?

YOUNG RUSALKA (Looking after NIKODIM, softly) I'm afraid of him, Grandfather.

FATHER PAFNUTY That enough now, what is there to be afraid of? He wouldn't do evil to anyone. You and I are not wise enough to understand God's word, but he does. To us it is not given, but it is to him.

YOUNG RUSALKA (Thoughtfully) I don't know about that, Grandfather. It's just that his eyes are like two wax candles, like the ones you have in the chapel, they hardly give any light. But your dear eyes, Grandfather, are like the dear little stars at night. I'm not afraid of you, but I am afraid of him.

FATHER PAFNUTY You're afraid of God.

YOUNG RUSALKA I'm not afraid of God either. You yourself have said so many times that God is kind, kinder than any humans. If He is even kinder than you – why should we be afraid of him? (She sits down next to FATHER PAFNUTY and begins sorting the flowers. Then suddenly she jumps up with the wreath of yellow globeflowers in her hands.)

YOUNG RUSALKA Grandfather! I forgot! This is what I wove for you at the lake. Look, isn't it pretty?

FATHER PAFNUTY Oh, yes, very pretty. It's beautiful. God's blossoms.

YOUNG RUSALKA Try it on! Let me put it on you.

FATHER PAFNUTY (Laughs) What are you

up to, you little rascal? A wreath on my skullcap!

YOUNG RUSALKA   You said yourself – God's flowers. Look how pretty they are! When you wear flowers, you're all mine! And I can see the skullcap, too. All around the cap, around the rim, globeflowers from the lake. Can you smell them?

FATHER PAFNUTY   They smell of water and mire. Never mind, it's a nice smell.

YOUNG RUSALKA   And now I'll sing you a song. Shall I? The water and the grasses made me want to sing. . . .

(She gets up and stands before him.)

Here's a song, Grandfather. I've never sung it for you before. And you sing along with me. . . .

(She sings, at first softly and then steadily louder, making slow, flowing movements, like a rusalka in a round dance.)

The water sways in the rushes.
In the sky greenish stars have begun to
   blaze.
The moon rises over the forest.
Look, little sisters, the stars are burning
   out!
The fog twists and twines like a living
   thing. . . .
The fog – is our water-born soul.
   It starts to dissolve and, melting,
   vanishes. . . .
The fog is our water-born life and death.
   On this night we are all alive and joyful,
   our merriment is like the moonlight.
Come, let us call to one another,
let's all give voice for one another!
   We, of the lake, the river, the forest,
   the valleys, the deserts,
   underground, and on the earth,
   great and small,
   shaggy and naked,
let's make ourselves known to one
   another!
   O-ye! O-ye!
Answer, brothers! Answer, sisters!

(Toward the end of the song we hear
NIKODIM *singing as he comes back with the buckets. At first* FATHER PAFNUTY *and the* YOUNG RUSALKA *do not hear him.)*

NIKODIM   *(Offstage)*

To our one and only Lord,
righteous and stern,
   eternal praise and glory!
Blessed is His grace that tests us,

blessed is His right hand that punishes us,
Your slaves serve You, Heavenly King,
they sing praise and glory to You.
To the Father – Who sent his Son to
   death,
to the Son – Who created ill will and
   division,
to the Spirit – Who comes down to the
   foolish –
      praise forever and ever.

(The YOUNG RUSALKA *falls silent and listens.)*

YOUNG RUSALKA   *(Timidly)* Is he singing about that God you're always telling me about?

NIKODIM   *(Closer)*

To You who bring not peace but a sword,
to You who conquer death with blood,
in the power and glory to come,
to you, Christ and our God,
praise from now and until eternity!

YOUNG RUSALKA   He conquered death with blood, Grandfather? Tell me again about Him and how He gave humans an immortal soul. Grandfather!

*(*NIKODIM *enters with full buckets. His eyes are lowered, but at the door to the cell, he raises them, looks at* FATHER PAFNUTY, *and stops.)*

FATHER PAFNUTY   What's wrong, Nikodimushka?

NIKODIM   Flowers. . . .

FATHER PAFNUTY   *(With a slightly trembling hand he takes off the wreath and smiles.)* It's just that she . . . the little rascal . . . decorated me. God's blossoms. She was singing songs for me the way a child would. And she decorated me.

*(*NIKODIM *looks in silence at the* YOUNG RUSALKA. *She presses close to the old man and hides her face on his shoulder.)*

NIKODIM   I heard the songs. I wasn't far off.

FATHER PAFNUTY   You heard? Well, that's a blessing. What's wrong, Annushka? What are you hiding from? That's enough, sit down. What I have to tell you. . . . And you, Nikodim, go with God about your business.

*(*NIKODIM *exits.* FATHER PAFNUTY *strokes the* YOUNG RUSALKA's *head. She straightens up a little and sits at the old man's feet.)*

FATHER PAFNUTY   *(After a silence)* Well, then. Don't be afraid, little girl. There's no sin in your singing. You're a foolish child. Whatever you can do – that's the way you praise God. *(After a silence)* It's just that those songs of yours, as far as I heard, are all somehow . . . for nighttime.

YOUNG RUSALKA *(Mournfully)* Yes, my songs are all for nighttime.

FATHER PAFNUTY But you're also learning your prayers. We'll start singing our prayers together. God loves those like you.

YOUNG RUSALKA *(Astonished)* Loves? What does that mean, Grandfather?

FATHER PAFNUTY What does that mean? Christ so loved the people that He shed His blood for them, in order to save their souls.

YOUNG RUSALKA I know about the blood, Grandfather, and you've told me many things about Christ; but I don't seem to have heard that word, and I don't understand it.

FATHER PAFNUTY *(Laughing)* You don't understand love! My foolish little blade of grass! Now then, to understand why Christ shed His blood for you is to understand love.

YOUNG RUSALKA *(Sadly and seriously)* He didn't shed His blood for me, Grandfather.

FATHER PAFNUTY What? What are you saying, you foolish girl? That is a great sin. Why didn't He shed it for you?

YOUNG RUSALKA *(Looking aside)* He shed blood only for blood.

FATHER PAFNUTY I don't understand you. Let's sing a prayer together, that'll be better.

YOUNG RUSALKA *(Decisively)* No, Grandfather! First you must tell me: if I weren't baptized, I wouldn't have an immortal soul?

FATHER PAFNUTY How can that be? Babies who die right after they're born? They fly up as angels to God's throne. A person is born with an immortal soul. By His death, Christ conquered human death.

YOUNG RUSALKA *(As if to herself)* Human! *(To* FATHER PAFNUTY*)* But all the same you would baptize me wouldn't you, Grandfather, if you knew that I wasn't a Christian?

FATHER PAFNUTY But you have been baptized. You make the sign of the cross, your name is Christian.

(The YOUNG RUSALKA *weeps.)*

FATHER PAFNUTY *(Alarmed)* What are you saying, Annushka? Eh? What's wrong,

child? As long as you've lived with us, you've seemed sad and yet I've never seen you shed a single tear. Why is that?

YOUNG RUSALKA *(Through tears)* Grandfather, I don't know why it is myself. Don't give up on me. Talk to me.

FATHER PAFNUTY *(Clumsily trying to wipe her eyes with his wide sleeve)* Now, now. Enough of that. Give up on you, child? I pity you so much, it's like you're my own kin. It just seems like a sin because we're hermits. Nikodim says that we have to renounce everything worldly. But I can't conquer my joy. And you, child, have made your way into my heart, my God-given little daughter! You have no human wiles, I'm not afraid with you. Don't cry, child. Tell me, where do you hurt? I'm ready to give up my soul for you.

YOUNG RUSALKA *(Suddenly hugging him impetuously)* Soul? A soul for me? Is that what you said, Grandfather?

FATHER PAFNUTY *(Smiling irresolutely)* And what do you need my soul for? You have one of your own.

YOUNG RUSALKA *(Softly)* I didn't understand you, Grandfather. I wasn't asking for your soul. I thought, now that you've been so kind to me, especially in the face of everything, I thought you would agree to give me a soul. Because I have no soul, Grandfather.

FATHER PAFNUTY No soul? Heavenly powers be with us! What's wrong, Annushka? What's wrong, dear one?

YOUNG RUSALKA I have no soul! None, don't you understand? The Man, Christ, God – came only for humans, but He didn't come for us. He forgot us! Or rather, He didn't forget because His death brought death to us! We were immortal, but as soon as His blood fell on us, we began to die. As if it burned us out! *(*FATHER PAFNUTY *looks at her in horror and crosses himself.)*

YOUNG RUSALKA *(Continuing)* Why are you afraid of me? Don't be afraid. You have an immortal soul, and I don't. Maybe I, too, just like you, would give my soul for you, because you're so dear to me, so dear that I have no word for it. . . . But I have no soul, and I can't give it up for anyone or anything. I don't have either an earthly or a heavenly father.

FATHER PAFNUTY I'm not afraid of you,

child. As I said, so it shall be. You have made your way into my heart. Tell your Father everything you think and know.

YOUNG RUSALKA Yes, I'll tell you. I must tell you. Just listen.

(NIKODIM *enters and stops by the tree. Neither the* YOUNG RUSALKA *nor* FATHER PAFNUTY *notice him.*)

The blood – burned out my soul, but it didn't burn out my desire. I was born there (*Indicating the distance beyond the cutting*), on the lake and I came out of the water and the mire. There are many of us, living creatures, dying our deaths, without blood. Humans despise us and call us unclean. We melt into the fog, you know, and that's the end of everything. Humans think the Lord despised them – how can we not despise them too? But just tell me, if God wanted to kill us, why did He leave us with a desire for an immortal soul? And so strong a desire, such a will for it, that we can't resist?

FATHER PAFNUTY (*Softly*) You can't? Then perhaps that is *His* will? Perhaps it's not your will, but His? Perhaps He is calling you to come meet Him? How could He, the Blessed One, arrange for there to be no response to His will? If it is His will for you to desire an immortal soul, it means that He wants to give it to you. Pray to Him, child.

YOUNG RUSALKA (*Joyfully*) Grandfather! That's what I thought! You told me about Him, and since then that's what I've always thought. You taught me to pray. I came to you from there, from the lake, so you could teach me to pray. But I was told – and it's true – that I won't have an immortal soul until a human – someone like you – makes the sign over me. As soon as he does – I will have warm blood, like his, and it will give me an immortal soul.

FATHER PAFNUTY (*Severely and seriously*) What sign are you talking about?

YOUNG RUSALKA Baptize me . . . Grandfather.

(NIKODIM *takes several steps forward.*)

NIKODIM The Lord is righteous and stern. His ways are inscrutable.

(*The* YOUNG RUSALKA *dodges away in horror.*)

FATHER PAFNUTY (*Dismayed*) Were you here, Nikodimushka? Did you hear what the foolish child was saying? Perhaps she

dreamed it. That must be it. Your deeds are miraculous, O Lord. But it's impossible to believe everything she said. She doesn't know what she's saying.

NIKODIM Father Pafnuty, everything she says about herself is the truth. It was revealed to me long ago. Don't you believe it?

FATHER PAFNUTY (*Making an effort*) Why not? If it's true, isn't our path clear? How can we not do the will of the One who sent it to her and to us?

NIKODIM What are you saying, Father? Who would dare to receive one rejected by the Lord? Do you think He didn't know what He was doing when he brought life to people and sent the unclean creatures into the darkness? How can we transgress heavenly laws? Would you dare to christen a dog? And a dog is purer than Satan's breed, which has been marked for death by the Lord Himself. Do you know what the sacred books say about that?

FATHER PAFNUTY I don't know, Nikodimushka. I don't know books. I don't have the wisdom to understand the sacred books. It seems to me that you just can't damn a soul that is begging to be born for God. You must save it.

NIKODIM It is said in the books of God's wisdom that he who transgresses the law will perish. And if you blaspheme over the sacrament of baptism – *your* soul will die its death. There is no forgiveness for one who transgresses the law.

YOUNG RUSALKA (*In despair*) Grandfather! What is he saying? You will destroy your soul? You won't have a soul? Grandfather, my dear sweet one. . . .

(*She wants to throw herself on him, but* NIKODIM *raises his hand and stops her.*)

NIKODIM In the Name of the One Heavenly King, who died for us on the cross and was resurrected on the third day – I adjure you, creature of Satan – go away into your own place. For you are unworthy of the Lord in body and soul. . . . It is not for us, His slaves, to judge and correct His deeds.

FATHER PAFNUTY (*Getting up*) Brother Nikodim! I have not released you from your vow of obedience, but you have willfully taken it on yourself. Your zeal is great, the books of wisdom are open to you. But why do you care so much about my soul? Am I not free to think about it myself? Free to lose it if I deem it just? I don't remember all of God's words, but I do remember these: whomsoever seeks to save his soul will lose it. Leave us now, brother. Go. In the name of the Father and the Son and the Holy Spirit.

NIKODIM *(After a silence, with an effort)* Amen.

(He exits slowly, never taking his eyes off the trembling YOUNG RUSALKA. FATHER PAFNUTY *watches him go and then, saddened, sits down on a rock and meditates.)*

YOUNG RUSALKA *(Simply)* Grandfather, don't be afraid of me. Just tell me, is it true?

FATHER PAFNUTY What, my dear?

YOUNG RUSALKA That God will take away your soul if you save me? He, Nikodim, said just now. . . .

FATHER PAFNUTY I don't know. Nikodim knows, the word of God has been revealed to him, he understands the scripture. And I judge by my simple understanding. It isn't given to me to read books. Maybe his is the truth.

YOUNG RUSALKA You believe it? Well, that means it's true.

FATHER PAFNUTY Maybe I will lose my soul.

YOUNG RUSALKA No, Grandfather. If that's true, it's best that I go. Where he told me – I'll go there.

FATHER PAFNUTY *(With a start)* Where, you silly girl?

YOUNG RUSALKA *(Waving her hand to the right)* There, into the lake. You musn't baptize me. You mustn't lose your soul.

FATHER PAFNUTY *(Distinctly)* Listen to me, child. Here is what I have to say to you in all my simplicity. I don't know where the truth is; I don't know, whether I will lose my soul – that's His holy will! But I just can't let you go. I pity you so much – that I don't have any more strength. And don't go against me, child. I cannot not give up my soul, if God takes it. I feel such sorrow for you. I am going to baptize you, child.

(YOUNG RUSALKA tries to say something, but weeps.)

FATHER PAFNUTY *(Continuing)* I told you about Christ, I taught you to pray to Him, it is not for me to chase you away from Him.

(The bell tolls. The YOUNG RUSALKA *flinches.)*

Now what's wrong? That's Nikodim ringing for vespers. It's time. Don't go into the chapel now, child, stay here. You can sit there in the cell. And afterwards, when the service is over, make your way with God to the chapel. Be careful not to be late. I'll wait for you. After vespers I will baptize you.

(He embraces and kisses her.)

There's no need to cry, daughter. We are going to rejoice. Let His sacred will be done. That's the way. Say "Amen."

YOUNG RUSALKA *(Barely audible)* Amen.

(She kneels and kisses his hand, weeping. When FATHER PAFNUTY *leaves, she falls prone on the ground. Her hair covers her face. The bell sounds rhythmically and intermittently. It grows dark. A young moon, still pink, is visible among the trees. The* WITCH, *wrapped up in rags, her long yellow face twisted in a grimace, comes through the clearing. In her arms she has a calico sack into which she puts the herbs that she occasionally bends down to pick. She comes closer to the prone rusalka, stops over her, and laughs soundlessly, shaking.)*

WITCH What fun I'm having! The fire is burning nicely, with smoke and crackling! *(Louder)* Greetings, little fish! Do you recognize me?

YOUNG RUSALKA *(Raising herself up and pushing back her hair, alarmed)* Who's there? Is vespers over? Is that you, Grandfather?

WITCH *(Laughing)* Not Grandfather but Granny Witch! You didn't get it quite right. What do you need Grandfather for? It's not time for the baptism yet. Nikodim hasn't rung the bell yet.

YOUNG RUSALKA *(Sits up and glances around)* Ah, it's you, Granny Witch. I didn't know it was you. It's gotten dark already. And I'm not going to be baptized. Vespers isn't over yet. I have time.

WITCH Time for what?

YOUNG RUSALKA To go away.

WITCH Where do you think you're going, girl?

YOUNG RUSALKA Into the lake.

WITCH You'll probably drown in the lake now. You're not the same, little fish. Your blood may not be warm, but your body is solid. You got it from the humans. Beware of that lake!

YOUNG RUSALKA But I don't care!

WITCH *(Laughs)* You're being naughty, but you can't fool me! Have you really decided that you don't want that immortal soul any more? Has someone told you for sure that your grandfather will lose his soul if he baptizes you? That, my friend, you can never know for sure. So you've stopped wanting that soul?

YOUNG RUSALKA *(In despair)* Why are you tormenting me? What do you get out of it? I don't want a soul, I can't, if I'm not sure he won't lose his soul, if there's even a chance he might lose it! Why didn't you tell me before?

WITCH Because if I had told you: be careful, the human who agrees to baptize you might lose his soul for you . . . you would have said to me: So what? That means he's kind! And now. . . . You're a silly goose! Do you think I don't see how tormented you are? I came to help you, and you scold me.

YOUNG RUSALKA *(Distrustfully)* Help? How can you help me?

WITCH Just see how proud you've gotten! You've learned about the Man from humans, so now you don't want to believe me.

YOUNG RUSALKA Well, hurry up if you have something to tell me.

WITCH Don't give yourself airs, girl. If it wasn't for my fun, I would leave you here half-way. If you bully me, I really will leave.

YOUNG RUSALKA Just say it, Granny Witch.

WITCH I see it, I see it all. He has agreed to baptize you. . . . And you would rather go back into the lake. But evidently you need an immortal soul even more now. . . .

YOUNG RUSALKA Why do you keep tormenting me in vain?

WITCH Well then, I'll stop, I'll stop. Remember, girl, I said that if the old man doesn't agree to baptize you – there's another method? You can get an immortal soul even without baptism.

YOUNG RUSALKA And Grandfather won't lose his soul?

WITCH Not at all! He'll even get a halo from Him, from . . . that Man. That's what all the humans will say.

YOUNG RUSALKA *(Clasping her hands)* Granny! Benefactor! Teach me! Now I'm not afraid. I'm ready for anything.

WITCH *(Laughs)* I see you've changed a lot, little fish. Only take care that you don't praise me too soon. Perhaps you'll be afraid. I saved that method for you. I have it here in my sack. Wait a minute, I almost forgot. This method isn't suitable for every occasion. Tell me first, do you truly love that old man?

YOUNG RUSALKA What . . . do I love?

WITCH Yes, the way humans love. They love their children, their fathers, mothers, brothers . . . and each other at times.

YOUNG RUSALKA But I don't even understand the word, Granny.

WITCH *(Astonished)* You mean the old man didn't explain it to you?

YOUNG RUSALKA No, he said the word. Christ, he said, loved humans. . . . I didn't understand.

WITCH Now now, don't you name that . . . that Man to me. What a stupid old fellow, not to explain a word like that. Now I'll have to have to explain it to you. Listen. Love – that's when someone becomes dearer to you than you are to yourself. When you look at him – you're joyful, and when he's fine and merry – you're fine and merry, too.

YOUNG RUSALKA *(Listening greedily)* Yes, yes!

WITCH *(Continuing)* And when you love someone, you don't begrudge him anything, you would take what is yours and give it to him. If something hurts him – the pain is greater for you than for him. And if death comes for him – you will accept death in order to save him.

YOUNG RUSALKA Granny! Dear one! Thank you! I understand it all. I know everything, that's it exactly. It was just the word I didn't know. And moreover, Granny . . . *(Softly and distinctly)* – moreover, when I love someone and hear that He wants me, that He is calling me . . . I cannot not go to Him!

WITCH *(Stopping short)* But. . . . There you are again . . . going on about that Man. I was talking to you about human love. So, now that you know, tell me, do you love the old man? Because if you don't love him – the way I told you, so that if a speck of dust landed on him, it would cause you pain – then that method won't work.

YOUNG RUSALKA I don't love Grandfather? You know I do, Granny Witch, so why do you ask! After all, I'm going back into the lake because if I don't his soul will die. I keep wanting to have a name to call him; I find comfort and peace when I sit and listen to him, but the only thing is, I don't know what to call him, and that's painful. I am all his, as if I had been born to him, and we have the same afflictions and the same blessings. If it happens that my affliction is a blessing for him – won't I be blessed if I take that affliction on myself?

WITCH   That's enough. You're full of happiness. I opened the dam for you. Phooh, you've really made yourself at home with those humans and come to love them. That's your affair. Here is the method, little girl.

(Slowly she pulls a knife with a very long, thin blade out of the sack. The steel blade is supple and casts a bright, reddish reflection.)

YOUNG RUSALKA   What's that?

WITCH   A knife. A splendid knife. It's simply astonishing. Take it now, and after vespers go to the chapel. When does the old man want to baptize you – after vespers? That means he'll be waiting for you on the porch. He's stubborn too. You won't change his mind. He said he wants to baptize you and he's going to do it without thinking twice. And who knows – maybe he will lose his soul because of you.

YOUNG RUSALKA   But I said that I won't let him baptize me! That's how it is, Granny. I don't understand. . . .

WITCH   Don't interrupt. Listen. Go up to your old man – don't give him a chance to speak, and strike him immediately with this knife. You have such strong hands. Strike him so that the knife goes in good and deep and when his blood spurts on you, everything about you will change all at once, you'll become warm, like humans, and you'll get a soul. Well, do you understand? What are you looking at? How slow-witted you are!

YOUNG RUSALKA   *(Slowly)* That's . . . so I . . . should kill Grandfather?

WITCH   Of course. Make sure his blood, shed by your hand, touches you. After all, you can't kill his soul with a knife. His soul will become even lighter. Perhaps yours will be heavy. Humans say that . . . the Man doesn't forgive anyone who sheds blood. He will torment your

soul as punishment. That's what humans say.

YOUNG RUSALKA   No . . . that can't be right. Why would He torment me? After all, His blood was shed for the sake of humans. . . . . But what if human blood is shed – for Him?

WITCH   Well, I don't know anything about that. Humans say it. I told you – that's not my business. Choose as you wish. Be baptized or else go back into the lake, without a soul. You know best.

YOUNG RUSALKA   *(Looking off to the side)* Very well, then. . . . But just. . . . Granny! Have pity on me! *(She is almost shouting.)* How can I kill him, when his pain hurts me more than my own? How can I bear such torment? After all, I love him; I feel like I was born of him, like I live inside him, like his blood is my blood! On no, that's not it! I don't have the words I need to express that kind of pain! *(She throws down the knife; it rings softly and harmoniously.)* No, it's better to go into the lake. *(After a moment of silence)* It's become easier now.

WITCH   *(With a soft laugh)* I know it's easier, little fish. It's so much easier in the lake. I told you so, you know, about the knife. I know what a labor this is; not one of the humans, nor any other creature either, could take it on themselves. Creatures like the kind you used to be in the lake couldn't, because they don't know love. Humans know – but they can't do it for the torment. And without love this method won't work.

YOUNG RUSALKA   *(Repeating)* Won't work?

WITCH   No. If you want eternal life – then you have to earn it through unbearable torments. Yes, maybe humans are right: torment is eternal if there's no absolution for blood.

YOUNG RUSALKA   I don't care about that. I don't know. If He wants my immortal soul in order to torment it – that doesn't matter, does it? He wants it.

WITCH   But didn't give you the strength. Because nobody has the strength to carry it out. But there is a method. A just one. Blood for blood. Blood wasn't shed for you, so you have neither blood nor life. If blood is shed – it will burn up your death. But earthly creatures don't have the strength for this.

YOUNG RUSALKA   *(Slowly picks up the knife*

and looks at it. She says softly, almost to herself). He gave me his blessing. . . . He said, I'm going to baptize you, child. And there's no need to cry. We're going to rejoice, he said. . . .

WITCH   Now give me back the knife. I must admit that I only brought it because I wanted to have a look at you. I've seen others like you. Give it to me. If you're going into the lake, it's on my way, too. Your little sisters and grannies can't have come out yet. *(She takes a close look.)* The moon has risen early. *(After a silence)* Or else go to be baptized. The bell hasn't rung for a long time.

YOUNG RUSALKA   *(Not listening, but still holding the knife, she takes several steps across the stage.)* And he said something else in farewell. He said it, and afterward he immediately gave me his blessing. He has such a thin little old hand. . . . What was it he said?

WITCH   *(Guffawing)* You've forgotten! You're really not yourself, girl. The devil knows what you're muttering. Hand over that knife, I tell you.

YOUNG RUSALKA   *(Crying out in joy)* I remember, I remember what he said! "Let His sacred will be done."
(She runs off to the right. The WITCH watches her in astonishment. She stops laughing.)

WITCH   What a feckless girl she is! What's gotten into her? She's going to use that knife somewhere, no joke about it. It's such a nice little knife. I'll wait and see if she comes back. What a treat! Now the old man will be sure to baptize her. If she didn't go back into the lake at once, she's not going. But she was just showing off. *(She sits on a tussock.)* I'll rest a bit and see if she comes back. I'd be sorry to lose that knife. It's a nice little knife, just like new. *(She stops laughing and sighs. Once in a while she wraps her rags tighter. The sky has grown quite dark, but there is light on the earth from the golden new moon, with its fresh shadows. Something white can be glimpsed fleetingly in the distance, over the lake. Something that might be singing or the rustling of leaves is barely audible, borne by the wind.)*

Song (very softly)

Arise now! Arise!
Hasten! Make haste!

Over the lake is the sky.
In the lake is the sky.
Where does the sky above end?
Where does the sky below end?
        Hasten! Make haste!

(The barely audible sounds are overpowered by NIKODIM's voice, also very far off but somewhat clearer, and on the opposite side. NIKODIM almost speaks rather than sings.)

NIKODIM'S VOICE
You are merciful, O Lord,
long-suffering and all merciful,
but the hour of Your wrath will come,
those who do not know You fall before Your face
and Your fury pours out onto them.
You stretch out Your right hand
and destroy earth and sky. . . .

(He falls silent. Immediately singing, like the rustling of leaves, is audible from the lake.)

Where does the sky below end?
Where does the sky above end?

WITCH   *(Wrapping herself up angrily)* There's no peace and quiet anywhere. And that crazy girl isn't coming back. What is she up to? I've started to have second thoughts. Good fun, to be sure! But it's so noisy. Is that an owl's cry? *(Silence)* She's slow about it. Let her disappear then, the crafty girl.
(The WITCH rises. The YOUNG RUSALKA comes out very slowly from the depths of stage right. Her face is peaceful, her arms lowered.)

WITCH   Where's the knife? Give me the knife!
(The YOUNG RUSALKA is silent. The WITCH peers at her and takes a step backward.) You. . . .

YOUNG RUSALKA   *(Peacefully)* I can't talk to you. Go away.

WITCH   I'm going. I'm going. *(Wrapping her rags around her and retreating)* The Man . . . has won.
(She crawls behind a tree and immediately disappears. The YOUNG RUSALKA stands motionlessly, listening. When NIKODIM enters, she turns to face him. NIKODIM comes quickly and stops suddenly, in the right corner of the stage, far from the YOUNG RUSALKA.)

NIKODIM   *(Loudly, in a breaking voice)* You . . . committed the evil deed? You shed the blood?

YOUNG RUSALKA I did.

NIKODIM You killed Father?

YOUNG RUSALKA His soul lives.

NIKODIM The blood of a martyr cries out to the heavens. Be you from now and forever da. . . .
(YOUNG RUSALKA raises her hand, NIKODIM stops.)

YOUNG RUSALKA Now I am like you. It was *not my will* that was done. The blood was shed for me.

NIKODIM The cup of the Lord's patience overflows. Sacred blood. . . .

YOUNG RUSALKA Yes, sacred blood. And that which God shed for you – wasn't that sacred?

NIKODIM There is no forgiveness for your soul. There is no limit to the Lord's wrath. Eternal torments await you.

YOUNG RUSALKA In return for torment will He Whose will I carried out give me eternal torments? Because for His sake I shed blood that was dearer to me than my own? He knows – dearer than His own! Where is the person who would fear torment after my torments? I fear nothing. I went to the One Who called me, Who set me on the most difficult of paths – and He came to meet me.

NIKODIM *(Turning away and covering his face, impassively)* My hand won't touch you. But tomorrow. . . .

YOUNG RUSALKA *(Joyfully)* Do you hear the bell? No? But I hear it. There's nobody to ring it. It's ringing by itself.
(The bell tolls weakly. The sound merges with the far-off singing on the lake, so far away that the words are not audible.)

NIKODIM Tomorrow people will find out about the saint's death, and they will come here. Blood cries out for revenge. The people will kill you. Torments await you – torments of your body and your soul.

YOUNG RUSALKA *(Looking straight at him, distinctly)* It's all the same to me.

Curtain

Notes

1 According to Simone de Beauvoir, "Otherness is a fundamental category of human thought," which is "as primordial as consciousness itself." "Otherness" is the expression of a duality – "that of the Self and the Other." For de Beauvoir, this duality characterizes the relationship of men to women: "She is defined and differentiated with reference to man and not he with reference to her; she is the incidental, the inessential as opposed to the essential. He is the subject, he is the Absolute – she is the Other." See Simone de Beauvoir (1974) *The Second Sex*, New York: Vintage Books, xix.

2 I am using "marginality" as it was defined by Sandra Gilbert and Susan Gubar in *No Man's Land*, New Haven: Yale University Press, 102. It is a place – or perhaps a consciousness – "outside culture, beyond the limits and limitations of the cities where men make history, one of those magical shores that mark the margin where nature and culture intersect."

3 In her aversion to feminism, Gippius resembles Rachilde. "Bourgeois feminism" in Russia was based on British and American models. The Russian movement, which was held in check by the autocracy, was much weaker than its western counterparts. Because the scope of its activity was confined largely to education reform and philanthropy, many *kursistki* and other women of the intelligentsia scorned the Russian feminist movement. For more information on Russian feminism, see Linda Edmondson (1984) *Feminism in Russia, 1900–1917*, Stanford, CA: Stanford University Press; Richard Stites (1978) *The Women's Liberation Movement in Russia: Feminism, Nihilism, and Bolshevism, 1860–1930*, Princeton: Princeton University Press; Barbara Alpern Engel (1983) *Mothers and Daughters: Women of the Intelligentsia in Nineteenth Century Russia*, Cambridge: Cambridge University Press.

Bibliography

Selected primary sources

Gippius, Z. (rpt. 1991) *Zhivye litsa*, Leningrad: Iskusstvo.

—— (rpt. 1972) *P'esy*, Munich: Wilhelm Fink Verlag.

—— (n.d.) *Siniaia kniga: Peterburgskii dnevnik*, Tel Aviv: "Archive."

Bezrodnyi, M. (ed.) (1990) *Zinaida Gippius: P'esy*, Leningrad: Iskusstvo.

Pachmuss, Temira (ed.) (1972) *Intellect and*

Ideas in Action: Selected Correspondence of Zinaida Hippius, Munich: Wilhelm Fink Verlag.

—— (trans. and ed.) (1972) *Selected Works of Zinaida Hippius*, Urbana, IL: Univerity of Illinois Press.

—— (trans. and ed.) (1975) *Between Paris and St. Petersburg: Selected Diaries of Zinaida Hippius*, Urbana, IL: University of Illinois Press.

Selected secondary sources

Heldt, B. (1987) *Terrible Perfection*, Bloomington: Indiana University Press.

Moyle, N. (1987) "Mermaids (*Rusalki*) and Russian Beliefs about Women," in A. L. Crone (ed.) *New Studies in Russian Language and Literature*, Columbus, OH: Slavica Publishers.

Pachmuss, T. (1971) *Zinaida Hippius: An Intellectual Profile*, Carbondale, IL: Southern Illinois University Press.

Rosenthal, C. (1992) "The Silver Age: Highpoint for Women?" in L. Edmondson (ed.) *Women and Society in Russia and the Soviet Union*, Cambridge: Cambridge University Press.

Schuler, C. (1995) "Zinaida Gippius: An Unwitting and Unwilling Feminist," in K. Laughlin and C. Schuler (eds) *Theatre and Feminist Aesthetics*, Cranberry, NJ: Associated University Presses.

Zlobin, V. (1980) *A Difficult Soul: Zinaida Gippius*, Berkeley: University of California Press.

11 Djuna Barnes, 1892–1982

The Dove
USA

Djuna Barnes, about 1920–21. *Reproduced by permission of the Archives and Manuscript Department of the University of Maryland, College Park, Libraries.*

Introduction

by Cheryl J. Plumb

The life and work of Djuna Barnes

In a feature, "The Washington Square Players," for the *Morning Telegraph* the youthful Djuna Barnes wrote:

> We all have our personal and artistic griefs. It is well to see them rendered with as much artificial beauty as possible, since we must inevitably accept the children of our hours of pain, as we must accept the children of our hours of joy – literature and art.
>
> (December 3, 1916)

This passage aptly summarizes the life and art of Djuna Barnes: for Barnes the artificial beauty of language transformed personal and artistic griefs to the joy of artistic production.

In 1912 when the youthful Djuna Barnes and her mother and three brothers came to Brooklyn from the family farm in Huntington, Long Island, they left behind a family in crisis, separated because of legal charges that had been raised about the family's living arrangements. The family included Wald Barnes and Elizabeth Chappell Barnes with four children including Djuna and three brothers. It also included Fanny Faulkner, whom Wald married after Djuna's mother divorced him in 1912, and the two children by Fanny and Wald, and Wald's mother, Zadel Barnes. Barnes's characterization of her childhood is recorded in Emily Coleman's Diary entry, June 16, 1936: "Violence, fights and horror were all she knew in her childhood, no one loving her except her grandmother – whom she passionately loved." Barnes told Coleman that her father "had not the guts to

face his beliefs (polygamy)" and married Fanny because he feared going to prison (Emily Holmes Coleman Papers).

In Brooklyn, Barnes briefly attended the Pratt Institute – her only formal schooling – before leaving in 1913 to earn her living as a newspaper journalist for the Brooklyn *Daily Eagle* and moving in 1914 to the New York *Press*, contributing numerous articles, drawings, and interviews of theater personalities. In 1916 her first newspaper dramas began to appear in the New York *Morning Telegraph*. Between 1916 and 1923, she wrote thirteen plays, more properly sketches, many intended only for newspapers or magazines like *Vanity Fair* or *Shadowland*. A few of the earliest are in Irish dialect. They focus on the artist, or women who are spiritually superior to the poverty of life around them. Others, some carrying the pseudonym Lydia Steptoe, are lightly satiric in tone, mocking social conventions, as well as the "precocious" young lady determined to live outside conventional expectations.

Three of her plays were introduced to the stage by the Provincetown Players in its fourth season: *Three from the Earth* (October 1919), *An Irish Triangle* (January 1920), and *Kurzy of the Sea* (April 1920). Helen Westley, actress, friend, and frequent subject of newspaper interviews, directed the latter two plays. In 1923 *A Book* appeared, Barnes's collection of drawings, short stories, and three plays: *Three from the Earth*, *To the Dogs*, and *The Dove*.

The Dove may have been written for production by the Provincetown, but Barnes's trip to Paris in 1920 on assignment for *McCall's* separated her from an active theater group and audience. However, while still living in New York on 14th Street, she had written *Ann Portuguise*, a play in three acts. Between November 1923 and April 1924 while at 73 Blvd. St. Germain, she wrote another full-length play, *The Biography of Julie Von Bartmann*. Neither play was published. *Ann Portuguise* was produced in Germany in April 1992.

An unknown contemporary reader of the plays, whose report Barnes saved along with the scripts, felt they would confuse audiences, but noted "the author's electric insight into human character," her "passionate commentary," and observed that *Ann Portuguise* "is the product of a mind of genius"; the reader concluded of *The Biography of Julie Von Bartmann* that the author's "vigorous and pungent writing style belongs to a form aside from drama" (Djuna Barnes Papers). Whether these comments influenced Barnes to abandon drama, or whether her journalistic success provided the finances and mobility that she desired after 1923, she devoted herself to fiction, publishing short stories and the novel *Ryder* (1928); *Ladies Almanack* (1928), a good-natured satire of Natalie Barney's literary salon, her lesbian life and friends; a collection of short stories, *A Night Among the Horses*, many of which had appeared in *A Book*; and the novel *Nightwood* (1936).

After her return from Paris in the 1940s, Barnes again turned to drama. *The Antiphon*, a verse play edited by T. S. Eliot and published by Faber & Faber in 1958 as part of *Selected Works*, attracted the attention of Dag Hammarskjöld, who became a co-translator. The last drama that Barnes wrote, it was performed in Stockholm in 1961.

Barnes and the modern theater

The Dove was performed in May 1926 at the Bayes Theater as part of the fourth annual little theater tournament where one-acts from across the United States and two entries from Europe competed for the Belasco Cup. Abroad at the time, Barnes had no role in the play's production. Its director was Samuel A. Elliot, Jr., who acted in a few Provincetown productions; it was produced by Studio Theater, Inc., a group which had won the Belasco Cup in 1925. Reviewers found *The Dove* puzzling: "a crisp little essay into abnormality, filled with Freudian significances and probably was completely incomprehensible to most of the audience" wrote one (*New York Times*, May 7, 1926, 23: 2, 3). The *New York Evening Post* reviewer commented that the "play was acted with a strained intensity that irritated," and characterized the play as a "talk orgy" that was over the "heads of most of the audience" (May 7, 1926). But in a review of *A Book*, a *New York Times* writer observed: "[F]or dramatic conception *The Dove* is worth the best concrete presentation of any theater" (6 January 1924). One comment that Barnes must have appreciated was that of Eugene O'Neill, who wrote her in 1924 that he liked the book. His play *The Dreamy Kid* had appeared on the same bill as Barnes's *Three from the Earth* (31 October 1919).

There is little to document any influence of O'Neill on Barnes (or of her on him); rather, they appear to have a common interest in Strindberg and expressionism, or what O'Neill referred to as "supernaturalism." In a prologue to Strindberg's *The Spook Sonata*, presented by Provincetown on 3 January 1924, O'Neill praised Strindberg as "the most modern of moderns, the greatest interpreter in the theater of the characteristic spiritual conflicts which constitute the drama – the blood – of our lives today." He credited Strindberg with carrying what had been regarded as Naturalism to such a "poignant intensity" that a play like *Dance of Death* must be called "super-naturalism." Both O'Neill and Barnes pursued a strained emotional intensity associated with expressionism. He argued that it is only by using some means of "supernaturalism" that "we can express in the theater what we comprehend intuitively of that self-defeating self-obsession which is the discount we moderns have to pay for the loan of life" (Deutsch and Hanau 1931: 193).

Strindberg's appeal was similarly strong for Barnes. Years after her involvement with Provincetown, in December 1935, she responded to Emily Coleman's inquiry about her thoughts on Ibsen: "His plays annoyed me because they are symbolic (I do not like symbolism) sort of matrimonial symbolism always throwing itself off high mountains or getting wind blown at some fjord." She confessed that her comment was "merely smarty" and added she "much preferred" the first half of *The Dance of Death*. She wrote that she had been instrumental in "getting it on at the Guild" with Helen Westley in the lead (Letter, Emily Holmes Coleman Papers). Barnes's preference for Strindberg over Ibsen suggests that she was not interested in social realism. In a *Theater Guild* article that treated the productive Rachel Crothers dismissively, Barnes concluded that her twenty-fifth play in a "long and methodical" career dealt with "the social problem of the moment, rather than that of the race" (May 1931).

The Dove

Both Barnes and O'Neill point to a desire for theater to speak to the human soul, to explore universal problems of spirit, the "behind-life" rather than representational social situations. Certainly, *The Dove* demonstrates Barnes's awareness of the spiritual conflict and marginality of Vera and Amelia's lives. The play sets in motion conflicting chords: its setting, its reds and pinks and reclining chairs, is feminine, but more like a whorehouse than the home of two virgin sisters. Another disconcerting chord is the presence of guns and swords on the walls and about the room. They suggest patriarchal influence, though the "education" and life of the two sisters mock the Victorian conventions they publicly observe. The "long, low" apartment seems to press in upon them, enclosing an emptiness of which they are aware. The picture of *Deux Courtesans* both symbolizes their desire for a wider life, i.e. to express their sexuality, but at the same time it prevents a wider life. For example, Vera sends Amelia out for butter, "I don't dare to let the grocer call."

The Dove understands their ambivalence: "You have cut yourselves off – just because you're lonely."

The sisters occupy a kind of middle ground: aware of their sexuality and aware of social expectations, they closet themselves. Their conflict is intensified further by the character of their desires, which are lesbian, further marginalizing them as "abnormal." Vera confesses to The Dove that she has imagined herself "beyond the need of the usual home and beyond the reach of the usual lover."

However, in the character of The Dove Barnes presents the possibility of change. The Dove wishes every man "were beyond the reach of his own biography," that is, able to live fully without fear. And in the play she polishes the sword, loads the pistols – actions that connect her with masculine power, and specifically, in polishing the (s)word, she is connected to the power of expression, the power that destroys the picture of the courtesans, a symbol of the objectification of women and of the public image that imprisons. In doing so, The Dove exercises the power to transcend traditional conventions.

Interpreters are divided over just how to characterize the play's meaning and tone. Ann Larabee characterizes the play as the story of three women in love: "In *The Dove*, Barnes exposes and celebrates the violence of latent feminism in a way unimagined by anyone else," concluding that the "destruction of artifacts, including the carefully created artifact of the public self, is a liberating drama of disintegration, providing a new ground for self-creation" (Larabee 1991: 44). Anne B. Dalton reads the play in the biographical context of the Barnes family story. After reviewing personal documents, Dalton has interpreted The Dove's final biting of Amelia "as a sign of Barnes's fury at her grandmother" who, Dalton argues, as have other feminists, sexually abused Barnes (Dalton 1993: 133). Both Larabee and Dalton find Barnes's fury and rage to be central to the play's subtext.

However, is there not also irony and humor in the play? Multiple chords? Are not Vera and Amelia also ladies who aspire to "decadence" and "art" because it is "fashionable"? Who lead vapid lives – "Eating makes one fat, nothing more, and exercising reduces one, nothing more." Is

Amelia's last speech only hysterical? Or bored as well – "The hands too fat to wander"? The Dove's actions and the anticlimactic conclusion interrupt Amelia's hysteria, leaving an audience to grasp the implications of Amelia's final line: what is "obscene" is the public image of female sexuality. James B. Scott, for example, finds the relief decidedly comic (Scott 1976: 59).

Not just rage, but mordant wit pervades the play. For her audience and readers, Barnes offers a feast of meaning.

The Dove*

Published 1923, performed 1926

Djuna Barnes

Characters

AMELIA BURGSON ⎫
⎬ Sisters
VERA BURGSON ⎭

THE DOVE, a young girl living with
the Burgsons

Time
Early morning

Place
The Burgson apartment, a long, low
rambling affair at the top of a house in the
heart of the city.

*The decoration is garish, dealing heavily in
reds and pinks. There is an evident attempt to
make the place look luxuriously sensual. The
furniture is all of the reclining type.*

*The walls are covered with a striped paper
in red and white. Only two pictures are
evident, one of the Madonna and Child, and
one of an early English tandem race.*

*There are firearms everywhere. Many groups
of swords, ancient and modern, are secured to
the walls. A pistol or two lie in chairs, etc.*

*There is only one door, which leads out into
the back hall directly back center.*

*Amelia Burgson is a woman rather over the
normal in height, with large braids of very
yellow hair, done about a long face. She seems
vitally hysterical.*

Vera Burgson is small, thin and dark.

*The Dove is a slight girl barely out of
her teens; she is as delicate as china with
almost dangerously transparent skin. Her nose
is high-bridged and thin, her hands and feet
are also very long and delicate. She has red
hair, very elegantly coiffured. When she moves
[seldom] the slightest line runs between her*

*legs, giving her the expectant waiting air of a
deer.*

At the rising of the curtain THE DOVE,
*gowned in white, is seated on the divan
polishing the blade of an immense sword. Half
reclining to her right lies* VERA *in a thin
yellow morning gown. A French novel has half
fallen from her hand. Her eyes are closed.*

THE DOVE   Yes, I'm hurrying.

VERA   That's best, she will be back soon.

THE DOVE   She is never gone long.

VERA   No, never very long – one would
grow old waiting for the day on which
she would stay an hour – a whole hour.

THE DOVE   Yes, that's true.

VERA   *(Wearily)* She says we live
dangerously; *(Laughs)* why, we can't even
keep the flies out.

THE DOVE   Yes, there are a great many
flies.

VERA   *(After a pause)* Shall I ever have a
lover, do you suppose?

THE DOVE   *(Turning the sword over)* No, I
suppose not.

VERA   Yet Amelia and I have made it our
business to know – everything.

THE DOVE   Yes?

VERA   Yes. We say this little thing in
French and that little thing in Spanish,
and we collect knives and pistols, but we
only shoot our buttons off with the guns
and cut our darning cotton with the
knives, and we'll never, never be perverse
though our entire education has been
about knees and garters and pinches on
hindquarters – elegantly bestowed – and
we keep a few animals – very badly –
hoping to see something first-hand – and
our beds are as full of yellow pages and
French jokes as a bird's nest is full of
feathers – God! *(She stands up abruptly.)*
little one, why do I wear lace at my
elbows?

303

THE DOVE You have pretty arms.

VERA Nonsense! Lace swinging back and forth like that, tickling my arms, well, that's not beauty –

THE DOVE I know.

VERA (Returning to her couch) I sometimes wonder what you do know, you are such a strange happening anyway. Well then, tell me what you think of me and what you think of my sister, you have been here long enough. Why do you stay? Do you love us?

THE DOVE I love something that you have.

VERA What?

THE DOVE Your religious natures.

VERA Good heavens!

THE DOVE You misunderstand me. I call that imagination that is the growth of ignorance, religion.

VERA And why do you like that?

THE DOVE Because it goes farther than knowledge.

VERA You know, sometimes I wish –

THE DOVE Yes?

VERA That you have lived all we pretend we have.

THE DOVE Why?

VERA I don't know, but somehow someone like you should know – everything.

THE DOVE Do I seem so young?

VERA I know, that's what's so odd. (Impatiently) For heaven's sake, will you stop polishing that infernal weapon!

THE DOVE (Quietly) She said to me: "Take all the blood stains off first, then polish it."

VERA There you are; she is quite mad, there's no doubt. Blood stains! Why, she would be afraid to cut her chops with it – and as for the rest of her manifestations – nonsense!

THE DOVE She carries a pistol with her, just to go around the corner for a pound of butter.

VERA It's wicked! She keeps an enormous blunderbuss in the corner of her room, but when I make up her bed, all I find is some Parisienne bathing girl's picture stuck full of pin holes –

THE DOVE I know, she sits beside me for hours making those pin holes in the borders of everything in sight.

VERA (With a strange anger) Why do you stay?

THE DOVE Why should I go?

VERA I should think this house and two such advanced virgins as Amelia and myself would drive you to despair –

THE DOVE No, no, I'm not driven to despair –

VERA What do you find here?

THE DOVE I love Amelia.

VERA Another reason for going away.

THE DOVE Is it?

VERA Yes, it is.

THE DOVE Strange, I don't feel that way about it.

VERA Sometimes I think –

THE DOVE Yes?

VERA That you are the mad one, and that we are just eccentric.

THE DOVE Yet my story is quite simple.

VERA I'm not so certain.

THE DOVE Yet you have heard it.

VERA There's more than one hears.

THE DOVE I was born on a farm –

VERA So you say.

THE DOVE I became very fond of moles – it's so daring of them to be in the darkness underground. And then I like the open fields, too – they say there's nothing like nature for the simple spirit.

VERA Yes, and I've long had my suspicions of nature.

THE DOVE Be that as it may, my brothers were fond of me – in a way, and my father in – a way – then I came to New York –

VERA And took up the painting of china –

THE DOVE Exactly. I was at that for three years, then one day I met you walking through the park, do you remember? You had a parasol, you tipped it back of your head, you looked at me a long time. Then I met Amelia, by the same high fence in the same park, and I bowed to her in an almost military fashion, my heels close together –

VERA And you never did anything wild, insane –

THE DOVE It depends on what you call wild, insane –

VERA (With great excitement) Have you ever taken opium or hasheesh?

THE DOVE (As if answering) There are many kinds of dreams – in one you laugh, in another you weep –

VERA (Wringing her hands) Yes, yes, once I dreamed. A dream in the day, with my eyes wide open. I dreamt I was a Dresden doll and that I had been blown down by the wind and that I broke all to pieces –

that is, my arms and my head broke all to pieces – but that I was surprised to find that my china skirt had become flexible, as if it were made of chiffon and lace.

THE DOVE You see, there are many dreams –

VERA Have you ever felt that your bones were utterly sophisticated but that your flesh was keeping them from expressing themselves?

THE DOVE Or vice versa?

VERA Yes, or vice versa.

THE DOVE There are many kinds of dreams –

VERA You know, I'm afraid of you!

THE DOVE Me?

VERA Yes, you seem so gentle – do we not call you The Dove? And you are so little – so little it's almost immoral, you make me feel as if –

THE DOVE As if?

VERA Well, as if your terrible quality were not one of action, but just the opposite, as if you wanted to prevent nothing.

THE DOVE There are enough people preventing things, aren't there?

VERA Yes – that's why you frighten me.

THE DOVE Because I let everything go on, as far as it can go?

VERA Yes, because you disturb nothing.

THE DOVE I see.

VERA You never meddle –

THE DOVE No, I never meddle.

VERA You don't even observe as other people do, you don't watch. Why, if I were to come to you, wringing my hands saying, "Amelia has shot herself," I don't believe you would stand up.

THE DOVE No, I don't suppose I would, but I would do something for all that.

VERA What?

THE DOVE I should want to be very sure you wrung your hands as much as possible, and that Amelia had gotten all there was to get out of the bullet before she died.

VERA It's all very well, but why don't you do something?

THE DOVE A person who is capable of anything needs no practice.

VERA You are probably maligning yourself, you are a gentle creature, a very girl –

THE DOVE If you were sensitive, you would not say that.

VERA Well, perhaps. *(She laughs a hard laugh.)* What can you expect of a lumber dealer's daughter?

THE DOVE Why are you so restless, Vera?

VERA Because I'm a woman. I leave my life entirely to my imagination and my imagination is terrific. I can't even turn to religion, for the *prie-dieu* inclines me to one thing only – so there you are!

THE DOVE You imagine – many things?

VERA You know well enough – sitting here day after day, giving my mind everything to do, the body nothing –

THE DOVE What do you want, Vera?

VERA Some people would say a lover, but I don't say a lover; some people would say a home, but I don't say a home. You see I have imagined myself beyond the need of the usual home and beyond the reach of the usual lover –

THE DOVE Then?

VERA Perhaps what I really want is a reason for using one of these pistols! *(She laughs and lies back.* THE DOVE, *having risen, goes up behind* VERA *and places her hand on her throat.)*

THE DOVE Now you may use one of those pistols.

VERA *(Startled, but making no attempt to remove* THE DOVE's *hand.)* For such a *little* thing?

THE DOVE *(Dropping her hand, once more taking up her old position, sword on knee)* Ah!

VERA Why do you say that? *(She is evidently agitated.)*

THE DOVE I suppose I shall *always* wait.

VERA What is the matter?

THE DOVE Always, always!

VERA What *is* the matter?

THE DOVE I suppose I'm waiting for the person who will know that anything is a reason for using a pistol, unless one is waiting for the obvious, and the obvious has never been sufficient reason.

VERA It's all hopeless, I am hopeless and Amelia is hopeless, and as for you – *(She makes a gesture.)*

THE DOVE I've never held anything against hopelessness.

VERA Now what do you mean?

THE DOVE It doesn't matter.

VERA *(After a long pause)* I wish you danced.

THE DOVE Perhaps I do.

VERA It might make me happier.

THE DOVE *(Irrelevantly)* Why don't people

get angry at each other, quite suddenly and without reason?

VERA Why should they?

THE DOVE Isn't there something fine and cold and detached about a causeless anger?

VERA I suppose so, it depends –

THE DOVE No, it does not depend, that's exactly it; to have a reason is to cheapen rage. I wish every man were beyond the reach of his own biography.

VERA You are either quite an idiot, or a saint.

THE DOVE I thought we had discussed that.

VERA (Dashed but not showing it) Yes, a saint.

THE DOVE (Continuing) I'm impatient of necessary continuity, I'm too sensitive, perhaps. I want the beautiful thing to be, how can logic have anything to do with it, or probable sequence?

VERA You make my hair stand on end!

THE DOVE Of course, that's logical!

VERA Then how is it you like Amelia? And how do you stand me?

THE DOVE Because you are two splendid dams erected about two little puddles.

VERA You're horrid!

THE DOVE Only horrid!

VERA Yes, I'm really afraid of you.

THE DOVE Afraid?

VERA For instance, when you're out of this room all these weapons might be a lot of butter knives or pop guns, but let you come in –

THE DOVE Well?

VERA It becomes an arsenal.

THE DOVE Yet you call me The Dove.

VERA Amelia called you The Dove, I'd never have thought of it. It's just like Amelia to call the only dangerous thing she ever knew The "Dove."

THE DOVE Yes, there's something in that.

VERA Shall I sing for you?

THE DOVE If you like.

VERA Or shall I show you the album that no one ever sees? (She laughs.) If we had any friends we would have to throw that book in the fire.

THE DOVE And you would have to clear the entry –

VERA True. It's because of that picture of the Venetian courtesans that I send Amelia out for the butter, I don't dare let the grocer call.

THE DOVE You have cut yourselves off – just because you're lonely.

VERA Yes, just because we are lonely.

THE DOVE It's quite wonderful.

VERA It's a wonder the neighbors don't complain of Amelia's playing that way on the violin.

THE DOVE I had not noticed.

VERA No, I presume not, but every one else in the house has. No nice woman slurs as many notes as Amelia does! (At this moment AMELIA enters the outer room. She is wearing a cloak with three shoulder-capes, a large plumed hat, and skirt with many flounces.)

AMELIA (From the entry) You should come and see Carpaccio's Deux Courtisanes Vénitiennes now, the sun is shining right in on the head of the one in the foreground. (She begins to hum an Italian street song.) Well, I have brought a little something and a bottle of wine. The wine is for you, my Dove – and for you, Vera, I've a long green feather. (Pause in which THE DOVE continues to polish the blade of the sword. VERA has picked up her book.)

AMELIA (Advancing into the room, shrugging) It's damp! (Seeing THE DOVE still at work) What a sweet, gentle creature, what a little Dove it is! Ah, God, it's a sin, truly it's a sin that I, a woman with temperament, permit a young girl to stay in the same room with me!

THE DOVE (In a peaceful voice) I've loaded all the pistols –

VERA (With suppressed anger) Shined all the swords, ground all the poniard points! Attack a man now if you dare, he'll think you're playing with him!

AMELIA (In an awful voice) Vera! (She begins pacing.) Disaster! disaster! – wherever I go, disaster! A woman selling fish tried to do me out of a quarter and when I remonstrated with her, she said with a wink: "I, too, have been bitten by the fox!"

THE DOVE If you'll sit down I'll make some tea.

AMELIA No, no, we'll have a little lunch soon, only I never can get the corks out of bottles.

THE DOVE I can.

VERA Rubbish! (She gets up and goes out.)

AMELIA Well, has anything happened since I went out?

THE DOVE No.

AMELIA   No, no it never does. *(She begins to walk about hurriedly.)* Aren't there a great many flies in here?

THE DOVE   Yes, the screens should be put up.

AMELIA   No, no, no; I don't want anything to be shut out. Flies have a right to more than life, they have a right to be curious.

THE DOVE   A bat flew into the room last night.

AMELIA   *(Shuddering)* Some day I shall look like a bat, having beaten my wings about every corner of the world, and never having hung over anything but myself –

THE DOVE   And this morning, early, before you got up, the little seamstress' monkey walked in through the window –

AMELIA   *(Stopping short)* Are we to become infested?

THE DOVE   Yesterday the mail-man offered me some dancing mice, he's raising them.

AMELIA   *(Throwing up her hands)* There! You see! *(Pause)* Why should I wear red heels? Why does my heart beat?

THE DOVE   Red heels are handsome.

AMELIA   Yes, yes, that's what I say. *(She begins to dance.)* Little one, were you ever held in the arms of the one you love?

THE DOVE   Who knows?

AMELIA   If we had not been left an income we might have been in danger – well, let us laugh. *(She takes a few more dance steps.)* Eating makes one fat, nothing more, and exercising reduces one, nothing more. Drink wine – put flesh on the instep, the instep that used to tell such a sweet story – and then the knees – fit for nothing but prayers! The hands – too fat to wander! *(She waves her arm.)* Then one exercises, but it's never the same; what one has, is always better than what one regains. Is it not so, my little one? But never mind, don't answer. I'm in an excellent humor – I could talk for hours, all about myself – to myself, for myself. God! I'd like to tear out all the wires in the house! Destroy all the tunnels in the city, leave nothing underground or hidden or useful, oh, God, God! *(She has danced until she comes directly in front of* THE DOVE. *She drops on her knees and lays her arms on either side of* THE DOVE.*)* I hate the chimneys on the houses, I hate the doorways, I hate you, I hate Vera, but most of all I hate my red heels!

THE DOVE   *(Almost inaudibly)* Now, now!

AMELIA   *(In high excitement)* Give me the sword! It has been sharpened long enough, give it to me, give it to me! *(She makes a blind effort to find the sword; finding* THE DOVE's *hand instead, she clutches it convulsively. Slowly* THE DOVE *bares* AMELIA's *left shoulder and breast, and leaning down, sets her teeth in.* AMELIA *gives a light, short, stifled cry. At the same moment* VERA *appears in the doorway with the uncorked bottle.* THE DOVE *stands up swiftly, holding a pistol. She turns in the doorway hastily vacated by* VERA.*)*

THE DOVE   So! *(She bows, a deep military bow, and turning goes into the entry.)*

THE VOICE OF THE DOVE   For the house of Burgson! *(A moment later a shot is heard.)*

AMELIA   *(Running after her)* Oh, my God!

VERA   What has she done?

AMELIA   *(Reappearing in the doorway with the picture of the Venetian courtesans, through which there is a bullet hole – slowly, but with emphasis)* This is obscene!

Curtain

Selected bibliography

The Papers of Djuna Barnes are in The McKeldin Library, Special Collections, University of Maryland, College Park, MD.

The Emily Holmes Coleman Papers are held by Special Collections, University of Delawark, Newark, DE.

Barnes, D. (1915) *The Book of Repulsive Women: 8 Rhythms and 5 Drawings* New York: Bruno's Chap Books, II, 6; rpt. (1989) Los Angeles, CA: Sun & Moon Press.

—— (1923) *A Book*, New York: Boni & Liveright.

—— (1928) *Ryder*, New York: Liveright; rpt. (1979) published with additional materials: New York: St. Martin's Press.; rpt. (1990) published with addional materials: Normal, IL: Dalkey Archive Press.

—— (1928) *Ladies Almanack*. Paris: Edward Titus; facsimile edition, New York: Harper & Row, 1972; Elmwood Park, IL: Dalkey Archive Press, 1992; New York: New York University Press, 1992.

—— (1929) *A Night Among the Horses*, New York: Liveright.

—— (1936) *Nightwood*, London: Faber & Faber; New York: Harcourt, Brace & Co., 1937; New York: New Directions, 1946.

—— (1995) *Nightwood, The Original Version and Related Drafts*, ed. Cheryl J. Plumb, Elmwood Park, IL: Dalkey Archive Press.

—— (1958) *The Antiphon: A Play*, London: Faber & Faber.

—— (1962) *Selected Works of*, New York: Farrar, Straus & Cudahy.

—— (1962) *Spillway*, London: Faber & Faber; rpt. (1972) New York: Harper & Row.

—— (1982) *Smoke and Other Early Stories*, ed. Douglas Messerli, College Park, MD: Sun & Moon Press.

—— (1985) *Djuna Barnes: Interviews*, ed. Alyce Barry, Washington, DC: Sun & Moon Press.

—— (1993) *Poe's Mother: Selected Drawings*, Los Angeles: Sun & Moon Press.

Dalton, A. (1993) "'*This* is obscene': Female Voyeurism, Sexual Abuse, and Maternal Power in *The Dove*," *The Review of Contemporary Fiction* 13.3: 117–40.

Deutsch, B. and Hanau, S. (1931) *The Provincetown*, New York: Farrar & Rinehart.

Larabee, A. (1991) "The Early Attic Stage of Djuna Barnes," in M. Broe (ed.) *Silence and Power*, Carbondale: Southern Illinois University Press.

Scott, J. (1976) *Djuna Barnes*, Boston: Twayne Publishing.

The Purple Flower
USA

Marita Bonner. Photograph reproduced from *The Crisis* magazine, December 1925 by permission of *The Crisis*.

Introduction

by Esther Beth Sullivan

Bonner and the Harlem Renaissance

With the recuperative projects of scholars such as Kathy Perkins, Nellie McKay, Bruce Kellner, and James Hatch, women writers of the Harlem Renaissance are finally receiving attention within the field of theater studies. This attention is long overdue. While the Harlem Renaissance is a slippery historical category, no scholar would dispute African-American women's significant contributions to the artistic milieu that existed in northern U.S. cities of the 1920s. Marita Bonner was one such woman. Bonner published essays, short stories, and plays in *The Crisis* and *Opportunity* from the early 1920s through 1941. She earned many awards from those publications as well as the regard of fellow writers such as Georgia Douglas Johnson, Langston Hughes, and Willis Richardson. Her one-act play, *The Purple Flower*, was the prize-winner in *The Crisis*'s 1928 playwriting contest. Decades later, this "non-realistic," "expressionistic," or "allegorical" piece has been hailed by critics as "possibly the most provocative play" by an African-American woman in the first part of the twentieth century (Wilkerson 1986: xvii), and as "one of the most unusual plays ever written on the subject of black liberation" (Hill 1986: 419).

Bonner's work resists generic classification. Like many of her contemporaries, she wrote across genre, producing mostly short stories, but also contributing drama, poetry, songs, and essays. Moreover, within particular pieces, she blurs genre markers. Her plays feature second-person narration, while her essays often sound like dramatic monologues. Her distinctive use of some formal features lies in pragmatic rather than aesthetic concerns. She wrote short pieces, of a length appropriate for magazines, newspapers, and publications like *The Crisis* and *Opportunity*. In a manuscript notebook of her never-published stories, running word-counts appear in the margins as well as notations about possible publication venues. Scholars have surmised from these notations that Bonner was thinking about "conformity of length specifications of some magazine or newspaper," and making "preparations for submitting stories or songs to various contests" (Roses and Randolph 1987: 170). All three of Bonner's published plays seem to have been written specifically for magazines. Each is a one-act characterized by stage directions that are as central as any of the dialogue, and dramatic action that "may have been intended for reading rather than performance" (Flynn 1987: xviii). Bonner's first published play, *The Pot Maker*, is even subtitled "a play to be read" (17). Whether by intention or not, none of her plays was produced in her lifetime.

Bonner's style

Introducing Bonner's collected works, Joyce Flynn highlights a distinctive aspect of her style. Whether Bonner is writing short stories, essays, or plays, she regularly employs second-person narration (Flynn 1987: xiii–xiv). Describing the Sundry White Devils in her stage directions for *The Purple Flower*, she writes, "You are amazed at their adroitness. Their steps are intricate. You almost lose your head following them" (9). The implication of a "second person," or the "you" of direct address, is found in each of her plays. *Exit, An Illusion* begins with the phrase, "The room you are in is mixed" (47), and similarly, *The Pot Maker* is scenically set with statements such as, "You know there is a garden because if you listen carefully you can hear a tapping of bushes against the window" (17). This feature of Bonner's work foregrounds the participation of the reader. At the same time that she represents the controversies of "passing," "the color line," and "color-consciousness," she implies that the reader is already there, involved, and implicated in the problem.

Allegory is another characteristic feature of Bonner's writing. *Exit, An Illusion* involves the arrival of Mann, who turns out to be Death. *The Pot Maker* focuses on "the Son, called of God, Elias Jackson" (17). However, while most of Bonner's plays and short stories include an allegorical character, component, or theme, *The Purple Flower* is allegorical in all aspects, to the point that it is described as a "morality play" (Flynn 1987: xviii), "cast in an abstract, symbolic mode" (Hill 1986: 419), "employing expressionist techniques" (McKay 1987: 142). It is the drama of "Us" and "Them"; it takes place in "the Middle-of-Things-as-They-are"; and, it deals with the desire to get "Somewhere," a place where "the purple Flower-of-Life-at-its-Fullest" grows. From start to finish, the play proceeds as an allegory of race relations in which a character might be a personified quality ("Average" and "Sweet"), inanimate object ("Cornerstone"), or group ("All the Old Us"), and the story deals with the precarious state of affairs on the "Thin-Skin-of-Civilization."

The allegorical form of *The Purple Flower* can be explained by proximity to modern art movements such as "expressionism" and "symbolist drama." Certainly, such movements were part of the mix of artistic impulses in American cities of the time. But other more direct influences resonate within and help to explain the allegorical nature of *The Purple Flower*. Bonner's association with Georgia Douglas Johnson's "salons" in Washington DC, her involvement with the Krigwa Players in Washington, and her regular writings in *The Crisis* and *Opportunity*, connect her allegorical style to issues and formal considerations represented by writers such as W. E. B. Du Bois, Langston Hughes, and Willis Richardson.

The Purple Flower as allegory

By 1930, Willis Richardson had published an anthology of plays and pageants dealing with "the life of the Negro," bringing together pieces "written primarily for use in schools" (Richardson 1930: vii). Having worked with the Krigwa Players of Washington and citing the fact that similar plays and pageants had been staged in Washington public schools, Richardson praises this group of dramas as "suitable for every reasonable need of School, Church, or Little Theatre" (vii). In this volume, the "pageants" are remarkably similar to Bonner's *The Purple Flower*. They are allegorical, featuring characters reminiscent of morality plays (Art, Imagination, Truth, Justice, Leniency, etc.), and focusing on broad concepts or issues like "the rape of a continent" (307), "the spirit of Africa" (312), "the temple of service" (334), and "the bar of justice" (346). Richardson's introduction indicates that the pageant form was prevalent enough in schools and little theaters to have produced a large body of work from which he could select examples for his book. While none of these pageants presents imminent bloody revolution as does Bonner, nevertheless they resemble Bonner's play in treating race relations as a "moral" for the times. Like *The Purple Flower*, these dramas employ allegory to make perfectly apparent the fundamental concerns at issue "in the face" of racism and in the process of reclaiming a lost African heritage.

Richardson was not alone in his attention to the emergence of a twentieth-century African-American drama. W. E. B. Du Bois used his editorship of *The Crisis* to investigate the representation of "Negroes" in art, and to prescribe an agenda for African-American theater. In a series of articles entitled, "The Negro in Art: How Shall He Be Portrayed?", artists, producers, and publishers attempted to assess artists' responsibility in the continuing racial biases of American culture. The series was published in *The Crisis* from March through November of 1926. During that period, Du Bois formulated his own response in two articles dealing with "criteria for Negro art" (July and October, 1926). Du Bois argued that, for the most part, black folk were represented only in gross and distorted stereotypes. He called for a new "Negro art" that would address black history, noting that black writers would necessarily need to assume this task because white writers couldn't portray the fullness of black experience. Du Bois concluded this argument saying that "Negro art" must be propagandistic with a vengeance: "Thus all Art is propaganda and ever must be. . . . I do not care a damn for any art that is not used for propaganda" (Du Bois 1926a: 296). To produce such art, he listed "four fundamental principles" in a kind of manifesto for the theater: black theater must be "about us," "for us," "by us," and "near us" (Du Bois 1926b: 134). In what would seem a direct response to Du Bois's call for a new black theater, Bonner dramatizes the story of "us" and propagandistically represents the struggle of a people oppressed by the institutionalization of racism. Without apology and in the boldly literal form of allegory, the play sets forth a context of unmitigated racial uprising, and calls for its audience to position themselves for the radical change to come.

In this allegory of uprising, the setting is imagined around a mountain: the scene is "an open plain. It is bounded distantly on one side by Nowhere and faced by a high hill – Somewhere" (9). Two years earlier, Langston Hughes had used the metaphor of the "racial mountain" to explain the kinds of hardships facing the "Negro artist." He exemplified this mountain of "sharp criticism" in hypothetical dialogue: "'O, be respectful, write about nice people, show how good we are,' say the Negroes. 'Be stereotyped, don't go too far, don't shatter our illusions about you, don't amuse us too seriously. We will pay you,' say the whites" (Hughes 1971: 85). Like many of his contemporaries, he advocated a kind of theater that would confront the "racial mountain" seriously and unflinchingly. Whether or not such art "pleased" either white or "colored" audiences was of no matter: "We build our temples for tomorrow, strong as we know how, and we stand on top of the mountain, free within ourselves" (86). As in Hughes's essay, Bonner uses the "racial mountain" to symbolize the struggle that faces "us." While the dramatic action involves the conflict between "us" and "them," the dynamic of the play has to do with the movement of "all us" up to the top of Somewhere. She employs a recognizable political image, "the racial mountain," which in turn connotes a particular struggle, uprising, and ascendancy. Bonner uses other contemporaneous political images and metaphors: White Devils, the Leader (with reference to Booker T. Washington), and the New Man (with reference to the "new Negro"). Her allegory speaks directly to and about the metaphors that "populate" the "race questions" of the time.

As pageant, propaganda, and political imagery, *The Purple Flower* evokes issues and artistic concerns of its time. Its form is its content, as the author embodies the struggle of "us" against "them," dramatizes the "racial mountain," questions the words of the Leader, and speaks on behalf of the New Man. The allegory is bald-faced in purpose, "arguing" that nothing less than blood will give birth to new possibilities and ending with one question: "Is it time?" "You" are left "listening, listening" for the response (29).

The Purple Flower

1928

Marita Bonner

Characters

SUNDRY WHITE DEVILS (They must be artful little things with soft wide eyes such as you would expect to find in an angel. Soft hair that flops around their horns. Their horns glow red all the time – now with blood – now with eternal fire – now with deceit – now with unholy desire. They have bones tied carefully across their tails to make them seem less like tails and more like mere decorations. They are artful little things full of artful movements and artful tricks. They are artful dancers too. You are amazed at their adroitness. Their steps are intricate. You almost lose your head following them. Sometimes they dance as if they were men – with dignity – erect. Sometimes they dance as if they were snakes. They are artful dancers on the Thin-Skin-of-Civilization.)

THE US'S (They can be as white as the White Devils, as brown as the earth, as black as the center of a poppy. They may look as if they were something or nothing.)

Time

The Middle-of-Things-as-They-are. (Which means the End-of-Things for some of the characters and the Beginning-of-Things for others.)

Place

Might be here, there or anywhere – or even nowhere.

Setting

The stage is divided horizontally into two sections, upper and lower, by a thin board. The main action takes place on the upper stage. The light is never quite clear on the lower stage; but it is bright enough for you to perceive that sometimes the action that takes place on the upper stage is duplicated on the lower. Sometimes the actors on the upper stage get too vociferous – too violent – and they crack through the boards and they lie twisted and curled in mounds. There are any number of mounds there, all twisted and broken. You look at them and you are not quite sure whether you see something or nothing; but you see by a curve that there might lie a human body. There is thrust out a white hand – a yellow one – one brown – a black. The Skin-of-Civilization must be very thin. A thought can drop you through it.

Scene

An open plain. It is bounded distantly on one side by Nowhere and faced by a high hill – Somewhere.

Argument

The White Devils live on the side of the hill. Somewhere. On top of the hill grows the purple Flower-of-Life-at-Its-Fullest. This flower is as tall as a pine and stands alone on top of the hill. The Us's live in the valley that lies between Nowhere and Somewhere and spend their time trying to devise means of getting up the hill. The White Devils live all over the sides of the hill and try every trick, known and unknown, to keep the Us's from getting to the hill. For if the Us's get up the hill, the Flower-of-Life-at-Its-Fullest will shed some of its perfume and then there they will be Somewhere with the White Devils. The Us's started out by merely asking permission to go up. They tilled the valley, they cultivated it and made it as beautiful as it is. They built roads and houses even for the White Devils. They let them build the houses and then they were knocked back down into the valley.

Scene

When the curtain rises, the evening sun is shining bravely on the valley and hillside alike.

THE US'S *are having a siesta beside a brook that runs down the Middle of the valley. As usual they rest with their backs toward Nowhere and their faces toward Somewhere.* THE WHITE DEVILS *are seen in the distance on the hillside. As you see them, a song is borne faintly to your ears from the hillside.* THE WHITE DEVILS *are saying:*

"You stay where you are!
We don't want you up here!
If you come you'll be on par
With what we hold dear.
So stay – stay – stay –
Yes stay where you are!"

The song rolls full across the valley.

A LITTLE RUNTY US   Hear that, don't you?

ANOTHER US   *(Lolling over on his back and chewing a piece of grass)* I ain't studying 'bout them devils. When I get ready to go up that hill – I'm going! *(He rolls over on his side and exposes a slender brown body to the sun.)* Right now, I'm going to sleep. *(And he forthwith snores.)*

OLD LADY   *(An old dark brown lady who has been lying down rises suddenly to her knees in the foreground. She gazes toward the hillside.)* I'll never live to see the face of that flower! God knows I worked hard to get Somewhere though. I've washed the shirt off of every one of them White Devils' backs!

A YOUNG US   And got a slap in the face for doing it.

OLD LADY   But that's what the Leader told us to do. "Work," he said. "Show them you know how." As if two hundred years of slavery had not showed them!

ANOTHER YOUNG US   Work doesn't do it. The Us who work for the White Devils get pushed in the face – down off of Somewhere every night. They don't even sleep up there.

OLD LADY   Something's got to be done though! The Us ain't got no business to sleep while the sun is shining. They'd ought to be up and working before the White Devils get to some other tricks.

YOUNG US   You just said work did not do you any good! What's the need of working if it doesn't get you anywhere? What's the use of boring around in the same hole like a worm? Making the hole bigger to stay in?

(There comes up the road a clatter of feet and four figures, A MIDDLE-AGED WELL-BROWNED MAN, A LIGHTER-BROWN MIDDLE-AGED WOMAN, A MEDIUM LIGHT-BROWN GIRL, beautiful as a browned peach, and a SLENDER TALL BRONZY BROWN YOUTH who walks with his head high. He touches the ground with his feet as if it were a velvet rug and not sun-baked, jagged rocks.)

OLD LADY   *(Addressing the OLDER MAN)* Evenin', Average. I was just saying we ain't never going to make that hill.

AVERAGE   The Us will if they get the right leaders.

THE MIDDLE-AGED WOMAN – CORNERSTONE   Leaders! Leaders! They've had good ones looks like to me.

AVERAGE   But they ain't led us anywhere!

CORNERSTONE   But that is not their fault! If one of them gets up and says, "Do this," one of the Us will sneak up behind him and knock him down and stand up and holler, "Do that," and then he himself gets knocked down and we still sit in the valley and knock down and drag out!

A YOUNG US   *(Aside)* Yeah! Drag Us out, but not White Devils.

OLD LADY   It's the truth Cornerstone. They say they going to meet this evening to talk about what we ought to do.

AVERAGE   What is the need of so much talking?

CORNERSTONE   Better than not talking! Somebody might say something after while.

THE YOUNG GIRL – SWEET   *(Who just came up)* I want to talk too!

AVERAGE   What can you talk about?

SWEET   Things! Something, father!

THE YOUNG MAN – FINEST BLOOD   I'll speak too.

AVERAGE   Oh you all make me tired! Talk – talk – talk – talk! And the flower is still up on the hillside!

OLD LADY   Yes and the White Devils are still talking about keeping the Us away from it, too.

(A drum begins to beat in the distance. All the US stand up and shake off their sleep. THE DRUMMER, a short, black, determined-looking Us, appears around the bushes beating the drum with strong, vigorous jabs that make the whole valley

echo and re-echo with rhythm. Some of THE US *begin to dance in time to the music.)*

AVERAGE Look at that! Dancing!! The Us will never learn to be sensible!

CORNERSTONE They dance well! Well!!
(THE US *congregate at the center front. Almost naturally, the* YOUNG US *range on one side, the* OLD US *on the other.* CORNERSTONE *sits her plump brown self comfortably in the center of the stage. An* OLD US *tottering with age and blind comes toward her.)*

OLD US What's it this time, chillun? Is it day yet? Can you see the road to that flower?

AVERAGE Oh you know we ain't going to get up there! No use worrying!

CORNERSTONE No it's not day! It is still dark. It is night.
(For the sun has gone and purple blackness has lain across the Valley. Somehow, though, you can see the shape of the flower on top of Somewhere. Lights twinkle on the hill.)

OLD US *(Speaking as if to himself)* I'm blind from working – building for the White Devils in the heat of the noonday sun and I'm weary!

CORNERSTONE Lean against me so they won't crowd you.
(AN OLD MAN rises in the back of the ranks; his beard reaches down to his knees but he springs upright. He speaks.)

OLD MAN I want to tell you all something! The Us can't get up the road unless we work! We want to hew and dig and toil!

A YOUNG US You had better sit down before someone knocks you down! They told us that when your beard was sprouting.

CORNERSTONE *(To YOUTH)* Do not be so stupid! Speak as if you had respect for that beard!

ANOTHER YOUNG US We have! But we get tired of hearing "you must work" when we know the old Us built practically every inch of that hill and are yet Nowhere.

FIRST YOUNG US Yes, all they got was a rush down the hill – not a chance to take a step up!

CORNERSTONE It was not time then.

OLD MAN *(On the back row)* Here comes a Young Us who has been reading in the books! Here comes a Young Us who has been reading in the books! He'll tell us what the books say about getting Somewhere.
(A YOUNG MAN pushes through the crowd. As soon as he reaches the center front, he throws a bundle of books and cries –)

YOUNG MAN I'm through! I do not need these things! They're no good!

OLD MAN *(Pushes up from the back and stands beside him)* You're through! Ain't you been reading in the books how to get Somewhere! Why don't you tell us how to get there?

YOUNG MAN I'm through I tell you! There isn't anything in one of these books that tells Black Us how to get around White Devils.

OLD MAN *(Softly – sadly)* I thought the books would tell us how!

YOUNG MAN No! The White Devils wrote the books themselves. You know they aren't going to put anything like that in there!

YET ANOTHER OLD MAN *(Throwing back his head and calling into the air)* Lord! Why don't you come by here and tell us how to get Somewhere?

A YOUNG MAN *(Who had been idly chewing grass)* Aw, you ought to know by now that isn't the way to talk to God!

OLD MAN It ain't! It ain't! It ain't! It ain't! Ain't I been talking to God just like that for seventy years? Three scores and ten years – Amen!

THE GRASS CHEWER Yes! Three score and ten years you been telling God to tell you what to do. Telling Him! And three score and ten years you been wearing your spine double sitting on the rocks in the valley too.

OLD US He is all-powerful! He will move in his own time!

YOUNG US Well, if He is all-powerful, God does not need you to tell Him what to do.

OLD US Well what's the need of me talkin' to Him then?

YOUNG US Don't talk so much to Him! Give Him a chance! He might want to talk to you but you do so much yelling in His ears that He can't tell you anything.
(There is a commotion in the back stage. SWEET *comes running to* CORNERSTONE *crying.)*

SWEET Oh – oo – !

CORNERSTONE What is it, Sweet?

SWEET There is a White Devil sitting in

the bushes in the dark over there! There's a White Devil sitting in the bushes over in the dark! And when I walked by – he pinched me!

FINEST BLOOD *(Catching a rock)* Where is he, sister? *(He starts toward the bushes.)*

CORNERSTONE *(Screaming)* Don't go after him son! They will kill you if you hurt him!

FINEST BLOOD I don't care if they do. Let them. I'd be out of this hole then!

AVERAGE Listen to that young fool! Better stay safe and sound where he is! At least he got somewhere to eat and somewhere to lay his head.

FINEST BLOOD Yes I can lay my head on the rocks of Nowhere.

(Up the center of the stage toils a new figure of a square-set MIDDLE-AGED US. He walks heavily for in each hand he carries a heavy bag. As soon as he reaches the center front he throws the bags down, groaning as he does so.)

AN OLD MAN 'Smatter with you? Ain't them bags full of gold?

THE NEWCOMER Yes, they are full of gold!

OLD MAN Well why ain't you smiling then? Them White Devils can't have anything no better!

THE NEWCOMER Yes they have! They have Somewhere! I tried to do what they said. I brought them money, but when I brought it to them they would not sell me even a spoonful of dirt from Somewhere! I'm through!

CORNERSTONE Don't be through. The gold counts for something. It must!

(AN OLD WOMAN cries aloud in a quavering voice from the back.)

OLD LADY Last night I had a dream.

A YOUNG US Dreams? Excuse me! I know I'm going now! Dreams!

OLD LADY I dreamed that I saw a White Devil cut in six pieces – head here *(Pointing)*, body here – one leg here – one there – an arm here – an arm there.

AN OLD MAN Thank God! It's time then!

AVERAGE Time for what? Time to eat? Sure ain't time to get Somewhere!

OLD MAN *(Walking forward)* It's time! It's time! Bring me an iron pot!

YOUNG US Aw don't try any conjuring!

OLD MAN *(Louder)* Bring me a pot of iron. Get the pot from the fire in the valley.

CORNERSTONE Give him the pot!

(Someone brings it up immediately.)

OLD MAN *(Walking toward pot slowly)* Old Us! Do you hear me. Old Us that are here do you hear me?

ALL THE OLD US *(Cry in chorus)* Yes, Lord! We hear you! We hear you!

OLD MAN *(Crying louder and louder)* Old Us! Old Us! Old Us that are gone, Old Us that are dust do you hear me? *(His voice sounds strangely through the valley. Somewhere you think you hear – as if mouthed by ten million mouths through rocks and dust – "Yes – Lord! – We hear you! We hear you!")* And you hear me – give me a handful of dust! Give me a handful of dust! Dig down to the depths of the things you have made! The things you formed with your hands and give me a handful of dust!

(AN OLD WOMAN tottering with the weakness of old age crosses the stage and going to the pot, throws a handful of dust in. Just before she sits down again she throws back her head and shakes her cane in the air and laughs so that the entire valley echoes.)

A YOUNG US What's the trouble? Choking on the dust?

OLD WOMAN No child! Rejoicing!

YOUNG US Rejoicing over a handful of dust?

OLD WOMAN Yes. A handful of dust! Thanking God I could do something if it was nothing but make a handful of dust!

YOUNG US Well dust isn't much!

OLD MAN *(At the pot)* Yes, it isn't much! You are dust yourself; but so is she. Like everything else, though, dust can be little or much, according to where it is.

(THE YOUNG US who spoke subsides. He subsides so completely that he crashes through the Thin-Skin-of-Civilization. Several of his group go too. They were thinking.)

OLD MAN *(At the pot)* Bring me books! Bring me books!

YOUNG US *(Who threw his books down)* Here! Take all these! I'll light the fire with them.

OLD MAN No, put them in the pot. *(YOUNG US does so.)* Bring me the gold!

THE MAN OF THE GOLD BAGS Here take this! It is just as well. Stew it up and make teething rings!! *(He pours it into the pot.)*

OLD MAN Now bring me blood! Blood from the eyes, the ears, the whole body! Drain it off and bring me blood! *(No one speaks or moves.)* Now bring me blood! Blood from the eyes, the ears, the whole body! Drain if off! Bring me blood! *(No one speaks or moves.)* Ah hah, hah! I knew it! Not one of you willing to pour his blood in the pot!

YOUNG US *(Facetiously)* How you going to pour your own blood in there? You got to be pretty far gone to let your blood run in there. Somebody else would have to do the pouring.

OLD MAN I mean red blood. Not yellow blood, thank you.

FINEST BLOOD *(Suddenly)* Take my blood! *(He walks toward the pot.)*

CORNERSTONE O no! Not my boy! Take me instead!

OLD MAN Cornerstone, we cannot stand without you!

AN OLD WOMAN What you need blood for? What you doing anyhow? You ain't told us nothing yet. What's going on in that pot?

OLD MAN I'm doing as I was told to do.

A YOUNG US Who told you to do anything?

OLD MAN God. I'm His servant.

YOUNG US *(Who spoke before)* God? I haven't heard God tell you anything.

OLD MAN You couldn't hear. He told it to me alone.

OLD WOMAN I believe you. Don't pay any attention to that simpleton! What God told you to do?

OLD MAN He told me take a handful of dust – dust from which all things came – and put it in a hard iron pot. Put it in a hard iron pot. Things shape best in hard molds!! Put in books that Men learn by. Gold that Men live by. Blood that lets Men live.

YOUNG US What you suppose to be shaping? A man?

OLD US I'm the servant. I can do nothing. If I do this, God will shape a new man Himself.

YOUNG MAN What's the things in the pot for?

OLD MAN To show I can do what I'm told.

OLD WOMAN Why does He want blood?

OLD MAN You got to give blood! Blood has to be let for births, to give life.

OLD WOMAN So the dust wasn't just nothing? Thank God!

YOUTH Then the books were not just paper leaves? Thank God!

THE MAN OF THE GOLD BAGS Can the gold mean something?

OLD MAN Now I need the blood.

FINEST BLOOD I told you you could take mine.

OLD MAN Yours!

FINEST BLOOD Where else could you get it? The New Man must be born. The night is already dark. We cannot stay here forever. Where else could blood come from?

OLD MAN Think, child. When God asked a faithful servant once to do sacrifice, even His only child, where did God put the real meat for sacrifice when the servant had the knife upon the son's throat?

OLD US *(In a chorus)*

In the bushes, Lord!
In the bushes, Lord!
Jehovah put the ram
In the bushes!

CORNERSTONE I understand!

FINEST BLOOD What do you mean?

CORNERSTONE Where were you going a little while ago? Where were you going when your sister cried out?

FINEST BLOOD To the bushes! You want me to get the White Devil? *(He seizes the piece of rock and stands to his feet.)*

OLD MAN No! No! Not that way. The White Devils are full of tricks. You must go differently. Bring him gifts and offer them to him.

FINEST BLOOD What have I to give for a gift?

OLD MAN There are the pipes of Pan that every Us is born with. Play on that. Soothe him – lure him – make him yearn for the pipe. Even a White Devil will soften at music. He'll come out, and he only comes to try to get the pipe from you.

FINEST BLOOD And when he comes out, I'm to kill him in the dark before he sees me? That's a White Devil trick!

OLD MAN An Old Us will never tell you to play White Devil's games! No! Do not kill him in the dark. Get him out of the bushes and say to him: "White Devil, God is using me for His instrument. You think that it is I who play on this pipe! You think that is I who play upon this pipe so that you cannot stay in your bushes. So that you must come out of your bushes. But it is not I who play. It is not I, it is God who plays through me – to you. Will you hear what He says? Will you hear?

He says it is almost day, White Devil. The night is far gone. A New Man must be born for the New Day. Blood is needed for birth. Blood is needed for the birth. Come out, White Devil. It may be your blood – it may be mine – but blood must be taken during the night to be given at the birth. It may be my blood – it may be your blood – but everything has been given. The Us toiled to give dust for the body, books to guide the body, gold to clothe the body. Now they need blood for birth so the New Man can live. You have taken blood. You must give blood. Come out! Give it." And then fight him!

FINEST BLOOD I'll go! And if I kill him?

OLD MAN Blood will be given!

FINEST BLOOD And if he kills me?

OLD MAN Blood will be given!

FINEST BLOOD Can there be no other way – cannot this cup pass?

OLD MAN No other way. It cannot pass. They always take blood. They built up half their land on our bones. They ripened crops of cotton, watering them with our blood. Finest Blood, this is God's decree: "You take blood – you give blood. Full measure – flooding full – over – over!"

FINEST BLOOD I'll go. *(He goes quickly into the shadow. Far off soon you can hear him – his voice lifted, young, sweet, brave and strong.)* White Devil! God speaks to you through me! – Hear Him! – Him! You have taken blood: there can be no other way. You will have to give blood! Blood! *(*ALL THE US *listen. All the valley listens. Nowhere listens.* ALL THE WHITE DEVILS *listen. Somewhere listens. Let the curtain close leaving* ALL THE US, THE WHITE DEVILS, *Nowhere, Somewhere, listening, listening. Is it time?)*

Bibliography

Bonner, Marita (1928) *The Purple Flower*, in *The Crisis* 35.1 (January): 9–11, 28–29.

—— (1987) *The Pot Maker* (1927), *The Purple Flower* (1928), *Exit, An Illusion* (1929), in Joyce Flynn and Joyce Occomy Stricklin (eds), *Frye Street & Environs: The Collected Works of Marita Bonner*, Boston: Beacon Press.

Dictionary of Literary Biography 51: Afro-American Writers from the Harlem Renaissance to 1940 (1987), Detroit: Gale Research.

Du Bois, W. E. B. (1926a) "Criteria of Negro Art," *The Crisis* (October): 290–97.

—— (1926b) "Krigwa Players Little Negro Theatre," *The Crisis* (July): 134–36.

Flynn, Joyce (ed.) (1987) "Introduction," *Frye Street & Environs: The Collected Works of Marita Bonner*, Boston: Beacon Press.

Hill, Errol (1986) "The Revolutionary Tradition in Black Drama," *Theatre Journal* 38.4 : 408–26.

Hughes, Langston (rpt. 1971) "The Negro Artist and the Racial Mountain," in Raymond F. Betts (ed.), *The Ideology of Blackness*, Lexington: D. C. Heath & Co.

Kellner, Bruce (ed.) (1984) *The Harlem Renaissance: A Dictionary for the Era*, Westport, CT: Greenwood Press.

McKay, Nellie (1987) "'What Were They Saying?': A Selected Overview of Black Women Playwrights of the Harlem Renaissance," in Victor A. Kramer (ed.), *Harlem Renaissance Re-Examined*, New York: AMS Press.

Richardson, Willis (1930) *Plays and Pageants from the Life of the Negro*, Washington: Associated Publishers, Inc.

Roses, Lorraine Elena and Randolph, Ruth Elizabeth (1987) "Marita Bonner: In Search of Other Mothers' Gardens," *Black American Literature Forum* 21.1–2: 165–83.

Wilkerson, Margaret (1986) "Introduction," *Nine Plays by Black Women*, New York: New American Library.

Notes on translators and contributors ___

Anne-Charlotte Hanes Harvey

Born in Sweden, Anne-Charlotte Hanes Harvey was educated in Sweden and in the United States. Currently Professor of Drama and Teaching Associate in Women's Studies at San Diego State University, she also works as a translator and dramaturg, with Strindberg, Ibsen, and the works of Unga Klara as special interests. Other translating credits include the symphonic cycle *The Jewish Song*, the opera *Animalen*, and the play, based on Strindberg's poems, *Helluvaguy!!!*

Natalia Costa-Zalessow

Natalia Costa-Zalessow, Professor of Italian in the Department of Foreign Languages and Literatures at the San Francisco State University, received her Ph.D. in Romance Languages and Literatures from the University of California, Berkeley. Among her publications are *Scrittrici italiane dal XIII al XX secolo. Testi e critica* (Women Writers from the Thirteenth to the Twentieth Century, Texts and Criticism), the Italian section of *Longman Anthology of World Literature by Women (1875–1975)*, ed. by M. Arkin and B. Shollar, and articles in *Italica*, *Forum Italicum*, *Italiana*, *Italian Quarterly*, *Ausonia*, and others.

Susanne T. Kord

Susanne Kord teaches German at Georgetown University. She is the author of *Ein Blick hinter die Kulissen* (1992), the first extensive study of women's drama in eighteenth- and nineteenth-century Germany, and articles on German women playwrights, children's theater, re/definitions of the canon, gender and literature, and infanticide in literature.

Joanne E. Gates

Joanne E. Gates is an Associate Professor of English at Jacksonville State University, where she teaches Shakespeare and Women's Literature. Her biography of Elizabeth Robins (University of Alabama Press, 1994) was awarded the Elizabeth Agee Prize in literature. In connection with her work on Robins, she received Jacksonville State University's Faculty/Scholar Lecture Award for 1994–95.

Melanie C. Hawthorne

Melanie Hawthorne, an Associate Professor of French at Texas A&M University, works primarily on the French novelist Rachilde and the *fin de siècle*. Her translation of Rachilde's novel *The Juggler* was published by Rutgers University Press in 1990, and she is currently completing a critical biography.

Evelia Romano Thuesen

Evelia Romano Thuesen is a permanent faculty member at The Evergreen State College, Olympia, Washington. She specializes in Latin American Colonial and Contemporary Argentine Literatures. She has worked on authors such as Oviedo, Piglia, and Saer, and published articles in *Nueva Revista de Filología Hispánica*, *Literatura Mexicana*, and *Latin American Literary Review*. She is preparing an annotated edition of her translations of Alfonsina Storni's four major plays for publication.

Ritva Poom

Ritva Poom's translations from the Finnish and Estonian have been widely published. Among the authors she has translated are Paavo Haavikko and Ilpo Tuomarila

(Finnish); Mati Unt and Paul-Eerik Rummo (Estonian). Her translation of *Fog Horses*, a selection from Eeva-Liisa Manner's poetry, was awarded the Columbia University Translation Prize. She is the editor and translator of Juha Y. Pentikinen's *Kalevala Mythology* (Indiana University Press, 1989) and the recipient of fellowships from the National Endowment for the Humanities and the National Endowment for the Arts. In 1993, Ritva Poom won the American Scandinavian Foundation Translation Prize for her translations of Raija Siekkinen's prose.

Pirkko Koski

Pirkko Koski has been an Associate Professor at the University of Helsinki since 1989. Prior to 1989, she served for three years as a general director of the Central Union of Finnish Theatre Associations. From 1980 to 1989, she held the position of director of the Theatre Museum of Finland. She has published books on Finnish theater history as well as chapters in books and journals. She wrote as a theater reviewer from 1979 to 1993, and participated in international, especially northern, associations for theater researchers and documentarists.

Carole Cavanaugh

Carole Cavanaugh is Assistant Professor of Japanese at Middlebury College. She has published in the areas of early twentieth-century Japanese literature, film, and women's writing in Japan. Her current research is on Japanese film and cultural memory.

Kiki Gounaridou

Kiki Gounaridou is Assistant Professor of Theater and Performance Studies at the University of Pittsburgh. She has translated plays from the Ancient Greek and French and has published and presented papers on Ancient Greek theater, contemporary German theater, and translation theory.

Frazer Lively

Frazer Lively is a doctoral student in theater at the University of Pittsburgh. Her article on the staging of *Madame la Mort* is forthcoming in *Nineteenth Century Theatre*, and she is co-translator (with Kiki Gounaridou) of seven plays by Rachilde. Her dissertation examines Rachilde's theater career.

Catherine Schuler

Catherine Schuler is an Associate Professor of Theater History at the University of Maryland, College Park. She has published articles on women in theater in *The Drama Review*, *Theatre Survey*, *Theater History Studies*, and *Theatre Topics*. Her book, *Women in Russian Theatre: The Actress in the Silver Age*, is forthcoming from Routledge, and she is the co-editor (with Karen Laughlin) of *Theatre and Feminist Aesthetics*.

Mary F. Zirin

Mary F. Zirin is co-editor (with Marina Ledkovsky and Charlotte Rosenthal) of *Dictionary of Russian Women Writers* (Greenwood, 1994), translator of Nadezhda Durova's *The Cavalry Maiden* (Indiana University Press, 1988), and founder-editor of the newsletter *Women: East–West* sponsored by the Association for Women in Slavic Studies.

Cheryl J. Plumb

Cheryl J. Plumb, Assistant Professor at Penn State York Campus, has published *Fancy's Craft*, a study of the early work of Djuna Barnes. She has also published *Nightwood, The Original Version and Related Drafts*, a critical edition of Barnes's *Nightwood* (Dalkey Archive Press).

Esther Beth Sullivan

Esther Beth Sullivan is an Associate Professor of Theater at the Ohio State University. She is currently working on a book, *Plot Points: Feminist Readings of Narrative Onstage*, which examines theories of narrative in the work of contemporary women playwrights. Her articles have appeared in *Upstaging Big Daddy: Directing Theater as if Gender and Race Mattered*, as well as in *Theatre Journal*, *Theatre Studies*, and *Literature in Performance*.

319